THE BIRTH OF BEBOP

A Social and Musical History

Scott DeVeaux

D1235919

University of California Press   *Berkeley*   *Los Angeles*   *London*

The publisher gratefully acknowledges the
contributions toward the publication of this book
provided by the Sonneck Society for American
Music and by Sukey Garcetti and Michael Roth
and the Roth Family Foundation.

University of California Press
Berkeley and Los Angeles, California

University of California Press, Ltd.
London, England

Library of Congress Cataloging-in-Publication Data

DeVeaux, Scott Knowles.
  The birth of bebop : a social and musical history
  Scott DeVeaux.
    p. cm.
    Includes bibliographical references and index.
    ISBN 0–520–20579–0 (alk. paper)
    ISBN:13 978–0–520–21665–5 (pbk. : alk. paper)
  1. Bop (Music)—History and criticism.
  2. Jazz—1931–1940—History and criticism.
  3. Jazz—1941–1950—History and criticism.
  4. Music and society.   I. Title.
  ML3506.D48   1997
  781.65'5—dc21   96–46887
                                              CIP
                                              MN
Printed in the United States of America

08 07 06
9 8 7 6 5

The paper used in this publication meets the minimum requirements of ANSI/NISO Z39.48-1992
(R 1997) (Permanence of Paper). ∞

THE BIRTH OF BEBOP

To A., F., and V.—the women in my life

Contents

Illustrations

Photographs follow pages 160 and 280

Mal Braveman and Milt Shaw
Present
FOUR SOLID HOURS OF

MAD MUSIC
☆
Featuring
Our Guest of Honor
DIZZY GILLESPIE
World's Most Outstanding Trumpeter
DON BYAS
New King of the Tenor Sax
CHARLIE PARKER
Alto Saxmania
AL KILLIAN
Great Basie—Barnet Trumpeter
MOREY FELD
Benny Goodman's Ace Drummer

AL HAIG	**LEONARD GASKIN**
Piano	Bass
AL COHEN	**FREDDIE RADCLIFFE**
Tenor	Drums

Plus Plenty of Name Guests from the
T. Dorsey - Barnet Bands
☆
SUNDAY AFTERNOON, Sept. 16th, 1945
4 to 8 P. M.   Admission $1.50
☆
SPOTLITE CLUB, 56 W. 52 St. New York
(Bet. 5th and 6th Aves.)
Call EL 5-8148, Sun. Aft. bet. 2-4 P.M. for Best Table Reservations

MONTE KAY
presents a
MODERN JAZZ CONCERT
Starring 3 of America's Greatest Trumpeters
BUCK CLAYTON
Esquire's #1 Musician in the Armed Forces
DIZZY GILLESPIE
Esquire's New Trumpet King of 1945
HARRY EDISON
Dynamic Trumpeter with Count Basie
Featured in "Jammin' the Blues" at the Hollywood
DON BYAS
One of the Country's Finest Tenor Saxists
DEXTER GORDON
World's Weirdest Tenor Man - Out of Uniform
ERROL GARNER
Brilliant Young Pianist—A 1945 Jazz Discovery
SHELLEY MANNE
Driving Drummer formerly with Les Brown

SAMMY BENSKIN	**LEONARD GASKIN**
Piano	Bass

And Guests From Every Top Band In Town
SUNDAY AFTERNOON, FEB. 4, 4 to 8 P.M.
$1.50 Cover Charge—No Other Charge at Table
For Reservations: Call MAL BRAVEMAN
ELdorado 5-8148, Sunday after 2 P.M.
SPOTLITE CLUB 56 W. 52nd STREET
Bet. 5th and 6th Aves.

MONTE KAY presents a
MODERN JAZZ CONCERT
Starring
DIZZY GILLESPIE
Esquire's New Trumpet King of 1945
AL KILIAN
Skyrocket Trumpeter with Count Basie
HARRY EDISON
Driving Trumpeter of the Basie Band
DEXTER GORDON
Great Tenor Man — Ex Hampton and Eckstine
EDDIE DAVIS
Frantic New Tenor Saxist with Louis Armstrong

ERROL GARNER	**KEN KERSEY**
Two Brilliant Young Pianists	
SHELLY MANNE	**LEONARD GASKIN**
Drums	Bass

And Our Guests of Honor
BUDDY RICH
The World's Fastest Drummer
GEO. SCHWARTZ   HERB STEWART
Terrific Trumpet and Tenor Men with Artie Shaw
SUNDAY AFTERNOON, FEB. 11, 4 to 8 P.M.
$1.50 Cover Charge—No Other Charge at Table
For Reservations: Call MAL BRAVEMAN
ELdorado 5-8148, Sunday after 2 P.M.
SPOTLITE CLUB 56 W. 52nd STREET
Bet. 5th and 6th Aves.

MONTE KAY & PETE KAMERAN
PRESENT

AN OPEN HOUSE JAM SESSION
STARRING
Coleman Hawkins

THE MASTER OF THE TENOR SAX

DON BYAS — BENNY HARRIS — DENZIL BEST
THELONIOUS MONK — EDDIE ROBINSON
CLYDE HART — JACK PARKER
BOB DORSAY — *LEN GASKIN*
and other famous Guest Stars
RAYMOND SCOTT — COSY COLE
BUSTER BAILEY — RAY NANCE
EARLE WARREN — LESTER YOUNG

★ *Friday May 19th - 9 to 4* ★

DOWNBEAT CLUB 66 W. 52ND ST.
NEW YORK CITY
ELdorado 5-8773
No Cover — No Minimum — No Cabaret Tax

Promotional bills for jam sessions at
the Spotlite and the Downbeat clubs,
1944–1945. (Courtesy of Leonard
Gaskin.)

Acknowledgments

A project that has gestated for as long as this one necessarily has many midwives. First, I want to thank those who helped me during the writing of my dissertation, the research for which served as the foundation for this book.

During my years in Berkeley, I had the good fortune to meet Tom Hennessey, who was in town attending a National Endowment for the Humanities seminar. He generously shared his dissertation research with me and inspired me to take on a project combining a passion for music with the rigors of historical scholarship. I received help of a different sort from Richard Hadlock, author of *Jazz Masters of the Twenties;* in addition to providing me with access to many obscure recordings, he reminded me through his superb saxophone playing of the importance of simplicity and expression in music. I also wish to acknowledge the formative influence of my various music teachers, especially Bill Bell of the College of Alameda; C. K. Ladzekpo, leader of the African Music and Dance Ensemble; and—to reach back even further—Frank Cunimondo of Pittsburgh, who first awakened my curiosity about bebop.

Much of the research was carried out in New York City. I am grateful to various hosts over the years, including Kuni Yavneh, Jim Marketos, Pearl Seril Pell, and Andy Kaye. I also benefited from the relaxed atmosphere and expert assistance of the staff at the Institute of Jazz Studies at Rutgers-Newark, which at various times included Dan Morgenstern, Ed Berger, Ron Welburn, and (informally) Phil Schaap. I am particularly grateful to the late Howard McGhee, who put up with my persistent questioning on several occasions in the early 1980s and provided me with much of the inspiration to focus this book on the experiences of musicians such as himself.

The actual writing of the dissertation—which was supported by a generous grant from the Martha Baird Rockefeller Fund for Music—was strongly influenced by the three members of my thesis committee at the University of California at Berkeley. Through his teaching and his writings, Lawrence Levine convinced me that the most satisfying approach to scholarship comes from a desire to give voice to those "too largely neglected and too consistently misunderstood." Joseph Kerman worked carefully with me on both small- and large-scale aspects of prose, instilling in me the values of clarity and concision of expression. Finally, the chair of my committee, Olly Wilson, provided me with the support I needed to get the job done. He was—and is—an inspiration, both as a scholar of African-American music and as a fount of common sense and uncommon wisdom.

Once settled into Virginia, I found a new set of allies. As I expanded the scope of the project, the staff at the Music Library at the University of Virginia—Diane Parr Walker, Jane Penner, Pam Howie—made sure that I was supplied with all the microfilms, books, and other research tools I needed. Marita McClymonds, chair of the music department for much of my time here, shepherded my tenure case through to a successful completion. A grant from the National Endowment for the Humanities allowed me to take a year's leave from my teaching duties. While on the job, I enjoyed the company of my colleagues, especially Suzanne Cusick, Elizabeth Hudson, Fred Maus, and the current chair, Judith Shatin, all of whom have contributed to an unusually stimulating intellectual environment. On the bandstand, I had the pleasure of working alongside John D'Earth, Robert Jospé, James Rubin, LeRoi Moore, Clarence Seay, Carter Beauford, Tim Reynolds, Jeff Decker, Pete Spaar, Mike Cogswell, and other superb musicians who deepened my insights into jazz. Close friendships made life more pleasant: at the risk of neglecting some, I wish to particularly remember three friends who have subsequently moved elsewhere—Anne Newman, Tannis Gibson, and Mark Rush. I also must express my thanks to all of the folks at the Thomas Jefferson Memorial Church, Unitarian-Universalist, including members of the choir and the dream workshop, for nurturing my awareness of things spiritual and social.

Help also came from outside. Rich Crawford, Guy Ramsey, Mark Tucker, the late Martin Williams, Susan Cook, Ron Radano, Gene Lees, and Liane Curtis all read portions of the book in manuscript at various stages. I am particularly grateful to Krin Gabbard for his encouragement and many thoughtful comments; to my good friend Tom Brothers, whose trenchant observations at every stage have helped to make the book stronger; to Martha Bayles, for suggesting most of the chapter titles; and to Doug Richards, for checking the musical examples and offering sage advice on matters of notation. I learned a great deal by talking with musicians, many of whose words have found their way into these pages: Ray Abrams, Wilbert Baranco, Thelma Carpenter, Dizzy Gillespie, Al Haig, Al Hall, "Big Nick" Nicholas, Max Roach, Kermit Scott, and especially Leonard Gaskin, a true gentleman and one of the few musicians in my experience to have a historian's temperament.

My experiences with the University of California Press have been another source of gratitude. Alain Hénon took on the project initially and guided me toward a contract longer ago than I care to remember. The remainder of the work has been ably carried on by Doris Kretschmer, whose enthusiasm for the project helped to keep my spirits from flagging during the long months when it seemed I could find no time for the arduous tasks of writing and revising; Rachel Berchten, who shepherded the book through various obstacles; and Sue Heinemann, who gave it a painstaking and informed copyedit. The final shape of this book owes a great deal to their vision, persistence, and patience.

Finally, there is my family. I do most of my work at home, and for Amelia (born 1988) and Flora (born 1991), the sight of their father hunched over a computer has been a permanent part of their lives. I hope they are surprised and pleased to see that all that work has resulted in something gratifyingly tangible. Needless to say, the time I have spent away from the computer playing with them, reading to them, and watching them grow up has meant more to me than words can express. And of course, I owe more than can be repaid in words to my wife, Vivian Thomson. She was with me at the very beginning, when I took her to see Howard McGhee's band in a drafty street-front New York bar on a frigid New Year's Eve. She has been with me ever since, adapting and adjusting her own career to make it possible for our marriage to be a true partnership. For that I am truly grateful. To her, and to the girls, this book is dedicated with love and affection.

INTRODUCTION

Stylistic Evolution or Social Revolution?

There is a trick to balancing a yardstick. Hold the yardstick out flat, with one index finger under each end. Then bring these fingers in slowly toward the center. They will not slide in evenly: one will be held up by friction while the other spurts ahead until it, too, is caught. But inevitably they will meet at the pivot point of the span and come into balance.

Imagine for the moment that the history of jazz is a solid, linear object, like a yardstick. One endpoint marks the origins of jazz, somewhere in the mists of the early twentieth century; the other, the present. As of this writing, at least, the point at which the yardstick comes into balance falls somewhere in the mid-1940s.

By any measure, this is a crucial period for the history of jazz. During the years 1940–45 the first modern jazz style, shaped by Charlie Parker, Dizzy Gillespie, Thelonious Monk, and others, came into being. This music was known as bebop, or simply bop: "a most inadequate word," complained Ralph Ellison, that "throws up its hands in clownish self-deprecation before all the complexity of sound and rhythm and self-assertive passion which it pretends to name." But this music was crucial for the evolution of jazz and American music. For Ellison, bebop marked nothing less than "a momentous modulation into a new key of musical sensibility; in brief, a revolution in culture."

As the twentieth century comes to a close, bebop lies at the midpoint

1

of what has come to be known as the jazz tradition. It also lies at the shadowy juncture at which the lived experience of music becomes transformed into cultural memory. Inevitably, there will be fewer and fewer witnesses to contribute to—or contest—our ideas about the past. The recent passing of Dizzy Gillespie (1917–93) and Miles Davis (1926–92), among others, underscores our closeness to the physical and psychic reality of that history. In their absence we will be left with the image of bebop and jazz that we construct for ourselves.

Even as bebop recedes further into the past, it is unlikely to be dislodged any time soon from the heart of jazz discourse. Tradition, after all, is not simply a matter of cherishing the past, holding its memory sacred. There is some of that in jazz, but not much. What counts, as the musicologist Carl Dahlhaus has argued, is the continuing existence of the past in the present.

In this sense, bebop has a more legitimate claim to being the fount of contemporary jazz than earlier jazz styles. The large dance orchestras of the Swing Era and the improvised polyphony of the early New Orleans groups may hold a place of honor, but musicians no longer play that way. The nuances of the past have largely disappeared, along with the social contexts of nightlife and dancing that shaped and gave them meaning. A jazz orchestra of fifteen or more musicians suggests either nostalgia, the specter of superannuated bodies shuffling to yesterday's dance music, or the academic sterility of the university "lab band." The small New Orleans or "Dixieland" combo was long ago ceded to enthusiastic and atavistically minded amateurs. Even the most accomplished modern jazz repertory groups only drive home how difficult it is for a contemporary musician to inhabit the musical sensibility of King Oliver, Jelly Roll Morton, or Jimmie Lunceford.

By contrast, ask any member of the current generation of jazz musicians to play Charlie Parker's "Anthropology," or Gillespie's "A Night in Tunisia," or Monk's "'Round Midnight." It may not be their preferred avenue of expression, but they will know the music and how to play it. Bebop is a music that has been kept alive by having been absorbed into the present; in a sense, it *constitutes* the present. It is part of the experience of all aspiring jazz musicians, each of whom learns bebop as the embodiment of the techniques, the aesthetic sensibilities, and ultimately the professional attitudes that define the discipline. A musical idiom now half a century old is bred in their bones.

The perennial relevance of bebop is thus not simply a tribute to its enduring musical value. After all, the music of Louis Armstrong or Duke Ellington enjoys a critical esteem equal to that of Parker, Gillespie, and Monk, *and* it is better known and loved by the general public. But bebop is the point at which our contemporary ideas of jazz come into focus. It is both the source of the present—"that great revolution in jazz which made all subsequent jazz modernisms possible"—and the prism through which we absorb the past. To understand jazz, one must understand bebop.

As its title suggests, *The Birth of Bebop* concerns itself primarily with the question of origins. It is less the chronicle of a musical movement than an accounting of the various social and musical factors that culminated in its emergence. It devotes much of its attention to the period usually known as the Swing Era and ends where a more conventional approach to the subject, such as Thomas Owens's *Bebop*, would begin: with the first stirrings of bebop as a public phenomenon, signaled by the first commercial recordings by Parker and Gillespie, in 1945.

This unusual narrative structure is designed to force certain underlying assumptions to the surface. An approach to bebop that focuses more narrowly on musical style, exemplified by Owens's recent study, tends to avoid issues with racial, political, or economic ramifications or, indeed, anything that might distract from the real business at hand—the tracing of stylistic development. Other issues are so basic to the discipline that they are taken for granted.

Few authors, for example, critically examine the basic tenet that bebop belongs to a larger category known as jazz. They assume that bebop is best viewed not as an isolated phenomenon of popular culture, but as one phase of an artistic tradition whose history can be expressed as a coherent progression encompassing nearly a century of continuous innovation, from New Orleans dance music to avant-garde experimentation. The "jazz tradition" (to use the title of Martin Williams's influential book) is an internally consistent art form, distinct from other twentieth-century American music (to say nothing of the European art music tradition) and governed by its own logic.

This assumption places clear constraints on historical inquiry. If one accepts "jazz" as the overarching framework, the question of bebop's origins recedes to the more delimited (and manageable) problem of *transition* from one phase of jazz to another—as the title of another book

puts it, from "swing to bop." Not surprisingly, this view of history privileges continuity over discontinuity. Although the distinctive identity of
each jazz style cannot be entirely glossed over, resemblances must take
precedence over differences if jazz is to cohere as a whole. The process of
change that links these styles is seen as a gradual, linear evolution, con-
serving essential qualities even as it introduces innovations, thus continually affirming the integrity of the whole.

In contrast, consider the trope of *revolution:* bebop as a rejection of
the status quo, a sharp break with the past that ushers in something
genuinely new—in a word, discontinuity. This aspect of bebop, so evident in the phrase "the bebop revolution," seems to contradict the
evolutionary flow of the jazz tradition. Yet any disjunction may be accounted for by the rhetoric of modernism, which by its insistence on the
necessity of ongoing, radical innovation suggests that the process of
growth in an artistic tradition is likely to be punctuated by many such
"revolutions."

Characteristically, however, the revolutionary qualities of bop are sit-
uated not within but outside the jazz tradition, in the collision between
jazz as an artistic endeavor and the social forces of commerce and race.
Thus, bebop is often construed as a protest against commercialism:
through the uncompromising complexity of their art, bop musicians are
said to have asserted their creative independence from the marketplace.
Bebop is also frequently cast in explicitly racial terms: as a movement by
young African-American musicians (Parker, Gillespie, Monk) seeking to
create an idiom expressive of the black subculture, not the white mainstream. While separable, these themes of revolution tend to intertwine
as a rebellion by black musicians against a white-controlled capitalist
hegemony.

There are thus two quite different avenues to understanding bebop as
a historical phenomenon. The evolutionary approach is widely favored
by critics, music scholars, musicians—indeed, all whose primary focus is
on music itself, and for whom bebop lies at the core of the "jazz tradition."
Those who prefer instead to see music as evidence of broader social or
political currents in American culture tend to find the trope of revolution
a more congenial and powerful mode of explanation.

My purpose is not to try to resolve this apparent contradiction. Instead,
I hope to open up avenues of interpretation that move beyond the limiting simplifications of "evolution" and "revolution." In this introductory
chapter I examine each approach in turn as a useful starting point for a
deeper exploration of the social and musical meanings of bebop.

Organicism and the Jazz Tradition

Like most pedagogical simplifications, the concept of a jazz tradition seems natural, even inevitable—more common-sense description than theoretical abstraction. As a model for historical narrative, it is accepted virtually without question as the paradigm that defines the field. Anthologies like the *Smithsonian Collection of Classic Jazz* (a chronologically arranged collection of exemplary recordings judiciously balanced between pre- and post-bop styles), jazz textbooks, and the college survey courses they support—all embody a vision of jazz that, in the words of a jazz critic from the 1940s, extends "across the time and space of twentieth-century America, and back into the roots of African culture."

Yet any historical narrative as sweeping as the line that links the ur-jazz of New Orleans with avant-garde experimentation is necessarily vulnerable to fragmentation. Such a narrative links musics that are radically different in musical techniques and social circumstances, while excluding other musics on constantly shifting and emotionally charged grounds. Its forging has been a noisy process, characterized by bitter disputes pitting advocates of one vision of jazz against another, of which the tumultuous reception of bebop during the latter half of the 1940s is but one example.[1] If peace now reigns and the very idea of rejecting bebop as jazz, as the French critic Hugues Panassié continued to do as late as the 1960s, seems improbable, that is not because bebop has satisfied some a priori claim to be called "jazz," but because the definitions currently in circulation have been shaped in bebop's image.

The challenge of writing a coherent history of jazz has always been to prevent this fragile consensus from shattering under the pressure of internecine debate. The usual strategy is to retreat from the contentious world of historical particularity into the security of abstractions and essences—forces such as the evolution of style that seemingly operate outside human agency and ambition.

As with so much writing on the arts, jazz writing is permeated by the metaphor of organicism, conceiving of art forms as living entities. Like a great tree, the art form matures and branches out through impulses internal to itself. The proper focus of historical study is the art form itself, which acts as its own explanatory force. "Jazz" is an essence that "maintains its identity throughout the vicissitudes of change, thereby guar-

---

1. My argument here is drawn in large part from my article "Constructing the Jazz Tradition: Jazz Historiography" (DeVeaux 1991).

anteeing an unbroken continuity that prevents our picture of the past from disintegrating into unrelated fragments." To search for this essence, then, one looks not at any one style or cultural or historical context, but for that which binds all these things into a seamless continuum. The disparate styles must be understood not as isolated expressions of particular times and places, but as organically connected, as branches of a tree—the individual parts relating more to each other than to the world outside of art. The process of growth is ineffable, internal, and curiously static: the variegated manifestation over the course of time of a central, unchanging essence.

Can this essence be defined? Such a question is typically parried with mystification—"If you've got to ask, you'll never know." But semantic ambiguity is a necessary consequence of a historical narrative that swallows so much territory. There is no single workable definition of *jazz*, no single list of essential characteristics. Attempts to base a definition even on such seemingly unassailable musical fundamentals as improvisation and "swing" inevitably founder. Exceptions overwhelm and trivialize the rule. All that remains is the principle of continuity itself—the unbroken evolutionary succession of musical styles from turn-of-the-century New Orleans to the present. The writing of jazz history is accordingly obsessed with continuity and consensus, even—perhaps *especially*—when the historical record suggests disruption and dissent.

Nowhere is the disparity between the smooth certitude of evolutionary narrative and the "noise" (to use the French cultural critic Jacques Attali's term) of upheaval that signals social and cultural change clearer than in the jazz of the mid-1940s. If any movement in jazz can be said to reflect and embody the political tensions of its time, the aspirations, frustrations, and subversive sensibilities of an elite group of African-American musicians, it is bebop. "We were the first generation to rebel," remembers pianist Hampton Hawes, "Playing bebop, trying to be different, going through a lot of changes and getting strung out in the process. *What these crazy niggers doin' playin' that crazy music?* Wild. Out of the jungle."

But in many histories of jazz, the turmoil that accompanied bebop is almost reflexively subordinated to the seamless unfolding of musical style. Even the most radical departures from previous practice can be celebrated as an affirmation of a larger continuity—in a word, *tradition*. The following excerpt from a best-selling jazz textbook may be more blatant in this regard than most, but it is not unrepresentative:

Modern jazz did not burst upon the jazz scene as a revolution. It developed gradually through the work of swing era tenor saxophonists Lester Young and Don Byas, pianists Art Tatum and Nat Cole, trumpeter Roy Eldridge, guitarist Charlie Christian, the Count Basie rhythm section, bassist Jimmy Blanton, and others. Parker and Gillespie themselves began their careers playing improvisations in a swing era style. They expanded on this music and gradually incorporated new techniques; their work eventually became recognized as a different style, which, though departing appreciably from swing era approaches, was still linked to the swing era. Rather than being a reaction *against* swing style, modern jazz developed smoothly *from* swing styles.

This approach begs the question: if the birth of modern jazz was the result of a gradual and altogether unexceptionable progression of musical style, why was it *perceived* as revolution? Some explanations emphasize the vagaries of circumstance—the cultural static that garbled communication between musicians faithfully laboring within their tradition and the public. The war, for instance: youthful jazz fans called overseas after Pearl Harbor missed out on the crucial intervening developments (the "gradual incorporation" of "new techniques") and failed to recognize the continuity of the new jazz style on their return. Those at home were stymied by the ban on recording called by the musicians' union in mid-1942 (see chapter 8), which effectively blocked the production of new recordings for nearly two years.

But the bebop furor need not be chalked up entirely to poor logistics. Paradoxically, the perception of revolution can be seen as the natural by-product of evolution. The pace of evolutionary growth demanded of jazz at this juncture proved too brisk for the average listener to understand. As bebop "spurted beyond" received categories of style, its rightful audience was left gasping for breath. "Although the beginnings of bop can be traced back quite a way," explained Marshall Stearns in a 1958 book that traced jazz from its African roots to the most up-to-date expressions, "the new style evolved with terrifying suddenness."

This headlong pace is typical for twentieth-century modernisms—a point critics sympathetic to the new movement did not hesitate to make in bebop's favor. Developments in the European sphere provided a handy frame of reference. "Any contemporary style, whether that of a James Joyce or an Arnold Schönberg, remains controversial, and bebop is no exception," explained Ross Russell in 1948. This line of argument was not especially new: as Bernard Gendron has recently noted, the criteria by which jazz would be promoted as a modernist art form for decades to come had already been shaped by the "battle of jazz ancients and moderns" in the early 1940s, a noisy dispute that pitted defenders of New Orleans jazz against "progressive" swing music.[2] Bebop was simply the latest and most obvious wave of newness for jazz fans to absorb.

The artistic novelty of bop was such that its defenders felt obligated to educate audiences to shoulder their responsibilities as consumers of modern art. To the disgruntled or skeptical, they did not hesitate to point out that a studied disregard for audience sensibilities is the modern artist's prerogative. "The critics and jazz amateurs," noted Russell imperiously, "should bear in mind that it is not they but the working musicians who create jazz and authorize style changes."

Such high-handed mystification, ruling out any grounds for objection by the laity, only underscores the widening gulf between artist and audience. Bebop may well have been, in a narrow musical sense, a logical and seamless continuation of swing, but the consequence of musical innovation seems to have been social disruption. After all, jazz enjoyed no privileged status as high art before 1945. As a music created for immediate consumption through commercial channels, it had depended directly upon audience approval. Suddenly, with bebop, the terms of the relationship seem reversed: artists, acting on their own initiative, force radical and disorienting innovations upon a reluctant and bewildered audience, in this way guaranteeing a minority role in American culture for jazz as "avant-garde" art.

Is this an accurate representation of bebop? If so, what can account for this dramatic reversal? The answers to these questions depend very much on one's assumptions about the normal functioning of art in a capitalist economy.

Jazz and Commercialism: Improvisers in the Marketplace

The "jazz tradition" focuses on works of art: in this case, musical performances made permanent through the twentieth-century miracle of recording. While it is theoretically possible to write a history that restricts

2. Gendron argues that the "discursive formation" that resulted from this war of words in the early 1940s—the "concepts, distinctions, oppositions, rhetorical ploys, and allowable inferences, which as a whole fixed the limits within which inquiries concerning the aesthetics of jazz could take place, and without which the claim that jazz is an art form would be merely an abstraction or an incantation"—was adopted, consciously or unconsciously, by sympathetic critics wishing to make the case for bebop (1995, 34).

itself to aesthetic products (i.e., the development of musical language and style), few would find such a skein of abstractions to their liking. Instead, we seek linkages between the works of art and their creators—such jazz musicians as Louis Armstrong, Duke Ellington, and Charlie Parker. We celebrate, literally, these musicians' *authority:* their ability to create artworks that embody their expressive intent, and their freedom to do so without interference from external restraints. We treat them, in short, as composers. The parallel with European art music is obvious. A recent jazz textbook bluntly sums up the prevailing critical strategy: "Jazz is a classical music, and improvising jazz musicians are, in fact, composers."

Yet this assessment is at odds with the cold realities of modern capitalism. With few exceptions (Ellington being the most obvious), jazz musicians have not primarily been composers but "mere" performers—a status several notches lower in economic and social prestige. The issue here is not intrinsic artistic worth: the accomplishments of an Armstrong or a Parker are beyond question. But in a music industry designed to funnel profits to the owners of copyrights, improvisers have found themselves in an anomalous and frustrating position. The history of jazz can be read, in part, as an attempt by determined musicians to close the gap between artistic ambition and economic reward.

We tend to take for granted the division of labor that separates composer from performer. In a recent survey of American music, for example, the musicologist Richard Crawford outlines the economics of music-making in this way: "All pieces of music must be created in the first place, and musical creation is the province of the *composer.* Before a composer's music can be experienced, someone must sing or play it, and that's the province of the *performer.*" The composer, in other words, is given creative priority ("pieces of music must be created in the first place") and ownership ("a composer's music"). The performer is an intermediary, a "productive laborer" (to use the Marxist jargon) whose skill is called into play because the published score is not itself musical sound, but only a legally certified blueprint to be realized according to the composer's intentions.

This division of labor, however, does not characterize all music-making. Many music cultures around the world have not placed this kind of weight on the social category of composer—if, indeed, they recognize it at all. Nobody knows who first created the ballad "Barbara Allen," or a North Indian raga, or the intricate repertory of West African drumming ensembles. Such knowledge is irrelevant. Creative priority and ownership of music are not reserved for any one individual, but are placed in the hands of all who perform it.

The ethnomusicologist John Chernoff, probing into the musical history of the Dagbambas of Ghana, once asked a venerable *dondon* drummer who had introduced a particular genre. The response was a carefully considered paradox: "Any time you hear a dondon beater beating, and someone is dancing, then you must know that the dondon beater introduced the playing. He is the one who introduced the beating of the drum." The concept of composer has little weight in such societies because music is evanescent, subject to continuous change—even for musicians who understand themselves to be playing the "same" piece. "If an old man says that at the time they were drumming, the beat was good," the drummer continued, "I don't know what the beat was at that time, so I feel that what we are doing at present is good. And in the future they will feel that what they are doing is better than what we have been doing now. That is what will keep on happening."

The Western notion of composer is made possible only by the characteristically Western technology of music notation: a system of symbols for capturing music on the printed page specifically designed to remove music from the flux of orality. Notation imposes upon music the idea of a permanent text to which authorship can safely be ascribed and ownership securely established. Such fixity is a necessary precursor to commodification. As early as the sixteenth century, the invention of music printing transformed music into a fungible commodity, paving the way for its mass production and distribution. The intervening centuries have seen the systematic exploitation of this market for composed music, resulting in a specialized economy of music that has at times quite overshadowed the customary service-for-hire basis for performance.

The oral tradition of continuous re-creation of music has by no means disappeared, however. Even within European art music, which over the course of the nineteenth century gradually but emphatically established the principle that the author's intentions as embodied in print are to be strictly obeyed, performers have considerable autonomy. Their work is known as interpretation, but it is better understood as co-creation. In the popular sphere, the relationship between score and performance in the early years of jazz was even more hypothetical. Authors and publishers in the early twentieth century controlled only the rights to reproduction, not performance. As long as the sheet music sold briskly, they did not care that a published song would be realized very differently by fumbling amateurs, lucky to play it straight, and charismatic professionals, capable of making the song "their own."

It is to this latter sphere, of course, that jazz has always belonged. Although jazz musicians may avail themselves of notation, they are not bound by it. Their performance of copyrighted material often departs so radically from the legally recognized text that it is known by a different name: not *interpretation*, but *improvisation*.

Improvisation is typically set apart from both composition and the performance of composed music, as if this mode of creation were somehow peculiarly anomalous. But upon more careful consideration, these distinctions erode. The ethnomusicologist Bruno Nettl has argued that "we must abandon the idea of improvisation as a process separate from composition and adopt the view that all performers improvise to some extent. What the pianist playing Bach and Beethoven does with his models—the scores and the accumulated tradition of performance practice—is only in degree, not in nature, different from what the Indian playing an alap in *Rag Yaman* and the Persian singing the *Dastagh* of *Shur* do with theirs."

Similarly, one might say that what distinguishes improvisation from composition in a modern capitalist economy is that the improviser, almost by definition, renounces the intention of transmuting creativity into published commodity. Improvisation is process, not product. It is a way of reasserting creative autonomy within the normally circumscribed role of the performer, but without pursuing the rewards and privileges available to creators who become composers.

Except, of course, for recording. With the widespread introduction of recording technology into the popular market in the first decades of the twentieth century, music sound itself became a tangible object. In the process, the nuances of performance—which included African-American techniques of timbral variation, pitch bending, and swing as well as European rubato and expressive phrasing—could finally be made permanent. This had the potential to greatly expand the reach and prestige of the performer. In particular, recordings made possible the rise of the improvising jazz soloist, whose powers of on-the-spot creation are so compelling that the copyrighted music nominally performed seems to recede into irrelevance. As Evan Eisenberg has argued, "records not only disseminated jazz, but inseminated it . . . in some ways they created what we now call jazz."

But while recording (and radio) helped to make some performers famous, it did not necessarily make them rich. Even as sheet music steadily lost ground to recordings in the marketplace, economic power remained stubbornly in the grip of music publishers, who insisted (with the help of copyright law) that all financial benefits to creativity must flow to officially recognized composers. Since royalties for performance per se were relatively rare (contracts typically dictated a modest one-time fee), "mere" performers saw very little of this money, unless they somehow managed simultaneously to claim the role of composer. As before, most of their income came from the daily grind of live performance. Although improvising musicians began to win aesthetic acclaim for their work, they continued to strive for comparable economic reward well into the bebop era.

Moreover, the new technologies only deepened performers' involvement with and dependence upon the burgeoning popular music industry. As recording and radio systematically interposed themselves between performer and audience, musicians had no choice but to try to gain access to this highly centralized, capital-intensive technology. Such access was granted only on terms favorable to the industry. In practice, this often meant that the musicians most fully integrated within the system yielded control not only over repertory—over what tunes could be recorded and broadcast—but also over the way they performed them. Conversely, those who insisted on determining their own fate regularly found themselves pushed to the periphery. This ongoing struggle—between musicians' desire for artistic and economic autonomy and the logic of centralized control of mass-market capitalism—determined the dynamics of the emergence of bebop and gave rise to the commonplace perception of bebop (and jazz in general) as anticommercial.

One of the most striking aspects of the writing on jazz is a reluctance to relate the history of the music to the messy and occasionally sordid economic circumstances of its production. Not that this absence necessarily reflects ignorance of the subject. Many of the most prolific proselytizers for jazz—Leonard Feather, Martin Williams, Dan Morgenstern, Stanley Dance, John Hammond, Gene Lees, Gunther Schuller—have been intimately familiar with the business side of music, having observed jazz not as disinterested scholars but, variously, as journalists and editors for the trade press, publicists, concert promoters, record producers, writers of liner notes, and composers. These experiences, however, seem to have made them more determined than ever to present jazz as something other than a form of entertainment music shaped by mass consumer preferences: in short, as an autonomous art form (the "jazz tradition"). And if jazz is an art, subject to its own aesthetic principles and laws of development rather than to forces of the marketplace, it follows that its creators are (or ought to be) similarly high-minded, pursuing their artistic vision in serene disregard of commercial considerations.

This perspective underlies one of the most persistent themes in writing about jazz: the demonizing of "commercialism" as a corrupting influence. Thus the jazz historian Rudi Blesh declared in 1946: "Commercialism [is] a cheapening and deteriorative force, a species of murder perpetrated on a wonderful music by whites and by those misguided negroes who, for one or another reason, chose to be accomplices to the deed. . . . Commercialism is a thing not only hostile, but fatal to [jazz]."

Such heated rhetoric was especially popular with atavistic defenders of New Orleans–style jazz who, like Blesh, narrowly identified jazz with a romanticized notion of folk culture, untouched by commodity capitalism. But ultimately it mattered little whether jazz was labeled "folk" or "art." In either case it was claimed as an intrinsically separate sphere, staked out by those who dauntlessly resisted the crass manipulations of the mass market.

Indeed, the anticommercial stance proved particularly congenial to champions of jazz as a form of modernism. All modernist art forms stoutly declare their independence from the marketplace and zealously patrol their borders with mass culture. The more blurred the boundaries, the greater the effort required to maintain them. And no one can deny that in the early years of jazz, the boundaries were very blurred indeed. "The very omnipresence of the jazz element in American popular music, and especially dance and show music, after the First World War meant that for most Americans it had no precise location or independent existence," notes the historian Eric Hobsbawm. Jazz "was . . . so deeply embedded in popular entertainment in the cities of the U.S. that it was almost impossible to separate it out as a special kind of art." By the height of the Swing Era in the late 1930s, when jazz (or swing) had become clearly visible to at least a determined minority as both an artistic activity and the object of cultish enthusiasm, the ties that bound jazz musicians to the networks of the culture industry were even more obvious.

Envisioning jazz as a privileged sphere necessitated a heroic effort by critics to lift it forcibly from this context, to reassert its autonomy in the face of co-optation. Hence the shrill rhetoric that occasionally surfaced in the defense of bebop. Bebop could not claim the mantle of folk purity, but it could be said to carry on the fight against commercialism on its own terms. When bebop was itself attacked by conservative critics as shallow intellectual posturing masquerading as jazz, its advocates depicted it as the latest phase in the ongoing battle to fight the encroachment of popular culture:

> The story of bop, like that of swing before it, like the stories of jazz and ragtime before that, has been one of constant struggle against the restrictions imposed on all progressive thought in an art that has been commercialized to the point of prostitution.
>
> The war against the horrible products of the tunesmiths, which began with Fletcher Henderson in the 1920's, has been brought to a successful conclusion only by the beboppers. . . .
> Bebop is the music of revolt: revolt against big bands, arrangers, vertical harmonies, soggy rhythms, non-playing orchestra leaders, Tin Pan Alley—against commercialized music in general. It reasserts the individuality of the jazz musician as a creative artist, playing spontaneous and melodic music within the framework of jazz, but with new tools, sounds, and concepts.

The contrast in tone with Blesh's pronouncement is significant. Much of the early anticommercial rhetoric in jazz has a distinctly resigned and elegiac undercurrent, as if the efforts to reconstitute a folk music that had already been corroded by several decades of ruinous exposure to commodity capitalism were doomed to futility. Bebop, by contrast, is seen as heroic, affirmative, and deeply rooted in notions of progress. "What [Charlie] Parker and bebop provided," asserts Martin Williams, "was a renewed musical language . . . with which the old practices could be replenished and continued."

In many accounts of the circumstances leading to bebop, commercialism plays an important, if curiously passive, role. By the early 1940s, the story goes, jazz had reached an impasse. The reigning jazz style, swing, had become "threadbare" and "aging," a "harmonic and melodic blind alley" incapable of further development, a formulaic popular music undergoing "death by entropy," a "richly decked-out palace that was soon going to be a prison," a "billion-dollar rut."

These metaphors, sampled from the secondary literature, echo what the musicologist Leo Treitler has identified as the "crisis theory" of twentieth-century European music. Textbook after textbook imputes the eruptions of modernity in classical music at the beginning of the century

(Arnold Schoenberg, Igor Stravinsky) to the stubborn failure of musical style to move decisively beyond the language of tonality that had become worn out from overuse in the nineteenth century. Something similar is implied about jazz in the early 1940s. Musicians should have moved on to the next step, extending the rhythmic, harmonic, and melodic language of jazz in directions plainly indicated by the music itself. Their failure to do so built up the pressure that resulted in an eruption of a new musical modernism.

But as phrases like "billion-dollar rut" clearly suggest, the real culprit is commercialism—the commingling of art and commerce that for a time allowed swing to be both an authentic jazz expression and a lucrative national fad. Even after the swing style had run its course, the machinery of the popular music industry continued to prop up the "threadbare" and "aging" idiom, seducing musicians into going through the motions long after they had any legitimate artistic reason to do so. In other words, mass-market capitalism contributed to a logjam in the path of musical evolution, which could be removed only by explosive force. Bebop provided the resolution to this crisis. It was, in Leonard Feather's words, a "new branch of jazz . . . born of the desire for progress and evolution."

Bebop thus figures as a crucial moment of definition. In the telling of the story of jazz, there is an implicit entelechy in the progress from New Orleans through swing to bebop: the gradual shedding of its associations with dance, popular song, and entertainment; the dawning awareness by musicians and audience alike that jazz could aspire to greater things. Bebop is the logical culmination of this process—the moment at which jazz became "art," declaring its autonomy by severing once and for all its ties to commercial culture. Once this goal is clearly in view, the temptation to cast the entire history of jazz to midcentury as the story of its inexorable realization is irresistible.

So important a goal could not have been achieved by accident. It must have been the conscious aim of those in the best position to effect the necessary changes: the creators of bebop themselves. Such, at least, is the conclusion of one musicologist in a widely distributed jazz textbook: "Bebop musicians were trying to raise the quality of jazz from the level of utilitarian dance music to that of a chamber art form. At the same time, they were trying to raise the status of the jazz performer from entertainer to artist."

One can certainly agree that bebop musicians were trying to do *some-*

thing. But should they be counted among the charter members of the effort to legitimize jazz as art? We ought to keep in mind that the subsequent success of this effort has understandably influenced our perspective. A half century after the birth of bebop, the status of jazz as an art form has been affirmed by such august entities as the National Endowment for the Arts, Lincoln Center, and numerous degree-granting institutions. As such, jazz has joined its well-heeled European cousins, "classical" music and opera, as a nonprofit enterprise regularly vying for private and public subsidy on the grounds that it is incapable of surviving in the open market.

The insistence that bebop is anticommercial may well continue to suit the needs of contemporary jazz discourse. (Apart from its usefulness for fund-raising, one may cynically note that an image of artistic incorruptibility helps to boost sales.) But it is a singularly poor basis for historical inquiry. It idealizes the circumstances of artistic creation and asks us to repress the unpleasant reality that, as the cultural critic Andrew Ross reminds us, "commercial and contractual relations enter into *all* realms of musical entertainment, or at least wherever music is performed in order to make a living." One may well ask: Were the creators of bebop so disdainful of their lot as "utilitarian" dance musicians? Were they so convinced of the desirability or the necessity—to say nothing of the possibility—of aspiring to the nebulous status of "artist"?

I argue that they were not. For the black jazz musicians of the 1930s and 1940s who are at the center of this book, mass-market capitalism was not a prison from which the true artist is duty-bound to escape. It was a system of transactions that defined music as a profession and thereby made their achievements possible. One need not romanticize the exploitative aspect of the music industry to see that it served as an extraordinary mechanism for social and economic advancement, especially for African Americans. For musicians who saw themselves first and foremost as *professionals,* such advancement was a necessary prerequisite (or corequisite) to artistic achievement.

A good deal of this book is accordingly devoted to economic issues— not as something external to the process of musical change, but as an essential component of it. To understand bebop, it is necessary to situate its creators within the economic landscape they inherited, inhabited, and hoped to transform. Their professional world was defined by a complex and tightly integrated system of cultural production with the entertaining dance orchestra, or swing band, at its core. Economic pressures, coupled after 1941 by the disruptions of war, painfully constricted some opportunities, while underscoring the urgent need to develop new ones. By 1945 Charlie Parker and Dizzy Gillespie had indeed willed something like a new musical subculture into being. But they were not trying to disengage from the "commercial" music world so much as to find a new point of engagement with it—one that would grant them a measure of autonomy and recognition.

But this is only half the argument—as I have already let on by specifying "*black* jazz musicians" as the focus of this study. Economic issues are inseparable from the issue of race: a topic no less contentious, no less pervasive, and no less central to an understanding of bebop.

Bebop and Race

What role should race be assigned in the history of jazz? Few doubt that jazz is in some fundamental sense an African-American music; the consensus on this point is a common ground for various historical narratives that otherwise diverge sharply in their assumptions, approaches, and interpretations. But ethnicity remains an inherently slippery, not to say controversial, issue. Jazz is a music that lies squarely on the fault line of race relations. From the beginning it has counted among its practitioners white musicians as well as black. It has thrived by satisfying the tastes of the larger and vastly more affluent white audience as well as the black community. How one construes the importance of race for the historical development of the music is not simply a matter of marshaling the evidence: it depends very much on who is speaking and what that speaker wants to prove.

Within the jazz tradition, the ethnicity of jazz—its "blackness"—is primarily a way of positioning it as an art form with unique and internally consistent features. The musical techniques that set jazz apart from European art music are precisely those that derive from black American musical folkways (and ultimately from Africa): swing, call-and-response patterns, vocalized timbre, "blue notes," improvisation, and so forth. These qualities can be identified and analyzed in and of themselves, but they are also deeply embedded within the historical narrative: histories of jazz typically begin not with its putative origins in New Orleans but with the rich context of blues, spirituals, and work songs in the late nineteenth century, underscoring the connections between an ageless black folk aesthetic and the nascent art form. These musical markers of ethnicity are usually treated as *essentials:* they are part of jazz's development but are *not themselves subject to development.* Their presence throughout all the varied manifestations of jazz is a guarantee of authenticity. Conversely, their absence is a warning sign: music that doesn't swing, isn't improvised, and bears no obvious influence of the blues is in danger of being read out of the jazz tradition altogether.

But what is the relationship between this ethnically derived musical language and the musicians who play it? If musical technique resides in the realm of culture, not genetics, the two are separable. It should be possible for anyone with the requisite determination, sensitivity, and talent to master the distinctive nuances of jazz. "A note don't care who plays it—whether you're black, white, green, brown, or opaque," trumpet player Clark Terry has been quoted as saying, echoing a commonly voiced belief in the independence of music from petty, divisive racial politics.

This faith in the separability of the essential "black" musical qualities of jazz from the *political* circumstances of those who create it is the basis of the consensus liberalism that pervades so much historical jazz writing. One may readily grant that jazz is an ethnic music, deeply rooted in black traditions; that its most important innovators have been black; and that subsequent innovators may continue to be black, if only because mastery of ethnic nuance comes more easily to those absorbing it from birth. But the rapid spread of jazz away from its initial racial base, encompassing not only white Americans but Europeans, Latin Americans, and Asians, has suggested to many a transformation from a provincial folk expression to an art form with universal appeal. In the process of becoming a modern art, jazz ceases to be exclusively, or even primarily, an African-American music. It is, instead, "America's classical music"—a category into which racial difference and the political turmoil it entails finally disappear.

Bebop seems to affirm this view. At first glance, it is an unassailably African-American phenomenon. Even James Lincoln Collier, who has stridently attacked the automatic tendency to identify jazz with African-American culture, readily concedes the black character of the revolution: "Black musicians dominated bop in a way that they had not dominated other forms of jazz since the early days in New Orleans. Black musicians devised the music without any help from whites, and they were its stars for a considerable period thereafter: Parker, Gillespie, Thelonious Monk, Bud Powell, and somewhat later, Fats Navarro, Clifford Brown, and Sonny Stitt were the quintessential boppers and they were all black." When one considers that bebop emerged against the background of the Swing Era, a time in which jazz-oriented white dance bands flooded the marketplace and Benny Goodman was crowned King of Swing, the racial quality of the bop movement is all the more striking.

Yet the bebop pioneers seemed unmotivated by racial exclusivity. Quite the contrary: Dizzy Gillespie and Charlie Parker made a point of hiring white musicians for some of the earliest bop bands. Admittedly, George Wallington, Stan Levey, and Al Haig are peripheral figures, but their very presence in otherwise all-black bands was a powerful statement—a deliberate breaching of the artificial barriers imposed by segregation. By admitting whites into the inner circle, Parker and Gillespie affirmed music to be a meritocracy rather than a racial privilege. If the initial creative impulse for bebop was rooted in an ethnic sensibility, musicians of both races quickly mastered the style, making it possible for Leonard Feather, writing in 1960, to assert the ultimate irrelevance of race: "As soon as the rigid segregation under which [black jazz musicians] had lived began to relax, it became clear that given a freer interchange of ideas anyone could play jazz, according to his environment, his ability and his value as an individual, not as white or Negro."

The explosive potential of race—its capacity to divide rather than to unite—is not entirely purged from this optimistic, color-blind narrative, however. One need only consider the implications of the process by which (to quote Feather again) "jazz, originally the music of the American Negro and the American white, now simply the music of the American, will become more than ever a music of the human being." To attain this transcendent universality, jazz must abandon its origins in a particular subculture. It must exchange an idiosyncratic provincialism ("[jazz] stemmed from a specific social environment, originally conditioned by slavery, in which a group of people largely shut off from the white world developed highly personal cultural traits") for the abstractions of style and technique, available to all.

Is this development both inevitable and welcome—a gift from black Americans to the world? Or is the exchange more sinister? Is it, in fact, an act of theft—yet another instance of the co-optation of black creativity in the interests of white hegemony that Amiri Baraka has called "the Great Music Robbery"? The bland assertion that jazz has become "America's classical music," Baraka argues, carries

> no warm welcome of blacks as full citizens into the American mainstream (complete with democracy and forty acres and a mule). No, this late mumbling is another attempt to deny the peoplehood and the lives and history of black Americans. . . .
>
> There can be no inclusion as "Americans" without full equality, and no legitimate disappearance of black music into the covering sobriquet "American," without consistent recognition of the history, tradition, and current needs of the black majority, its culture, and its creations.

And, by extension, there can be no history of jazz that does not take fully into account how deeply bound up the music is in the political implications of ethnicity—the gross imbalance in power relations between the races that has kept black Americans from enjoying the full citizenship nominally guaranteed them by law.

No serious advocate for jazz needs a lecture on these painful realities, least of all the white critics and historians who labored on behalf of the music in the years before the civil rights revolution. To insist on the dignity and inherent worth of the black expressive arts was in itself a risky political act in the 1940s and 1950s. Most writers, to their credit, went much further. Feather included a chapter on "Jazz and Race" in *The Book of Jazz*, detailing the head beatings and petty humiliations that still beset famous black musicians in the late 1950s. Potential jazz fans were offered this depressing litany on the grounds that "no study of jazz can be complete without a consideration of the socio-racial factors that determined the associations and the frustrations of the men who created it."

The point of this exercise, however, is not to connect the expressive power of the music to oppressive social conditions, but to exorcise them so that the rest of the book may be safely devoted to the development of musical language. Far from being bound up in the creative act, "socio-racial factors" remain in Feather's reading inherently external to it. They are obstacles to free expression, not causes; the role of art is to transcend them.

Bebop and Revolution

By way of contrast, consider the account of the genesis of bebop given by Langston Hughes. It takes the form of a dialogue with his fictional Harlem man-on-the-street, Jess B. Semple. "Simple," as he is known, is first spotted wildly scat-singing to a bebop recording on the stoop of his Harlem apartment. When upbraided by his nameless interlocutor for the patent meaninglessness of his "nonsense syllables," Simple reacts testily:

> "You must not know where Bop comes from," said Simple, astonished at my ignorance.
> "I do not know," I said. "Where?"
> "From the police," said Simple.
> "What do you mean, from the police?"
> "From the police beating Negroes' heads," said Simple. "Every time a cop hits a Negro with his billy club, that old club says, 'BOP! BOP! ... BE-

BOP! ... MOP! ... BOP! ... ' That's where Be-Bop came from, beaten right out of some Negro's head into those horns and saxophones and the piano keys that play it. ....

"That's why so many white folks don't dig Bop," said Simple. "White folks do not get their heads beat *just for being white*. But me—a cop is liable to grab me almost any time and beat my head—*just* for being colored.

"In some parts of this American country as soon as the polices see me, they say, 'Boy, what are you doing in this neighborhood?'

"I say, 'Coming from work, sir.'

"They say, 'Where do you work?'

"Then I have to go into my whole pedigree because I am a black man in a white neighborhood. And if my answers do not satisfy them, BOP! MOP! ... BE-BOP! If they do not hit me, they have already hurt my soul. *A dark man shall see dark days*. Bop comes out of them dark days. That's why real Bop is mad, wild, frantic, crazy—and not to be dug unless you've seen dark days, too. Folks who ain't suffered much cannot play Bop, neither appreciate it. They think Bop is nonsense—like you. They think it's just *crazy* crazy. They do not know Bop is also MAD crazy, SAD crazy, FRANTIC WILD CRAZY—beat out of somebody's head! That's what Bop is. Them young colored kids who started it, they know what Bop is."

Amiri Baraka (then LeRoi Jones) was a "young colored kid" in Newark when a cousin brought over a stack of new recordings to his house. "They were Guilds, Manors, Savoys," he recalls, "with groups like Charlie Parker's Reboppers, Max Roach and the BeBop Boys, Stan Getz, Dizzy Gillespie's 'Pooopapadow,' 'Hot House,' 'Ornithology,' 'The Lady in Red,' and waboppadapaDam! my world had changed!! I listened to BeBop after school, over and over. At first it was strange and the strangeness itself was strangely alluring. BeBop! I listened and listened." Gradually, the sounds began to take on meaning:

BeBop. A new language a new tongue and vision for a generally more advanced group in our generation. BeBop was a staging area for a new sensibility growing to maturity. And the BeBoppers themselves were blowing the sound to attract the growing, the developing, the about-to-see. Sometimes even the players was carrying about the end of another epoch as they understood it. Though they knew they was making change, opening a door, cutting underbrush and heavy vines away to make a path. And where would that path lead? That was the real question. It is the real question of each generation. Where will the path you've shown us lead? And who will take it?

The path, Baraka concluded years later, led to revolution: a radical transformation of American society with black activists, their revolutionary awareness awakened by the clarion call of bebop, in the vanguard. That revolution has still not come. As of this writing, Baraka is still waiting for the "single upward stroke to socialism" that will finally set to right the injustices suffered by African Americans under a white-dominated capitalist system. But bebop, according to his analysis, was created in the consciousness, however inchoate, of the revolution to come.

In this sense, Baraka's interpretation of bebop corresponds more closely to the concept of the "historical avant-garde" analyzed by the theorist Peter Bürger than to the high modernism of the jazz tradition. The terms *modernism* and *avant-garde* are often used interchangeably with reference to the radical innovations of twentieth-century art, and both have been applied to bebop.[3] But modernism, in Bürger's reading, is by definition disengaged from social relations. Although its continuous and rigorous attack on artistic convention strongly suggests a stance of alienation from society and antagonism toward its audience, modernism nevertheless accepts the place in bourgeois culture that has been reserved for it: an autonomous art carefully segregated from the "praxis of life." The modernist artist content to occupy a separate and privileged sphere has no connection to the world of power relations and is therefore powerless to effect meaningful change.

By contrast, the "historical avant-garde" of the early twentieth century (i.e., such movements as futurism, Dada, and surrealism) actively resisted the totalizing control of bourgeois culture by assaulting the category *art* itself. Exhibiting a urinal with the mock-delicate title *Fountain* and signing it "R. Mutt," or scrawling a mustache on a reproduction of the Mona Lisa (to cite two of the most notorious examples of Marcel Duchamp's shock technique), negates the sanctity of individual artistic creativity at the core of bourgeois notions of art and derides the institutions—galleries, museums, the academy—that support and justify art as a world unto itself.

Bürger's interpretation of the avant-garde has limited applicability to jazz, if only because the black American musician has (until very recently) been granted no privileged position in officially sanctioned culture

3. According to Grover Sales, bebop was "the first genuine avant-garde movement in jazz" (1984, 127). For Bruce Tucker, the creators of bebop were "steeped in the rhetoric of modernist avant-gardism and determined to turn jazz into an art music" (1989, 273). Eric Lott has characterized bebop as "one of the great modernisms" (1995, 249), while Mark Harvey has referred to it as both "the first authentically modern phase in jazz" and "the avant-garde style" (1991, 136, 137).

from which to carry out such an assault. "The substantial distance that has always existed between jazz and high art," Krin Gabbard has argued, "makes the old avant-garde stance unavailable to the contemporary jazz artist." Yet the distinction between an autonomous modernism and a politically engaged avant-garde remains useful in jazz. It takes the form of resistance, not from above but from below—a defiant assertion of ethnic consciousness in the face of efforts by a white-controlled culture industry to co-opt and contain its subversive potential. Baraka wishes to rescue the ethnicity of jazz from domestication as merely the constituent elements of musical language. He offers the example of the reduction of the "life tone and cultural matrix" of the blues to its formal, twelve-bar outline: "Without blues, as interior animation, jazz has no history, no memory. The *funkiness* is the people's lives in North America as slaves, as an oppressed nation, as workers and artists of a particular nationality! To think, as one critic has argued, that the blues is merely a particular twelve-bar form is to think dancing is those footprints in the Fred Astaire newspaper advertisement!"

In this struggle, race is inextricably linked to economics. "Commercialism" is a continual threat to jazz—not to its autonomy as an art music, but to the political and economic power due its black creators. As Andrew Ross has suggested, "a discourse about color ('whitened' music) is spliced with a discourse about commercialization ('alienated' music)" so consistently in writing on American popular music that "it is often assumed that the two are necessarily aligned; that commercialized music = whitened music, that the black performance of uncommercialized and therefore undiluted black music constitutes the only truly genuine form of protest of resistance against the white culture industry and its controlling interests, and that black music which submits to that industry automatically loses its autonomous power."

The thrust of the bop revolution, according to Baraka, was directed not just against white America, but also against those blacks who had yielded their birthright of cultural autonomy in pursuit of the fraudulent goal of assimilation. In his reading, swing was a hopeless dilution, sacrificing whatever connection it may have once had to the lives of the "blues people" for the sake of an illusory commercial success. (That this leaves Duke Ellington, Count Basie, and other black swing musicians in a tenuous position does not seem to trouble Baraka unduly.) Bebop was the antidote: a "willfully harsh, *anti-assimilationist*" music that sought to "restore jazz, in some sense, to its original separateness, to drag it outside the mainstream of American culture again."

The problem with the avant-garde stance is that it is doomed to failure.

The shock of seeing a urinal in an art gallery quickly wears off, its in-your-face gesture absorbed into the narrative of "official" modern art that it was designed to explode. The bebop movement, as Baraka characterizes it, was similarly fraught with internal contradictions, not least of which was the rapidity with which black *and* white musicians eagerly mastered its stance of alienation as well as its musical language. As Ralph Ellison has acerbically noted, "nothing succeeds like rebellion (which [Baraka] as a 'beat' poet should know)." The most visible signs of resistance—the subcultural wardrobe, the impenetrable lingo, the refusal to play the expected role of entertainer—defined a place for bop in the marketplace. "Today the white audience expects the rudeness as part of the entertainment," Ellison points out in an essay originally published in 1958. "If it fails to appear the audience is disappointed."

Indeed, the hoped-for "separateness" of bop falls apart because the "original separateness" of jazz from the entangling web of white-controlled capitalism was an illusion. From the necessity of forming a continuous engagement with the culture industry—recording companies, radio, publishers, booking agents, journalists, critics, historians—there is no escape short of socialist revolution. Perhaps the beboppers were only seeking, as Ellison has suggested, "a fresh form of entertainment which would allow them their fair share of the entertainment market." Otherwise, wondered one black pianist, if the idea was to keep the music out of the hands of white mass culture, "why go to a white recording studio and record it then? . . . The music was progressive, just the minds, the political thinking was a little absurd."

If I have lingered over Baraka's interpretation, it is because his work is one of the few examples of historical explanation not beholden to the narrative of the "jazz tradition," and because (not surprisingly) he gives race its proper place in the unfolding of the music. I am in strong sympathy with his insistence that jazz, and bop in particular, must be viewed through the prism of history. My criticism is with his reading of history, which typically is sketchy, unnuanced, and too transparently a prisoner to ideology.[4]

4. Bebop is crucial not simply to Baraka's vision of the march toward socialist revolution, but to his personal history as well. As John Gennari has noted: "Having grown up with bebop and having derived from it a sense of the possibility of an assertive black male ego, Baraka very much wanted this music to be seen as a threshold in black-white relations, as a cultural fault line marking the distinction between slavery and freedom. Among other

Baraka is at his most persuasive when his discussion of bebop is firmly grounded in historical detail—the ambivalent but highly charged reaction of African Americans to the transition between Depression and war. "Between the thirties and the end of World War II," he writes, "there was perhaps as radical a change in the psychological perspective of the Negro American toward America as there was between the Emancipation and 1930." On the one hand, the war economy widened "the bridge into the mainstream of American society," with tangible advances in income, educational opportunity, and geographic mobility. But these gains only sharpened "the sense of resentment Negroes felt at the social inequities American life continued to impose upon them."

Rising expectations met by intransigent racism, leading to a new sense of militancy: this history lesson is absent from most accounts of bop, which focus instead on the young musicians' supposed grievances about the commercialization of their art. But then, little attention is paid in general to what one historian has called the "forgotten years of the Negro revolution"—the powerful stirring of black political consciousness in the 1940s.

Compared with the achievements of the civil rights revolution of the 1950s and 1960s, the tangible results of wartime activism may seem paltry. A. Philip Randolph's threatened march on Washington in 1941 has been overshadowed by the real march two decades later; race riots in Detroit and Harlem in 1943 have been superseded in memory by the "long hot summers" of the 1960s and Los Angeles in 1992. By contrast, bebop survives as a cultural project that succeeded brilliantly in articulating the mood and energy of its time. "Bebop was intimately if indirectly related to the militancy of its moment," argues the contemporary scholar Eric Lott. "Militancy and music were undergirded by the same social facts; the music attempted to resolve at the level of style what the militancy combatted in the streets."

But what, exactly, constitutes the "intimate if indirect relationship" of music to politics? For while the bebop pioneers and the zoot-suit-wearing rebels of the urban underground shared certain experiences—most notably the arbitrary threat of the white policeman's billyclub—the two groups are by no means identical. This is a distinction that politically sensitized readings of bebop tend to ignore or gloss over. As highly skilled

---

things, this enabled Baraka, at the very moment when he was emerging as a prophetic figure in black letters and politics, to claim a personal history that coincided with a liberationist thrust in the black arts" (1991, 491).

artists, the members of the bebop generation had "raised themselves by their talents and achievements above the level of the ordinary labourers from whom they had sprung." They carved out a professional world that isolated them, physically and psychically, from the mass. The usual attempt to cast them as self-conscious revolutionaries or anarchistic hipsters fails to take into account the unique privilege and distinctive ethos of their profession.

It may be exaggerating to call them, as Ralph Ellison does, "the least political of men." Black entertainers necessarily kept provocative opinions to themselves (unless, like Paul Robeson, they deliberately courted disaster). In private, they were better able to speak their minds. Bassist Milt Hinton remembered lengthy conversations with Charlie Parker "about politics and race and really deep things like the solution for blacks in America." Parker and Dizzy Gillespie shared an admiration for Vito Marcantonio, the fiery radical congressman from Spanish Harlem. Still, Gillespie's sense of political involvement was clearly informed by professional concerns that can only be called parochial: "We liked Marcantonio's ideas because as musicians we weren't paid well at all for what we created."

The bebop musicians' relationship to politics was oblique at best, and certainly very different from that of their counterparts on the street corners. If bop was a revolution, it was hardly a revolution aimed directly at the black masses, who insisted on a music that satisfied their taste for bluesy dance and entertainment.[5] Rhythm and blues, not bebop, became the soundtrack for the urban black experience of the late 1940s and 1950s. If, as the subway graffiti proclaimed on Charlie Parker's death in 1955, "Bird lives," it is not in the streets but in the music studios. Drummer Art Blakey's chilling epitaph for Parker is instructive: "A symbol to the Negro people? No. They don't even know him. They never heard of him and care less. A symbol to the musicians, yes."

5. This is a point that Gerald Early makes even more forcefully in his discussion of the later phase of Louis Armstrong's career. Armstrong, he argues, was doubly isolated by losing both the "finger-popping, "good-timing" black audience to rhythm and blues *and* the young intellectuals to bop. "Bebop musicians, despite their stance as militant, socially aware, artistically uncompromising professionals, were no more in tune with the black masses than the older Armstrong and, in some sense, were probably less so. The beboppers' insistence on seeing themselves as artists and not entertainers pushed them much closer to viewing their cultural function in more European terms. To Armstrong and to the black masses, the concept of the artist and of art as it is generally fixed by Euro-American standards is, quite frankly, incomprehensible. Armstrong saw himself as an entertainer who must, by any means, please his audience. And to the black masses generally there would scarcely be a reason for the public performer to exist if he did not feel that pleasing his audience was the prime directive" (Early 1989, 296–297).

Nevertheless, the "social facts" that sparked the Harlem riots also gave bebop its unmistakable edge of resistance—one that perhaps makes most sense when the successes of music professionals are set against the usual backdrop of frustration and despair. In the latter half of the 1930s, black musicians had good reason to feel optimistic. The triumph of swing held out the tantalizing possibility of a new prosperity in which black talent would play a leading role. Advances were dramatic and tangible: for the next several years the entertainment industry expanded rapidly, providing steady and lucrative employment for a small but influential elite of black musicians—the men who staffed the bands led by Ellington, Lunceford, Basie, and Cab Calloway. Hundreds more entered the profession, eager to be rewarded by a level of material gain, social freedom, and respect from white America that could not even have been imagined a few decades earlier. Within the black community, no single musician enjoyed the prestige of Joe Louis, the heavyweight boxing champion who from 1937 to 1949 literally beat white contenders to their knees. But as a class of skilled professionals who had proved their worth in open competition with their white counterparts, musicians were uniquely positioned to further the cause of black social and economic progress.

All this began to change in the 1940s. As the Swing Era inevitably cooled off, competition stiffened and the underlying inequities of race were felt with renewed force. Entrenched patterns of segregation, both in the music industry and in society at large, automatically gave white musicians a nearly insuperable advantage in the mainstream market, blunting black ambition and forcing it into new channels.

Bebop was a response to this impasse, an attempt to reconstitute jazz—or more precisely, the specialized idiom of the improvising virtuoso—in such a way as to give its black creators the greatest professional autonomy *within* the marketplace. Bop was the twin child of optimism and frustration, of ingenuity and despair.

"People Made Bebop"

Throughout this book I have sought to avoid the tendency either to reduce bebop to a textbook example of stylistic evolution or to represent it as a social upheaval expressed through music. My quarrel with these narratives is not that they fail to address important issues. To the contrary, any analysis of bop that ignores either the nuances of musical language or the political context for its creation is manifestly incomplete. But each approach tends to exclude the other. They operate from different assumptions and cherish their own characteristic modes of discourse—

the smooth evolutionary lines of style history on the one hand, the dialectical confrontations of black nationalism on the other.

There *is* a point, however, at which the apparently irreconcilable lines of the musical and the social meet: the professional musician. It is the day-to-day, year-by-year decisions made by the musicians of the bebop generation in the pursuit of their careers that constitute the real focus of this book. As Amiri Baraka once put it: "People made bebop. The question the critic [or historian] must ask is: *why?*"

If this obvious frame of reference has all too often been overlooked, that is because the usual narratives for jazz history remain largely suprapersonal. To be sure, jazz writing remains fixated on charismatic, idiosyncratic personalities. But beneath the surface of anecdotes, the real agents of change are abstractions to which individual will is subordinated. Even the "Great Man" school of historical writing, with its apparent focus on the individual exercise of genius, falls into this category. When Martin Williams speaks of Charlie Parker being *"called upon"* (like a minister receiving the call to preach) to "change the language of jazz, to reinterpret its fundamentals and give it a way to continue," Parker seems to have no choice in the matter. Or more precisely, questions of choice become irrelevant: had he declined, or proved unfit to the task, the call would have passed down the line to someone else. There is something to this view, of course. Currents in history are often larger than individuals. But the habit of telling history this way sacrifices the complexity and ambiguity of lives lived in a particular historical moment.

Bringing the focus of jazz history back from lofty abstractions to quirky contingencies not only restores a measure of common sense to jazz; it helps to heal the rift between the two main master narratives. For the young black men who created bebop, musical and social issues were not warring abstractions, but conjoined elements of their adult identities. They were, of course, *artists,* and as such enjoyed a degree of autonomy from society. Distinguished from the masses by their special gifts and absorbed with the details of their craft, they carried out their work with a certain disregard for their immediate environment. But at the same time they were *professionals:* ambitious and opportunistic, eager to exchange their specialized skills for monetary advantage in the service of their careers. And their experience as *African Americans* permeated their music as well as every aspect of their personal and professional lives.

My concern in this book is to understand bebop as the result of the decisions these musicians made. Why did the young professionals of the bebop generation choose to abandon swing and create a new musical genre? The answer depends on how the inquiry is framed. If *swing* and *bebop* are reduced to abstract stylistic categories, the transition from one to the other means merely the exchange of one set of musical procedures for another, with musical texts the only permissible evidence. But *genre* is a concept that, in Leo Treitler's words, "overlaps 'style' . . . [with] the additional coordinate of function." Swing was more than a constellation of techniques and procedures to be altered at will by strong-minded artists. It was an integral part of the burgeoning entertainment industry, a genre of dance music embedded within an elaborate network linking musicians with booking agents, dance-hall and theater operators, songwriters, publishers, journalists, radio broadcasters, record companies—and of course, the public. It was a system that made musicians' careers possible and that defined their place within the whole. All of the bebop musicians began their careers within this system. Their decision to break, or at least radically revise, their relationship to it was no casual act. Nor, given the realities of power in American society, could it hope to be entirely successful.

The overall narrative structure of *The Birth of Bebop* is tripartite. The first part, "College of Music: Coleman Hawkins and the Swing Era," examines the Swing Era from a multitude of perspectives—musical, economic, cultural—with particular attention paid to the singular position of African-American musicians. Its chief protagonist is Coleman Hawkins, the preeminent tenor saxophonist of his generation and one of the most intriguing figures in the early history of jazz. As the title of the opening chapter suggests, he was a progressive, committed to a vision of social advancement in which the black jazz musician, through the disciplined exercise of talent in one of the few professional avenues open to African Americans, would find a place in the world commensurate with his skills.

The trajectory of Hawkins's career provides one pathway through a complex and rapidly changing landscape. Through the mid-1930s, he achieved a degree of fame as the featured soloist in the prominent black dance band led by Fletcher Henderson. In 1934 he exchanged his status as a salaried dance musician for the liberating uncertainties of life as a solo act in Europe. In 1939, at the height of the Swing Era, he returned from Europe to try his luck as the leader of his own dance orchestra. When that enterprise failed in 1940, he put aside hopes for success on a grand scale, concentrating instead on gaining a more modest niche for himself as a freelance virtuoso. After a few discouraging lean years, he found himself once again thriving, this time in the clubs on New York's 52nd Street.

There, during the early 1940s, he came into contact with the corps of young musicians, roughly ten to fifteen years his junior, who were at the heart of the nascent bop movement. The second part of the book, "Professionals After Hours: Young Black Musicians in the 1940s," is the portrait of this generation. As one might expect, the early careers of Charlie Parker and Dizzy Gillespie, bebop's central figures, are given special prominence. But their life stories were interwoven with those of numerous other aspiring musicians, some now well known, others still obscure, with whom they shared certain formative experiences. Most entered the profession during the initial heady years of the Swing Era boom and continued to make their way even as professional advancement became more difficult. Their professional world was bounded on the one side by public exchanges with their audience through live performance and the mass media, and on the other by the struggle for recognition within the musicians' community in the private sphere of the jam session. All felt the limits imposed on their aspirations and personal freedom by institutionalized racism—an experience only exacerbated by the upheavals of life on the home front. Gradually, their commitment to the professional world as they knew it (although not to professionalism per se) eroded, as they became alert to alternative tacks for pursuing their careers.

The third and final part of the book, "Taking Advantage of the Disadvantages: Bop Meets the Market," traces the complicated history of the formative years of bebop. During the war years, the economic structures of the Swing Era remained firmly in place. Common sense dictated that many young musicians (Dizzy Gillespie and Charlie Parker among them) continue to work through the entertaining dance orchestras toward something like conventional success. But new opportunities, however modest, pointed in a different direction. Jazz aficionados created a market, both in live performance and on recordings, for small-combo jazz, pulling the distinctive aesthetic and procedures of the jam session out of the private and into the public sphere. The resolution of the union ban on recordings in 1943 indirectly encouraged the creation of scores of small independent record companies, providing an outlet for the commodification of new strains of improvised music. As a well-established freelance, Coleman Hawkins was an early beneficiary of these developments. But the bop generation, spearheaded by Gillespie's determination and entrepreneurial instincts, was not far behind. The 1945 recordings matching Gillespie with Parker mark the beginning of a new genre.

This, in broad outline, is the story line of *The Birth of Bebop*. To answer the "how" and "why" of bebop, I consistently try to place the actions of musicians within the context of their professional world, an approach that entails close attention to the interpenetration of music-making and economics. At the same time I rely heavily on biography—drawing in large part from the rich resources of oral history that a living tradition provides. Wherever possible, I link the issues at play within the jazz world to broader trends in American, especially African-American, history and culture.

At times I address questions of musical style, sometimes in considerable technical detail. As a musicologist and a jazz performer, I feel a particular responsibility to do so. Music scholars have always faced the daunting challenge of explaining musical intricacies to a lay public and bringing the specialized jargon of music theory in line with the plainer prose of historical narrative. With jazz, the challenge is even greater. There is no widely accepted theoretical discourse to fall back upon, no scores to adduce as evidence in print, nor even substantive agreement on the aesthetic and technical principles that distinguish jazz from the tradition of European "classical" music. I cannot claim to have developed a more coherent or convincing approach to jazz analysis, but I have tried to draw music into the historical discussion in a way that does not do violence to its distinctive qualities—the qualities that make it worth caring deeply about in the first place. Although those without musical training may find a few passages difficult, I hope they will persevere, and that the coherence of the overall narrative will guide them to the conclusion.

The Birth of Bebop is not meant to be a comprehensive record of the beginnings of bebop. Any number of areas touched upon here—music, politics, economics, race, historiography—could be explored in more depth and detail. My aim is to explore how these varied considerations relate to one another in the birth of a musical genre some fifty years ago. My guiding principle has been that jazz must be understood as an integral part of American history and culture.

PART ONE

COLLEGE OF MUSIC:
COLEMAN HAWKINS
AND
THE SWING ERA

1 · PROGRESS AND THE BEAN

*In spite of all that is written, said and done, this
great, big, incontrovertible fact stands out,—the
Negro is progressing, and that disproves all the
arguments in the world that he is incapable of
progress.* JAMES WELDON JOHNSON

*There's no such thing as bop music, but there's
such a thing as progress.* COLEMAN HAWKINS

Alto saxophonist Cannonball Adderley remembered it later as a child-
hood moment that set the direction for his life. His father took him to
see the Fletcher Henderson band at the City Auditorium in Tampa, Florida. Featured in the band was the imposing tenor saxophonist Coleman
Hawkins. "Man, it was a great day for me," said Adderley. "I think he
was the most interesting looking jazz musician I've ever seen in my life.
He just looked so authoritative. I kept looking at him. I never did look
at Fletcher. I said, 'Well, that's what I want to do when I grow up.' "

Adderley was neither the first nor the last musician to be impressed
by Coleman Hawkins. In a field in which charismatic figures were no
rarity, Hawkins had a special quality. Hawk, or Bean—as he was affec-
tionately nicknamed—was not a particularly striking or flamboyant
man. And yet his quiet dignity and utter confidence in his abilities commanded respect, even awe—at least from musicians, who were in the
best position to judge Hawkins's artistic achievement. In a familiar anecdote, a younger musician encountering Hawkins for the first time in
the 1960s reportedly told Adderley that the older saxophonist made him
nervous: "Man, I told him Hawkins was *supposed* to make him nervous.
Hawkins has been making other sax players nervous for forty years."

Hawkins's place as one of the founders of jazz is secure. He was among
the earliest generation of jazz musicians, the men and women who un-

selfconsciously created a new art form. He is often called the father of the tenor saxophone, the first to discover the expressive potential of an instrument previously thought to have a limited emotional range, and therefore the patriarch of a lineage that extends through John Coltrane, Sonny Rollins, and other moderns to the present.

In the sweep of jazz history, Hawkins is usually classified as a swing musician. This label not only narrows the focus to a particular phase of his career, but also suggests that the artistic attitudes and techniques he acquired during that time served as his compass for the remainder of his life. It also strongly implies that his moment of significance was limited to a specific historical moment: the Swing Era, when his distinctive approach to improvisation was widely accepted as the model for all saxophonists and the standard against which they were measured.

"Body and Soul," recorded in 1939, shortly after his return from a self-imposed five-year exile in Europe, remains Hawkins's best-known record and a landmark in the history of jazz recording, not least for the fact that it was simultaneously a commercial success and admired and studied by musicians. But Hawkins is represented by hundreds of other recordings, from his pre-1934 solos with Fletcher Henderson to the flood of records for various independent labels in the early 1940s. Each combines a confident and assertive manner with a bracing, complex harmonic language that anticipated many of the innovations later associated with bebop, including the so-called flatted fifths. With each recording, his reputation as an innovator grew. "Coleman Hawkins was *the* saxophonist then," remembers pianist Billy Taylor. "Hawk was most highly respected," agrees bassist Milt Hinton. "He seemed to be the most creative man of the era. Everybody just thought he was the top man."

This stature, however, did not long outlive bebop. After 1945 Hawkins's influence declined, and his standing in jazz history automatically became problematic. Even in his last years, as he matched himself against John Coltrane, Thelonious Monk, and Sonny Rollins, he was considered less a full participant in contemporary musical life than an icon—a living legend—of the art.

Hawkins's decline in status is not unexpected. A history of style usually boils down to a history of innovation: novel techniques that stand out against the background of common practice and can be shown, after the fact, to point to the future. Only stylistic "advances" give shape and momentum to such a historical narrative. It follows that the cutting edge must be kept sharp. With jazz, the pace of change has been particularly brisk. Major artists are routinely and unsentimentally shunted from the vanguard to obsolescence before they reach middle age, their later work marginalized or forgotten, their historical role diminished.

Such seems to have been the fate of Coleman Hawkins. In 1944, as he approached his fortieth birthday, his prestige and influence were at their peak. This moment of glory was overshadowed, however, by the onslaught of bebop, and with it, his reputation as innovator vanished. He is now remembered as making only a brief appearance on the periphery of the bop revolution, despite having been very much on the scene. Even the comforting role of paterfamilias to the younger generation has been denied him. The swing tenor saxophonist universally acknowledged to have served as source and inspiration for the emergent idiom is not Hawkins, but Lester Young.

The frequent rhetorical pairing of Coleman Hawkins and Lester Young has the air of a cautionary tale, with Young's rise coming at the expense of Hawkins's decline. The issue is rhythm: specifically, the "logical rhythmic change" that Martin Williams saw as the mainspring of stylistic evolution in jazz. If evolution in jazz is about rhythm, then the "cool" rhythmic language pioneered by Young is a touchstone. As "the most gifted and original improviser between Louis Armstrong and Charlie Parker" (in Williams's reading), Lester Young is the conduit between the path-breaking innovations of early jazz and the revolution of the 1940s. His improvised solos, full of ironic understatement and witty, unpredictable manipulation of phrase lengths and rhythmic motives, contrasted starkly with the earnest effusions of Hawkins's playing. Young's rhythmic approach anticipated the future, as Hawkins's more ponderous idiom did not. As tenor saxophonist Dexter Gordon, who came of age in the mid-1940s, put it: "Hawk was the master of the horn, a musician who did everything possible with it, the right way. But when Pres [Lester Young] appeared, we all started listening to him alone. Pres had an entirely new sound, one that we seemed to be waiting for."

Some musicians date the passing of the mantle even earlier, to an incident in 1933 in which Hawkins, still a soloist with the Fletcher Henderson band, found himself locked in a marathon after-hours jam session at the Cherry Blossom in Kansas City with Ben Webster, Herschel Evans, and Lester Young. Mary Lou Williams was rousted from her sleep at four in the morning to relieve the exhausted piano players: "Get up, pussycat, Hawkins has got his shirt off and is still blowing." The event, now a staple of jazz folklore, found Hawkins struggling for hours to shake off the competition until finally giving up, tearing off in his Cadillac to make the next job in St. Louis. Mary Lou Williams, herself a historian (she devoted much of her later life to jazz education) had no trouble drawing the moral from this ritual combat: "Yes, Hawkins was king until he met those crazy Kansas City tenor men."

As the critic Jed Rasula has noted, jazz historians are fond of such "primal torch-passing scenes": colorful anecdotes that seem to embody the abstract workings of history. In this case, the story is all the more compelling for being somewhat in advance of events. Hawkins, after all, remained king for a good while longer, his reputation hardly damaged by this obscure encounter in the provinces. But the handful of participant-observers at the Cherry Blossom had seen the future. Through the telling and retelling of the story, later generations have joined them as privileged insiders, better attuned to the true workings of history than the majority of those who lived through it. Hawkins's day had passed almost before it had begun.

Thus, Hawkins's encounters with the bebop revolution have been reduced to mere historical curiosity. Dizzy Gillespie has put it more generously than most: "Hawkins had the great taste in music to understand my generation and to come with us." But the image is still oddly skewed—deliberately so, perhaps, given Gillespie's penchant for self-mocking humor: the young unknowns as the leaders, the forty-year-old "most creative man of the era" as the follower. In early 1944, when Hawkins became increasingly involved with the bop generation, the word *bebop* did not yet exist. Over the course of the year, Hawkins systematically employed musicians from the emerging underground. A recording session under Hawkins's leadership in February of that year featured Gillespie and Max Roach, while his working bands for 1944 included such well-known bebop pioneers as Thelonious Monk, Kenny Clarke, and Oscar Pettiford, as well as others now more obscure: Howard McGhee, "Little Benny" Harris, Vic Coulsen.

For his early encouragement of bebop musicians, Hawkins has been given his due. Unlike others of his generation, whose attitude toward bop ranged from hostility to resentment to bemused indifference, Hawkins championed the music, earning him a degree of loyalty (Thelonious Monk remained a lifelong friend) and respect. The title of a tune from a 1946 recording session, which included J. J. Johnson, Milt Jackson, Fats Navarro, and Max Roach, pays tribute to the relationship between the older saxophonist and his young protégés: "Bean and the Boys."

To make sense of this relationship, one must move beyond the compelling simplifications that dominate jazz history. Music cannot be reduced to a narrative of stylistic development, just as the complexity of a life lived in music cannot be flattened into a set of musical characteristics. This dictum is especially true for bebop, a movement that reflected the totality of the artist's consciousness.

For the bop musicians, Hawkins had a special relevance. As keen-eared aspiring artists, they paid close attention to Hawkins's musical legacy, appropriating some elements while rejecting others. But they also understood these details of craftsmanship as part of a broader picture, inseparable from the qualities of personality and intellect that informed the achievements of an extraordinary elite: black jazz musicians in midcentury America.

Hawkins shared many traits with the Dukes and Counts of that elite: the unshakable confidence of the successfully self-taught man, a tireless professional ambition, and a sense of dignity, tending toward inner reserve, under even the most trying of circumstances. Still, even among his peers, Hawkins stood out. The quality that arrested the attention of the youthful Cannonball Adderley was Hawkins's sense of *purpose*. This quality found its most obvious manifestation in his restless exploration of technical resources, but it cannot be reduced to them. It was both social and musical. The peculiar combination of personal traits and musical abilities that marked Hawkins—steely ambition, a strong intellect, and virtuosity—characterized the bebop revolution as well. He was, as Sonny Rollins has recently put it, one of its most prominent "role models": the prototypical progressive jazz musician.

Jazz and Progress

The word *progressive* makes many people in the late twentieth century uncomfortable. It calls to mind an ideology of continuous and irreversible betterment, one singularly out of sync with contemporary thought and experience.

In particular, it is grating to find notions of progress applied to the arts. To claim progress in the fields of science and technology is one thing. Some may argue whether such "advances" actually improve life, but few disagree that new solutions to old problems have rendered previous efforts obsolete. Old technologies are discarded without a second thought: the slide rule and the typewriter may have equipped one generation, but to the next, they become puzzling curiosities. In the arts, however, such wholesale dismissal of the past seems unthinkable. As museums attest, the old retains its power and actively shapes the sensibilities of the present.

Within the arts, music is a special case. Compared with the tangible objects of the visual arts, music is an inherently evanescent art, more process than product. Music notation, of course, was invented centuries ago as a corrective. Written music embodies musical structure independent of any given performance and makes the category of a "work" possible. But it took time for the reification of music as composition to take effect. The museum-like quality of the "classical" European repertory dates back no earlier than the nineteenth century. Only in the past hundred years has the music of the past, the canon of "timeless" masterpieces, come to dominate the present and undermine any notion of music's evanescence. Before this time, music was created primarily for current value: to be used and discarded. No one gave much thought to what generations beyond the reach of memory might have done, or to what future generations might think.

For jazz, the more modern technology of recording served a function parallel to that of notation. Jazz was a music created, like any other, for immediate consumption. Through recording, particular performances of music were transmuted into durable artifacts capable of outlasting the particular circumstances of their creation. Recordings were not necessarily treated with reverence: like other products of mass-market capitalism, they were meant to be used up. But some survived, in attics and junk shops, to be picked over in later years by eager record collectors.

Jazz history itself grew out of discography, a rational system of classification devised to help collectors sort the "classic" jazz recordings from the ephemera of popular culture. This process led to the wholesale rescue of jazz recordings from planned obsolescence and gradually to the jazz consumers' consciousness of the music as an art form. Today recordings are seen as jazz's museum, housing works of lasting value. It follows that new additions to the museum do not displace the old. The innovations of subsequent decades, whether by Charlie Parker or Ornette Coleman, do not diminish the value placed on contributions by King Oliver or Duke Ellington, but rather furnish another wing in the museum. The process is value neutral: growth, not progress.

It would be a mistake, however, to read this ideology back into the circumstances of the musicians who created the recordings. At the outset of Hawkins's career, jazz was not art music, but dance music. While record collectors shivered in private ecstasy listening to their favorite treasures, others gathered in large public spaces to enjoy dancing to the finest music they could find. Dance music is by nature ephemeral—which does not mean that it is unimportant or inartistic, but simply that it tends not to survive its time. In popular music, continual change is essential, as in sartorial fashion. It is a marker of generational identity, and every generation has the privilege of mocking its predecessor as hopelessly outdated and unhip. For those growing up in the first half of the century, surrounded by the ongoing triumphs of technology, it was virtually irresistible to associate change with progress.

Hawkins broke into the music business in the early 1920s as a callow teenager in rumpled, ill-kept clothes that earned him the nickname "Greasy," but quickly evolved into a dapper sophisticate, keenly sensitive to the imperatives of fashion. To his horror, his involvement with the dance music of the Jazz Age, captured on dozens of recordings with the Henderson band, later became the fetish of jazz collectors and critics. They delighted in playing these recordings in his presence, and the mortified Hawkins acted as if he had just been shown faded photographs of his youthful self in clownishly outmoded attire. The mature Hawkins thought of himself as perpetually young, perpetually in step, and hated admitting to a past. Confronted with evidence of it, he immediately countered with the notion of progress.

That Hawkins was not alone in this regard is evident in the French critic André Hodeir's complaint, from the mid-1950s, that musicians of the swing generation "naively believed their music better than that of their predecessors, just as they would have judged a 1938 automobile faster and more comfortable than a 1925 model." Hawkins, who insisted on owning the latest-model Cadillac, would have appreciated the analogy, but would probably have objected to being characterized as naive. His sense of progress in music was grounded not simply in a chauvinism of the up-to-date, but in an awareness of undeniable improvements in things that could be objectively measured. Musicians played faster, extended the ranges of their instruments, had better control over intonation and timbre (which is not to say that they conformed to European standards, but that any deviations from those standards were *intentional*). They had, on the whole, a sounder grasp of the intellectual components of music: the ability to translate musical notation into sounds and sounds into musical notation, a working knowledge of the syntax of tonal harmony, and a carefully calculated rhythmic assurance that made the dance music of the 1920s seem comparatively awkward and stiff. All of these skills had become the minimum professional equipment for musicians in the 1930s and 1940s, and counted as progress—real, hard-won achievement.

Jazz critics continually held up earlier jazz for admiration, but Hawkins was pained at the thought. "It's like a man thinking back to when he couldn't walk, he had to crawl," he complained after rehearing one of his solos twenty years later. That art, out of all areas of human endeavor, should be singled out and denied the possibility of systematic improvement made him indignant: "That's amazing to me, that so many people in music won't accept progress. It's the only field where advancement meets so much opposition. You take doctors—look what medicine and science have accomplished in the last twenty or thirty years. That's the way it should be in music—that's the way it has to be."

The analogy between science and art that Hawkins suggests seems improbable, but as generations of scholars have discovered, the work of science historian Thomas Kuhn offers some intriguing points of comparison. In science, entire fields are occasionally transformed, or brought into being, by new organizing principles: the discovery of antibiotics in medicine, plate tectonics in geology, quantum mechanics in physics. In *The Structure of Scientific Revolutions*, Kuhn identified such breakthroughs as new "paradigms" and saw in them the basis for understanding revolutionary change in science. Similar breakthroughs have characterized the arts; indeed, the animating purpose of Kuhn's study was to adapt concepts of revolution already widespread in the humanities for use in the sciences. What have come to be known as paradigm shifts in both the humanities and the sciences are the disjunctures dramatized in the telling of history—the sudden irruption of a new sensibility, a fresh way of seeing things, embodied in a particular set of techniques and procedures that becomes the model for all to follow.

Still, as Kuhn emphasizes, the dramatic, paradigm-shattering breakthrough is not characteristic of scientific activity as a whole. What he calls "normal science" is the unglamorous but necessary work that uses the prevailing paradigm to pose problems and systematically solve them. Progress—the incremental accumulation of knowledge—is made possible only by such unremitting labor. Scientists do not seek revolutionary insights for their own sake (although the achievements of a handful of radical innovators are properly lionized). Most simply extend the existing framework further and assume, for want of any evidence to the contrary, that it will go on indefinitely.

The analogy with jazz seems straightforward and helps in part to explain Coleman Hawkins's preoccupation with progress. One of the most influential truisms of recent historical writing is that jazz was given something like an initial paradigm by "the first great soloist," Louis Armstrong. According to Martin Williams, "jazz musicians spent the late twenties and early thirties absorbing Armstrong's rhythmic ideas, the basis of his swing." Armstrong's performances, especially his recordings from the 1920s, defined the exacting discipline of the improvised solo and provided concrete examples of the rhythmic principle of swing.

For the next two decades, hundreds of musicians applied themselves to the task of absorbing and extending Armstrong's example. The "problems" they sought to "solve" (both words crop up frequently in the secondary literature) differed from a scientist's experiments in that their ultimate goals were aesthetic. But, like a scientist, these musicians systematically applied principles inherent in the original paradigm to novel contexts. Specifically, they learned from Armstrong's example how to construct a solo and how to swing, and they learned to do this within their own musical personalities, on their own instruments, and in the context of changing fashions in dance music. The process can be viewed as intuitive and holistic (learning how to "tell a story"), or intellectual and reducible to such technical problems as range, speed, and articulation. Responsibility for achievement was individual: personal improvement. But, as Coleman Hawkins proudly saw, the net result for the discipline was progress.

Bebop, to continue the analogy, figures as a major paradigm shift. Through the transformative example of Charlie Parker and Dizzy Gillespie, jazz in the 1940s experienced a "reconstitution of the field from new fundamentals." All the familiar symptoms of revolution, the world turned upside down, are there: the youth of the revolutionaries; the startling, unexpected nature of the new insight; the specter of an older generation clinging to the old paradigm, even as hordes of new practitioners rush to embrace the new; and finally, the triumph of the new paradigm and the recasting of the field in its image.

But what is the relationship of the new order to the old? How and why do such revolutions arise? As Kuhn emphasizes, a paradigm is not lightly set aside. It is the foundation of a field, and those who run counter to it risk no longer being recognized as members of the discipline. New paradigms emerge only in moments of great crisis, when the usual ways of doing things prove wholly inadequate. At such times, practitioners are forced, almost against their deepest instincts, to devise radical new ways of constructing their professional world. It is not enough for historians to admire the originality and brilliance of the new paradigm, as if originality and brilliance were sufficient explanation. They must also understand the extraordinary pressures that turned dedicated practitioners into revolutionaries and pushed them to the reckless step of abandoning the old paradigm.

What, then, was the crisis that provoked the bebop revolution? As we have seen, something like a "crisis theory" is already in place in the bebop story. It suggests that by the beginning of the 1940s, jazz musicians found themselves frustrated by the prevailing paradigm. The encouragingly brisk pace of development that had characterized jazz to this point slowed, as if something were impeding musicians from progressing further. Some have imputed the difficulty to musical style per se. "I do not think that one can hear the impeccable swing of a player like Lionel Hampton," wrote Martin Williams, "without sensing that some sort of future crisis was at hand in the music, that. . . . a kind of jazz as melodically dull as a set of tone drums might well be in the offing." But this is not a comfortable argument, since it suggests that the musical language itself is somehow at fault. The more usual approach, as I have already noted, is to deflect the blame for the crisis away from the music toward external forces (such as commercialism). Bebop thus emerges as a musical solution to a social problem—or more precisely, a reassertion of the autonomy of music-making in the face of social pressures.

I would frame the argument differently. At the risk of overextending the analogy between art and science, one further aspect of Kuhn's analysis deserves to be mentioned. The revolutions he describes happen not to science in the abstract, but to communities of professional scientists. Insofar as the concept of paradigm "stands for the entire constellation of beliefs, values, techniques, and so on shared by the members of a given community," it is sociological: a "disciplinary matrix" that grounds the putatively autonomous pursuit of science in social realities. To understand fundamental change in science, one must account for its social dimension—not just its institutions (degree programs, journals, scholarly associations), but the cultural values that underlie informal behavior: how information is disseminated, reputations made, and conflicts between competing paradigms resolved.

I would argue that fundamental change in music must similarly be understood as social and cultural as well as musical. The proper analogy for a paradigm in jazz is not musical style, but something like Kuhn's "disciplinary matrix": the sum total of practices, values, and commitments that define jazz as a profession. The romantic myth of the artist working in isolation from (or even in opposition to) the outside world may seem congenial or convenient to jazz critics. But myth it is. All activity in the arts takes place within what the sociologist Howard Becker has called an "art world": "the network of people whose cooperative activity, organized by their joint knowledge of conventional means of doing things, produces the kind of art works that art world is noted for." Only within this context can the decisions of individual jazz musicians to effect dramatic changes not only in musical style, but also in their social role as professional musicians, be properly interpreted.

In focusing on Coleman Hawkins, one of the most influential musicians of the Swing Era, I hope to provide one vivid, concrete example of how that social role was constructed. In emphasizing the social, I do not mean to neglect or diminish the musical. I will deal separately, and at some length, with technical musical issues in the chapters that follow. My first task, however, is to situate Coleman Hawkins as a musician within his historical context. What did it mean for a young African-American man to pursue the career of professional jazz musician in the first several decades of the century? In particular, what did it mean for him to be *progressive?*

Music as Career

"Progress," "advancement," "improvement": this is the rhetoric of black self-help, articulated at the turn of the last century by spokesmen for "the race" such as Booker T. Washington and internalized by hundreds of thousands of African-American households eager to escape the cycle of poverty and despair.

The America faced by a youthful Coleman Hawkins (born 1904) was a bleak landscape. Hopes raised by Reconstruction had been dashed by race riots, lynchings, disfranchisement, the spread of Jim Crow laws, declining educational opportunities, and the systematic exclusion of black labor from many skilled industries, making it clear that white America had renounced any responsibility for the welfare of the black population. In difficult times, black Americans had historically turned away from overt political agitation and demands for social equality to the themes of self-help, racial solidarity, and economic advancement. Booker T. Washington's philosophy emphasized the responsibility of the individual for ameliorating his or her condition and, by extension, the responsibility of black Americans as a community for their own social and economic progress. Self-improvement, through the diligent mastery of specific marketable skills (with an eye carefully turned toward what white society would tolerate), was the only way to improve their lot and take their places as productive citizens of the twentieth century.

Washington's efforts centered on what is commonly called industrial education, which left little room for artistic pursuits. Music was a frequent target of his scorn, a symbol of unrealistic cultural pretensions: the sixty-dollar organ owned by a family that shared a single fork, the rosewood piano in the tumbledown shack. His views accorded with a general American view of music as either a genteel accomplishment of limited economic utility or a socially suspect form of entertainment. Folk music stood outside this sphere. But among the genres of black folk music, only the spiritual, emblematic of the religiosity and deep expressiveness of the black experience, was made palatable to middle-class tastes by college choirs. The rest—field hollers, work songs, ballads—was too redolent of agricultural peonage to be attractive to those desperately trying to escape it.

More broadly, only a modest percentage of the vast numbers who pursued music as an avocation before the turn of the century—from folk traditions to marching bands to parlor music—could expect any economic advantage from it. Full-time professional musicians of any race were relatively rare before 1900. The kind of expensive training in music that socially aspiring black families of even limited means sometimes provided for their children (one thinks of Scott Joplin's lessons with a German music teacher in Texarkana or the cello lessons young Hawkins received) might well have been viewed by Washington as pretentious indulgence.

Still, had Washington been a more astute reader of trends, he would have installed a conservatory at Tuskegee. Music-making in the black community had never been entirely without tangible social or economic benefits. Since the colonial period, slaves and free blacks had frequently been used as dance musicians. In towns throughout the country black men and women with some skill at an instrument supplemented their earnings by performing or teaching. Many early jazz musicians came from families in which one or both parents gave lessons, or they grew up (as Lester Young did) as a member of a "family band." As opportunities in the cash economy expanded, so did the number of African Americans who devoted their energies to music. By the beginning of the twentieth century, the profession of musician was taking its place alongside barber, caterer, and Pullman porter as one of a handful of occupations outside unskilled manual labor open to blacks.

Like these other professions, music allowed blacks access to the larger white market. In this sense, it was just another form of service. But music played to one of the greatest strengths of black culture: the power of African-derived rhythm to animate people's bodies and draw their minds, even against their conscious will, into a distinctively African-American cultural orbit. Music was a cornerstone of black cultural identity, so musicians could count on prestige, respect, and a degree of economic support from within their own communities even as they reached outside for a larger economic reward. All of this combined with the slippery status of music in the culture at large—was it merely functional entertainment for the masses, a social adornment for the middle class, or great art?—to make music a particularly effective avenue for escaping the limitations routinely imposed on black talent.

By the time Coleman Hawkins was old enough to think about becoming a professional musician, playing dance music had emerged as a promising career for the exercise of youthful black ambition.

In the years just before the First World War, a craze for dance music swept aside Victorian prejudices against dancing in public places, opening up the vast middle-class market for economic exploitation. The democratization of dance music shifted the center of gravity from a narrow base of patronage by the social elite to the anonymous workings of the marketplace. James Reese Europe's Clef Club, founded in 1910, was an intermediate step: a self-help organization designed to secure as much of the trade as possible for Harlem musicians by pooling resources and rationalizing business practices. But Europe and others continued to aim for a relative handful of lucrative and exclusive hotel and society dance gigs. As late as the early 1920s, the cornetist Rex Stewart keenly felt the social distance between the Clef Club "clique"—now-forgotten names like Ford Dabney, Will Vodery, and Tim Brymn, who were the "aristocracy" of the black musical world, the "bigwigs who played Miami Beach, Piping Rock, Bar Harbor and all the other posh resorts"—and the "rank and file" of musicians toiling in dime-a-dance halls and disreputable cabarets.

Such distinctions would soon vanish. The comfortable society jobs were eventually skimmed off by white dance orchestras like Meyer Davis's. Meanwhile, in the 1920s, "every hamlet had its dance hall and the big cities all had dance emporiums." The larger venues offered the pleasures, as well as prestige, of conspicuous consumption to the masses. The marble staircase of the Savoy Ballroom in Harlem (which opened for business in 1926) led to "fancy wall decorations all over, thick patterned carpets on the floor, soft benches for sitting, round tables for drinking, and a heavy brass railing all around the long, polished dance floor. . . . Even the bouncers wore tuxedos." The pleasure of dancing to music performed by sophisticated professionals was no longer the exclusive privilege of the moneyed classes, but available to anyone who could pay a modest admission charge. The result was a boom in employment: "In New York you had a whole bunch of dance halls that had fifteen- to eighteen-piece bands. Then all the dancing schools would have six- or seven-piece bands. There were a million nickel dance halls that all had bands. When you'd go to work on the train, it would be loaded with people and when you'd come back in the morning, there'd be nothing but musicians on it."

Even so, the professional category of jazz musician associated primarily with dance orchestras took time to emerge. Black musicians entering the profession in the 1920s were attracted, in part, by the glamour and raw vitality of the entertainment world. Their careers often overlapped with theatrical entertainment. Much of Jelly Roll Morton's early professional experience, for example, came on the vaudeville stage. A 1914 review commented: "As a comedian, Morton is grotesque in his makeup and sustains himself nicely through the work. . . . He does a pianologue in good style."

Even as vaudeville entered its decline, black show business continued to attract talented instrumentalists. For a young Rex Stewart, vaudeville acts "were very important due to their year-long contracts." His "introduction to the big time" came with the 1921 show *Go-Get-It*, followed by a stint with the Five Musical Spillers. Hawkins escaped from provincial St. Joseph, Missouri, in 1922 as a member of a band accompanying blues singer Mamie Smith in a touring variety show, in which he slap-tongued his saxophone while lying on his back with his feet in the air. Count Basie, who broke into professional life in 1924 with a show called *Hippety Hop*, later wrote, "At that time, I didn't really think of myself as a jazz musician. I was a ragtime or stride piano player, to be sure, but I really thought of that as being an entertainer, in other words, just another way of being in show business."[1]

The link between jazz and the broader world of show business persisted

---

1. Other examples documented in autobiographies include trombonist Clyde Bernhardt with the Whitman Sisters (Bernhardt 1986, 70–79) and Garvin Bushell with Mamie Smith and other vaudeville shows (Bushell 1988, 21–27, 41–47).

for many black musicians of the 1930s. As the dance orchestra moved closer to the center of popular culture, musicians with the requisite talent and temperament moved decisively into the role of entertainer. The meteoric rise of Louis Armstrong from dance musician to pop icon is merely the most celebrated example; others included Fats Waller, Cab Calloway, and Lionel Hampton. Especially as stage shows featuring swing bands displaced vaudeville, hundreds of musicians with some gifts for singing, comedy, or sheer physical exuberance gained a modest amount of time in the limelight.

Taking center stage had its risks. For black artists, it meant coming to terms with the corrosive stereotypes inherited from the minstrel show. Few had this distasteful legacy thrust on them quite so literally as did Billie Holiday, who, as the vocalist with Count Basie's band in 1937, was required to put on blackface for a theater show in Detroit (the chorus line was dressed in plantation "mammy" dresses). But every public career up through the bebop era required some accommodation to white expectations of a black performer's persona, whether it was Armstrong's transfiguring ebullience or Dizzy Gillespie's mischievous barbed wit.

Those who sought to make their mark solely as instrumentalists, however, could generally enjoy some of the benefits of show-business life without these risks. Like theater people, successful dance musicians dazzled the lay public with the sophistication and elegance of their attire. Many took advantage of the access their work afforded to wild nightlife and glamorous showgirls. On the whole, however, their work entailed the routine and anonymity of playing in any orchestra, demanding the same unglamorous traits of dependability, versatility, and unobtrusive competence. These work requirements, as much as anything, fostered values that could only be called middle-class where one would least expect to find them—at the heart of the jazz world.

A Matter of Class

The stereotype of the jazz musician as wastrel and deviant, content with a life on the fringes of respectable society, has proved remarkably durable over the years. So, too, has the related image of the black jazz musician as the product of the urban ghetto. The former has its roots in the sensibilities of white rebels like Bix Beiderbecke, for whom the very choice of popular music as a career, let alone open admiration for black music, was an act of rebellion. The latter corresponds to the experiences of many early New Orleans musicians—Louis Armstrong being the outstanding example—for whom music was an escape from a life of manual labor. "That's why so many kids in New Orleans took up music," recalled the guitarist Danny Barker. "If they were thick in the head, they'd end up doing stevedore work on the levee in the hot sun."

Yet nearly forty years ago, the jazz historian Hsio Wen Shih pointed out that the "typical" black jazz musician from the 1920s and 1930s was quite different:

> He was born about 1900, into a Negro family doing better than most, possibly in the Deep South, but more likely on its fringe; in either case, his family usually migrated North in time for him to finish high school. If he had gone to college, and he often had, he had gone to Wilberforce or a fringe school like Howard or Fisk. He might have aimed at a profession and fallen back on jazz as a second choice. He was, in any case, by birth or by choice, a member of the rising Negro middle class; he was Fletcher Henderson, or Don Redman, or Coleman Hawkins, or Duke Ellington.

Despite Hsio's consistent use of the male pronoun, his most fully developed example is a woman: Lil Hardin, the Memphis-born pianist who married Louis Armstrong in 1924 and added the iron of ambition to the gold of his talent. Hardin exemplifies the qualities that Hsio ascribes to a generation: not only musical skills, but ambition ("both musical and in the larger sense, social") and "an engaging mixture of shrewdness and adventurousness."

This analysis would seem to place achievement in jazz squarely within the realm of black bourgeois respectability: a discomfiting notion, perhaps, for those who automatically equate the black middle class ("surely one of the most disparaged social groups in all of modern history," in Andrew Ross's phrase) with craven assimilationism and selling the birthright of culture for a mess of pottage. It is all the more important, therefore, to situate the middle-class aspects of jazz as a profession within a broader social and economic context.

The black bourgeoisie of the early twentieth century was a relatively tiny elite, dominated by the professions needed to service a segregated community: teachers, lawyers, doctors, ministers, undertakers. Since even skilled professionals could not count on earning more than a fraction of what their white counterparts earned, social standing had traditionally been defined more by skin color, family background, and educational attainment than by income, although as time went on income began to matter more and more. It was a world isolated from the rest of society, limited and hampered by segregation but also curiously dependent on it for its modest prosperity. For as long as white professionals were unwilling to serve a black clientele, black professionals enjoyed a monopoly, a freedom from competition that has been called "taking advantage of the disadvantages."

By the very nature of their work, black professionals were integral to their community and worked hard for the advancement of the race as a whole; from their ranks, political leadership came. But even as they rubbed elbows with the masses in the workplace, they took pains to distinguish themselves from their social inferiors in other spheres. From this stems the contempt for African-American folk traditions and the corresponding exaggerated admiration for white gentility for which the black middle class has been roundly criticized. As the sociologist and economist Gunnar Myrdal noted in the early 1940s, the cultural orientation of the black elite lay not within the black community, but across the color line, toward their putative peers in the white upper class, on whom they modeled their elaborate social life, with its debutante balls and cotillions, its rigid social hierarchies, and its unrelenting emphasis on conspicuous consumption. Their musical tastes were correspondingly genteel. "Waltzes was popular then in Harlem," remembered one black musician who played in the mid-1930s for "high-powered colored associations" at the Renaissance Ballroom in Harlem. "If you didn't play any at colored social affairs, you didn't play for that club anymore."

Several black jazz musicians belonged to this world by birthright and probably inherited some of its snobbery as well as its prerogatives. The Creoles of New Orleans are a classic example of a shabby aristocracy that clung to privilege based on "good family." They wielded their fierce pride, so characteristic of the privileged black classes, as a weapon in the struggle to assert themselves in the world, even at the expense of their darker-skinned colleagues ("The worst Jim Crow around New Orleans was what the colored did to themselves," recalled the bassist Pops Foster). Duke Ellington is another, perhaps more instructive example. As numerous biographers have pointed out, he grew up on the periphery of what was then the "center of Negro 'society,' " the large and relatively prosperous black community of Washington, D.C. In his youth, he skillfully negotiated its complicated social hierarchies: "I don't know how many castes of Negroes there were in the city at that time," he later wrote, "but I do know that if you decided to mix carelessly with another you would be told that one just did not do that sort of thing." From this environment, Ellington absorbed an unshakable confidence, folding an air of effortless superiority into his aristocratic public persona.

Most musicians, however, made their way without such advantages. Music was a wide-open field, attracting those who, according to Tom Hennessey (whose research has confirmed and extended Hsio's insights), saw in jazz "an opportunity for artistic exploration and economic and social advancement." Music appealed to African Americans of all classes and offered opportunity where other avenues were blocked or nonexistent. For someone like J. C. Higginbotham, born in rural Alabama, it was a skilled profession that provided an alternative to life on a farm or to the blue-collar trades he explored before settling on a career as a trombonist. For others, ironically, music was more practical than the educated professions. Fletcher Henderson's decision to pursue music rather than chemistry (in which he had a degree from Atlanta University) is the best-known example, but there were many others with ambitions in law and medicine.[2] Expediency was the rule. Pianist Jimmy Jones prepared diligently for a career as a doctor, studying physics, botany, and zoology in high school. But with the onset of the Depression, "the music took over because that was a thing right at my fingertips to make some money. Then I got into that and had to stay in it. I was locked into it. . . . It just took money to go to med school, and we didn't have it. It was that simple."

Music could never hope to rival law or medicine in respectability. Families of musicians often expressed deep reservations about their children's chosen path, whether out of religious conviction or fear of the general unsavoriness of a show-business career. But their resistance tended to soften or vanish once the wage-earning potential of music-making became clear. Dramatic successes were not uncommon, in part because the relatively narrow range of earning power within the black community made any success seem a meteoric ascent. (As Myrdal noted, "It is not uncommon for a Negro . . . to rise from the lowest to the highest social status in one generation.")

The relatively obscure career of Clyde Bernhardt provides as good an

---

2. A few examples: the parents of Sy Oliver, who were music teachers (Knauss, 150–177), and those of Sid Catlett, who were domestic servants in upper-class households (Balliett 1986, 181), had planned for their sons to study law. Adolphus "Doc" Cheatam's father wanted him to go to medical school, like several of his elder male relatives, and distrusted Cheatam's eventual choice of profession because "musicians drank a lot" (Adolphus Cheatam, National Endowment for the Arts / Smithsonian Institution Jazz Oral History Project).

example as any. Born in rural North Carolina but moving to Harrisburg as a teenager, he struggled with several unskilled or semiskilled jobs (Western Union messenger, street sweeper) before carefully nurturing his talent for the trombone. Against all odds, he managed to break into the music profession. His mother, who had always regarded him as a ne'er-do-well, greeted his first professional successes with quiet praise: "You are making a start now, Clyde. Playing for all those big colored people, doctors, and lawyers. Doing something that everybody can't do." Bernhardt had no particular liking for the middle class, the "big colored people" whom he disdained as "nothing but phonies, putting up a front." But he had no need to accommodate himself to that world, since he had surpassed it. By 1930 he was earning fifty dollars a week, "during the time some black doctors was pulling twenty-five a week and thought they doing good." Music proved singularly effective as, in Hennessey's words, "a way to 'make it' into the mainstream."

The emergence of music as an avenue for African-American aspiration was, in part, another example of "taking advantage of the disadvantages." It depended on the existence of a segregated black market whose entertainment needs were met primarily by black musicians. Patterns of migration relocated a previously rural proletariat in the heart of northern cities, where they flocked to the slicker mass entertainment available to them: dancing, vaudeville, recordings. These audiences were overwhelmingly working class and retained a strong orientation to African-American folk traditions. Many musicians came from this class themselves, of course. They provided examples of the kind of artist that Eric Hobsbawm found characteristic of working-class communities throughout the Western world: rising from its ranks and exemplifying its values, wholly lacking the pretensions of the middle class:

> The artist sprung from the unskilled poor, and playing for the poor is in a peculiar social position. In the world from which he comes and in which he works "entertainment" . . . is not merely a way of earning a living, but far and away the most important way of making one's individual path in the world. . . . The star musician, dancer, singer, comedian, boxer, or bullfighter is not merely a success among this sporting or artist public, but the potential first citizen of his community or his people.

But even those who came from unarguably bourgeois backgrounds had little difficulty satisfying the tastes of the black working class, just as they learned to adapt to socially diverse white audiences. Unlike others

of their class, however, these professionals developed, as a necessary re-
quirement of the job, a healthy respect for the durability and artistic
integrity of black folkways. That respect was reciprocated. Far from re-
senting professional musicians for their prosperity and their highly developed skills, the black mass public celebrated them. After all, there were
few enough arenas in which black talent could openly and fairly compete
with white. Jazz musicians were unqualified successes, conquering the
broader world outside as well as satisfying deep-seated aesthetic needs
within the black community. It may be true, as Hobsbawm argues, that
in the pursuit of ever higher professional standards (appreciated only by
their peers), black jazz musicians gradually receded in importance for
the black community. But to a remarkable extent, jazz in the 1930s resulted from a symbiotic relationship between an artistic elite and plebeian
taste.

I emphasize the middle-class orientation of black jazz musicians primarily to counter the persistent stereotypes of dissipation and bohemian
excess. How many jazz aficionados suspect, for example, that a New York
bank in the 1930s preferred to hire black musicians as messengers because
they "know how to talk to people, how to wear a tie and collar. Disciplined. They do their work"? In their own way, jazz musicians were
hardworking, solid citizens, but there was nothing of the "make-believe"
(in the sociologist E. Franklin Frazier's phrase) of the black bourgeoisie
about them.

Malcolm X had as keen an eye as any social critic for the grotesque
disparity between social ambition and the realities of racial caste. While
still a teenager in Boston, he noted with contempt the airs put on by
"anyone who could claim 'professional' status—teachers, preachers,
practical nurses. . . . Foreign diplomats could have modeled their conduct
on the way the Negro postmen, Pullman porters, and dining car waiters
of Roxbury acted, striding around as if they were wearing top hats and
cutaways." By contrast, he had nothing but open-jawed admiration for
Duke Ellington, Count Basie, Lionel Hampton, and other "professionals"
who graced his shoeshine chairs. He even once allowed Johnny Hodges
to walk away absentmindedly from a shine without paying: "I wouldn't
have dared to bother the man who could do what he did with 'Daydream'
by asking him for fifteen cents."

One quality that jazz musicians shared with the black socioeconomic elite
was a respect for education. As Gunnar Myrdal observed in 1942, "the
Negro class system has its most characteristic feature in the fact that, on

the whole, capitalist business and wealth mean so relatively little, and that general education and professional training mean so relatively much, as criteria for attaining upper class status." Many of those who did attend college undoubtedly claimed automatic social superiority. According to one disgruntled musician, Jimmie Lunceford's attitude could be summed up as "If you don't come from Fisk [Lunceford's alma mater], you ain't nothing." But unlike their counterparts in law and medicine, musicians could not acquire specialized skills by enrolling in officially accredited programs. The peculiar nature of the "progressive" mindset in jazz arises from the basic problem of education in jazz, succinctly framed by Hobsbawm: "The jazz business deals in the distribution of an available product: musicians. It does not deal in their production. Like all show business, it has always assumed that saleable players will just appear on the scene. Nothing like the conservatoire, or the classical ballet-school, has ever existed in jazz. Musicians have got their elementary education in playing instruments wherever they found it and their secondary and higher education by playing with other musicians."

The inescapable challenge for those, like Hawkins, who wanted to break into the music game was that of acquiring professional competence. This is not to say that jazz musicians, especially black ones, were necessarily unschooled when they entered the profession, or that none of their schooling related to conventional music curricula. Efforts to extend the benefits of education to the black masses after the Civil War usually included music. For the socially aspiring, European music remained the lodestar, although efforts were made to accommodate African-American traditions within it (as with the concert arrangements of spirituals pioneered by the Fisk Jubilee Singers). An active tradition of black involvement on the concert stage extends back well into the nineteenth century. Although sharply circumscribed by racism, it boasted a few celebrated public careers: the soprano Sissieretta Jones (1869–1933), the pianist Thomas "Blind Tom" Bethune (1849–1909), the violinist Joseph Douglass (1871–1935, grandson of Frederick Douglass).

But the early twentieth century saw a crucial shift, as the leading edge of trained black musical talent moved decisively away from concert music into the popular arts and frankly embraced aspects of the African-American folk tradition previously shunned as "lower class," even as it retained its basically middle-class orientation. That pioneering generation included Scott Joplin (born in 1868), whose *Treemonisha* attempted to reconcile ragtime with grand opera; Will Marion Cook (born in 1869), the Joachim-trained violinist who turned to musical theater and wrote such songs as "Who Dat Say Chicken in Dis Crowd?"; W. C. Handy (born in 1873), the prim bandmaster who "discovered" the blues; and James Reese Europe (born in 1881), whose work with the Clef Club cemented the relationship between black musicians and dance music.

The following generation found it easier to inhabit the world of dance music and popular song, but still tended to receive at least some formal training, either through the public schools or from their families (a substantial number of jazz musicians were second- or even third-generation professionals). In the reminiscences of many musicians, teachers figure prominently, such as the formidable Major N. Clark Smith, who hammered the rudiments of music into hundreds of young boys in Kansas City before moving to Chicago. Lionel Hampton, who played under his leadership in the band sponsored by the *Chicago Defender*, remembered him as a portly, mustachioed man of considerable presence, as likely to wear a military cape and hat (in honor of his service with Teddy Roosevelt's Rough Riders) as his more ordinary outfit of morning suit, vest, and striped pants. Such instructors encouraged an association between musical precision and discipline and emphasized the qualities their young charges would need to advance in the world. The symphony director at Chicago's Wendell Phillips High, Dr. Mildred Bryant Jones, punctuated her rehearsals with discussions about manners and even set a table in front of her students to demonstrate the proper use of silverware. Musicians with access to this kind of music education played in conventional marching bands and school orchestras, eventually mastering such workhorses of the light classic repertory as Franz von Suppé's ubiquitous *Poet and Peasant Overture*.

The trick was to square this conventional training with the emergent world of jazz and blues. Those who specialized in orchestral instruments like the violin or the cello had to learn some other instrument, because there was no possibility for employment in an orchestra. Benny Carter remembered being aware even as a child that "as a black, or Negro, as I termed myself at that time, . . . there was no future in being a symphonic musician." Marshal Royal progressed far enough on violin to become a member of the Junior Philharmonic of Los Angeles, but on graduation from high school, his uncle presented him with a clarinet and the terse advice: "Go out and make some money." Hawkins's mother may have pushed him to practice his cello, but he unerringly aimed for the saxophone and left home at the age of seventeen to play the blues with Mamie Smith.

Those musicians with training imaginatively mined it to further their later careers. Pianists generally had it easier. Stride pianists were fond of interpolating famous passages from opera and the light classics into their stomps, and Earl Hines was pleased to discover that the Czerny exercises he had practiced so diligently at home could be slipped into his improvisations.[3] Other instruments had only the sketchiest of traditions. Drummers, for example, were almost entirely on their own. The modern drum set—a complicated and technologically ingenious amalgam of existing percussion instruments—did not even exist before the beginning of the century. Flams, paradiddles, and other rudiments of military parade-ground technique contributed to dance band drumming, but other essential skills, especially the dexterity required to work the foot pedals for the bass drum and high-hat cymbal, had to be developed on the job through experimentation.

Even players of more established instruments could not always count on a ready-made body of instruction. As guitarist John Collins remembers, "Nobody taught guitar then. You couldn't get a teacher. Everybody was groping, so you just had to have some ingenuity and imagination and do these things yourself." Highly personal combinations of ingenuity, hard work, and a determined eclecticism contributed to nearly all of the major technical advances in jazz. By whatever means, the goal was to expand in any direction from a limited technical base, leading not just to instrumental facility in its narrow sense but also to those felicitous discoveries of style and technique that have given jazz its originality. James "Trummy" Young's experience at learning trombone both within and outside his school's marching band is characteristic:

> We used to jazz up the marches sometimes. They'd get after us and tell us to tone it down. . . . When we were on our own, we'd try anything with those instruments. . . . We'd get together and anything we heard, we tried

3. In the lengthy interview recorded by the Library of Congress in 1938, Jelly Roll Morton demonstrated how he transformed the "Miserere" from Verdi's *Il Trovatore* into a ragtime piece with a "Latin tinge." James P. Johnson "once used Liszt's *Rigoletto Concert Paraphrase* as an introduction to a stomp" and performed "rag paraphrases" on Rossini and Grieg (Davin 1964, 52–53). Earl Hines explained his use of Czerny in a series of lectures at the University of California in 1983: "Sometimes, I'd go back to some of the classic numbers that I learned, and some of the exercises that I did—Czerny books, and all that. And sometimes I'd relate back to those things, and I'd be playing and all of a sudden a passage in there would come before me, and I'd stick that in and see how it would work out. And that's why guys never knew where I was—I didn't know where I was myself!" (Earl Hines, Bloch Lectures, University of California, Berkeley, Spring 1982).

EX. 1.
Trombone imitation, Trummy Young.

to play it. If we heard an operatic singer, we'd try to play what they were singing. It was just a challenge to us. . . .

There was no road to go on. We had to make our own road. Really, because all a trombone player did back then was: [imitates simple trombone part; see music example 1]. That's the only way they played. They didn't know any other way to play. In fact, the first trombone player I ever heard in my life that didn't play like that was Arthur Pryor [the star trombone soloist with the John Philip Sousa band]. He played all these intricate parts in a band. And I said, "Wow, I sure want to play like that," you know. And I don't want to play all this [resumes trombone imitation] on this thing. . . . And this is what made me pick up in jazz before I ever got a lesson, because I wanted to get around a little bit on the horn and do some different things than what I had been hearing.

Technical progress therefore demanded not merely diligence and discipline, but also imagination, intellectual curiosity, and the willingness to find inspiration from any source, no matter how unorthodox. With "no road to go on," even youthful optimism could not disguise the difficulty in carving out a new path. When Will Marion Cook suggested to the young Duke Ellington that he pursue his musical training in a formal academic setting, Ellington's response summed up the dilemma of a generation: "I don't want to go to the conservatory because they're not teaching what I want to learn."

Part of the education of any artist is a painful awareness of how much there is to be learned. Aspiring black musicians in the early twentieth century, already mindful of their own technical inadequacies, were often caught in a double bind. Such training as they received was sometimes excellent, but more often spotty, and in any case usually stopped short of what would constitute a sound foundation for professional life. At the same time, no existing school could teach how to improvise, or swing, or arrange for a dance band, or coax new timbres from trombones and saxophones. All this contributed to the characteristic preoccupation of Swing

Era musicians with technique—a preoccupation passed on to the bebop generation and beyond.

As more and more musicians jostled for positions in the top bands, the greater was the tendency to sort out specialized skills—soloing, speed, sight-reading, section leading, range (especially for trumpet players), arranging—and to rank musicians according to their proficiency in these skills. The responsibility for technical improvement may have been individual, but the effort was more often than not collective. Self-improvement, in early-twentieth-century black thought, went hand in hand with ideals of racial solidarity and cooperation. Progress for the individual was a prerequisite for progress for the race as a whole; any help that could be offered could only benefit those who offered.

This interrelationship was especially true in music, where the basic economic unit—the band—was an aggregate of individuals. Black musicians correctly saw in the acquisition of basic music skills the same key to power and prestige within the profession as education and literacy were for the society as a whole. They were quick to realize that the fortunes of a band would rise or fall on the skills of each member. Cooperation thus tended to override competition as a motive for experienced musicians to share what they knew with the novices in their midst. The pianist Cliff Smalls remembers failing miserably at his first attempt at arranging because he didn't understand that trumpets and saxophones are transposing instruments. Members of the band threw the parts down in disgust, until a trombone player said, "We've got to help him. Maybe he's the guy that's going to save us one of these days." After the mysteries of transposition had been explained to him, Smalls became the band's regular arranger.

The schooling bands provided could hardly be described as formal—although one Kansas City band prefaced its rehearsals with an hour-long period of classroom-style instruction in scales, chords, and other essentials of music theory. Still, many musicians referred to bands they played in as "colleges" and "universities," for it was there that they completed their professional education, gaining advice and tips, as well as a chance to closely observe their section mates. Since the schooling of musicians from white immigrant families did not differ markedly from that of black musicians, clarinetist Artie Shaw's experience of playing in a theater orchestra in 1925 is probably typical:

> There were a number of trade tricks you weren't apt to learn unless you got them from people who'd been around in the business for some time. I began

to learn a new method of sight reading. The idea was to read three or four, or even more, bars ahead of where you were playing. I found out about new methods of tone production, and the various kinds of tones that could be used in different types of ensemble playing—dry tone, warm tone, the use of vibrato—wide and narrow—and when to avoid vibrato altogether. I was introduced to the whole matter of dynamics. . . . In short, I had to learn so many technical and non-technical aspects of the seemingly simple procedure of blowing a horn in a dance band, that after a few weeks of it my head buzzed. I remember that I used to go home nights and have a terrible time getting to sleep at all. Round and round in my mind would go the "lessons" of the day.

What was acquired in this way was not simply the rudiments of music, but a whole complex of behavior patterns that defined the experience of a working musician:

The most important thing I learned from that whole job had less to do with music itself than with the way a professional musician was supposed to behave. All the kid-stuff I had been indulging in up to now [Shaw was only fifteen at the time], not necessarily in my playing but in my attitudes toward myself and the men I worked with—all that was out. . . . In time I began to learn to conduct myself more in accordance with my status as a professional musician working with other professionals who took their means of livelihood fairly seriously.

"Technique" must therefore be seen as more than instrumental facility—the nuts and bolts of mastering an instrument, or what musicians call "chops." For musicians hoping to make their way into the new world of jazz, it also meant mastering the characteristic expressive devices of the African-American tradition—the smears, bent notes, and varied timbres by which instrumentalists approximated the nuances of black song, and the sense of rhythmic momentum known as swing. "What [these abilities] represent," the novelist and critic Albert Murray reminds us, "is not natural impulse but [that] the refinement of habit, custom, and tradition have become second nature, so to speak. . . . Indeed on close inspection what was assumed to have been unpremeditated art is likely to be largely a matter of conditioned reflex, which is nothing other than the end product of discipline, or in a word, training. . . . As a very great trumpet player, whose soulfulness was never in question, used to say, 'Man, if you ain't got the chops for the dots, ain't nothing happening.' "

To the extent that these techniques "become second nature," they are likely to be invisible. Their acquisition is normally a matter of acculturation, which is a largely unconscious process, rarely verbalized. The difficulty in defining *swing* points to the problem. Rhythm is intimately bound up with body movement (kinesics), which in turn is an integral part of the nonverbal communication that underlies verbal discourse and is, in anthropologist Edward Hall's words, "the essence of ethnicity."

To be sure, many black musicians growing up in middle-class households in the North and Midwest in the early days of jazz lacked the kind of contact with black folkways, urban or rural, that informed the sensibilities of artists as disparate as Louis Armstrong, Charlie Parker, and Ornette Coleman. For them, the nuances of the tradition were techniques to be learned in what amounted to a crash course in acculturation. The New Jersey–born James P. Johnson got his grounding in African-American rhythm in 1913 by learning what satisfied recent migrants from South Carolina ("Breakdown music was the best. . . . the more solid and groovy the better. They'd dance, hollering and screaming until they were cooked"). A decade later, Ethel Waters got the "damn-it-to-hell bass" she wanted out of Fletcher Henderson (who in her opinion leaned "more to the classical side") by playing piano rolls of James P. Johnson's music over and over until Henderson was finally able to match his fingers to the movement of the keys.

Through whatever avenues, a distinct aesthetic, and the techniques to manifest it, became thoroughly diffused in the black jazz musicians' community. Even a musician as inclined to the "classical side" as Coleman Hawkins understood the value of folk techniques and the priority of an African-American aesthetic. In 1956 he insisted that the Henderson band became "too sophisticated" in later years: "I think it should always have been a stomp band. I think they should have stomped all the bands out of existence. . . . If you ever heard [the band] at the Roseland playing 'King Porter Stomp' . . . we used to rock those walls, and the place would shake when we played the thing." Turning to "folk music," he gave it an urbane professional's endorsement by underscoring its inherent technical challenges: "Don't think for a minute that it's easy, because it's not. And it's as musical as it can be. If you don't believe me just listen to anybody's folk music . . . and you'll think of folk music as being something from barrels, earth music, you know, and right away you'll say to yourself, 'Oh well, that's mean,' 'It's got to be elementary,' or something, but it isn't. That music is some of the hardest that there is to play."

Perhaps because a folk sensibility was fundamental to jazz, it tended not to be the focus of what musicians meant by "progress." African-American folk traditions provided an anchor—as the foundation for individual black musicians' sense of ethnic identity, as the main means of communicating with black audiences, and as the distinctive selling point for black music in the white mass market. Although folk sensibility certainly did evolve (the blues of Charlie Parker could not be mistaken for the blues of Bessie Smith or Charley Patton), the continuity and stability it provided were perhaps more important. Black jazz musicians assumed that their music would swing, that it would speak in the culture-specific accents of the blues. Progress involved expanding technical resources within that context—better (and different) ways to swing, better (and different) ways to get people moving on the dance floor. The challenge was to absorb new musical elements without dislodging the African-American aesthetic from its central place.

Progress also meant *versatility.* Long after the minstrel show proper faded into oblivion, public representations of black musical folkways were indelibly associated in the white eye with the Sambo image—the smiling, shuffling darky clown. As black musicians traded on their musical culture for personal gain in the marketplace, they inevitably found themselves boxed in and belittled by pervasive racial stereotypes. The Sambo image was immune to direct assault, for to renounce the stereotype was to risk renouncing the black cultural identity it mocked. Besides, it was useful as a form of protection, a mask that could be worn to deflect white hostility. The most effective strategy, as the cultural critic W. T. Lhamon, Jr., has suggested, was versatility: "The trick was less to transcend the common ground of American racism than to speed the Sambo figure across it, showing him in alternative contexts, indicating to each audience how the others viewed him. By putting the figure in the light of many audiences, his many facets would become apparent."

Musicians in early jazz were careful to foreground their distinctive mastery of swing and blues, as much to stake a claim to cultural leadership within the black community as to satisfy the white market's appetite for black cultural products. And yet they maintained a careful, ironic distance from overt enactments of the Sambo archetype in music: "As urbane jazz musicians," Lhamon notes, "they absorb their primitive sources complexly but simultaneously insist that audiences notice their spit-shined shoes." They were particularly anxious to show that such skills were not, as it were, hard-wired. The most satisfying way to undermine, in the pianist Teddy Wilson's words, "the picture of the Negro in the white world as a clown, a buffoon, an illiterate happy person who jammed all day" was to incorporate elements of what the white world respected as musical knowledge and literacy *into* the cultural practices that fueled the stereotype. A form of swing that was both earthy and erudite, both down-home and in touch with "advanced" musical currents far beyond the ken of the average white square—*that* was a goal worth reaching for.

The results, in any case, spoke for themselves. On the eve of bebop in 1944, Leonard Feather used the pages of *Esquire* to sound the praises of contemporary swing: "Never before has any branch of music made such rapid progress, and never before have there been so many superlative jazzmen, or so many first-class bands. . . . Their great strides in technique, range, and harmonic feeling have given them greater means to express the inspiration they inject into their improvisations. Today you may find a tenor sax man in Joe Doakes' band who can make music just as great as anything Coleman Hawkins did in 1929."

Hawkins probably would have taken a quiet satisfaction in this assessment: not only the general affirmation of progress in his chosen field, but also the implication that contemporary saxophonists had only just caught up with where he had been in 1929. He, meanwhile, had spent the last fifteen years ensuring that the Coleman Hawkins of 1944 had left the Hawkins of 1929 far behind.

One Step Ahead of the Pack

Jazz has been around long enough for us to see its most respected practitioners become gray, paunchy, and venerable. The precocity of a Wynton Marsalis—already famous at twenty-three—is startling. But during the Swing Era, youth was the norm and the advent of middle age a potential symptom of stagnation. Nearly all the prominent jazz musicians active in the 1930s (with the notable exception of Duke Ellington, born in 1899) were born in the twentieth century. Most had established their reputations before they reached thirty and steadily rose in their field even in the midst of the Depression. As each entering wave of professionals raised the stakes for technical proficiency, they also raised the specter of obsolescence for older musicians. The bassist Oscar Pettiford jokingly proposed a fund for a "comfortable retirement" for musicians over forty: "Styles are changing very fast in jazz. By the time they're forty, life should have ended for them professionally." "Jazz is like baseball," according to pianist Eddie Heywood. "It's a young man's game."

Coleman Hawkins was among a handful of aging progressives (Ellington, Basie, and Hines were others) pointedly excluded from this grim assessment. "He's been around twenty years," Heywood allowed, "but he's brought his style up to date; time will never catch up with him." If Hawkins managed to retain the respect of the younger generation even as he pushed forty, it was because his most impressive accomplishments, like those of Duke Ellington, lay in areas that could not easily be imitated and exhausted. As his colleagues recognized, his achievements reflected not mere trained athletic reflex, easily dulled by the advent of age, but a progressive temperament that inspired him to continually reshape his music.

The first of Coleman Hawkins's accomplishments, and the one that had the most immediate impact on his fellow saxophonists, was his prodigious, full-bodied tone. Initially, this was a matter of expediency. Playing alongside such powerful brass soloists as Louis Armstrong in the Henderson band of the early 1920s made Hawkins acutely aware of the inherent limitations of reed instruments in the pre-microphone era. "I always did want to be heard," he later remembered. "I used to say to myself: it's foolish to be blowing if nobody can hear you. . . . I wanted a strong tone." He turned to musicians' technology, experimenting with unusually hard reeds and customized mouthpieces: "I always did work with kind of a stiff reed. I used to work on those reeds all night to make them sound."

One source of inspiration was operatic singers, whose recordings he listened carefully to on his prized Capehart phonograph at home. His compact, sturdy frame made him ideally suited physically to the discipline of tone production. His long and sinuous melodic phrases, ranging widely over the available registers, revealed a stamina and breath control that would be the envy of any singer. Yet Hawkins could turn in an instant from operatic elocution to the hard, percussive bite of the African-American dance band.

The saxophone is ideally suited for speed. In the hands of a smooth virtuoso like alto saxophonist Rudy Wiedoeft (1893–1940), who earned fame in the 1920s through vaudeville appearances and recordings, it seemed to have found a light, fluid style appropriate to its nature. By deciding to make his tenor saxophone compete in volume and tone with Louis Armstrong's trumpet, Hawkins seemed to set himself a perversely difficult challenge. Hawkins's ultimate success was all the more dramatic. More than anything it was an expression of sustained will. One time in 1927, Rex Stewart vividly remembered, Henderson's lead trumpet player, Russell Smith, was injured in an automobile accident. "Coleman—on tenor—took over the first trumpet book and not only played the parts so well that we scarcely missed the first trumpet but also carried the orchestra with volume such as I had never heard coming out of a tenor sax." Such an anecdote resides in the realm of folklore, but recordings from the period, such as "The Stampede," show enough of a penetrating tone, commanding presence, and unusually good control of the extreme upper register to make it credible.

By the 1930s and 1940s, Hawkins's sound had become the standard against which all other saxophonists of the time were measured and found wanting. "You either had more or less tone than he did," observed pianist Billy Taylor. "Well, no one could have more, I guess, so I should say you had varying degrees of tone less than he did." The richness of tone and the volume of his playing forcibly impressed his preeminence on would-be rivals. Tenor saxophonist George "Big Nick" Nicholas, soon to play in the Earl Hines band with Dizzy Gillespie and Charlie Parker, was overwhelmed on hearing Hawkins for the first time in 1941: "I heard that sound. Now, what actually I heard was that every note that he played—they were all the same bigness, *all* the notes. I says, 'Ohhhhh, ohhhhh!' because the other tenor players, they had certain notes that they petted and they became bigger, but *all* of [Hawkins's] notes were big. And it was really something. When they did the show, he came out from the kitchen playing his solo on 'Body and Soul.' I think he had an eight-piece band, but, Jesus Christ, his sound was bigger than everybody put together."

At the same time, Nicholas saw Hawkins's sheer physical force and control as indistinguishable from other, more intellectual dimensions of musical accomplishment: "[He] seemed to have everything. All of his notes were clear and beautiful, and he had an evenness about his horn; and then his brain, he seemed to have such a deep knowledge of sound and chord structure and he just seemed to have everything."

Hawkins's curious nickname, Bean, suggests the cerebral as well. "I used to ask, 'Why do you call him Bean?' " remembered Nicholas. "What they meant was—'The Brain'!" Tenor saxophonist Budd Johnson concurred: "We called him Bean . . . because he was so intelligent about music and the way he could play and the way he could think and the way his chord progressions run. We'd call him Bean, instead of 'egghead,' you know."

Hawkins's store of knowledge about music was such that impressionable young musicians who worked alongside him in the 1940s reached for academic metaphors to describe the experience. "In the three to four months that I was [with Hawkins]," recalled bassist George Duvivier, "it was like two years in the university"; while for alto saxophonist Johnny Board, "a year with Hawkins was like working four years in a doctoral program in one of the best universities in the world." For pianist "Sir" Charles Thompson, Hawkins was a "college of music": "The greatest musicians, the ones who were the leaders . . . like Coleman Hawkins and Roy Eldridge and many other great jazz players during that time, they were proficient inasmuch as they could read music, sight-read music, and they could play chord progressions. And they were ahead of everybody else in that department. . . . Coleman Hawkins . . . was involved in the highest form of progressions and music interpretation that there was around in those days."

Such testimonials repeatedly stress Hawkins's command of harmony: both a firm grasp of its theory and the ability to translate that knowledge fluently into improvisation ("play[ing] chord progressions"). Hawkins's use of harmony was particularly impressive because it was dynamic and open-ended, exemplifying the progressive attitude. Throughout the 1930s and 1940s, Hawkins continued to explore chromatic harmony, demonstrating with each recording new ways to introduce startling dissonances and rich layers of harmonic complexity into his improvisations. Each step seemed an advance in knowledge—not just for Hawkins personally, but for the musicians' community as a whole.

Because harmony is a subject steeped in the specialized terminology of European music theory, black jazz musicians of the era often found it intimidating as well as fascinating. Hawkins was among the relative few who had been exposed to it systematically as part of their early music education. With some pride, he described his youthful study of piano and cello as "scales, exercises, study, theory, harmony in the thorough but dull old-fashioned way. When I took up the tenor, I knew music." Even a thorough grounding in conventional music theory, however, did not shield would-be professionals from the challenge of adapting it to the new realities of popular music and improvisation. As Milt Hinton, who had gone to the trouble of taking courses in harmony at a junior college in Chicago, complained: "Nobody had taught me anything about using music theory in a practical way. Just like all the others, I had to learn how to play on a chord by experimenting myself."

The willingness to experiment was more important than prior educational attainment. "Untrained" musicians were perfectly capable of learning by trial and error how to make their improvisations fit within chord progressions, even if they could not articulate what they were doing.

"There [were] many musicians that at that period could improvise very well, and still didn't know a C⁷ from an F diminished," Benny Carter explained. "They would know it by sound, but not by name, necessarily." Unless they also harbored the ambition to become composers or arrangers, improvising soloists tended to defer to pianists and guitarists, whose business it was to know the right chord: as one pianist remembered, they "depended on you playing the right chord progressions for them to hear what they were to play." As experienced a soloist as trombonist J. C. Higginbotham claimed, "I don't know anything about chords."

Nevertheless, there were undeniable advantages to conscious control over harmonic materials. For one thing, the harmonic language of popular music was steadily growing more chromatic. Musicians who had learned by ear to play simple harmonic progressions in familiar keys might find the complex chord structures and internal modulations of Jerome Kern's "Yesterdays" (1933) or "All the Things You Are" (1939) difficult to take in. The same may be said of the work of jazz arrangers and pianists: the startling harmonic originality of Duke Ellington's idiom and the bristling complexity of Art Tatum's, to choose two well-known (if extreme) examples, were beyond the ken of even seasoned professionals. In negotiating this new harmonic landscape, some continued to rely on the more informal aural approach to harmony, even preferring its flexibility. Lester Young, for example, once told his brother, Lee, that too detailed an awareness of each chord in a harmonic progression "confines you too much. . . . you start thinking of the only notes that will go in that chord, and [Lester] would say that's not what he would hear." But many others became fascinated with harmony for its own sake and were eager to explore it consciously and systematically.

Hawkins exemplified this trend. A skilled pianist himself, he drew on other pianists for inspiration. "I just listen to piano players," he once noted. "I hear a lot of things that they are making that I like, [and] I try to make that on my horn, that's all." The keyboard was for him a way to externalize and rationalize the harmonic relationships that he absorbed from his musical environment. "He was a very studious person, musically," according to the bassist Leonard Gaskin. "He had, like, a photographic mind, and anything anybody played, he'd amble over to the piano long after and fish around to see what kind of change this fellow was playing."

The pursuit of "advanced" harmonies was perhaps the most important way Hawkins stayed one step ahead of the pack. Years later, he enjoyed telling of his return to New York in the summer of 1939 after his self-imposed exile in Europe. He was worried, he said, that he might have lost ground to some of his rivals in the meantime. After making a tour of Harlem jam sessions, however, he concluded there was nothing to fear: his colleagues had failed to progress. Drummer Cozy Cole recalled him complaining: "Oh, yeah, it sounds good, but man, when I went away, they were playing those same changes. Nothing changed. Maybe a little faster, but they're playing them same changes." Hawkins himself elaborated:

> They didn't make the changes good. You know, the changes were kind of sad. And I listened, I went around and I heard all the musicians, and I used to go to all the sessions and everything, you know? [pause]. I was *surprised*, you know, 'cause I'd been over there for so long, you know. And I thought by the time I came back I thought the musicians here would be much further advanced, you know? But they—it was just like—just like when I *left*. I didn't see any—nothing, hadn't advanced it, hadn't done anything.
>
> I used to go around—I'd go in there, I'd hear everything I was going to hear in there. I thought to myself, They're not going to cut me playing that, not what I just got through listening to—I mean, there must be something they're holding back. I know what this is—[laughs]—they're just *waiting* for me! You know, they think I'm stale or something, I've been away too long, and all that. But if *that's* the best they're going to play—not like that, they won't, you know? So, that was the funniest thing: I said, it'll be *easy*. It'll be *easy* to play with that. That ain't going to be too much strain at all. 'Cause all you got to do is play a couple of off notes, here! Make a couple of off notes, and you got it made! [guffaws] I knew *that*, 'cause they *never* made any! You know?

Hawkins's natural affinities lay with a younger generation of progressives, for whom he was often an inspiration and model. Recalling saxophonists Hawkins and Benny Carter, Roy Eldridge, seven years Hawkins's junior, emphasized, "They really inspired me. I'd listen to them and be stunned, man. I didn't know the right names for anything at first, but I knew what knocked me out.... Changes, man. I dug." By age sixteen, he had memorized Hawkins's solo on "The Stampede" and learned to play it on the trumpet. The few trumpet players he heard who knew "the right changes," like the now-forgotten Cuban Bennett,[4]

4. Theodore "Cuban" Bennett, a cousin of Benny Carter's, earned a reputation as an accomplished trumpet soloist within the New York black jazz musicians' community of the 1920s, but apparently declined to be heard outside this community. He made no recordings

"played more like a saxophone did. . . . [They] would run changes, would run through all the passing chords." Along the way, Eldridge found the "right names" for things: "I was full of ideas. Augmented chords. Ninths."

The early education of Dizzy Gillespie, seven years younger in turn than Eldridge, was similarly shaped by a fascination with harmony. If Eldridge initially groped his way toward understanding, Gillespie (who after all had the examples of both Eldridge and Hawkins before him) approached his study more systematically. A friend remembered working with the teenaged Gillespie on George Gershwin's "Liza": "We would try running these chords as we were playing. Running them up, running them backward, running them upside down, and all kinds of ways. And then we would take a tune like 'I Can't Get Started' . . . and we would try to make different chords off of almost every note there was in the tune." "Body and Soul," a popular song with a particularly challenging chord progression, was also grist for Gillespie's mill. The Philadelphia-based Frankie Fairfax band, for which Gillespie worked in the mid-1930s, used to practice "Body and Soul" by modulating up a half step with each chorus until returning, a dozen choruses later, to the original key. "That was supposed to be one of the hardest things," recalled a colleague. "Dizzy would take 'Body and Soul' and run over it like a rabbit running over a hill. Any key, it didn't make no difference. . . . So you had to say, damn, what's with this cat?" In this way, the progressive musical temperament passed down, intensified, to bebop.

A fascination (not to say obsession) with harmony provided common ground between Hawkins and the young progressives. Here Hawkins could assume an attitude of peremptory leadership: there was very little by way of chromaticism in the playing of Gillespie or Charlie Parker that he had not already done or could not easily absorb, and both he and they knew it. But harmony in and of itself was never quite the point. Hawkins was not admired simply because his music was more chromatic: his self-consciously "advanced" forays in composition—"Queer Notions" (1933), with its chains of whole-tone chords, or the tritone-laden "Night Ramble" (1945)—are intriguing curiosities, but do not explain his preeminence. Hawkins was admired because his harmonic erudition made his solo improvisations that much more compelling. The ultimate effect was *gestural* or *dramatic:* an idiosyncratic way of inhabiting the role of jazz

---

and performed only in small Harlem clubs (Berger, Berger, and Patrick 1982, 9; Barker 1986, 114).

soloist, as carefully constructed over the course of his long career as was his unmistakably individual tone.

But in the rhythmic sphere, the younger generation held the upper hand. And if one accepts Martin Williams's reading of things, rhythm necessarily takes priority over harmony. To quote again from *The Jazz Tradition:*

> The crucial thing about the bebop style is that its basis came from the resources of jazz itself, and it came about in much the same way that innovation had come about in the past. That basis is rhythmic, and it involves rhythmic subdivision. . . . We should not talk about harmonic exactness or substitute chords and the rest before we have talked about rhythm.
>
> Like Louis Armstrong, Charlie Parker expanded jazz rhythmically and, although his rhythmic changes are intricately and subtly bound up with his ideas of harmony and melody, the rhythmic change is fundamental.

There is certainly something to this point. The new rhythmic language of bebop—its discontinuities, its elusive ebb and flow, its sudden spurts and stops—is strikingly original, and in retrospect the most important musical contribution of the bebop generation. The presence or absence of the rhythmic sensibility found in the improvising of Charlie Parker is a crucial factor separating premodern (swing) and modern (bebop) jazz. Viewed from this perspective, the contemporary preoccupation with harmony may seem irrelevant. What if the bebop generation occasionally picked the pockets of Swing Era progressives like Hawkins for pungent dissonances, as long as they slipped these harmonic innovations into a rhythmic manner of their own creation?

Still, harmony and rhythm cannot be so easily separated. Hawkins's rhythmic approach did have a strong influence on the new idiom. His solos from the late 1930s and early 1940s, with their long, undifferentiated strings of eighth notes (or sixteenths, depending on tempo) and their strikingly regular accentuation patterns, are less varied rhythmically than those of many of his contemporaries (or for that matter, even his own solos from a decade earlier), but they swing nevertheless, and in a way that made a deep impression on the coming generation of musicians. Hawkins demonstrated that rhythmic effectiveness could be achieved through the sophisticated deployment of harmonic resources.

All these stylistic transactions were occurring not in the abstract, but within the "disciplinary matrix" that Hawkins, as much as anyone else, helped to define. What bound Hawkins and the bebop generation together was the shared experience of finding a satisfactory place in the music business, and in American culture generally, for that most anomalous of professional categories: the African-American virtuoso instrumentalist.

2 · THE MAKING OF A VIRTUOSO

By all accounts, Louis Armstrong made a bad first impression on Coleman Hawkins and the rest of the Fletcher Henderson orchestra when he arrived on the job in 1924. With his old-fashioned, thick-soled shoes fastened by hooks ("the kind that policemen wear"), long underwear showing at the ankles, a thick New Orleans accent, and a bashful manner, the twenty-three-year-old Armstrong could only have come off as a bumpkin—a social embarrassment to the cool, sharply dressed New Yorkers, who spent a good deal of their discretionary income to ensure that their physical appearance alone stamped them as an elite. Hawkins himself was only nineteen, but already a seasoned professional. As a highly skilled dance musician, able to adapt smoothly and efficiently to a variety of performing situations and well paid for it, he had climbed to the top and was settling in for a long stay. His distinctive persona had already begun to emerge: sophisticated, reserved, with more than a touch of condescension. From Armstrong's perspective, Hawkins and the rest of "the boys" looked "a little stuckup."

First impressions can be deceiving. Within months, the New Yorkers were busy imitating the guileless, awkward newcomer—even to the point, as with the awestruck teenager Rex Stewart, of clomping around in heavy policeman's shoes. The catalyst, of course, was Armstrong's music. He may have struggled with the arrangements put before him at that first rehearsal (in one account, a "medley of beautiful Irish waltzes"; in another, "By the Waters of Minnetonka"). But given the opportunity to "cut loose," his reputation was made: "all of the band boys just couldn't play for watching me."

Armstrong's approach to the role of African-American musician proved so compelling that it effected a subtle but crucial shift in the way his fellow musicians thought about what they were doing. Largely through his example, the "hot solo," formerly a moment of incidental excitement in a dance band arrangement, became the focus of a new discipline, both deeply satisfying and unexpectedly prestigious (at least within the burgeoning circle of jazz aficionados). Armstrong himself emerged as the exemplar: the improvising virtuoso, the "mere" performer who captures for himself some of Prometheus's fire as a creative artist.

Hawkins may have been caught off balance, but he quickly adjusted his ambitions when confronted with the tangible evidence, artistic and commercial, of Armstrong's triumphs. If Hawkins, like many others, had initially thought of music mainly as the exercise of a skilled craft, the deep impression that Armstrong left on his audiences raised the stakes. Several decades later, asked to describe his greatest experience as a jazz musician, Hawkins cited the following epiphany at the Roseland Ballroom in 1925: "There were thousands of dancers, all yelling and clapping. . . . The high spot came when Louis Armstrong began 'Shanghai Shuffle.' I think they made him play ten choruses. After that piece a dancer lifted Armstrong onto his shoulders. Fletcher Henderson kept on beating out the rhythm on his piano and I stood silent, feeling almost bashful, asking myself if I would ever be able to attain a small part of Louis Armstrong's greatness."

This concession from the fiercely proud Hawkins is, admittedly, anomalous; in its profession of humility, perhaps even disingenuous. The relationship between the two men who shared the spotlight in the Henderson band was never warm. Their inevitable rivalry, exacerbated by differences of class and temperament, was fueled afterward by Armstrong's well-deserved rise to celebrity. To say simply that Armstrong "influenced" Hawkins is to reduce a complex relationship to genealogy. Anyone eager to apply literary critic Harold Bloom's agonistic notion of the "anxiety of influence" to yet another field need look no further. "I don't think Louis influenced Coleman Hawkins, except unconsciously, because Coleman hated Louis," remembered trumpeter Cootie Williams. "It was when I was in the Fletcher Henderson band [in 1929] that I learned about this. I knew Hawk then, and he just couldn't even stand the name Armstrong." It is perhaps stretching things too much to cast Armstrong, who was only three years older than Hawkins, as a father figure in an oedipal drama (although musicians did call him Pops), but Hawkins was certainly faced early on with the unpalatable task of escaping his shadow. By some evidence, he actively resisted his debt to Armstrong and spent the better part of a decade searching for his own distinct musical and professional identity.

It is unlikely, in any case, that Hawkins could ever have imagined following directly in Armstrong's footsteps. To be sure, they had quite a bit in common. Both were opportunistic and ambitious young African Americans from the provinces who rose, on the strength of formal musical training (in Armstrong's case, the tutelage of Peter Davis at the Waif's Home in New Orleans), on-the-job experience, imagination, and self-promotion to prominence in New York. But Armstrong had already staked out a different career path beyond being a trumpet player. Like many other black musicians of the 1920s, he saw instrumental virtuosity less as a discipline unto itself than as one of several skills that might be cultivated by the professional entertainer.

Jazz criticism tends to focus on Armstrong as an instrumentalist, emphasizing his contributions to the nascent art of jazz. Gunther Schuller's characterization of Armstrong as the new music's "first great soloist," an improviser whose "inventiveness and musical integrity" rose naturally above the "crass entertainment" of the time to take its place alongside "the highest order of previously known musical expression," has been echoed by many other writers. Armstrong was, of course, also a singer. As with Fats Waller, Nat "King" Cole, and George Benson to follow, his turn away from instrumental jazz per se to popular song and entertainment has been routinely regretted in jazz circles as a betrayal of art to commercial taste. It is better understood as the fulfillment of an ambition, however inchoate, to "make it" in show business. Noting Armstrong's startling self-description as "actor" on a 1932 passport application, Gary Giddins explains in his biography, *Satchmo:* "He undoubtedly used the term in the same generic sense that every vaudevillian, minstrel, and cabaret performer of the day did. . . . From the time he sang for pennies in a boys' vocal quartet in the streets of New Orleans, Armstrong was a showman as well as a musician."

Giddins does not dissent from Schuller's characterization of Armstrong as a revolutionary instrumentalist of great artistic import. He seeks instead to situate this accomplishment in its proper context—as an artistry that took on greater meaning *from* its context. Armstrong, he writes, discovered his métier when he "figured out how to make his music part of a larger presentation." He was "an artist who happened to be an entertainer, an entertainer who happened to be an artist—as much an original in one role as the other. He revolutionized music, but he also revolutionized expectations about what a performer could be." In the heat of live performance, the boundaries between abstract musical logic and the physical spectacle of entertainment melt away. Consider this eyewitness description of Armstrong in action from 1933, quoted at length by Giddins:

> He announces "When You're Smiling" and this time he has a new act. He backs off, downstage left, leans half-way over like a quartermiler, begins to count, (swaying as he does) "one, two, three" . . . he has already started racing toward the rear where the orchestra is ranged, and he hits four, executes a slide and a pirouette; winds up facing the audience and blowing the first note as the orchestra swings into the tune. It's mad, it's meaningless, it's hokum of the first order, but the effect is electrifying. No shabby pretenses about this boy! He knows what his audience will take to their hearts, and how he gives it to them. His trumpet virtuosity is endless—triplets, chromatic accented eerie counterpoints that turn the tune inside out, wild sorties into the giddy stratosphere where his tone sounds like a dozen flutes in unison, all executed with impeccable style and finish, exploits that make his contemporaries sound like so many Salvation Army cornetists. Alternately singing choruses and daubing with the handkerchief at throat, face, forehead (he perspires like a dying gladiator) while a diamond bracelet twinkles from his wrist, he finally gets off the stage to rest.

Needless to say, such talents are not normally conjoined in a single individual, leaving the question that must have shaken even the self-confident Coleman Hawkins: how am I to compete with all *that?* The obvious answer is to play to one's strengths. As he stood in silent witness to Armstrong's charisma at the Roseland in 1925, his thoughts may have turned not just to *whether* "a small part of Louis Armstrong's greatness" was attainable, but to *what part.*

Some choices were easy to make. Hawkins lacked the extroverted temperament of the entertainer. He typically played his instrument with eyes closed, oblivious to his audience. Nor did he have any particular gift as a singer, as he demonstrated on an obscure 1936 recording from Switzerland, bluffing his way through a pop song of his own composition,

"Love Cries." The results, however embarrassing, are revealing. Clearly, Hawkins listened carefully to Armstrong and admired his singing enough to mimic accurately some of its more salient mannerisms: the genially gruff delivery, slurred pronunciation, and vocalized syllables ("mmmmm") familiar from any number of Armstrong recordings from the 1930s. Had the experiment been more successful, Hawkins might have developed singing as a sideline—an obvious advantage to anyone in show business. Instead, he let it lapse. Any singing he did would be, like his piano playing, for his private gratification.

His only option, then, was to continue to be a professional instrumentalist, aiming for "greatness" within a public persona that Armstrong instinctively eschewed: the "studied virtuoso" who "walks to center stage, plays God's music, bows again, and leaves." If the ultimate goal was to carve out a niche as distinct from Armstrong's as possible, Hawkins nevertheless found Armstrong's example useful—but only after abstracting and refining it through more than a decade's hard work into an idiom unmistakably his own.

"One Hour"

Just how close, and how far apart, Hawkins was from Armstrong by the end of the decade can be gauged by recordings that each made, within half a year of each other, of the same pop song: James P. Johnson's "(If I Could Be with You) One Hour Tonight."

Throughout the 1920s, Coleman Hawkins prospered in Fletcher Henderson's steady employ. He enjoyed his role as star soloist with New York's premier black dance band, with its pied-à-terre at the Roseland Ballroom on Broadway in midtown Manhattan. Now out of Armstrong's shadow, he had ample opportunity to play solos, both in performance and on recordings. Indeed, his services had become so valued that his was the only salary in the band that Henderson guaranteed during periods of slack employment.

One sign of his rising stature was that he began to take more jobs in the recording studio independent of the Henderson band. Among these was a recording date on 14 November 1929, with a group called the Mound City Blue Blowers. Rather daringly for the time, the Blue Blowers was an interracial group, matching Hawkins and black New Orleans bassist Pops Foster with (among others) Glenn Miller, Eddie Condon, and Pee Wee Russell. It is in this context that "One Hour" was recorded. Hawkins's full-chorus improvisation on this recording is routinely cited in jazz criticism as a landmark in the maturation of his style: "the first important example of Hawkins as a ballad player, perhaps that aspect of his art which was more imitated than any other."

Armstrong's version came in quite another context. Since leaving the Henderson band, he had immersed himself in the turbulent musical life of Chicago's South Side, with lasting effects. As the historian William Kenney has noted, the emphasis on visual spectacle in Chicago cabarets and floor shows encouraged black musicians to develop a "self-conscious act" to fit the "structured world of night-club entertainment." Armstrong's stage persona proved particularly compelling, in part because it resolved the tensions of the black migrant experience. On the one hand, his indisputable professional success underscored the possibility of upward mobility. Despite his humble southern roots, he had risen on the strength of his instrumental facility and music-reading skills. He even earned the grudging admiration of *Chicago Defender* columnist Dave Peyton, the self-appointed guardian of bourgeois values of hard work and discipline, who routinely excoriated jazz musicians for "faking" and "bad habits" and dismissed their music as "sloppy New Orleans hokum."

At the same time, Armstrong's performances embodied the African-American folkways that were denigrated by Peyton and threatened by widespread transplantation to the urban North. In Armstrong's stylish blues phrasing, rhythmic nuances, and body language, South Side audiences recognized themselves, and they took comfort in the successful integration of these down-home modalities into sophisticated entertainment. Milt Hinton remembered hearing Armstrong at the Vendome Theater, which was crowded on Sundays by black audiences in formal dress:

> It was like we were emulating white folks, like it was a big white theater.
> . . . We were going to be just like downtown. And we'd sit there, my mother
> would have me by the hand, and we'd sit and listen to this overture which
> had a European environment. Then the people would be a little restless, and
> say "Well, that sounds nice," and applaud it. Then somebody would say
> "Hey baby, play so and so," and when Louis stood up and played one of his
> great solos, you could see everybody letting their hair down and say "Yeah,
> that's the way it should be. This is it."

In the spring of 1929, Hawkins's and Armstrong's paths briefly crossed—surprisingly, in the world of mainstream musical theater. Fletcher Henderson had been hired as the musical contractor for a new musical comedy, Vincent Youmans's *Great Day*. Louis Armstrong had just returned to New York, and his new manager, Tommy Rockwell, eager to set him to work, recommended him for the first trumpet chair. What seemed to be a promising opportunity to appear on Broadway for all concerned turned to disaster when the management began arbitrarily replacing black musicians, including Armstrong, with white ones. Hawkins survived the first cut, but as the production lurched toward Broadway, even Henderson was displaced. This may have been a blessing, for *Great Day* flopped after only thirty-seven shows.

Armstrong himself had better luck in the theater. Later in the year, he earned a spot in the all-black revue *Hot Chocolates*, moving "out of the pit and on the stage" to sing and play Fats Waller's new hit song, "Ain't Misbehavin'." This performance convinced Rockwell to promote Armstrong as a "single act"—a front man for large dance orchestras—and to begin a series of recordings that received extraordinarily wide distribution through both "race" record and mainstream pop catalogs. Thus it was that shortly after relocating to California to play at Frank Sebastian's Cotton Club in Culver City in July 1930, Armstrong recorded his own version of "If I Could Be with You One Hour Tonight," with a full-chorus trumpet solo preceding the vocal.

If one places transcriptions of Armstrong's and Hawkins's solos side by side (with Hawkins's transposed to match Armstrong's key of E-flat for easy comparison; see music example 2), the similarities are striking. The two solos share the same basic rhythmic vocabulary (e.g., the pervasive double-time feeling) and characteristic melodic contours (e.g., the upward arpeggios in measure 5). In some places, they share the same idiosyncratic note choices. Had Hawkins's solo not been recorded first, one might assume that he had consciously modeled his solo on Armstrong's. Instead, the similarities are strong evidence of an underlying commonality of approach.

Both solos exemplify the technique known as *harmonic improvisation*. Roughly speaking, this is the practice of deriving notes for an improvised line from the underlying chord progression. Such a technique is impressive in its own right for adding an air of sophistication or technical polish to a performance (or at least avoiding unpleasant clashes between melody and harmony). But it also contributes to the rhythmic effectiveness of the improvised line. Properly handled, harmonic improvisation is a subtle but essential component of the sense of rhythmic momentum in jazz usually known as swing.

EX. 2.
Top line: "If I Could Be with You One Hour Tonight" (1930), Louis Armstrong solo, mm. 1–6. Bottom line: "One Hour" (1929), Coleman Hawkins solo, mm. 1–6 (transposed from original key of A-flat).

Harmony and swing may not seem to have much to do with each other. They even claim different pedigrees: as the musicologist Thomas Brothers has noted, the "fusion theory" of the origins of jazz ascribes chromatic harmony to Europe and its distinctive rhythms to Africa. But harmony is linked to rhythm through *dissonance,* as the following brief digression into elementary music theory should make clear.

In common parlance, dissonance connotes harsh and unpleasant sounds. Its meaning in music theory is less judgmental and more technical. A dissonance is any combination of tones that is understood to be unstable and therefore requires resolution to a stable sonority, or consonance. This is the basic principle of tension and release in the tonal system, and it operates on many different levels. Notes that clash against the prevailing harmony at any given moment—nonharmonic tones, or what Hawkins would call "off notes"—are the most obvious and immediate generators of tension; but within a key, any chord other than the tonic, no matter how internally consonant, is inherently unstable and therefore dissonant. Dissonance implies forward movement, a drive toward resolution. It is in this sense that we speak of a harmonic *progression*. In the repertory that jazz musicians of the 1920s and 1930s played, the forward momentum of the harmony is unambiguous and an important constituent of rhythmic drive.

A harmonic progression is commonly thought of as a succession of discrete and independent entities called chords, but this description is a kind of shorthand. When we say, for example, that G^7 moves to C (V^7 to I in the key of C), we are really describing the aggregate melodic movement of several different voices. Some implied melodic motions are more highly charged than others: the note F, when forming the dissonant seventh of the dominant seventh chord G^7, has a particularly strong tendency to resolve downward, by half step, to E, the third of C. These unstable melodic tones are known as tendency tones (or in modern jazz theory, guide tones). Each tendency tone contains potential energy, like a coiled spring, which can be unleashed by the proper voice-leading. Any jazz musician with sufficient understanding of harmony to incorporate these dissonances smoothly into an improvisation can draw upon that energy for an extra dimension of rhythmic drive. Louis Armstrong, whose grasp of harmony was as sure and confident as his command of rhythm, relied on this principle as one of many dimensions of swing.

In both Armstrong's and Hawkins's solos on "One Hour," the tendency tones are fairly easy to spot. More often than not, they are chromatic aberrations that stand out against an otherwise diatonic background. Knowing how to "run the changes" thus meant more than being able to spell out the notes of the chords through arpeggiation (although for many musicians of their generation, that was challenge enough). It meant singling out the most active tones in the underlying harmony, absorbing them into the improvised line, and riding the momentum of their melodic resolution to the next chord. In "One Hour," both Armstrong and Hawkins pounce upon the dissonant augmented fifth (f-sharp') in the second measure of "One Hour" and lead it to resolution on g' at the beginning of the next phrase (rather more explicitly in Hawkins's case than Armstrong's). "Running the changes" could also mean introducing chromatic tones where none is implied by the harmony—as when both Hawkins and Armstrong choose to intensify a diatonic melodic motion (c'–d' in measures 5–6) with an interpolated chromatic passing tone (c-sharp').

This much the two solos have in common, but there is a difference in rhythmic sensibility, which is less evident here because it is disguised by the medium of transcription. The printed page cannot begin to convey the authority and eloquence of Armstrong's musical gestures and the relative inadequacy of Hawkins's by comparison.

A crucial source of this authority for Armstrong, as for many other jazz musicians, was the blues. As one of the constitutive elements of African-American cultural identity, the blues is not easy to define. But in narrowly musical terms, it may be thought of as a modal system that coordinates several different dimensions simultaneously: pitch collections (the "blues scale"), characteristic melodic contours, a subtle manipulation of intonation ("blue notes"), vocalized timbres, and an elusive, floating rhythmic quality. It is the latter quality that is relevant here. Armstrong's rhythmic gestures have the paradoxical and unmistakably bluesy property of seeming at once completely free from the meter *and* grounded in the foundation dance pulse.

Such gestures, immediately apparent to the ear, translate poorly to the printed page, for the simple reason that ambiguity cannot easily be conveyed in a linear system of notation. To choose one small but revealing example: at the beginning of his solo, Armstrong places the note e-flat" (the third note of measure 1) just fractionally after the beat. He does so, however, with such absolute authority that one is almost convinced that it *is* on the beat. This expressive manipulation of time is similar in principle to the Western notion of rubato, in which time is momentarily suspended, or stretched, to underscore a particularly important moment of arrival. The difference is that in jazz, the suspension of time occurs in one rhythmic layer while the steady foundation pulse is rigorously maintained in another, so that one experiences the expressive time-stretch and the unchanging framework as a disconcerting *simultaneity*. To convey this characteristically African-American multiplicity of interpretations in a single melodic line, I have resorted to a kind of notation idiosyncratic to jazz transcription. The rhythm on the page is what Armstrong implies by stress accents—a reality that Armstrong momentarily creates and persuades us to accept. But these rhythms are modified by an arrow in brackets, a reminder that the phrase is simultaneously perceived as clashing with the underlying foundation pulse.

This subtle ambiguity is clearly recognizable as part of the initial statement of James P. Johnson's melody. Eight bars later, the melody returns— as anyone familiar with the symmetries of popular song form might predict—and Armstrong's response (music example 3) is richer and more complicated: still a telling of the original, but stretching it almost to the

EX. 3.
"If I Could Be with You One Hour Tonight," Louis Armstrong solo, mm. 9–10.
Top line: transcription by the author. Bottom line: transcription from Schuller
1989, 168.

breaking point. I have chosen one way of rendering this juncture in musical notation; Gunther Schuller, in *The Swing Era*, another. The point is
to underscore the deliberate ambiguity that makes it impossible to come
up with a single accurate representation. The critic Stanley Crouch speaks
of the essence of the black aesthetic as a "sense of infinite plasticity." For
Armstrong, time is elastic, capable of infinite reshaping, unbound by
artificial divisions into equal beats. Such gestures are the essence of his
art. Like a master elocutionist, Armstrong builds intensity through an
accumulation of well-timed and expertly shaped phrases. His eloquence,
as with the black preacher in James Weldon Johnson's *The Autobiography
of an Ex-Colored Man*, "consists more in the manner of saying than in
what is said."

A bluesy approach to improvisation was by no means foreign to Coleman
Hawkins's experience. He had ample opportunity to hear and learn the
blues throughout his early career, from Mamie Smith to the blues-
oriented trombonists in the Henderson band like Charlie Green, Dicky
Wells, and Claude Jones, who shaped their solos through an artful use of
idiomatic timbres, slides, and melodic contours. Still, perhaps because he
continued to associate it with the uncouth theatrical entertainment of his
youth, Hawkins openly disdained what he once called the "plain blues."
On rare occasions (as, for example, on Horace Henderson's 1931 "Hot
and Anxious," where he toots out an aggressively bluesy chorus on the
clarinet), Hawkins abstracted from the blues a certain rough tone and
forceful, percussive manner, and demonstrated his mastery of some of its

simpler and more obvious phrases. Otherwise, he showed little affinity for the idiom.

As a result, Hawkins lacked Armstrong's sense of timing, his feeling for the note placed "in the cracks" of the beats, disrupting and enriching the underlying metrical framework. Where Armstrong soars in the ninth measure of "One Hour," Hawkins stumbles. He begins the phrase with a strong cross-rhythm (accents on the fourth note of each sixteenth-note grouping), but he cannot maintain it and quickly succumbs to the gravitational attraction of the downbeat. By the phrase's end (measure 10), the rhythmic shape has flattened out into even sixteenths and the line trails off into the musical equivalent of an embarrassed mutter.

Still, for all these flaws, Hawkins's "One Hour" is convincing and deserving of the critical acclaim it received. Its success points unmistakably in the direction of Hawkins's later achievements. In essence, Hawkins isolated the one aspect of Louis Armstrong's musical persona—the mastery of harmony—that was most congenial to his talents and temperament and subjected it to an intense, and highly personal, development.

In the hands of a skilled instrumentalist, "running the changes" could serve as the basis for an idiom that owed little to either the blues or to the melodies of popular song. Armstrong was certainly aware of this possibility, for he had heard it in the clarinet obbligatos of the New Orleans jazz ensemble. Early in his career, as he later told an interviewer, he tried the style on for size, only to retreat to the musical language dictated by his received role in the ensemble: "I was just like a clarinet player, like the guys run up and down the horn nowadays, boppin' and things. I was doin' all that, fast fingers and everything, so [King Oliver] used to tell me: 'Play some lead on that horn, boy.' "[1]

For Armstrong, harmonic improvisation was never the main focus. His use of it in "One Hour" is unobtrusive. It is as if two levels were operating simultaneously: the unfolding of the diatonic "lead" in the upper register in long note values and an open, singing tone, and the articulation of the underlying harmony in sixteenth-note asides that im-

---

1. Trombonist Clyde Bernhardt tells a similar story about his experiences with King Oliver in the early 1930s. Thrilled to be playing with the famous bandleader, Bernhardt put his prodigious technique on display: "I took some long solos, got off some extra triple tongue passages, all that fast stuff. I was showing the King all my tricks and that I was worthy of him." Oliver's laconic response was: "Son, you don't have to do all that shit to impress me. You got a good swinging style and all them snakes [i.e., long chromatic passages] you makin', loses the flavor. It don't mean a damn thing" (Bernhardt 1986, 95).

ply a double-time feeling. The distinction between the two layers begins to dissolve after measure 9, as the solo begins to heat up: the melody is stretched almost beyond recognition, and a purely harmonic event—the e-natural" associated with the chord C⁷—irrupts into the melodic register in measures 11–12. But the overall rhetoric is still that of melodic paraphrase.

Hawkins, by contrast, seized on the idea of harmonic improvisation and made a specialization of it, wearing his intellectual and technical control over the process as a badge of honor. While still with the Henderson band, he made a show of mocking his band mate and close friend, trombonist Jimmy Harrison, for his alleged ignorance of harmony: "I used to tell him, 'Doggone shame the way you're fooling people. You ain't doing nothing! You're not playing your changes, you're missing changes. Look at this. You just play this—you see this change right here? This change makes this other one sound better, because it *resolves* into the other one.' "

By the early 1930s, Hawkins had moved decisively beyond Louis Armstrong as an immediate inspiration. If his earlier model had been the trumpet, he now took advantage of the greater agility of his instrument and adopted the rapid, fluid playing of fellow reed players, such as Jimmy Noone and Johnny Hodges. He underscored his virtuosity by the simple one-upmanship of playing more notes. As he later bluntly explained, "When I was playing one note, it was because I couldn't play but one note . . . When I can make two, I make two. That's how it's always been with me." In recording after recording from the 1930s, one can hear the conscious strategy of saturating the available musical space—a kind of rhetoric of abundance. Of course, this approach also took advantage of his unusually well-developed grasp of harmony, which allowed him to *hear*, as well as execute, two notes where others heard only one. He paid close attention to piano players and, in particular, to a virtuoso pianist he heard in Toledo in the late 1920s. According to Rex Stewart,

Hawk, like the rest of us, was greatly impressed by a young fellow named Art Tatum, who displayed such a wealth of talent on the piano. His then-new conception of anticipating the chord changes within the framework of a tune left us numb from the experience. . . .

[Hawk] was so taken by Tatum's playing that he immediately started creating another style for himself, based on what he'd heard Tatum play that night.

Nowhere was this more evident than in Hawkins's specialty: the romantic ballad. His impassioned playing on such tunes as "It's the Talk of the Town," "The Day You Came Along," or "I've Got to Sing a Torch Song" (all from late 1933) stood curiously apart from the contexts of either dance music or popular song. The dance-inspired double-time feeling of many of his recordings disappeared. In its place was a dramatic, almost theatrical attitude that belonged less to the cadences of popular music than those of coloratura or instrumental bravura. Beginning with relaxed triplets, Hawkins typically accelerated to note values that hovered ambiguously between sixteenths, sixteenth-note sextuplets, thirty-second notes, or even faster note values as he plummeted toward a melodic goal. The intent was to overwhelm: no other saxophonist of the time could begin to match the brilliant surface of these improvisations—which came, remarkably enough, at no sacrifice to his stentorian tone.

But this rhapsodic style had obvious limitations. It implied a role set apart from the dance band, and therefore dangerously anomalous. For no concert hall of the time—except occasionally the Salle Pleyel in Paris—would accept Hawkins as a concert artist, receiving his bravura variations on popular songs with the same reverence accorded to violinist Jascha Heifetz or coloratura soprano Amelita Galli-Curci. Hawkins's entrance into the concert hall would come much later, with jazz promoter Norman Granz's imaginary (and portable) "Philharmonic" devoted to jazz. For the moment, Hawkins had to inhabit the world of dance music.

At more ordinary tempos, when swinging *with* the groove of a dance band rather than apart from it, Hawkins had more difficulty distinguishing himself from the herd. His notorious tendency toward rhythmic uniformity—a steady stream of eighth notes (actually "swing" eighth notes, with the first note of the pair slightly longer than the second), later caricatured by one writer as a "machine-gun style"—was only exacerbated by his ongoing project of crowding as much of the underlying harmony as possible into his improvised line. "It is as if," Martin Williams has written, "in making all the chords, Hawkins also became determined to make all the beats." Even as he solidified his control over range, speed, and tone and intimidated rivals with his erudition, he struggled with the overall rhythmic effect of his improvisations.

One response was to seek relief in rhythmic gestures that, in Gunther Schuller's words, fell "between the rhythmic cracks." There are passages in many of Hawkins's most celebrated solos with Fletcher Henderson—"Honeysuckle Rose," "Underneath the Harlem Moon," "New King Porter Stomp" (all 1932)—that seem willfully perverse in their refusal to settle into the groove. Such gestures, like many of Armstrong's, are rhythmically elusive and virtually impossible to translate into notation. But Hawkins's gestures often seem arbitrary and extravagant, even impatient, their relationship to the ground beat deliberately obscure.

Throughout the 1930s Hawkins's usual aggressive confidence had an edge of restiveness and unease. Looking back some twenty years later, Hawkins claimed to see no value in his music from this period: "Back in the 'thirties—I can't think of nothing I particularly like from then. Not now! As I said, your ears change!" Even as compelling a landmark as Hawkins's solo on "Honeysuckle Rose" calls to Schuller's mind "a giant, wrestling with a large problem." The problem may have been, as both Schuller and Hawkins imply, largely aesthetic. Ever the perfectionist, Hawkins was always looking for a better way to swing, a more convincing way to construct a solo. But it may also be construed as social. His restless dissatisfaction was part of an ongoing search for a professional role more suited to his talents, temperament, and ambitions.

Virtuoso in Exile

On March 23, 1934, Hawkins set sail from New York for London on the *Île de France*. In so doing, he became perhaps the most prominent musician of his generation to attempt a declaration of independence from the dance bands.

There had always been jazz musicians whose careers intersected only glancingly with dance orchestras, of course: pianists like Fats Waller or Art Tatum, New Orleans survivors like Sidney Bechet, white rebels like Eddie Condon or Pee Wee Russell. But Hawkins's decision was particularly striking because his career had been virtually coeval with the growth of the big bands. For more than a decade, his fortunes and those of the premier black dance orchestra of the time were intertwined. As Fletcher Henderson's prospects brightened, so did his: by the beginning of the 1930s he was earning an average of $150 a week and was billed as "Cole Hawkins, World's Greatest Saxophonist." Henderson's band was a secure source of employment that gave Hawkins the framework he needed to develop as a musician. Recordings document year by year his striking progress from journeyman saxophonist to mature and confident virtuoso.

The Depression abruptly flattened the upward curve of the booming 1920s, and rising expectations hit the hard wall of reality. With prospects dimming at home, Europe offered an intriguing alternative. Through their highly publicized tours of Britain and the continent in the early

1930s, Duke Ellington and Louis Armstrong had already shown that black jazz musicians were welcome in prestigious theaters and concert halls. Fletcher Henderson himself tried to set up such a tour toward the end of 1933. After it fell through, Hawkins decided to act. A terse telegram of inquiry ("I am interested in coming to London") gained him an invitation from Jack Hylton, a prominent British dance bandleader. What was originally intended as a tour of a few months' duration stretched out to five years. By age thirty, Hawkins was on his own.

The assumption that jazz was better appreciated and supported in Europe than at home has recently come under sharp attack by the critic and historian James Lincoln Collier. Among other things, Collier argues that the actual audience for jazz in Europe was insignificant compared with the vast market in the United States. In a purely quantitative sense, this is certainly correct. Hawkins gained no particular financial advantage from what amounted to a detour in his career, a lateral escape from the American music industry. Indeed, it is more than likely that his removal from the American scene shortly before the dance band business embarked on a dramatic expansion worked to his disadvantage. Had he been on the scene just a year or two later, in 1935 or 1936, he would have been a logical candidate to lead his own band and might well have ridden the crest of the swing wave to considerable financial success.

But life as an expatriate offered other rewards. Hawkins settled into a pleasantly nomadic routine—shuttling between engagements in England, France, Belgium, Holland, Denmark, and Switzerland, returning to the United States only when threatened by the rumblings of war. As a freelance musician, he enjoyed a new professional autonomy. Whether on the variety stage and in concert halls, as the star soloist with dance bands ranging in size from seven to sixteen pieces, or as the leader of groups ranging from a trio to a ten-piece band, he was very much his own man: imposing his own tastes on the repertory, negotiating performing conditions, exercising his right to move on whenever an extended engagement became tiresome.

As the center of attention, Hawkins played for as long as he liked and as often as he liked. His solos took up most of the space on many of the recordings from Europe, and even ensemble passages were frequently interrupted—and quite overwhelmed—by his improvised obbligatos. By the same token, he also played as little as he liked. On many engagements, his appearances were carefully limited to a handful of featured numbers (the better to capture the attention of an admiring public), leaving him ample time to indulge his taste for fine liquor and women in pleasant surroundings. The black trumpeter Arthur Briggs, who hired Hawkins for a brief residency in Brussels in 1938, recalled:

> When we were working at the Casino, he would drink a bottle of brandy a day. He was featured at the tea dance. He did three numbers, so most of the time he was free in the baccarat room. He didn't gamble, he'd just be at the bar, and when I sent someone to fetch him to play he'd come straight as ever. . . . I think Europe was a rest cure for him. Think of the work he'd done in America with Fletcher Henderson. In Europe he was playing an hour a day maximum.

Along with professional freedom came a heady degree of social freedom. Collier is right to point out that Europe, then as now, was hardly free from racism, that admiration for black musicians was mixed with condescension and founded on a good deal of ignorance about jazz and black Americans in general, and that the enlightened social attitudes of a small core of enthusiasts were far from representative of the European population as a whole. Still, for African Americans inured to the numbing inescapability of racial caste in their own country, the respect and attention they received abroad was startling, and ultimately healing. Ellington found in his 1933 European tour the "kind of thing [that] gives you the courage to go on. If they think I'm *that* important, then maybe I have kinda said something, maybe our music does mean something." Rex Stewart remembered his arrival in Europe with Ellington six years later with simple eloquence, as "the first time in my life I had the feeling of being accepted as an artist, a gentleman and a member of the human race."

Perhaps because he preferred to project an unflappable image of worldly sophistication, Hawkins left no such record of emotional transformation. But it is hard to imagine him being unmoved by the enthusiasm with which he was greeted all over Europe. On a tour of Scandinavia in 1935, he basked in the kind of adulation associated more with opera stars than dance musicians. In Oslo he was presented with a bouquet of flowers. In Copenhagen an estimated crowd of 5,000 fans met him at the train station, carrying him to his taxi on an ornate chair. Everywhere he went he was revered by European musicians and enjoyed the company of European women. "Girls were his hobby," one Dutch jazz fan remembered.

"He used to serenade them with his sax. . . . The tenor saxist Johnny Russell once said to me, 'Every goddamn town I ever played had a girl there chasing Hawkins.' " According to Tommy Benford, who played drums with Hawkins on a 1937 Paris recording session, "Europe was really Europe then. We couldn't do wrong. The pianos were *always* in tune and everything was always clean, and every club, no matter how small, had a room for the musicians to go between sets—not like it is here, where you have to walk up and down the sidewalk when you're not playing."

Although he continued to work primarily as a dance musician, Hawkins found ample opportunity to explore other possibilities. With concerts and theater engagements, he was thrust into a new role, for he had to justify his appearance onstage as a "featured attraction." Although he could have fallen back on the role of entertainer—what Lionel Hampton once called "a long, honorable tradition of clowning in black performing"—Hawkins had no particular taste for that kind of stage business, his youthful acrobatics with Mamie Smith notwithstanding. Instead, he drew almost by default on the obvious model of the European concert tradition, which demanded little of the performer beyond a confident, dignified manner; a well-groomed countenance; and an air of total concentration on the matter at hand.

Hawkins was not naive enough to believe that in adopting its manners, he had somehow become a concert artist in the European tradition. But he relished situations that challenged the boundaries separating jazz and classical music, and by extension, the social limitations that prevented a black man of talent from experiencing the wider world. When a young woman who had heard him perform over the radio told him his improvisations "sounded as classics," he was flattered. Characteristically, he was sensible enough not to be seduced by such praise into superficial borrowings from European music. It was enough that his virtuoso abstraction of a pop song like "Sweet Sue" be judged independent of the socially limiting associations of entertainment and dance. Recounting a concert appearance in Roubaix, France, in 1937, in which he performed one of his favorite tunes—"It's the Talk of the Town"—to the accompaniment of a symphony orchestra, he noted with an engaging mixture of pride and self-mockery:

They jotted the chorus down, that's all—a chorus with an ending, you know what I mean. They fixed for me to make my little breaks and things to bring the ending in, and the director just brought them down on this long, big, heavy ending chord, and that's all there was to it. It was real funny. [emphatically:] I was the *only thing* on the program like this. I mean, like, they had an opera singer. There was a—well naturally, at these concerts, they always have these soloists. Like they had a cello soloist that night on the program, things like that. Imagine—I'm on this program, and the concert-iest thing, I mean [laughs]—the long-hairedest thing I played was "It's the Talk of the Town"! [laughs].

This gradual shift in Hawkins's public persona—from dance band musician to concert virtuoso—was striking enough to discomfit some of his longtime supporters. Jazz journalist Walter Schaap happened to hear Hawkins at the Negro Palace in Amsterdam in 1937. Shortly before Hawkins's return to the United States in 1939, he felt compelled to warn his American readers about what he saw as troubling new undercurrents: "Five years abroad have done Hawkins no good. The adulation of critics and public has tended to bring out the exhibitionist in him, while playing as the featured soloist with inferior orchestras accustomed him to consider himself as the star, not as a fully integrated member of the band."

Similarly, Spike Hughes, the British bassist and arranger who five years earlier had served as Hawkins's patron by organizing a series of recording sessions that strongly featured him, found grounds for complaint in some of his 1938 appearances: "Hawkins's performances on stage had something of the demonstration in a lecture hall about them. They were in a curious way unreal. . . . From tempo-less, rhapsodic introductions and codas, Hawkins grew more and more into the star performer, less and less the inspired artist."

To some extent, these criticisms reflect circumstances peculiar to Hawkins's European years. The shortage of jazz musicians of his own caliber in Europe certainly encouraged Hawkins to view himself as the center of attention. As Schaap remembered, "Most of the time, except for a piano chorus or two or maybe a drum break, Hawkins was out there alone, uncorking four or five choruses in a row to the plaudits of the crowd." At the same time, the strong, even moralistic, tone of disapproval (Europe has "done [him] no good") suggests something more: that in positioning himself as a "star," Hawkins had transgressed some fundamental aesthetic boundary, imperiling his own artistic integrity—and perhaps that of the idiom as a whole.

Indeed, the very notion of a jazz virtuoso ran counter to the strain of primitivism that permeated much contemporaneous writing on jazz, especially (but not exclusively) in Europe. Winthrop Sargeant, for example, argued in his book *Jazz: Hot and Hybrid*, originally published in 1938, that the aesthetic power of jazz was grounded in its social reality as the expression of the African-American folk community. Like all folk music, he claimed, jazz "exhibit[ed] no intellectual complexities" and made "a simple, direct emotional appeal." It was distinguished from fine art by the evident lack of "the creative ingenuity and technique of an unusual, trained musical mind." Jazz arose from an illiterate folk culture, according to this view, and any inroads of education or training threatened its primitive effectiveness. So long as individual members of that culture remained unconscious exponents of a folk sensibility, its artistic power was virtually guaranteed. But, Hugues Panassié contended, a mere taste from the tree of knowledge—even the mere awareness that music might be the key to social mobility—was enough to cut musicians off from their source, as the subsequent development of jazz showed:

> For years jazz musicians had played as much for their own pleasure as to make a living. They enjoyed playing at dances and provoking the enthusiasm of the dancers and any musicians who came to hear them. They played by instinct, without thought of technique, and felt elated when the orchestra was "in the groove."
>
> But when jazz orchestras began to appear in theaters as "an attraction," when the magazines and reviews began to speak of jazz as an art . . . the Negro musician became increasingly aware of his own importance, or at least the importance of his music. That music which had been up to then an amusement took on the aspect of a fine art. And the inevitable occurred. These musicians who had infallibly played in a perfect manner, and had never digressed for an instant from the pure tradition of their art as long as they blindly followed their instincts, now swerved from their tradition and began to reason and to "improve" their music.

To the extent that Hawkins was even aware of such blanket condemnations of the foundations for his life and career—and Collier reports that the few blacks who were aware of Panassié's work found it an "oddity"—he did not let them interfere with his work. (Nor, for that matter, did Panassié's convictions prevent him from sponsoring, as codirector of the Hot Club of France, an elaborate concert at the Salle Rameau with Hawkins as its main "attraction.") Hawkins's challenge, as always, was to find a way to remain true to certain African-American aesthetic principles (e.g., playing "in the groove") while continuing to "improve" his art and adapt it to new circumstances, *and* advancing his career as a professional instrumentalist. As both Schaap and Hughes correctly (if unsympathetically) observed, this involved crafting a musical persona that projected him forcefully as a "star performer." Such a persona could accurately be described as "unreal" if what is meant is that it deliberately challenged the usual "realities" defining the ways in which jazz could be heard. The elaborate, unaccompanied introductions and codas—devices that Hawkins continued to use long after his return from Europe—were one way of setting his performances starkly in relief from these contexts. They established his credentials as a virtuoso as surely as vocal *fioritura* distinguish the operatic diva from the average chorus singer or the gospel soloist from the choir.

Another device Hawkins used to set himself apart was his ongoing exploration of harmonic improvisation. The results of his fascination with chromaticism were less obvious to the untrained observer than his stage manner, perhaps, but more directly relevant to the "intellectual complexities" supposedly alien to true jazz. Throughout the 1930s, and especially during his years in Europe, he continued to refine and redefine the art of harmonic improvisation, steadily increasing the level of dissonance in his solos.

To be sure, many of the dissonant tones in his improvisations hardly called attention to themselves. They were a basic constituent of the style, a way of preventing the monotony of unrelieved consonance. A passage from the bridge of Hawkins's famous solo on "Crazy Rhythm," recorded with Benny Carter and Django Reinhardt in 1937, illustrates the manner. In measure 19 (see music example 4), where the harmony turns (for the first time) to the subdominant, the core of Hawkins's line—a scalar descent in the implied new key of B-flat—is encrusted with nonharmonic tones. These dissonances are typically combined in double neighbor motions that converge on a point of resolution. The e-flat"–c-sharp" in the second half of the measure is a good example, as is the a"–f-sharp" pair at the beginning, which leads to a note (g") that is itself a passing tone in need of resolution (on f"). Such nonharmonic tones add color and variety to an improviser's palette and turn routine scales into elegant arabesques.

The continuation of the phrase illustrates a subtler and more interesting phenomenon. In measure 21, the harmony changes to the minor

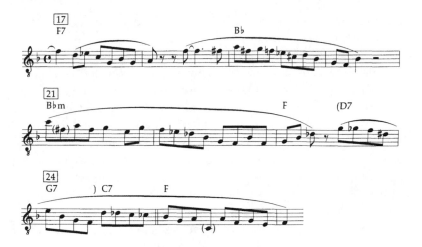

EX. 4.
"Crazy Rhythm" (1937), Coleman Hawkins solo, mm. 17–26.

subdominant (B-flat minor), with the tendency tone D-flat faithfully reflected in Hawkins's line in the following measure. D-flat aims at a resolution on C—presumably in measure 23, the beginning of a standard
cadential formula (the "turnaround") that prepares for the return of the
tonic. But Hawkins's phrase pauses briefly in measure 23 on d-flat", leaving the broader harmonic dissonance (the minor subdominant) for the
moment unresolved. Instead, he steers the line toward a strong arrival
on the leading tone, e", on the downbeat of measure 24, thereby establishing the dominant. The dangling d-flat" is picked up by the chromatic
descent at the end of the measure, part of a lengthy stepwise motion that
finally falls to f' in measure 26. The e", itself left hanging, is resolved by
the f" that begins the new phrase on the third beat of the measure (not
shown).

There is nothing particularly dramatic about this passage, but the effect
of deferring resolution is to spill the energy of the harmony slightly over
its boundaries into the next measure. This rhythmic intensity, generated
by harmonic resources, is an essential characteristic of Hawkins's approach to improvisation. One has to only compare this treatment of the
end of the bridge with the Benny Carter solo that preceded it (music
example 5) to see how differently this harmonic juncture could be handled. Carter—a man who preferred to "present things neatly packaged"—articulates the harmonic arrivals with elegant understatement

and precision. His line has little of the urgency or the aggressiveness with which Hawkins assaults the bar line.

A more striking use of chromatic dissonance can be heard in "Sweet Georgia Brown," recorded on the same day. Hawkins has two solos on the recording. The first is a kind of warm-up, restrained in volume, timbre, and register, and restricted primarily to chord tones. Benny Carter's elegant muted trumpet solo follows, with Hawkins's second solo coming in on its heels (music example 6). Hawkins's competitive spirit immediately inspires him to a more aggressive manner. He marks his entrance with a burst of intensity, leaping upward to d''' (the peak of the entire solo) to emphasize the mild but striking dissonance of the thirteenth against the prevailing F⁷ harmony.

When the same harmony returns at the halfway point of the chorus

EX. 5.
"Crazy Rhythm" (1937), Benny Carter solo, mm. 17–25.

EX. 6.
"Sweet Georgia Brown" (1937), second Coleman Hawkins solo, mm. 1–3.

(music example 7), the rhythm is flattened out to even eighth notes. At the same time, the level of dissonance increases noticeably. The nonharmonic tones in measure 18—g-flat', b-flat', c-flat'—can be quite sensibly understood as contrapuntal elaborations of the underlying F^7 harmony, which are not fully resolved until the next measure, or perhaps not even until the appearance of an unadorned F^7 arpeggio at the end of measure 20. But by deferring resolution for so long, Hawkins leaves open the possibility of a second interpretation: that these dissonant notes are the constituent tones of an interpolated or "substitute" harmony—ii^7 (E-flat, G-flat, B-flat, C) in a presumed ii^7–V^7 formula in the key of B-flat minor, or even a C-flat major triad, its root a tritone away from the root of the F^7. How much one should make of this example is not clear: the passage flies by at such a clip that the implied harmonies are ambiguous. Nor is Hawkins entirely in control. The spilling over of dissonant tones into measure 21 seems simply to be a miscalculation.

It did not take Hawkins long to learn how to handle more sophisticated chromatic dissonances, however. Although documentation is spotty, extant recordings suggest that this must have occurred in his last years in Europe. Compare, for instance, performances two years apart of "My Buddy," a 1920s sentimental song transformed from waltz-time to a danceable swing 4/4. In the first version, recorded in The Hague in 1937, the only chromatic notes in Hawkins's solo are passing tones or tendency tones implicit in the harmonies. The climax of the solo (apparently carefully planned out, for in an unissued take it happens in the same spot) comes three-fourths of the way through, in measures 25–26 (music example 8): a fortissimo rip upward to peak of pitch (c'''), followed by an emphatic descending chromatic scale.

By the time of the second version, recorded shortly after his return to New York in the winter of 1939, Hawkins used chromatic interpolations to strike an ingenious balance between the vertical dimension of harmony and the horizontal logic of the melodic line. This led him to tinker with the harmonic progression for the sake of an unorthodox bit of voice-leading. In measures 5–8 (music example 9), as part of a melodic descent (g"–f-sharp"–e"–d"), Hawkins offers an arpeggiated dominant seventh chord based on F-sharp in place of the B-flat diminished chord in measure 6. This implied clash is not particularly harsh, since F-sharp^7 has three tones in common with B-flat diminished; but it is unorthodox, and probably would have puzzled most musicians of the time who happened to think about it. In the solo that immediately follows Hawkins's (music example 10), Lionel Hampton briefly tries out an F-sharp triad, only to quickly retreat, apparently unable to see how it resolves.

A more characteristic harmonic embellishment occurs three-fourths of the way through (music example 11). As with the earlier version, Hawkins announces a climax of sorts with an emphatic chromatic descent from the tonic. But before the implicit goal of the descent (d″) is reached, one of the notes—e-flat″—emerges as the seventh of a new chord, F⁷. F⁷ is easily understood as a chromatic passing chord filling in the space between I (G) and VI⁷ (E⁷). However, its continuation into measure 27,

EX. 7.
"Sweet Georgia Brown," second Coleman Hawkins solo, mm. 17–22.

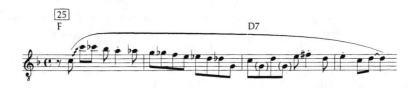

EX. 8.
"My Buddy" (1937), Coleman Hawkins solo, mm. 25–28.

EX. 9.
"My Buddy" (1939), Coleman Hawkins solo, mm. 5–8.

EX. 10.
"My Buddy" (1939), Lionel Hampton solo, mm. 9–10.

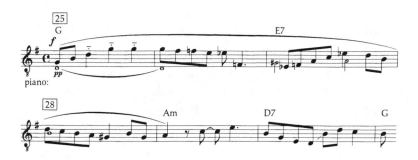

EX. 11.
"My Buddy" (1939), Coleman Hawkins solo, mm. 25–31.

where the E^7 is not only expected, but sounded in the rhythm section (note the countermelody played quietly by pianist Joe Sullivan), is a sharp dissonance, characteristic of Hawkins's mature style. It works because each dissonant note finds its downward resolution, either as soon as the E^7 harmony arrives in the following measure, or—in the case of e-flat' and f-natural'—the next time Hawkins happens to pass through that particular register (i.e., several measures later, in measure 30). It is logical, forceful, and uncompromisingly complicated—three essential elements of Hawkins's style.

While Hawkins's imaginative and unorthodox approach to chromatic harmony impressed and intimidated his fellow musicians, it is doubtful that such details of craft would have moved audiences had he not learned, like Armstrong, to "make his music part of a larger presentation." Eventually, Hawkins integrated his dissonances into an overall rhetorical plan.

His way of "telling a story" through his improvised solos was uncomplicated and emotionally direct. It was a continuous, carefully controlled crescendo of intensity on several fronts at once: a gradual thickening or hardening of timbre, a steady increase in volume, and a climb to a melodic peak carefully withheld until very near the end. The relentless linear logic of harmonic improvisation served as the connecting thread. None of this, it might be added, was particularly Hawkins's property. The general scheme was so obvious, so rooted in musical common sense, that it was widely imitated. Hawkins was simply better at it than anyone else, more adept at building seamlessly to a shattering climax. No recording better exemplified this formula, and its potential appeal, than his famous "Body and Soul."[2]

Passionate Virtuosity

Later in life, Hawkins liked to tell the story of "Body and Soul" as if its extraordinary success mystified him. The tune had meant nothing to him before 1939; the circumstances of its recording were accidental; and the performance was nothing out of the ordinary:

> I don't think I started playing "Body and Soul" until—let me see—'39. . . . And then I never thought of it seriously—you know, I never thought of "Body and Soul" as being anything big for me. I used it as an *encore*, something to get off the stage with, now you know how much I thought of it! I call myself getting off the stage, I want to ease off! [chuckles] You know what I mean? *Through*, you know? And I'd play this thing, you know, and I never thought anything of it. Playing down at Kelly's [Stable, on 52nd Street], when Victor asked me to record it. I was surprised that they even thought about it! But what they'd done, some of the boys had come in, you know, and had heard me play it in the club. So they ask Leonard Joy to get me to record it, you know. So I said, [puzzled] "What is this? I don't even have an arrangement on it!" . . .
>
> What we used to do, at nights I used to play—you know, I'd be—after a couple quarts of Scotch, I'd sit down there, killing time, I'd perhaps play about ten choruses on it, and the boys, every so often they'd come in with me and play harmony notes, you know what I mean, and I'd finish it up, and that was all there was, you know. So naturally, when we got ready to do the date, they couldn't play but two choruses, 'cause the three minute record won't take over that. So we did it the same way, and I thought nothing of it. . . . [emphatically] And I didn't even bother to listen to it afterwards! Got through playing it, and packed my horn up and walked out! . . .
>
> Gracious, I play like that all the time! You know what I mean, I made a

---

2. For a full transcription of Hawkins's solo on "Body and Soul," see Schuller 1989, 442–443.

thousand pieces of that same thing, played in the same vein and everything else! But they didn't mean nothing—you know?

In fact, as the research of Hawkins's biographer, John Chilton, has made clear, "Body and Soul" was one of only a handful of standard pop songs that Hawkins felt comfortable enough with to make a regular part of his repertory during his European years.[3] On his return to the United States in the fall of 1939, he continued to feature it regularly. "The boys" at Victor Records were not the only ones to notice. Something about the song seemed to inspire Hawkins to new heights of sustained eloquence. A reviewer for *Variety* who saw Hawkins at Kelly's Stable commented appreciatively on his ability to play "Body and Soul" for "chorus after chorus and no two alike." A photograph of Hawkins in *Down Beat* ran with a caption that described him as "going into his seventh straight chorus of 'Body and Soul.' " For a visitor to a Long Island jam session, the "highlight" of the evening was Hawkins's inspired playing, in particular "his ten-minute solos of 'Body and Soul.' "

The recording of "Body and Soul" enjoyed surprising success in the marketplace. Its sales, estimated at nearly 100,000 copies in the first six months, did not approach the magnitude of such hits as "One O'Clock Jump," "Begin the Beguine," and "Tuxedo Junction." But for a record without vocals, catchy riffs, or a hard-swinging dance tempo, it did remarkably well. Hawkins expressed puzzlement at the widespread appeal of a lengthy, uninterrupted improvisation that had little in common with the language of popular song and made few overt concessions to popular taste:

> Thelonious Monk said to me . . . he used to say it quite often back in the 52nd Street days, but about six months ago he mentioned to me, "You know, you never did explain to me," he said, "*how* did these people, these *old folks* and everybody, go for your record of 'Body and Soul'? . . . 'Cause I've listened to the record, and I can understand if you played melody, 'cause that's

---

3. Before a concert in Belgium in 1937, Hawkins wrote to the promoter, informing him that his program would "consist of all the old favorites," specifically mentioning "Blue Skies" and "Body and Soul" (Chilton 1990, 136). He performed "Body and Soul" nightly at the Negro Palace in Amsterdam in early 1939 (Chilton 1990, 150), and just before leaving for America he wrote to a close female friend: "Thanks so much for liking the way I played 'Body and Soul,' you know that's always been one of my favorite tunes" (Chilton 1990, 154).

what they like, those kind of people, that's what they like, they like melody."
He said, "They sure won't listen to anything else that's jazz!" He said, "I
can't understand how you got—how they listen to it."

So I just told him, I said, "That's just one of those cases." You know? . . .
[laughs] That's all! 'Cause you know I didn't play no—where's the melody
in "Body and Soul"? So I've talked to these people—hm!—[imitates thin,
affected voice]: *You can just hear the melody all through it!*" [returning to
his natural voice] Now these are the people that don't know anything about
music. I mean, these people I'm talking about, you know—the people you've
got to please, you know? They hear the melody! [forcefully] Where is the
melody? They didn't play no melody—ain't no melody, ain't no real melody
in the whole piece!!

Again, his remarks seem disingenuous. Anyone listening to the opening bars of the recording can immediately "hear the melody," for the
good reason that Hawkins states it. His version is delicately ornate and
rhythmically elusive, but quite recognizable. Hawkins establishes a lan-
guorous, intimate mood at the outset by allowing his phrases to lag
slightly behind the beat. Transcriptions tend to misrepresent this effect
by rendering the rhythms too literally. The late arrival on d-flat' in measure 3 is often shown as a busy syncopation (music example 12), but
Hawkins invests it with the weight of an important arrival—which, as
the goal of a chromatic descent to the tonic, it is—and makes it *sound*
like a downbeat (music example 13). The ambiguity of the gesture—a
characteristic African-American clash of rhythmic interpretations—gets
things cooking without disturbing the larger strategy of giving the "old
folks" a melodic frame of reference.

This introductory section passes imperceptibly into a restless double-
time, with the underlying quarter-note pulse subdivided into sixteenth
notes (in effect "doubling up" the pulse). At this point, melodic paraphrase yields to harmonic improvisation, again without disruption, per-

EX. 12.
"Body and Soul" (1939), Coleman Hawkins solo, mm. 1–3, transcription from
Tirro 1993, 65.

EX. 13.
"Body and Soul" (1939), Coleman Hawkins solo, mm. 1–8.

haps because "Body and Soul" is one of those relatively rare tunes recognizable from the chord progression alone. (As Miles Davis once said of Hawkins, "he plays all of the chords and you can still hear the ballad.")

"Body and Soul" had long been notorious among jazz musicians for its difficulty. The "bridge" (i.e., the "B" section of the thirty-two-bar AABA form) of a popular song is typically an area of harmonic contrast, often establishing a new key area. In "Body and Soul" those modulations are unusually distant: to D major and C major, a half step above and below the tonic of D-flat major. Even the A section has a restless quality. Its characteristic sonority, heard in the first and fifth measure of each eight-bar unit, is not the tonic but the relatively unstable ii^7 chord. This chord eventually resolves to the tonic, through a standard ii^7–V^7–I cadence (which, as we shall see, is inflected chromatically). But even at the "final" cadence in the last measure of the eight-bar phrase, any sense of arrival is undercut by the necessity to immediately move on either to ii^7 (on the repetition of the A section) or to the new key of D major (at the beginning of the bridge).

This restlessness suited Hawkins's purposes perfectly. Each note he plays articulates the local harmony, but is also part of a polyphonic web, in motion toward some resolution. The general tendency of the line is downward: an ebbing in energy, a tailing off in dynamics and timbre, as it subsides toward its goal. Hawkins uses all the means at his disposal to defer the moment of resolution—elaborating the descent through chromatic passing tones, dividing the linear motion among several implied voices. But he relies on the chord progression to call new dissonances into play at regular intervals, thus setting the whole process into motion once again. In "Body and Soul," the opportunities for fresh beginnings come along quite often. The sinking quality of lines is periodically counterbalanced by sudden *forte* entries in the upper register, usually corresponding to moments of harmonic instability: the ii^7 chord at the beginning of the A section, the diminished chord in the A section's fourth measure, the temporary tonicization of D major in the bridge.

The climax, which comes at the beginning of the last eight-bar phrase of the second chorus (music example 14), is unmistakable—and not simply because of the *fortissimo* entrance and the upward thrust of the line through two octaves. The progression from ii^7 to I had previously always involved a chromatic descent: either E-flat–E-double-flat–D-flat or B-flat–B-double-flat–A-flat. At the climax, the voice-leading is reversed: e-flat''' moves upward, through harshly dissonant tritones (b-flat''–e''') to the peak of the entire solo on f'''. After such a dramatic expenditure of energy, a rapid falling off is nearly inevitable. Even the heartbeat-like pulse of the accompaniment is dismissed in the final measures, as Hawkins gently winds down to the register and softened timbre of the opening.

The overall plan of "Body and Soul," then, is essentially tripartite: a gentle introduction, lingering on the melody; a restless central section in double-time, relying on Hawkins's apparently inexhaustible invention; and a climactic final passage, the simultaneous peak of dynamics, pitch, and timbral intensity, which yields to an unaccompanied cadenza. The listener is left with the impression of seamless continuity—beginning soft and slow, gathering intensity, climaxing with an impassioned outburst before gently subsiding. Hawkins's ability to conceive and execute this plan finds a parallel in narrative: as Martin Williams has suggested,

EX. 14.
"Body and Soul" (1939), Coleman Hawkins solo, chorus 2, mm. 26–27.

in "the special declamatory drama of the concert singer and the concert stage," or, in the jazz argot, telling a story.

But what kind of story was he telling? Hawkins indirectly supplied an answer when he counseled the vocalist in his 1940 big band, Thelma Carpenter, on the proper way to convey a song. "First, you have to tell them the story," he told her. "Then it's like making love. Suppose you get in bed with a woman. You jump on her—and that's it. No! You must romance her." On another occasion, he clarified, "You greet the song, then you slowly get closer to it, caressing it, kissing it, and finally making love to it." Hawkins used his recording of "Body and Soul" as a point of reference. Of the climax, he said: "that's when you're having the orgasm"; of the unaccompanied coda—"well, now that's the satisfaction."[4]

The image is intriguing, in large part for what it reveals about how Hawkins may have conceptualized his new public persona. The implicit fusing of head and heart—of the technical logistics of playing over difficult chord changes and the broader challenge to touch people's deepest emotions—calls to mind an old saw about the similarity between the role of technique in art and in lovemaking. Well-meaning fumbling has its charm, as does a certain heartless skill, but what we *really* want is passionate virtuosity. Hawkins is here the passionate virtuoso, an unabashedly romantic temperament informed by an unquestioned mastery of craft, as well as a thoroughly professional insistence on getting the job done right.

The imagery raises other questions. What, one wonders, is the point of this sexually charged spectacle? Is it self-advertisement? Hawkins was a notoriously successful ladies' man, and like many other male musicians, he undoubtedly relied on a demonstration of musical mastery onstage to project the promise of sexual potency after hours. (As James P. Johnson once observed, a jazz pianist's music was designed to "put the question in the ladies' minds: 'Can he do it like he can play it?' ") But the fact that Hawkins performed pieces like "Body and Soul" not just occasionally but on a regular basis to anonymous, paying customers suggests something rather different. In Hawkins's mind, the average, unhip listener (the "people you've got to please") came to popular music expecting to hear "the melody." His job, therefore, was to draw their patronage by touting his specialized services as a professional purveyor of pleasure. In place of

---

4. "And the funny thing was," Carpenter remembers, "I was still a virgin, I didn't know anything about making love! But he came right out and was very graphic about the whole thing" (Carpenter, interview with author, 1986).

romantic popular song—product—he offered process, a *way* of playing that privileged the virtuoso over the composer. The jazz lovers who crowded Kelly's Stable presumably understood this. The mystery for Hawkins was why "Body and Soul" appealed so strongly to the "old folks," and perhaps even more relevant for the future course of his career, whether he could count on it ever happening again.

If the general audience was attracted to "Body and Soul" by its hint of erotic drama, musicians came away deeply impressed by Hawkins's erudite use of chromaticism. "Body and Soul" was, if not the first, then certainly the most famous jazz solo to use the device now known as a tritone substitution—the replacement of a chord (usually the dominant) by a chord with a root a tritone distant from the original. Most musicians in 1939 would have expected the tonic chord (D-flat major) of the opening bars of "Body and Soul" to have been preceded by a V⁷ (A-flat⁷) chord. Instead, Hawkins strongly suggests a chord with its root on the lowered second degree of the scale—technically, an E-double-flat, but sounding the same as a D. This device puzzled Hawkins's contemporaries, as he delighted in recounting later:

> I started to play, and a lot of them used to say I was playing wrong notes. And it used to be funny to me, I used to laugh about it. I couldn't understand that. Like, the first time I played "Body and Soul"—when the record first came out? Well, everybody, including [tenor saxophonist] Chu [Berry] and everybody said I was playing wrong notes. . . .
>
> At that time, you make some type of a D change, or anything, going into a D-flat—that was *wrong*. Mm-*mmmm*. At that time, you had to make a A-flat seventh to go into a D-flat. If you didn't make A-flat⁷—*strictly* A-flat⁷, now they don't know that that's a relative chord to D anyway. But I mean, they just didn't know these things, and they couldn't see it any other way. They heard that D, it had to be—"Ooooh, that's terrible." [chuckles] You know? Which is nothing but a flatted fifth form, and things like that, that's all, an augmented change, or something like that. But—they couldn't hear it. But I mean, of course, that's *extremely* common now, you know. But that just became common after that. It certainly wasn't common before I made "Body and Soul," I can tell you that now! No. Mm-mmm.

Hawkins exaggerated his contemporaries' aversion to progressive harmonic ideas. In fact, a variety of chromatic alterations were already widely in circulation by 1939. In an earlier version of "Body and Soul" featuring Chu Berry and Roy Eldridge, recorded in 1938 while Hawkins was still in Europe, the tritone substitution—a D chord in the third measure—is plainly audible in Clyde Hart's stride piano accompaniment. Hart, who later lent his talents to the bebop movement, was one of many pianists and arrangers familiar with such up-to-date harmonic side-stepping.

The fact that a seventh chord with its root on the flatted second degree of the scale can substitute effectively for the dominant seventh is not simply an oddity, but a doorway to a new tritone-based chromatic language. Again, a digression to elementary music theory may prove helpful.

The tritone (so called because it is made up of three whole steps, or tones) is a dissonant, and therefore highly unstable, interval with peculiar properties. Every other interval, when inverted, forms a different interval: a fifth (C–G) becomes a fourth (G–C); a third (C–E) becomes a sixth (E–C); and so forth. The tritone divides the octave evenly, so that its inversion is yet another tritone. A diminished fifth (C–G-flat) and an augmented fourth (G-flat–C) are both tritones. Similarly, a diminished fifth (C–G-flat) and an augmented fourth (C–F-sharp) starting from the same note sound identical, even though they are "spelled" differently and are normally associated with different harmonies. (Intervals that, like homonyms, are spelled differently but sound alike are called enharmonic.)

The tritone is not an exotic interval found only in esoteric art music, but an integral part of every major and minor scale. For its subversive qualities, it was shunned by medieval theory as the "devil in music," but in subsequent centuries, it worked its way into the center of tonal harmony as part of the dominant seventh chord, where its instability became crucial to concepts of tension and release. In a dominant seventh chord— say, A-flat^7—the tritone is formed by the third degree (C) and the seventh (G-flat). The notes forming the tritone are, in a sense, the "working parts" of the dominant seventh, for it is these notes that resolve strongly to chord tones in the tonic harmony: in the A-flat^7 chord (music example 15), the C moves up to a D-flat, while the G-flat moves down to an F.

The situation becomes more complicated when one takes advantage of the fact that a tritone is enharmonically identical to its inversion. A dominant seventh chord based on A-flat and a dominant seventh based on D have the same tritone: the third and seventh of the A-flat^7 chord (C–G-flat) sound the same as the seventh and third of the D^7 chord (C–F-sharp). The D^7 chord therefore fits smoothly into a V^7–I cadence in

D-flat (music example 16), even though the root and the fifth (D, A) are foreign to the key.

What did Hawkins's would-be competitors make of this chord? When Clyde Hart plays a D⁷ in the 1938 "Body and Soul" (music example 17), Chu Berry, surprisingly, avoids the notes D and A. Instead, he emphasizes

Ab7 Db

EX. 15.
Standard resolution of V⁷ to I.

D7 Db

EX. 16.
Tritone substitution for V⁷ in V⁷–I cadence.

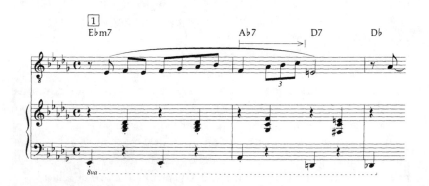

EX. 17.
"Body and Soul" (1938), Chu Berry solo with piano accompaniment, mm. 1–3.

E-natural, suggesting that he understood the chord as some kind of augmented dominant chord—a dominant seventh with an augmented fifth. The augmented dominant was quite common: as we have seen, it was prominent a decade earlier in the Hawkins and Armstrong solos on "One Hour" (this is probably what Hawkins meant in his interview by an "augmented change"). The augmented fifth adds another dissonance to the chord—another tendency tone that leans strongly toward resolution to the tonic.

But Chu Berry doesn't use it that way. He treats it as an opportunity to slip into a well-worn chromatic device: the whole-tone scale. A whole-tone scale is, simply, a scale made up entirely of whole steps. (There are, in fact, only two such scales: one comprising the pitches C–D–E–F-sharp–A-flat–B-flat, the other the pitches B–C-sharp–D-sharp–F–G–A.) In a whole-tone scale, the usual building blocks of harmony—perfect fifths or fourths—are absent. The symmetry of the scale prevents any one note from emerging as a tonal center. As a result, whole tones are extremely ambiguous in their harmonic implications—a convenient device for escaping, at least temporarily, the network of dissonance and resolution.

Whole-tone scales entered jazz through the music of Debussy and Ravel (the famous piano prelude "Voiles" by Debussy, for example, is made up almost entirely of whole tones). As an easily grasped and indisputably "modern" effect, they were eagerly adopted by American composers, songwriters, and arrangers. Dance band arrangements from the 1920s abound in whole-tone interludes and modulations, and adventurous jazz musicians exploited whole-tone scales either to induce a kind of chromatic reverie, as in Beiderbecke's "In a Mist," or aggressively for their harsh dissonance, as in Hawkins's own "Queer Notions" from 1933.

As virtually everyone who has tried to use them has discovered, it is difficult to proceed beyond such superficial effects with whole-tone scales (unless one is willing, as in the music of Debussy or Monk, to displace received chord formations with a virtually new harmonic language). The augmented dominant seventh was simply a convenient way of inserting a whole-tone scale into a conventional harmonic progression: the root, third, augmented fifth, and seventh of the chord already contain four of the six notes of the scale. In the tenth measure of his solo on "Body and Soul" (music example 18), Chu Berry combines these notes with yet another (B-flat); Clyde Hart's D-natural in the bass completes the scale. The result is less an independent harmony than a mildly dissonant, and pleasantly ambiguous, pathway from ii^7 to I.

By contrast, Hawkins's new harmony—the D chord substituting for the expected A-flat⁷—emerges as a logical outgrowth of Hawkins's fondness for chromatic passing tones. The F-sharp (or G-flat) is already part of an A-flat⁷ chord; the A-natural (or B-double-flat) is part of a chromatic passing motion from ii⁷ to V⁷ (music example 19). Even the introduction of D-natural (E-double-flat) can be understood as part of a chromatic double neighbor converging on D-flat (music example 20). But taken together, these notes clearly imply a chord with its root on the lowered second degree. In European theory, this would be called a Neapolitan chord, but Neapolitan chords typically appear in first inversion, with the bass line outlining the familiar cadential pattern 4–5–1. Hawkins's pseudo-Neapolitan chord is in root position and therefore more frankly chromatic, with the half-step slide downward (2–flat2–1) clearly audible in the bass (music example 21).

EX. 18.
"Body and Soul" (1938), Chu Berry solo, mm. 9–11.

EX. 19.
"Body and Soul" (1939), Coleman Hawkins solo, mm. 10–11.

EX. 20.
"Body and Soul" (1939), Coleman Hawkins solo, mm. 26–27.

In the interview quoted above, Hawkins refers to the D chord as a "flatted fifth"—an imprecise description that requires clarification. If the new chord (D⁷) simply replaces the dominant, there is no flatted fifth. This is the case in the tenth measure of the first chorus of "Body and Soul," for example: the bassist, anticipating Hawkins's substitution, simply plays a D root (E-double flat in the transcription) in place of the A-flat (music example 22), filling in the root movement between E-flat and D-flat chromatically. As Dizzy Gillespie said of a similar passage in an arrangement he heard in 1938, "We always looked on that simply as a half-step, not as a 'flatted fifth.'" But should the tritone substitution be actually *superimposed* on an A-flat root, the root of the implied chord (D) would form the dissonant interval of a diminished fifth (or flatted fifth) with the root of the A-flat⁷ chord—as it in fact does in measure 31 of the first chorus of "Body and Soul" (music example 23).

The distinction between these two practices is subtle, at least in this instance: it is more a matter of what the bassist chooses to play than of what the soloist does. But the distinction is important nevertheless. In the first case, the tritone substitution is a normal dominant seventh chord

EX. 21.
Left: Neapolitan cadence. Right: ii–V–I cadence with tritone substitution for V.

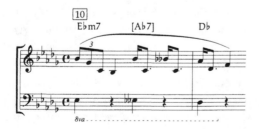

EX. 22.
"Body and Soul" (1939), Coleman Hawkins solo with bass accompaniment, mm. 10–11.

EX. 23.
"Body and Soul" (1939), Coleman Hawkins solo with bass accompaniment, mm. 31–32.

in an unusual context. It requires some erudition to know that such a dominant seventh belongs there, but the chord itself is nothing out of the ordinary. For Hawkins, a D⁷ chord in place of the dominant was the only way to play "Body and Soul" ("That *is* 'Body and Soul,' actually!"). In the second case, the resultant chord (with the flatted fifth) is a rich, complex hybrid. Dominant seventh chord and tritone substitution become ambiguously commingled, raising the level of dissonance and pointing unmistakably toward a new harmonic *sound*—the characteristic sound of bebop.

Pleasant Ambiguities: Lester Young's Alternative

"Body and Soul" contributed other seminal musical ideas to bebop. Such advanced chromatic harmonies as the flatted fifth were in the air, but Hawkins demonstrated their usefulness to solo improvisation more convincingly than anyone else. Even his tendency toward rhythmic uniformity had its uses in the blindingly fast tempos that many bop musicians favored, as well as in their penchant for double-time in ballads.

Beyond this, Hawkins's "Body and Soul" represented an intellectual approach to music that the following generation found compelling. Anyone listening to it with an ear for technical detail would understand, if they hadn't understood before, that intellectual rigor was not incompatible with jazz's well-known emotional expressiveness—a lesson the younger musicians took to heart. As Sir Charles Thompson later remembered: "It was through ['Body and Soul'] that everybody recognized that Coleman Hawkins was a leader of jazz saxophonists and musicians, with a modern sense. Now it was through this that these people . . . like Dizzy Gillespie, Charles Parker, who were just starting out on their own, they were inspired by him."

Of course, even as Gillespie, Parker, and other "moderns" looked to Hawkins as the model of the progressive jazz improviser-as-virtuoso, they were far from Hawkins epigones. There remains the musical generation gap of the 1940s, the great rhythmic divide that left "old-fashioned" Hawkins on the far side of history, while bolstering Lester Young's credentials as musical revolutionary. Before setting the issue of musical rhetoric and improvising style aside, then, one may ask: what, precisely, about Hawkins's style was found to be inadequate and discarded? And in what sense did Lester Young's example provide the alternative?

Coleman Hawkins's music was built on the principles of continuity and certainty. The certainty derived from the precision with which he understood the workings of tonal harmony. Each note of his improvisations finds its place within the framework of tonal relations implied by the tune. Whether the notes are derived literally from the harmony, or imposed as an alternative to it, makes little difference: in either case, the resolution of dissonance, the movement of tendency tones toward their implicit goals, is inexorable. The appropriate rhetorical mode is thus continuity: an earnest, relentless building of intensity.

Bebop relied on these principles as well—at least as the underlying thread for most passages. But more broadly, it made striking use of the contrary principles of ambiguity and discontinuity. These qualities are notably absent from Hawkins's music but salient in the music of Lester Young.

It must be remembered that Hawkins's approach to improvisation, however logical (and handy to explain via conventional means), represents a narrowing of the possibilities open to a soloist. This is the inevitable result of specialization. The harmonically oriented improviser reduces a tune to its chord progression, looking for voice-leading possibilities to exploit in a solo line. Where too few opportunities present themselves (i.e., where the harmonic progression is static), passing chords can be implied or new harmonic pathways can be created. But the tendency is always to fill in, to flesh out, to maintain the illusion of harmonic movement even where it is absent.

There are alternatives, of course. I have already spoken of the blues, a mode of playing that most musicians avail themselves of frequently, and some make the focus of their style. As a modal system—a system of *melodic* organization—the blues tends to downplay harmonic difference. The same blues riff can fit over the three basic chords of the harmonic accompaniment: tonic, subdominant, and dominant. Lester Young was a bluesy player, and some of the more effective moments in his solos come from gestures, usually subtle bends in intonation, that suddenly evoke a blues frame of reference. These gestures stand out because they are projected against a background that is largely diatonic and *unbluesy*—the bright, open sound of the major scale.

Young's method required thinking of the chord progression of a tune from a rather different angle. Where Hawkins's competitive spirit was stimulated by viewing the detailed progression of chords as a set of hurdles to be run, Young preferred to move in the opposite direction: to *reduce* the harmonic implications, often to the point of appearing to ignore harmonic movement altogether. Gunther Schuller has referred to this as "the superimposition of a *single* harmonic zone (to which the melody is then confined) on several chords or an entire chord progression"—a view that has the advantage of positing a process on the opposite side of the spectrum from the "substitute" chords of the harmonic improviser. But I prefer to think of this practice not as an artificial "superimposition," but as the revealing of bedrock reality—a cooling of the harmonic temperature to a state approaching absolute repose.

One might expect such harmonic stasis to be inherently lacking in interest. But it is not, for it is only one dimension in a multidimensional experience. The real interest lies in the ambiguous relationship among the different layers. The harmonic cycle—the ticking away of chords in strict rhythmic succession—continues in the accompaniment. Every gesture made by the soloist from the cooled-down perspective thus has singularly rich implications: Is the improviser articulating the harmony? Or are the notes simply part of the deep background—a projection of the overall tonality?

A good example comes from Lester Young's first recording session in 1936 (music example 24). The tune "Lady Be Good" provided the kind of open-ended chord progression that appealed to him—capable of being either tricked out with substitute harmonies or emptied of all but the most rudimentary tonal landmarks. Walter Page's bass line in the first chorus (lightly fleshed out by Count Basie's piano) suggests the former, with a harmonic rhythm of two chord changes per measure. (But even this has an element of ambiguity, since the bass line could easily be understood *linearly* as an uncomplicated elaboration of tonic and dominant. Page once told fellow bassist Gene Ramey, "Now, there's a whole lot of things I could do here, but what you must do is play a straight line, because that man out there's waiting for this food from you, you know.

EX. 24.
"Lady Be Good" (1936), Lester Young solo with bass accompaniment, mm. 1–8.

. . . You could run changes on every chord that's going on. . . . But if you do, you're interfering with that guy. So run a straight line.") Young prefers for the most part to move in the opposite direction, retreating for long stretches to a bluesy G-major pentatonic scale (bluesy because of the occasional interpolation of a lowered seventh degree). At times, he seems simply to ignore the harmonies, but he is never unaware of them. There is always a subtle and complex relationship between the linear and the horizontal—between the static simplicity of the solo line and the constantly shifting harmonic accompaniment.

All of this has two main effects. First, it gives Lester Young a remarkable degree of rhythmic leeway. There is nothing in Hawkins's playing (or anyone else's of the time, for that matter) like the supple asymmetries of Young's phrasing. Whereas Coleman Hawkins is bound by the logic of resolution of dissonance into near-continuous movement, Young floats through the harmonies "by the devious means of omission, implication and suggestion." He is free to stop and start as he pleases. Instead of rushing ahead toward some goal, he seems poised at any time to pull back, as if to savor the pleasant ambiguities of the moment. This love for discontinuity and unpredictability had an immediate and long-lasting effect on the bop generation.

Second, in Young's music a much greater importance is attached to pitches that, in Tom Brothers's words, "occupy an ambiguous place be-

tween consonance and dissonance." These idiosyncratic pitch choices are not just harmonic effects—i.e., sixths, ninths, and other mildly dissonant accretions to the triad—but a bridge between the linearity of the improvised solo, with its relatively static modal (pentatonic or blues) orientation, and the underlying harmonic accompaniment.

The sixth degree of the scale is particularly useful in this respect. Linearly, it is part of the pentatonic scale that includes tonic triad pitches, but not of the tonic triad itself. Harmonically, it is a chameleon note, equally at home in combination with the tonic (as an added sixth), dominant (an added ninth), or subdominant, representing the modal independence of melodies from their harmonic foundation. Young exploits these qualities to telling effect in "Lady Be Good" (music example 24). In measures 4–5, he lingers over the pitches e'–g', isolating them through repetition and subtle variation in their rhythmic shape. Gradually, he "resolves" the wayward sixth degree (e') downward to the fifth degree, neatly coinciding with the V^7–I cadence in measures 6–7 (although ignoring the usual voice-leading of that cadence). In measure 7, however, the sixth degree suddenly pops up again. This time, it receives peculiar emphasis—not merely by register or articulation (in both respects, it recalls the opening gesture of the solo), but because it comes at the *end* of the phrase. This unexpected rupture in the continuity of the line calls into question all previous interpretations. Is the sixth degree part of the tonic triad (to which it seems attached through arpeggiation)? Does it articulate the even more detailed harmonic movement, or the "turnaround," that begins at precisely this point (i.e., the VI^7 chord implied by Page's bass line)? Is it an anticipation of the dominant harmony to come in measure 8? Or is harmony irrelevant here, the sixth degree being merely part of the underlying pentatonic scale? There is, of course, hardly time to formulate such thoughts, let alone sort them out. The listener is simply "sent." The irony is that such a welter of conflicting interpretations is triggered by the *absence* of information, in artfully placed discontinuities. This, too, was a lesson that left a deep impression on bebop.

The bebop pioneers were, on the whole, too deeply invested in the orthodoxies of the time—the "progressive" fascination with chromatic harmony, the professional advantage associated with overt displays of virtuosity—to model their style directly on Young's understated approach. (It was not until considerably later, in the 1950s, that a younger generation of musicians would do so.) Nevertheless, they saw in Young's example a way of extending the legacy of Coleman Hawkins and other harmonic improvisers in new and unexpected directions.

But in 1940 all this lay in the future. Bebop was still several years away, and Coleman Hawkins's famous recording was rapidly finding its way into jukeboxes and record collections across the country. "Body and Soul" established Hawkins as the preeminent improviser of his generation. Its success in the marketplace held out the possibility that an African-American instrumentalist, presented without the trappings of entertainment or even the surrounding context of a dance band, offering little to the general public beyond a superbly polished virtuoso idiom, could nevertheless find favor. For the next several years, Hawkins labored to make the most of the opportunity. The broad-based acceptance he hoped for as a swing bandleader was not to materialize. But the more specialized territory that he eventually staked out as compensation became the fertile ground out of which bebop sprang.

3 · OUT OF STEP WITH SWING

*The truth is that the public will absorb only a
very limited number of Negro bands.*
PAUL EDUARD MILLER

*Few colored bands of today are getting rich,
anyway.* COLEMAN HAWKINS

During the years that Coleman Hawkins lived in comfortable isolation in Europe, the professional world he had left behind was transformed almost beyond recognition. In 1934 the entertainment industry as a whole was reeling from the Depression, and portions of it—recordings, vaudeville—lay in ruins. While black musicians continued to ply their trade and a few bands (Ellington's, Calloway's) did quite well, working conditions for most were poor and horizons limited. The once-prosperous Fletcher Henderson band teetered on the brink of insolvency.

On Hawkins's return just five years later, jazz-oriented dance bands (rechristened "swing bands") were not only restored to health, but took their place at the leading edge of a full-scale recovery. Dance music, once on the periphery of the entertainment industry, now reaped unprecedented profits and moved forcefully to the center of American popular culture. This transformation lasted barely a decade, from the mid-1930s to the mid-1940s, but it looms so large in the history of American popular music that it is universally known by the portentously inflated title the Swing Era.

From the musicological standpoint, *swing* is a stylistic category, and a rather ill-defined one at that. Unlike bebop, it was neither a revolution nor a movement. There are few sharp dividing lines between preceding styles ("early jazz" or "New Orleans jazz") and the common practice of

116

the 1930s. The obvious distinction is in instrumentation and sheer size of the ensemble: the aptly named big bands, with their sections of trumpets, trombones, and saxophones, versus the informal New Orleans style combo. But the trend toward larger and more organized bands was really a product of the 1920s, fueled by the early examples of Paul Whiteman, Fletcher Henderson, and other bandleaders.

In strictly musical terms, the most that one can fasten onto is a subtle but decisive shift in rhythmic sensibility—a quality first evident, perhaps, in the soloing of Louis Armstrong and in the relaxed lope of a good New Orleans band, but by the beginning of the 1930s increasingly pervasive in dance bands. One useful marker of this shift is the widespread and rather sudden replacement of the tuba by the string bass in most bands in 1930, as well as the roughly contemporaneous surfacing of "Harlem's newest dance craze," the lindy hop, beyond its home territory. As the jazz scholar Howard Spring persuasively argues, the two factors are intricately interconnected. The string bass facilitated, and the lindy hop depended on, a rhythmic foundation of an even four beats to the bar—a radical departure from the 2/4 feeling of most dance music before swing.[1] Soloists found the new rhythmic framework congenial, as did arrangers. One could argue that the arrival of swing was announced more by the shift from verb to noun, as in Ellington's "It Don't Mean a Thing (If It Ain't Got That Swing)" of 1932, than by Benny Goodman's successes some three years later. As Gunther Schuller has recently contended, "Jazz had by 1932 evolved aesthetic, stylistic, technical criteria which were to govern its future for some years without major changes or radical breakthroughs." It is this plateau—André Hodeir's "classic period," marked by the "equilibrium which comes with maturity"—that

1. In 1942 bandleader Shep Fields discussed the changes in dance music over the previous decade for the readers of *Down Beat*. Before Goodman introduced a "smashing powerhouse style with its flat 4/4" to the dance world, Fields said, dance music was in 2/4. The second and fourth beats of the measure were "an upbeat—it was much easier to dance to because it indicated to the average guy when to go and when to stop. Technically speaking, the sort of beat a good swing band plays is better dance music, but only for a good dancer. He takes the unvarying accent, and dances *against* it, instead of just following along the way an ordinary dub does. . . . If you've ever really watched the dancing at the Savoy up in Harlem, that's the essential difference between the dancing done there and by the average goon. Uptown, they know what's happening, and can use counter and cross beats. Downtown they just got to follow along—and when you play straight 4/4, they don't know what to do with themselves—someone took the signpoles down." Fields cautioned against "sweet" bands drifting into a 4/4 feeling without being aware of it: it's "worthless for dancing or anything else unless it has the power of a really good swing band behind it" (" 'Too Little Dance Music'—Shep; Bounce of Lunceford Recommended for Style," *Down Beat* 9 [1 July 1942]: 17).

defined the musical language of jazz until the bebop revolution more than a decade later.

Yet in certain respects, the Swing Era was a genuine revolution—if not in musical language, then certainly in the economic and cultural basis for musicians' careers. The indelible images of the revolution—Benny Goodman's breakthrough engagement at the Palomar Ballroom in Los Angeles in 1935, the frenzied crowds of bobby-soxers dancing in the aisles of the Paramount Theater in 1937—suggest a nexus with two complementary components. On one side was a new mass audience: mostly white, youthful, and relatively affluent, filling theaters, ballrooms, and even Carnegie Hall to overflowing. On the other side was the figure of bandleader-as-celebrity. Both were unprecedented. The jitterbugs' enthusiasm for their "new" dance music and their willingness to express that enthusiasm through consumer spending (recordings, attendance at dance halls and theaters) set off an explosion within the entertainment business that had the music industry scrambling to meet the spiraling demand. In the process, previously anonymous bandleaders were elevated to icons of consumerism. A few dance band musicians had attained some fame before, but now Goodman, Artie Shaw, Harry James, and others became stars—identifiable by first name alone—rivaling the Hollywood pantheon (and through screen appearances and marriages to movie stars, even blending in with it). If only a handful attained this lofty status, a degree of glamour now touched the entire profession.

The cult of personality, carefully nurtured by publicity machines, obscured the fact that the Swing Era was above all a *system* of economic interdependence in which individual musicians played clearly defined roles. This is perhaps true of any art form in a modern capitalist economy. But with the Swing Era, the integration of dance music with other forms of mass-market entertainment was carried out on a scale and with a degree of technological sophistication never seen before. New media— radio, recordings, film—began to tie the vast American continent together into networks of production and dissemination controlled from New York and Los Angeles. Each step brought new efficiencies that increased the potential for profit, while requiring the individual to yield more and more autonomy to the system. By the 1930s these networks had matured to the point that they were virtually inescapable, even at the local level. Just a decade or two earlier the careers of dance musicians, especially black musicians (the pioneers of jazz in New Orleans come to mind), could unfold almost untouched by the emergent popular music industry; indeed, it required conscious effort and ambition to find a place within it. By the Swing Era, the system, with its booking agencies, radio broadcasts, and record contracts, was pervasive and all-inclusive. To exist outside of it was either an admission of incompetence or an act of rebellion.

The role played by African Americans within the system during the Swing Era was also revolutionary—or at least, potentially so. Their mere presence in popular culture is hardly surprising. From the minstrel show to ragtime to early jazz, black music and dance had proven an irresistible product, and black artists increasingly became more directly involved, as entertainers, instrumentalists, and songwriters, in its production. With the opening up of markets aimed at the rapidly expanding black population in the North, their public careers in show business became even more secure. The early twentieth century even saw some of the first black celebrities—Bert Williams, Bill "Bojangles" Robinson, Louis Armstrong, Duke Ellington—drawing support in equal measure from black and white audiences. While the ability of even the most famous black musicians to reap a reward appropriate to their efforts was inevitably constrained by racism, the penetration of jazz-oriented dance music into the popular mainstream promised to reward a much wider stratum. If black musicians remained on the periphery of economic power during the Swing Era, they were nevertheless closer to the center than ever before. Skeptical as they may have been of any opportunities offered by white society, they must have been tantalized by the possibility for change.

During the boom years, from 1935 to about 1939, what black jazz musicians hoped to get out of the new prosperity often split along generational lines. Seasoned veterans already at the top of the profession (such as the members of Cab Calloway's bands) tended to accept success as their due, a welcome if belated confirmation of their life's achievement. Younger musicians like Dizzy Gillespie entered the profession brashly expecting to storm their way to the top through talent and determination. Yet after 1939 such hopes would be frustrated by the subsiding of the swing craze and by the racial barriers erected by white society. The story of Coleman Hawkins's brief career as the leader of his own swing band is a cautionary tale—at once the fulfillment of Hawkins's dreams and the thwarting of his ambition. His disappointments had a particular resonance for musicians of the bebop generation, for if Coleman Hawkins couldn't make it, who could?

The Swing Boom

The economic structure of the Swing Era had its roots in the gradual concentration, over several decades, of economic power in popular entertainment into large, impersonal institutions. It started with the mass production of popular song, centralized as early as the 1890s in the New York publishing firms known collectively as Tin Pan Alley. (Music publishing and songwriting remained the nominal center of the music business until the mid–twentieth century, even as new technologies rapidly eroded the power of the printed page: through the formation of the American Society of Composers, Authors, and Publishers [ASCAP] in 1914, publishers and composers shrewdly extended their control into live performance, forcing payment of licensing fees wherever their songs were performed, including, eventually, radio and film.) In the early years of the century, giant vaudeville circuits controlled the movements of large numbers of musicians (as well as comedians, dancers, and entertainers of all kinds) across the country. These enterprises were dominated by whites, but black artists and entrepreneurs eventually managed to gain a foothold, sometimes through ordinary channels (as with black songwriters and such headline acts as the nonpareil comedian Bert Williams), but more often through parallel institutions that, by catering to a specifically black clientele, "took advantage of the disadvantages" of segregation. Examples include the chain of black theaters known as the Theater Owners Booking Association (TOBA) and "race recordings" marketed exclusively in the black community.

Revolutions in communications technology in the early twentieth century transformed this landscape and hastened the process of consolidation. Sound recordings of popular song and dance music gained steadily in popularity and, by 1920, began to rival, and in some cases exceed, sheet music in sales. (Publishers and composers were protected: by virtue of the 1909 copyright law, they automatically received royalties for "mechanical reproduction.") The first radio stations were rapidly absorbed into national networks, beginning with NBC in 1926, permitting broadcasts to be coordinated on a vast scale. The burgeoning giants of the motion picture industry meanwhile developed their own chains of hundreds of movie theaters, often at the expense of vaudeville chains.

The onset of the Depression only deepened the reliance on new technologies and on economies of scale. There were winners and losers. Vaudeville fell into an irreversible collapse: its theaters either folded or were absorbed into the movie chains, and its stars fled to radio and film.

The recording industry, surprisingly, was another apparent casualty. Sales plummeted from a peak of $106 million in 1921 to $5 million in 1933, and dozens of small companies went bankrupt. Although the industry recovered handsomely by the end of the decade (helped, in large part, by the swing boom and by the new technology of the jukebox), the multiplicity of companies that had flourished in the 1920s was reduced to three (the "Big Three," or the "majors"): Victor, Columbia, and newcomer Decca.

Black musicians gradually became absorbed into these nationwide networks. In the 1920s most dance music remained stubbornly local in scope. While the most famous dance orchestras performed and recorded in New York and Chicago, the remainder—"territory bands"—were regional, operating in "territories" that were within a day's travel over rough roads by automobile from the home base. Like circuit preachers, these bands brought dance music to large areas too distant from major cities to have access to the best-known bands and too small to support a local music scene. Business arrangements tended to be decidedly casual and personal; bookings were handled in most instances by the bandleader (although a number of bands operated as cooperatives).

Fletcher Henderson's band both fit this pattern and showed the way for black musicians to take advantage of the emerging national system. During Hawkins's years with the band, Henderson participated in some of the most important transformations of the music business. Henderson's home base was the Roseland Ballroom in midtown Manhattan, at the very center of the entertainment industry. Nearly from the outset, the Henderson band was a national band, with influence far beyond its local "territory." Although Henderson was frequently criticized for his lack of business acumen, his was probably the first black dance band to establish a national reputation through a skillful combination of media exposure and touring. In this respect, as contemporary commentators noted, the Henderson band resembled the prominent white bands of the era—those led by Paul Whiteman, Ted Lewis, Vincent Lopez—more than its black counterparts. Henderson recorded prolifically—nearly two hundred individual titles in the 1920s alone—and broadcast frequently on powerful New York stations. During its summer vacations from the Roseland, the band reinforced its popularity through tours, at first concentrating on neighboring New England and Mid-Atlantic states but by the end of the decade regularly extending to the Midwest as well. Such touring was made possible by the rapid improvement of highways in the 1920s. Many of the Henderson musicians developed a fondness for fast, expensive automobiles, including Hawkins's Cadillac Imperial and Henderson's Packard roadster. They made something of a sport of racing from job to job, resulting in not a few accidents, including the 1928 incident that seriously injured Henderson. But in one important respect, these high-tech tours remained old-fashioned: Henderson and his wife, Leora, continued to handle all the engagements themselves, coordinating their travels through a tedious round of letter writing, telephoning, and telegraphing.

Even this modest degree of autonomy in business affairs had to be jettisoned in the early 1930s. To survive during the Depression, black dance bands needed to gain access to the increasingly centralized resources of the entertainment industry. This meant placing their fate in the hands of professional intermediaries.

The first important agencies, like the William Morris Agency, were organized at the beginning of the century to handle the theatrical and vaudeville trade, and in time branched out into radio and film. By the late 1920s, similar services were offered for dance orchestras, and the Music Corporation of America (MCA) emerged as the leading agency. Professional intermediaries rapidly became the norm. Personal managers and booking agents (the latter characteristically employees of large agencies) represented the bands to "buyers" in the business and coordinated the various aspects of the bands' business. Large institutions like theater chains, record companies, and radio networks found working with professional agents more congenial and efficient than working with individual bandleaders. By the end of the 1930s, a handful of giant booking agencies (MCA, General Amusements Corporation, William Morris) controlled access to nearly all major venues.

At first, these agencies handled only white bands. But black bandleaders proved to be particularly in need of professional services, if only because as black men they had a doubly difficult time gaining the attention of white corporations. Mavericks like Irving Mills, Joe Glaser, Harold Oxley, and Moe Gale specialized in black music. The difficulty of the task only spurred their ingenuity. Duke Ellington's rapid rise to national prominence, for example, depended not only on his strikingly original music, but also on the shrewd strategy of his manager, Irving Mills. In a pattern that would become standard during the Swing Era, Ellington established his reputation in the late 1920s through radio broadcasts from the Cotton Club (over the CBS network), recordings (for Columbia and Victor as well as numerous smaller labels), and aggressive press releases (a Mills specialty). He then cashed in on that reputation through extensive tours of theaters and ballrooms far from his New York base. All of this came at a price, of course: for large agencies, the customary 10 percent; for personal management, "a piece of the action" (Mills, for example, became a partner in Ellington's business and regularly added his name to Ellington's compositions). Bandleaders also relinquished considerable control over where and what they would play, and under what circumstances. But such were the sacrifices musicians were willing to make to assure professional survival.

Bands like Henderson's that adapted imperfectly to the new system were doomed, in John Hammond's words, to be "exploited by the small timers." In the lean years of the Depression, Henderson's band was frequently shortchanged by cash-poor club owners, who found it easier to alienate an individual band than a professional agency. Longtime band members, accustomed to the relative security of the 1920s, complained bitterly. ("You know what used to happen during the depression?" Hawkins recalled. "We used to play a lot of jobs and didn't get paid. Everybody belonged to the union and everything, but it seemed like there wasn't anything we could do about it.") Henderson finally gave up and signed up with an agency in early 1934 (a press notice bluntly described him as the "property" of Irving Mills), but the damage had already been done: Hawkins had left on the *Île de France*.

Economic consolidation altered the structure of the dance band business from a loose patchwork of regional music-making to a tightly controlled pyramid. The broad base of the pyramid comprised the "B" bands, including the former territory bands, now resigned to a subsidiary role in a national system. Musicians with ambition who hoped to escape this level had no choice but to shoot for the top: the handful of "name" bands (so called because the name of the bandleader alone provided what marketers call product recognition), all headquartered in New York. Among black bands, Duke Ellington, Cab Calloway, and perhaps a few others (Henderson certainly, despite his fading fortunes) had attained name band status by 1935.

What changed as a result of the swing boom? One important change was psychological and cultural: the breaching of the unspoken boundaries that had separated musical repertory along racial lines. Benny Goodman's youthful listeners may not have been aware, or have cared, that the core of his repertory was provided by prominent black arrangers, including Fletcher Henderson (and his brother, Horace), Edgar Sampson, and

Jimmy Mundy. But through these arrangements—and more important, the performance practices the arrangers took for granted—white musicians brought the rhythmic sensibility that had for several years been the stock-in-trade of the black dance orchestras to a vast new audience, one at the center of all subsequent dance crazes in the twentieth century: the white adolescent market.

Admittedly, such racial boundaries had been breached before. The titillating effect of much African American–influenced popular entertainment, from the minstrel show through ragtime and the cakewalk to the Jazz Age of the 1920s, had depended on the slightly scandalous specter of white bodies inhabiting the distinctive gestures of black dance and music. Yet these transgressions only underscored the indelible association of "hot" rhythm in the public mind with black musicians. This association was embedded in a racial stereotype—the "Sambo" image—and assumed to be a permanent characteristic of the race, as in the minstrel-show-era axiom that all blacks were possessed of "natural rhythm" (updated in the twentieth century to include the conviction that blacks were "naturally" more libidinal). Although they might prefer for social reasons to have their musical needs satisfied by musicians of their own race, white audiences before the Swing Era were more inclined to believe that black bands could authentically deliver the "hot stuff," and perhaps were ultimately more comfortable seeing blacks rather than whites engaged in such a subversive activity.

Black musicians worked quietly to undermine the limiting aspects of this stereotype. As the dance band business expanded in the 1920s and 1930s, the nature of the job pushed every band, black or white, in the direction of an eclectic musical policy. Successful black bands performed all kinds of dance music, hot and square, as well as specialized accompaniments for theatrical productions. Those that didn't had to learn. The Count Basie band, nurtured in the isolation of black Kansas City, nearly fell apart in its initial bid for national recognition in 1936 when confronted with the challenge of playing for the floor show of the Grand Terrace in Chicago and for the dancers at the Roseland in New York. "I don't think we even had a waltz in the book," Basie recalled. "I don't think I even knew what a goddamn tango was." But such provincialism was more the exception than the rule. Even a musician as emblematic of the autonomy and integrity of black folk traditions as the New Orleans cornetist King Oliver understood the advantage in reaching as many different audiences as possible. As early as 1917, he was (by one eyewitness account) "adapting . . . to the white dances more and more." In the early

1930s his repertory included "My Wild Irish Rose," "Danny Boy," and "'O Sole Mio.'" "[Other black bands] can't get nowhere near them big white ballrooms I play," he gloated.

Earl Hines was just as practically minded a dance musician. "My idea of a band is one that can play all types of music, not just one certain style," he explained in 1938. "I try to adapt myself to whatever the dancers demand. In California, for example, it's rhumbas. . . . To be successful you have to be commercial."[2] He delighted in the fact that his coast-to-coast broadcasts from the Grand Terrace made it impossible for listeners to pigeonhole him: "I used to get letters from people in schools, and [they'd] say, 'what are you, white or black?' They didn't know what nationality I was. I'd play a waltz, and I'd play a ballad, and I'd play a ragtime thing. They didn't know what I was . . . and I did that because—you had to do that on the air, because you had a lot of competition. And I was in competition with Guy Lombardo, Paul Whiteman, the Dorsey boys."

Little of this is reflected in the recorded output of black bands—or in their public image. "It seems to be congenitally impossible for Negro dance musicians to play *straight*," reported *Fortune* in 1933. In the recording studio they were encouraged—or required—to conform to the stereotype. Black musicians naturally resented this, if only because dignity seemed to lie in versatility—the ability to play hot *and* straight. As one industry observer wrote in praise of Fletcher Henderson, "The contrast of jazz and erudition is what makes for the effect." "Somewhere in the vaults of some record company," noted Rex Stewart, "there may still exist recording gems which the Henderson band made and that were rejected because they were considered too perfect musically for a negro orchestra. . . . Few people remember how extensive and beautiful [Henderson's] waltz book was. No band of that era could cut the group playing waltzes."

Yet the stereotypes, by establishing a kind of monopoly on hot music, also provided a degree of protection for black bands. "The highest grade of Negro entertainment," continued *Fortune*, "always has a market of its own." Essentially excluding black musicians from performing or recording certain kinds of repertory (romantic ballads, for example) may have

---

2. Another musician, the violinist Stuff Smith, explained: "I try to give the public a combination of entertainment, comedy, novelty, and swing. . . . We can, and do, play rhumbas, fox trots, waltzes, boleros, swing, corn (if our patrons insist), and light classics" ("Critics in the Doghouse: Stuff Smith Examines Stuff Smith," *Down Beat* 6 [August 1939]: 9).

hampered their ability to participate as fully in the entertainment network as their white colleagues. But by playing a kind of music that clearly lay within a racially defined area of expertise, Henderson, Ellington, and other black bands gained access to white theaters, ballrooms, and college proms in the 1920s.

The onset of the Swing Era irrevocably shattered the isolation that had ensured a modest prosperity for black bands. One might have expected the encroachment of white bands into the musical territory of black musicians to work to the latter's disadvantage, and in the long run, it did. ("The Swing Era didn't open up ballrooms for colored bands," trombonist Dicky Wells reflected sourly, "because they were already playing them. They were playing for white audiences even in the Deep South.") In the short term, however, the mania for swing combined with other factors against a background of gradual economic recovery to spark a vigorous expansion of the entertainment industry with new opportunities for all parties. These factors included the widespread introduction of the jukebox, which provided a new public forum for recorded music and helped to revive a moribund recording industry (by 1938 jukeboxes accounted for over half of all record sales), and the repeal of Prohibition at the end of 1933, which rid jazz of unsavory underworld associations and gave restaurants, nightclubs, and ballrooms a steady source of revenue with which to begin hiring live music.[3]

Goodman's hysterical reception at New York's Paramount Theater in March 1937 highlighted another crucial trend: dance orchestras had become a kind of theatrical entertainment, filling the void left by the demise of vaudeville. Major urban movie theaters had always lured audiences into their cavernous auditoriums by offering live entertainment: by the late 1920s a hybrid form, known in the trade as vaudefilm, filled in the time between film showings. Dance bands played a supporting role, appearing as one of a succession of acts or as accompaniment to an elaborate revue. But theater owners soon discovered that music was the attraction. After 1935 the swing band evolved into "a virtual show in itself": bands entertained with their instrumental numbers, singers, and occasional

3. At the end of 1937 *Variety* noted that "liquor opened up innumerable spots to music and dancing" (John Hurley, "$80,000,000 Dance Cost," *Variety* 129 [29 December 1937]: 1, 40). By 1941 an estimated 25,000 venues used live music. "In most key cities, the number of spots with music, liquor and food have doubled since repeal": in New York, for example, the number of cabaret licenses jumped from 600 in 1933 to 1,300 in 1941 ("25,000 U.S. Night Spots," *Billboard* 53 [8 March 1941]: 3, 17).

comedy turns by band members. Old-timers found dance bands a poor substitute for the glories of vaudeville. "Nearly all of them have jamming, jaw-grinding trapmen; pale-faced and blue-jowled musicians (all without makeup); and an always-smiling leader, to whom none of the musicians pay attention," complained *Variety.* "That's the core of what was once vaudeville." Nevertheless, what one observer called a "compromise version of vaudeville, with the entertaining orchestra as its keystone," kept movie theaters full, while adding lucrative week-long engagements to dance bands' touring schedules.

In a short time, dance music became astonishingly big business. Only a few years after the initial swing craze, dance orchestras generated nearly $100 million annually, employing some thirty to forty thousand musicians, as well as another eight thousand managers, bookers, promoters, and other support personnel. The very breadth of the music business, now extending into every corner of the entertainment industry, required those who hoped to prosper to be versatile, responding to widely divergent performing situations: "The bands of today differ markedly from the old units in that invariably the better ones can step from night clubs, to hotel, to cafe, to one-night ballroom dates, and then skip into a film theater for appearances either on stage, or—more recently—on the hydraulic orchestra pit platform."

Any band that could meet these exacting criteria was likely to flourish. The most spectacular successes were white, but many black bands did well enough in the latter half of the 1930s. Fletcher Henderson's band saw a revival in 1936, thanks to an extended engagement at the Grand Terrace and a hit recording ("Christopher Columbus"). Other long-established bands, such as Ellington's or Cab Calloway's, enjoyed renewed visibility and prosperity. As the market continued to expand, the music industry scrambled to develop new bands to meet the skyrocketing demand. This expansion did not necessarily increase the total number of musicians in the profession, since access to the national media and publicity networks remained limited to a few, and since the emphasis on national success led to declining opportunities at the local level.[4] Com-

4. Figures from the United States Census show a decline in the number reporting their occupation as "musician or music teacher" from 165,218 in 1930 (10,583 of whom were black, or 6.4% of the total) to 133,399 in 1940 (9,157 of whom were black, or 6.9%). Only a very small fraction of these musicians were involved as full-time professionals in the dance band business (U.S. Census Bureau, *Fifteenth Census of the United States: 1930; Sixteenth Census of the United States: 1940*).

petition for the lucrative positions at the upper end of the spectrum became all the more intense, and the stakes for success were suddenly raised beyond all previous expectations.

The new boom economy for music hinged on an elaborate network of publicity and the skillful marketing of personality. Before the swing boom, dance musicians were "more or less in the same category as the waiters in the locations where they appeared—necessary but unglorified." After Goodman's breakthrough, bands led by formerly obscure white jazz musicians—Artie Shaw, Tommy Dorsey, Harry James, Glenn Miller—became money-making machines. Their meteoric rise to fame at a level comparable to the stars of stage, screen, and radio could hardly have been anticipated, but each occurrence was immediately exploited for its value in the marketing of dance music as entertainment. Publicity networks created demand not simply for dance music, but for a particular band and—more important—for a particular bandleader, who projected a distinctive and compelling "personality." In this, dance music was simply conforming to the rest of the entertainment world. As Abel Green, veteran reporter for *Variety*, noted: "By 1934, it was axiomatic in radio that if you wanted to stamp your personality unforgettably into the consciousness of listeners, you had to develop a trademark—just like soap or coffee—and hammer it over the airwaves mercilessly. It was the rare star or show . . . which didn't have its aural mark of identification."

To a point, that "trademark" could be musical—especially when the bandleader had earned a reputation as a virtuoso instrumentalist (as with Benny Goodman, Louis Armstrong, Harry James, Artie Shaw, or Gene Krupa) or when (as with Ellington or Glenn Miller) a band could be distinguished by its unusual orchestration. And of course, every name band was closely identified with its hit recordings and tried to develop a concise, immediately recognizable theme song. But even a musical personality could be a gimmick, as with the "Rippling Rhythm" of Shep Fields—a silly bit of business involving blowing bubbles in front of a microphone. In other cases, the ploy to distinguish a bandleader in the open market followed familiar models from popular entertainment: Kay Kyser's quiz show, the "Kollege of Musical Knowledge," or Cab Calloway's exuberant singing and street-smart elegance. Where personality was not part of a calculated strategy, it could be extracted through voyeurism; as with movie stars, fans carefully followed the love lives and personal idiosyncrasies of their music idols. In short, it was not even necessary for a bandleader to be a musician—a complaint made forcefully by Artie Shaw in 1939: "As it is now, musical worth is measured not by how well a man handles his instrument or directs his orchestra, but by his personality, his love life and his glibness of tongue. Mountebanks have cheapened popular music to such an extent that a wisecrack or a catch phrase becomes more important to their success than the music they play."

The marketing of celebrity only accelerated the concentration of power in the national networks. At every step, the name bands headquartered in New York enjoyed an overwhelming advantage over local music makers. The process began with media exposure. Name bands recorded prolifically, and record companies made sure that their products found their way into jukeboxes across America—but there was no way to know in advance whether a particular recording would even be heard. Radio was a surer bet. During the months that bands typically played extended engagements (or "location jobs") in big-city hotel ballrooms and nightclubs, their music was sent across the continent through late-night broadcasts on network radio. Night after night, these "sustaining" broadcasts (so called because the location, rather than the radio network and its commercial sponsors, paid for the cost of remote transmission) brought some of the glamour of Manhattan nightlife into small-town middle-class homes and engendered a hunger to see and hear favorite bands when they conveniently happened to pass through the area. Count Basie, who got his big break in 1938 by getting on the CBS network several times a week from the tiny Famous Door on 52nd Street, was amazed at the response in the heartland: "We still didn't realize how big a reputation we were building up until we went back out on the road and out to places like Cleveland, Dayton, and Cincinnati again. . . . When you went out to all those other towns and everywhere you went there were all those people who knew about you from those broadcasts and your records and were just waiting to see the band live. . . . There were a lot of very good bands that couldn't get work in many places outside of New York."

It was a salient fact of the Swing Era that the real money was to be found on the road. Location jobs paid relatively little, barely enough to cover operating expenses in most cases. But outside New York lay a vast audience growing increasingly restive with local offerings and readily crowding ballrooms and nightclubs on a Saturday night for a chance to dance, to listen, or just to gaze at a famous band. It required the resources of a large booking agency to patch together one-night private parties and proms, weekends at local clubs, and week-long residencies at major urban theaters into a nationwide tour. It also required fortitude on the part of musicians, who found themselves driving (only a bus or private automobile provided enough flexibility to reach out-of-the-way locations) for months on end across the American continent. But the rewards were considerable: ever higher fees for engagements, with ballroom and nightclub owners willing to pay whatever it took to bring a name band to town. "Spots which never before went in for name strength are suddenly seeking top monikers to stretch across their ads in bold type," reported *Variety* in June 1937, adding the following month:

> Sudden spurt in one-nighter business during the past six or seven months has sent the band business line up to a new high. . . . Claim is that many of the smaller spots, including those far off the beaten path, turn in better grosses than recognized city palaces. Reason is that radio buildups have made even the bare-footed population recognize band names when they hear 'em. . . . [Attendance] records are being broken practically every night of the week. . . . General bettering of business conditions has also helped to increase admission prices and attendance, but most of the credit is given to radio buildups and booking competition.

As the system continued to expand, however, a new problem emerged: there were not enough orchestras with proven national reputations to go around. This dilemma encouraged frenetic speculation. The expense involved in starting up a new band—not only the initial investment in uniforms, transportation, and arrangements, but an opening phase in which income would inevitably fail to cover operating costs—were hardly insignificant. But the potential rewards were too great to be ignored. Besides, one could minimize the risks by drawing candidates for stardom from the ranks of already famous dance orchestras. Among the first of these defectors was Gene Krupa, the flamboyant drummer with the Benny Goodman band. Goodman acknowledged the importance of Krupa's charismatic presence to his band in 1937 by paying him the handsome salary of $275 per week (supplemented by $75 for each broadcast and $20 for each recording); by the following spring, that base salary had reportedly risen to $500. Still, Krupa's ambitions to "cash in on the name he has built for himself" were not to be deterred. While Krupa's band was never an overwhelming success, his popularity allowed him to hold the band together until well into the 1940s. The glory, as well as the profit, came to him in greater share as bandleader.

In 1939 the stream of new bands had become a flood. By February the number of Goodman alumni leading their own bands had grown to seven (Krupa, Harry James, Jack Teagarden, Bunny Berigan, Vido Musso, Teddy Wilson, and Toots Mondello). By the summer, these aspirants to fame and fortune had been followed by Bob Zurke, Ray McKinley, Will Bradley, and Bobby Byrne, all members of other name bands, in what *Variety* called "hysterical activity in the forming of new orchestras." "Never before in the history of dance bandom have so many new orchestras sprung up as now," editorialized *Metronome* in its September 1939 issue. "The enthusiasm of former side-men who are willing to take a risk for greater glories is exceeded only by promoters in booking offices who see newer ways toward bigger shekels without the risk." As an example, it cited Teddy Wilson, the black pianist who had broken the color barrier as a member of Benny Goodman's Trio and Quartet: "For years, mild-mannered Theodore was a high-priced star in the Goodman organization. Benny showed him off plenty so that musicians the world over finally recognized him as swingdom's greatest pianist. 'You're great, you're terrific, you can't miss!' exclaimed friends and bookers excitedly. 'Start your own band, you'll be a sensation!' "

The Rise and Fall of a Swing Band

Hawkins's return to New York City on August 1, 1939, thus seemed perfectly timed. As a seasoned professional with a long track record as a virtuoso soloist, he was a good prospect for success. Almost immediately, he was courted by booking agents. Some sought to hire him as a featured soloist to enhance the value of established bands, like Ellington's—or more daringly, a white band (to replace some of the talent that had been siphoned off by expansion). Others hoped to establish Hawkins as a bandleader in his own right. Among the latter was the prominent William Morris Agency, which had belatedly seen the advantages of moving into the dance band field, hiring Willard Alexander, the far-sighted agent who had shepherded Benny Goodman to his first successes, away from MCA. The energetic Alexander contacted Hawkins before he even left Europe. It did not take much to persuade Hawkins that becoming a bandleader was the next logical step in his career.

Hawkins, undoubtedly enjoying the flattering attention, moved slowly, unhurriedly. With characteristic imperiousness, he assumed that he would be able to surround himself with many of his former associates from the Fletcher Henderson band: saxophonist Benny Carter, trombonist Benny Morton, trumpeter Henry "Red" Allen, and bassist John Kirby.

The idea of an "all-star" band was one that he had apparently formulated while in Europe, and he was not easily dissuaded.[5] Booking agents had to tactfully inform him that Carter was leading his own band and that Morton, Allen, and other top-flight soloists were already gainfully employed and not at all eager to sign up as Hawkins's employees in a precarious new enterprise. The same situation pertained to the best new talent. Hawkins had first heard the teenaged Roy Eldridge while with Henderson and had expressed admiration for his recordings while in Europe ("that young guy is blowing up a storm," he told a Swiss jazz fan in 1936). His reaction to hearing him again in 1939 was immediate and proprietary: "That boy's wonderful! I want him in my band." The affinity between the two musicians was natural, eventually blossoming into a lasting partnership in the 1950s. But in 1939 Eldridge was already a bandleader, having led a modest ten-piece band since earlier in the year. Irritated agents began to doubt whether they would ever be able to bring Hawkins down to earth. "Hawk had been away a long time," a report in *Down Beat* concluded, "and had lost track of American music activity, and had no conception as to how swing music had become so universally popular of late." Like an expansion team in sports, the fledgling Hawkins band would have to make do with seasoned, if unremarkable, veterans and promising, if untried, prospects.

An embryonic version of the Coleman Hawkins Orchestra opened at Kelly's Stable on 52nd Street on October 5. It comprised two trumpets, a trombone, three saxes (including Hawkins), a rhythm section (piano, bass, and drums), and a vocalist—not much smaller than the Fletcher Henderson bands of the 1920s and large enough to require written arrangements, but well below the contemporary standard of fifteen or sixteen pieces. The trade press referred to it as a "jam outfit" or a "small combination," a pointed reminder that the band would have to expand before being taken seriously by the music industry. That Hawkins intended to be taken seriously as a commercial dance band was signaled by the presence of vocalist Thelma Carpenter, an eighteen-year-old who had been one of two singers for the struggling Teddy Wilson band. Her hiring was decidedly casual: "I just thought I'd take a chance—you know, just go over there and see what's going on. ... He looked at me and said, 'Ohhhh, they're making 'em like you now. OK, you got the job.' And I

---

5. Swiss jazz writer Johnny Simmen, who spent an evening playing American jazz records with Hawkins in late 1937, quotes Hawkins as saying: "John Kirby is my favorite bass player. He's another one that I'll hire for my band when I'm home" (in Chilton 1990, 144).

just sort of walked out of Teddy Wilson to go sing with Coleman Hawkins."

Another young "find" was the nineteen-year-old trumpet player Joe Guy, who had recently left Teddy Hill's band. Guy's extroverted solo style, showing the clear influence of Roy Eldridge, compensated for his inexperience and occasionally shaky technique. In a revealing error, a jazz newsletter referred to Hawkins's new trumpet player as Joe "Dizzy" Guy. The slip was logical. Joe Guy and the slightly older John "Dizzy" Gillespie (who had just turned twenty-two) were both musicians with obvious technical gifts and a penchant for advanced harmonies. (Hawkins later said, in reference to Gillespie and Charlie Parker, "Joe Guy was playing their way when he started with me in 1939.") Both Gillespie and Guy were struggling for a place in the music business, although Gillespie was already on his way up, having just been chosen to fill a vacancy with Cab Calloway, one of the few black name bands.[6] Joe Guy remained with Hawkins for the life of the big band as one of its principal soloists, his thin, crackling trumpet serving as a foil to Hawkins's booming tenor on up-tempo swing tunes.

Hawkins's band did a brisk business in the cramped confines of Kelly's Stable, but it needed to secure an audience beyond the club's walls. So, on the morning of October 11, less than six hours after finishing at Kelly's at 4 A.M., the band straggled into the studios of Victor Records. Hawkins himself "showed up almost an hour late with a giggling young blonde on his arm." Two of the tunes recorded that day were up-tempo dance numbers composed by Hawkins, their titles redolent of in-group humor: "Fine Dinner" was slang for a good-looking woman, while "Meet Doctor Foo" referred to the nickname of drummer Harold "Doc" West. The arrangements strive for the sound of a much larger band, but the thinness of the nine-piece instrumentation undercuts that impression. Hawkins's booming tone overpowers the ensemble, and the inexperienced Joe Guy's fluffs in the upper register are mercilessly exposed. The other arranged tune on the recording session, "She's Funny That Way," is a gentler affair, a ballad focusing as much on Thelma Carpenter's singing as on solos by Hawkins and pianist Gene Rodgers.

A fourth tune may have been planned, but recording executive Leonard

---

6. Through his connection with Calloway, Gillespie had earned a spot with Hawkins on a small combo recording date led by Lionel Hampton in September: "Man, I was so scared, I was nervous as a sheep shitting on shingles." He was still obscure enough that Hampton's wife misunderstood his name and made out his check to "Charles" Gillespie (Gillespie 1979, 102).

Joy asked Hawkins to record instead a tune that he had been playing at Kelly's Stable. "[Hawkins] reached over some place and got a bottle of Cognac, took a good healthy sip, laid it down, and then he got right under the middle of the microphone and he said, 'Make an introduction on "Body and Soul," ' " remembered pianist Gene Rodgers. "He just played with no interruption, flat-footed, and he probably didn't even hear the accompaniment. His eyes were closed and he just played as if he was in heaven." Hawkins's career as a bandleader was launched, but in a direction he could hardly have anticipated.

The success of "Body and Soul" was, on the surface, a good omen for Hawkins's ambitions as a bandleader. Before, his fame had been restricted to the community of musicians, to the audience for pre–Swing Era black dance music (i.e., those who still remembered the old Fletcher Henderson band), and to the growing but still modest number of jazz fans. "Body and Soul" suggested an opening to a much broader and less specialized audience. Once it became clear that this casually conceived recording was the hit record he had been hoping for, the "aural mark of identification" every aspiring bandleader needed, it was diligently exploited for publicity value. "Body and Soul" was the band's official theme song—radio broadcasts from the Savoy Ballroom in the summer of 1940 always began with Hawkins's paraphrase of the original melody over a ponderous orchestral background—and Hawkins himself was referred to in print advertising and over the radio as the "body and soul of the saxophone."

Yet the popularity of the record underscored a fundamental flaw in Hawkins's strategy. Jazz improvisation may have been the crucial element that distinguished swing from earlier forms of dance music and elevated it to an unprecedented popularity. But even when a swing band was led by an acknowledged jazz virtuoso (as in the case of Benny Goodman, Earl Hines, Harry James, or Lionel Hampton), improvisation was only one part of a carefully balanced package of entertainment. Extraordinary instrumental technique by itself counted for something, but it still needed to be packaged somehow for public consumption. Those who managed to make their mark concentrated on finding some distinguishing trademark. Harry James, one of the most brilliantly successful of the instrumentalist bandleaders, provides an interesting example. As Gunther Schuller notes, his "radiantly brassy tone, combined with an overbearing vibrato, was totally original and *instantly recognizable*. . . . On purely commercial terms, it is that kind of nervy authority, technical perfection, and unequivocal recognizability that succeeds. It succeeds because it is clearly identifiable, therefore precisely labelable and therefore, in turn, marketable." But even at that, the James sound was only a hook that drew the listener into a world of entertainment: prodigious displays of trumpet technique complementing ballad crooners like Frank Sinatra and lush string arrangements.

It is striking in retrospect how many bands, black bands especially, were led by musicians of relatively modest talent as instrumentalists—Fletcher Henderson, Jimmie Lunceford, Andy Kirk, or even Basie and Ellington. The real virtuosity of these soft-spoken men, one might say, lay in organizing, channeling, managing, and even "selling" the talents of others. Perhaps this skill was particularly crucial for a black musician, who had to appear as unthreatening as possible so as not to offend the sensibilities of either the white-controlled music industry or the white public. In any case, the central responsibilities of a Swing Era bandleader—working in coordination with more than a dozen other musicians to develop a collective musical personality, presenting the appropriate persona to the public, cooperating with industry professionals in a strategy to find a niche in the market—seemed to escape Hawkins. He was notoriously oblivious to his musical surroundings, a quality that may have helped him survive in Europe, where the unevenness of musical personnel might have driven another musician to distraction, but that made it very difficult for him to parlay his considerable artistic achievement into real popular success. Hawkins's solo on "Body and Soul" works *in spite of* its haphazard accompaniment. Aside from the marvelously appropriate piano introduction, the only place where the band stands out is the performance's only glaring flaw: the poorly balanced, poorly timed final chord that follows Hawkins's cadenza.

The end of 1939 found the band in a delicate position. Hawkins's reputation among professional dance musicians was unquestioned, and even his limited round of activities in the fall was enough to rekindle enthusiasm among dedicated jazz fans. As *Down Beat* noted when he won first place in the tenor saxophone category of its annual poll, "Coleman Hawkins is the surprise of the entire poll; several years in Europe haven't dimmed his popularity." And yet to reap the rewards of the Swing Era, a jazz musician, no matter how well respected by the readers of *Down Beat*, needed to function effectively as the leader of a *dance band*. For a black musician, this was even harder, since the white public expected at least some conformity to the stereotype of black artist as entertainer. There were various ways of satisfying that expectation while avoiding the most corrosive aspects of the stereotype: the sophisticated suavity of Ellington (backed, of course, by an orchestral sound of startling originality); Cab Calloway's zoot-suited jivester persona; the slick, polished, versatile stage shows of the Lunceford band; the sheer enthusiasm and motor drive of Lionel Hampton; the casual, back-room flavor of the Basie band; and the total conviction with which Louis Armstrong inhabited the entertainer's role.

None of these suited Hawkins. Had he been content to remain a famous soloist in someone else's band—Basie's, for example (and rumors that Hawkins would join the tenor section alongside Lester Young, perhaps to replace the recently deceased Herschel Evans, were circulating in the fall of 1939)—he might have postponed some difficult choices. But he had left that role behind years before when he cut his ties to the Henderson band. In the boom atmosphere of 1939, he felt fully entitled to his share in the financial gain and glory, and forged ahead with his plans.

By November, Hawkins was preparing for the plunge into the wider market. Dutifully, he began expanding his group. Within a few months, the band grew to sixteen pieces. More important, the number of wind instruments doubled: from two trumpets to four, one trombone to three, and three saxes to five. On the October recordings, Hawkins easily dominated the small group—not just when he took a solo, but throughout the performance. It is possible—just possible—for a saxophonist of Hawkins's power to do this with a nine-piece group. But by expanding, Hawkins delegated much of that musical authority to other professionals.

Among his new acquisitions was Bill Dillard, a veteran first trumpet player in Teddy Hill's band from 1934 to 1938. As in any orchestra, the first-chair musicians were crucial. They were typically chosen not as soloists but for their excellent tone and ability to mold the disparate timbres of their section into an acceptable sound. Dillard's experience helped to compensate for the rawness of some of the other new talent. Dizzy Gillespie, who was taken under Dillard's wing after joining Teddy Hill's band in 1937 as a teenager, attested to Dillard's effectiveness as a musical educator: "He'd show me how to hold notes out, how to sing on the trumpet, and how to use a vibrato. I was young and fly and could play . . . but I didn't know a lot of the fine points of music. Bill helped me change the little things that I did that weren't professional."

Unlike Dillard, tenor saxophonist Kermit Scott came to the band with almost no big-band experience, although a few years later, at ground zero of the bebop revolution, he would lead the house band at Minton's Playhouse alongside Joe Guy, Thelonious Monk, and Kenny Clarke. Scott had arrived in New York in 1936, after playing with a territory band from Texas. By 1940 he was a regular at after-hours clubs in Harlem (including Monroe's Uptown House). His track record in New York, however, was limited to a few recording dates for Billie Holiday and helping Fats Waller expand his small combo to full band size for an engagement at the Apollo Theatre. He reacted with bemusement that Hawkins had chosen him for the band over more seasoned professionals: "Why he took me I can't understand. . . . Someone told me, 'Man, Hawk is auditioning, so why don't you go down?' So I went down there and man, you had guys who could transpose faster than I could read, actually, you know what I mean? And all those good guys—I didn't figure I had a chance, man."

Scott probably impressed Hawkins with his sound, not his reading and transposing skills. "He used to sound like Hawk," tenor saxophonist Budd Johnson remembered. This resemblance proved to be convenient for Hawkins, who set Scott up as a surrogate for his frequent absences from the bandstand: "He had me sit up right next to him. . . . During the time, leaders would stand up in the front. His stand was facing mine, man, and he would sometimes ask me what tempo to play tunes with, you know? And then when he'd go off and wouldn't be there, I took his solos and things."

Having finally built up his band to a size that could be taken seriously by the industry professionals, Hawkins set to work finding a place for it to play. He needed some kind of extended residency, to give his new band time to settle in—to learn their repertory, acquire new arrangements, and let the haphazard mix of musical personalities and temperaments gel. With any luck, the band would also get some radio exposure. Finding a residency could have been a challenge, for Hawkins was bucking the seasonal flow of the band business. Had he picked up a copy of *Metronome* that fall, he might have noticed an editorial with the stern title "Don't Start a Band Now!" warning that October marked the beginning of the "Sterile Season." Reputations, *Metronome* explained, were made in the summer months, when resorts, parks, and other seasonal entertainments increased the demand for dance music. By the fall, when bands scurried for the shelter of extended ballroom jobs, booking agents had already decided which bands were worth investing in. "Suppose you started a band and a month from now walked into one of the booking offices," the editorial conjectured. "They might hear you and might even be impressed. 'But look,' they'll say, 'we have all these bands under contract already, and we haven't placed them. Why should we take on additional headaches?' "

The enlarged version of the band made its debut with a brief engagement at the Arcadia Ballroom in downtown Manhattan, where the band mixed rhumbas and tangos into its swing repertory. But for the long term, Hawkins looked uptown. This normally would have meant the Savoy Ballroom, owned by Moe Gale and his Harlem business partner, Charlie Buchanan. Gale, a luggage manufacturer from the Lower East Side who made a sudden lateral move into show business by building a ballroom in Harlem in 1926, had long wielded considerable influence over the professional fortunes of black musicians. "It seems to be a custom for most of the really good colored bands to get started at the Savoy," wrote critic George Simon in 1935.

With the onset of the swing boom, the Savoy only grew in importance, because it remained one of the few "location jobs" available to black musicians with regular nationwide radio broadcasts. "Gale affects the life of every Negro maestro, even those not under his wing, because most of them can't come out ahead without playing six to twelve weeks a year at the Savoy," claimed the *Saturday Evening Post*. Over the years, Gale gradually took a more active role in shaping the destinies of his black charges, sponsoring the careers of the Ink Spots and drummer Chick Webb. "Because the average Negro musician is emotionally stormy," the *Post* patronizingly explained, "it requires years of patience and discipline to develop them. Gale has mastered the art of gently cracking the whip, and over the years he has turned countless colored folk into box-office celebrities."

As it turned out, Hawkins was lucky enough to be shopping his band around just as one of Gale's former business partners decided to challenge the Savoy's hegemony in Harlem. In October 1939 a new ballroom opened its doors there. The Golden Gate Ballroom (formerly the State Palace Ballroom) was a cavernous, 25,000-square-foot spot with room for five thousand on the dance floor (as well as several thousand more spectators) that doubled as a roller-skating rink. The Golden Gate was the latest project of Jay Faggen, the Broadway promoter who had been one of the original owners of the Roseland Ballroom. Faggen sold out his share of the Roseland to launch the Arcadia in 1924, and in 1926 had joined forces with Moe Gale to build the Savoy. Gale eventually bought out his partner. The opening of the Golden Gate represented an aggressive bid to capture a share of the Savoy's business. Faggen spent his money freely, attracting large crowds by hiring as many as five orchestras at once—a tactic considered by the trade press to be "one of the most ambitious ballroom policies undertaken anywhere." In the words of the local Harlem newspaper, the *New York Amsterdam News,* the battle for Harlem's dancing public promised to keep "the hope of work alive in the breasts of hundreds of musicians, and [to] stimulate competition in Harlem where it is most needed." Hawkins became an early beneficiary of this competition, earning a spot in the Golden Gate's roster of house bands in mid-December alongside Count Basie and Teddy Wilson.

By this time Hawkins had acquired professional management. He became a client of Consolidated Radio Artists (CRA), where his business was handled by Joe Glaser. Glaser is best known for his close partnership with Louis Armstrong, although he served as manager for a number of other prominent black bandleaders, including Andy Kirk and Roy Eldridge. Glaser knew that Hawkins's band was not ready yet to go on the road. After a brief tour of black theaters in the Northeast to test the waters (the Howard in Washington, the Earle in Philadelphia, and the Royal in Baltimore), the band settled into its residency at the Golden Gate. February found Hawkins fully involved in the ballroom's hectic activities. On the seventh, he teamed with Count Basie to provide the music for the 1940 Miss Harlem contest. The next week he was part of a massive, five-band celebration (a "Rhythm Rodeo") on Lincoln's birthday. And in a gimmick commemorating Leap Year Day, two couples were married on the dance floor while Hawkins played a wedding march. Hawkins later remembered his time at the Golden Gate as one of the biggest "kicks" in his career. After nearly twenty years as a musician's musician, he had finally come into his own as a bandleader at the height of the Swing Era.

But just as Hawkins seemed positioned to take advantage of the crest of popularity of the "Body and Soul" recording, his fortunes began to unravel. In March the Golden Gate was dealt a fatal blow: the loss of the ballroom's beer license. The official reason given in the press for the revocation was the violation of regulations governing the serving of hard liquor, but it is hard not to suspect the influence of Faggen's powerful competitors. The volume of business dropped off sharply, and in short order the ballroom went into bankruptcy, only to be snapped up by the owners of the arch-rival Savoy Ballroom. The Golden Gate quickly assumed a decidedly subsidiary position as a "social ballroom," rented out to civic and society organizations for private affairs. "It's Czar Moe Gale in Harlem Now," trumpeted a headline in the trade press.

Lacking Gale's sponsorship, Hawkins had a difficult time regaining a foothold in New York. For a period of several weeks after the closing of the Golden Gate, he was forced to "lay off," freeing his musicians to find whatever work they could. Finally, in May, he landed a job as one of two house bands at the Fiesta Danceteria on Times Square. The Danceteria, which had just opened for business the previous November, was a peculiar hybrid of cafeteria-style fast food and nightlife. Described by *Billboard* as a "self-service nightclub catering to the great middle class," it offered an inexpensive (sixty-cent) all-you-can-eat smorgasbord, with music by popular dance orchestras as a kind of side dish. As the manager explained: "Since the Danceteria is primarily a restaurant, we must keep our dance music toned down so that table conversation may be carried on. Some of the name bands we booked had a tendency to blast the roof off, most of them having just returned from a tour of one-nighters, where they played in huge structures with the acoustics of an armory. But when they found out that the Fiesta fans wanted their swing on the soft side, they muted their instruments."

The Danceteria proved to be a challenge that Hawkins cared not to meet. Although the plan was for a lengthy engagement, he abruptly pulled his band out after only a week in protest. He had been asked to play stock arrangements of such ephemera as "The Woodpecker Song," instead of being allowed to choose from his normal repertory. For the late-night crowd, the management requested its usual "swing on the soft side" with muted brass. Hawkins's reaction was blunt and uncharacteristically vehement—reflecting, no doubt, his own irritation at having to play for the squares on Times Square. "Mine isn't a Mickey Mouse band," he complained, "and if I can't play the music I want, I'd rather not have the job." For Hawkins, the conditions imposed by the Danceteria were an affront to his reputation and to his struggling band: "If they want that kind of music, let them hire Blue Barron or Reggie Childs. That place was ruining the morale of my men. You can't expect to develop a swing band by having your men held under wraps. I have to play the music that I feel, and I can't feel the kind the Fiesta asked me to play."

Time was running out. It was now June 1940, more than half a year since the band had been launched, and the band had yet to earn a reputation. After the Danceteria fiasco, Hawkins gave up on CRA and Joe Glaser, joining Moe Gale's fold instead. Gale worked hard to raise Hawkins's profile, using his Harlem connections and his flair for publicity to ensure that the bandleader (if not always his band) was seen and heard in the right places. When Count Basie appeared at the Apollo Theatre in Harlem, Hawkins joined fellow bandleaders and celebrities Charlie Barnet, Benny Carter, and Erskine Hawkins in an opening-day jam session. The *Amsterdam News* helpfully reported that Hawkins "nearly started a riot as he played some of the greatest music of his long career." The next week, Hawkins himself opened with his band as the featured attraction at the Apollo. On the morning of the first show (June 14), another jam session was held, to which an impressive display of "name" bandleaders, both black and white, were invited, including Harry James, Bunny Berigan, Tommy Dorsey, Gene Krupa, Count Basie, and Charlie Barnet. In addition, Gale gained invaluable radio exposure for Hawkins as a guest star on nationwide broadcasts by other prominent orchestras, including those of Gene Krupa, Tommy Dorsey, and Jimmie Lunceford.

All this was prelude to the main event: a make-or-break engagement at the Savoy Ballroom. At the Savoy, bands had the luxury of performing for discriminating and supportive black audiences while gaining badly needed nationwide radio exposure. Throughout the summer, Hawkins's band could be heard three nights a week on sustaining broadcasts from the Savoy over the NBC network. But even for a location job, the pay was unusually meager. For many years, the well-connected Gale had kept the standard salary for musicians at about $33 a week (with $50 for the bandleader), an astonishingly low wage for top-rank professional musicians even during the Depression. (Gale supposedly paid out the salary to Chick Webb's band in 1934 with one-dollar bills, "on the theory that a Negro with thirty one-dollar bills is happier than a Negro with six five-dollar bills.") Gale's standard salary was well below the minimum wage supposedly required by the New York local of the musicians' union, a circumstance that bassist George Duvivier blamed on an "unholy alliance" between the union and the Savoy management. By Hawkins's time, the wage had probably drifted upward to about $36 a week. Not until late 1943 did a storm of public pressure force Gale to match the $50 salary at the downtown ballrooms. For this, the musicians worked long, hard hours: from 9 P.M. to 4 A.M., Tuesday through Saturday, with a four-hour afternoon matinee on Sunday, followed by six more hours in the evening.

Musicians were told to be grateful for the chance to play at the Savoy: "They used to say to us: 'What are you complaining about? You're home, you're not on the road. This is your home.' " As Benny Carter recalled, "The idea was that playing the Savoy was expected to lead to other things, so a band was supposed to be glad to be there. In fact, the owners and managers felt they were doing the bands a favor. They thought of us—in management and remuneration—as maybe a cut above the waiters." But few musicians were fooled. As one musician acerbically noted, "To work the Savoy would lift up the status of your band for your agent 100%, but you would *never* see that money."

Hawkins struggled to make the most of the opportunity. He juggled his personnel: those who had left, discouraged by slack employment or lured away by higher wages, were replaced. On August 9, he took the full band into the studio for its first and only recording session, producing three instrumental numbers (all carrying Hawkins's name on the composer credits) and a vocal ballad. By all accounts, Hawkins did well at the Savoy, pleasing the dancers and impressing listeners with his powerful playing. But the audience that mattered lay outside the Savoy's walls. The only way for Hawkins to cash in on his new status on radio and recording was to take his band on the road. Just how difficult that might be was underscored by the annual popularity contest in the August issue of *Metronome:* out of approximately 5,800 votes cast in the "best swing band" category, Hawkins received exactly five, earning him thirty-first place in the poll.

In mid-September, Hawkins took the plunge. Moe Gale arranged for his band to tour in conjunction with the house band, Al Cooper's Savoy Sultans, who pestered Gale for opportunities to get away from the Savoy and go out on the road. The two bands traded sets, as they had done for the past several months at the Savoy. The tour unfolded with little publicity, and surviving musicians are hazy on the exact details. "I think we went all through the South," remembers Kermit Scott. "We covered a lot of miles on that tour, mostly ballroom dates, I seem to recall," comments drummer J. C. Heard. The trade press reported two appearances: a "race [i.e., all-black] prom" in Kansas City on October 18 and a night at the Savoy Ballroom in Chicago on October 20. Finally, Hawkins straggled home to New York in November with a tired, dispirited group of musicians. With no work forthcoming, and not enough money to meet the payroll, Hawkins was forced to dissolve his band.

By the end of the year, Hawkins was back where he had started: on 52nd Street, at the new Kelly's Stable, with a "small jam band" of seven pieces. The band gathered together a number of seasoned professionals—Clyde Hart, Peanuts Holland, Eddie Barefield—in addition to the few remaining members from his big band, Sandy Williams on trombone and J. C. Heard. Hawkins still commanded attention as a soloist: according to

George Duvivier, the audiences were so enraptured that "you could hear a pin drop." But his status as a bandleader had vanished. Nothing short of a full-size dance orchestra made much of an impression on the music industry. The disparity between Hawkins's former ambitions and his current situation was an irony not lost on observers of the scene: "Now Hawk is playing with five [sic] men in a little dimly-lighted club on 52nd Street, where the pay is meager and the chances for becoming nationally prominent—with an uninterested public—negligible."

When this band, too, dissolved in mid-March, Hawkins remained optimistic: as *Down Beat* noted, "He doesn't seem concerned about his status and says Joe Glaser, the booker, will 'fix me up with something good when I'm ready.' " Within a couple of months, Hawkins had given up on New York, heading instead for Chicago. Over the next several years, he worked with a number of small combos of varied quality, but he was never again to lead a large dance orchestra.

Ruinous Competition

The unimpressive trajectory of Hawkins's dance band, from promising beginnings to extinction in less than a year, was scarcely noticed in the music industry. Had they been asked, his contemporaries could have come up with any number of reasons for the band's failure, ranging from the riskiness of any venture in popular entertainment to specific shortcomings in tactics and execution on the part of the bandleader or his management. (Some of these will be considered below.) But in retrospect, it is apparent that Hawkins chose to launch his band just as the giddy expansionary phase of the Swing Era was coming to a halt.

The end of the decade seemed to mark a turning point. By early 1940 industry observers began noting that the swing craze was ebbing: the teenage and college crowd drifted on to other fashions, while the adult public, tiring of frenetic rhythms, retreated to the comfortable certainties of such tried-and-true dances as the waltz. Although reports on the "death" of any fad often substitute wishful thinking for objective analysis, in this case the bets were noticeably hedged: the new trend was dubbed "sweet-hot" or "swing-sweet"—a "white man's style of swing, retaining the Negroid bounce but coupling it to more respect for the melody." Some people in the industry already realized that the speculative bubble on which the prosperity of the Swing Era rested was about to burst. Swing was no longer a spontaneous cultural force. It had "degenerated into a cold business proposition": kept alive by the investment already made in creating celebrity bandleaders and subject to the inflexible law of supply and demand, but no longer stimulating new enthusiasm. *Variety* described the underlying economic forces bluntly in its 1939 year-end roundup: "Every new band that's formed, whether making money or not at the start, tends to bring down prices. Maybe not now, but eventually. It's elementary logic that when the market is drugged, the values skid. Sooner or later, if the present pace is maintained, that's just what will happen to the band business."

By the beginning of the new decade, several disturbing symptoms were evident. For one thing, payroll costs skyrocketed. Every successful band needed its featured soloists, some of whom (like Gene Krupa) became nearly as famous as the bandleader. While the number of bands increased, the supply of experienced, highly skilled musicians remained relatively constant. Unlike baseball players of the time, musicians were under no contractual obligation to remain with their employers. The most desirable became free agents, jumping from band to band and extracting higher salaries at each stop—or they decided to become bandleaders themselves, further diluting available talent. "The practice is drawing a knife across the throats" of even the most prosperous bands, reported *Variety*, "because sooner or later they find themselves with so top-heavy a payroll the band can't grow enough profit if the bookings aren't right."

At the same time, new bands entered into a potentially ruinous competition for employment. "Where are all those bands going to work?" editorialized *Metronome* in the fall of 1939. "There's not even a semblance of a proportional increase in the number of spots into which they can be booked." Agents began offering their clients at abnormally low prices, just to get gigs. Venues with "wires"—the local radio hookup that allowed them to serve as broadcasters for the evening—took advantage of the situation to lower their fees, knowing that desperate bands (or their agents) would be willing to sacrifice income for media exposure. A few bandleaders even offered to absorb the cost of the "wires"—surreptitiously, because the powerful musicians' union considered the extra expense to be "unfair competition" and "working under scale," and threatened punishment accordingly.

The most prosperous bands, like Benny Goodman's or Harry James's, were insulated from the worst effects of these pressures. The brunt of the tightening economic conditions was borne by lesser bands, especially the new entrants into the field. In many cases, starting up a band proved to be an ill-conceived gamble—not so much for the booking agents (who had plenty of other irons in the fire) but for the unlucky would-be bandleader, whose ambitions were preyed upon with increasing efficiency and cynicism. Drawing on his conversations with a booker, Dave Dexter described the pattern in *Down Beat:*

> "We take a young guy with a new band . . . and shoot him out in the sticks on one-nighters to break in his band. Then we set him in a location with airtime. Sure he loses $100 to $500 a week while on location, but we mark that off, for we'll get it back after a few months of airtime by going into a theater at anywhere from $3000 to $4500 a week. Once we hit theaters, the money rolls in."
>
> Yep, it rolls in. But after theaters, what? Go back on location and lose all the profits fast. The young leader can't go from theaters to the road (one-nighters) because the band hasn't been on the air while doing vaude[ville theaters], and hence, means nothing as a b-o [box office] attraction.
>
> That's when it gets tough, and unless the young maestro luckily makes a hit record . . . he's on the skids already. For by this time the booker who got him heated up about leading a band has milked him good and is now working on some other young sideman.
>
> It's a brutal circle, a vicious dead-end street which not only demoralizes the leader, but also his men.

In certain respects, Coleman Hawkins's fate resembled this hapless neophyte's. He, too, had once been enthusiastically courted by booking agencies and encouraged to make a full-fledged bid for stardom, only to be dropped once it became clear that the enterprise was foundering. Indeed, the band's disastrous final tour in the fall of 1940 may have been a deliberate attempt to run it into the ground. As *Metronome* had reported that summer:

> Since the supply of dance orchestras now far exceeds that of spots, the easiest way to keep up the price (and thus also the commission collected by the office) is to kill off competitive bands. And the new outfits, so often playing for mere scale, not only are competition, but cannot hope to bring in lucrative returns. . . .
>
> The system might be termed "travelling the band into submission." The offices arrange road tours which they know in advance are likely to be financially ruinous to the leader. One tremendous jump follows another, resulting in blistering expenses. On top of that, each job brings in a ridiculously small sum, often little more than mere scale for the spot. Few leaders can survive such a system for long. . . .
>
> That such tours are arranged by bookers knowing that they might lead

to the breaking up of bands has been readily admitted by more than one representative, one of whom laughed at the plight of some leaders who recently had to give up under the strain.

But in other respects, Hawkins's experience differed markedly from the "young guy" of Dexter's anecdote. Although nowhere is race mentioned, the hypothetical bandleader is unmistakably white: he enjoys automatic access to crucial areas of the entertainment world, such as lucrative theater engagements and months of radio exposure, that were routinely closed off to black musicians. It is an inescapable fact that for every problem facing new bands in the competitive climate of the late 1930s, black bands had to deal with the additional handicap of racism. As a result, the very musicians on whose musical contributions the Swing Era rested found themselves increasingly unable to compete for its economic rewards.

The Wages of Discrimination

The fault lines of racial caste that ran deep through America of the pre–civil rights era divided the music world into two distinct and unequal spheres. In all but the most extraordinary circumstances or the most informal settings, black musicians performed only with blacks and inevitably suffered the social and economic stigma of segregation. Even the musicians' union, supposedly representing the interests of all musicians as workers, maintained separate "colored" locals in every city (with the notable exception of New York and Detroit). Mass-market capitalism in theory rewarded anyone who struck a responsive chord with the public. In reality, patterns of discrimination systematically denied black artists the opportunity to compete fairly for those rewards.

As long as the Swing Era remained at high tide, the disadvantages of institutionalized racism were minimized. Indeed, John Hammond went so far as to contend in the heady days of 1936 that "the acceptance of swing music, which is fundamentally Negroid, has improved the bargaining power of the black musician immeasurably. . . . People of all classes are demanding guts and swing in their music." But with the encroachment of white bands on their territory, black bands soon found that their race was a liability, not an asset. The first signs of difficulty began to appear as early as 1938, with "competition from the Dorseys, Benny Goodman, Larry Clinton, Bunny Berigan, Artie Shaw, Gene

Krupa"—few of whom were in business before 1935—leading to a slow but steady erosion of theater engagements and one-nighters available to black bands.

As business conditions worsened, black bands were inexorably squeezed to the margins. A report in *Billboard* at the end of 1940 noted that employment for black entertainers generally had declined some 25 to 30 percent from the peak levels of two to three years earlier. Several reasons were adduced: out-and-out racial prejudice, the general backlash against the "blary music" of swing (the article refers to the "passing of the swing era"), and—perhaps as a result of these factors—a steep decline in the number of establishments offering employment to black musicians. The famous Cotton Club, home base for first Ellington and then Cab Calloway, had closed its doors in June. All-black theaters, once numbering two dozen, had dwindled to a handful (the Apollo in New York, the Howard in Washington, the Royal in Baltimore). Equally disturbing was the tendency for venues that had previously relied heavily on black bands to shift to white entertainment. The *New York Amsterdam News* applauded the racial liberalism represented by the appearance of white bands at Harlem theaters and ballrooms, but wondered, "when a Negro band is on the sidelines during an engagement of a white outfit, does it have the chance to work in the big hotel spots downtown left by the white band that came to Harlem?"

That rhetorical question was addressed in a surprisingly frank manner in a survey of the dance band business that appeared in *Harper's Magazine* in 1941 with the provocative subtitle "A Study in Black and White." Its author, Irving Kolodin, began by discussing at some length the business fortunes of various well-known white bands, but then noted:

> It is rather . . . curious that [one] group of names has been . . . less conspicuous in this inquiry, for it embraces musicians who are in no sense moribund and very much a part of the contemporary jazz picture. It is a list which begins with the name of Duke Ellington, and continues with those of "Count" Basie, [Jimmie] Lunceford, Louis Armstrong, Fletcher Henderson, Ella Fitzgerald, Cab Calloway, Teddy Wilson, Andy Kirk, John Kirby, Coleman Hawkins, Erskine Hawkins, Lionel Hampton, Roy Eldridge, and sundry others. They are names with a familiar echo even to a public unfamiliar with this subject; but *they are almost never to be encountered in a prominent hotel, and never on a commercial radio program.*
>
> They are of course all Negro musicians—and rigorously excluded, as if by Congressional decree, from these two principal sources of prestige and

financial reward. Thus, though each enjoys a serious repute among students of jazz music, and substantial income from records and theater engagements and dance-hall appearances, they can never hope to equal the fabulous earnings of Goodman, Shaw, or Glenn Miller.

There were exceptions—the Hotel Sherman in Chicago, for example, employed black bands. Moreover, the optimistic could take comfort in the gradual eroding of barriers. Louis Armstrong's appearance on a radio broadcast sponsored by Fleishmann's Yeast in 1940 and the hiring of Count Basie by a major New York hotel in 1943 were hailed as breakthroughs. But to overcome ingrained habits of prejudice required both courage and a sense of moral outrage—traits conspicuously absent, then as now, in the entertainment world. Radio networks and hotel operators typically professed no racial animus, deflecting responsibility to a distant and more intractable source: the South. Southerners entering a hotel dining room where black musicians were employed would take offense, the hoteliers claimed. Similarly, radio executives deferred to the sensitivities of the sponsoring companies, who worried that the appearance of black musicians on their programs might spark boycotts of their products below the Mason-Dixon line.

Just how damaging were these racially based restrictions? The absence of black bands from prime-time programs—such as Coca-Cola's "Spotlight Bands," the "Camel Caravan," or the "Fitch Bandwagon"—certainly deprived them of an important source of income upon which many white name bands depended, although only the most prestigious could have expected to appear on such shows.[7] The exclusion from prominent hotels was far more deleterious. The issue here was not income: as we have seen, major white bands, such as Glenn Miller's or Tommy Dorsey's, actually *lost* money over the course of an extended engagement. But it was from hotels and ballrooms that bands could be heard week after week over the radio—invaluable publicity that could then be exploited in nationwide tours. This strategy, pioneered by Irving Mills with Ellington at the Cotton Club, still worked beautifully for black bands with access to radio broadcasts. In 1937, for example, Calloway followed a winter

7. Figures published in mid-1940 detailing the sources of income for one fairly successful white band—Bob Crosby's—showed commercial radio accounting for $37,249, or 13.8% of the total. This was more than records and royalties (9.1%), but less than theaters (31.1%), one-nighters (29.4%), and even location jobs (16.5%) ("Theaters Most Profitable in '39," *Down Beat* 7 [1 June 1940]: 19).

season at the Cotton Club with six months of solid bookings in theaters and ballrooms, earning more than $6,000 a week on average in net profits. In the summer of 1943, thanks to a rare extended stay at a downtown location (the Hurricane Club) with nearly six broadcasts a week, Ellington was able to charge at least two to three times more for one-nighters than the season before. However, the places from which black bands could broadcast (the Savoy Ballroom in New York, the Grand Terrace in Chicago) were pitifully few.

To reach their audiences, black bands counted more heavily on recordings—a medium that allowed black musicians to engage in remunerative transactions across racial barriers without the inconvenience of social contact.[8] Records could, and frequently did, make black bands prosperous in and of themselves. Several broke into the national ranks primarily on the strength of their hit recordings: Count Basie with "One O'Clock Jump" (1937), Erskine Hawkins with "Tuxedo Junction" (1939), Lionel Hampton with "Flying Home" (1942). But recordings were a decidedly uncertain source of income. No one could predict which records would become hits, and there was always a considerable lag time between the actual date of a recording and its release. Appearances on radio programs, by contrast, could be regularly scheduled, and the fees were paid up-front. Nothing matched the power of radio to blanket the entire country simultaneously with the same broadcast.

Lack of airtime was only one of the problems posed by the unwritten ban on black bands in hotel ballrooms. Extended engagements at major hotels provided a badly needed interval of rest in a band's hectic schedule. After the busy summer season, the top white bands normally counted on being able to spend the winter months in New York. Musicians could unpack their bags, spend time with their families or girlfriends, leave their instruments at the gig, enjoy the delights of the late-night music scene in Manhattan, and otherwise settle into a comfortable routine after months of continuous travel. Bandleaders could break in new personnel, plan the next season's tours, and try out new arrangements—all while

8. When pianist and bandleader Teddy Wilson was asked how racial discrimination had hindered his career, he replied, "the biggest handicap is in radio. Radio and records are the lifeblood of a band, so that means that a colored band has to rely mainly on records" (Leonard Feather, "Jazz Symposium: How Have Jim Crow Tactics Affected Your Career?" *Esquire* 22 [September 1944]: 93). Jimmie Lunceford tried to put an optimistic spin on the situation: "Is air time essential? Not on my life!" But the bottom line was the same: to stay continuously before the public, the Lunceford band counted on an output of approximately twelve records a year (Jimmie Lunceford, "Is Air Time Essential? Not on My Life—Lunceford," *Metronome* 58 [October 1942]: 9, 26).

continuing to reach the entire country through late-night broadcasts. Black musicians were afforded none of these luxuries. Even the most prestigious bands were forced into a year-round succession of exhausting tours, with only brief interludes in New York at the Savoy or the Apollo Theatre. Musicians complained bitterly about the lack of places to "sit down and play."

Meanwhile, the road became a less hospitable place. One factor, ironically, was the passage of equal-rights laws in many northern states, prohibiting discrimination in attendance at public functions. Club owners could no longer keep black patrons away. Fearing a potentially explosive racial mixture (or lawsuits if they continued to discriminate), clubs shied away from hiring black bands. Some bandleaders even went to the extreme of sending musicians into black neighborhoods when they did land an engagement at a "white" club, asking the local population not to come to their show. More and more, black bands were forced into tours of the South, where racial divisions could be more efficiently policed. There, of course, they encountered the Jim Crow system—the inadequate housing, the obstacles to obtaining a decent meal, the fear and hostility that pervaded every waking moment.

Finally, the old stereotypes came back to haunt them. White bands, having proven their ability to play hot, were prized for their versatility. Tommy Dorsey, for example, was praised for his ability to mediate between the "blare of the jam cellar" and staid parties, pleasing the "cats" and conservative customers at the same time.[9] Although black bands, as we have seen, were equally adaptable and sensitive to changing currents in fashion, white audiences continued to regard them as one-dimensional. An article appearing in the spring of 1940 put the matter bluntly: *"The truth is that the public will absorb only a very limited number of Negro bands."* Only a handful had attained any measure of financial stability. Of these, Calloway sold on the basis of his "personality," Armstrong on his "high-note appeal," while Ellington was *sui generis*. The remainder struggled to establish an identity separate from straightforward swing: "Basie's high-powered jump style caught on, but if public reaction means

9. Dorsey elsewhere carefully distinguished between "swing" and "jamming," making clear where his sympathies lay: "Swing is smooth, easy to listen to and calm enough for the most conservative dancer—there are no extraneous flourishes or 'out-of-the-world' take-offs by individual instrumentalists. While soloists are featured and the music does not follow any standard arrangement, the basic melody is always distinguishable. On the other hand, jamming is an admixture of blaring trombones, wild tom-tom tones, improvised saxophone runs, and plenty of loud vocalizing" (Tommy Dorsey, "Swing It—Sweetly!" *Billboard* 50 [31 December 1938]: 71).

anything, there's room for only one band of that caliber." Earl Hines, Andy Kirk, Roy Eldridge, Ella Fitzgerald (inheriting Chick Webb's band on the drummer's death the previous year), Benny Carter, Teddy Wilson, Jimmie Lunceford, Claude Hopkins, Don Redman, and Coleman Hawkins—all were "practically out of the picture so far as the general public [was] concerned."

Both onstage and off, through flashy uniforms and hyperbolic press releases, black bands did their best to project an image of prosperity. But while they managed for the most part to disguise their precarious existence, black musicians could only be painfully aware of their declining economic position.

Even Count Basie's band, one of the most conspicuous success stories of the late 1930s, hit a bump in the road with a bitter dispute between Basie and the booking agency Music Corporation of America (MCA) at the end of 1940. Basie's affairs had previously been handled by Willard Alexander, but with the latter's defection to William Morris in mid-1939, Basie no longer had a champion within the giant corporation. The immediate issue was the size of the fee charged by the agency. According to one report, MCA took in $19,000 in commissions for a year in which Basie showed a net loss of nearly $11,000. But the allegations went deeper. Basie's longtime road manager, Maceo Birch, charged MCA with failing to meet its basic responsibility to find extended engagements with radio exposure and to devise tours that kept the band steadily employed with a minimum of transportation expense. "We haven't had a location job with air time in a year. Some weeks we work every night, jumping 500 miles a night. Other weeks we lay off." Despite Basie's popularity, the overhead for the continuous, punishing travel wiped out any profits. In a desperate move, Basie threatened publicly to dissolve his band—or even to join Benny Goodman as a featured soloist—in an effort to force MCA to lower its commissions and improve the quality of its bookings. MCA refused to concede, citing the "natural limitations" to finding work for a black band. Basie finally paid a $10,000 penalty to annul the contract with MCA before rejoining Willard Alexander at the William Morris Agency.

Other bands found themselves skimming below the surface of prosperity, unable to escape a decidedly secondary status. The Kansas City–based territory band led by Andy Kirk broke into the national ranks in 1936 with its hit recording of the ballad "Until the Real Thing Comes

Along." Kirk signed with Joe Glaser and settled into a steady routine of touring, especially through the South ("because that's where our records had sold best"), averaging 50,000 miles a year. Glaser apparently promised extended engagements with radio exposure at the Savoy Ballroom and the Grand Terrace, but nothing materialized. Instead, the band labored on, playing gig after gig for its modest share of the revenue. "People may wonder if we were exploited by agents," Kirk wrote later. "We all were. In contracts. The bookers and managers had their own lawyers who were ours, too. That didn't make sense. Glaser got his cut, the territory booker got his cut, the ballroom or location got their cut. We had what was left. But we were happy to be playing, so we didn't think too much about the money."

The optimistic Kirk consistently put an upbeat spin on the situation: "You always hear about one-nighters, how awful they were: 'Man, those one-nighters are killing me. They're a drag, man.' I want to talk about how *good* one-nighters were. If it hadn't been for one-nighters, I wouldn't have met Mrs. Mary McLeod Bethune, and Dr. George Washington Carver. . . . I wouldn't have known there were any other people but rednecks in the South." His musicians, however, were less sanguine. "Kirk is still playing one-nighters," *Down Beat* reported in 1939. "His boys call them 'turkey tours' because they're tough as hell to work." The situation had not changed at the end of 1940: "How long can Kirk, Mary Lou Williams and the boys continue jumping from 200 to 450 miles every night, night after night, year after year, without air time, without a location job, and without the rest they as human beings must have? There's a limit to that kind of work and Kirk knows it."

The unacknowledged champion of the road was Jimmie Lunceford, a sometime saxophonist from Fisk University with a martinet's flair for organization, who parlayed a territory band known as the Chickasaw Syncopators into one of the most stylish black dance bands of the 1930s. Lunceford's career was launched by radio exposure from an extended residency at the Cotton Club in 1934 and maintained by a steady stream of recordings thereafter. Lacking any subsequent opportunities to play extended engagements, Lunceford earned a reputation as a bandleader willing to accept any one-nighter, including those that other name bands would have rejected as too unremunerative or inconvenient. As a result, the band's work schedule was legendary. In a typical month, May 1940, they played eighteen jobs, as far west as St. Louis and as far north as Toronto and Boston. The distance between successive jobs was often extraordinary. On May 30, the band performed in Providence, Rhode Island; the next night, in Martinsburg, West Virginia; on June 1, in Clemson, South Carolina—all this, needless to say, in an age before airplanes or interstate highways.

By the early 1940s the strain of continuous travel began to wear on his musicians, some of whom had been with Lunceford for more than a decade. "We were out there all the time on the road," Trummy Young remembered. "You had no kind of life because you were just moving year in, year out, all the time. . . . You were riding from the time you left the job the night before until not too much time before you went on the next job." In 1942 Lunceford's sidemen called a meeting at a Harlem YMCA, ostensibly to complain about the terrible condition of the buses they rode in (Lunceford drove a Cadillac). According to Trummy Young, "We were full of cold from leaking buses out there in the winter and freezing in the buses, rain, had to move over that the rain don't get on you, you know." The sidemen also used the occasion to press for a pay raise, a demand that caused Lunceford to bristle: "He called it mutiny and everything else, and he got angry in the process. 'You see my name up in front of this band,' he told us, 'not that of any of you guys.' He said he couldn't do any better, and that was that. The trouble started there and the guys began leaving one by one."

If bands as well established as Basie's, Kirk's, and Lunceford's struggled by the end of the 1930s, new black bands faced almost insurmountable obstacles. The brief career of Teddy Wilson as a bandleader is instructive, for in many respects it paralleled that of Hawkins. Both were veteran instrumentalists who commanded great respect within the musicians' community, and who had attained a modest degree of celebrity. If anything, Wilson was better known to the public through his association with the Benny Goodman Trios and Quartets.

In the spring of 1939, Wilson started his own band, using the money he had carefully saved from his years with Goodman to buy the necessities: uniforms, a PA system, arrangements, music stands. By fall, his investment already looked shaky. An in-progress report by *Metronome* pinpointed the crucial weakness of the band: the inability—or unwillingness—of Wilson's booking agency, MCA, to get him enough work: "During one month, [the band] worked a total of nine days. Wilson was having a devil of a time holding his men together. He had to pay them out of his own pocket so that they could live. He kept hounding his bookers for work, sitting endless hours in waiting rooms, often never even getting in [to] see them. 'We'll try,' they explained simply via their secretaries. And so Teddy waits."

Metronome did not specify why jobs were so scarce for Wilson's band, other than to point out the difficulty in keeping so many new bands employed. But for Wilson, as for other black bandleaders, racial discrimination was a factor. The year before, *Variety* noted that "Pennsylvania, [the] country's prime dance date location, has all but turned thumbs down on Negro bands. This season had been most notable with hardly any bookings. Ohio is acting similarly." Wilson was fully aware of the situation, as he later explained in an interview: "They had an equal rights law in Pennsylvania, and promoters were scared to hire colored bands because it might attract Negro patrons and they'd be risking lawsuits by refusing them admittance. That means that where a white band doing a road trip out of New York could break it up into short, convenient transportation jumps, a colored band could not break the journey until it got to Pittsburgh, the first town large enough to hold a strictly colored dance."

To add to his problems, Wilson resisted the usual pigeonholes. His was not, as he later put it, "the typical black jazz band of the time," hot and raucous. "Perhaps it needed more flash to attract a public that associated excitement with colored bands," suggested George Simon years later. "The Teddy Wilson band was so polished that it was ridiculous," remembered bassist Leonard Gaskin, who heard the band at the Golden Gate. "They were just too smooth for words—with power." Not only did the controlled elegance of a Teddy Wilson not fit the stereotype, it threatened the stylistic territory staked out by white bands in whom the music establishment had a considerable investment. Thelma Carpenter, who sang with the band at the Famous Door on 52nd Street, overheard insiders complain that "Teddy's band was too white. They were saying that because everything was so pretty. And even when they swung—well, you know how Teddy was. And if the song publishers and booking agents couldn't maneuver you to where they wanted you to be. . . . Well, Teddy was adamant about how *he* wanted his band to be, not how you *thought* it should be."

In October 1939 Wilson was lucky enough to be chosen by the new Golden Gate Ballroom as one of its two house bands. In between engagements at the Golden Gate, he tried to take the band on the road, but found only sporadic bookings at amusement parks and college campuses. When his best musician, tenor saxophonist Ben Webster, left him to join Duke Ellington in January, "that broke the spine of the band," according to bassist Al Hall. By April 20, when the band was scheduled to end its term at the Golden Gate, Wilson had tentatively decided to dissolve the band. He described his plight to Leonard Feather in an interview: "Things look so bad, I don't know what else I can do. We only have four scattered one-nighters lined up for a whole month. Outside of that, I'm losing so many of my key men. . . . The way things are going, it's hardly worthwhile trying to hold the band together. Maybe I'll get a small band and take a club job."

That was precisely what Wilson did do. In July, through the influence of John Hammond, Wilson landed a job at the nightclub Café Society as the leader of a seven-piece band—"the type of band his advisers have always felt he should have" (apparently not the same advisers who had told him the year before that he "couldn't miss"). With a small group, he could finally hire veteran musicians like trombonist Benny Morton, whose salary would have been too great an expense for his big band. Wilson earned only $100 a week at the Café Society, but that was $100 that he could count on, month after month, to meet his expenses and pay off his debts. He remained at the Café Society for four more years.

Benny Carter was another veteran black musician who struggled to find a niche in the music business commensurate with his talent. Like Hawkins, Carter spent the mid-1930s in Europe, returning in 1938 to form a dance orchestra that used the Savoy Ballroom as its base for the next several years. The inability of Carter's band, routinely praised by critics and musicians as extraordinarily sophisticated and polished, to gain much of a reputation beyond the Savoy puzzled observers, who called Carter a "mystery man." One report argued that "Carter could be the best of all the colored front men if conditions were identical with those of three, five, or even seven years ago," but that "[Carter's manager] can't land Benny a good location date with air time. Benny can't keep his men together because they leave after the band has gone jobless a few days." By late 1941, with jobs few and far between, Carter pared his band to a sextet. While he re-formed his large band the next year and kept it active throughout the war, he never achieved the success many had predicted for him.

What did it take, then, to make it in this climate? Lionel Hampton's success provides one answer. As with Teddy Wilson, his career as a bandleader was launched by years of association with Benny Goodman's small groups. But Hampton was as ebullient and uncomplicated a public personality as Wilson or Hawkins was withdrawn and enigmatic. A born entertainer, Hampton was determined to please the public with the sort of athletic exuberance they expected from black performers: "The audiences wanted good music, but they also wanted a show. I gave it to them. . . . We never forgot that we were supposed to be entertaining an audience, not just playing a jam session in front of a bunch of strange people."

Hampton also had the good fortune to have a hard-headed wife, Gladys, whose shrewd business skills impressed even the misogynist Malcolm X.[10] Gladys Hampton ruthlessly kept expenses as low as possible by hiring only young, inexperienced musicians, paying them as little as she could get away with—$10 a night, to be paid out *only* when the band was working. The Hamptons were not above using the limited opportunities available to their young charges as a way of keeping them in line. "[Lionel Hampton] sort of had an attitude towards the fellows in the band that you can't work any place, because there are so few places for black musicians to work, and if you don't like the way I treat you, you're out of a job," remembered Joe Wilder, who played with Hampton in the early 1940s. "It was sort of a reverse slavery in a way." Trumpeter Hal Mitchell described the Hamptons' philosophy as, "Why should you give it up to them when you can always get somebody else?" Hampton's boundless energy and his wife's steely resolve saw the band through endless grueling tours and kept the band working when others were folding.

As it turned out, the slump of 1940 was not the end of the Swing Era. Within a year or two, the business climate for live entertainment would be affected, mostly for the better, by the approach of war. As early as 1941, increased defense spending put money in the pockets of potential customers, giving a badly needed boost to the entertainment industry. The artificial stimulation of a wartime economy temporarily disguised the structural problems in the music industry and postponed the inevitable collapse of the Swing Era until shortly after the troops returned home in 1945. During the war years, shortages of critical materials, restrictions on transportation, inflated salaries, a manpower shortage caused by the draft, and a frenetic "live-for-today" atmosphere created a wholly new environment for those musicians fortunate enough to remain behind on the home front. The war years were a time of barely controlled chaos,

10. "My boss's wife and Gladys Hampton were the only two women I ever met in Harlem whose business ability I really respected" (Malcolm X 1964, 116). Malcolm X's boss at the time (c. 1943) was a numbers runner.

ripe with opportunity for those not averse to risk. Not coincidentally, they were also the years when the bebop movement took shape.

The disillusionment of the difficult years 1939 and 1940, however, left its mark on the leading lights of the black jazz community. Precisely those who had the most legitimate claims for success—virtuoso instrumentalists, arrangers, veteran bandleaders—found themselves boxed in by an economic system that gave insuperable advantages to white musicians who were frankly imitators, however accomplished, of a black idiom. It is remarkable, in the face of these difficulties, how many prominent black musicians tried to remain bandleaders when they could have enjoyed a more secure and profitable existence working as arrangers, or even star soloists, for white orchestras. Teddy Wilson could have earned a higher income and rid himself of the aggravations of self-employment by returning to Benny Goodman's band as a featured artist. Benny Carter could have commanded high fees for his stylish arrangements instead of reserving them for his own use. Even Earl Hines, who had been leading dance bands since the 1920s, admitted that in late 1940 he had nearly dissolved his band: "Goodman offered me a job with a nice guaranteed salary and it took a lot of pro'ing and con'ing before I made my decision."

Hines, of course, was able to remain as a bandleader for many more years. Wilson, Hawkins, and other equally talented musicians were not. As the 1940s began, a number of black musicians held anomalous positions in the band business: as failed bandleaders or disgruntled former soloists, these veteran performers had no clearly defined way of cashing in on their economic potential. They clung to their prerogatives, refusing to return to the lesser status of an employee in someone else's dance orchestra. The only format open to them was the small combo. With varying degrees of enthusiasm, they put their hopes of celebrity aside and occupied a more modest niche in the music industry, performing irregularly in small nightclubs such as those lining New York's 52nd Street.

"I'm Tired of a Big Band"

How did Hawkins himself adjust to this change of status? To more fully understand the road he took, and to see how his example may have influenced or inspired a younger generation of musicians, it is necessary to shift from impersonal economic forces to the man himself—his temperament, his attitudes.

Hawkins projected an enigmatic presence. He was a difficult man to get to know, even for his friends and colleagues. As trumpeter Rex Stewart, who knew Hawkins well from Fletcher Henderson days, observed: "Hawkins differs from the usual public conception of a musician. He is not the prototype of the affable extrovert. Coleman presents a dignified facade that often borders on the cool side, something that can be unnerving to people who do not know him." "He was a person people were afraid to talk to," according to Roy Eldridge. Friends described him as shy, private. "To get him to talk was an effort," remembered tenor saxophonist Eddie Johnson, who played with Hawkins in 1941. Undoubtedly, there was an element of conscious strategy in his detachment. Hawkins found it more convenient and congenial to remain on the sidelines, leaving it to others to guess what *he* was thinking. "You could sit with him for hours, and he wouldn't say nothing," Thelma Carpenter recalled. "He would just be observing." "Hawkins was a very taciturn man," reflected Sonny Rollins, who had ample opportunity to observe Hawkins as a young musician in Harlem, "but that was sort of a mask." To again quote Rex Stewart: "In him we have a person who, despite his facade, actually enjoys life but paradoxically goes to great lengths to conceal his enjoyment and even his admiration for the work of others."

In itself, a reserved, detached, and ironic personality posed no handicap for leading a band. The same description, after all, fits Count Basie, with whom Hawkins had a special affinity. Remembering the two of them sitting together, Thelma Carpenter remarked: "They were good friends. They always had a thing. It was always, like, 'Mm-hmmmmmm' and 'Oh, yeahhhhhh.' And they could spend *hours* like that. 'Mmmm-hmmmm.' 'Oh, yes.' And you light your cigarette and sit there, and there's this long silence."

Hawkins was not completely uninterested in the human comedy. As with Basie, his impassivity often concealed a sly wit and a mischievous streak. He was particularly adept at needling his cronies through indirection—the time-honored African-American art of "signifying." Stewart tells a story from the 1920s of how Hawkins used to rattle trombonist Charlie Green, a fellow soloist with Fletcher Henderson. Green was a jealous husband, and Hawkins would drive him to distraction by saying to another band member, just loud enough for Green to hear, "Well, I guess I'd better call my old lady. It's not that I don't trust her, but I want her to know that I'm thinking about her." Hawkins pulled the same trick with trumpeter Henry "Red" Allen when he joined the band in 1933, explaining to him later that it was a kind of rite of initiation.[11] In later years, when Hawkins was traveling by air with Jazz at the Philharmonic, Stanley Dance reports that he enjoyed disconcerting band members who were afraid of flying by parading up and down the aisle of the plane, head buried in a tabloid announcing a fatal air crash.

But in the long run, Hawkins had no taste for being one of the boys. He was, by temperament, a loner. Friends remember a particularly close relationship with trombonist Jimmy Harrison during a time when he was but one ambitious, hard-drinking soloist among many. After 1934, however, he left the communal atmosphere of the big band for the more rarefied role of concert virtuoso. On his return from Europe, he often struck his colleagues as distant and faintly exotic. To Howard McGhee, Hawkins was "a very strange man, in the sense that him being in Europe made him stand out from the rest of the fellows. . . . It meant he acted differently and he lived different." While Basie rode with the band on the bus, kept an eye on the endless games of poker and craps, and generally stayed as near the band's collective nerve center as possible, Hawkins drove off in his Cadillac, priding himself on being the last to leave and arriving just in time to make the gig. In the waning days of his big band, he shared his car with trombonist Sandy Williams, whom he knew from the Henderson days. Irritated band mates greeted their arrival on the gig with, "There come the two bosses."

Over his long career, Basie proved to be a master at establishing authority through an understated presence that masked an iron determination. "He was the first leader I ran into who used jokes as hints, along with nicety, to whip you back into line," said Dicky Wells. "His motto was: 'I'm not going to fire you—you're going to fire yourself.' " The ostensibly laid-back, laissez-faire atmosphere of his band was a shrewd strategy by which Basie took advantage of the fire and spirit of musicians who genuinely liked each other and had honed a collective sensibility night after night in jam sessions. Basie ran the show, but sensibly stayed out of the way in other spheres to allow the magic to take place. He depended on "head arrangements"—loosely conceived collections of riff backgrounds and solos that could be extended on the spur of the moment, building in intensity and overwhelming bands that looked to elegance and precision for their effects. As Teddy Wilson ruefully remembered: "I

---

11. Stewart himself was the victim of signifying on the occasion that the Henderson band came to Pittsburgh and encountered the young, still-unknown Roy Eldridge. Hawkins and the rest convinced Eldridge "to play against Rex Stewart, to get Rex mad, because I was only a kid. They didn't call it carving in those days, they called it 'signifying' " (in Chilton 1990, 157).

was concentrating on written arrangements, and we were trying to make written notes swing. . . . And [we] were lax on the good head arrangements which you need for crowd pleasing—when you play a battle of music, it's the head arrangements that you could play for about ten minutes and get the dancers going, like Basie's 'One O'Clock Jump.' . . . That was the end of the dance!"

In contrast to Basie, Hawkins projected only himself. Judging by the few surviving live broadcasts from the Savoy, he was featured prominently on nearly every arrangement. One review from late 1940 noted, "the 'Hawk' seemed to bear the brunt of putting the band over. . . . Hawkins solos at every opportunity." Onstage, Hawkins undoubtedly cut an impressive figure. He carefully cultivated a public image of dignity and elegance—his handsomely tailored suits, his saxophone with five gold platings to make it sparkle and shine.[12] "He had such great confidence in himself," Bill Dillard remembered. "The moment he came on stage everyone was aware of this. He had his own style of walking on stage. You knew and the audience knew before he'd blown a single note that he was a master."

But this confidence may not have been enough to satisfy audiences that looked to swing bands to provide a more flamboyant kind of entertainment. Hawkins's main experience of bandleaders had been the diffident, unassuming Fletcher Henderson. In the meantime, the music business had been taken over by bandleaders who offered the public something more. In 1937 *Variety* noted that in the new competitive atmosphere, "aggressive, progressive, showman-minded maestros have climbed with the help of ideas, stunts, taglines, etc., to sell themselves and their crews with more than 'just music.' " Hawkins's attitude, however, suggested not the eager-to-please show business entertainer, but the noblesse oblige of the concert artist. While his music spoke unmistakably in the accents of African-American culture, he showed no interest in playing the traditional role of black entertainer. Onstage, he forgot himself in the world of his playing. Thelma Carpenter, who as vocalist sat near the front of the stage, would grow alarmed as she watched Hawkins, eyes closed and deep into a ballad, wander perilously close to the edge. "I'd have to say:

12. Hawkins, on the appearance of his saxophone: "I'll make a frank confession to you—when I buy a sax I'm always very impressed by the looks. That's a fact. I like it to strike the eye as smart and shining—that's why I play a highly-burnished, gold-plated model with a lot of engraving. My present instrument had five platings to make it sparkle like it does" (Coleman Hawkins, "Playing Tenor," *Melody Maker* 10 [14 April 1934]: 11).

Coleman Hawkins, with characteristic
impeccable dress and enigmatic smile.
(Courtesy of the Institute of
Jazz Studies.)

Opposite, top: Tenor saxophonist Lester Young strikes a characteristic pose on an engagement with Clyde Hart (piano) and Danny Barker (guitar) at Kelly's Stable, c. 1940. (Courtesy of the Institute of Jazz Studies.)

Opposite: Vocalist Thelma Carpenter in a publicity shot from the 1950s. (Courtesy of Thelma Carpenter.)

Above: Cab Calloway: athleticism and style. (Courtesy of the Institute of Jazz Studies.)

Opposite, top: The irrepressible Lionel Hampton, shown here playing one of several instruments to which he applied his talents. (Courtesy of the Institute of Jazz Studies.)

Opposite: The Cab Calloway band of 1941, with a young Dizzy Gillespie (*top row, far left*). (Courtesy of the Institute of Jazz Studies.)

Above: Charlie Parker relaxing on stage. (Courtesy of the Institute of Jazz Studies.)

Above: A gathering of bebop pioneers under the awning of Minton's Playhouse (*left to right*): Thelonious Monk, Howard McGhee, Roy Eldridge, and the club's manager, Teddy Hill. (Photo © William Gottlieb. From the collection of the Library of Congress, Ira and Leonore S. Gershwin Fund.)

Trumpeter Howard McGhee, sporting the shades that became his generation's trademark. (Courtesy of the Institute of Jazz Studies.)

Guitarist
Charlie Christian
concentrates
intently on his
music. (Courtesy
of the Institute
of Jazz Studies.)

The bassist
Leonard Gaskin
in 1945.
(Courtesy of
Leonard Gaskin.)

Above: Bandleader Charlie Barnet (*right*) towers above the four young African-American musicians in his employ in the early 1940s (*left to right*): Howard McGhee, James "Trummy" Young, Oscar Pettiford, and Peanuts Holland. (Courtesy of the Institute of Jazz Studies.)

On the road with the Charlie Barnet Orchestra: Trummy Young (*left*) and Howard McGhee. (Courtesy of the Institute of Jazz Studies.)

[in an undertone] 'You're at the edge of the stage. Get back a little bit.' Because he'd just get so *wrapped up.*"

In a business that expected its bandleaders, especially black ones, to act as entertainers or at least congenial masters of ceremony, Hawkins's lack of involvement was a distinct liability. The unexpected success of "Body and Soul" may have deceived him into thinking that an unvarnished presentation of his music would be enough. But small-group recordings that Hawkins periodically made in 1940, although equally representative of his improvisational skills, were greeted coldly by the commercial trade press: "limited market stuff"; "for swing collectors . . . not a true interpretation of recognized tunes"; "good, but not for average pop consumption." A review of Hawkins at the Howard Theater in Washington in January 1940 flatly declared his band a "dud," with most of the blame placed explicitly on Hawkins: "Many of his admirers were disappointed, except for his 'Body and Soul.' His attitude was listless, taking much of the edge off the appetite of his admirers." "To hep cats used to the guttier styles of Georgie Auld, Henry Bridges, and other hot experts of today, Hawkins's improvisations may seem uninspired," wrote another reviewer. The intimate mood of the jam session, so vivid on the recording of "Body and Soul," was difficult to translate to the stage of theaters, and the intricacies of his style could be lost in the vast ballrooms of the Swing Era. "He was giving them a show," according to Thelma Carpenter, "but they didn't know what a show it was!"

A swing band was, of necessity, a group effort. Hawkins seemed never to understand or accept the responsibility of a bandleader to set an example. In the Henderson band he had played the role of the star soloist, regularly exercising his prerogative to make a grand entrance by showing up late to rehearsals and recording sessions. Yet as he made the transition from employee to employer, he retained the same destructive habits. "His biggest problem was getting to work on time," remembered guitarist Lawrence Lucie. "When he had his own big band he was always late for the rehearsals—and he'd called them. Everyone would be waiting and Hawk would come in and say, 'Sorry, I've been jamming all night and I just couldn't get up in time.' " Musicians remember him as something less than a disciplinarian. "The most he'd do on the bandstand was to glance back at a musician or at a section if something did go wrong, just to let you know he knew," according to Bill Dillard. In a pattern that was to become more regular in later years, he frequently left performances early, letting Kermit Scott take over his solo spots. One reviewer complained of paying "the better part of a dollar" to hear Hawkins on a one-nighter, only to have him play for only ninety minutes: "He disappeared entirely for almost two hours, letting his badly rehearsed band take over."

Hawkins's lack of concern for the day-by-day responsibilities of running a swing band were most glaringly evident in the business sphere. Pianist Gene Rodgers described him as "always up in the clouds. Sometimes pay-nights you couldn't find Coleman. He'd gone off somewhere. He wouldn't even say goodnight to anybody. He's in a cab surrounded by floosies." Rodgers finally convinced Hawkins to give him power of attorney so that someone was legally authorized to collect the money at the end of the job and pay the musicians. Hawkins was notoriously tight with money; while insisting on the best in everything for himself—clothes, cars, food—he was a man who, in Rex Stewart's memorable phrase, "wouldn't give a quarter to see the Statue of Liberty do the twist on the Brooklyn Bridge at high noon." The payroll for fifteen-odd musicians was a drain on his resources that he must have found painful. According to Thelma Carpenter:

> He didn't care about the band. I don't think the band concerned him. As a matter of fact, I think he hated the responsibility. I know one thing, that he hated to pay. *Very* tight with his money. 'Cause I'd have to say, "Where's my salary?" "Oh, I thought I paid you." You know, like the joke now is, "The check is in the mail"? Well, that's the way it was. Because he was still thinking of getting that money all for himself. He wanted the best musicians, but he didn't want to have to be bothered with all that.

In short, Hawkins's heart wasn't really in it. He liked the music, enjoyed the fame and prestige associated with show business, but was unwilling to make the adjustments in his personal behavior or compromises in his music necessary to make his band a real success. The experience must have been frustrating, and perhaps infuriating, but characteristically, he didn't let it show. "He was a very sensitive, a very proud man," observes Thelma Carpenter. "He'd get mad. He'd get *real* mad. But he would suppress it. Because he had so much gentleman in him." When success did not accrue to him automatically as a reward for his achievements as the greatest living virtuoso of the tenor saxophone, he withdrew to the pleasures available to him, the jazz musician's "kicks": women, liquor, and the endless round of jam sessions. When the band came to an end, he still had his pride.

Rex Stewart offers an amusing anecdote about Hawkins that has little to do with music, but reveals a good deal about the man's character. The Henderson band had been challenged to a baseball game, and after the game had already been under way for several innings,

> a weird sight ambled across Boston Common. I looked blinking my eyes from left field, at the spectacle of a fellow wearing a panama hat, tuxedo, and patent-leather shoes, Coleman Hawkins' uniform for participating in the national pastime. The ensemble was set off by an even funnier note— the tender way he carried a new first baseman's mitt.
>
> When he announced that we were in the presence of the world's greatest shortstop, Jimmy [Harrison] laughed until tears came to his eyes and said, "Hawk, that's a first baseman's mitt you've got there." This made Coleman quite indignant, and he replied, "Any damn fool knows that, Stringbeans, but I've got to protect these valuable fingers or *you* won't eat." So, to keep peace, Fletcher put Bean [Hawkins] in at shortstop. Batter up. And the first ball was hit right to Hawk. He fielded the ball, threw the man out, stuck his mitt into his hip pocket, and walked off the field. That was the end of Coleman's baseball career, as far as I know.

Hawkins showed as little tolerance for the conventional rules of behavior in the dance band business as he did for baseball. His appearance with his big band at the Fiesta Danceteria in the spring of 1940 is a good example. The venue was far from ideal (Thelma Carpenter remembers it bluntly as a "shitty place"), but arguably, it was a make-or-break job for the Hawkins band. An extended stay there would have brought in badly needed income and added to the band's thin résumé. Instead, as we have seen, Hawkins pulled his band out of the club rather than compromise what he saw as his artistic sensibilities and his sense of dignity.

Hawkins's replacement was Jimmie Lunceford. The Lunceford band had a long and prosperous engagement at the Danceteria, and (judging from critic George T. Simon's description of the band's performance as "swing brilliance personified") faced few restrictions on repertory. It is possible that the ballroom, on the heels of the Hawkins fiasco, gave the next band greater leeway, or that Lunceford, with his bigger name, was treated with more circumspection. But it is equally likely that Lunceford, a consummate professional with a sharp business sense, dealt with the situation more diplomatically, conceding the validity of the complaints while insisting that everyone would benefit from having the band play its usual repertoire.

After 1940 Hawkins never worked again with a large dance orchestra. In a feature article in *Down Beat* in January 1942, shortly after his relocation to Chicago, Hawkins explained why, at age thirty-seven, he was willing to settle for less:

> I'm tired of a big band, of one-nighters and long hops, and I want to settle down in one place with my own small combo and relax. I believe I can play better that way. I know it's all right for youngsters to travel with bands on the road every night of the year. They can take the grind and besides, they're getting better experience. But me, I'm happier blowing my horn in one spot all the time!
>
> I think the majority of rising colored bandleaders would be smart to concentrate on smaller outfits. The number of places where big Negro bands can go on location is becoming limited but there are any number of spots open to jumpy small bands—such as the Cafe Society and Famous Door in New York, for instance. And few colored bands of today are getting rich, anyway.

Hawkins's decision to cast his lot with small combos was partly personal, but it also came from a realistic appraisal of the band business and his likely place in it. For in the years ahead, more opportunities did open up for "jumpy small bands." After a brief but difficult period of transition, Hawkins returned to New York, only to stumble onto a leadership role of a different kind, as the most prestigious freelance jazz soloist around. There his paths crossed with younger musicians, many of whom were coming to essentially the same conclusion: that a "rising colored bandleader" would do well to look toward the burgeoning small club/jam session scene in New York City.

PART TWO

PROFESSIONALS
AFTER HOURS:
YOUNG BLACK
MUSICIANS
IN THE 1940s

4 · SPITBALLS AND TRICKY RIFFS

*With bop, you had to know—not feel; you had
to know what you were doing.*
HOWARD MCGHEE

*The older musicians did what they had to do. But
in the age that we came up in we didn't have to
do those things, you know? We just figured, we
felt like we were liberated people, and we* acted
like liberated people. DIZZY GILLESPIE

When Leonard Feather assembled a group portrait of the bebop movement for his 1949 book *Inside Be-bop*, the bop revolution had reached
its crest. The place of honor was given to the two "living legends" of
bebop, Dizzy Gillespie and Charlie Parker. Crowding the picture were
their musical progeny—the even more youthful wave of musicians
drawn to the movement by the 1945 recordings. Parker and Gillespie,
still at the beginning of potentially long careers (Parker was not yet
thirty), had already attained the status of founding fathers. Their revolutionary exploits earlier in the decade were painstakingly documented
and celebrated in Feather's prose, supplying the raw material for an official history of the insurgency, now successful and settling in for a long
stay.

As events receded further into the past, the utility of revolutionary
fervor vanished. Even the word *bebop* became an embarrassment, linked
as it was to social eccentricity and drug abuse and the planned obsolescence of fashion. Within a few years, Feather's publisher convinced him
to change the title of the book to *Inside Jazz*. The change, in retrospect,
is significant. Bebop has become yet another style of jazz, yoked in an
ironic embrace to the traditions it fought so hard to displace. In the process, the early history of bebop is reduced to a period piece, nostalgia for

those unwilling to relinquish their glimpse of a time when the "world was swinging with change."

It is a challenge, therefore, to return to the beginning of the 1940s, to the earliest point at which it is possible to imagine a bebop movement, and try to understand just what sent the bop pioneers on their unorthodox path. A group portrait taken sometime in 1942, although featuring many of the same faces, would look quite different from the successful, cocksure revolutionaries several years later. It would be a snapshot, not a formal portrait, since the various parties would not necessarily know one another, and certainly would not understand why they were being assembled. They would be a raffish, heterogeneous bunch, some mugging for the camera, others standing indifferently with their backs turned. Most would have a professional identity with one or another of the large dance bands, although some, like the reclusive Thelonious Monk, would not. Dizzy Gillespie and Charlie Parker would already be recognizable as figures to be reckoned with, although it would be hard to foresee how their divergent temperaments and musical proclivities could be bridged. Others now familiar to jazz fans would be ranged alongside them (Kenny Clarke) or just edging into the picture frame (Max Roach, Bud Powell). But the group would include many now largely lost to obscurity: Howard McGhee, Joe Guy, Leonard Gaskin, Allen Tinney, Vic Coulsen, Benny Harris, Kermit Scott.

It is misleading to speak of the "typical" bebop pioneer: the sample is too small, the spiky sense of individuality too prominent. Nevertheless, some sense of the forces drawing this disparate group together may be gleaned by examining their salient collective characteristics.

First, the bebop revolution was distinctly African-American—a movement with a firm base in the musicians' community of Harlem. There were, to be sure, a few white faces in the crowd from the start: Johnny Carisi sat in frequently at Minton's, while as early as 1944 bop bands on 52nd Street used pianists Al Haig and George Wallington and drummer Stan Levey. Racial mixing was no casual public gesture in the early 1940s, even in relatively tolerant New York City. The willingness of blacks like Gillespie to accept and even encourage white musicians in their midst proves that there was no conscious policy of racial exclusion behind bebop. If anything, these transgressions were a deliberate and provocative attempt to extend the relaxed social spirit of the musicians' community, within which personal relations between blacks and whites were more collegial than in perhaps any other professional sphere of the time, into the broader public sphere of commerce.

But if bebop cannot be easily tied to a conscious expression of a separatist sentiment, it was nevertheless rooted deeply in the uncomfortable realities of race in America. For jazz musicians, the situation was particularly poignant, for music was manifestly capable of transcending racial barriers. Yet there is no escaping the fact that black musicians lived and worked in a separate and unequal world, facing obstacles and enduring indignities that set them apart from their white counterparts. Even as they enjoyed a degree of social freedom and prosperity known to few others of their race, they were acutely aware of their precarious status as second-class citizens. Bebop was shaped and to an extent stimulated by these social facts. Without the omnipresent pressure of racial hostility, musicians of such divergent talents and temperaments might not have found themselves forced into the same narrow space, and they would not have had the same incentives to forge a new path.

Second, the bop pioneers were young—in their teens or early twenties in 1942. Their ranks were occasionally peppered with older musicians, who either sponsored their activities (Earl Hines, Coleman Hawkins, both nearing forty) or recorded with them (Sid Catlett, Clyde Hart, Cozy Cole, Budd Johnson, Don Byas, all in their early thirties). But on the whole, the bebop generation falls within a strikingly narrow age range. With the exception of Kenny Clarke (born in 1914), nearly all were born between 1917 and 1924, and entered professional life sometime between 1935 and 1942.[1]

The formative years of the bop pioneers' careers were therefore bounded by two crucial historical events: the boom and bust cycle of the Swing Era and the outbreak of the Second World War. The Swing Era defined the "art world" within which they would live and work. As we have seen, the startling expansion of the music industry shattered the older, more static role of the dance musician, holding out the tantalizing prospect of unprecedented reward (even as it systematically constrained the possibility for individual action). Those coming of age after 1935 naturally had higher expectations than their predecessors, for they could

---

1. A partial list of bebop pioneers, by birth date, would include Kenny Clarke (1914); Dizzy Gillespie, Thelonious Monk, Tadd Dameron (1917); Howard McGhee, Tommy Potter, Charlie Christian (1918); Art Blakey (1919); Charlie Parker, Gil Fuller, Leonard Gaskin, Joe Guy, Curley Russell (1920); Allen Tinney, Billy Taylor (1921); Oscar Pettiford, Duke Jordan, Cecil Payne (1922); George Wallington, Dexter Gordon (1923); Max Roach, Bud Powell, J. J. Johnson, Benny Harris, Al Haig, Sarah Vaughan (1924); Stan Levey (1925). Older musicians often associated with bop, either by performing and recording with bop groups or as leaders of bands that employed bop musicians, include Earl Hines (1903); Hawkins (1904); Sid Catlett, Budd Johnson, Clyde Hart (1910); Don Byas, Trummy Young (1912); and Billy Eckstine (1914).

see firsthand the vast profits being made. They were predictably frustrated when the economic contraction after 1939 forced them into unequal competition with both their white counterparts and older, better-connected black musicians for a share of the shrinking pie. The onset of war partially salvaged the situation, by stimulating the economy with new defense spending and creating a nearly hysterical demand for entertainment on the home front. But the fabric of American life was warped by war into unpredictable new patterns. The resultant chaos undermined the status quo, making it easier for the imaginative and ambitious to challenge it.

Finally, the majority of bop pioneers were committed to careers as commercial dance musicians. They fit Howard Becker's category of "integrated professionals"—participants in an art world whose contributions mesh smoothly and efficiently with those of other professionals (whether performers, creators, logistical support, or middlemen) to create artistic products.

This point requires reiterating because the beboppers have so often been caricatured as disgruntled and marginalized rebels, alienated by the "tasteless commercialism" of swing and bent from the outset on creating an avant-garde movement that would "drag [jazz] outside the mainstream of American culture." Disgruntled and alienated they may have become, even colorfully so (the bohemianism that has figured so prominently in popular accounts is not entirely an exaggeration). But the early history of bebop suggests that they originally saw themselves—if only for the want of a realistic alternative—as dedicated and even enthusiastic participants in a system that offered, at least in theory, a reasonable reward for artistic excellence. Their reaction to the Swing Era, to both its music and its business arrangements, was not revulsion that art and commerce had promiscuously been allowed to mix, but frustration that things could no longer be made to work to their advantage.

To construe the bop revolution as "anticommercial" is naive. Bebop proposed a revised relationship between artist and audience that tried to avoid the most debilitating or distasteful consequences of the cash nexus; but significantly, "the political economy of jazz in the 1940s . . . was not appreciably different from that of earlier decades. . . . Bebop was produced, distributed, and consumed within the same network of capitalist social relations as '30s swing and '20s early jazz." The boppers had no particular quarrel with their profession per se, but by virtue of the restless energy of youth they had few inhibitions against reshaping it as circumstance seemed to dictate. In this, they resembled Thomas Kuhn's revolutionaries: "Almost always the men who achieve these fundamental inventions of a new paradigm have been either very young or very new to the field whose paradigm they change. And perhaps that point need not have been made explicit, for obviously these are the men who, being little committed by prior practice to the traditional rules . . . are particularly likely to see that those rules no longer define a playable game and to conceive another set that can replace them."

The particular form that bebop took, in short, resulted from the explosive combination of broad economic opportunity with the realities of racial inequality. The music industry gathered young musicians of extraordinary skill together from across the country and concentrated them in New York City. Racial inequality ensured that their efforts would be underrewarded and their talents would go underutilized. The peculiar dynamics of the jam session suggested a new shape and purpose for their intellectual and artistic aspirations. Without these circumstances, it is unlikely that there would have been a bebop movement.

A Spectrum of Possibilities

The careers of the bebop pioneers tended to follow a predictable pattern, beginning with a period of apprenticeship. From their diverse points of geographic origin, they rose rapidly through the ranks of various local or territory bands, making their mark as soloists, arrangers, or reliable sidemen. By 1942 most had reached the level of the national or name dance bands, spending much of their time on the road but returning often enough to New York to establish a reputation in the musicians' community there. In various after-hours clubs and jam session spots, they fell into the company of others who shared their interests and attitudes. Their training was likely to have been haphazard, mostly a matter of self-education. In their fascination with technical virtuosity and harmonic complexity, fueled by an engaging combination of restless curiosity and guileless ambition, they were self-consciously progressive.

To this point, the broad outlines of their experiences differed little from those of hundreds of other black musicians over the previous decade. It is the subsequent phase that sets the bebop generation apart: a period of disillusionment, coinciding with the beginning of the war, in which they gradually began to disengage themselves from the art world of the Swing Era. Exactly when a given musician began imagining an alternative to the usual career path is impossible to say. The process was a subtle one, perhaps perceivable only in hindsight. Some factors—thwarted ambition, a weary disgust with working conditions—conspired to dislodge musicians, at least temporarily, from their usual career paths. Others pulled them toward the after-hours jam session, a shadow world closely associated with the professional world of the dance musician and yet set apart from it. These factors and their effect on the bop generation from 1942 to 1945 will be described and analyzed in more detail in subsequent chapters: the jam session in chapter 5, the disruptions of the war years in chapter 6.

For now, the focus is on explicating the pattern that brought the bebop pioneers to 1942. Within the general pattern, of course, there was ample room for individuality. The two most important musicians of bebop—Charlie Parker and Dizzy Gillespie—show with particular clarity how sharply divergent temperaments and personal goals within the bebop movement could be.

In their public personalities as well as in their personal lives, Parker and Gillespie were a study in contrast. As his nickname indicates, John Birks "Dizzy" Gillespie cultivated a mischievous persona. "I was all-ways bad, you know," he once told an interviewer. Onstage, he was constantly in motion, animated by a barbed humor that drew most of its edge by signifying on the traditional role of the black entertainer—keeping the squares amused at their own expense. Offstage, he was a shrewd and sober businessman who was as responsible as anyone for the direction the bebop movement ultimately took. He was, according to Miles Davis, the "head and hands" of bebop, "the one who kept it all together." Gillespie's progress from brash outsider to establishment figure (chosen by the State Department to represent America on overseas tours at the height of the cold war) is the progress of bebop itself, from fringe movement with bohemian overtones to as near the center of American culture as jazz is likely to get.[2]

2. Which, apparently, is not very far. Gillespie's sensitivity to being on the outside as a black jazz musician was amply demonstrated during a televised musical evening at the Reagan White House on 4 December 1982. The hapless Itzhak Perlman, acting as master of ceremonies, turned at one point to the white saxophonist Stan Getz to ask him about the origins of bebop (Gary Giddins, "Jazz and the Reagans: They Don't Call It the White House for Nothing," *Village Voice* 27 [21 December 1982]: 1, 105). Getz had the sense to duck the question, but Gillespie, already infuriated at his treatment by the White House staff ("they sent me down some fried chicken, a couple of pieces of watermelon"), vented his anger afterward to the press: "Perlman asked what bebop was. Getz didn't know what to say. Here was a guy asking him about the music when I was really one of its creators. Getz should have pointed to me and said, 'Ask him.' . . . I'm mad. And don't let me get

Charlie Parker's life, by contrast, was a painful mixture of steely determination and sordid excess. Even as he helped Gillespie steer bebop into the mainstream in the 1950s, his descent into a personal hell was a public spectacle—"like a man dismembering himself with a dull razor on a spotlighted stage," as Ralph Ellison has written. He became entangled with drug abuse as a teenager, and for all the brilliance of his musical achievements, never strayed far from the underworld of pushers and the shadow of drug-induced psychosis. His tragicomic and self-destructive behavior, amply documented and even celebrated in books such as Robert Reisner's *Bird: The Legend of Charlie Parker* and Ross Russell's *Bird Lives!*, have become part of jazz folklore—the dark underside of bebop. "Bird was great and a genius musician, man, but he was also one of the slimiest and greediest motherfuckers who ever lived in this world," remembers Miles Davis, who knew Parker well enough to judge. And yet Parker is also known for his fierce and uncompromising dedication to music. He stood unnervingly still while he played, all of his mental and physical energy concentrated on the task at hand. "No jazzman, not even Miles Davis, struggled harder to escape the entertainer's role than Charlie Parker," Ellison declares. Trumpeter Howard McGhee makes the following pointed comparison: "See, Dizzy was a comedian. He's funny, he likes to be funny and laugh and so forth. Bird wasn't like that, he was a serious man. And he figured, when you hit that bandstand, you supposed to be serious. You ain't supposed to be making people laugh and all that bullshit, like Dizzy would be doing. And he would get mad when he'd see Dizzy do that."

Parker and Gillespie were polar opposites in other ways as well. Parker came across as a "natural" musician, whose creations, rooted in the blues tradition, seemed effortless. He had the knack of making the most radical innovations seem instantly understandable, masking both the bristling complexity of the musical language and the disciplined intellect behind it. "He'd play a phrase," remembers Gillespie, "and people might never have heard it before. But he'd start it, and the people would finish it with him, humming. It would be so lyrical and simple that it just seemed the most natural thing to play." Parker's ability to absorb the musical world around him into his playing—as evidenced in his lifelong habit of peppering his solos with ingeniously apposite quotations from popular

---

mad. . . . Man, it was a travesty" (Leah Garchik, "A Breezy Afternoon with Dizzy," *San Francisco Chronicle*, 20 February 1983, Datebook, 37).

songs—astonished his colleagues. Pianist John Malachi recalls that musicians in the Billy Eckstine band used to gather in Parker's room to listen to the saxophonist play along fluidly with whatever was being broadcast on the radio. "The alto saxophone was just a metal pipe with keys to him. Whatever he heard, he played."

Gillespie, by contrast, was more visibly a striver. "Bird paid strict attention to what people did," according to Buddy Anderson, the trumpeter who first introduced Parker and Gillespie in 1940, "and if he found anything that they did that struck him, he brought that into his thing. . . . But Diz is damn near all Diz, and it's a little bit studied, but nobody could do it but Diz." By his own admission, Gillespie lacked bluesy intensity: "I'm not what you call a 'blues' player," he wrote in his autobiography. "I mean in the authentic sense of the blues. . . . My music is not that deep—not as deep as Hot Lips Page or Charlie Parker, because Yard [Parker] knew the blues." But he made up for that lack with conscious study, ultimately becoming as at home at the piano and the orchestral score as at his trumpet. Like Hawkins, he was fond of externalizing harmonic relationships at the keyboard. He was a born teacher, working tirelessly to impart his hard-won knowledge to other musicians: coaching drummers like Max Roach and Art Blakey in the fundamentals of bop drumming, pounding out chord voicings for novice bop pianists like George Wallington, singing the proper phrasing to horn sections in Billy Eckstine's band. According to Eckstine, "[Bird] was so spontaneous that things which ran out of his mind—which he didn't think were anything—were classics. But Dizzy would sit there, and whatever he played, he knew just what he was doing. It was a pattern, a thing that had been studied."

John Malachi has related an anecdote from the Billy Eckstine band that neatly sums up their different attitudes. Malachi had just learned the popular song "All God's Chillun Got Rhythm," a tune with a challenging chord progression that later became absorbed into the bebop repertory. As he ran through it on the piano, Gillespie walked in, heard the song and liked it, grabbed his horn, and asked Malachi to call out the chord changes as he played. After several choruses, Gillespie had memorized the chords and was playing fluently when Parker walked in. As Parker got out his horn, Malachi once again began calling out the chord changes. But Parker asked him not to: "Just play the tune." Musicians of any temperament could find their bearings somewhere between the tenaciously analytical approach Gillespie championed and the fluid command of oral tradition exemplified by Parker.

Thus, Charlie Parker and Dizzy Gillespie encapsulate the spectrum of possibilities for the bop generation. Gillespie represents one end—the diligent, hardworking, self-disciplined careerist who saw in bebop the opportunity to carve out a new path for professional advancement when the old paths became blocked. Parker symbolizes another extreme: brilliant talent combined with a diffidence toward conventional success that verged on self-destructiveness. These characterizations are simplifications, of course; in Parker's case especially, the romantic myth of artist as prophet or martyr is all too evident. But these extremes show with particular clarity the challenge the bebop generation faced. On the one hand, they risked perpetuating the black artist's limited role within the music industry if they replicated its existing structures too closely (as we shall see, one of Gillespie's first acts on attaining a measure of celebrity in 1945 was to form his own big band). On the other hand, if they "dropped out" to savor the social freedom of the jam session scene, they might all too easily enter a nightmare of narcotic excess, which still left the black musician exploited and unempowered.

Apprenticeship in the Provinces

In the earliest part of their careers, the commonalities between Parker and Gillespie were more striking than their differences. Like most musicians active in New York in the early 1940s, they were immigrants from the heartland: Parker from Kansas City, and Gillespie from Cheraw, South Carolina. Both started out as callow, largely self-taught amateurs, initially lacking the discipline and determination that would become their professional trademark. For each, the entry into professional life was marked by incidents that forced them into the progressive mold by bringing them face to face with their own inadequacies and making them keenly aware of what was required to pursue music in the public sphere.

At age thirteen, Gillespie had earned the reputation as the top trumpet player in Cheraw. But because his musical mentor, a third-grade music teacher, could play the piano only in one key, Gillespie's accomplishments were limited to the key of B-flat. His epiphany came when Sonny Matthews, the son of a local music teacher and a relatively experienced musician, returned to Cheraw for a visit. Matthews heard about the local hero and invited Gillespie to jam with him. When Matthews called for the tune "Nagasaki" in the key of C, Gillespie, not surprisingly, fumbled ineptly. "Oh, oh, I've got to learn it," Gillespie managed to blurt out, but his youthful confidence was shattered. "I felt so crushed, I cried," he remembered in his autobiography, "because I was supposed to be the town's best trumpet player. That incident taught me that there were other keys in music besides B-flat."

Embarrassment hardened a diffident adolescent into a disciplined artist. His failure to negotiate the key of C sent Gillespie into a self-imposed regimen of sight-reading and scales to ensure that he would "never . . . be embarrassed again by key changes." Within two years he had learned enough to sit in with the territory bands that passed through Cheraw. Although still short enough that he had to play standing on a box, Gillespie now easily passed over the threshold of competence, playing two choruses of "China Boy" in the key of F: "Sonny Matthews had shamed me once, but now, my ideas flowed beautifully." That night, he went to a neighbor's to listen to the remote broadcast from the Savoy Ballroom and dream of escaping Cheraw for New York.

He had never before seriously considered music as a profession, but having tasted some hard-won triumphs it now emerged as a realistic alternative to manual labor. After graduating from the ninth grade, Gillespie spent part of the summer of 1933 digging ditches on a WPA road gang alongside grown men who couldn't write their own names. "It really hurt me to see my brothers . . . walk up to the table to get their pay and have to make an X," Gillespie remembered. "That made a deep impression on me." When he was offered a full scholarship to the nearby Laurinburg Technical Institute to play in the school band, it came "like a blessing from the blue." Soon, "music was the only thing I was serious about."

A similar moment of truth came for Charlie Parker at about age sixteen, shortly after he had graduated from the baritone horn he played in school marching bands to the saxophone. With the brashness of youth, he set out to conquer the Kansas City music scene. "I knew how to play, I figured," he later recalled. "I had learned the scale and I'd learned how to play two tunes in a certain key—the key of 'D' on the saxophone [i.e., concert 'F']. And I had learned how to play the first eight bars of 'Lazy River' and I knew the complete tune of 'Honeysuckle Rose.' I had never stopped to think about different keys or nothing like that." One night, he dropped in at the High Hat Club to sit in with a practice session, where the musicians (only a few years older than Parker) tested the newcomer with a difficult tune. "The first thing they started playing was 'Body and Soul,' so I got to playing my 'Honeysuckle Rose' and it was an awful conglomeration. They laughed me off the bandstand. They laughed so hard it killed me." During this time, Parker worked irregularly with a local nonunion band, Lawrence Keyes's Deans of Swing, but failed to make headway in the rigid Kansas City musical hierarchy. A series of similarly painful experiences only confirmed Parker's status among Kansas City jazz musicians as an annoying interloper, a "nothing saxophone player" who had to be chased out of clubs and told to go home. "Bird couldn't play much in those days," recollected bassist Gene Ramey, "and was mad about it, too. In that respect he was just an evil, spoiled kid."

Lacking a Laurinburg Institute to shore up his professional credentials, Parker turned instead to more experienced musicians, like alto saxophonist Buster Smith and guitarist Efferge Ware, to guide him through the intricacies of music theory. He then applied himself with characteristic vigor to the task of mastering scales and keys, practicing so hard (by his own account, over twelve hours a day) that the neighbors complained. Gradually, he laid claim to professional status, astonishing the skeptics with his newfound virtuosity. Gene Ramey heard Parker again in 1937, after Parker's return from an extended summer gig in the Ozarks: "Bird . . . startled everybody." Greeted by cries of "Yeah, here comes this guy, he's a drag," Parker not only played "Lady Be Good" fluently, but expertly mimicked the intricate Lester Young solo recorded only the year before. "Played it note for note," according to Ramey. "And from then on, Bird was gone."

"That Dizzy Little Cat"

Both Parker and Gillespie aimed unerringly at New York as the fulfillment of their professional dreams. By 1942 each had already made the difficult leap from local music-making to national status by becoming members of a top-rank dance orchestra. But their trajectories were quite different, each revealing different facets of the bebop experience.

Dizzy Gillespie's path to New York ran through Philadelphia, where his family had moved in 1935. Within three days of his arrival, he had landed a job paying eight dollars a week and celebrated by "getting sharp"—buying three suits on credit. "Pinstripes, pegged pants, drapes, beautiful stuff, made me feel like a million wearing it. Finally, I got some clothes of my own." The next step on the ladder was a position in a local big band, led by Frankie Fairfax, where in addition to invaluable professional experience he acquired his nickname, Dizzy—as in "that little dizzy cat's from down South."

In 1937, emboldened by the success of some of his band mates, he decided to make his move. He heard that there was a spot in the trumpet section of Lucky Millinder's band and "cut out like a real musician" for New York. The job fell through, but he stayed anyway. "Trying to survive in New York without any job was risky, but it was the only way to make the big time in jazz." He set about making a name for himself in the big city with characteristic hustle and determination, making himself visible (and audible) in jam session spots night after night, and frequenting the Savoy Ballroom so often that its manager, Charlie Buchanan, began letting him in free. It was at the Savoy that bandleader Teddy Hill gave Gillespie his first big break, inviting him to join the band as a substitute for a recording session (his first) and a tour of Europe.

Gillespie was, at the time, only nineteen. His band mates were not that much older—most were in their late twenties—but in a profession dominated by youth, they counted as seasoned veterans. Having put at least a decade of professional experience behind them, including the lean years of the Depression, they were protective of their status as members of a leading dance orchestra and understandably skeptical that a teenager was qualified to join their ranks. Word that Teddy Hill was about to hire Gillespie for the prestigious European tour set off protests. Key members of the band threatened to quit unless a more experienced trumpet player were hired. The threat was never carried out, but the lingering animosity clouded Gillespie's enjoyment of his achievement. "Being able to read and play well wasn't enough to keep some of the older, gloomier guys in the band off of my ass," he later commented. "I couldn't hardly sit down before they started on me."

What Gillespie went through in his first days with Teddy Hill was probably no different from what any number of musicians experienced when joining a new band. Bands were tight-knit social units, and newcomers were frequently made to feel unwelcome, at least initially. But in Gillespie's mind, the hostility signified something more serious: a determination on the part of the older generation to hold on to their status in the face of youthful competition. More than forty years later, the bitterness he felt toward the "older" twenty-six- and twenty-seven-year-olds in the band was still vivid:

> Shad Collins, Dicky Wells, and some other guys had worked with other big bands, like Fletcher Henderson, and none of them believed in giving young guys a break. They had an *old* clique. In New York when the big bands of Chick Webb, Fletcher Henderson, and Teddy Hill were in their heyday, a young musician couldn't get in those bands. That was a drag because it kept a whole lot of guys out. If you were lucky enough to get into a band, some guys felt it was their duty to make it hard for you.
>
> Shad Collins was very nasty. During my solos, he and Dicky Wells tried

to act like I was playing absolutely nothing and looked around at me sneering. . . . The older musicians are the guardians of the music, but that's not an excuse to keep people down and try to destroy their talent. Those guys were just keeping our music motionless, trying to stop it from moving forward so somebody old could sit there and hold a horn.

Revealingly, he gloated over his eventual triumph: "Today, I'm a world-renowned trumpet player and Dicky Wells is a bank guard. . . . Shad Collins is a cabdriver. When I get to be his age, I'll still be where I am now."

The first several years in New York tested Gillespie's resolve. On his return from Europe, he found himself out of work. He was still not a member of the powerful New York Local 802 and had to endure a three-month waiting period designed to protect New Yorkers from outside competition. Even when he was allowed to rejoin Hill's band, work was sporadic and Gillespie, who refused to compromise his professional status by taking a day job, struggled to make ends meet. His future wife, Lorraine, then a dancer at the Apollo Theatre, remembered him as a hungry musician too poor to buy a bowl of soup. Girlfriends advised her, "Get yourself somebody like Rex Stewart, a real boyfriend, that's working."

Eventually, word of Gillespie's varied talents got around, and he began to get more work. For one thing, he was an excellent sight-reader. He had failed to get a job with one band in Philadelphia some years earlier because of his alleged inadequacies at reading music (the fault actually lay with an idiosyncratic notation that only members of the band could decipher), and undoubtedly he took special pride in his skills in New York. His audition for the Edgar Hayes band was made with characteristic flair. Hayes had grown exasperated with his third trumpeter's inability to play a particularly difficult passage in an arrangement of "Bugle Call Rag." The drummer Kenny Clarke suggested Gillespie as a substitute. At rehearsal, Hayes tested Gillespie's mettle by calling immediately for the difficult arrangement. Gillespie read the part flawlessly on sight. A second run-through only confirmed that the first was not a fluke. Finally, Gillespie, sensing the opportunity to make a point, asked for a *third* run-through: "Fess, now take it down again for *me*. I think I got it now." Turning his back to the music stand, he played the part from memory. Needless to say, he got the job.

Gillespie was a valued employee because he combined several useful skills. He was a reliable section man, as his dramatic demonstration of sight-reading shows. He was a fiery improviser, who modeled himself directly on Roy Eldridge, one of the most influential soloists of the time. Perhaps most important—for those who could appreciate it—he was a musical "progressive," far better grounded in music theory than most horn players of the time and able to translate his hard-won understanding of harmony to his improvising. While a student at the Laurinburg Institute in South Carolina, he had taught himself enough piano to allow him to manipulate harmonic progressions: "I'd play chord changes, inverting them and substituting different notes trying to see how different sounds led naturally, sometimes surprisingly, into others. I'd take them and play them on my horn, and used to surprise people with new combinations." He continued these explorations during his first professional years in Philadelphia, paying particular attention to the chromatic side-stepping in Eldridge's solos, which he carefully parsed on the piano. His experience with harmony laid the groundwork for his eventual success as an arranger. But those attuned to such things were excited by the grasp of the more advanced developments in harmony evident in his soloing. "Edgar Hayes really respected my knowledge of music," Gillespie remembered. "He made an arrangement on 'Body and Soul' just for me. He wrote it himself and asked me what changes I wanted to play."

For these reasons, bandleaders were willing to tolerate Gillespie's notoriously "dizzy" behavior. His idiosyncrasies were less irresponsible breaches of professional behavior than a not-so-subtle tweaking of authority, transmuting his restless ambition into humor. Sometimes, when in the middle of attempting a difficult high-note solo he hit a wrong note, he would stop and laugh out loud. "Like a mischievous kid, he be doing devilish things on the job," recalled trombonist Clyde Bernhardt. "One time during a number he slid off his seat and sat on the floor, blowing and turning his horn all kinds of funny ways. Another time, he rose from his chair while playing, came down, and pushed Hayes halfway off the piano bench. With his right hand he chorded some extra harmony, then slowly walked back to his seat and sat down, not missing a note the whole time. 'That's the biggest fool I ever saw in my life,' Hayes said. But the audience loved it, thought it was part of the act, and had a good laugh." If pushed, however, Gillespie was quick to retaliate, even violently. When he left the Hayes band, he was still owed a few days' pay. After being put off by Hayes on a number of occasions, he pulled Hayes's glasses off his face while the pianist was performing at a nightclub, saying, "if you want your glasses, give me my money." Hayes followed him outside the building, and in the ensuing fight, Gillespie knocked the bandleader down with the glasses still clenched in his fist. "Man, my hand was bloody. . . . I could have really hurt myself and messed up my playing hand for life, but I just hate somebody taking advantage of me, so I donated that money to his coffin."

Gillespie's next move landed him near the top—as a member of Cab Calloway's band. The raucous singer, dancer, and entertainer had been among the biggest names in black show business since 1930, when he took over from Duke Ellington as the house band at Harlem's Cotton Club. Broadcasts from the Cotton Club established Calloway and his trademark scat-singing theme song, "Minnie the Moocher" (with the catchphrase "hi-de-ho"), across the nation. Throughout the worst years of the Depression, Calloway's band worked regularly, alternating Cotton Club shows with lucrative tours of theaters and dance halls. By mid-decade, Calloway began to adjust his strategy. The Cotton Club abandoned its Harlem location for midtown Manhattan in 1936 (only to close altogether four years later); the Swing Era brought with it a public less attuned to glamorous floor shows and more focused on jazz-oriented instrumental dance music. "I saw the handwriting on the wall," Calloway later wrote. "When the Cotton Club closed . . . we continued the road tours, but bands were beginning to play more jazz, which the people seemed to want to listen to. . . . I began to move in that direction. The only problem was that jazz is much more demanding than show and dance tunes. It requires a greater degree of musicianship. So I made changes in personnel."

From 1936 on, Calloway ensured that his bands featured top-flight jazz improvisers. By the time Gillespie joined in 1939, the band boasted the talents of Chu Berry, Cozy Cole, Hilton Jefferson, Keg Johnson, Danny Barker, and Milt Hinton, among others. As Gillespie remembered, "Cab could get anybody he wanted because he had the money to pay them." The standard salary for Calloway sidemen in the late 1930s was $100 per week—more than virtually any other black band, except perhaps Ellington's, could afford. Calloway himself was a singer of considerable gifts and a brilliant entertainer—bassist Gene Ramey described Calloway single-handedly winning a battle of the bands against Jay McShann with an athletic display of somersaults and chair-vaulting, all while singing. But Calloway was virtually untrained as a musician. Although he studied saxophone briefly in the 1920s, he was a singularly mediocre instrumentalist (Chu Berry reportedly joined the band on one condition: "As long as I'm with you, don't never play that damned sax of yours"). Calloway held his bands together not by musical authority, but by an iron will: he was, in his own words, an "unrelenting, stubborn black son of a bitch." "Discipline! That was the word—and with no deviations from it," according to Gillespie. "On the stand he was a tyrant," remembered Garvin Bushell. "He ran his orchestra with an iron hand, not giving much room for your decisions, your concept. We began calling him Simon Legree. At rehearsals he'd scream and holler at you into submissiveness—he thought by acting that way he could make up for his limited knowledge of music."

Being hired by Calloway in 1939 was simultaneously the fulfillment of Gillespie's ambition and the last straw that sent him searching for something new. On the one hand, playing with Calloway represented a major improvement in working conditions—an antidote to the sporadic employment and primitive transportation that plagued most black bands of the time. "It was the best job that you could possibly have, high class," Gillespie later asserted. "Cab's band always traveled in the best way, by private railroad car or chartered bus, and I remember how we would go on the road then for eight, nine, or twenty weeks, in those private cars, and know where we were going to be for the next three years. Boy!" The private railroad car shielded the musicians from the petty humiliation of Jim Crow. The band still followed a rigorous travel schedule, but Calloway's staff (including three valets) did its best to make the musicians comfortable (they even got a two-week paid vacation for Christmas). Working under such conditions gave band members a sense of belonging to an elite. "There's never been any band, black or white, that traveled any finer than Cab's band did," confirms Milt Hinton. "We were the tops and we knew it and we acted it. Arrogant as all get out. The guys dressed to kill—all the time. The first thing I did [on joining the band] was to take $600 and buy a whole closet full of suits. I had to."

Yet once again, Gillespie's enjoyment of his achievement was poisoned by a sense of frustrated ambition. Once again, older musicians stood in his way. The average age of the band members in 1941 (excluding Gillespie) was over thirty-three; some had been with Calloway since the Cotton Club days. Working with Calloway offered a degree of security, comfort, and prestige unusual for black musicians. (When fired by Calloway, Danny Barker reports, musicians would typically become hysterical, inconsolable, as though expelled from their families.) Younger musicians on the make found the atmosphere of self-satisfaction stifling. Milt Hinton describes his reactions on joining the band in 1936, three years before Gillespie: "I was out of Chicago, out of the rat race. I was fresh and trying to still be creative, and I came into this organization a kid, off the streets, you know. . . . And then I was amazed at the complacency." As Hinton explains:

> We were in this big social band that played the big time theaters. Except for Ben [Webster] and Cozy [Cole] and me—these guys wouldn't even go across the street to hear somebody else. . . . These guys had been making money for years. And they were thinking about chicks and dressing—they didn't go around to dig a guy playing. Ben was the only one who did that, and he took me with him. . . . These guys never went around to any club and sat in with anybody. They went in a club, dressed up, and got a table and ordered a steak and applauded the show. But they wouldn't sit in. And that's why they got stale.

Calloway's relevance to Gillespie would not be evident until much later. When Gillespie stepped into the public arena in his own right as a celebrity bandleader in the late 1940s, he borrowed liberally from Calloway's book: reliance on exuberant physical comedy, nonsense syllables, and more generally, the idea of entertainment as the expression of a hip, urban, and unmistakably black sensibility. Gillespie differed, however, in his insistence that such entertainment derive its legitimacy from the specialized accomplishments of professional instrumentalists. "Musical nothings," in his formulation, had no business standing in the way of their betters.

Accordingly, Gillespie was disdainful of Calloway, who "wasn't interested in developing any musicians. He always hired established musicians, who were already of high caliber." Gillespie considered his time with Calloway as part of his apprenticeship—one more step toward his full realization as a musician. He was, in Danny Barker's words, "young, vigorous, and restless," seizing every opportunity to further his musical explorations. He convinced Hinton to lug his bass up a narrow spiral staircase to the roof of the Cotton Club so that they could work out alternative harmonizations together during breaks in the show: "Dizzy would take me up there to blow with him, and he would show me the hip changes—substitution chords as we call 'em—and so I was very happy 'cause I'm learning now. I'm progressing. . . ." He "raved" to fellow trumpet player Jonah Jones about substitute chords and talked the trumpet section into inserting double-time passages in conventional arrangements, amusing the musicians while disconcerting the bandleader. His soloing was equally experimental.

He would play a solo and he would get involved in it, "ba-do-ba," and he didn't have the chops he acquired later. He had the ideas but his chops weren't always up to his ideas in those days. He was making an attempt at something, and he'd get about two-thirds of the way through it and just run right out of chops completely, and it wouldn't be nothing but hot air coming out. The trumpet players, mostly, would be in awe because they would be admiring him for even attempting this. And even if he didn't make it all, they could envision what it would sound like if it had been finished. Of course, Cab, not being that kind of musician, all he heard was the last two measures were just hot air. And he'd say, "Man, why can't you play the solos like all the other cats who just play what's on the paper? And play the thing nice instead of going all up there and missing all them notes." And Diz would hang his head while Cab bawled him out.

What survives on recordings is a good deal more calculated, if still defiantly progressive in its ostentatious use of chromatic dissonance. A good example is Gillespie's brief solo on "Cupid's Nightmare" (music example 25), a remarkable (if somewhat shapeless) free-floating chromatic piece by Don Redman. (The solo was carefully worked out, as a comparison between the commercial version and a 1940 broadcast shows.) Few soloists of the time could have parsed the challenging harmonies so accurately, and fewer still would have included a tritone substitution, as Gillespie does in measure 6 of the broadcast version.

Off the bandstand, Gillespie worked continuously to improve his skills, including a lengthy round of jam sessions at the end of a night's work:

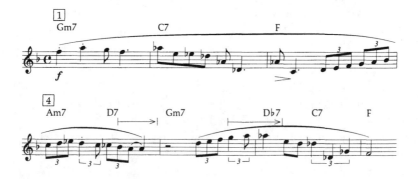

EX. 25.
"Cupid's Nightmare" (aircheck, 1940), Dizzy Gillespie solo, mm. 1–7.

I was always into something else outside. Playing with Cab was my job. Cab frowned on the idea of guys going out blowing, but I went anyway. In the different towns we'd visit, I'd go out and blow. People would say, "He's with Cab Calloway." Cab didn't like that. But I'd sneak out anyway. Shit, fuck Cab! I was thinking about my own development. When we were in New York, after the show, I'd go to Minton's and then to Monroe's Uptown House and jam until 7:00 in the mornings.

These jam sessions were documented on a few occasions on a portable disc recorder operated by jazz enthusiast Jerry Newman. On a version of the standard "Exactly Like You" (anachronistically titled "Kerouac" by Newman when the recordings were later made available to the general public), Gillespie diligently takes chorus after chorus, restlessly honing his craft (music example 26). The jagged contours of his lines—the habit of plunging suddenly from the upper to the lower register—owe an obvious debt to Roy Eldridge. So, too, at this point, does the kind of chromaticism he explores. As Gunther Schuller has noted, the filling in of the diatonic scale with chromatic tones (leaving aside for the moment the "blue" third and seventh degrees) began, in solos by Eldridge and Lester Young, with the lowered sixth and ninth. This led Gillespie, as it did Eldridge, to substitute for the dominant, not the chord with a root a tritone distant (the tritone substitution—in this instance, C-flat^7 for F^7), but a chord with a root a half step higher (G-flat^7). Compare, for example, measures 4–5 of Gillespie's solo with the opening of Eldridge's 1938 solo on "Body and Soul" (music example 27). A more systematic use of flatted fifths would come later.

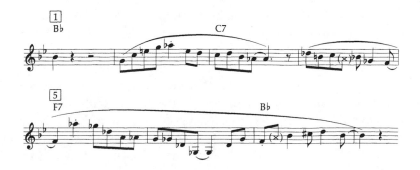

EX. 26.
"Kerouac" ["Exactly Like You"] (1941), Dizzy Gillespie solo, chorus 2, mm. 1–8.

EX. 27.
"Body and Soul" (1938), Roy Eldridge solo, mm. 1–3 (transposed from original key of D).

None of this experimentation, by Gillespie's account, made much of an impression on his colleagues: "I worked hard while I played with Cab, and practiced constantly. I could seldom get much encouragement from the guys in Cab's band. Mostly, they talked about real estate or something, never talked about music. That atmosphere kept me acting wiggy and getting into a lot of mischief."

Gillespie sublimated his hostility and frustration into a variety of ingenious antics, designed to drive his short-tempered employer to distraction. While Calloway was singing a romantic ballad, Gillespie would pantomime throwing a football across the bandstand. When trombonist Tyree Glenn pretended to catch it, drummer J. C. Heard signaled the impact with a subtle "boom" on the bass drum. The audience, naturally, broke up in appreciative laughter, leaving Calloway to wonder what was going on behind his back. "And of course, when he came off," Milt Hinton has revealed, "he would bawl the daylights out of us. 'Well, fellas, something is happening back there, and I don't like it at all!' And nine times out of ten, he would finally find out it was Dizzy. And he would bawl Dizzy out, and Dizzy would take it."

Tensions finally came to a head in the fall of 1941, while the band was playing at a theater in Hartford, Connecticut. Gillespie was apparently fond of throwing spitballs, although he was careful to keep them within the perimeter of the band. "The spitballs would go *ping* off the trombones and everybody would crack up, but Dizzy would just sit back there with that innocent look of his on his face." In Hartford, a spitball landed in the spotlight during a performance by the "band-within-the-band," the Cab Jivers. When the curtain closed at the end of the show, a furious Calloway confronted Gillespie. This time, however, Gillespie was blameless, and refused to take his tongue-lashing. (The spitball had in fact been thrown by Jonah Jones.) A heated exchange of words predictably escalated to violence.[3] A contemptuous slap by Calloway prompted the streetwise Gillespie to bring out his knife.

The scuffle was quick. What exactly transpired is unclear. Gillespie may well have cut Calloway, or the injury may have been an accident. According to Jonah Jones, the incident took place along a hallway crowded with heavy touring trunks, and Calloway, maneuvering for advantage, jabbed his thigh against the sharp edge of a lock on one of the trunks. In any case, Calloway hardly felt the wound, and the combatants were separated. On his return to the dressing room, he saw that his white band-leader's suit was soaked with blood. Gillespie was fired immediately.

In the short term, the spitball incident was a setback for Gillespie's career. He had lost the financial security and prestige that came with one of the best jobs in New York, and he had reinforced a reputation for reckless, "dizzy" behavior, which made other employers reluctant to use him. (A guilt-stricken Jonah Jones recommended Gillespie for a job with Charlie Barnet, but the bandleader responded, "That's the guy who cut Cab, right?") On the surface, the next several years were unsettled, even chaotic. But in the long term, the loss of the job with Calloway only strengthened Gillespie's determination to make his own way in the music business.

> Despite losing the "good job" with Cab, I was quite self-assured. . . . I felt I had something new, a real chance of creating some beautiful music and gaining the proper payment, respect, and recognition for it. Realizing that I had something very imaginative and unique going for me, *I stopped accepting jobs where the salary was too low and unreflective of my talents and contributions as a soloist* [italics added]. Jazz musicians were paid some pitifully low wages at that time, as sidemen, and since I had no group of my own established, people considered me a sideman. That status—and the little money that went along with it—I refused to accept. I ended up working at a furious pace for about a year with over *ten different bands* [italics in original], trying to make each one give me what I wanted. I refused to stay in any one place for too long, demanded special treatment, and if I didn't get it, I'd leave and go someplace else.

By 1942 Gillespie had, in effect, embarked on a freelance career: supplementing short-term jobs with dance orchestras by playing in small com-

---

3. According to Rex Stewart, "Cab Calloway wanted to settle things with a fight—he'd invite the problem man to go outside" (Stewart 1991, 117).

bos on 52nd Street, writing arrangements, and performing for union scale at public jam sessions. This new round of activities lacked the security of a regular job with a dance band, but it gave him the independence to pursue his own interests and ambitions. In time, he came to look upon leaving the Calloway band as "the best thing in the world, my most significant move."

Bird in Flight

Charlie Parker's entry to New York musical life was decidedly more subterranean. He made some headway while in Kansas City, playing with a sextet led by pianist Jay McShann at Martin's-On-The-Plaza, a "conservative" white nightclub where the clientele demanded a repertory of soft, romantic ballads as well as jazz-oriented dance music. But he left Kansas City under a cloud: he apparently cut a taxi driver with his knife in an argument over the fare and landed in jail. On his release, sometime in 1938, he hoboed his way on a freight train to Chicago; when he walked into a nightclub and asked to sit in, he struck Billy Eckstine as "the raggedest guy you'd want to see." His arrival in New York sometime in 1939 was equally inauspicious. Unable to land a musical job at first, he washed dishes at Jimmy's Chicken Shack in Harlem, slaking his ambition by gazing up at the sign for the Savoy Ballroom, "just digging New York, period." He eventually found work as a musician, but while Gillespie was beginning his two-year stint with Cab Calloway, Parker was playing on the fringes of the music business, in seedy dime-a-dance halls.

During this time he was barely recognizable as a member of the musicians' community. Successful musicians spent a good deal of time and money on sartorial sharpness (or looking "clean")—as much as anything to make their affluence apparent to passersby. Parker's disheveled appearance made him immediately suspect. When guitarist John Collins, then playing with the Roy Eldridge orchestra, first met Parker in 1940, he thought Parker was just a hanger-on who made some money by selling marijuana. "I didn't even know Bird played saxophone. We used to call him the Shadow because Bird would wear this dark cap and this long black overcoat, and he was a man, you know. He sold pot." When Collins finally did hear Parker, he was, like so many others, astonished at the saxophonist's virtuosity. Parker was gradually accumulating a reputation. On the basis of his encounter with Parker in Chicago, Billy Eckstine had begun telling musicians, "You got to hear this guy play . . . man, this cat will outplay Benny Carter."

But there were not many opportunities to hear Parker play. Musicians remember him joining the jam sessions at Monroe's Uptown House and Dan Wall's Chili House in Harlem. These occasions have taken on a heightened significance in retrospect. It was at the Chili House, late in 1939, while jamming with guitarist Biddy Fleet, that Parker supposedly suddenly saw the possibilities of improvising with the upper partials of chords.[4] Unlike Gillespie, Parker was not familiar with the keyboard. But by listening closely to harmony instruments like Fleet's guitar, he learned how to draw unexpected melodic lines out of the fabric of voice-leading in the chord progression. According to Fleet,

> Bird liked my playing, and it wasn't because I played that much. Lot of
> guitar players was playing more guitar than I. But the voicing of my chords

4. The source for this assertion is an article about Parker by John Wilson and Michael Levin:

> Charlie's horn first came alive in a chili house on Seventh avenue between 139th street and 140th street in December, 1939. He was jamming there with a guitarist named Biddy Fleet. At the time, Charlie says, he was bored with the stereotyped changes being used then.
> "I kept thinking there's bound to be something else," he recalls. "I could hear it sometimes but I couldn't play it."
> Working over Cherokee with Fleet, Charlie suddenly found that by using higher intervals of a chord as a melody line and backing them with appropriately related changes, he could play this thing he had been "hearing." Fleet picked it up behind him and bop was born ["No Bop Roots in Jazz: Parker," *Down Beat* 16 (9 September 1949): 12].

In the original, only a small portion of this passage is attributed to Parker directly. The technical explanation, with its vague, pedantic air ("appropriately related changes"), seems clearly to be a summation by the authors of what they could glean from Parker. This excerpt was reprinted in Nat Shapiro and Nat Hentoff's oral history compilation, *Hear Me Talkin' To Ya.* To heighten the impression that the book was (as its subtitle claimed) "the story of jazz as told by the men who made it," all of the material was presented in the first person. Accordingly, the entire passage, including the technical explanation, was put in Parker's voice. This is the version that has entered jazz folklore:

> I remember one night before Monroe's I was jamming in a chili house on Seventh Avenue between 139th and 140th. It was December, 1939. Now I'd been getting bored with the stereotyped changes that were being used all the time at the time, and I kept thinking there's bound to be something else. I could hear it sometimes but I couldn't play it.
> Well, that night, I was working over Cherokee, and, as I did, I found that by using the higher intervals of a chord as a melody line and backing them with appropriately related changes, I could play the thing I'd been hearing. I came alive [Shapiro and Hentoff 1955, 354].

The last sentence—culled, apparently, from the opening of the original excerpt—substitutes effectively for the rather pedestrian "and bop was born," and adds an irresistible touch to what is now taken, on Parker's own testimony, to be the "great epiphany" (Giddins 1987, 54) in his career.

had a theme within themselves. You could call a tune, and I'd voice my chords in such a way that I'd play the original chords to the tune, and I'd invert 'em every one, two, three, or four beats so that the top notes of my inversions would be another tune. . . . And Bird had a big ear, and he listened. He say, "Biddy! Do that again!"

Nevertheless, Parker does not seem to have made much of an impression at the time. At the Chili House, he kept his horn in the corner and had to be prodded into playing: "he used to come out in the spotlight in raggedy clothes." At Monroe's, he was mainly noticed for his evident stylistic debt to Lester Young. "Nobody paid me much mind then except Bobby Moore, one of Count Basie's trumpet players," Parker himself recalled in 1949. "He liked me. Everybody else was trying to get me to sound like Benny Carter."

Parker left New York early in 1940, returning to Kansas City, where he reestablished a relationship with Jay McShann. With the sponsorship of jazz journalist Dave Dexter and the financial backing of Walter Bales, a local insurance executive, McShann had expanded his band to a full-size dance orchestra. By 1940 the McShann orchestra was playing the best of the local jobs and had begun to tour within the broader Kansas City territory. One of the jobs was a "walkathon," a grueling endurance contest at the Pla-Mor Ballroom lasting several months. "When we came out of there," according to McShann, "we had a heck of a big band. We had, I bet you, seven hundred head arrangements and maybe two hundred and fifty written arrangements." The numbers are undoubtedly exaggerated; but the proportion of head arrangements to written arrangements in the McShann band—somewhere between 3:1 and 2:1—is probably accurate. Head arrangements were the McShann band's specialty, and it is in this context that Charlie Parker was especially valuable to the band.

Head arrangements are arrangements that exist only in the players' heads: they consist largely of riff figures that serve as a background for solo improvisation. For the sake of timbral clarity, if a brass player took a solo, the riff figures would be played by the saxophones, and vice versa. The riffs could be worked out in advance, harmonized, and memorized, or the entire process could be collapsed into the heat of the moment, with the riffs "set" by one player in the band and instantaneously harmonized. The practice was not exclusive to Kansas City. Trombonist Clyde Bernhardt remembered developing head arrangements in tandem with a trumpet player in Newark, New Jersey, as early as 1928: "He set a riff, I took the thirds, and he took the tonic." But Kansas City musicians refined the technique and proved its applicability to the modern dance band.

As Bernhardt's description indicates, a head arrangement depended on a kind of reflex by which a musician automatically complemented a line at a set harmonic interval. With only three horns, the harmonization could consist of simple triads (root, third, fifth). As horn sections gradually expanded to four or five, musicians faced with the dilemma of doubling someone else's part ("You playin' my note? Get off my note!") began to add sixths and ninths to the sonority. In Kansas City jam sessions, where ten saxophonists might be waiting their turn, the trick was to come up with a graceful background behind the soloist by spontaneously harmonizing riffs. The roots of this practice in African-American vocal traditions—the spontaneously conceived spirituals of the black church, for example—are evident enough: bassist Gene Ramey compared the atmosphere of Kansas City jazz to a "camp meeting—completely imitated from one of those revival meetings, where the preacher and the people are singing, all that living, and there's happenings all around." But the growing professionalization of jazz put a sharply competitive spin on collective music-making and made it part of a musician's training. Alto saxophonist Buster Smith, a mentor to the youthful Charlie Parker, was renowned for setting rhythmically intricate riffs that stumped all but the most experienced:

> The other guys would have to harmonize with that, and if they didn't get the harmonic notes to every one of those things he made, they just [got] eliminated. . . . And Buster would do that in a jam session, especially when it got to be too many horns in there. He'd set some of them heavy riffs and the guys would just get their horns and go away and sit down. . . . It showed a young guy that came in there, that he didn't only have to learn how to play a solo, he had to learn how to team. . . . [how to] breathe at the same time and all that. . . . And this was the thing that was most inspiring to Bird, was that he learned so many different kinds of riffs, tricky riffs.

In the McShann band, Parker led the saxophone section on head arrangements. Normally a "lead" saxophonist was chosen for tone, sight-reading skills, and the ability to shape a section's phrasing. For written arrangements, McShann depended on alto saxophonist John Jackson, a fluent sight-reader. "But when we did a head tune, Bird phrased . . . and Bird set most of the riffs." He was, in short, a team player, an invaluable part of McShann's effort to mold his fledgling dance orchestra into a unit that could survive competition on the national scene. In McShann's own words: "He was an *interested* cat in those days. . . . I always say his peak was when he was with my band."

Parker made his first commercial recordings with McShann for Decca in the spring of 1941—recordings that have been pored over by fans and scholars looking for bebop antecedents. His twelve-bar solo on "Hootie Blues" (music example 28) in particular is a marvel of rhythmic fluidity. From the opening pair of phrases, lagging far behind the beat, to the almost imperceptible gradations between an easygoing triplet feeling and double-time sixteenth notes, Parker's rhythmic language is continually in flux, but always precisely controlled and nuanced. It is also completely integrated with the traditional melodic gestures and intonational subtleties of the blues, on the one hand, and a modern harmonic outlook, on the other. Examples of the former are everywhere; examples of the latter are sprinkled strategically throughout the solo: the knowing use of nonharmonic tones (some bluesy, some not) in the third phrase (measures 3–4), ending with a perfectly timed resolution of the dissonant dominant seventh (d-flat), or the confident spelling out of the ii^7 harmony in measure 9. And yet it must be emphasized that while this remarkable solo clearly foreshadows the musical language of bebop, there is nothing in it that implies the coming divorce of the bebop generation from the big bands. Parker's sensibility was as naturally suited to the relaxed and swinging Kansas City sound of the McShann band as Lester Young's was to Basie.

Unfortunately, only a small and unrepresentative sample of Parker's playing in the McShann band has been preserved on recordings. On that first recording date, McShann played a variety of tunes, including a Charlie Parker arrangement of "What Price Love," a variation on Earl Hines's "Rosetta," later titled "Yardbird Suite." But Decca executive Jack Kapp was unimpressed. With his eye on the lucrative "race market," he insisted on narrowing McShann's recorded repertory to the blues, to be marketed on Decca's Sepia Series. McShann resented not being allowed to display more of the band's versatility, which had greatly contributed to the band's successes in live performance. But Kapp's hunch proved to be correct. A hastily concocted head arrangement, "Confessin' the Blues," featuring singer Walter Brown (who had joined the band only days before), proved to be the best-selling record of the date. (Parker was not featured on the number, although he came up with some of the background riffs in the

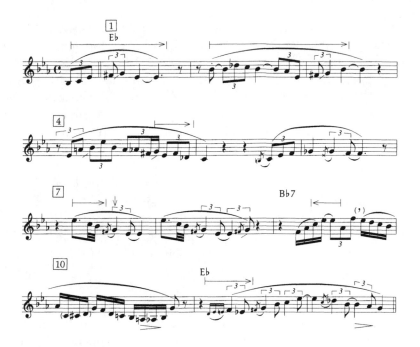

EX. 28.
"Hootie Blues" (1941), Charlie Parker solo.

recording studio.) "Confessin' the Blues" helped to establish McShann's credibility as a national bandleader. McShann then came under Moe Gale's management and secured a New York debut at the Savoy Ballroom in January 1942.

The musicians in the McShann band were painfully lacking in urban sophistication. In their Sears and Roebuck suits, they made a poor impression on New Yorkers. Charlie Buchanan, manager of the Savoy, taunted them on their arrival: "What in the hell have we got here? This is the raggediest looking band I ever saw in my life! This is New York City, boy, this isn't Kansas!"

The band alternated sets with the Lucky Millinder band, a seasoned New York group. In the competitive spirit of the Savoy, musicians from Millinder's orchestra mischievously sent McShann a note: "We're going to send you hicks back to the sticks." But the McShann band won the crowd with its hard-driving swing and its flexible head arrangements, which could be extended indefinitely to send the dancers into an ecstatic frenzy. "When Jay turned his boys loose, he had hellions working. Just roaring wild men . . . unknown stars, guys I was sure was going to make names for themselves some day," remembered Clyde Bernhardt, who played opposite McShann at the Savoy a month later with the Edgar Hayes orchestra. One of those young hellions was Charlie Parker, who was frequently turned loose on a head arrangement of "Cherokee" lasting up to half an hour. McShann's men eventually acquired sharp uniforms— tan jackets, brown pants, tan shoes, dark green bow ties—and a reputation in New York.

By 1942 Parker had arrived at roughly the same professional niche as Gillespie: a featured soloist with a national dance band (although McShann's band was a notch or two below Calloway's in prestige). The same year saw the erosion of Parker's commitment to the big bands as the arena for his professional and artistic ambitions. One reason, surely, was his involvement with drugs, which eventually poisoned his professional relationship with McShann. As Clyde Bernhardt, who joined the McShann band in late 1942, said, "Jay didn't give a damn what anybody in his band did as long as it didn't get in the way of the job." But Parker's breaches of professional behavior became more and more intrusive. The final straw came at an engagement at the Paradise Theater in Detroit, where Parker, who liked to take off his shoes while playing, walked out into the spotlight to take a solo in his stocking feet. By one account, he passed out cold onstage. McShann fired him, and Parker had to make his way back to New York on his own. The juxtaposition of his discipline and drive with such self-destructive behavior is part of the Parker paradox. "I know it's gonna out me one of these days," he once told a band mate about his drug use, "but man, I'm not a bad cat, this is just my life and I can't do without it."

But the erosion of commitment was also more subtle, more grounded in Parker's aesthetic sensibilities. Parker was attracted to the bohemian pleasures of New York's famous nightlife, and he came to prefer the liberating informality of playing in after-hours joints to steady work on a bandstand. McShann watched this shift in attitude with regret:

> When Bird started getting into this other thing [i.e., heroin] . . . all he wanted to do was put his horn under his arm and just go down to Monroe's, Minton's, and just like, "I go in there and get me a taste, little couple of tunes, get off, come back in another hour and get a couple of tastes, go blow a tune." He didn't have his heart like it was with that big band.

Parker put it differently:

> When I came to New York and went to Monroe's, I began to listen to that real advanced New York style. . . . At Monroe's I heard sessions with a pianist named Allen Tinney; I'd listen to trumpet men like Lips Page, Roy, Dizzy and Charlie Shavers outblowing each other all night long. And Don Byas was there, playing everything there was to be played. I heard a trumpet man named Vic Coulsen playing things I'd never heard. . . . That was the kind of music that caused me to quit McShann and stay in New York.

What seemed from the outside to be a descent into sordid obscurity was, to Parker, the beginning of a new kind of professional life—fraught with insecurity and vulnerable to the undertows of addiction, but also full of possibilities. By the end of 1942 he, like Gillespie, had started to define his career in his own terms and was forming working relationships with like-minded musicians.

"McGhee Special"

The experiences of Dizzy Gillespie and Charlie Parker were echoed in the careers of many other musicians who would constitute the front line of the bop revolution. To document the passage of each bebop pioneer to professional maturity around 1942 would be an exercise in tedium. Instead, I will briefly present a lesser-known career that shows how the general pattern accommodates yet another talented and idiosyncratic musician: trumpet player Howard McGhee.

Like so many others, Howard McGhee came from the provinces. His musical education was spotty and opportunistic. His first exposure to organized music came from the marching band at a boys' school in the historically all-black town of Boley, Oklahoma. He came to the band already knowing a few rudiments on the cornet, having been inspired by hearing Louis Armstrong on the radio to teach himself a few simple scales. The bandleader, in an effort to put all the young students on an equal footing, handed McGhee a clarinet instead. He ended up learning both instruments, and later attributed his agility as a trumpet player to his early experience as a clarinetist.

McGhee's climb up the ladder of the music business was slow and uncertain. In his early teens he left school to work as a trumpet player in small itinerant carnival bands in Oklahoma. Gradually, he drifted into larger and more accomplished bands. His family moved to Albuquerque, New Mexico, where he joined a seven-piece combo led by the young Jay McShann, who taught him the rudiments of keyboard harmony and gave him some guidance in writing arrangements for the small group. In 1935, while still only seventeen, he left Albuquerque to join several larger territory bands working in the mountain states and the upper Midwest, bands with such improbable names as Gene Coy's Black Aces and Art Bronson's Bostonians, and one led by Harriet Calloway, who did her best to cash in on the misleading impression that she was related to Cab Calloway.[5] The teenaged trumpet player struggled to survive in the depths of the Depression on starvation wages. Gene Coy, he remembers, "didn't pay nobody. We go play, and play, and play, and he wind up probably giving you two dollars. I said, 'Jiminy, *this* ain't it!' " After Harriet Calloway's band broke up in Grand Forks in September, McGhee endured the ravages of a North Dakota winter. While working in Minot, he contracted a near-fatal case of pleural pneumonia. Later, in a Fargo nightclub, when the pianist was fired, he found himself playing trumpet with one hand and piano with the other. "It was kind of mean," he recalls. "But I was lucky because I always kept getting jobs. I didn't know much about the music business at that time. I was just trying to learn how to play."

Gradually, McGhee drifted east, following various jobs to Minnesota, Wisconsin, Michigan, and Ohio, playing with now-obscure midwestern territory bands led by Leonard Gay, Tommy Fox, and Jimmy Raschel. He remained attuned to developments in modern jazz, listening to Roy Eldridge's broadcasts from the Three Deuces club in Chicago beginning in 1936. Like Gillespie, he was fascinated with Eldridge's facility—"I got so I could play as *fast* as Roy, and eventually even faster because I studied clarinet in school"—and his experience with the piano keyboard helped him absorb the more chromatic harmonic language. Tenor saxophonist Big Nick Nicholas heard McGhee in the Cotton Club in Cincinnati: "His feature was 'Body and Soul,' and he was playing like Roy Eldridge at the time." His income steadily rose, from $18 to $35 a week.

In 1941 McGhee was hired by the Club Congo in Detroit—a job that

---

5. As obscure as these bands are, many well-known musicians passed through their ranks. Art Bronson's band is best known today for providing Lester Young with one of his earliest jobs; alumni of the Gene Coy band include Ben Webster, Dick Wilson, and Junior Raglin (McCarthy 1977, 106).

brought him, finally, from the margins to the mainstream of the entertainment business. The Club Congo was a nightclub on a national touring circuit, featuring top acts in black show business (the Mills Brothers, Buck and Bubbles). For $70 a week, McGhee was responsible for organizing and rehearsing a band that accompanied the floor show and played for dancing. Because the headline acts changed weekly, McGhee was constantly learning new music, as well as writing interludes and accompaniments for acts that didn't specify their own music.

The job at the Club Congo gave McGhee a new visibility. He made contacts with musicians passing through Detroit with the national dance orchestras, such as Dizzy Gillespie (still working for Cab Calloway). He also wrote a piece for trumpet soloist and dance band entitled "McGhee Special"—"a thing that featured me, so I could be down in the front of the band." In addition to being a reliable staple of his band's repertory, it called attention to McGhee's multiple talents as a composer, arranger, and soloist. Eventually, the advertisement paid off. In the summer of 1941, Lionel Hampton, who had left the Benny Goodman Quartet to form his own band the year before, heard McGhee performing his personal showpiece at the Club Congo and was impressed enough to offer him a position in the trumpet section. Hampton's band in 1941 was neither particularly well known nor prosperous, but it did rank among the national orchestras, offering McGhee a new level of professional experience. As McGhee tells it, "[Hampton] came through and he heard me playing 'McGhee Special' and he said, 'Maggie, you got to come join my band, you gotta come join my band.' Well, I did. 'Yeah, O.K., I'll do that,' I said. 'That's one step a little higher.' "

His association with Hampton was remarkably brief. For one thing, he was uncomfortable in the narrow role of high-note specialist: "He wanted me and Ernie [Royal] to be hitting high F's and G's on every end of every song, and I said, 'Ain't no use in workin' for this cat 'cause he's gonna blow my lip out!' . . . and Hampton would hold the chord till you turned blue in the face." More to the point, McGhee's hopes that joining a national band would increase his income were quickly shattered by the stingy wage schedule imposed by Gladys Hampton: no guaranteed salary, just $10 per gig.

> Me, like a dummy, said, "Yeah, I guess I will [join]." I figured, this is a big name, I'll probably get into something. Boy, you never know. When Gladys paid me off . . . she handed me 2 ten-dollar [bills]. I said, "What is

this?" She said, "This is your salary." I said, "Salary! I was making $70 a week in Detroit, and I quit that to come out here! I can't go for this kind of money." So she said, "Well, you'll either have to go back or forget it, 'cause we don't pay no more than that." I was so amazed, because I didn't think—I just took it for granted that they paid well.

McGhee had seen Hampton as his ticket to New York and the big time, but "Shit, I ain't goin' to New York *broke.*"

McGhee retreated to Detroit, but soon received a telegram from band-leader Andy Kirk. Unlike Hampton, Kirk "was working *all* the time." This, of course, had its downside: the inevitable grueling schedule of one-night stands in the southern states.

McGhee never liked the southern tours: "I don't like to talk about it, because I get angry when I think about it." Indeed, from a black musician's standpoint, there was little to like. In the South the lines of segregation were clearly drawn, and black musicians from the North were dangerously anomalous. Even casual social interaction had to be treated with extreme caution. As McGhee remembers: "We played a lot of white dances, and the girls used to hit over me, and down there I was scared to take a breath! Let alone talk to a girl."

At this stage in his career, however, McGhee was too taken up with the novelty of his new responsibilities to linger on the bitter side. Performances of "McGhee Special," backed by a full-size dance orchestra in theaters and ballrooms all across the country, helped to establish his reputation as a virtuoso instrumentalist. Gradually, McGhee became aware of his full potential within the music business. While playing with Kirk, his salary increased from $17 a night to a peak of $35 a night. Kirk, who had no pretensions to instrumental virtuosity, generously encouraged him to spotlight his talents:

> You know, cause sitting back there in the trumpet section, they don't anybody know who's back there. But if you come out in front [to take a solo], they at least will give a *mention* of you. "Oh, yeah, they had a trumpet player there by the name of Howard McGhee," or something. And [Kirk] said, "Well, that's good, because you got to make a name for yourself." But I didn't know what he was talking about. You know, I was a dummy, I didn't know what was happening about making a name for myself.

But McGhee quickly learned. He also adapted quickly to the varied requirements of the entertaining dance orchestra, mastering a number of marketable skills and proving to be a resourceful and valued employee. When Mary Lou Williams, who had been the principal arranger for Kirk for more than a decade, left the band early in 1942, McGhee filled in. On one occasion, the Kirk band arrived in Austin, home of the University of Texas. The song "Deep in the Heart of Texas" was then at the height of its popularity, and a desperate Kirk came to McGhee with a copy of the sheet music:

> He said, "Maggie, can you write this up for the band tonight so we can play it?" So after riding all day I went in my room and wrote it up for the band, and we run it down when we got to the hall. And that night it was the hit thing. Andy was tickled to death. He said, "You can write anything you want—I don't care. Just whatever you write is all right, and tell the manager that I said OK." So I used to write and take the bill to Billy Shaw, the manager of the band, and I would write anything I wanted. I made a lot of extra money that way.

Kirk appreciated McGhee's up-to-date-ness. He counted on the young trumpet player to add streamlined riff tunes like Charlie Christian's "Seven Come Eleven" to his repertory. Before veteran pianist and arranger Mary Lou Williams left the band, McGhee took advantage of her expertise and learned something about substitute chords ("I didn't know you could do that with music"). He also cultivated a relationship with June Richmond, a raucous, bluesy vocalist and entertainer he greatly admired. He tailored arrangements to her needs and even joined her as a singer and comedic straight man on a few feature numbers.

By 1942 McGhee, like Parker and Gillespie, had carved out a position for himself as a top-rank soloist and arranger with a national dance band. His arrival in New York in July of that year only confirmed that status. A lengthy tour of theaters and ballrooms culminated in a three-week engagement at Loew's State Theater on Broadway, where McGhee's impressive versatility was noticed by the trade press. He made his recording debut in the same month, with "McGhee Special" eventually released on Decca.[6] He was twenty-four—not particularly young by the standards of the business, but young enough that the possibilities for future achievement must have seemed endless.

6. "McGhee Special" is discussed at length in Schuller's *The Swing Era:* its internal modulation from F major to A-flat major is the occasion for a remarkable technical digression on the harmonic relationships among minor-third-related chords (1989, 360–367).

The ultimate direction of his career was determined by the musical contacts he made in New York in that first year. He renewed his acquaintance with Dizzy Gillespie; the trumpeter came to hear him at Loew's State and invited him uptown to the jam sessions at Minton's. There he heard a more chromatic harmonic language: "raised ninths and flatted fifths and so forth." The sonorities were not surprising to him—he recognized them from various arrangements he had heard and played—but their applicability to soloing was a new and unexpected twist. "I said to myself, this is where I belong, because I fit in."

The turning point came later in 1942. McGhee had left the Kirk orchestra at the end of the summer for work as a featured soloist with white bandleader Charlie Barnet. In October the Charlie Barnet band concluded a brief tour of theaters in New England with an engagement at the Adams Theater in Newark. McGhee remembered the incident vividly:

> I had just come in after we came off the stage. I turned on the radio and Charlie Parker came [on the] air playing "Cherokee." I had never heard anything like that in my *life.* I had never heard anybody play *that* much horn, you know. And hearing Charlie [Barnet] play and hearing Charlie *Parker* play was like day and night. So that night, we all went up—the whole band went up to the Savoy Ballroom to hear Jay McShann's orchestra with this cat Charlie Parker. I asked Jay, I said, "Jay-Jay, who's the cat [who] played the solo on the radio today?" So he said, "That cat sitting right there in the third seat." And I looked at Charlie, and he was a little skinny guy, and I said, "Jiminy, that's the guy that played all that horn?" I said, "Will you play that for us? 'Cause we came all the way over here to hear this guy." So he says, "Yeah." So about three numbers later he played "Cherokee" and Charlie got up and played, and I never—we all stood there with our mouths open because we hadn't heard anybody play a horn like *that.*

From the moment of that broadcast, Parker had a tremendous impact on McGhee. Parker served as a catalyst, sharply focusing McGhee's self-awareness as a progressive jazz musician. Because he was an arranger and sometime pianist, McGhee was more attuned than the average jazz musician to harmonic theory and was astounded by Parker's complete command of this aspect of improvisation: "I could hear what he was doing, and I knew what he was doing was right [harmonically]." McGhee found Parker's command of technique and expression nothing short of overpowering: "I mean, here's a guy who's playing everything that he wants to play and *playing* it, you know. And I was sitting there thinking, 'Jiminy, listen to *this.*' And he was playing all the changes, and playing them fluently, like they were just meant for to be there. . . . And I said, 'What am I doing out here fooling around with this horn? I don't even know what's happening.' . . . I never heard nobody play a horn like that—that *complete.*"

Like most other jazz musicians of his generation, McGhee continued on the usual path for a dance band musician. He was in no position in 1942 to even imagine using Parker's example as the foundation for a dramatic change of career. The disillusionment would come soon enough—as would the opportunities to patch together a new kind of career on the margins of the music business. In the meantime, he took advantage of every occasion to play with and learn from like-minded progressives. It was at Minton's and Monroe's, at clubs on 52nd Street like the Onyx and the Three Deuces, and at a host of jam session spots in Harlem now lost to obscurity, that the paths of Gillespie, Parker, McGhee, and all of the other bebop pioneers crossed. The musicians' community was relatively small and clannish, but continually in motion. Even in New York, their time was often consumed with physically demanding performing sched-ules—four to five shows a day in theaters, for example. The after-hours scene served as a magnet, drawing musicians together in relaxed circum-stances that encouraged experimentation and the cross-fertilization of ideas. The associations that had begun to develop by 1942 grew stronger year by year. By 1944 or 1945 a recognizable new jazz idiom emerged—one that in musical style and performance ambience owed a great deal to the informal atmosphere of the after-hours jam session.

5 · THE JAZZMAN'S TRUE ACADEMY

Wherever there was good musicians, there was after-hours jam joints. It was almost part of the business. CLYDE BERNHARDT

No aspect of the jazz world has been the object of more fascination than the jam session—or the locus of more misunderstanding. Its flexibility and lack of pretension, its offhand displays of virtuosity, its apparent disregard for everything outside of its own charmed circle—all seem to sum up that which is attractive and liberating in the jazz aesthetic. This peculiar constellation of qualities lies at the heart of the "modulation into a new key of musical sensibility" that bop has come to represent. For in adopting the characteristic attitudes and procedures of the jam session and making them the central focus of public presentation, bebop radically revised the prevailing definition of jazz. In place of the often tawdry transactions between artist and audience summed up by the words *entertainment* and *showmanship,* bebop offered the spectacle of musicians playing for their own enjoyment, capturing some of the dignity and autonomy of the concert stage without losing the informal atmosphere that tied jazz to a vernacular social context. The shift to the format and spirit of the jam session suggests any number of compelling dichotomies: between ponderous big bands and fleet, flexible combos, in which each individual voice is heard; between constricting written arrangements and free-flowing improvisation; between demeaning conventions of popular entertainment and a format free of associations with comedy or dance. The jam session, in short, underlies all claims for the legitimacy of bebop—not simply as a jazz idiom, but as the decisive step toward jazz as art. It is at the heart of our after-the-fact conviction that the emergence of bebop was both right and inevitable, a confirmation of underlying principles.

If at first bebop appeared to be an impenetrable subculture, operating according to unseen codes, that is only to be expected. The jam session offers few clues to the uncontexted outsider. There is little or no written music in evidence, and certainly no rehearsal. There is no "band": musicians come and go as they please, even during the middle of the number. They may not even know one another, although they usually have at least a passing acquaintance and may use the bandstand (if indeed the performance space is physically set apart at all) to socialize. There is no frame for the performance, no spoken introductions or attention-getting silences. Hardly a word is exchanged beyond a few cryptic phrases— "blues in B-flat," "rhythm changes," a quick countdown to set the tempo—and they are off, into a performance that may last anywhere from a few minutes to an hour. Everybody seems to know what to do without being told. The listener is left face to face with the mystery of improvisation—an alchemy that creates music out of nothingness. It is creativity without artifice.

But, of course, there is artifice. The jam session would not be possible without certain procedures with which every competent jazz musician is presumed to be familiar. The repertory is reduced to a handful of structures: the blues, Gershwin's "I Got Rhythm" (the "rhythm changes" referred to above), and other pop song "standards." The only fixed personnel is a rhythm section of piano, bass, guitar, drums (although one can make do with less: in hotel rooms, drummers often spread a newspaper on a briefcase and played it with brushes); they serve as accompaniment for whoever cares to participate. The format is a string of solos—each instrumentalist playing for as many cycles, or choruses, as desired. The other "horns" either wait their turn or improvise background figures behind the soloist. Members of the rhythm section, if they are to take a solo, wait patiently until the end. Introductions are usually the responsibility of the pianist, with the rest of the band straggling in as needed. Endings—the one obvious weak spot—are notoriously formulaic or chaotic. These routines are so thoroughly internalized by the musicians that they are virtually invisible.

That the codes are not made explicit comes from the fact that jam sessions were never intended to be public spectacles. They were physically and temporally separate, usually taking place late at night in out-of-the-way places known only to the cognoscenti. They were also carefully set apart from the monetary economy. Even the most highly paid professionals played for free or for the simple barter of food and drink. Precisely because of this, jamming was officially condemned by the musicians' union, whose firmest rule was that any performance must be remunerated at the union-mandated minimum wage. Jamming was tolerated only to the extent that it could be demonstrated to be a strictly internal affair—for the private pleasure of musicians, carefully shielded from the general public.

This history accounts for the striking indifference toward the outside world that has always marked the jam session. If in a conventional performance energy is directed outward, beyond the stage, in the jam session all attention is focused inward. Rather than being ranged linearly on a bandstand for maximum visibility, musicians tend to cluster, leaving those on the margins to strain to look over their shoulders. The musicians themselves are the audience. All others present—which may include other musicians waiting their turns or simply listening and digging, as well as the inevitable hangers-on—form concentric circles (or semicircles) around the core. As the jam session has become adapted to public spectacle, this distinctively cloistered ambience has made its way into concert settings. Audiences are invited to look in, to enjoy the private gestures of the musicians without disturbing them by more than polite applause at the end of each solo; or, if the atmosphere is rowdier, they may masquerade as insiders, exhorting the musicians to greater and greater levels of intensity. Bebop emerged in this atmosphere, its practitioners impassive and intent rather than genial entertainers.

Ironically, the ultimate viability of bebop as a *commercial* genre depended on many jazz enthusiasts' conviction that the jam session represented jazz in its purest state—an uncorrupted, unmediated, and uncommercial form of musical expression. This conviction predated bebop; it was at the core of most "primitivist" interpretations of jazz as a species of folk music struggling to survive in a ruthless market economy. The Swing Era, bringing with it the appropriation of jazz improvisation as one element in an eclectic package of entertainment, increased the enthusiasts' insistence on the isolation of "real" jazz from the broader world of commerce and the celebration of the jam session as a privileged space free from external pressures of all kinds. "Many a big-time commercial sideman likes to get away from all the phony music he plays for a living, and get down to earth with some genuine jazz," wrote a correspondent for the jazz trade press in 1941. "When you're playing for yourself you discover the really good ideas that are inside of you. There's no audience, no crowd, no hot fans. Thank god, there are no messy jitterbugs, no critics to mutter under their breath."

It is a short step from here to the jam session as symbol of alienation. If "genuine jazz" is incompatible with the marketplace and can be played only in deliberate isolation from it, then the sincere artist's association with such commercial enterprises as the dance band is just a marriage of convenience. Jazz musicians submit to the indignities of commercial entertainment to support themselves, so that they will be free—on their own time and away from the public eye—to reconstitute the music on their own terms. The jam session is not simply a form of escape, but an act of defiance.

How that defiance was interpreted depended on the ideology of the observer. For those who saw jazz musicians as displaced folk artists, the jam session recaptured the innocence of a precapitalist economy. In his book *The Real Jazz*, Hugues Panassié, writing in 1942 on the eve of the bop revolution, described the jam session this way:

> This is the music they are not permitted to play in the large commercial orchestras which they have been forced to join to earn their living. . . . The jam session overflows and is carried away with an enthusiasm for which one would search vainly elsewhere. During these hours, the musicians play out of a love of music, without attempting to create a "work" but simply because the music makes them feel intensely alive. Here certainly music is returned to its natural state and is delivered of all preparations and artifice.

Panassié, of course, was notoriously hostile to bebop. Its self-conscious complexities were antithetical to his ideal of jazz as a "natural" folk idiom.

A different reading of the jam session, however, fit the new style perfectly: bebop as the jazz avant-garde. The privileging of the jam session as the province of embattled, marginalized artists—an artistic domain of unquestioned integrity in stark contrast to the hopelessly philistine commercial sphere of the bandstand or theater—became central to the bebop myth. Much has been made of the bebop pioneers as insurgents, alienated from the commercial music scene. Frustrated by the clichés of the swing bands and the lack of opportunity to perform their own music, the story goes, they withdrew to the obscurity of the jam session to plot a new music, defiant in its autonomy. In particular, the late-night sessions at Minton's Playhouse in Harlem have been caricatured to the point that, as Leroi Jones (Amiri Baraka) has complained, they sound "almost like the beginnings of modern American writing among the emigrés of Paris."

It is unfortunately all too easy to project back onto the formative years of bebop attitudes that did not find full expression until much later or were more characteristic of one segment of the musicians' community than another. William Bruce Cameron's study "Sociological Notes on the Jam Session" puts an academic sanction on the antagonism of jazz and commercial music and the importance of jam sessions as a refuge for marginalized jazz musicians. Published in 1954, but based on the author's prior professional experience (he began playing "dance music for money and jazz for pleasure in 1939"), it explicitly defines the jam session as a "recreational rather than a vocational activity"—in the words of one musician, "a chance to get the taste of commercial music out of my mouth." Over and over, Cameron emphasizes the insuperable gulf between the two worlds in language that echoes Panassié's: "For outsiders, the intensity of distaste the jazzman feels toward money-making commercial dance music surpasses belief. In a very real sense the session is a ritual of purification for him. . . . He resides somewhere; he works somewhere else; but it is in the session that he most meaningfully lives. This is what he practices and learns for. This is the focus of his life."

Throughout his study, Cameron implies that the attitudes he has observed are universal—true of jazz musicians from the beginning and extendable into the foreseeable future.[1] But this is a questionable assumption. For one thing, Cameron fails to indicate whether his observations were made before or after the war years—a crucial point, since only in the wake of bebop, a genre no longer directly dependent on conventional dance music or entertainment, would musicians be so likely to put up a hostile front to the outside world. More troubling, he fails to specify whether the musicians he studied were white or black—although the ease with which he moved in their circles and his characterization of jazz as a form of rebellion against bourgeois norms strongly suggest the former ("Jazz is at once radical and idealistic and suffused with the glam-

---

1. In discussing the word *square* as a designation for the nonjazz outsider, for example, Cameron states: " 'Square' is a contemporary jazz term denoting disapproval; the word will change, but the attitude it expresses will remain to be expressed by a new term" (1954, 181).

our of Promethean artistry and the raw vulgarity of the brothel. . . . To become a great jazz artist when one is sixteen is a wonderful way of running away from the triple tyranny of home discipline, school discipline, and financial dependence").

The distinction is crucial. White musicians were far more likely to take on the role of "jazzmen as romantic outsiders," to use Neil Leonard's phrase—becoming artists as an expression of their contempt for middle-class culture, living only for "kicks" and aesthetic pleasure. With conventional paths to success open to them, their choice of music—especially a cross-racial music tainted with vice—and their embrace of a "deviant" lifestyle marked them as defiantly bohemian. For their counterparts in the black community, on the other hand, the music profession offered one of the few consistent means of social advancement. As we have seen, many had abandoned their earlier intentions to enter medicine, the law, or other skilled professions for the immediate prosperity available in the 1920s and 1930s to those with the requisite musical talents. Black musicians had little taste for romanticizing poverty, even in the service of art, and were far less inclined to disparage the virtues of a steady wage. As Charles Nanry once summed it up, "jazz selects blacks; whites select jazz."

In any case, Cameron's irritable deviants, clearly ill at ease with the very idea of music as a profession, bear little resemblance to the bebop pioneers. For black musicians at the height of the Swing Era, public performance and after-hours improvising were not separate and antagonistic spheres, reflecting an unbridgeable gulf between the need to put bread on the table and artistic self-respect, but interrelated parts of a larger whole. The jam session was an integral part of the "art world" that constituted their professional life. It was both recreational *and* vocational. The element of escape and recreation is obvious: the jam session was a part of nightlife, a window onto the varied entertainments of the city for young and energetic men with some money to burn. But it was also a kind of work. Musicians counted on having this time to practice, to work out new ideas and techniques, to exchange information, to network with their colleagues, to establish a rough-and-ready hierarchy of competence—all useful and necessary activities that could not practically be carried out on the bandstand. Far from protesting their status as professional musicians, the emergence of bebop evidenced its creators' deep commitment to the music profession and the peculiar discipline it entailed.

Friendly Competition

From the outset, jazz musicians have spent time playing for their own amusement. With the emergence of a class of professional dance musicians in the 1920s, informal music-making became a central feature of life off the bandstand. As Alan Merriam and Raymond Mack, who wrote a sociological study of the jazz community in 1960, have noted, the very nature of jazz musicians' work led them to form an isolated, self-sufficient subculture. Jazz musicians worked while others played, played while others slept, and slept while others worked. Like railroad workers, their routine was one of near-continuous travel, punctuated by occasional returns to a home base. Their recreation took on the form of a busman's holiday—a return to the pleasures of music under more relaxed circumstances, but still informed by their avocational interests.

In Harlem before the Swing Era, the most important jam session spot was the Rhythm Club (formerly the Band Box) on 132nd Street. The Rhythm Club was operated by Bert Hall, a racketeer and sometime trombonist who had earned the respect of his peers by instituting reforms in Local 802 of the American Federation of Musicians to ensure that black musicians were promptly paid. According to trombonist Dicky Wells, it was "strictly a musicians' club," offering an all-purpose venue for whatever they wanted to do after hours. They could play cards, shoot pool, have a meal, gossip, joke, size each other up or put each other down, and otherwise enjoy a comforting sense of community. A parallel scene for white musicians emerged at the Onyx, a 52nd Street speakeasy where the password was, "I'm from 802."

Like James Reese Europe's Clef Club before it, or the union headquarters downtown (which black musicians considered "primarily for whites"), the Rhythm Club served as a clearinghouse for employment. On Monday afternoons, knowing that all the major bandleaders would be hanging out, musicians would come by to collect their wages for the previous weekend's work and make themselves as available as possible for the next. "The guys used to gather [there]," remembers bassist Al Hall. "You go with your shoeshine, your dark suit, maybe with your instrument, maybe not. They had a slate on the wall, and you write your name on it for availability." "You could call at any hour of the day or night and hire a musician," according to Milton "Mezz" Mezzrow. Saxophonist Ben Webster, when he first came to New York, was counseled by Count Basie to head straight to the Rhythm Club. According to Basie, "A lot of guys used to bring their instruments with them . . . just in case somebody came by there looking for somebody to go out on a job. Which happened quite often. So there were always some of them around, and then in the late morning and after midnight, when the other joints were closing, you'd see all those cats dropping in there on their way home from work, and most of them would be carrying their instruments too."

And of course, they made music at the Rhythm Club. As was typical for jam session clubs, there was a house band; but as Count Basie remembered, "the thing about the Rhythm Club was that somebody was always sitting in." On the day that Danny Barker first arrived in New York in 1930, his musician uncle Paul Barbarin took him to the Rhythm Club. "What I saw and heard I will never forget," wrote Barker in his autobiography. "A wild cutting contest was in progress, and sitting and standing around the piano were twenty or thirty musicians, all with their instruments out waiting for a signal to play choruses of Gershwin's 'Liza.' " First came a competition among banjo players, dominated by a left-handed man known only as Seminole; then drums (with Chick Webb "washing away" the novelty playing of a vaudeville drummer); then a "trumpet battle" involving Rex Stewart, Bobby Stark, and Cuban Bennett.

The atmosphere was playful and festive, with musicians spilling out onto the sidewalk and shouting approval and encouragement. But like the professional baseball players recently studied by George Will, these were men at work. Through these "cutting contests," musicians established and maintained a hierarchy of professional competence. The particular spur for the jam session that Danny Barker witnessed that Monday afternoon was the arrival in New York of a well-known band, McKinney's Cotton Pickers—a prime opportunity to reshuffle the deck and see how the outsiders stacked up against New York's finest. As Barker noted with pop-eyed wonder, the occasion attracted a representative sampling of bandleaders and virtuoso sidemen: Benny Carter, Don Redman, Claude Hopkins, Jelly Roll Morton, Johnny Hodges, Red Allen, Sonny Greer, John Kirby—and Fletcher Henderson, who observed the scene with studied nonchalance while playing pool. These were men whose business it was to know who the best performers were, either to size up competitors or to keep track of potential employees. "On the New York gossip scene, musicians were appraised, discussed," recalls Barker. "Generally the verdict of your appraisal concerning tone, technique, facility was just about correct. . . . You would, in a musician's absence, in a gathering mention a question on his ability and be sure to get a total analysis."

At the highest echelon, the mechanisms for sorting out the pretenders from the elite were particularly well oiled. At one Harlem club, Mexico's, special evenings were devoted to particular instruments: "trumpet night," "saxophone night," "trombone night," and so forth. The sessions were intended only for the most experienced musicians, who would "always wash you away if you were from the second division." At the Hoofer's Club—a basement room on 132nd Street—the jam sessions, called "suppers," were by invitation only, via formal announcements printed on special cards ("You Are Invited to a Trombone Supper"). According to Dicky Wells, "You had to graduate to get down there": only "those *bad* cats"—musicians of the stature of Coleman Hawkins and Jimmie Harrison—were expected to play:

> Anyone could go, but mostly performers went, mostly musicians. There was no admission charge and we weren't paid. No money was involved at all.
>
> All the musicians would be sitting around the walls, all around the dance floor. Maybe there would be forty guys sitting around there. The floor was for dancers only, and they would be cutting each other, too, while we were cutting each other on the instruments. Everybody would be blowing— maybe six trombones. Now Hawk (Coleman Hawkins) would always come by the session, whether it was a Saxophone Supper or not.
>
> "I just happened to stop by and had my horn," he would say.
>
> You knew he'd come by to carve somebody.

For Hawkins, such apparently aggressive behavior could be justified as sheer self-defense:

> What you're calling today a jam, we used to call them cutting contests. Like I hear about regular tenor players playing down there, and I had to go down and cut them, you know. But they used to come and get me. A lot of times they'd come and find me. . . .
>
> They tried to catch me ever since I've been a kid. I don't know *why* they never leave me alone—they never *did* leave me alone! They got to cut *me*—if possible, and all that.

The focus in jam sessions was on competition; its specialized vocabulary—cutting and carving—suggestive of hand-to-hand combat. This ritual of competition was deeply ingrained in African American culture. It found its parallel in verbal contests such as the dozens, where quick-witted, aggressive responses and spontaneous creativity were highly valued. While the competition was serious, the atmosphere was congenial and supportive. Individual reputations might be made or broken, but the ultimate purpose was to raise the quality of performance all around. "Through all these friendly but lively competitions," wrote white jazz saxophonist Mezz Mezzrow, a close observer of the Harlem scene in the 1920s, "you could see the Negro's appreciation of real talent and merit, his demand for fair play, and his ardor for the best man wins and don't you come around here with no jive. . . . The Negro audience is extra-critical when it comes to music and won't accept anything second-rate."

Jam sessions provided affirmation for those at the top of their game and a formidable barrier to those trying to reach the highest levels. According to Count Basie, "The Rhythm Club sessions were a good way for a new musician to get himself some quick recognition if you were somebody with something special. And if you didn't [have something special] and didn't have any better sense than to go in there and tangle with them cats, that was the quickest way to get yourself embarrassed. They didn't have any mercy on upstarts in there." The point, however, was not to humiliate and discourage beginners but to spur them on by giving them a taste of the highest standards. As Mezzrow pointed out:

> These contests taught the musicians never to rest on their laurels, to keep on woodshedding and improving themselves. Dancers had the same kind of competitions, and so did most other kinds of entertainers. Many's the time some hoofer would be strutting his stuff in the alley outside the Lafayette Theater, with a crowd around him, and [tap dancer John] Bubbles would wander up and jump in the circle and lay some hot iron that lowrated the guys, then walk off saying, "Go on home and wrastle with that one, Jim." There wasn't any room for complacency. Bubbles wasn't just showing off. He was making that cat work harder.

For younger musicians still learning their craft, the trial by fire of the jam session was as much a part of their training as practicing scales. As trombonist Trummy Young once said, "If a guy came into town, [and] he could play—well, everybody was after this guy. Man, let's try to catch old so-and-so. . . . They'd invite him, 'Come out, man, you know.' And everybody'd get up there and take shots at him. Some of them we could handle and some of them we couldn't. But every time you do that you're sharpening your knife, see."

In this way, the after-hours jam session became an integral part of an aspiring musician's musical education. As Ralph Ellison has put it, the jam session was "the jazzman's true academy":

> It is here that he learns tradition, group techniques and style. For although since the twenties many jazzmen have had conservatory training and were well grounded in formal theory and instrumental technique, when we approach jazz we are entering quite a different sphere of training. . . .
>
> In this his instructors are his fellow musicians, especially the acknowledged masters, and his recognition of manhood depends upon their acceptance of his ability as having reached a standard which is all the more difficult for not having been rigidly codified. This does not depend upon his ability to simply hold a job but upon his power to express an individuality in tone. Nor is his status ever unquestioned, for the health of jazz and the unceasing attraction which it holds for the musicians themselves lies in the ceaseless warfare for mastery and recognition—not only among the general public, though commercial success is not spurned, but among their artistic peers. And even the greatest can never rest on past accomplishments, for, as with the fast guns of the old West, there is always someone waiting in a jam session to blow him literally, not only down, but into shame and discouragement.

The jam session academy was not for everyone. It did not test such crucial professional skills or specializations as sight-reading, leading a section, or the endurance required to be the high-note man in a trumpet section. Many successful dance band musicians, even in jazz-oriented organizations, made their reputations without ever having to improvise. Others, having found their professional niche, felt no need to subject themselves to continuous competition. But for the young soloist on the make, the late-night jam session scene was a necessity. Although the most celebrated sessions were held in New York and featured established stars, jam sessions could be found across the country and were just as much the province of the less well known and unemployed. At the margins of the profession and during difficult times, playing in a jam session provided the only tenuous link to professional status that a musician might have. Of the famous nightlife in Kansas City during the 1930s, trumpeter Buck Clayton has written: "The young musicians could be found jamming at the Union during the day. The unemployed musicians were to be found at night jamming at different clubs just to keep in shape to be ready when they did find a job, then at night the pros took over after they had finished their work in various clubs."

Bassist Al Hall remembers: "We had a session going at all times, all hours, you know. That was our life. We had nothing else to do. We didn't have employment, that's for sure! [laughs]. . . . It's the same as a soldier with a gun. If he doesn't get to shoot it, he isn't much of a soldier, and an instrumentalist with an instrument [who] doesn't get to play it isn't a musician, right?"

Challenging the "No-Talent Guys"

"In those days we had several means of access to experience," writes Dizzy Gillespie, neatly summing up the division of his professional world into two complementary spheres. "Big bands were one, jam sessions were another. I tried to get plenty of both." As a teenager in Philadelphia, he observed cutting contests between Roy Eldridge and Rex Stewart from the sidelines, too intimidated to participate. But during his first restless year in New York as a professional in 1937, Gillespie remembers going to "ten or twelve places a night" to jam: "We'd go down to the Village to a lot of places, then finish off uptown: George's in the Village; the Yeah Man, and the Victoria, the Britwood [sic], and Hollywood on 116th Street; Smalls', the Big Apple and another place over on 111th Street. We'd play at the 101 Ranch on 139th Street, and then Monroe's Uptown House and Dicky Wells' [not the trombonist]."

The number of clubs reflects not only Gillespie's enthusiasm and determination, but also the practical need to keep one step ahead of the union "walking representative," whose thankless task was to patrol clubs, fining any performers not officially working under contract: "We'd go in a place and find out if the union man had been there. If he hadn't been there, we'd cut that one aloose and go to someplace where he'd already been and play there. 'Cause if he'd catch us there, he'd want to fine you. Fifty or a hundred dollars, that was a whole lot of money—and fine the whole band too—but they'd run you out most of the time."

The clubs Gillespie mentions were nightclubs, some operating during conventional hours but most flourishing "after hours"—after the 4 A.M. curfew nominally enforced on New York nightlife. Jamming was far more casual in these circumstances. Clubs like the Brittwood (conveniently located on the same block as the Savoy Ballroom) and Monroe's Uptown House provided a good place for "lightweights"—musicians of modest talent or fledgling reputations—to gain invaluable experience sitting in with a small combo. Some, like Smalls' Paradise, were well established, featuring elaborate entertainment, music, and dancing, and regularly recommended by the New York police to white people looking for a "safe" place in Harlem. Others were far less prepossessing—basement rooms or "holes" (in Dicky Wells's phrase), often accessible only through a dingy boiler room.

In such environments, musicians rubbed elbows not only with fellow musicians, but also with entertainers from all areas of show business, gamblers and racketeers, and big spenders coming up to Harlem from downtown. These were the "night people"—a "conglomeration of artists, taxi drivers, . . . radio people, prostitutes, actors, musicians, adventurers and entertainers" who formed the natural constituency for the breakfast dances of Harlem and Kansas City. "The average musician hated to go home in those days," Sonny Greer, longtime drummer with Duke Ellington, remembered. "He was always seeking some place where someone was playing something he ought to hear. Ten o'clock in the morning, someone would come by and say, 'Man, they're jamming at so-and-so's,' and over he'd go."

While nightclubs and after-hours clubs were nominally open to all paying customers and not explicitly designated as the province of professionals, musicians still imposed on them a fine sense of professional hierarchy that outsiders or naive newcomers violated at their own risk. "When you were in this category you played into this club," according to Jo Jones. "You did not go over here and play into this club until you qualified. Then you begin to move up and you sit in over here." Jones was not above acting as the enforcer of this stern dictum. In a moment now celebrated in the pretentious central image of the movie *Bird*, he threw his high-hat cymbal on the floor of the Reno Club in Kansas City to make it clear to a struggling teenaged Charlie Parker that he most emphatically did *not* belong—yet.

But for the most part, musicians preferred subtler means of putting an interloper in his place. It was far more to the point if the untalented or insufficiently trained realized on their own that they were in over their heads. So jam sessions gradually accumulated special musical procedures to be called into play whenever someone's "qualifications" needed to be challenged.

One of the simplest and most effective of these devices was to play in keys outside the ken of ordinary musicians. Self-taught musicians typically felt most comfortable playing in a handful of favorite keys, and at the lower reaches of the profession nothing more might be required. But a rising professional was sure to encounter situations that demanded a fluid grasp of almost any key: accompanying singers, reading difficult charts for floor shows, or playing tunes with sudden, distant modulations, such as "Body and Soul" or "Cherokee." Mastery of key signatures bristling with sharps—especially foreign to those playing E-flat and B-flat wind instruments (musicians used to call them "oriental keys")—was mandatory for advancement in an increasingly competitive and specialized field.

The irascible and flamboyant pianist Willie "the Lion" Smith, who like many pianists learned the trick of transposing while accompanying cabaret singers in their favorite keys, was particularly well known for insisting that the young musicians who dared to jam with him negotiate his whimsical modulations to unfamiliar keys. Benny Carter used to try to cheat, pulling out his mouthpiece to force the tune from A or E to an easier key. This dodge earned him a scolding from Smith. "After I finally had gotten a little better control of the keys," Carter recalled, "he would just play in any key. You never knew what he was going to do. He caught himself sometimes trying to trick you, you know, just for fun. And it was a very valuable musical experience for me." After listening to Smith play at a Harlem nightclub for several months, the teenaged Rex Stewart finally worked up the nerve to ask to sit in:

> "Mr. Smith, I know this tune. Would it be okay for me to play it with you?" The Lion growled, "Yeah, kid, if you know your tonics." For all the musical education I had had by then, I didn't have a clue what he meant by "tonics." Nevertheless, I hopped on the stand. Then I found out as Willie played on, each chorus in another key: [A flat to A natural,] B flat to B natural, and so on. But I struggled on. . . . And I'll never stop thanking Willie "the Lion" Smith for his important part in my musical education.

At the Rhythm Club and at various other small clubs in Harlem and on 52nd Street, harmonic obstacles were a way of keeping the unqualified at arm's length while providing a useful challenge for those with the talent and courage to remain behind. Modulating up a half step each chorus was one widespread device. Another was choosing a tune in an unfamiliar key and a brisk tempo:

> If a guy came in [to Monroe's Uptown House] that played very bad or wasn't adequate enough on his horn, instead of playing something in B-flat that he knew (and we knew he played it in B-flat) we would play it in B-natural—

and at a faster pace—and this guy would say, "They did it to me again." And he'd pack up his instrument and leave. You see what I mean. He'd go home and practice it in B-natural. [Laughter] He'd come back and we've moved it up to C-sharp or something like that, you see. [Laughter] We kept doing this, and these guys also made us more proficient, you know . . . We didn't actually discourage musicians. But if you was gonna sit in, we didn't want you to be half, you know, I don't want to use the other half of that word! [Laughter]

"Guys used to come in when we were playing at the Onyx Club," remembered drummer Cozy Cole, "and want to sit in, and Stuff Smith would tell them right quick, 'No, don't jump up on this bandstand if you can't play, 'cause we're liable to play anything.' "

Devices of this sort were sometimes part of a game of one-upmanship. Fletcher Henderson early on helped to position his band at the top of the profession by pitching his arrangements in intimidating keys. Count Basie vividly recalled one humiliating occasion in the 1930s when he sat near the bandstand at the Roseland Ballroom to listen to the Henderson band. The bandleader noticed Basie and slyly asked him to sit in as pianist while he ran a quick errand:

> I got up there and looked at the sheet music on the piano *and everything I saw was in D or B-natural or something like that!*
>
> So I just got right back down and sat on those little steps where I had been in the first place. Then I realized that Fletcher could see every move I had made because he was looking out through the window of a little room that must have been used as a control booth during broadcasts and he was laughing his can off. . . . But I didn't fool around up there because I knew that pretty soon there was going to be a piano solo in one of those hard keys, and something like that was the last thing I wanted to get tangled up with.

Henderson's most famous alumnus, Hawkins, used unusual keys to particularly devastating effect. One night at Kelly's Stable in 1941, while Hawkins was backstage enjoying a drink of Calvert's, he allowed a "phalanx of tenors," including Ben Webster, Corky Corcoran, and Lester Young, to jam on a blues in B-flat. When he emerged, he called for the blues in G-flat. "He lost quite a few people at that point," remembers bassist George Duvivier. When he called for "East of the Sun" in B-natural, "he lost *everybody*." The jam session ended with Webster sighing loudly and slamming his saxophone case shut. Even the famous show-down with Lester Young in Kansas City in the early 1930s conformed to this pattern, if the testimony of Count Basie is to be taken seriously. "I don't know anything about anybody challenging Hawkins in the Cherry Blossom that night. . . . The way I remember it, Hawk just went on up there and played around with them for a while, and then when he got warmed up, he started calling for them bad keys."

Jam sessions therefore encouraged techniques, procedures, attitudes—in short, the essential components of a musical language and aesthetic—quite distinct from what was possible or acceptable in more public venues. Admittedly, the results were not always dramatically different. As surviving recordings from Minton's and Monroe's demonstrate, sometimes the only difference between what one might hear in a jam session and in a ballroom or public nightclub was that the jam session soloists played for as long as they liked without fear of interruption. When established stars like Benny Goodman or Count Basie dropped in, the house band was deferential, careful to accommodate their tastes (some musicians even brought their own rhythm sections with them when they went jamming). But where the restless energy and imagination of ambitious young progressives were given free rein, a startling new music took shape. The fast tempos and deliberately convoluted harmonic progressions, obstacles thrown up to disorient the "no-talent guys"; the pursuit of virtuosity for its own sake; the shift of focus away from the mass audience to the personal struggle of musicians to master the art of improvisation: all fed directly into the emergent bebop style.

Minton's

Until 1942 these innovations remained in the shadowy backstage world of the jazz community. It was musicians' business, not intended for public consumption. In retrospect, it is easy to see how the pattern emerged, and tempting to imagine young bebop musicians plotting their revolution step by step. But the components of the bebop style either emerged from the pressures on professional musicians to "advance" in predictable directions—range, speed, facility with chromatic harmony—or from idiosyncratic, even accidental discoveries, whose implications were not clear until much later, when the conditions for transmuting the jam session into a distinct genre emerged.

The development of modern jazz drumming by Kenny Clarke—the first piece of the bebop musical puzzle to fall into place—provides a telling example of how musical ideas and personnel tended to drift from the public sphere to the private world of the jam session, where an experimental bent could be given more latitude. By the late 1930s Clarke was already an experienced big-band drummer, content with his specialized professional role. "I always concentrated on accompaniment," he told an interviewer. "I thought that was the most important thing, my basic function as a drummer, and so I always stuck with that. And I think that's why a lot of the musicians liked me so much, because I never show off and always think about them first." He began studying arrangements carefully, playing rhythms along with the brass: "I knew exactly what they were playing because I saw it on the music, and I put what I thought was a good support for them, a special passage." Where there were "holes" in the arrangement, he filled them with drum interpolations. This practice provoked criticism from musicians used to a steady rhythmic foundation. "They said, 'Oh, that little guy is crazy. He's always breaking up the tempo.' But I stuck with it. I liked it, so I wasn't about to change something that I had found, you know."

But Clarke's most important innovation—shifting the pulse away from the bass drum to the ride cymbal—was more fortuitous:

> It just happened sort of accidentally. . . . We were playing a real fast tune once with Teddy Hill—"Old Man River," I think—and the tempo was too fast to play four beats to the measure, so I began to cut the time up. But to keep the same rhythm going, I had to do it with my hand, because my foot just wouldn't do it. So I started doing it with my hand, and then every once in a while I would kind of lift myself with my foot, to kind of boot myself into it. . . .
>
> When it was over, I said, "Good God, was that ever hard." So then I began to think, and say, "Well, you know, it worked. It worked and nobody said anything, so it came out right. So that must be the way to do it." Because I think if I had been able to do it [the old way], it would have been stiff. It wouldn't have worked.

Clarke's technique of keeping a shimmering pulse on the ride cymbal, occasionally punctuated by vigorous accents on the bass and snare drums, earned him the onomatopoeic nickname Klook-mop, or Klook. It was greeted enthusiastically by some younger musicians, including band mate Dizzy Gillespie. But it angered one of Hill's veteran trombonists, who complained to Hill, "Man, we can't use 'Klook' because he breaks up the time too much." Hill reluctantly fired his drummer in 1940.

Ironically, Hill's own band failed shortly thereafter, and the former bandleader took on new responsibilities at a Harlem club called Minton's Playhouse. Minton's Playhouse was started in 1938 by Henry Minton, a tenor saxophonist and the first black delegate to Local 802 of the musicians' union. It was located on 118th Street, adjacent to the Hotel Cecil, a frequent temporary residence of musicians passing through New York. In late 1940, to bolster sagging business, Minton hired Hill to organize the music policy for his club. As Clarke remembered, "After he became manager of this club, he came and got me. He said, 'Now, Kenny, I'm managing this place. I want you to be the bandleader. You can drop all the bombs, all the re-bop and the boom-bams you want to play, you can do it here.' So I said, 'Oh, this is wonderful,' you know! [laughter]" For the remainder of the group, Clarke chose trumpeter Joe Guy, who had been left unemployed by the collapse of Coleman Hawkins's orchestra; bassist Nick Fenton (also a veteran of the Hawkins band); and a local pianist named Thelonious Monk.

Minton's was an understated place: a bar in front, a back room for music, tables with white linen tablecloths and flowers in glass vases. But it offered a kind of sanctuary. Like the Rhythm Club, it was intended primarily for the use of professional musicians. Because of Minton's connections to the union, musicians could sit in without fear of being fined by the union delegate for playing without pay. Unlike many other jam session spots, the self-described "Showplace of Harlem" was a legitimate nightclub, staying open only until the official curfew of 4 A.M. It was ideal for musicians working with a big band at a theater like the Apollo or the Paramount, as they could drop by after their job was through for the night (which might be as early as eleven o'clock). It was also popular with out-of-work musicians (a category that, by 1942, included what one might call the *deliberately* underemployed—those like Parker or Gillespie who used their time in between jobs to explore the jam session scene). Everybody was welcome on Monday night, the traditional night off—dubbed "Celebrity Night" because Hill invited the entire cast of the Apollo Theatre for a buffet dinner. As always, the evening culminated in a jam session. "Teddy Hill treated the guys well," according to Gillespie. "He didn't pay them much money—I never got paid—but he treated the guys nicely. There was always some food there for you." The music and socializing would go on until closing time, when Hill would shatter the cozy ambience by lowering a garishly bright streetlight that he had installed on a rope for just this purpose.

Even though it barely paid a living wage, Minton's was a pleasant and stimulating environment in which to work. Like most jam session locales, it provided Clarke with the space to refine new and unusual techniques and the opportunity to parade these skills before his peers nightly. Fragments of this phase of Clarke's career have been preserved, almost by accident, on acetate recordings from Minton's made on a portable machine by jazz enthusiast Jerry Newman in 1941. They include one of the most remarkable documents of early bebop—the electrifying interaction of Clarke and guitarist Charlie Christian on the tune "Topsy" (later retitled "Swing to Bop" when issued on LP).

Christian—whose premature retirement from public performance in mid-1941 at age twenty-five robbed jazz of one of its most compelling voices (he was dead of tuberculosis by 1942)—provided the perfect foil for Clarke's disjunct rhythms. Thanks to the timely intervention of John Hammond, who convinced Benny Goodman to hire the guitarist in 1939, Christian had bypassed the usual phase of struggle for a young black musician, leaping directly from regional obscurity to a position of high visibility in the Goodman Sextet. Throughout much of 1940 and early 1941, the Goodman band remained headquartered in New York, leaving Christian free to sit in regularly with the band at Minton's.

Although not a progressive from the standpoint of harmony, the guitarist's sense of rhythm was startlingly supple. Most soloists of the time (Hawkins certainly among them) relied heavily on the unflagging momentum of the underlying dance pulse, even as they actively resisted it in places with syncopation. Christian's lines dissolved the usual hierarchical distinctions between strong beats and weak beats (and strong and weak *parts* of the beat), allowing him to shift effortlessly between sharply contrasting rhythmic grooves. Although the downbeat retained its overall structural importance as a frame of reference—it was still the place at which the listener (or dancer) begins to count "one, two, three, four"— Christian treated the rhythmic flow as an undifferentiated stream of eighth notes that could be shaped instantaneously into unpredictable patterns. These deliberate discontinuities invited a rhythmic partnership with Clarke's drumming. Within the confines of Minton's, Clarke and Christian quickly adopted a mode of playing that owed little to the chugging 4/4 foundation of dance music.

The final chorus of "Topsy" (music example 29) begins with an unexpected example of synergism: Christian's emphatic off-beat entrance matched precisely by Clarke's snare drum accents. (This kind of telepathic empathy happens more often than one might think in jam sessions.) From this point, Clarke retreats to a more supportive role, tending to

EX. 29.
"Swing to Bop" ["Topsy"] (c. 1941), Charlie Christian solo with Kenny
Clarke drum accompaniment, final chorus, mm. 1–17.

emphasize the "backbeat" (beats 2 and 4) with accents on the snare. But
as Christian raises the temperature with disorienting cross-rhythms in
the remarkable passage that begins in measure 9, Clarke responds in kind
on the snare, returning to the downbeat just as Christian does in measure
13. "Topsy" shows Clarke to still be a sensitive accompanist, but now,
outside the fixed structures of the big-band context, he is free to engage
in an open-ended and continually evolving dialogue.

    At the time all this was essentially an ingenious form of musical exercise, delighting the crowd at Minton's, but not readily extendable to any other venue. Still, Clarke's self-advertisement of his formidable skills eventually paid off in more conventional terms. The veteran swing drummer Sidney Catlett began telling other drummers, "Man, that little cat is modern, if you listen to him." According to Clarke, "That was the biggest sendoff. That was the stamp I needed." When Catlett, who had been working in Louis Armstrong's dance band, decided to leave to join Benny Goodman, he took Clarke aside, set up his drums, and taught him Armstrong's entire repertory. Needless to say, Clarke got the job—leaving Armstrong shaking his head, wondering how Clarke learned his parts so fast.

For the most part, bebop pioneers were drawn to the jam sessions as the arena in which they could work out their audacious ideas, but they did not—yet—think of these ideas as an end in themselves. The immediate goal was still to get a job—a job that would, with any luck, be artistically rewarding, financially remunerative, or both, but in any case would not simply be a jam session. Not until jam sessions (or something like them) moved into the public arena and became a viable source of income, and it became clear that the dance bands offered neither acceptable working conditions nor opportunities for advancement, did some young musicians begin to move, tentatively, toward the idea of creating a new genre of music.

For a few musicians, however, the pressure to make it in the music business was less urgent. Thelonious Monk was not, like so many others, a recent migrant to New York struggling to gain a foothold in the big city; he was a native New Yorker, living at home with his family. Although Monk was born in Rocky Mount, North Carolina, in 1923, when he was still a small child, his family had moved to an apartment on West 63rd Street in the San Juan Hill district of Manhattan. He left New York for several years as the accompanist for a touring evangelist, but by the late 1930s he was back in the city, playing "every kind of job you can think of . . . non-union jobs, $20 a night, seven nights a week; and then the boss might fire you at any time and you never got your money."

For Monk, the job at Minton's was not so much a stepping-stone to the big time as the fulfillment of his own, more modest ambitions: "I wanted to play my own chords. I wanted to create and invent on little jobs." Minton's became a second home, where he was free to work out his ideas on the piano without interruption. "He'll come in here anytime and play for hours with only a dim light," Teddy Hill noted in 1948. "Many times he's gone on so long I've had to come back and plead with him to quit playin' the piano so I could close up the place." Asked about Monk's reputation for eccentricity, Hill mused: "One reason for it, I guess, is that he was living at home with his own people. Maybe if the guy had to stand on his own two feet it might have been different. But knowing that he had a place to eat and sleep, that might have had a lot to do with it. Dizzy had to be on time to keep the landlady from saying, 'You don't live here any more.' Monk never had that worry."

It was during his first few years at Minton's that Monk began composing in earnest: "'Round Midnight," "Ruby My Dear," "Epistrophy," and "Well, You Needn't" are among the tunes that date from this period. His compositions attracted the attention of Minton's clientele and drew him at least tangentially into the orbit of the large dance orchestras. When Joe Guy joined Cootie Williams in 1942, he brought several Monk tunes into the band's repertory: "Epistrophy," a collaboration between Monk and Kenny Clarke, was used by Williams as his radio theme song and recorded by him in April 1942 under the title "Fly Right," with Guy as the main soloist. In the same year, Monk was hired briefly by Lucky Millinder, apparently at the urging of Gillespie, who was working with the band at the time: "He got me hired on piano so's he could be around me."

But Monk had a more profound influence on the small coterie of musicians at Minton's. He introduced them to the half-diminished chord, then still a "freaky sound" on or beyond the boundary of most musicians' knowledge. Modern jazz theory places the half-diminished chord securely within a conventional tonal framework, as the characteristic form of ii^7 in the minor mode. Its interpolation into a major context (i.e., substituting for the ii^7 in a ii^7–V^7 progression) provides a way to "borrow" the lowered sixth and seventh degrees from the minor scale. Bebop musicians learned to use the chord that way, in chains of chromatically related ii^7–V^7 progressions. But for Monk, it was a sonority that had a certain fascination in and of itself. "The first time I heard [the chord]," Gillespie remembers, "Monk showed it to me, and he called it a minor-sixth chord with a sixth in the bass. . . . What Monk called an E-flat-minor sixth chord with a sixth in the bass, the guys nowadays call a C-minor seventh flat five." One can see this ambiguity by comparing the striking opening bars of "'Round Midnight" as it is usually parsed today in jazz "fake books" (music example 30) with the way that Monk usually played it (music example 31, drawn from a 1957 recording).

EX. 30.
'Round Midnight," standard "fake book" arrangement, mm. 1–3.

EX. 31.
'Round Midnight" (1957), Thelonious Monk solo piano, mm. 1–3.

The ultimate fascination of the half-diminished chord lay in the tritone buried in its interior. Monk's harmonic language was centered around the tritone: it showed up in his fondness for augmented chords, whole-tone scales, and the infamous "flatted fifth." Although this territory had already been explored by a number of jazz musicians, including Coleman Hawkins, Monk's compositions isolated the characteristic sonority of the tritone more systematically than any music then in circulation. In addition to writing his own compositions, Monk also reharmonized jam session standards. Indeed, many of his "originals," like "The Theme" and "Rhythm-a-Ning," were transparent reworkings of "I Got Rhythm," the hoariest of the jam session warhorses. But in the process of translating these tunes to his own harmonic sensibilities, Monk radically defamiliarized them.

One example, vividly caught by a Jerry Newman recording, demonstrates the uses to which Monk's unorthodox harmonies were typically put. The tune is "Sweet Lorraine," a 1928 pop song that had gained new currency on the basis of a 1940 Nat "King" Cole recording. Monk starts off the tune with an unaccompanied eight-bar introduction (music example 32). The melody is faithfully stated, but the harmonization veers off in unexpected directions—sometimes by the tritone substitutions that eventually became standard practice (e.g., the A-flat[7] and D-flat[7] chords in measures 1–2), sometimes by idiosyncratic chromatic inter-

EX. 32.
"Sweet Lorraine" (c. 1941), Thelonious Monk introduction, mm. 1–8.

polations (measures 6–8). Monk is joined for the tune statement proper by co-conspirator Joe Guy and by an unidentified bassist. The bassist may have been Nick Fenton, but he was more likely an interloper, to judge by his almost comical struggle to find a foothold in Monk's slippery harmonies. After thirty-two bars, this fruitful chaos is over. The drummer enters, and order is restored, just in time for the first of several instrumentalists to begin their solos over more conventional harmonic accompaniment.

Monk's approach proved to be an ideal update of an old trick: the harmonic barrier to keep out the "unqualified." It could take the form of Monk's compositions, guaranteed to be familiar only to Minton's regulars. Or it could involve imaginative reharmonization. While working through chords on the roof of the Cotton Club, Dizzy Gillespie and Milt Hinton used to plan their strategy for the coming night at Minton's: "Let's change the changes to 'I Got Rhythm,' and we'll play B-flat to D-flat to G-flat to F. . . . When we go in there, I won't say anything— I'll just stomp off and you'll go through these changes with me and we'll blow, and these cats don't know the changes and they can't get in." Danny Barker only joined in on occasion: "I couldn't see going up there and wasting energies on something not commercial." But he was interested enough to go to Minton's to hear the results:

[Monk] generally started playing strange introductions going off, I thought to outer space, hell knows to where. . . . Somewhere in Monk's intro there was the melody of the song to be played. In Minton's there was complete quiet: very little talking, no glasses clinking, no kinds of noises. [Note: This is contradicted by the few existing recordings, which contain a good deal of background noise.] Everybody intense in observing and figuring out the music and the behavior of the players, especially of the musicians who dared to jump into the arena. Those who dared and played . . . were now free to talk and join the small, but gradually building bebop fraternity.

In this context, the elements of the bop style took shape. Monk's reharmonizations provided a focus for harmonic exploration and laid the foundation for a new repertory. Dizzy Gillespie continued to focus and refine his virtuoso style, which added to his luster as a featured soloist: the results can be heard plainly in the blisteringly fast double-time passage on his solo in the 1942 recording of "Jersey Bounce" with Les Hite (music example 33).

Gillespie also took charge of developing a new sense of ensemble in the rhythm section. According to Kermit Scott, "Diz was there *every night*. And he would get *on* drummers, man. He'd get back there—say, 'man, play boot-d'-ding, boot-d'-ding.' They was playing another kind of way, man, and he'd tell them how to play the cymbal because our kind of swing was a little different." The sharper young musicians, like Howard McGhee, could tell the difference:

EX. 33.
"Jersey Bounce" (1942), Dizzy Gillespie solo, mm. 1–9.

That was about the best rhythm section in them days to be had. . . . 'Cause I was playing with Kirk and he had Johnny Young on piano, and he's a damn good piano player; Booker Collins was the bass player—fair; drummer—fair. They wasn't playing, like, "ch'bop" [imitating smooth bop groove]; they wasn't playing no shit like that. They'd just play "bang, bang, bang, bang, bang, bang," you know, all the way.

I mean, 4/4 is all right—it's for people when they're dancing. But for solo work, it just doesn't swing, man; it leaves you like you got to be right there on the beat all the time, and that ain't the way music is supposed to be played. You're supposed to play music whatever way you feel, and if it doesn't entail that kind of rhythm section, you don't need it.

[In small combos] you have more freedom. Because if you played something a drummer could fit in things behind it and so forth. So you do that enough times and you got something happening. But with a dance band, if they wasn't dancing, what do you play when they play four beats to the bar?

McGhee recalls a conversation in the early 1940s with Roy Eldridge as the two shared a taxi to Harlem. Eldridge, who had been challenged by Gillespie in cutting contests, was baffled by the rapidly changing style:

He said, "Hey, Maggie, do you really dig this?" I said, "Yeah, I dig it, Roy. It's something new, it's something a little different from what has been played." And he said, "Well, I don't dig it." I said, "Yeah, I can understand you saying that. I mean, because you done put your foundation down, and you got to what you got going." And I say, "Dizzy's *playing*, man, I tell you, I can't say nothing wrong with what he's doing. . . . You heard Charlie Parker?" He says, "I *really* don't understand him." I say, "Yeah, that's what I'm talking about. You really don't *understand*. . . . "

See, [musicians like Eldridge] had come up in an era [with] Louis Armstrong and all the guys that played back in those days. They figured, well, if they played a little bit more than that, that they *had* something. But that wasn't the idea of playing bop. Bop, you had to *know*—not *feel*, you had to *know* what you were doing. . . .

Like Charlie Parker—I think the thing that happened to him, he came out to play with people and he didn't know music, period. He didn't know "Body and Soul" and all those things that had chord changes to it. So he tried to play and everybody laughed at him. So he went back home and stayed in the house about three months and learned all the changes and all the things, so when he came back out he knew what he was doing. And that's what you had to do in bebop, was to *know* what you were doing.

Monroe's Uptown House

All the attention given to Minton's in the mythology of bebop has tended to obscure the importance of any other venue. But the band at Monroe's Uptown House deserves no less to be called, in pianist Allen Tinney's words, "the nucleus of bop." Minton's was a comfortable but unglorified musicians' hangout, offering little to those not part of the inner circle. The Uptown House was heir to a long tradition of late-night Harlem entertainment extending back to the glory days of Prohibition. Located at 198 West 134th Street, it lay at the heart of the nightlife district dominated to the south by the Apollo Theatre on 125th Street and to the north by the Renaissance Ballroom on 138th Street and the Cotton Club (closed since 1935) and the Savoy Ballroom on Lenox Avenue, just above 140th Street. Smalls' Paradise, a posh nightclub dating back to 1925 and still open in the early 1940s, when a teenaged Malcolm X worked there as a waiter, lay just around the block on Seventh Avenue and 135th.

Since the mid-1920s, the area between 133rd and 135th Streets in particular had been a favorite for speakeasies and small nightclubs designed to attract curious white pleasure-seekers from downtown. Such clubs as the Nest Club on 133rd and Pods' and Jerry's on 132nd offered a lively, more intimate alternative to the larger venues, one that cashed in heavily on the image of Harlem as a round-the-clock playground. The sole purpose of these clubs, according to Malcolm X, was "to entertain and jive the white night crowd to get their money":

> Especially after the nightclubs downtown closed, the taxis and black limousines would be driving uptown, bringing those white people who never could get enough of Negro *soul*. The places popular with these whites ranged all the way from the big locally famous ones such as Jimmy's Chicken Shack, and Dickie Wells', to the little here-tonight-gone-tomorrow private clubs, so-called, where a dollar was collected at the door for "membership." Inside every after-hours spot, the smoke would hurt your eyes. Four white people to every Negro would be in there drinking whisky from coffee cups and eating fried chicken. The generally flush-faced white men and their makeup-masked, glittery-eyed women would be pounding each other's backs and uproariously laughing and applauding the music. A lot of the whites, drunk, would go staggering up to Negroes, the waiters, the owners, or Negroes at tables, wringing their hands, even trying to hug them, "You're just as good as I am—I want you to know that!"

Whites were encouraged to feel that they had stumbled onto an all-night party—an illusion that was carefully nurtured by the seasoned professionals who staffed the joints. As Danny Barker describes it, a certain amount of play-acting was involved:

> I first saw the drama cleverly enacted at the old Nest Club, where there was not much action until after the big joints closed at the curfew time. . . . It was a night when the place was empty. Everybody sat around like half asleep. At the door upstairs there was Ross the slick doorman. When he rang three loud rings on the upstairs door buzzer (it rang loud), it meant some live prosperous-looking people, a party, were coming in.
>
> Like jacks out of a box the band struck up *Lady be Good.* Everybody went into action; the band swinging, waiters beating on trays, everybody smiling and moving, giving the impression the joint was jumping. . . . The unsuspecting party entered amid finger-popping and smiling staff. ('Make believe we're happy.') This was kept up until the party was seated and greeted and their orders taken. Then on came the singers, smiling and moving; then another singer, a dancer. Then it was off to the races—action—'Let's get this money.' "

By the late 1930s Harlem nightclubs were visibly in decline. On March 19, 1935, the rumor that a black teenager was being beaten sparked a night of violent rioting, which confirmed in most New Yorkers' minds the decline of Harlem from the center of exotic nightlife—"America's Casbah"—to a dangerous slum. The larger clubs, such as the Cotton Club, either closed or relocated downtown. At the same time, an alternative strip of jazz-oriented nightclubs emerged on 52nd Street, prompting some black musicians to wonder whether the widely publicized dangers of wandering through Harlem at night were simply a ruse to frighten white customers away from Harlem after-hours clubs to a more convenient midtown location. For whatever reason, by the mid-1940s the center of gravity had gradually shifted away from Harlem to 52nd Street. But during the early years of bebop, enough Harlem clubs remained in operation to provide the adventurous with late-night entertainment and musicians with sporadic employment. Among the most prominent of these was Monroe's Uptown House.

The owner of the Uptown House, Clark Monroe, was a "man about town" who harbored ambitions to become a major nightclub operator. Monroe's roots were in the entertainment business: at one time he had worked as a tap dancer. "The guys used to kid him a great deal about that," remembers Leonard Gaskin. "We used to call him a 'one-leg dancer,' because he had a couple of one-foot licks." Like his younger brother

Jimmy, who dazzled Billie Holiday into marrying him in 1941 ("he was the most beautiful man I'd laid eyes on since Buck Clayton"), Clark was a handsome man, known locally as "the Dark Gable." "He was an outspoken, dapper, colorful dude, and one that the women loved, because he was a handsome guy. He had a way about him. He was really a ladies' man. The fellows seemed to like him too." The feeling was mutual. "Clark Monroe had a warm feeling for musicians," Dizzy Gillespie has said. Like Henry Minton, he would greet them warmly, offer them a bite to eat, and otherwise create a sense of community.

Monroe's gregarious nature not only made him the ideal host for an evening's entertainment, but also allowed him to ingratiate himself with the powers that could keep an enterprise of dubious legality in operation. The club was periodically raided, but only as a formality. "Clark was very business-like," according to Danny Barker. "He was in cahoots with the mob and the people who run that business. He was well liked." He was also shrewd enough to realize that his future lay outside of Harlem and ambitious enough to try to work his way into the new networks that were taking shape. Later, in the mid-1940s, he followed the flow of capital out of Harlem, opening a club on 52nd Street. But during the formative years of bebop, the center of his entrepreneurial energies was in the Uptown House.

Like most after-hours clubs, the Uptown House was an unprepossessing basement club with no awning or sign to attract the attention of passersby. It depended on the trade of those in the know: well-off socialites with a taste for adventure, professionals in the entertainment business and their hangers-on. Harlem may have become a more dangerous place, but women could still stroll the streets late at night in their mink coats. Movie stars like Lana Turner and John Garfield frequented the club, as did the musicians from prosperous white swing bands like Glenn Miller's or Harry James's. The club opened for business in the late evening, but things didn't really get rolling until the curfew hour of 4 A.M. approached. Closing time came when the last crowds dissipated, usually well past dawn.

The entertainment was more informal than the tightly choreographed shows of the larger cabarets. Singers and dancers, including female impersonators performing raunchy parodies of current popular songs, followed one another in a flexible, semi-improvisational format called ups (as in "You're up," "I'm up next"). The house band was expected to provide accompaniment for these acts, as well as to produce "some kind of noise" to keep the entertainment more or less continuous. Since musicians in particular made a habit of coming to the Uptown House after hours, the "noise" more often than not featured the patrons themselves. Monroe's became famous for its jam sessions, pitting established soloists from name bands against hungry up-and-comers. The famous musicians gave Monroe's its reputation, but the young upstarts gave it its energy. "Musicians used to go there and battle like dogs," remembered Budd Johnson. As Ray Abrams, a young Brooklyn saxophonist who eventually became part of the house band, recalled:

> When those guys came in to play, they wouldn't play one number or two numbers and get up and go. They'd be there all night long. And you know how it is when you're nineteen, twenty years old. You couldn't get rid of them sometimes! I've seen it happen up there where they're playing a number about this tempo [he taps a tempo of ♩ = 290], and the piano would change, like Bud [Powell] would get up and Duke [Jordan] would sit down. But the number is still going on! And the drummer has to go through all of that. And when they'd finish, man, they'd be soaking wet.

Because he knew he could count on the jazz community to enliven the proceedings on any given night for free, Monroe invested relatively little in music. The pool of musicians he drew upon were not highly competitive and unionized professionals, but local talent, teenagers mostly, willing to put up with the demanding schedule for the sake of breaking into the nightclub scene. Most had already found their way to his club, and as Monroe came to realize, they offered something quite different for relatively low cost.

One of these upstarts was Allen Tinney, whose family moved to New York in 1923, when he was only two. His interest in music came from his father, who was a professional saxophonist, but his early professional experience in the entertainment world came at the prompting of his stage-struck mother, who pushed Tinney and his siblings into parts as child dancers in numerous Broadway theatrical performances. Tinney started playing piano at an early age and was skilled enough to play in an onstage band in a Gershwin production as well as in various local dance pickup groups. For his nineteenth birthday in May 1940, Tinney went to Monroe's to celebrate, and there he was encouraged to sit in with the house band. Afterward, to his astonishment, Monroe asked him to join the house trio as the regular pianist. Tinney was working in a production of *Sing Out the News* at the time, and like the other entertainment professionals, he realized that he could come to Monroe's after his regular evening's work was finished.

Tinney's presence attracted other musicians his age to come into Monroe's to play. They came from Harlem, Brooklyn, and Newark, and included the trumpeter George Treadwell, the saxophonist Ray Abrams, and the drummer Max Roach. The trio regularly swelled to a seven- or eight-piece group, and Monroe, seeing the possibilities, asked Tinney to hire some of these musicians regularly. The pay was low—about two dollars a night. The paltry salary could be augmented by tips, which depending on the whim of Monroe's free-spending clientele, could be extravagant. "You had these people coming in from everywhere," remembers Leonard Gaskin, "and suppose they said to the trio, 'Play "Flying Home!,' " and this dude's got a little bread and throws you a $50 bill—you're making some bread!" But such windfalls could not be counted on. If any of the musicians could get a job for higher wages, they took it. The band personnel was shuffled and reshuffled almost every night, although enough of a core remained to provide some continuity. In this way, the young New Yorkers gained some valuable experience, and drifters like Charlie Parker found their way into a stimulating and refreshingly unstructured environment.

Tinney's importance lay in imposing order on this chaos: "When I put my foot in the door, things started to happen because I always like organization. I didn't care if I had one guy playing, I wanted him to play something definite. . . . We would play different melodies on the same chord changes as an existing melody on top, which would make it our song now. We'd put some sort of—not an obbligato, but you could use it as an obbligato to the actual melody. . . . And as everything became organized, and the guys that came in would learn the things that we were doing . . . it was really no more of a jam session."

The group began developing its own repertory, with Tinney as its arranger. They listened closely to the light, propulsive swing of the Count Basie band: "When 'Every Tub,' and 'Swinging the Blues,' and later 'One O'Clock Jump' came out, we wore them out listening to them. And we tried to emulate them." They applied this rhythmic sensibility to a careful selection of obscure tunes from the recent repertory of Artie Shaw ("Zigeuner," "This Time the Dream's On Me") and Duke Ellington ("Chocolate Shake" from *Jump for Joy*, "Main Stem," "Hayfoot, Strawfoot"), to popular songs with challenging chord progressions like "Cherokee" and "How High the Moon," and even to some early Monk compositions

("Well, You Needn't," "Epistrophy," "'Round Midnight"), brought up to Monroe's from Minton's after the four o'clock curfew. " 'How High the Moon' was a ballad, for crying out loud, until it was played there," according to Gaskin. "That's how the music was born. Looking for different tunes that were not conventional. . . . All those tunes were very strange, and we used to play them all in a muted, swinging way. And so that's where Dizzy heard of us, and Cootie and Monk and all of those other fellows, they heard of this little band, and they all came around to listen to it."

Another musician who had a hand in shaping the musical direction of the house band was a now-obscure cornetist named Victor Coulsen. Coulsen frequented Monroe's as early as 1940 and became a regular member of the band under Tinney's leadership. "He was really the innovator of our little ideas," Gaskin asserts. "He didn't have a big propelling tone, but gems would come out of that instrument." Aside from the 1944 session for Apollo Records led by Coleman Hawkins (see chapter 8), where he played in a three-man trumpet section, Coulsen never recorded, so it is impossible to know exactly what he sounded like. But all who heard him agree that he played with a delicate, understated tone, frequently with a mute, and that his musical ideas were finely shaped. "He didn't have a lot of range, I don't think," pianist Al Haig reflects. "His playing was rather impeccable in a way. He did what he wanted to do. He played a little bit like beginning Miles."

Coulsen was an introverted, enigmatic man who, as Tinney says ambiguously, "had a tendency to be very evil at times." He was a sharp dresser who, like Charlie Parker, enjoyed living on the fringe between legitimate professional life and the underworld of drug addicts and hustlers. Unlike Parker, he sank into that underworld before making his mark with his music. "He did have one problem," remembers Gaskin. "He was fooling around with the stuff at the time. That *had* to be a problem." Tinney was drafted into the army in 1943, and on his return to civilian life shortly after war, he was shocked to see that the dapper Coulsen had become a "wino." Nothing more is known of him.

Most of the other musicians at Monroe's were firmly grounded in family life. Ray Abrams, Leonard Gaskin, Cecil Payne, and Max Roach lived at home in Brooklyn with their parents and involved themselves in professional life only insofar as it suited them. They began playing in nonunion bands in Brooklyn, but soon were making the trip to Manhattan to sample the music. According to Gaskin, "Ray always had a piece of junk car, or Max's father used to take us in a Model T, or Model A, or something. And we'd all pile in and go to the city." Various nonunion engagements gave them a toehold in Manhattan musical life. Gaskin found a job at a small after-hours club called Covan's Morocco, a ground-floor brownstone on 133rd Street across from Dickie Wells's, and occasionally subbed at Monroe's. Abrams got a job at the 78th Street Tap-room, a tiny Upper West Side club that offered a floor show with dancers and comedians seven nights a week. There Clark Monroe, ever the extroverted impresario, made a big show of "conducting" the band. When Monroe found the drummer inadequate, Abrams recommended Max Roach. Charlie Parker also played in the band in 1942. After the conclusion of the job at three in the morning, the musicians would head to the Uptown House. "Naturally, we were eighteen, nineteen years old," remembers Abrams. "We didn't have nothing but energy and pep, vim and vigor, get up and go!"

The teenagers' families were understandably discomfited by this bohemian lifestyle, which lacked even the clear career path and tangible accomplishments of the dance band musician to compensate for the outlandish hours and disreputable company. Gaskin was enrolled at Brooklyn College, and his father had saved enough money for him to go on to Cornell University, but such ambitious plans seemed incompatible with staying up until eight in the morning night after night: "I was undecided about what I wanted to do. I knew I liked the music, but my parents weren't particularly keen, based on what they saw. These people were always in my house, and they all seemed to be, as they put it, 'ne'er-do-wells.' I'd get up in the afternoon, and they're angry! 'Why don't you do something decent with your life?!' "

But parental support, no matter how ambivalent, gave Gaskin and other young musicians the freedom to pursue their unorthodox and vaguely articulated musical goals: "We used to kid each other all the time: 'You actually think you'll amount to anything?' . . . Those of us who were natives, we didn't push, primarily because we didn't have anything to *prove*. . . . We were all people from established families. We weren't nomads. . . . As you look back, we were lucky because we had homes, so consequently if we were hungry, it was of our own choice."

Some of the experimentation was not for public consumption. "We used to have mental rehearsals, more or less, to try to screw each other up," remembers Gaskin. "We would try to play things in five, and think in five, and solo in five, and even seven. . . . We'd do this amongst ourselves. We used to do it every afternoon, as a matter of fact." But enough found its way into the music to make Monroe's a place for musicians in the know. "Actually, what we were doing was swinging so hard, it was ridiculous, man." Musicians—especially those who were not working regularly—made a habit of coming to Monroe's directly from Minton's.

Unfortunately, documentation of the band at Monroe's is nearly non-existent. Jerry Newman's recordings capture something of the flavor of the club, with appearances by Billie Holiday and Count Basie, and lengthy solos by Dizzy Gillespie (see chapter 4). A recently uncovered version of "Cherokee," featuring Charlie Parker soloing against a simple arranged backdrop, provides a pale reflection of Parker's moment of glory at the Savoy Ballroom with Jay McShann earlier in the year. Nothing else remains of the labors of Tinney's crew of youthful musicians.

Nevertheless, Monroe's Uptown House holds a place of special importance alongside Minton's in the early history of bebop. By 1942 the Harlem music scene was changing rapidly. The onset of the war and the continuing economic decline of Harlem forced the bebop pioneers to look downtown, to the clubs on 52nd Street, for similar opportunities. In the process, the music also changed—becoming more codified, more commodified, more sharply focused. But the sense of community nurtured in the jam sessions of Harlem helped to sustain musicians in the difficult transition ahead.

6 · WARTIME HIGHS—AND LOWS

Hard as it may be for Europeans and Asians to imagine, the world-consuming conflagration that was World War II is remembered in the United States with an unmistakable tone of nostalgia. It was, in Studs Terkel's phrase, "the good war." Those fighting the war faced a fascist enemy that was irremediably evil, throwing the virtues of American representative democracy into sharp relief. Victory, when it came, was clearcut and decisive. Of all the major combatants, only America was spared devastation. Life on the "home front" required sacrifice, but the kind that builds a sense of community, a putting aside of personal ambition in the service of a larger, nobler goal. Despite shortages and rationing, Americans enjoyed a new prosperity. As the war machinery swung into action, the unresolved crises of the Depression were superseded. "Hard Times, as though by some twentieth-century alchemy, were transmuted into Good Times," wrote Terkel later. "War was our Paracelsus."

For African Americans, the record was, predictably, mixed. On the one hand, the boom in the defense industries combined with a worsening labor shortage to give black workers their first firm foothold in the industrial economy. Opportunities for wages far beyond the reach of black men and women before 1940 lured hundreds of thousands to industrial centers, completing the transformation, begun several decades before, of the black population from a rural peasantry to an urban proletariat. In

Detroit or Los Angeles or Norfolk, black workers found access to skilled and semiskilled work that had been systematically closed off before. Where barriers still remained, Roosevelt's 1941 executive order creating the Fair Employment Practices Committee (FEPC) at least affirmed the principle that the federal government had a commitment to eliminate them. Moreover, these tangible advances were inseparable from a new strategy of assertiveness: it was A. Philip Randolph's bold threat to mobilize the black masses for a march on Washington in 1941 that wrested this commitment from the Roosevelt administration. "We shall not call upon our white friends to march with us," Randolph said. "There are some things Negroes must do alone."

Still, the dissonance between the democratic principles for which the war was being fought and the reality of entrenched bigotry at home was too great to ignore. Black advances were everywhere checked by racism, which enjoyed both the weight of social custom and the political protection of powerful southern Democrats. In a cold but simple calculation, the need to enlist the cooperation of industry and transportation in the war effort overrode any commitment on the part of the federal government, explicit or implicit, to change attitudes toward black labor. "There is no power in the world," announced the first head of the FEPC, "not even in all the mechanized armies of the earth, Allied and Axis, which could now force the Southern white people to the abandonment of the principle of social segregation." The FEPC became "the Wailing Wall for minorities, virtually powerless to act but handy as a safety valve."

While defense work brought African Americans new economic and social freedoms, it placed them cheek by jowl with transplanted white southerners, with the result that overburdened cities became new racial battlegrounds. At the same time, northern blacks who wanted to demonstrate their commitment to the country by fighting in the war found themselves subject to the extremes of Jim Crow in segregated boot camps in the Deep South. Interracial violence reached a peak in 1943: incidents of pushing and shoving on public transportation, gang warfare, brutalities against black soldiers in the South, explosive riots in Detroit and Harlem. Rising expectations (rooted in firm economic reality) collided with a bitter awareness of the hypocrisy of white America—its refusal to yield more than an inch of its racial privilege even as it spoke of fighting for freedom. It was during these years that militancy began to take root, that "the seeds of the protest movements of the 1950s and 1960s were sown." As James Baldwin later put it: "The treatment accorded the Negro during the Second World War marks, for me, a turning point in the Negro's relation to America. To put it briefly, and somewhat too simply, a certain hope died, a certain respect for white Americans faded."

The place of black musicians in this picture is not easy to draw. The several hundred musicians who staffed the major dance orchestras were anomalous in any reckoning of black labor in the early 1940s. By virtue of their special skills and their unique access to the broader white market, they constituted a tiny and privileged professional elite. They lived and worked in a world apart. While the mass of black people were undergoing an enormous and often painful economic transformation, black jazz musicians preserved, and even strengthened, a status they had earned years before. The vast changes in the economy and the social fabric affected them mainly insofar as it changed the nature of their audiences and the conditions of their work.

At the same time, their very visibility, prosperity, and social freedom made black musicians lightning rods for social change. During a time when the status of black men and women was threatening to change more rapidly than at any time since Reconstruction, successful black musicians became volatile symbols: rallying points of pride for the black community (and its white supporters) or targets for abuse and violence by those desperately trying to preserve the old order. The growing acceptability of jazz as an "indigenous American art" represented the first possibility. Duke Ellington's highly publicized appearance at Carnegie Hall in 1943 underscored the extent to which black achievement could gain the attention, if not the wholehearted embrace, of the establishment.[1] Innumerable instances of repression illustrated the second possibility. This explosive combination—the relatively successful and isolated world of the black musician, and the vulnerability of *any* black American to the slings of racial hatred—provided the unique and potent social subtext for bebop.

Business Not as Usual

The effects of the war on the music industry were unpredictable and contradictory. Some of the changes stimulated the business; others undercut its profitability. Still others added nightmarish logistical difficulties to the already complicated task of providing entertainment on a national scale. On the large scale, these factors tended to cancel out, creating a vigorous but unstable wartime prosperity for the business as a whole.

1. Hollywood, under pressure by the NAACP to improve the image of blacks in movies, turned to Ellington, Basie, and Armstrong during the war years (Naremore 1995, 103).

For individual musicians, however, each of the changes had a distinct impact, many of which proved especially significant for the young bebop musicians-to-be, active between 1942 and 1945.

During a time when many domestic industries were suspended or converted to war use, the music business enjoyed a relatively privileged position. Even as Americans set about the grim task of arming their country for a global struggle, they expected radio, popular song, motion pictures, and dance music to flow unimpeded through their usual channels. In many respects, musicians were allowed to go about their business undisturbed—although, as individuals, they were expected to report for military duty or to contribute voluntarily to morale-building efforts. Indeed, their services were more "essential" than before, as a safety valve for an overwrought populace. A former postmaster general declared, "Entertainment and sports are the greatest antidote against hysteria, and we need them to win the war!"

Industry observers had always expected the entrance of the country into war to redound to the benefit of the entertainment industry. A hardworking, well-paid population on the home front would need diversion. "Normal moral repressions may vanish," speculated *Down Beat* in the immediate aftermath of Pearl Harbor. "A fatalistic spending spree will appear. Flesh and blood entertainment will be most appealing. Money and jobs will be more plentiful. IT WILL BE OUR JOB TO KEEP EMOTIONS NORMAL AND HEALTHY."

After the initial shock over the Japanese sneak attack (which prompted many cities, fearing an imminent assault on the mainland, to institute curfews and blackouts), these predictions came true. Defense spending put money in the pockets of a broad swath of the population, and wartime shortages ensured that entertainment was one of the few things the money could be spent on. The result was a sharp increase in the earning power of dance bands, both black and white. The sheer numbers of people patronizing music venues, and the inflated prices they could afford or were willing to pay, remained unprecedentedly high for the duration of the war.

The shape of this artificially stimulated economy, however, was distorted by shortages of crucial raw materials needed for the war effort. The tentacles of war production reached into the most mundane activities and required the music industry, like every other phase of American life, to adjust and improvise. Shellac, for instance, the main ingredient of phonograph records, was needed for such military applications as bullet coatings and electric wiring. The main supply for shellac was East Asia.

Japanese advances early in the war caused the War Production Board to impose stringent quotas on its use by domestic industry. Thanks in large part to a vigorous campaign to recycle shellac from old, worn-out records, these restrictions never entirely choked off the production of new recordings—although, inevitably, the quality suffered. By the end of the war, records by the Billy Eckstine band on the DeLuxe label were made of such poor material that they felt like cardboard.

More far-reaching in its implications, for the general public as well as musicians, was the shortage of rubber. Like shellac, rubber had been imported from areas of the southwest Pacific cut off by early Japanese victories. Rubber was crucial for almost all aspects of a mechanized armed forces, and the government scrambled to speed up research and development into the production of synthetic substitutes. In the first years of the war, however, rubber remained in critically short supply. The public was encouraged to recycle rubber from everything from automobile tires to girdles, but both the quantity and quality of recovered material fell far short of demand. As a result, the first draconian government decrees for conservation of crucial materials fell on motorized travel. New tire production was stopped, and recapping tires forbidden. Gasoline rationing was instituted on the East Coast by May 1942, largely in response to a localized shortage of fuel, but also to conserve rubber. Rationing was extended to the nation as a whole by December (conveniently after the 1942 congressional elections), and a ban on "nonessential" driving instituted by January 1943, lasting until the following September.

These regulations had an immediate impact on dance orchestras. The elaborate network of one-nighters, reaching into the remotest areas of the country, had been designed with the inherent flexibility of automotive transport in mind. As travel by highway became more and more impractical, bands were forced to shift to fixed railroad routes, with predictably unsatisfactory results. Trains did not service many communities; their schedules were infrequent and inconvenient; and wartime routes were crowded, so that musicians often had to travel standing in the aisles, cradling their instruments. Nevertheless, trains did manage to deliver passengers and their cargo to the centers of most major cities, where the nation's most prestigious theaters and ballrooms were located. Managers and bookers quickly learned to tailor their bands' schedules to the exigencies of the moment, and they kept their intricate operations running smoothly throughout the most disruptive circumstances.

In any case, the very transportation difficulties that tied bandleaders' hands tended to concentrate their audiences into urban areas. To tap into the new prosperity, all that musicians needed to do was to place them-selves where the people were. "The best bet," *Down Beat* counseled its musician readers at the onset of the war, "is a hotel or nitery location in a business section of a metropolitan area. A spot which can be reached by street car, subway, bus or elevated." Urban entrepreneurs, it turned out, were all too eager to accommodate potential customers. Hotel ball-rooms expanded their music offerings, paying substantially above their usual fees as they competed for the best-known bands. Theaters displaced one-nighters as the most important (and profitable) leg of a band's itin-erary: the number of full-week engagements in major theaters grew from a peak of thirty to forty at the start of the war to over fifty by the end of 1942, while fees rose an estimated 25 percent over the same period. The "out-and-out seller's market" continued to be fueled by restless, entertainment-hungry urban crowds. When full-scale travel restrictions went into effect at the beginning of 1943, cities became "even more fan-tastically crowded on weekends."

The main beneficiaries of this windfall were the most prosperous white dance bands. As always, operators of nightclubs, ballrooms, and theaters were particularly eager to hire bands that already had a proven reputation for drawing large audiences. Glenn Miller, Harry James, Tommy Dorsey, and a handful of other "super-names" were able to pick and choose their jobs, reaping the benefits of inflated wages while effectively shielding themselves from the inconvenience of wartime travel. James, for example, avoided the first wave of gas rationing by spending the latter half of 1942 in midtown Manhattan: with successive jobs at the Hotel Astor, the Par-amount Theater, and the Lincoln Hotel, he didn't even have to leave the block. Bands in James's class continued to draw on their income from network radio contracts, while Hollywood beckoned with new opportu-nities for lucrative appearances in motion pictures. Buoyed by their af-fluence, the top tier of bands expanded their rosters, with bands like James's and Dorsey's employing as many as thirty instrumentalists and singers, including string sections.

For most of the war, demand outstripped supply. "Band bookers are constantly complaining these days re the shortage of orchestras available for bookings," reported *Variety* in the summer of 1942. These circum-stances might have sparked frenetic attempts to form new bands, as in the first years of the Swing Era—were it not for the draft. At the onset of the war, the preponderance of professional musicians were young men between the draftable ages of twenty-one to thirty-five. As the war ma-chine got into high gear, eligible musicians were continuously siphoned off into the military. Bandleaders struggled to keep their ranks constant. This manpower shortage led, among other things, to the infiltration of teenagers into professional ranks and to some increased opportunities for women (usually as members of "all-girl orchestras," such as the International Sweethearts of Rhythm). In addition, it fostered a gradual (if incomplete) erosion of the taboos against racially mixed bands.

As the pool of experienced professionals dwindled, the demand for skilled soloists and section men provoked a bidding war for their services. Government regulations tried to keep wage inflation under control, but ambitious musicians could evade wage limits simply by exchanging one job for another at a higher salary. Bandleaders were troubled by the unprecedented autonomy their employees enjoyed. "An independent attitude . . . is giving many a leader a constant headache," noted *Variety* in 1942. "Few sidemen want to travel; they'll hand in [their] notice the minute a band is scheduled to leave a key city location and immediately wire a rival leader for a job." Wages rose steeply: according to *Variety*, a musician earning $75 a week at the beginning of the war could expect to earn at least $125 a year later. The increase in the cost of labor undermined the surface prosperity of the wartime music business, effectively wiping out the profit most bands enjoyed from higher fees during the war and, according to some industry observers, presenting an insuperable obstacle to the formation of new bands. But at the same time, the dearth of bands made it easier for existing bands to stay continuously employed.

No Buses for Black Bands

What was true for the music business generally was also true for black musicians, but with the usual qualification: entrenched patterns of racism ensured that every dislocation, every inconvenience worked more sharply to their disadvantage.

For one thing, black bands were poorly positioned to take advantage of the ephemeral wartime boom. As we have seen, most location jobs were off-limits to them: very few hotels and only a handful of theaters offered employment to black musicians.[2] As a result, since the beginning of the Swing Era black bands had spent most of the year on the road,

2. Fifty-three theaters offering a full-week engagement to dance bands were available as of the fall of 1942. Of these, only the Apollo in New York, the Paradise in Detroit, the Royal in Baltimore, the Howard in Washington, D.C., and the Regal in Chicago were "colored" theaters, providing black entertainment to black audiences. Engagements for name black bands in other theaters were possible but relatively rare (Joe Schoenfeld, "Bands at Theatre B.O. Peaks," *Variety* 148 [7 October 1942]: 41).

deriving the bulk of their income from lengthy tours made up of one-nighters. Not surprisingly, disruptions to the transportation network had disproportionately severe consequences for their economic survival. The controversy over buses in 1942 illustrates this perfectly.

In June 1942, six months after Pearl Harbor, the Office of Defense Transportation (ODT) issued a preliminary edict eliminating the use of buses, both to save rubber and to commandeer the limited supply of vehicles for transporting troops. The ruling was immediately protested by bookers Moe Gale and Joe Glaser, both of whom worked almost exclusively with black bands; by Cab Calloway, who made a special trip to Washington accompanied by Walter White, executive secretary of the National Association for the Advancement of Colored People (NAACP), to plead with the ODT; and by the record producer and social activist John Hammond. Arguing that the unintended effect of the ruling would be to threaten the economic survival of black bands, these parties tried to negotiate a compromise arrangement that would allow the bands to tour.

The case was compelling. The private automobile, the usual mode of transportation for white musicians, was out of the question for black musicians. Traveling in small groups left them vulnerable to harassment and intimidation in the South, and the sight of prosperous black professionals driving late-model automobiles tended to enrage the local white population. Fats Waller's Lincoln sedan, for example, became a frequent target for resentment: its tires were slashed, and sand was poured in the crankcase. For those who could afford it—Cab Calloway and Duke Ellington—private Pullman railroad cars were the answer. But a more practical and economical solution was the bus. A bus made it obvious to the casual observer that black musicians were traveling as a professional group rather than as private individuals (in addition, white drivers were usually used). These buses were normally chartered, although a few bands, such as Les Hite's and Fletcher Henderson's, owned theirs. During the Swing Era, the band bus had become the symbol of life on the road for black musicians. It was their rolling home on wheels: the locus of good conversation and endless card games in the involuntary camaraderie of constant travel, and—all too often—a place to eat and sleep when no accommodations were available.

The threat to buses caught black bandleaders and their managers and bookers by surprise and left them with few options. As *Variety* sympathetically reported, "Without busses to play one-nighters these [Gale's] outfits will be seriously injured since there are few hotels, only a handful of theaters, and perhaps a dozen weeks of location work open to them. Other Negro bands like Count Basie, Cab Calloway, Duke Ellington, Andy Kirk, Louis Armstrong, are in a similar fix."

Booking agencies scrambled to meet immediate commitments by switching to rail transportation. A logistical nightmare under any circumstances, this task was made even more difficult in wartime by the periodical commandeering of rail lines for troop movements. The switch to rail had serious financial consequences as well. Tickets for each member of the band were only part of the expense. To get from the railroad station to the dance hall or theater, trucks had to be hired to haul instruments and equipment, while musicians called cabs. The additional expense— increasing the bill for transportation by anywhere from 25 to 50 percent—further eroded black bands' already fragile profit margin, with the result that bands found themselves enduring grueling tours for little financial gain.

In the short term, a compromise on buses was hammered out. At a September meeting at the New York headquarters of the NAACP, the government agreed to lend five buses for the use of black bands for a three-month period, beginning in October. The buses were to be pooled among approximately forty-five bands; in exchange, the bands were required to entertain the troops under the auspices of the United Service Organizations (USO) at least twice a week while on tour in the South. A similar deal was eventually worked out for white territory bands, as tire shortages ultimately made travel by automobile equally impossible. But by January 1943 the short-term compromise expired, and buses were denied to all bands. This technically put black and white bands on the same footing until the ban on driving was lifted in September 1943. But since white bands were less dependent on travel for income, the difficulties of rail travel fell disproportionately on black bands.

"Crazy Enough Not to Want to Fight"

The prospect of being inducted into the military also had distinctly different implications for blacks than for whites. Throughout the war, the attitude of the black community toward military service was decidedly ambivalent. On the one hand, black political leadership loudly insisted that African Americans had the right to fight for their country: as the title of an article by Walter White in the *Saturday Evening Post* put it, "It's Our Country, Too!" On the other hand, the pull of patriotism was undermined by the memory of the First World War, when black Americans went off to France with the full backing of even such ardent critics of American racism as W. E. B. Du Bois, only to return to the racial hostilities of the 1920s. Few could justify an open antagonism to the war effort, especially given the Nazi threat. Instead, they called for a war on two fronts: victory over fascism abroad and victory over racism at home.

One of the most racist institutions in American life was the military. At the outset of the war, blacks were barred entirely from the marines and air force and allowed to enlist in the navy only as messmen. Their participation in the army was restricted to four segregated units left over from World War I. The onset of war found the military largely unprepared to absorb large numbers of black draftees, and during the first half of 1942 induction proceeded slowly. But new segregated facilities were rapidly put in place. The policies governing the handling of black personnel placed a premium on protecting white sensibilities at the expense of any modification to racist practices of the past. As General George Marshall put it, "The War Department cannot ignore the social relationships between Negroes and whites which have been established by the American people through custom and habit." Black soldiers were assigned to segregated units, where black officers could rise no higher than the lowest-ranking white officer. More often than not, they were shunted into menial labor—the Quartermaster Corps, for example, which dealt with what one black recruit described as glorified stevedore work. Both during training and in combat, they were carefully segregated and routinely denied such basic privileges as use of the PX.

For most white Americans, military service was a force of democracy, the great leveler. Men from all parts of the country and from all walks of life found themselves forced together in life-and-death situations that compelled cooperation. Reminiscences of the war are filled with stock characters—the Brooklyn Jew, the Italian American, the boy from Arkansas—who learn to replace their provincial suspicions of one another with a deep and hard-won respect. Across the racial divide, however, the leveling process seemed mainly aimed at bringing all black Americans down to the lowest common denominator. Training camps were often located in the Deep South, where every action by a black soldier was under the grip of Jim Crow. Black recruits typically found themselves under the command of white southerners whose contempt for their charges was unmistakable and whose instinct was to suppress even the hint of insolence with violence. Race riots broke out on or near military facilities from California to South Carolina. For some blacks, the military may have been no worse than civilian life, and it at least offered a chance to acquire skills and experience that would lift them out of agricultural labor. But for urban blacks from the North and West with some education or professional skills, the right to fight for one's country left a bitter taste.

Black musicians in particular had a great deal to fear. They were accustomed to far greater social freedoms than most black Americans. They also knew that they were less likely than their white counterparts to be placed in a military band, an assignment that at least acknowledged their special skills. Many simply ignored their draft notices as long as possible, hoping that their itinerant lifestyle would provide a plausible excuse. Lester Young avoided induction until 1944, when a friendly zoot-suiter ("big chain down to his knees like Cab Calloway") turned out to be an FBI agent serving his notice. When all else failed, a number of traditional dodges were available. Buck Clayton, the veteran trumpet player with Count Basie, tried eating soap and imbibing a mixture of Benzedrine and Coca-Cola before reporting for his induction. His only reward was a splitting headache and boot camp sergeants who tried to "make an example" of him, assigning him to clean latrines and expecting him to report for duty a few hours after playing for an officers' party (for no pay). Clayton finally ended up in an army band in New Jersey, thanks to the intervention of friends in the clerical pool, who persistently scratched his name off assignments to southern camps. Few others were so lucky.

The most effective dodge, ironically, was to play into stereotypes of Harlem jivester behavior. Malcolm X showed up at his physical in his wildest zoot suit and yellow shoes, professing great enthusiasm for his induction. Once behind closed doors with the psychiatrist, he confided conspiratorially: "I want to get sent down South. Organize them nigger soldiers, you dig? Steal us some guns, and kill up crackers!" Few musicians played the role with such deliberate perfection, but the basic strategy—an open (and honest) expression of hostility—was the same. Howard McGhee told the army psychiatrist, "Man, why should I fight? I ain't mad at nobody out there. . . . I wouldn't know the difference. . . . If he's white, I'm going to shoot him. Whether he's a Frenchman, a German, or whatever, how the fuck would I know the difference?" McGhee was informed, "We can't use you." Later, he reflected: "I wasn't ready to dodge no bullets for nobody. And I like America. But I didn't like it *that* much. I mean, it's all right to be a second-class citizen, but shit, to be *shot* at, that's another damn story." Dizzy Gillespie (who drew the attention of the psychiatrist by carrying his trumpet in a paper bag) had a similar reaction:

They started asking me my views about fighting. "Well, look, at this time, in this stage of my life here in the United States whose foot has been in my ass? The white man's foot has been in my ass hole buried up to his knee . . . ! Now, you're speaking of the enemy. You're telling me the German is the enemy. At this point, I can never even remember having met a German. So if you put me out there with a gun in my hand and tell me to shoot at the enemy, I'm liable to create a case of 'mistaken identity. . . . ' "

They finally classified me 4F because I was crazy enough not to want to fight, in anybody's army.

Drug use provided another way out. The pianist John Malachi, who was reluctantly inducted in 1944 ("I felt like if I was going in the military, I should've been going down to Mississippi to fight somebody down there!"), found himself at the Great Lakes Naval Center under the thumb of a racist sergeant. After enduring a week of an intolerable situation, he was sent to a psychiatrist for a routine interview. The psychiatrist asked him whether he knew about heroin. Malachi was not a drug user, but sensing an opening, he "let 'im have it with both barrels." With the psychiatrist urging him to open up, he confessed to every drug-related depravity he could imagine. A few weeks later, he was back on the street.

Not surprisingly, the young black musicians who managed to avoid induction and were therefore free to pursue their careers during the war were likely to have an "attitude." They instinctively distrusted authority and looked for ways to undermine a system they could not entirely escape. The veteran bandleader Andy Kirk complained that his wartime charges (including Howard McGhee) "came in with their own thinking. They'd be drinking and clowning and were not accustomed to the decorum and standards I thought were right." They irritated a reviewer for *Billboard* by wearing sunglasses on stage ("even those called for featured spots at the mike wear them"). Out of exasperation, Kirk once called the band into the dressing room during an intermission to ask, "What's the matter with you fellows?" Tenor saxophonist J. D. King raised his hand like a kid in school and said, "You know something's wrong with us. We're all 4Fs."

Such insouciance was shared by thousands of young black men, who paraded their defiance in elaborate zoot suits that openly subverted the War Production Board's rationing of fabric. Like the zoot-suiters, black musicians were horrified at the prospect of being drafted to fight a white man's war, and they faced the same daily threat of random racial violence. But the musicians had more than their stance, their attitude: they had a finely honed expressive discipline and, during the war years, an unprecedented degree of professional freedom. The manpower shortage gave them greater choices than ever before—to move from one band to the next, to go on the road or stay behind in New York. More and more talented musicians disengaged from the touring dance orchestras, finding temporary refuge in small-combo jobs or disappearing from the business for a time. Some were aware of the "progressive" idiom taking shape at Minton's and Monroe's, or had begun to see the possibilities for an alternative music scene, and formed a conscious decision to be a part of it. But for many more, dropping out was a visceral reaction to things as they were, unpremeditated and impervious to rational argument. This state of frustration, anger, and weariness was the necessary precondition for the emergence of bebop.

"We're Going Down South, Man!"

Of the forces that alienated musicians from dance bands, none was more immediate than the working conditions they regularly endured. Sheer exhaustion played a large part. Black bands were on the road continuously, and the strain of travel wore out even the most robust constitutions. Taft Jordan, who played trumpet with Duke Ellington for four years in the mid-1940s, recalled that on leaving the band he "slept almost a whole year. . . . For a long time I actually slept two or three times a day, and not cat naps, but for two or three hours. I hadn't realized how tired I was." Clyde Bernhardt, plagued by headaches, swollen feet, and chronic exhaustion after a grueling nine-month stretch of one-nighters with Jay McShann in 1942–43, left the band on his doctor's orders. Trumpeter Adolphus "Doc" Cheatham, a veteran of the Cab Calloway, Teddy Wilson, Benny Carter, and Fletcher Henderson bands, grew so fatigued by the early 1940s that he was briefly hospitalized. His wife, frustrated when he wouldn't go back to work, finally left him. These and other musicians drifted into small group work not out of any artistic revolutionary impulse, but because they were simply too worn out to carry on.

This physical toll was only augmented by the psychological effects of travel through the segregated South. To eat, bands had to search out the black section of town or depend on their white managers or bus drivers (or even light-skinned musicians) to order take-out meals. "They'd take all the prices down and charge us three times as much. And then the pièce de résistance: the promoter would let people in for half a buck apiece to watch us eat!" Proud musicians, accustomed to thinking of themselves at the top of their profession, wolfed down "'axle-grease fried chicken' or dried-up ham sandwiches on even more dried-up bread" on the bus or at the back door of a restaurant. Their hard-won economic status counted for nothing. "We traveled through the South all day and have a pocketful of money and couldn't get a glass of water," recalled Art Blakey, who toured with Fletcher Henderson during 1943–44. "And if you did, they'd sell it to you a dollar a glass. And it would be hot as panther piss."

For lodging, musicians were forced to rely on the local black community. "In that whole section of the country there weren't more than six black hotels, and that's probably being generous," remembered Lionel Hampton. Musicians have warmly acknowledged the many families that housed them and fed them with home-cooked meals, often forming friendships that would last for life. But the darker side of human nature was also evident:

> We had a hard way to go with the local black people. We got robbed by all the local hotel owners and people who ran these rooming houses. They knew that they had us, that we couldn't go to white hotels, and they ripped us off worse than if we were being refused at a white hotel. They would charge you three or four dollars for a night. To stay in somebody's house, you know. And a hotel might charge you five or six dollars, and man, it was terrible. One bathroom 'way down the hall. They wouldn't even change the sheets on the bed sometimes. Bed bugs, roach-infested places that they didn't clean up. And they just figured, the hell with it. They didn't have to clean them up, because we had no other place to go. And they were all black-owned. And we really resented this highly, because they knew that they had us. And our same brother white bands were staying in hotels, and the guys were paying two or three dollars a day, in nice white hotels.

Beneath such routine discomforts and indignities lay the omnipresent threat of violence—a threat all the more terrifying for being arbitrary and unpredictable. To catalog all the incidents in which black musicians legitimately feared for their safety would be a numbing exercise. Suffice it to say that as strangers, as blacks, and as northerners (even native southerners had acquired a certain New York patina in the course of their professionalization), they were lightning rods for any resentments or arbitrary expressions of authority by the white population. Even the local black population could be aroused to vengeful envy by mischievous whites ("Look, them niggers are from New York and they come down and take your women. . . . They think they're smart because they live in New York").

Black musicians often found themselves in an uncomfortably ambiguous position. On the one hand, they were celebrities of a sort, having appeared on radio and recordings, and they carried with them the unmistakable swagger of show business. But at the same time, they were, in effect, servants, subject to peremptory commands underlaid with the implicit threat of violence. Black musicians everywhere were expected to conform to the Sambo stereotype, and the more sadistic among the white population felt entitled to punish those who refused to comply. Once, when playing with Fletcher Henderson on the Eastern Shore of Maryland, Rex Stewart was asked by a white woman (in the company of a "big red-faced man") to play "Pink Elephants." Her demands began to accelerate: "Blackie, that was all right. Now I want you to sing 'Pink Elephants.' . . . I bet he'd even dance like a pink elephant if I ast him, wouldn't you, boy?' " Something told Stewart to comply ("my first command performance," he called it). On driving out of town, a badly unnerved black gas station attendant exclaimed, " 'My gawd! Didn't you know they lynched a man there just two days ago?' "

What the historian Burton Peretti has called the "public, *theatrical*" expression of racism in the South changed very little from the early 1930s, when black bands began touring the South in earnest, to the war. Older black musicians did not feel humiliation any less keenly, and more than a few were prepared to protect themselves if necessary. "In those days, when we were traveling in the South, most cats had firearms somewhere, somehow," according to Dicky Wells. "When I was with Fletcher Henderson, I found out he never approved of it, but the guys would say: 'We're going down South, man! We've got to have our artillery!' " In the main, however, the absence of any realistic alternative to southern tours dictated a stoic and stringently self-monitored regimen of behavior. As bandleader Horace Henderson recalls advising his young employees: "You just be a gentleman and do your thing. You were there to play; you were there for one night. Play your little riffs, get your bread, mind your own business, and get out. And be careful if you are lonesome. Be careful who you're talking to and who you're with."

The possibilities for protest remained severely limited in the early 1940s. Members of the rising bebop generation were not eager to become martyrs, and they were not above using time-honored strategies for deflecting hostility when necessary. (Charlie Parker reputedly played the stuttering Negro rube to perfection on occasion to get out of tight scrapes with the law.) But these young musicians sensed that the time was ripe for change. The war was stirring up the sediments of racial and class hierarchies. Black men had once again been asked to die for a democracy that declined to treat them as full citizens. Musicians may not have been overtly political, but they sensed their responsibility as African Americans with a rare opportunity to act freely. "There was a message to our music," asserted Kenny Clarke. "Whatever you go into, go into it *intelligently*. . . . The idea was to wake up, look around you, there's something to do." At times, the only intelligent thing to do seemed to be to refuse to go along.

To the routine degradations for black musicians, the wartime ban on buses added a new one: travel by rail in the South in segregated cars. Poorly heated in winter, suffocating in summer, and traditionally located immediately behind the engine, where soot poured in the windows, the Jim Crow car was a ritual of humiliation that black musicians from the South had not had to put up with for years, and that black musicians from the North may never have experienced at all. Dan Burley, columnist for the *New York Amsterdam News*, conveyed to his urbane readers just how vivid a reminder of second-class status this particular trial by transportation was:

> Remember how Cincinnati and Washington used to be the Big Change terminals? . . . How conductors were said to have hollered (under their breath, of course) "Every pig to his own pen," or words to that effect, and how your ancestors and mine and some of our own relatives dutifully toted their shoeboxes loaded with fried chicken, pigsfeet, cake and cornbread, blankets and squealing kids into the Jim Crow Car?
>
> . . . Remember the soot, the grime, the almost unbearable heat of these American "steerages" on rails? . . . Remember how the Jim Crow Car used to be on the end of the train and how the white folks changed all that and put it up behind the engine after several accidents in which engines collided and all the white folks in the Pullman behind the engine were hurt or scared to death? . . .
>
> The Jim Crow Train, its car, has been through history one of the real reasons people say to themselves, why in the hell should I worry about them when they treat me this way? . . . The ignominy of it, the idea that this is your place and in it you'll stay has stuck with Negroes down through the years in the South, and much of it has come because of the Jim Crow Train.

If the Jim Crow car eroded the dignity of every black American, it was a particular affront to musicians. The Jim Crow car made it clear how little their singular achievements counted in the face of state-enforced racism. "Of course, the whites were sitting back in the passenger cars in air-conditioned comfort," remembered Johnny Young, the pianist with Andy Kirk's band in 1944. "Whenever the assistant train engineer would shovel coal, all of the coal dust and cinders would fly back on us. Of course, the irony of the thing was when we would get off the train, white folks would look at us and say, 'Look at those filthy niggers.' But there was no other way for us to look because we had been sweating and felt stinky and dirty from the subhuman treatment we had received on the train."

For band mate Howard McGhee, the Jim Crow car proved to be the last straw:

> You had to ride in the first car of the train, and it wasn't air-conditioned, so you had to put the windows up; you put the windows up, and all the cinders came in from the engine into the car. Which was a *drag*, you know. I mean, shit, I didn't need to be going through this kind of thing, not as well as I'm playing, because I know that people liked what I was doing—I could tell that from the audience, you know?

McGhee had rejoined the Andy Kirk band in early 1944, traveling cross-country from New York to California and back. The band had finished an engagement at the Royal Theater in Baltimore when Kirk made an announcement that caused McGhee's blood to run cold:

> He gives us a list of one-nighters where the band was going. And they ain't nothing but Alabama and Mississippi and Florida and Georgia and all that shit. . . . They had told me before the band's going back to New York, which would have been all right with me. I mean, I like New York. . . . So I said, "I don't want to be down there, man, I don't want to go. Andy, I ain't going." He says, "Well, you can't leave just like that." I said, "Yes, I can—I ain't going." "Well you know I could file charges [with the union]." I said, "Do what you have to do, but *I'm leaving.*"

But where could a musician go?

During the war years the bebop pioneers had several alternatives. The course of action that led most directly into bebop involved reshaping the music at Minton's and Monroe's for public consumption in nightclubs, taking advantage of the new opportunities for small combos (discussed in subsequent chapters). But this was still a fairly radical step, taken only after other, more conventional career options had been exhausted.

With the Big Bands—Again

Dance bands remained central to the music industry as a whole. Even by war's end, it was by no means clear that they would soon be supplanted. It is therefore hardly surprising that most of the bebop pioneers spent some time in their employ. Younger, struggling musicians continued to rely on dance bands as the main point of entry to the profession, even as an increasing number began to drift to the small-club scene in New York. Older, more experienced musicians had their pick of jobs and sometimes took band gigs in part to satisfy their musical curiosity. Dizzy Gillespie spent a "very strange" four weeks trying to penetrate the inner world of the Duke Ellington band during an engagement at the Capitol Theater in late 1943. During the same time, Howard McGhee joined the Count Basie band (replacing the recently drafted Buck Clayton) during its landmark engagement at the Hotel Lincoln, accepting a lower salary than he had been accustomed to for the privilege of playing with his musical idol, Lester Young.[3] ("I'd hang out with him all night . . . and we'd go up to Minton's, because that's where we found Dizzy, Don Byas, and Monk, and Kenny Clarke.") But when the Basie band went on tour at the beginning of 1944, McGhee stayed behind. Not even the thrill of playing for Basie could motivate him to go back on the road.

One dance band stands out against this background and figures prominently in the folklore of bebop. In November 1942 Earl Hines was persuaded by some of his younger musicians, including vocalist Billy Eckstine, to hire Dizzy Gillespie, who had temporarily given up on New York and relocated to his adoptive hometown of Philadelphia, and Charlie Parker—on tenor saxophone, because of the departure of veteran tenor saxophonist Budd Johnson. For the next nine months, until the end of the summer of 1943, Parker and Gillespie worked alongside one another, cementing their musical relationship in the enforced comradeship of continuous travel. In Gillespie's words, "Out on the road with Earl, things started happening between Charlie Parker and me. . . . We were together all the time, playing in hotel rooms and jamming." At the same time, the

---

3. "Basie wouldn't pay no money, man. I think he paid ninety bucks for a week to work at the Hotel Lincoln. I didn't think that was so hot because I had been making more than that with Andy Kirk" (Howard McGhee, interview with author, 1984).

difference in their temperaments became apparent. "His crowd, the people he hung out with, were not the people I hung out with. And the guy who pushed dope would be around."

These backstage musical developments had little direct relevance to the day-to-day goings-on of a major dance band, however. To Hines, Charlie Parker and Dizzy Gillespie were exciting young soloists, if a little weak on tone. Each had a role to play in Hines's organization, and they fulfilled their roles admirably, but those roles were necessarily delimited. Parker, Hines later testified, was "a very good section man, and a very good reader. . . . I mean, he was a *musician!*" Gillespie was "one of the fastest guys as far as execution on his horn. . . . the man that played all of the fast numbers and numbers that had a punch to it." Hines did avail himself occasionally of Gillespie's talent as an arranger: "A Night in Tunisia" and "Down Under" entered his repertory, and Gunther Schuller, who heard the band as a teenager, vividly remembers "flatted fifth chords and all the modern harmonies and substitutions and Dizzy Gillespie runs in the trumpet section work." The absence of commercial recordings of the Hines band throughout this period—the result of the American Federation of Musicians ban on recordings (see chapter 8)—has frequently been lamented as a lacuna in the early history of bebop. But the beboppers-to-be had little overall effect on Hines's offerings, which, like those of most jazz-oriented dance bands, mixed up-tempo swing tunes with ballads, blues, and such unabashedly sentimental pop fare as "Down by the Old Mill Stream" and "Easter Parade." When Gillespie, Parker, Eckstine, and other young musicians left in the summer of 1943, Hines struck out in a completely different direction, adding an all-female string section (the better to protect himself against the vagaries of the draft).

For Gillespie, playing with Hines was another in a series of dead-end jobs, made tolerable by the opportunity to work regularly with Parker. Not that he held any particular animus against the bandleader. Although Hines was "a black entertainer from the old school," he was also an endlessly inventive virtuoso whose unflappability earned Gillespie's grudging respect. When the band would mischievously test Hines by refusing to come back in at the end of one of his piano solos, "he'd look up and keep playing and grinning. You couldn't flush him, no matter what you did. . . . He'd be sweating, man, and he's so cool. He is the epitome of perfection." But Gillespie would be satisfied only with a similar opportunity to prove his own mettle. He needed to be in charge musically— and that, with as strong a personality as Earl Hines at the helm, was an unlikely prospect.

For Charlie Parker, playing with Hines proved to be, in conventional terms, the apogee of his career—his only extended association with a name band. Because this period coincided with the ban on recordings called by the musicians' union, it seems today nearly as shadowy and obscure as his activities at Minton's or Monroe's. Yet for the better part of a year Parker performed regularly before large, paying crowds across the country. As his experience with McShann showed, Parker clearly had the potential to be an integral part of a dance band. Hines sensed this and felt that he, unlike McShann, could overcome Parker's personality flaws and "make a man of him." His failure to do so has become part of the Parker legend: the strung-out Bird, hiding behind dark glasses, learning to fall asleep on the bandstand with his cheeks poked out, as if he were still playing. Parker's inability to maintain minimal professional standards was a source of frustration for his fellow band members, who periodically ganged up on him backstage to intimidate him into straightening out. Nevertheless, in his more lucid moments Parker clearly relished the professional responsibilities of his day: reading his parts flawlessly, blending with a section, playing intriguing but supportive obbligatos underneath Sarah Vaughan's vocal lines. As with any other ambitious young musician, it was important for him to prove that he could play in the big leagues—even as his behavior made it impossible for him to do so much longer.

Joining a white orchestra was another alternative that intrigued a handful of black musicians during the war years, for it offered a chance to experience firsthand professional life on the other side of the racial divide. For the most part, the music business was governed by a strict apartheid, broken only by the occasional interracial recording session (where the identities of the musicians could easily be obscured) and by light-skinned blacks "passing" for white. Black and white musicians might mingle after hours in jam sessions, but on the bandstand they were understood to occupy distinct and separate spheres. The first open assault on the system came with Benny Goodman's celebrated hiring of first Teddy Wilson and then Lionel Hampton (in 1935 and 1936 respectively), but even that radical step was carefully hedged: Wilson and Hampton were billed not as regular members of the band, but as "guest artists" with the Goodman Quartet—a ruse that apparently satisfied conservative sponsors and audiences. Goodman continued to hire black musicians for his small groups, but few bandleaders seemed willing to follow his lead. The hard-headed

Artie Shaw was one: he hired Billie Holiday as vocalist for most of 1938 and the trumpeter Hot Lips Page in 1941. Charlie Barnet was another.

Barnet was a maverick whose disregard for conventional opinion was legendary. Born into a wealthy railroad family, he inherited a degree of financial independence ("I frankly admit that I never had to worry about eating, sleeping, or most of the nice things in life") that allowed him to give full expression to the rebellious side of his nature. The general public knew him as the "Mad Mab," a hard drinker and gambler who married no fewer than eleven times. But the core of his rebellion was an admiration for black music, which shaped his musical career. At an early age he became infatuated with jazz; even before the Swing Era helped break down stylistic barriers between black and white bands, Barnet openly modeled his music on his favorite black bands, especially Duke Ellington's and Count Basie's. His success at assimilating black styles may be judged by his following with black audiences, beginning with his 1933 appearance at the Apollo Theatre—the first time a white band played there. No less an authority than Malcolm X, who worked as a shoeshine boy at the Roseland Ballroom in Boston in the late 1930s, credited Barnet's ability to reach the black masses: "The fact is that very few white bands could have satisfied the Negro dancers. But I know that Charlie Barnet's 'Cherokee' and his 'Redskin Rhumba' drove those Negroes wild. They'd jampack that ballroom, the black girls in wayout silk and satin dresses and shoes, their hair done in all kinds of styles, the men sharp in their zoot suits and crazy conks, and everybody grinning and greased and gassed."

Barnet began quietly using black musicians on an occasional basis in the mid-1930s. Lena Horne was his vocalist in 1940. Dizzy Gillespie worked for him for a few weeks in late 1941, shortly after the spitball incident with Cab Calloway. Early in 1942 Barnet added Herbert "Peanuts" Holland, a veteran black trumpet player and vocalist, to his roster. Characteristically, Barnet downplayed his role as an instrument of racial progress: "I never made a point of hiring black musicians to change the social order. I hired them because of how well they played, not with any idea of starting a racial revolution." But in the early 1940s, the real impetus to challenge racial orthodoxy was the manpower shortage caused by the war. Barnet's racial liberalism made him naturally turn to the pool of black musicians as a resource—as he freely admitted in the case of Peanuts Holland: "We were losing more and more men to the draft and good trumpet players were especially hard to find. One day I ran into Peanuts Holland. . . . Peanuts had a bad foot and was in no danger of being drafted. I asked him how he felt about joining a white band. . . .

Peanuts said okay, so once again I had a mixed band." During the war, Barnet relied heavily on top-flight black musicians, including trumpeters Howard McGhee, Dick Vance, Al Killian, and Joe Guy; trombonist Trummy Young; and bassist Oscar Pettiford.

For black musicians, working with a white band usually meant improved working conditions and increased earnings. While a band like Andy Kirk's had to work long strings of one-nighters in order to stay afloat financially, Barnet's itinerary consisted primarily of lucrative theater and ballroom engagements in major urban areas. During the three months after McGhee joined the band in the fall of 1942, Barnet traveled exclusively in the Northeast, going no farther west than Ohio; the band stayed at each location at least three days, more commonly a week. This schedule came as a revelation to McGhee: "White bands, you got better gigs. [Laughs.] You know what I mean? They had better jobs. . . . [Before joining Barnet] I thought everybody played the same places, but it ain't like that. 'Cause with Charlie I played more theaters, and more white dances than Andy [Kirk] ever played. But I mean, it was just one of those things."

Another advantage to working with white bands, as Gillespie discovered during his brief time with Barnet, was that they typically paid musicians a guaranteed weekly salary. Black bands usually paid by the job—during slack weeks, musicians suffered. McGhee admitted to joining Barnet for the money. When Barnet's black arranger, Andy Gibson, approached McGhee about joining the band, his reply was, "Yeah, of course. For money I'd go with King Kong." McGhee actually ended up earning less with Barnet than with Kirk—probably because of his status as a relative newcomer and the fact that his salary with Kirk had been augmented by arranging fees. More experienced musicians saw a sharp increase in their salaries: Trummy Young, who left the Jimmie Lunceford band for Barnet, earned about $50 more per week. McGhee, however, keenly felt the disparity between Barnet's cavalier display of wealth and the meager salary he paid:

When you work for a millionaire, you see what kind of money *this* guy's [got], and you say, "Jiminy, this is the chicken feed I'm making? It ain't saying too much." So I got the image, I said, "I'd like to have *me* some money." Charlie got his from his railroad family. . . . And Charlie, he could do what he wanted to do. And he was the *tightest* sonofabitch I ever seen. . . . But I mean, people that got money don't spend—I mean, they'll spend for what *they* want, but that's *all* they spend. People that work for them, they don't give them nothing. "You're just a musician." Boy, I said, "Oh, yeah, OK." That put me wise to having money.

The potential for financial reward aside, black musicians stood to gain in publicity at the vanguard of integration. But they also were subject to extraordinary pressure. Billie Holiday bitterly noted, "I hardly ever ate, slept, or went to the bathroom without having a major NAACP-type production. . . . I got tired of having a federal case over breakfast, lunch, and dinner." She finally quit the Artie Shaw band out of nervousness and exhaustion. Roy Eldridge's experiences as a featured soloist with both Barnet and Shaw were particularly traumatic. Once, when refused admission to a dance hall where his name was up in lights, he broke down:

> When I finally did get in, I played that first set, trying to keep from crying. By the time I got through the set, the tears were rolling down my cheeks. . . . I went up to a dressing room and stood in a corner crying and saying to myself why the hell did I come out here again when I knew what would happen?
>
> Man, when you're on the stage you're great, but as soon as you come off, you're nothing. It's not worth the glory, not worth the money, not worth anything.

Even the more subtle forms of racism were debilitating. Shortly after joining the Barnet band as Peanuts Holland's replacement, McGhee discovered that he was expected to fulfill the stereotype of black man as entertainer. One of Holland's featured numbers had been a Duke Ellington novelty tune, "Oh! Miss Jaxson"—a mugging ode to Miss Jaxson's "fine barbecue" that Holland had sung in a rough, quasi–Louis Armstrong style.

McGhee had clowned and sung with vocalist June Richmond during his time with Andy Kirk, and Barnet expected more of the same. But that was with a black band. As the sole black artist in an otherwise all-white group, he felt exposed and embarrassed: "Charlie Shavers heard me, when I first came into the theater, I did 'Oh! Miss Jaxson.' So Charlie Shavers never let me forget it. Everytime he see me, he say, 'Maggie, you got that barbecue?' . . . Oh, I hated that thing. He knew I didn't like it from the way I was singin'."

For all his fealty to the black musical tradition, Barnet still acted from a base of privilege with frequent disregard for the sensitivities of his black employees. He infuriated McGhee by gambling away large sums of money and then refusing to give his trumpet player a raise ("he used to take me with him [shooting dice] and let me see him doing it!"). He once fired the entire band in a drunken fit of pique on being told that it didn't sound like Duke Ellington's. (McGhee cannily used the occasion to demand a raise; the next time Barnet got drunk, he called out, "Everybody fired except McGhee!") Barnet was notorious for practical jokes, and he once stood by while a friend of his frightened the veteran black arranger Andy Gibson, who occasionally traveled with the band in the South, into thinking he was being ambushed by Ku Klux Klanners. As Barnet tells it, "[Gibson] came out of the car like Jesse Owens and made a beeline for me across the street." Even after being wined and dined in expiation, Gibson didn't find the prank amusing.

The "joke" on Gibson was particularly cruel, for absence from personal danger was one advantage of serving behind the scenes as an arranger. For many years, skilled black arrangers had discovered that they could earn far more money by crossing the racial divide. Fletcher Henderson, Benny Carter, Jimmy Mundy, and Edgar Sampson all contributed items from their book to the early successes of Benny Goodman; Henderson's association with Goodman propped up his own moribund career as a bandleader. Gillespie similarly relied on his arranging to tide him over while freelancing in the early 1940s, writing for Jimmy Dorsey, Woody Herman, and Boyd Raeburn: "Often, when I'd find myself strapped for vittles, I'd write an arrangement and fend off starvation. . . . Just when I needed some money, BOOM! I'd make an arrangement."

The monetary incentive was real enough: white bands could afford to pay more for good arrangements than black bands, and perhaps more than a black musician might earn as a performer during a comparable amount of time (especially if work were scarce).[4] But such transactions eased short-term financial difficulties at the expense of long-term interests. Arrangers received a flat, one-time fee (and composer royalties for an original composition), but they lost all control over their creative products. Arrangers were invisible to the public eye—which is why the en-

4. Budd Johnson earned $150 a week writing four arrangements a week for Gus Arnheim in 1937. When Arnheim retired, Johnson turned to writing for Earl Hines at $10 to $15 per arrangement (Budd Johnson, National Endowment for the Arts / Smithsonian Institution Jazz Oral History Project). Dizzy Gillespie charged somewhat more in the early 1940s, on the grounds that the complex harmonies took time for him to work out and that bandleaders like Jimmy Dorsey were willing to pay for "the latest things" (Gillespie 1979, 165). Gillespie's standard charge was $100 per arrangement, beginning with his work for Woody Herman in 1942 (Herman and Troup 1990, 39).

tertainment industry was so open in this instance to the flow of music across the color line. White bands were eager to pay for Gillespie's original musical ideas, but unwilling to enter into any other kind of partnership that might offer him more substantive reward or public recognition. "Boy, I'd love to have you in my band," Jimmy Dorsey once told Gillespie, "but you're *so* dark."

"Sweet Georgia Brown"

If dance bands remained the nominal focus of the bebop pioneers' careers, their musical interest shifted decisively to the controlled chaos of the jam session, where the disparate innovations of Gillespie, Parker, Clarke, and Monk began to solidify into a new common practice.

Hard evidence for this process is virtually nonexistent. But fortunately, a fragment of what was happening offstage with the Earl Hines band has survived on a recently rediscovered private disc recording from a Chicago hotel room on a Monday night in February 1943. For nearly eight minutes, Charlie Parker (on tenor sax) and Dizzy Gillespie trade choruses of "Sweet Georgia Brown" over Oscar Pettiford's bass line. The quality of the recording is terrible, and the music is interrupted in spots where the disc itself, made with shoddy wartime materials, has deteriorated. Nevertheless, in the grooves, one can faintly hear not just the notes but also something of the social atmosphere supporting them: encouraging shouts behind Parker's solo ("c'mon, Yard!"), handclaps on the backbeat where the unbroken flow of improvisation gathers irresistible momentum. This recording provides a unique opportunity to assess the behind-the-scenes changes in musical language.

At this point Parker's and Gillespie's approaches were still quite distinct. On the surface—the surface that is visible in transcription—it is Gillespie who is more conspicuously and self-consciously the progressive. His improvised lines are densely packed with chromatic dissonances— mostly simple passing tones, but also occasionally the flatted fifth (music example 34), in what might be called the "Night in Tunisia" cadence (compare music example 35).

Peppering Gillespie's solos are flamboyant and obviously well-polished gestures (they reappear verbatim both here and in later performances), in which chromatic dissonance is wedded to equally disruptive rhythms. These are the "hooks" of the nascent bebop style, naggingly memorable and attention-getting: off-center whole-tone scale fragments (music example 36), tricky polyrhythmic alternations of adjacent notes (music example 37), and Gillespie's trademark, complicated triplet patterns that fit easily into a variety of harmonic contexts (music examples 38, 39, and 40). They advertise both Gillespie's virtuosity and the modernity of his idiom, and point toward the music's ultimate commodification.

By these standards, Parker seems more conservative. There are no startling shifts into faster rhythmic note values or polyrhythmic interruptions of the flow of eighth notes—although this may simply be a constraint of the less familiar and more cumbersome tenor saxophone (he

EX. 34.
"Sweet Georgia Brown" (1943), Dizzy Gillespie solo, chorus 1, mm. 29–32.

EX. 35.
"Night in Tunisia" cadence: "A Night in Tunisia," theme, mm. 7–8.

EX. 36.
"Sweet Georgia Brown" (1943), Dizzy Gillespie solo, chorus 1, mm. 10–13.

EX. 37.
"Sweet Georgia Brown" (1943), Dizzy Gillespie solo, chorus 2, mm. 1–3.

EX. 38.
"Sweet Georgia Brown" (1943), Dizzy Gillespie solo, chorus 2, mm. 5–7.

EX. 39.
"Sweet Georgia Brown" (1943), Dizzy Gillespie solo, chorus 3, mm. 10–12.

EX. 40.
"Sweet Georgia Brown" (1943), Dizzy Gillespie solo, chorus 3, mm. 21–23.

once complained to Eckstine, "Man, this thing is too big"). More surprisingly, there are fewer harsh, disorienting dissonances. Parker proves himself here, as elsewhere, to be a superlative harmonic improviser in the Hawkins mold, parsing each chord cleanly and accurately as it flies by. There are enough passing dissonances to give his lines both interesting shape and an extra dimension of momentum, but the dissonances are generally less ostentatious than Gillespie's flatted fifths and whole-tone scales. Like Lester Young, Parker aims for the "pretty notes" (music example 41): ninths (g″ in measure 1, c″ in measure 5) and thirteenths (g″ in measure 6), which occupy a middle ground between dissonance and consonance and do not urgently require resolution.

EX. 41.
"Sweet Georgia Brown" (1943), Charlie Parker solo, chorus 1, mm. 1–9.

And yet it is Gillespie in this instance who is learning from Parker. Gillespie later insisted that the essentials of his style had "already developed" before he met Parker, but he readily conceded the central importance of Parker's manner of phrasing and articulation to the emergence of bebop:

> I think I was a little more advanced, harmonically, than he was. But rhythmically, he was quite advanced, with setting up the phrase and how you got from one note to another. How you get from one note to another really makes the difference. Charlie Parker heard rhythms and rhythmic patterns differently, and after we started playing together, I began to play, rhythmically, more like him. . . .
>
> The enunciation of the notes, I think, belonged to Charlie Parker because the way he'd get from one note to another, I could never . . . That was just perfect for me. I came from an age of Roy Eldridge, and Roy Eldridge got from one note to another much differently from Charlie Parker. What I did was very much an extension of what Roy Eldridge had done—Charlie Parker definitely set the standard for phrasing our music.[5]

How a performer "gets from one note to another" is one of those qualities that rarely surfaces in transcription, for the good reason that performance nuances are elusive, and conventions for notating them necessarily vague. Slurs, accents, staccato marks, and the like are available

5. Tenor saxophonist Benny Golson reported a similar pronouncement by Gillespie: "You know, I was talking to Dizzy last night about the time when he and Charlie Parker were together. He said, 'Do you know what Charlie Parker brought? Charlie Parker brought the rhythm. The *way* he played those notes'" (Lees 1991, 225).

to composers, but even at their most precise such markings are only suggestions to the performer. As descriptions of what has already been played, they are clearly inadequate to the task. Take, for example, dynamic markings: *forte* and *piano* are simply translations of the Italian words for "loud" or "soft" and usually provide nothing more than a general indication for the character of a given passage. There is no convenient way to specify the subtle variations of dynamic level from note to note *within* a line, short of labeling each note individually or indicating the relative increase or decrease in volume with crescendo and decrescendo marks. But dynamics are essential to Parker's conception of phrasing, which in turn is at the heart of the peculiar rhythmic effect of his playing.

One way to describe this effect is to say that the pattern of accents in a Charlie Parker line is in a constant state of flux—falling sometimes on the strong beats of the measure, but also (and quite unpredictably) on "weak beats" (beats 2 and 4) or on the weak half of the eighth note pair. Yet to speak of "accent" begs the question. The perception of accent in music is a complex affair (the ethnomusicologist Charles Seeger has called it a "compound function"). In Parker's case, a note often receives emphasis not because it is played with particular force, but because it is preceded by notes that are conspicuously *under*played. In jazz parlance, these are "ghosted" notes, usually notated with an *x* for the note-head. But deemphasized notes run the gamut from true ghost notes (those that are barely audible, or inaudible but implied by phrasing) to passages that contrast with their surroundings by a kind of terraced dynamics. Variations in dynamics allow Parker to suggest a highly varied rhythmic surface without abandoning the Hawkins-like stream of eighth notes so essential to continuous harmonic improvisation.

But there is more to it than this. The shifting pattern of accents is not a purely rhythmic device imposed on the flow of notes. The different kinds of accentuation and phrasing are associated with specific melodic shapes and pitch choices, used by Parker to heighten the rhythmic momentum that arises from skillful harmonic improvising: the resolution of dissonance to consonance.

One of the most distinctive and pervasive patterns—a consistent accenting of the second half of the eighth-note pair, slurring slightly from the upbeat to the downbeat—almost always occurs in descending stepwise passages (music example 42). Although the upbeat is accented, both notes are clearly played. The stepwise resolution from dissonance to consonance ("getting from one note to the next") is underscored by the

simple expedient of subtly emphasizing the dissonances (which are always on the upbeat).

More generally, the continually shifting patterns of accents—especially when effected by changes in dynamics—serve to differentiate the
various "voices" implicit in the single line. In music example 43, the
distinction between an upper voice (on beats 1 and 3) and a lower voice
(the remaining eighth notes, played at a distinctly lower level of volume)
is particularly clear. The same is true of any number of other patterns
that one can isolate from the fabric: upward-directed arpeggios, in which
the lower two notes are held back (music example 44), or the variety of
ways that Parker inserts a dissonant C-sharp (or D-flat) into the last bar
of the F⁷ harmony (music examples 45, 46, 47, and 48).

But the real effect is best heard over the broader sweep of a passage.

EX. 42.
"Sweet Georgia Brown" (1943), Charlie Parker solo, chorus 2, mm. 1–2.

EX. 43.
"Sweet Georgia Brown" (1943), Charlie Parker solo, chorus 3, mm. 11–12.

EX. 44.
"Sweet Georgia Brown" (1943), Charlie Parker solo, chorus 1, mm. 14–15.

EX. 45.
"Sweet Georgia Brown" (1943), Charlie Parker solo, chorus 1, m. 4.

EX. 46.
"Sweet Georgia Brown" (1943), Charlie Parker solo, chorus 2, mm. 3–4.

EX. 47.
"Sweet Georgia Brown" (1943), Charlie Parker solo, chorus 2, mm. 20–21.

EX. 48.
"Sweet Georgia Brown" (1943), Charlie Parker solo, chorus 4, m. 20.

Parker is a favorite of jazz analysts because of the clarity with which he articulates linear descents over the four- and eight-bar spans that make up the harmonic units of the jazz repertory. In music example 49, the descent of the upper line from g"[6] is reinforced by unexpected accents (the d-flat" in measure 27 or the b-flat' in measure 28). The movement is recapitulated in more condensed form in measures 29–32. Like Haw-

6. This excerpt is part of an octave descent from an a-flat" in the previous four-bar phrase.

EX. 49.
"Sweet Georgia Brown" (1943), Charlie Parker solo, chorus 2, mm. 25–32.

kins, Parker is not above altering the harmonic progression for a bit of chromatic voice-leading, as in the remarkable substitution for C⁷ in measure 26.

The resemblance to Hawkins is brought out, of course, by the instrument Parker is playing. If his timbre suggests Lester Young, his choice of notes owes a great deal to Hawkins. Indeed, shorn of its distinctive accentual nuances, many a Parker passage looks remarkably like something the older saxophonist might have played (music example 50; compare music example 7 in chapter 2). But Parker's playing leaves an entirely different impression. Hawkins is expansive, saturating the sonic space. Parker, for all the profusion of notes, is concise and streamlined. Hawkins spreads out into all registers, investing each note with the same rich, full tone and contrapuntal potential, continually deferring closure through a relentless flow of notes until he attains a simultaneous climax of timbre, register, and volume. Parker, by contrast, is perfectly willing to close things off. (He once told Howard McGhee, "I can play all I know in eight bars.") Nothing could be more elegantly closed off, for example, than the cadences in music example 49. Except, of course, that the trademark rhythmic ending—the eighth-note pair that is the onomatopoeic source of the word *bebop*—leaves one expecting something more: a new entrance in an unexpected rhythmic position, riding the ongoing momentum of the harmonic cycle, which never comes to rest as long as there is one more chorus to be played.

Fats Waller (who died in 1943) is said to have complained to unnamed musical tormentors at Minton's, "Stop that crazy boppin' and a-stoppin' and play that jive like the rest of us guys!" The bopping is inseparable from the stopping—the artful disruption of the natural expectation of

continuity. Coleman Hawkins's earnestness has one fatal flaw. Once
he has reached his climax, he has nowhere to go—no way of ratcheting
the level of intensity up another notch short of incoherent screaming.
Parker's rhetoric, on the other hand, allows for irony, the juxtaposition
of the unexpected. It may simply be a matter of ingeniously asymmetric
phrasing. Or it may involve the juxtaposition of different *kinds* of rhetoric. At one point in "Sweet Georgia Brown," after another superbly executed phrase, Parker lands on the tonic (music example 51). Four bars
of tonic harmony follow. Rather than generating momentum by superimposing harmonic movement over this passage, as he does in other
choruses, Parker momentarily celebrates being stuck: he thickens his tone
slightly and plays a brief Swing Era–type riff figure. On other occasions,
he is likely to suddenly shift to a blues mode, with all the idiomatic pitch
bending and rhythmic "playing in the cracks," or he may quote from the
vast store of popular songs in his memory.

It is this open-ended quality—the open-endedness of ambiguity—that
Parker shared with Lester Young, and that made both of them devastat-
ingly effective in a cutting contest. If Hawkins's art is monologic (Schuller
cites his ability to "creat[e] his Hawkins music in total independence of
his surroundings"), the art of Charlie Parker, and the bebop idiom he
helped call into being, is dialogic. So too, one might add, is much of jazz
and the blues. But bebop managed to *absorb* Hawkins's specialized "progressive" brand of virtuosity and bring it into a new relationship with

EX. 50.
"Sweet Georgia Brown" (1943), Charlie Parker solo, chorus 3, mm. 19–20.

EX. 51.
"Sweet Georgia Brown" (1943), Charlie Parker solo, chorus 3, mm. 13–16.

EX. 52.
"Sweet Georgia Brown" (1943), Dizzy Gillespie solo, chorus 3, mm. 1–3.

EX. 53.
"Sweet Georgia Brown" (1943), Dizzy Gillespie solo, chorus 1, mm. 5–8.

other kinds of rhetoric, especially the blues, and into a new rhythmic configuration that undermined its tendency toward sameness and continuity.

By early 1943 Dizzy Gillespie had gotten the basic hang of the new rhythmic idiom. He clearly relished the unexpected disruptions of the rhythmic texture: sudden outbreaks of fast triplets, or witty, punning riff figures like music example 52, in which a change in emphasis momentarily transforms a previously underemphasized chromatic neighbor note (g-sharp') into a blue note (notated here as a-flat'). (As the critic Francis Davis has written, Gillespie's solos "had a rich sarcasm about them that immunized them against excess abstraction.") And yet he still struggled to capture the idiom's more subtle nuances. In many phrases, he falls back on the habit of consistently ghosting the weak half of the beat (music example 53). But he was learning fast.

By the end of the year, Gillespie would be ready for the difficult task of creating a *genre* out of what was, as yet, only a way of playing. "Could the new style survive alone, commercially?" he asked rhetorically in his autobiography. "Could we all survive as modernists, without any further ties to the mother dance bands?" The experiences of Coleman Hawkins, who had been "surviving" as a progressively minded freelance instrumentalist since 1941, provided a revealing and instructive example.

PART THREE

TAKING ADVANTAGE
OF THE
DISADVANTAGES:
BOP MEETS
THE MARKET

7 · SHOWCASING THE REAL STUFF

*There was a warmness about New York, an
excitement. Your blood started circulating. That's
the only way I can describe it. There was Art
Tatum with his trio, and there was Dizzy
Gillespie across the street, and Erroll Garner
wasn't too far away from us. And Coleman
Hawkins and Don Byas, playing together, and
Thelonious Monk was playing piano. And we just
didn't see this in Chicago. . . .*

*When I first went to New York, I said, "I'm
not going back to Chicago, ever."* JIMMY JONES

The general sense of weariness and frustration experienced by many
African-American musicians at the start of the 1940s came from many
sources: poor working conditions, including endless travel; racially motivated humiliations and the omnipresent threat of violence; the initial
decline in public enthusiasm for swing, leading to a reduced share of the
market for black dance orchestras. One may think of these forces as *centrifugal.* They were the inescapable, unpleasant realities that gradually
pushed young and ambitious dance band musicians out of the only career
paths they had known, with no hint of an alternative. Centrifugal forces
swelled the numbers of the discontented and irregularly employed, and
were primarily responsible for the bebop generation's well-deserved reputation for alienation and rebelliousness.

At the same time, there were forces that might be better understood
as *centripetal:* subtle changes in the entertainment industry that pulled
like-minded musicians together into a new sense of community and purpose. *Centripetal* may be too strong a word. Many of these changes were
fortuitous, arising from circumstances far beyond individual control and
uncertain in their implications. The battles in the recording industry to
be discussed in the following chapter—for example, the war between

performance rights organizations and the 1942–43 recording ban—were fought over musicians' heads and, on the surface, seemed to bring as many inconveniences as new opportunities. The centripetal pull, then, came not from the changing circumstances themselves, but from the determination of a handful of musicians (most notably Dizzy Gillespie) to make the most of marginal advantages, gathering the frayed edges of the Swing Era and weaving them into new patterns.

This chapter focuses on new performance venues. By the early 1940s, many musicians could imagine making a living primarily, or even exclusively, with small, jam-session-style combos. This trend had been under way for some time. The gradual drift of the jam session out of the musicians' community and into the public sphere began in the mid-1930s, marked by the conversion of 52nd Street speakeasies into nightclubs and the emergence of the "jazz concert." The peculiar dynamics of wartime both accelerated the process and skewed it unpredictably. Some aspects of transformation, such as the rapid and irreversible deterioration of Harlem as an entertainment center, were painful. Others were more pleasant. Increasingly, musicians could count on the support of a well-organized and affluent subculture of jazz enthusiasts, most of whom relished the opportunity to hear music on terms dictated by the musicians themselves—that is to say, in the atmosphere of the jam session.

The existence of a market for small-combo jazz was a prerequisite for the birth of bebop. Without it, Gillespie, Parker, and others would not have been inspired to transform their backroom experimentation into a new form of concert-style entertainment. As it was, even the remote possibility of a career apart from the usual grind of dance orchestra touring provided sufficient incentive. Fortunately, there was a good precedent for such an alternative career. For nothing better illustrates the rapidly changing climate for jazz in the early 1940s than the decline, and rise, in the fortunes of Coleman Hawkins.

Exile in Chicago

The collapse of his dance band at the end of 1940 had left Hawkins with only a few options. He was now thirty-six—at the peak of his powers, but without the secure place within the music industry of contemporaries like Earl Hines or Count Basie. He could have easily worked in someone else's dance orchestra, but that was a possibility he apparently never seriously considered. Instead, determined to remain in charge of his own professional fortunes, he launched a career as a "single"—the industry's term for a musical act not associated with an established dance band. Unfortunately, the prospects for employment in 1941 for a small jazz band in New York were still limited. After only a few months, his seven-piece band had worn out its welcome at Kelly's Stable on 52nd Street. With the end of the contract, his sidemen scattered to better-paying and more prestigious jobs.

Undaunted, Hawkins decided on a change of scenery. Just a few years earlier, he had led a pleasantly nomadic life, trading residency in one European capital for another. Perhaps with this in mind, he relocated to America's "second city," Chicago. At Dave's Swingland, a South Side cabaret, he assumed leadership of a ten-piece band and took his place as the featured attraction on a bill that included comedians, singers, and a chorus line. Once again, as in Europe, he was greeted by crowds eager to see and hear the famous virtuoso. The initial six-week contract was extended indefinitely, and Hawkins reportedly received the highest salary of any musician working regularly in the city. Evidence of his local renown came with a year-end poll in the *Chicago Defender*, perhaps the most widely circulated black newspaper in the country. In the competition for "best band," Hawkins amassed nearly 50,000 votes—far fewer than poll leaders Ellington, Basie, and Lunceford, but more than Earl Hines, Lucky Millinder, and many others.

Buoyed by this reception, Hawkins decided to leave the Swingland in November 1941, taking his modest-size band on tour. It was a risky move by any standard. Bands rarely pushed their way into prominence on the basis of live performance; they were pulled by media exposure. Hawkins may have made a name for himself in Chicago and New York, but he had done nothing to attract attention in the heartland since "Body and Soul." Since 1940, he had not made any radio appearances or new recordings (other than a guest appearance with Count Basie in April).[1] In any event, Hawkins did not get very far with his tour before the attack on Pearl Harbor forced a hasty retreat.

Now Hawkins was stuck. Even well-established black bands struggled to meet their itineraries during wartime. Hawkins had little choice but to take up residency in another South Side cabaret, White's Emporium, where once again he was greeted by enthusiastic crowds. Chicago may have begun to feel like home. He had even met and married a local

---

1. Another recording session on 16 January 1941, for Victor records, featured Hawkins as part of the *Metronome* All-Stars. The proceeds went to charities supported by the musicians' union (Chilton 1990, 185–186).

woman, the twenty-one-year-old Dolores Sheridan, the previous October. In his public pronouncements he made the best of the situation: staying in one place was far preferable to the grueling tour schedule of a dance band, he said.

But the private story appeared to be different. There could have been little satisfaction in playing indefinitely with a mediocre band at a Chicago nightclub. During his stay at White's Emporium, Hawkins drank heavily to kill the boredom—so much so that he sometimes had to brace himself against the arch of the grand piano while he soloed. In his more constructive moods, Hawkins found ways of challenging himself—characteristically, through a strenuous regimen of modulation. Eddie Johnson, who played tenor saxophone in the band at White's, recalls: "I remember he detested playing 'Body and Soul,' but he had to play it because it was the tune that really made his name a household word. . . . So in order to avoid boredom from playing the same tune, he would actually change keys every eight bars. He might start off in F, go to D and then to A or go into a minor key. . . . You could hear the piano player modulating from one key to another, and Hawkins was gone."

By the middle of 1942, even the security of a regular gig had vanished. Poor business and political complications temporarily closed White's Emporium, along with several other South Side clubs. Hawkins moved briefly to Cleveland, where he fronted a floor show. On his return to Chicago at the end of the summer, he tried once again to lay the groundwork for a national comeback by arranging several recording dates. This time, his plans were thwarted by the ban on recordings called by the musicians' union on August 1.

Hawkins's public response to these difficulties continued to be a study in nonchalance. "Hawkins is now reportedly rebuilding his band," announced *Down Beat* in September. "Nothing lined up, but Hawk doesn't seem to be too worried about things in general." To drum up business, Hawkins turned to a Chicago promoter named Phil Shelley, who set to work publicizing his band in the decidedly less prestigious category of "cocktail unit." Shelley tried hard to make this sound like canny business sense: "Coleman Hawkins, in keeping with the times, has disbanded his larger orchestra and developed a new six-piece combo, which is being heralded as the smoothest musical sextette on the horizon." Reporters in the trade press tended to agree. Thanks to the wartime manpower shortage, the "cocktail lounge" (or, to use another euphemism, "miniature attractions") field was enjoying unprecedented prosperity at the end of

1942—a circumstance that ultimately provided a solid basis for Hawkins's prosperity.

In the short term, though, the only job of substance that emerged was a two-week engagement in the unlikely location of Cedar Rapids, Iowa. The band drew standing-room-only crowds. But for the cosmopolitan Hawkins, playing in a dry state where his favorite Calvert's whiskey was unavailable was an affront to his dignity. At job's end on Saturday night, he insisted on driving over two hundred miles back to Chicago because, as he told his saxophonist, he "didn't want to spend a weekend in a hick town." Even such second-rate jobs, whether in Iowa or Duluth, Minnesota, proved to be few and far between. By the end of November, *Down Beat*'s Chicago reporter laconically noted, "Hawkins is back in town out of work."

Finally, Hawkins decided to put an end to his self-imposed exile. By December he had returned to New York and yet another engagement at Kelly's Stable. This time, however, his career took an immediate turn for the better. For in the intervening years, several trends had converged to make an independent career as a jazz soloist more plausible. Far from being on the periphery of the music business, Hawkins found himself at the center of a new network: working continuously, recording prolifically, and—perhaps most satisfying—surrounded by young musicians as dedicated to the progressive ideal as he was.

Jamming for Dollars

The public jam session was a curious hybrid. It arose in the 1930s from the contradictory impulses of the jazz enthusiasts, who celebrated the jam session as an inner sanctum of the jazz world known only to musicians and their close associates while yearning to penetrate that sanctuary and share its treasures with the outside world. Most jazz enthusiasts initially approached the music as collectors of commercially available recordings, quickly learning to distinguish between fodder for the masses and the "real jazz," known only to cognoscenti. Their hunger for the music soon expressed itself in a burning desire to experience the music firsthand: they avidly absorbed the idea that the most authentic jazz took place not in the glare of publicity, but in secret, subterranean places.

The more enterprising started befriending (and sometimes harassing) musicians and frequenting nightclubs and musicians' hangouts. But as difficult as it was to track down obscure 78s in piles of records in secondhand stores, it was even more difficult to gain access to the real music. Conventional public appearances were not authentic enough; even the conversion of 52nd Street speakeasies like the Onyx Club into nightclubs after the repeal of Prohibition did not satisfy the true jazz fan's desire for an unmediated artistic experience, free from the trappings of commercial culture. Since few jazz fans had the connections or the chutzpah to gain entry to the after-hours venues where musicians preferred playing, an artificial version of the jam session began to emerge, often as an outgrowth of activity at the grass-roots level. In cities such as Los Angeles, Detroit, Philadelphia, Boston, and San Francisco, "hot clubs" devoted to the playing of favorite jazz recordings began to incorporate informal music-making, with the occasional professional guest to authenticate the proceedings.

But the public jam session really got under way with the intervention of Milt Gabler in 1935. Gabler owned the Commodore Record Shop, a 42nd Street store that specialized in jazz recordings and quickly became a gathering place for musicians and fans. Gabler had built a small but loyal clientele for the retail and resale of obscure (and expensive) jazz recordings. He soon realized that sponsoring live music offered a way to simultaneously publicize and expand his business. Under the auspices of a newly formed umbrella group, the United Hot Clubs of America, or UHCA (which he formed "in an effort to promote the sale of jazz records"), he began organizing Sunday afternoon jam sessions. These were originally held in recording studios, carefully removed from the commercial sphere. Although the jam sessions were free, only Gabler's best customers, who had paid two dollars each to gain a place on the mailing list, knew about them. Eventually, Gabler wore out the hospitality of the record companies, who grew tired of having cigarette butts ground into their floors. By 1936 he moved the proceedings to the Famous Door, a 52nd Street club, and began paying the musicians and charging the audience admission.

Jazz enthusiasts may have hoped that they could somehow be absorbed into the jam session scene without distorting it. There had always been an assortment of nonmusicians in jam session venues, ranging from fellow entertainment professionals to those lucky or determined enough to stumble their way into the jazz musicians' after-hours world. Gabler's sessions tried to expand the inner circle just wide enough to admit new admirers without breaking it. But the growing popularity of swing after 1935 made it impossible for the jam session to retain its paradoxical position as a noncommercial sphere for professional musicians. When

Gabler's Sunday afternoon jam sessions were immediately imitated by 52nd Street club owners, who saw yet another opportunity to take advantage of the swing craze, an anonymous UHCA representative complained plaintively in (of all places) *Variety:* "The original idea was to give the fans genuine swing which they craved, and to give the great swing artists the recognition they deserved. There was no attempt or desire to make money for anyone."

But money was there to be made, and the jam session—or at least a simulacrum of it—quickly became an integral part of the swing craze. The latter half of the 1930s was the golden age of the "swing concert," exemplified by Benny Goodman's Carnegie Hall debut and John Hammond's "From Spirituals to Swing." Such large-scale events featured stylized versions of the jam session as well as mainstream fare by dance orchestras. On 52nd Street one could hear small jazz combos offering an irreverent mix of heady improvisation and slapstick humor. Jazz enthusiasts struggled to maintain their sense of higher artistic principles in the midst of this tumult. If the general public tended to treat jazz as entertainment, the true believers accorded it respect in the only way they knew: a painfully self-conscious aping of established concert etiquette. By 1937 the swing mania was at its height, and the appearance of Count Basie, Benny Goodman, and Artie Shaw, among others, at a UHCA jam session on March 14 drew a crowd of over five hundred people into the studios of the American Record Corporation. A correspondent for *Variety* duly noted the "correct method of listening to swing":

> There was naught but reverential quiet until each number was over, but over. Nobody made the horrible blunder of mistaking the break for the finish. Nobody shushed; nobody needed shushing. Latecomers came in on tip-toe, even if they happened to enter during a Chick Webb barrage. . . . Only by its mass tremor, a unanimous, controlled shiver whose particular tempo was established at the beginning of each number, and like the number, never wavered thereafter, was it possible to detect life in the audience at all.

The swing craze affected musicians, too, and in a different way disturbed the fragile equilibrium that had protected the jam session. For by celebrating a handful of brilliant soloists, swing underscored the importance of jazz improvisation within the musicians' community and sent musicians eager to hone their skills to nightclubs and after-hours spots, where they crowded the bandstands. Musicians in Pittsburgh picked up the habit of jamming from the Count Basie orchestra, fresh out of Kansas

City and on its way to New York in early 1937. After their gig at the William Penn Hotel ended at two in the morning, the Basie musicians made the round of clubs in the black Hill district until dawn, inspiring locals to adopt the same routine. A similar upsurge in after-hours music-making was reported in Philadelphia, Kansas City, and Chicago.

These subterranean musical developments have found their way into the historical record only because they were officially deplored—by the American Federation of Musicians. "There's always been a strict union rule against free playing," declared the head of the Philadelphia local in 1938, "and that's all jamming is." The union waged a vigorous counter-offensive against the jam session in the 1930s, threatening violators with fines and expulsion. These actions can be understood in part as a kind of muscle flexing by the resurgent union—the rigid enforcement of regu-lations for the sake of internal discipline. A 1937 notice from Cleveland read: "The local is really clamping down under their new administration. Election of officers has brought in new heads that are putting over a new deal to make the Cleveland Union one of the strongest. . . . Rules and regulations are strictly observed, so mind your P's and Q's, you gates, while in Cleveland. A Bob Crosby man was fined for sitting in on a jam session."

But the union was also responding legitimately to issues of exploita-tion. It was easy for anyone to take advantage of musicians' enthusiasm and naiveté: one need only hire a local rhythm section and send word to visiting musicians that they would be welcome for a jam session. Jazz fans would pack the club for top-rank entertainment, while musicians, true to the ground rules for jam sessions, received nothing. The ruse worked as well for established stars as for the unemployed jazz musicians who, as the *New York Amsterdam News* noted, were "as plentiful as fleas." At some point the line was crossed—usually when the club in question charged admission. Drummer Cozy Cole remembered an inci-dent in which a verbal promise to return to a nightclub in Seattle trans-lated into a newspaper advertisement brazenly announcing that he and Chu Berry would appear that night. In this case, there were two outraged parties—the musicians' union and Cab Calloway, Cole's and Berry's em-ployer at the time:

> We went out there that night, man, and played and had us a ball, we got a
> nice meal, you know. We came back and boy, Cab was raising hell—"What
> the hell you guys doing, playing competition against us"—and the union

Top: A daytime view of 52nd Street in the 1940s, looking east.
(Courtesy of the Institute of Jazz Studies.)

The debonair emcee and entrepreneur Clark Monroe (*center*) is
feted backstage at his "legitimate" Harlem Club, Murrain's, 17
July 1943, surrounded by some of his employees. Among those
visible are pianist Duke Jordan (*extreme left*), bassist Leonard
Gaskin (*right of Monroe*), drummer Max Roach (*right of
Gaskin*), and trumpeter Vic Coulsen (*bottom, second from
right*). (Courtesy of Leonard Gaskin.)

Opposite, top: Aftermath of the
Harlem riot, 2 August 1943.
(Bettman Archives.)

Opposite: Coleman Hawkins on a date
for Signature Records, 8 December
1943, shortly after the end of the ban
on recordings called by the musicians'
union: (*left to right*) Eddie Heywood,
Shelly Manne, Andy Fitzgerald, Al
Casey, Bill Coleman, Hawkins, and
Oscar Pettiford. (Courtesy of the
Institute of Jazz Studies.)

Above: Tenor saxophonist Don Byas
(with hat) on a 1945 recording session
with trumpeter Benny Harris.
(Courtesy of the Institute of
Jazz Studies.)

Opposite, top: Coleman Hawkins and band adjusting with good humor to the absence of Thelonious Monk for the opening set of the evening at the Downbeat Club, 20 October 1944: (*left to right*) Vic Coulsen, Eddie Robinson, Leonard Gaskin (substituting for Denzil Best on drums), Denzil Best (substituting for Monk), and Hawkins. (Courtesy of Leonard Gaskin.)

Opposite: A gathering of musicians and entertainers at the Yacht Club on 52nd Street, 2 April 1944 (*left to right*): Louie (of the dancing duo Pops and Louie), Sid Catlett, Scoops Carey, Trummy Young, Leonard Gaskin, Budd Johnson, Snags Allen, Dizzy Gillespie, and Harold "Doc" West. (Courtesy of Leonard Gaskin.)

Above: The young soloists in Billy Eckstine's "band-within-the-band," 1944 (*left to right*): Lucky Thompson, Dizzy Gillespie, Charlie Parker, and Eckstine. (Photo by Charles "Teenie" Harris. Courtesy of FPG International.)

Bandleader Woody Herman in a publicity photo from the 1940s. (Courtesy of the Institute of Jazz Studies.)

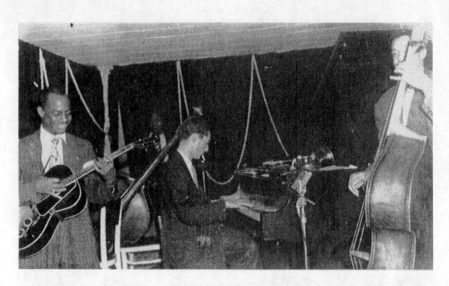

Top: The versatile jazz critic, publicist, and entrepreneur Leonard Feather sits in on piano with guitarist Tiny Grimes and Leonard Gaskin at the Downbeat Club, 12 October 1944. (Courtesy of Leonard Gaskin.)

Pianist Clyde Hart and Leonard Gaskin enjoy a private musical joke at the Downbeat Club, 25 May 1944. (Courtesy of Leonard Gaskin.)

Top: Howard McGhee leading one of the first bebop
bands in Los Angeles, 1945. Drummer Roy Porter is
on the extreme right. (Courtesy of the Institute of
Jazz Studies.)

By October 1945, Charlie Parker was leading his own
band at Clark Monroe's Spotlite Club on 52nd Street
(*left to right*): Stan Levey, Leonard Gaskin, Parker, Miles
Davis, and Dexter Gordon. (Courtesy of Leonard Gaskin.)

One of the last pictures of Coleman
Hawkins, showing his advanced state of
decline by 1969. (Courtesy of the
Institute of Jazz Studies.)

was going to fine us five hundred dollars apiece and had Chu and I frightened to death. That stopped us from going around jamming. . . . I don't mind jamming if there's not a paid audience, you know . . . but to go out there and sit in where people are paying to come in that door, all they giving you is a just a drink and a sandwich or a steak, whatever—you know, you got money, you can buy that.

By the early 1940s a compromise had emerged that satisfied the needs of both jazz fans for an "authentic" experience and musicians for protection against exploitation. Although informal jamming continued to spread throughout the country (in 1941, *Down Beat* reported jam sessions in such unlikely places as Stockton, California; Harrisburg, Pennsylvania; and Worcester, Massachusetts), public jam sessions remained concentrated in New York and a few other cities. Often called jazz matinees (to avoid the problematic connotations that "jam sessions" still held for the union), they were largely the province of jazz enthusiasts turned entrepreneurs. Djakarta-born jazz fan Harry Lim, later responsible for artists and development at Keynote Records, experimented with jam sessions in New York before starting a successful series at the Hotel Sherman in Chicago in 1940. Ralph Berton, brother of the drummer Vic Berton, graduated from swing radio programs on WNYC to jam sessions at the Village Vanguard. Milt Gabler initiated a long-running series at Jimmy Ryan's on 52nd Street in 1941.

Jazz matinees were openly commercial, but on terms that were guaranteed to make no one rich. Admission ranged from $.50 to $1.50, while musicians were paid the minimum union scale—anywhere from $8 to $14 per session. The personnel on any given occasion was necessarily flexible, shaped in part by promoters' tastes and personal connections to the musicians' scene, but highly dependent on the vagaries of musicians' schedules. New York in particular was a crossroads, where one could expect to see and hear prominent soloists from major dance orchestras, as well as a variety of freelancers more or less based in Manhattan. Racial mixture was common, but far less of an issue than in other spheres— perhaps because the free-floating nature of the jam session avoided any suggestion of permanent social association. White musicians were particularly prominent, especially the group of musicians around the colorful guitarist Eddie Condon. Condon saw the jam session format as a refuge against the highly arranged swing style and argued loudly for a defiantly noncommercial "Dixieland" jazz based on collective improvisation. But swing musicians were also welcome. Gabler's sessions featured two bands, divided roughly along racial lines: the predominantly white "Condon mob" and a "Harlem-type" group built around Red Allen, Ben Webster, and Don Byas.

Gabler relied on his Harlem-based group to attract other black musicians to his sessions. This was not an easy task at first. Although black musicians had been performing on 52nd Street since the mid-1930s, their social sphere remained uptown, and they knew they were still not entirely welcome in midtown Manhattan. ("The problem was to get [them] to bring their wives," as Gabler remembered. "They weren't used to socializing outside of Harlem.") In the early 1940s, however, connections were established between the Harlem scene and the new downtown venues. One group of promoters, led by Pete Kameron and Monte Kay, were particularly aggressive in recruiting black musicians. When Kay and Kameron began a series of jam sessions at Kelly's Stable in 1942, they immediately took advantage of their contacts with the younger black musicians congregating at Minton's. "We would go uptown to Minton's on Sunday night—that was when all the cats were out—and line up the guys for next week," remembers Teddy Reig, who worked for Kameron and Kay. "Monday morning we'd get postcards printed up and send them off." Dizzy Gillespie was among those who took advantage of the opportunity. Even when he relocated temporarily to Philadelphia in the fall of 1942 (before joining the Hines band), he would take the train to New York to earn eight dollars at the Sunday sessions. "There were sessions going on . . . in the Village and Kelly's Stables [sic] and you could always pick up a little change from them." The sessions at Kelly's ended abruptly in mid-1943, when the police put a padlock on the door. "Naturally, it had to do with the black-white thing," according to Monte Kay. "We drew an integrated crowd." The police action did little to stem the cultural tide. Harlem was coming downtown.

Hawkins's return to New York from Chicago at the end of 1942 immediately brought him into contact with the Minton's crowd. The Kelly's Stable house band, for which he assumed nominal responsibility, had been led by Kenny Clarke, who continued to play for Hawkins until inducted into the army some months later. Thelonious Monk played intermission piano. Meanwhile, the Sunday afternoon jam sessions were well under way. Hawkins played there at least once (it cost Kay and

Kameron $20, double the union scale, for the privilege), and probably stopped by on other occasions to check out the competition. He may have been amused by the spectacle of people paying good money to see a jam session, and perhaps he was intrigued by the prospect of getting a modest share of that money for a few offhand improvisations. He had played a few such gigs on his return from Europe years before and continued to do so when the opportunity presented itself (as with his appearance at a Boston jam session in February 1944). But he could not have failed to be impressed by the broader picture of which the public jam sessions were a part.

For one thing, the first glimmerings of the modern notion of jazz as concert music became evident in those years. There was some precedent: Benny Goodman's landmark Carnegie Hall concert of 1938, Paul Whiteman's 1928 "Experiment in Modern Music" in Aeolian Hall, and even the James Reese Europe Clef Club concerts in Carnegie Hall from 1912 to 1914. But these were splashy one-shot events, invaluable for prestige and publicity, yet usually operating at a loss. Not until the outbreak of World War II transformed the economics of entertainment did the concert format offer the potential for profit. Promoters were quick to realize that symphony auditoriums made ideal venues: vacant for much of the year, centrally located, and acoustically perfect. The prestige of the concert setting not only attracted new audiences, but made it possible to charge far more for a single evening than in theaters or ballrooms. Jazz concerts were part of a trend affecting all areas of vernacular music: if Duke Ellington proved surprisingly profitable in concert halls from New York to Chicago, so did acts as disparate as Frank Sinatra, Burl Ives, and Phil Spitalny and his All-Girl Orchestra.

Even the public jam session made the transition from smoky back room to concert stage. The pioneer in this regard was the hardworking, wise-cracking Eddie Condon. Condon's ambitious series of jam-session-style concerts in the spring of 1942 in New York's Town Hall consistently drew full houses, prompting surprise in the trade press that "pure and righteous jive may at last be emerging from the phenomenon stage into something resembling commercial stature." The low production costs associated with the jam session format made it attractive to the music industry, and Hawkins himself became a target for speculation. In the spring of 1943, the William Morris Agency announced plans to market five different combos, each offering a distinct style: Condon's "Chicago style," a Sidney Bechet–led New Orleans group, a "blues/barrelhouse" group, a Kansas City group, and finally, a group built around Hawkins, simply characterized as "All-American" or "All-Star." All five groups were to join forces for attention-grabbing concerts in major cities, enlisting the support of local hot clubs. After that, individual groups would be available for one-nighters—perhaps even spreading the public jam session far into the hinterland.

Hawkins's "all-star" septet was in fact staffed by relative unknowns—although daringly, the guitarist and trumpeter were white.[2] The band played nightclub residencies in Toronto and Boston before joining the other groups for a "monster jam session" in Springfield, Massachusetts, on June 20, 1943. Nothing much came of the experiment. Hawkins quickly retreated to Kelly's Stable and within a few months dissolved the band. The flaw in the plan, perhaps, lay in diluting the talent in so many different bands. Within a few years, Hawkins would tour the country in a genuine all-star jam session band—Norman Granz's Jazz at the Philharmonic. In the meantime, Hawkins continued to rely on the drawing power of his own name. He had no particular need to travel: he had found a comfortable home on 52nd Street.

Swing Street

In retrospect, it seems unlikely that former speakeasies on 52nd Street in midtown Manhattan would host such an astonishing concentration of jazz talent. Carved out of the basements of once-residential brownstones, they were cramped and unlovely. Kelly's Stable was typical: "long, low-ceilinged, narrow, and always looking more crowded than it is. . . . The management goes in for subdued lighting so enthusiastically that the place is practically blacked out half the time." "All the clubs were shaped like shoe boxes, and they had dingy canopies outside," recalls Leonard Feather. "The tables were three inches square and the chairs were hard wood. The drinks were probably watered. They were miserable places. There was nothing to them except the music." When Miles Davis first saw the Three Deuces on 52nd Street in 1944, he was astonished at its shabbiness: "It had such a big reputation in the jazz scene that I thought it would be all plush and shit. The bandstand wasn't nothing but a little tiny space that could hardly hold a piano. . . . I remember thinking that it wasn't nothing but a hole in the wall, and that East St. Louis had hipper-looking clubs."

2. The personnel included Lem Davis, alto saxophone; Roy Stevens, trumpet; Herman Mitchell, guitar; Danny Negis, piano; Wallace Bishop, drums; and Al Lucas, bass ("Bean Romps in Beantown," *Down Beat* 10 [1 July 1943]: 23).

But this was New York, and 52nd Street offered steady employment for the top rank of jazz virtuosos. Other nightclubs drew customers with elaborate floor shows, but clubs like the Onyx and the Famous Door offered instrumental jazz well before the swing craze made it fashionable to do so. On rare occasions, a club might squeeze an entire dance orchestra onto its tiny bandstand, as with Count Basie's landmark residency at the Famous Door in 1937 (or, a decade later, Dizzy Gillespie's big band at the Spotlite in 1946). But small jazz combos worked best and proved to be reliable money makers. Rather than simply offering an eclectic evening's entertainment, clubs wisely made prominent jazz soloists their main focus, proudly displaying their names on their awnings and relegating the ubiquitous comedians and dance teams to support status. As the headline act at Kelly's for most of 1943, Hawkins was required to make only a few magisterial appearances per show.

Wartime only strengthened the emphasis on jazz on 52nd Street. One factor, as Max Roach is fond of pointing out, was the infamous cabaret tax, a wartime measure imposed in the spring of 1944. The cabaret tax was a 30 percent (later reduced to 20 percent) surcharge on any venue that offered "a public performance for profit . . . in the way of acting, singing, declamation, or dancing." Instrumental music was by definition exempt, and this prompted some clubs along 52nd Street to advertise their strict jazz policy with large "NO TAX" signs in their windows.

But the trend away from elaborate entertainment had been in motion for some time. The wartime economy accelerated the prosperity of 52nd Street, confining recreational activities to the urban core and funneling defense money into the hands of the entertainment-hungry crowds thronging New York's midtown district. Moreover, that money increasingly passed into the pockets of African-American artists. "Since the decline of the one-nighter business due primarily to transportation difficulties," reported *Billboard* in late 1943, "Negro musicians have been deserting large bands to join or organize small units. . . . Money available in the cocktail field is far more attractive than the salaries paid them by the larger bands on the road." Booking agencies estimated that the number of new black combos exceeded the number of new white combos by three to one—and these included some of the biggest names in the business. Of the thirty acts listed as "sure-fire attractions" in 1944, twenty-four were black—including Coleman Hawkins, Art Tatum, Ben Webster, Billie Holiday, Cozy Cole, Maxine Sullivan, Oscar Pettiford, Roy Eldridge, Hot Lips Page, and Benny Carter.

To be sure, black artists were consistently paid less than their white counterparts, but they earned far more than they could have earned in any other venue. Billie Holiday earned $175 a week for her work at Kelly's Stable in the early 1940s (a few years later, thanks in part to wartime inflation, her reported weekly income was $1,250). Fats Waller drew $300 in 1943, his last year, and Art Tatum, playing with his trio, grossed over $1,000 a week. Pianists and vocalists were longtime favorites on 52nd Street: Tatum had played at the Onyx Club when it was still a speakeasy and musicians' hangout, and Holiday and Maxine Sullivan had been among the first of the post-Prohibition attractions. But others on the list were refugees from the dance orchestras, men who had made their reputation as soloists and even bandleaders, but who now found it more convenient and profitable to lead small combos.

For many black musicians, 52nd Street had its drawbacks—not the least of which was an uneasiness about working in white-dominated midtown Manhattan. Billie Holiday, whose career began in Harlem cabarets, bitterly complained about her treatment in 1935 at the Famous Door, where she and Teddy Wilson worked as intermission entertainment. Black musicians were rare at the time, and they were told in no uncertain terms not to fraternize with white patrons. Holiday sarcastically characterized all of 52nd Street as a "plantation. . . . It was supposed to be a big deal. 'Swing Street' they called it. . . . It was this 'new' kind of music. They could get away with calling it new because millions of squares hadn't taken a trip to 131st Street." By the time she returned to work on 52nd Street at Kelly's Stable in 1939, employment opportunities had improved dramatically: the "plantation owners . . . found they could make money off Negro artists and they couldn't afford their old prejudices. So the barriers went down, and it gave jobs to a lot of great musicians." But the social barriers remained. "I resented the exclusion of black people as customers," remembers Leonard Feather. "The clubs could not exclude black musicians with whom they were familiar. But by and large, they tried to keep as white as possible. . . . It was not until 1943–44 that the raised eyebrows began disappearing." Even during the war, when 52nd Street earned a reputation as a haven of relative racial harmony, the mere presence of black artists and audiences outside of Harlem was enough to spark unpleasant and occasionally violent harassment by white servicemen.

Still, working on 52nd Street was congenial enough. The clustering of a half dozen or more clubs within a city block encouraged the practice of "sitting in": musicians, on their intermissions, would stroll down the street to join their colleagues on the bandstand. Or if they were tired and in need of refreshment, the White Rose bar at the corner of 52nd Street and Sixth Avenue offered inexpensive drinks (twenty-five cents for a scotch), free hors d'oeuvres, and good company. "The tourists didn't have a chance to get in, the place was always so jammed with musicians." More important, a musician working on 52nd Street had access to mainstream audiences and living wages without having to leave home. It is little wonder that Hawkins made it his headquarters for the next several years. Nor is it any wonder that younger musicians began plotting how they could gain a foothold.

From Harlem to 52nd Street

The eve of war found Harlem in a tense and hostile mood. In November 1941, just a month before Pearl Harbor, reports of a "crime wave" in Harlem temporarily displaced headlines about the conflict in Europe in local newspapers. The murder of a fifteen-year-old white boy within ten blocks of Mayor Fiorello La Guardia's apartment on upper Fifth Avenue provided the occasion for the *New York Times* to detail "petty and sordid crime" in the area. Storeowners who refused to interfere with shoplifting for fear of sparking "another Harlem riot"; white schoolteachers who requested, and received, a police escort; the novel technique of "mugging," in which a victim was simultaneously choked from behind and thrown off balance, allowing a second "gang member" to strip him of his valuables and even his clothing: all reinforced the image of Harlem as a place that had sunk below the standards of civilization, a place where white people in particular were threatened.

Adam Clayton Powell, Jr., who had just won election as the first African American on the New York City Council, argued bitterly that the press coverage was misdirected. "The so-called recent crime wave is neither a crime wave, nor is it recent," he complained. "It is not a crime wave in the accepted sense because it is not being conducted by criminals. It is not recent because it dates to the beginning of the depression." But where Powell pointed to woefully inadequate facilities for recreation, education, and health, whose funding had failed to keep pace with the steadily increasing population, the mayor simply sent in more police and issued dire warnings. Predictably, the entertainment district of Harlem suffered, even though the highly publicized "crime region" lay some twenty blocks to the south. "Harlem night life . . . was experiencing the first glimmer of a comeback until last week's disclosures," reported *Variety*. "Great publicity given to tales of murder, rape, and robbery in Harlem and nearby northernmost part of Central Park has sent nitery biz into a cellar-spin."

Things only got worse. In the summer of 1942, Harlem was declared off-limits for servicemen on leave, ostensibly as a public health measure: too many men were contracting venereal disease uptown. In the spring of 1943, the Savoy Ballroom was closed for six months, on the grounds that it was a haven for prostitutes (according to Malcolm X, "the real reason was to stop Negroes from dancing with white women"). Finally, on a hot summer evening, the spark was set. On the night of August 1, 1943, a black soldier tried to come to the aid of an intoxicated woman who was arguing loudly with a white policeman in the lobby of the Braddock Hotel. A scuffle ensued; the soldier grabbed the policeman's nightstick and tried to run off; and the soldier was shot in the shoulder. Those who saw the incident assumed he had been killed and spread the word. Within hours, a riot had started. Shop windows along 125th Street were shattered, and after midnight, looters descended to reap the harvest of chaos. La Guardia sent in all available civilian and military police, who restored order—but only after six people, all Harlemites, had died in the crossfire.

Ralph Ellison, who observed the riot from his offices at the *Negro Quarterly*, later imaginatively re-created it in the closing pages of *Invisible Man*. Along the way, he offered a range of conflicting interpretations of its meaning, from spontaneous eruption ("Hell, man, it just exploded," says a bystander. "These is dog days") to purposeful, passionate action. Watching a group of men systematically torch their rat- and roach-infested tenement, Ellison's nameless protagonist marvels, "They did it themselves . . . planned it, organized it, applied the flame." But his pride shades into horror as he sees "the crash of men against things" yield inevitably to "the crash of men against men and with most of the guns and numbers on the other side."

In the end, the futility and destructiveness of the riot quite overshadowed the legitimacy of the deeply felt grievances it sought, however inchoately, to express. The city establishment stood side by side with black leaders and even the Communist Party in deploring the "hoodlums, vandals, and irresponsible elements" behind the destruction, applauding the swift police action, and expressing great relief that the unrest had never degenerated into an open race riot, as in Detroit. But the damage had been done. An elegiac editorial in the *New York Amsterdam News* summed up the tragedy:

Numerous stories have been told of the glamour and beauty of Harlem, and Harlem has become known through the world as the Negro capital of America. In every city of any size, its Negro community became a Harlem, and people everywhere, both here and abroad, grew to think of Harlem as a place of unlimited opportunity for Negroes.

Native Harlemites, who knew better, aided the conspiracy by pretending they believed Harlem was heaven. They bragged about having been born here, about not having been further south than the Bowery, all land beyond the Hudson River being the Hinterland, and about how every night spent outside Harlem was just another night camping out. Newcomers to Harlem soon discovered that Harlem was not heaven, but they, too, pretended that it was so, lest they might be called hicks and small-towners who didn't know the ways of the big city. . . .

It's time now for Harlem to quit kidding itself. Harlem is part of a great city, but Harlem is far behind. It has been given a grand build-up in song and story, but Harlem never has lived up to its reputation abroad. Not even in the days of the "golden era," sometimes called the "renaissance," was Harlem on a sound economic or political footing. Harlem is, and has been for years, in a bad way. It has refused to face the facts.

Just a few months before, Clark Monroe had made his bid to escape the dying after-hours world of Harlem. His first venture did not take him very far. Murrain's, a new nightclub at Seventh Avenue and 132nd Street, was only two blocks away from the Uptown House. But as a legitimate business, operating within legal curfew hours, it was worlds apart, and a first step toward bigger things. Murrain's offered a conventional floor show, with a chorus line. For the house band, Monroe gathered the corps of musicians who usually played for the Uptown House: Max Roach, Duke Jordan, Vic Coulsen, and Leonard Gaskin. The group was billed as Clark Monroe and His Funsters. "Being such a ham, he wanted to be in front of something. He saw an opportunity to take these young fellows, and front them—he would be out in the limelight." The shift from the Uptown House to Murrain's was equally important for his young employees. After a late adolescence spent on the margins of the music business, they were poised for a decisive commitment to a professional career. The job at Murrain's required that they belong to the union; so on June 10, they trooped down en masse to the union office to sign on as members of Local 802.

Monroe still had his sights set on downtown; the devastation of the riot must have dashed any hope he had for a revived Harlem nightclub scene. By early fall he had found his opportunity—on 52nd Street. The group at Murrain's found a new niche as the house band at Kelly's Stable, once again working under Monroe's nominal direction. There, they joined forces with Coleman Hawkins. Monroe's group provided accompaniment for Hawkins and vocalist Billy Daniels, alternated with the Clarence Profit trio, and filled in the remainder of the time with the same eclectic mix of Ellington, Basie, unfamiliar pop tunes, and original compositions they had perfected at the Uptown House. They were barely noticed in the trade press (one report pegged them as "strictly on an Ellington kick"), but their unusual repertory, bolstered by Max Roach's subtly polyrhythmic drumming, gradually attracted the attention of Hawkins and fed his curiosity about what was going on uptown.

Dizzy Gillespie, in the meantime, had found his way downtown as well. In September he left the Earl Hines band. Looking for work, he approached Coleman Hawkins for an engagement at Kelly's Stable.[3] It was not his first engagement on 52nd Street. In late 1941, shortly after being fired by Cab Calloway, he worked in a band led by Benny Carter, playing first at Kelly's Stable and later at the Famous Door. Gillespie enjoyed the gig, which reunited him briefly with Kenny Clarke ("it was just a long honeymoon"), but he left as soon as engagements with dance orchestras became available. Two years later, he was more experienced and confident, and looking to make a name for himself. Hawkins hired him, but their relationship immediately foundered in a dispute over salary. Gillespie was offered what the other musicians were making—union scale, $66 a week. " 'Look, you're gonna miss a trumpet player around here, because I want $75,' " Gillespie countered. "A little over scale, I figured, because I was a good musician, a soloist." In Gillespie's 1979 autobiography, he soft-pedaled the dispute. Hawkins was amenable, he said, and tried to persuade the management of Kelly's to give the young trumpeter a raise. This seems out of character with Hawkins's generally imperious attitude toward his employees. Gillespie set a more realistic tone slightly later: "They paid Coleman the money he asked for. . . . He was getting his money by saying, 'I want so-and-so for myself. Those other musicians work for scale.' " In any event, Gillespie took the $66 at the end of the week and quit.

3. This incident did not take place in 1941, as Gillespie has stated in his autobiography (1979, 152), or as John Chilton has stated in his biography of Hawkins (1990, 187). See Leonard Feather, "Dizzy Like a Fox," *Metronome* 61 (July 1944): 16, 31.

The First Bop Combo

In November, after a four-week stint as a substitute in Duke Ellington's band, Gillespie came back to 52nd Street. This time he sought not just employment, but a measure of control, as leader of his own band. He decided to join forces not with an established star, but with a younger musician whose rise had been even more meteoric than his own.

Oscar Pettiford emerged as one of the most remarkable success stories of 1943. Just a year before, the young bassist had become so discouraged with the prospects for playing music in his home town of Minneapolis that he had quit the profession altogether for nearly half a year to work in a defense plant. Howard McGhee had worked with the Pettiford family band several years earlier during his wanderings in the Midwest; when the Barnet band came through Minneapolis, he arranged for the band-leader to hear Pettiford play. Barnet was impressed with the twenty-year-old's obvious talent and hired him immediately to augment the band's cadre of black musicians. In May, Pettiford left the band and came to New York. Shortly afterward, he replaced Nick Fenton as the house bassist at Minton's Playhouse, working alongside Thelonious Monk. Later in the year, he gained experience on 52nd Street playing with Roy Eldridge at the Onyx Club. By year's end, Pettiford had attracted enough attention during his brief time in New York to win first place ("Gold") in a new critics' poll conducted by *Esquire* magazine.

Pettiford's rise is hardly surprising: then, as now, skilled and reliable bass players are in great demand. But Pettiford added an extra dimension. Like bassist Jimmy Blanton, whose powerful playing with Duke Ellington from 1939 until his untimely death in 1942 startled the jazz world, Pettiford was a confident soloist. Gillespie was struck in particular by his melodic imagination, his ability to free himself from the gravitational pull of the chord roots that bassists were required to provide. As it turned out, Gillespie got a niche on 52nd Street on Pettiford's coattails. Pettiford's personal manager called the Onyx Club and arranged for a combo co-led by his client to appear on a bill with Billie Holiday and guitarist Al Casey—all winners of the *Esquire* Gold Award. Gillespie, it was agreed, would be co-leader, but his name didn't even appear on the bill.

Although the group organized by Clark Monroe at Kelly's Stable preceded it by several months, the Gillespie-Pettiford band at the Onyx is generally regarded, with good reason, as the first bop combo to appear in a public venue—"the birth of the bebop era," as Gillespie has put it.

Gillespie had naturally hoped that it would represent the finest talent from the uptown scene. He wanted Charlie Parker to join him in the front line, but was apparently unable to contact him. Instead, Lester Young, who was familiar with many of the musicians from jamming at Minton's, worked with the band in its first several weeks. At the end of November, Count Basie, who was enjoying a rare midtown Manhattan residency at the Hotel Lincoln, fired tenor saxophonist Don Byas and convinced Young to return to his band. Byas was hired by the Onyx as a featured soloist, but drifted into rehearsals and eventually onto the bandstand with the Gillespie-Pettiford group.

On drums, Gillespie would have preferred his longtime compatriot Kenny Clarke, but Clarke was in the army. He may have used Harold "Doc" West, the drummer in the house band at Minton's, for a time, but he soon persuaded Max Roach to leave Kelly's Stable to join his band. Finally, Gillespie considered using Bud Powell as the pianist and on at least a few occasions reportedly used Thelonious Monk (who perhaps came down from Minton's with "Doc" West). But as Gillespie later noted, "We didn't need a strong piano player in there. We had Max and Oscar Pettiford. . . . Bud's importance was as a great soloist, not necessarily an accompanist. He was too much of a rebel for that. Bebop pianists didn't lay down the changes; some, like Monk, just embellished them." After working for some time without a pianist, the group finally settled on George Wallington, a more malleable neophyte, who dutifully studied modern chord changes with Gillespie.[4]

The shifting personnel was less important than the new repertory that took shape at the Onyx Club. Like Clark Monroe's group, the Gillespie-Pettiford band offered an eclectic mixture of traditional jam session war-horses, unusual popular songs, and originals. In the latter category were a few Monk compositions like "'Round Midnight," a pair of startlingly up-tempo pieces ("Max Is Making Wax," "Be-Bop"), a miniature concerto featuring Pettiford variously called "One Bass Hit" or "For Bass Faces Only," and reworkings of "I Got Rhythm" by Monk, Gillespie, and others ("Salt Peanuts," "Mop Mop," and what came to be known as the "52nd Street Theme"). With the exception of tunes like Gillespie's "A Night in Tunisia" (which betrayed in its elaborate structure its origins as a big-band arrangement [see chapter 10]), most of this repertory had been

4. According to Oscar Pettiford, "Wallington couldn't play a whole song through with the right changes. We had to teach him" (Pat Harris, "Oscar Pettiford Now on Cello Kick," *Down Beat* 17 [29 December 1950]: 20).

conceived and passed on orally. This had its advantages: the new rhythmic language was so intricate and elusive that it was easier to convey the sense of a passage by singing it with scat syllables ("Ooop bop ta oop a la doo bop doo ba") than by translating it into cumbersome Western notation. But the band was under pressure to solidify its repertory quickly, virtually demanding that some of it be written down. In January the veteran tenor saxophonist Budd Johnson replaced Don Byas in the combo. Johnson, a skilled arranger, soon found himself in the role of scribe:

> I put down a lot of things for Oscar Pettiford. . . . Most all of those tunes that we played on 52nd Street when I worked with Diz, damned near half of them were Oscar's tunes. He was writing tunes every day. "Hey, Budd. Put this down. Put this down. Put this down." 'Cause he couldn't notate it on paper. . . . I used to put things down for Monk. That was back in the 52nd Street days. . . . We'd get a bottle of wine. I'd go over to his mother's house where he was livin' over on the West Side. I would put things down for him.

Pettiford and Johnson were apparently also responsible for the distinctive way that the quintet presented those compositions. There were several previous models. A small combo could attempt to simulate the full-bodied homophonic texture of a dance orchestra. John Kirby's group, for example—which billed itself as "the biggest little band in the world"—featured three horns (saxophone, trumpet, clarinet) and voiced most of its ensembles with block harmonies. Or one could opt for a polyphonic ensemble—ranging from the multivoiced, independent counterpoint of the New Orleans style to a melody decorated with improvised countermelodies or supported by sustained whole notes. Pettiford and Johnson instead chose the stark, modern sound of two horns playing in unison or octaves, the better to throw the jagged lines of "52nd Street Theme" or Gillespie's "Be-Bop" into relief. This procedure, already in the air through performances by the Benny Goodman small groups and through the famous opening chorus of Duke Ellington's "Cotton Tail," became the standard for bebop and beyond.

During this time Hawkins began paying closer attention to the music being created by men some fifteen to twenty years younger than he. He had ample time in between appearances at Kelly's to walk less than a block down 52nd Street to the Onyx Club, and ample reason to be curious what his erstwhile trumpet player was up to. That he actually took the opportunity to do so was confirmed later by a young Gillespie fan in a letter to the editor of *Down Beat:* "I noticed that Coleman Hawkins was often present to hear Dizzy blow. Such recognition means Dizzy must be good."

Still, the real impetus for Hawkins to move beyond mere curiosity to active involvement with the Gillespie crowd came not from live performance on 52nd Street, but from new opportunities in the recording studio. These opportunities were the unexpected outcome of a prolonged and bitter battle between the recording companies and the musicians' union.

8 · THE RUSH TO RECORD

On August 1, 1942, James Petrillo, president of the American Federation of Musicians, engineered one of the most extraordinary coups in modern labor history. He had spent his prior two years in office securing a closed shop, forcing such independent organizations as the American Guild of Musical Artists and the Boston Symphony Orchestra to join the AFM fold. By 1942 almost every professional instrumentalist held a union card. Thus armed, Petrillo turned his attention to an issue that had long bedeviled him: the use of recordings—"canned music"—to replace the services of union musicians. Why, he argued, should a musician contribute to his own unemployment by making a recording? Since the Supreme Court had recently confirmed that artists had no control over the use of their own recordings after the point of sale, Petrillo had to devise a more roundabout strategy—a demand that record companies contribute a fixed fee from every recording to a union fund for unemployed musicians— and strong-arm tactics to make it work.

As early as 1937, Petrillo called for a ban on new recordings. Because he was head of only the Chicago local at the time, his leverage to make this action effective was limited. In 1942, in firm control of the entire organization, he revived the idea of a ban (technically, the licenses requiring record companies to use only union musicians were withdrawn, making it illegal for union members to record), and he made it stick. The few feeble attempts to evade the ban—records made entirely with vo-calists (who were not required to belong to the union) or featuring uku-leles, harmonicas, or other instruments not covered by union agree-ments—underscored the union's remarkable success at controlling the activities of thousands of members. One could criticize, as many did, Petrillo's Luddite attitude toward technology, as well as his blatant vio-lation of a general pledge by the American Federation of Labor leadership to forgo strikes "for the duration" of the war. One could also question the long-term effectiveness of his strategy, which did little to stop the inroads of prerecorded music into the lives of professional musicians. But from a purely logistical standpoint, it is hard to fault Petrillo for the execution of his plan. Thousands of loyal union members obeyed him, and for more than a year, the vast recording industry was silenced.

The recording ban is a convenient watershed in the history of jazz. On one side is the Swing Era, with the record catalogs dominated by the large dance orchestras. With the resumption of recording comes a new age and a new sensibility. Thus Brian Rust's two-volume discography, *Jazz Records*, ends in 1942, when "a whole chapter, even a whole volume of recorded history came to an abrupt close. By the end of 1944 . . . jazz had branched off in a new direction." For those interested in tracing the continuity of jazz throughout the period, however, the recording ban is a source of deep frustration. It is a black box through which the music passes and is transformed by unseen forces before it emerges on the other side. Somewhere in that enforced period of silence were the first elusive traces of the bebop movement, now lost to posterity. The recording ban falls like a curtain in the middle of the most interesting part of a play; by the time the curtain rises, the plot has taken an unexpected and in-explicable turn, and the characters are speaking a new language.

This sense of loss, of opportunities missed, has become an inextricable part of the telling of the bebop story. The recording ban is routinely cited as the reason why the pieces of the puzzle don't fit together. James Lincoln Collier writes, "By about 1942, it was clear to musicians that here was something more than mere experimentation. Here was a new kind of music. Unhappily, we cannot pinpoint these developments. . . . As a result [of the ban], there are few commercial recordings of any of the bop play-ers during the years they were working out their innovations." Similar remarks may be found in other textbooks or historical overviews. Such speculation is reinforced by the testimony of no less an eyewitness than Dizzy Gillespie. In his autobiography, he describes how he learned to interpolate chromatically descending chains of ii^7–V^7 into tunes like "I Can't Get Started": "We'd do that kind of thing in 1942 around Minton's a lot. We'd been doing that kind of thing, Monk and I, but it was never documented because no records were being made at the time."

Such claims are at best incomplete, overlooking the fragments of evidence that do exist. Private recordings by Jerry Newman of rambling jam sessions at Minton's and Monroe's, as well as the Bob Redcross "Sweet Georgia Brown" session in a Chicago hotel room in 1943, provide candid portraits of Gillespie, Parker, Monk, and others at this phase of their careers. But the existence of such recordings begs the question: what would established record companies have been doing there, anyway? It is decidedly naive to imply that in the absence of a ban, recording executives would have been inclined to "document" the goings-on in back rooms in Harlem. True, the three "majors," Decca, Columbia, and Victor, had been spurred into an awareness of a market for small-combo jazz by the success of upstart companies like Commodore and Blue Note in the late 1930s. Coleman Hawkins had benefited by this policy by 1940, as had other established names in the jazz field like Sidney Bechet, James P. Johnson, and Eddie Condon.

But even had talent scouts from the major record firms stumbled onto a new (and potentially marketable) musical style uptown, the prospects for Gillespie or Parker being invited into the recording studio in the early 1940s were decidedly slim. Ironically, improving business conditions were largely to blame for major record firms pulling away from the recording of small jazz combos in the year immediately preceding the AFM ban. By 1941 the recording industry had fully recovered from the lean years of the Depression. Sales of records reached new heights, and demand for such hit recordings as "Chattanooga Choo-Choo" (which sold over a million copies in six months) far outstripped existing production capacity. At the end of the year, war in the Pacific threatened supplies of shellac, a major ingredient in 78 rpm records. Both of these factors meant that by mid-1942, record companies were ready to dedicate all of their dwindling resources to best-selling pop recordings. As a trade correspondent put it, jazz records "take up shellac, sell slowly, and have a low margin of profit. They're out." Well before Petrillo's intentions to halt recording were made public, John Hammond warned: "Unless record fans rise up in arms immediately, there will not be any more good jazz on discs except by accident. Retrenchment necessitated by the shortage of shellac has already caused recording executives to go conservative in the extreme. . . . Reissues and small band dates are out for the duration. . . . All the companies are devoting themselves to tunes either on or slated for the hit parade."

To the extent that members of the bebop generation worked for mainstream dance orchestras, their work stood a reasonable chance of being recorded before August 1, 1942. This is what indeed happened with Charlie Parker's solos with Jay McShann and Dizzy Gillespie's solos (and arrangements) with Cab Calloway, Les Hite, and Lucky Millinder. It would certainly have happened with the Earl Hines band of 1943—the most obvious instance of the AFM ban robbing posterity of potentially invaluable "documentation." But this is not the same as capturing the bop style in its formative stages.

Before bebop could make its way into the recording studio, it had to become a viable commercial product. In its original Harlem setting, the new music, as yet unnamed ("the music wasn't called bop at Minton's," said Kenny Clarke, "we called ourselves modern"), was uncommodified. Its distinctive idiosyncrasies—a loose, improvisatory format and an eclectic repertory of standards studded with harmonic obstacles—were tailored to the specialized requirements of professional musicians, who pursued their commercial ambitions through other, more public channels. For all the energy and imagination poured into these late-night sessions, no one (apart from the house band, which drew a very modest wage) expected to make any money from their efforts.

The commodification of bebop thus required a conscious commitment on the part of musicians to reorient the music to existing commercial channels. This process was set in motion early in the 1940s by the lure of public jam sessions and the nightclubs on 52nd Street, both of which put jam-session-style jazz on a profitable footing. It accelerated as the war years unexpectedly opened up new opportunities, further encouraging young musicians to imagine using a novel idiom of their own invention as the means to achieve a degree of artistic and financial independence.

Along the way, the music would have to be deliberately transformed. The repertory would have to be converted into clearly defined economic units, preferably original compositions, for which authorship could be precisely established. The often chaotic atmosphere of the jam session would need to be streamlined and subtly redirected toward paying audiences. Reputation among musicians would have to be translated into commercial reputation, a name on a nightclub awning that would draw customers inside. The music would have to be given a label or tag, something akin to a brand name for marketing purposes.

Inevitably, something was lost and something was gained. Even if, as Miles Davis has insisted, "the *real* thing happened up in Harlem, at Minton's," black musicians needed to take the music outside of their own insular professional community to make it the basis of a career. Dizzy Gillespie, who saw this perhaps more clearly than anyone, spearheaded the transformation. With the Onyx Club combo settling for a long stay on 52nd Street, the process was well under way by early 1944. As Gillespie has explained: "Jamming at Minton's and Monroe's we had our fun, but with the level of music which we'd developed by 1944, it wasn't very profitable, artistically or commercially. We needed to play to a wider audience and Fifty-second Street seemed ready to pay to hear someone playing something new."

But the move to 52nd Street is only part of a broader picture. By early 1944, Gillespie suddenly had a host of willing partners in the business world: recording companies eager to add relatively unknown jazz musicians to their catalogs. Their eagerness is one of the nicer ironies of the period. For an unexpected outcome of the AFM recording ban—or more precisely, the way the ban was ended—was a shattering of the major record companies' monopoly on recorded music, providing a brief, but crucial, window of opportunity for the bebop generation.

Cracks in the Monolith

From the beginning of the century through the 1930s, the trend in American popular music had been toward a concentration of economic power at the center. Local music-making became inexorably absorbed into a handful of enormous enterprises controlled and coordinated at the national level: radio networks, the "Big Three" recording companies, national booking agencies, motion picture studios, publishing firms (fifteen publishing companies accounted for 90 percent of the hit songs in 1941), and the performance rights organization ASCAP. These highly efficient organizations worked in concert to create commodities that would appeal to as many people as possible: the Hollywood film, the hit song, the million-selling record, the name band. Twentieth-century technology blanketed the country with these entertainments, absorbing regional and ethnic differences into an increasingly standardized and homogeneous product. The result was something close to a unitary popular culture.

The music industry had long acknowledged the existence of minority tastes and organized these into specialty markets on the fringes of the music business—"race records," "hot" jazz, "hillbilly" music. But at the height of the Swing Era, these markets seemed anachronistic. Any profit derived from them counted for very little compared with the astonishing returns attainable in mainstream entertainment. The traffic was always from the margins to the center—as when "folk" boogie-woogie piano styles, championed by John Hammond and brought to the stage of Carnegie Hall in his "From Spirituals to Swing" concert in 1938, became commercially viable in dance orchestra performances of such tunes as Will Bradley's 1940 hit, "Beat Me Daddy, Eight to the Bar."[1]

The swing phenomenon itself was the result of this drive toward a unitary popular culture. We tend now to think of swing as a form of jazz and to reduce it to its music—the solos and arrangements carefully preserved on shellac. But this was only part of the package. Swing bands were still dance bands, playing in ballrooms to publics that might dance to Count Basie or Jimmie Lunceford one week and Kay Kyser or Guy Lombardo the other. Tin Pan Alley was still in full flower: throughout the formative years of bop, its great composers continued to produce new songs—Richard Rodgers ("People Will Say We're in Love," 1943), Cole Porter ("You'd Be So Nice to Come Home To," 1943), Irving Berlin ("White Christmas," 1942), and Jerome Kern ("Long Ago and Far Away," 1944)—and swing bands performed them. And by inheriting vaudeville's place in theaters, swing thrived on clowning and physical entertainment. Whether crisscrossing the continent, appearing over the airwaves, or providing the soundtrack for Saturday night good times on the local jukebox, the name band simultaneously embodied all of these delights, its appeal cutting across divisions of age, class, race, and region.

This approach to the marketing of entertainment did not long outlast the Swing Era. Control over the production and dissemination of popular music continued to lie in the hands of vast, impersonal networks, but eruptions from below mandated a degree of diversity. Cultural differences were allowed to become permanent rifts in the landscape. "Hillbilly" music became country, with its headquarters in the nation's heartland in Nashville. The youth market, so crucial to the success of swing, broke off its ties to the adult world of professional songwriters and singers and

---

1. Will Bradley was himself a good example of the necessity to downplay or disguise ethnicity, having changed his name from Wilbur Schwichtenberg before embarking on a career as a name bandleader.

embraced the raucous freedom of early rock 'n' roll. The black market served by race records, invigorated by the accelerated pace of postwar migration from country to city, reemerged as rhythm and blues and soul.

Viewed against this broad background, the emergence of modern jazz in the form of bebop may seem relatively insignificant. Many of its initial corporate sponsors (and not a few musicians) had clear hopes that it might emerge as a new and lucrative form of black vernacular entertainment. But bop quickly became eclipsed at the jukebox by an emergent rhythm-and-blues style that gradually shed its jazz roots, leaving bop to retreat to a precarious position on the margins of the business as an art music without portfolio. Nevertheless, it was the rebellious professionals of the bebop generation who were among the first to discover the incipient cracks in the monolith of popular entertainment in the early 1940s, and they found ways to turn the ensuing chaos to their advantage.

The first of these cracks came with a dispute between ASCAP and the radio networks, which led to the creation of an alternative performance rights organization, Broadcast Music Incorporated (BMI), at the beginning of the 1940s. ASCAP was probably the most flagrantly monopolistic organization in the music business, tenaciously extending the dominance of professional songwriters long after sheet music sales had ceased to be the principal measure of a song's success. ASCAP pooled the copyrights of its member composers and their publishers, and it demanded a sizable percentage of net receipts from radio networks for the privilege of broadcasting live performances of its catalog of songs. New members were continuously added to keep the catalog up to date, but payments were distributed by an arcane system that favored members of long standing, regardless of whether they continued to publish new hits. Membership was strictly controlled, which tended to exclude composers who did not fit the traditional Tin Pan Alley mold. Ellington was an early member, as were W. C. Handy and Maceo Pinkard (the African-American composer of "Sweet Georgia Brown"). But Jelly Roll Morton was kept at arm's length until 1939, losing (by his estimate) some $75,000 in performance royalties in the process. Boogie-woogie pianist Meade "Lux" Lewis, whose hit "Honky Tonk Train Blues" dated back to 1927, became a member in 1942 only after a public airing of his difficulties embarrassed ASCAP into admitting him. Scott Joplin was admitted in the same year — twenty-five years after his death.

BMI was formed by the radio networks not with an eye to righting these wrongs, but as a way of creating a body of published music not subject to ASCAP's control, for use over the radio. When their contract with ASCAP expired at the end of 1940, the networks broke off ties with the organization, allowing only BMI-registered music (or tunes in public domain) to be performed over commercial radio for most of the following year. Lawsuits by the Justice Department under the Sherman Antitrust Act against ASCAP, BMI, and the radio networks helped to bring about a truce, but only after exposing the performance rights organizations for the cartels they were. Among the charges were "the illegal pooling of most of the desirable copyright music available for radio broadcasting in order to eliminate competition and to monopolize the supply" and "illegal discrimination against composers who were not members of ASCAP."

BMI was here to stay, and its practices constituted a sharp break with the past. For one thing, in its efforts to build up its catalog quickly, BMI turned to grass-roots sources previously excluded from ASCAP—folk music, hillbilly (as country music was then known), Latin American music, jazz—and it remained committed to these marginalized genres after it was securely established. ASCAP had protected only live performance, but BMI paid its composers for any form of performance over the radio, whether live or recorded. Both of these considerations made BMI the performance rights organization of choice for the emergent country, rhythm-and-blues, and rock-'n'-roll fields, which came to dominate popular music during the 1950s.

The AFM ban was a second shock to the system. Not that Petrillo had any intention of challenging the monopoly of Columbia, Victor, and Decca in calling for a recording ban. All he wanted were concessions on behalf of union members, and it was far more convenient to assume for the purposes of negotiation that the record industry was synonymous with these three giant recording firms. Other, much smaller companies— the "independents"—were eager to come to terms with the union and start recording, but Petrillo ignored them, and regularly snubbed their efforts. As it turned out, Decca was far more vulnerable to Petrillo's strategy than its competitors. Unlike Victor and Columbia, which were associated with the radio networks NBC and CBS respectively, Decca was exclusively in the business of producing recordings and had no alternative source of income. Decca capitulated to the union's demands in September 1943. Once Decca had accepted the union's terms, all other companies were free to do so. Columbia and Victor, in the meanwhile, continued to hold out for another year (they finally surrendered on Armistice Day 1944). On its own Decca could not reestablish the monopoly of the Big Three, and so the door was opened to the independents.

The independents were a heterogeneous group. One large firm, Capitol, founded just before the ban, was soon taken seriously as a competitor to Decca, Columbia, and Victor. A few other labels (Hit, Musicraft) were also aimed at the mainstream pop or classical markets. The remainder were decidedly less impressive and had no intention of competing with the majors on their own turf. Most of the best-selling artists were still contractually obligated to a major label, and small companies could not in any case afford the performers' fees and associated high production costs. They tended instead to try to find a foothold in one or several marginal specialty markets: black gospel, rhythm and blues, hillbilly, Latin American music, polkas.

An obvious and attractive area of specialization for these companies was small-combo jazz. The jazz market had been staked out for several years before the ban by several small labels run by enthusiasts: Milt Gabler's Commodore, Alfred Lion's Blue Note, Bob Thiele's Signature. But even for companies with no deep-seated commitment to the music, jazz offered several advantages. The audience for jazz was small but dedicated with a disproportionate representation of high school and college-age consumers, who were willing to pay premium prices for records that satisfied their tastes. Recording artists could be easily drawn from a pool of skilled freelancers working on 52nd Street, eager for a chance to record and willing to work for union scale. The flexible jam-session-style performance format precluded the need for expensive arrangements.

The jazz market soon became crowded with new entrants. Before the ban, Keynote Records had offered an odd assortment of material: folk, classical, and music with a decidedly leftist slant (Paul Robeson, the Soviet Army Chorus). In late 1943, just as the ban was ending, Keynote made a bid for the "small but lucrative jive-loving and jazz-collecting field," hiring as its producer Harry Lim, the young jazz enthusiast who (as we have seen) had worked for the past several years organizing public jam sessions. In the next year alone, Keynote recorded nearly a hundred individual titles in some two dozen sessions.

One of Keynote's chief competitors was Savoy Records. Savoy was owned and operated by Herman Lubinsky of United Radio, a prospering record and radio parts store in Newark. Lubinsky began recording before the ban and maintained an eclectic catalog, including spirituals and war-time novelties. In 1944 he moved aggressively to establish a presence in the jazz market, hiring intermediaries to help him make contacts with prominent musicians. By year's end he seemed determined to record every musician on 52nd Street.

Savoy and Keynote were joined by other hastily organized companies struggling to find a niche in a disorganized and rapidly changing marketplace. "Apparently all that is required is an office, a phone, and a license," ran a report in the trade press. Such fly-by-night companies "rent a studio by day, hire talent, cut a master, and send it out of town for pressing."

The unseemly haste with which records were made was a direct result of the unsettled conditions. The appetite of the public for new recordings, exacerbated by the fifteen-month ban, remained at an all-time high, while wartime restrictions on materials and manpower continued to limit output. Record companies estimated that they could sell ten times more than they were currently capable of producing. Virtually any record they pressed and distributed could be immediately translated into profit. The smaller companies also feared that it was only a matter of time before Columbia and Victor settled with the union and began signing the better-known jazz artists to more lucrative contracts. They deliberately recorded more material than they could possibly produce, with an eye to creating backlogs that could be drawn upon later.

For the musicians themselves, recordings continued to be an invaluable source of prestige and publicity. The jazz fans packing 52nd Street in 1944 were "disk educated," "familiar with the great jazz recordings" and "name-conscious," spending good money for the chance to hear their favorite recording artists in person. But in and of themselves, recordings were not particularly profitable. Union regulations mandated a one-time fee of $30 ($60 for the leader) for a recording session lasting three hours and producing four tunes. (Union scale represented only the legal minimum, of course: Lubinsky reportedly paid "whatever the traffic would bear"—as little as $15.) This was the only income musicians were likely to see. Major bandleaders might command a royalty on the sales of recordings (as much as 5 percent), but freelance instrumentalists were left with their flat fee. As the jazz market heated up, the bargaining position of the best musicians improved: they demanded, and received, higher fees—double union scale for sidemen and as much as several hundred dollars for leaders.

The one-time fees and the absence of subsequent provisions for royalties encouraged musicians to record as prolifically as possible. This proved to be something of a headache for the record companies, who soon found the market for jazz recordings saturated by a handful of the most popular artists. But business arrangements were deliberately kept loose. "It was 'monkey see, monkey do' and nobody had a contract," remembered Teddy Reig, Herman Lubinsky's chief assistant. "Nobody really wanted one. The artist wanted to stay free in case he got hot and got an offer from a major label. The owners, on the other hand, didn't want to make a commitment either. . . . Everyone was watching everyone else."

One aspect of the new business climate that was to have a striking and immediate impact on the nascent bebop idiom was the value placed on original compositions. Part of the reason was marketing. The colorful, often whimsical titles of the originals offered at least the appearance of novelty and variety in a repertory that in fact consisted of innumerable thinly veiled reworkings of a few jam session standards, such as "I Got Rhythm," "How High the Moon," or "Whispering." But more important, originals offered a source of potential income. Under existing copyright laws, record companies were required to pay two cents per record to the owner of the copyright—one cent to the composer, one cent to the publisher. With the help of BMI, which had an interest in building up its own catalog, record companies set themselves up as "publishers" of the original tunes recorded on their own labels. BMI even agreed to buy a certain number of records and distribute them to affiliated radio stations for airplay.

The performance rights angle to this arrangement proved to be something of a disappointment. Jazz simply didn't get played over the radio often enough to generate much income. But by acting as their own publishers, the payments for which record companies were liable were cut in half. For their part, composers typically received an advance against future royalties. Depending on the ethics of the company, this might be the only money a composer would receive.[2] Indeed, the loose atmosphere provided ample opportunity for the unscrupulous to fleece the naive or careless. Leonard Feather, who was active in the 1940s as a record pro-

2. According to Teddy Reig (1990, 12), Herman Lubinsky of Savoy Records never paid royalties (beyond the advance at the time of recording), allowing his profit margin per disc to swell from sixty-five to seventy cents. The New York local of the musicians' union reportedly fielded a number of complaints about small companies, including false composer credits ("Small Wax Firms under 802 Eye," *Down Beat* 12 [15 February 1945]: 2). In 1945 the Music Publishers' Protective Association investigated several small record companies that it accused of not filing for royalty payments—among them Keynote Records ("MPPA Probes Payments of Royalties by Smaller Record Companies," *Variety* 160 [26 September 1945]: 49; "Small Diskeries Lax in Paying Pubs Royalties," *Billboard* 57 [1 December 1945]: 12).

ducer as well as a critic and publicist, described the sleazy side of the business through a fictional account of "Wrecker Records, Inc.":

> You don't read or write music yourself, and you don't want to pay anybody to write music for the session, so when the boys come into the studio they start noodling around with "I Got Rhythm" or "Honeysuckle Rose" and pretty soon they have a brand-new melody based on the same chords, and they decide to call the product "Jumpin' at Wrecker" or "Wreckerlection Stomp." The boys don't realize that in the course of their noodling they have created a new tune of their own, so you put yourself down as a composer without telling them. Next day, you copyright the number, place it with a music publisher, and land yourself a fat advance royalty. Oh yes, it's a nice game, the record business.

Hawkins in the Studio: The Apollo Recordings

Eventually, small firms like Savoy would turn to Dizzy Gillespie and Charlie Parker and provide the means by which the bebop generation would reach a public beyond 52nd Street. But in 1944 the greatest beneficiary of the new climate was Coleman Hawkins. Ironically, being an uncommitted freelance now suddenly worked to his advantage. In the three years following the demise of his dance orchestra in 1940, he had appeared in exactly one commercial recording session. By contrast, in the thirteen months from December 1943 to the end of 1944, he recorded nearly one hundred tunes, on two dozen separate recording sessions for nine different labels. On nearly all of these occasions he was listed as bandleader, and on all prominently featured as a soloist.

The first celebrated his winning the Gold Award for saxophone in the first critics' poll held by *Esquire* magazine. On December 4, 1943, he recorded for Commodore Records as part of an all-star group that included fellow Gold Award winners Art Tatum, Cootie Williams, Sid Catlett, and the twenty-one-year-old Oscar Pettiford. Later that month he continued his association with Pettiford, using him on three sessions for the fledgling Signature label, including "The Man I Love" (now anthologized on the *Smithsonian Collection of Classic Jazz*).

That Hawkins had begun to listen carefully to the younger generation of musicians is evident from one of the tunes recorded at the Commodore session. "Mop Mop" (music example 54) falls into the broad category of tunes based on Gershwin's "I Got Rhythm" that were a staple of jam session repertories. But the intricate nature of the melodic line clearly points to the new, disorienting rhythmic language of Minton's and Mon-

EX. 54.
"Mop Mop" (1943), theme, mm. 1–4.

EX. 55.
"Straight, No Chaser," theme, mm. 1–6.

roe's. The opening motive, taken by itself, is a standard swing riff, unambiguously in the groove. But subsequent repetitions dislodge it from its original metrical bearings until, by the third bar, it is precariously off-balance. The fourth bar provides the punchline: two quarter notes (reinforced by the bass drum), ponderously reaffirming the downbeat ("mop! mop!"). Hawkins listed himself as composer, but this in itself tells us little beyond the fact that Hawkins brought it into the studio first. Leonard Feather, trying to sort out the early bop repertory only five years after the fact, traced the figure to Charlie Parker, who in fact used a variant of the "mop mop" idea in a tune he recorded as "Red Cross" in the fall of 1944 (see music example 79 in chapter 10). But the rhythmic displacement is also reminiscent of Thelonious Monk, especially his "Straight, No Chaser" (music example 55). "Mop Mop" most likely traveled from Minton's to 52nd Street with Kenny Clarke; it was in Hawkins's repertory as early as the spring of 1943.[3] And "Mop Mop" was only the beginning.

3. Joe Gregory, a dancer and sometime drummer from Newark, was hired for the floor show at Kelly's Stable. He worked with Hawkins when the regular drummer took sick: "I remember they played 'Mop Mop' real fast." The incident took place shortly before Hawkins's trip to Toronto in May 1943, since Gregory remembers that he missed the opportunity to go to Canada for want of a union card (Kukla 1991, 70).

Hawkins's decision to align himself with the bebop generation at the onset of 1944 may seem on the surface to be a sudden, inexplicable shift in his career. His penchant for impulsive action was well known. When he took up a new hobby—model trains, fishing—he'd "dive in with all four feet," as one musician put it. Guitarist Tiny Grimes remembered taking Hawkins fishing once: "And the next thing I know this cat had about $500 worth of fishing stuff and he didn't even know which way it go. . . . He got all this stuff going on the fishing boat like he was going to catch Jaws or something." But even with his private enthusiasms, impulse was often preceded by a period of intense scrutiny. A *Down Beat* reporter who once followed Hawkins on a stereo-shopping expedition remarked: "Hawkins usually thinks about something new a long time before he acts. Then when he does, he acts so rapidly and with such economy of announcement or motion that others sometimes mistake it for haste or lack of proper consideration."

Hawkins had been thinking about the state of jazz and his place in it for some time. Ever since he got off the boat from Europe in 1939, he had been on the lookout for younger jazz musicians attuned to a harmonically more advanced style. By 1944 he was sure he had found them. When asked about bebop in a 1956 interview, he responded, "That's what they should've been playing when I came back in '39! That's what I mean, you know? When I came back—then I would've—I'd have gone around and listened, and I would have said, 'hmmmmmm—hmmm, oh yeah— yeah, boys are getting smart!' " As the grand old man of jazz—then pushing forty—he naturally expected to take "the boys" under his wing. "Charlie Parker and Dizzy were getting started, but they needed help. What they were doing was 'far out' to a lot of people, but it was just music to me." In 1944 he had a lot of help to offer them—especially access to recording studios.

One of the new labels eager to record Coleman Hawkins was Apollo Records. Apollo was the brainchild of Teddy Gottlieb, owner of the Rainbow Music Shop on 125th Street in Harlem. It was aimed generally at "the colored market," but Gottlieb decided to begin with a series of recordings featuring Hawkins. Gottlieb later claimed that he introduced Dizzy Gillespie to Hawkins and suggested that he use the trumpeter for the recording. But this is contradicted by the facts. Hawkins and Gillespie had appeared together at a four-hour Saturday afternoon "Swing Concert" sponsored by the Rainbow Music Shop at the Savoy Ballroom early in 1943, shortly after Hawkins had returned to New York; and as we have seen, Gillespie was briefly a part of Hawkins's band at Kelly's Stable at the end of 1943. Now Hawkins began to think about harnessing some of Gillespie's energy for the upcoming February recording date.

It was to be a more ambitious venture than usual. Most of Hawkins's recordings in 1944 featured small pickup groups—extremely distinguished pickup groups, to be sure (his band for a January 31 date for Keynote, for example, included Roy Eldridge, Teddy Wilson, and Cozy Cole), but decidedly casual in approach, requiring little advance preparation. For Apollo, Hawkins assembled a jazz orchestra, nearly the size of a dance band but with an asymmetrical distribution of wind instruments: three trumpets, no trombones, and no fewer than six saxophones (two altos, three tenors, and one baritone). The personnel reflected Hawkins's new 52nd Street acquaintances. Vic Coulsen, Ed Vanderveer, Leo Parker, Leonard Lowry, and Ray Abrams came from the Clark Monroe band at Kelly's Stable. From the Onyx Club band came Oscar Pettiford, Max Roach, Budd Johnson, Don Byas, Clyde Hart (who had recently replaced George Wallington as pianist), and Dizzy Gillespie, who served as Hawkins's foil as soloist on the date. The arrangements commissioned for the occasion turned out to be so challenging that two different recording sessions were needed to complete six tunes.

Taken as a whole, the recording sessions struck a balance between the older, established Hawkins and his new progressive image. Two of the tunes were out-and-out showcases for Hawkins, including "Yesterdays," a stentorian reading of the Jerome Kern ballad. A moody minor-mode piece with a rich harmonic foundation set in motion by chains of restless augmented dominant chords, "Yesterdays" was an ideal vehicle for Hawkins. Like "Body and Soul," it gave him the chance to link his virtuoso idiom to the drama and pathos of a superior popular song, his uninterrupted solo reaching a climax on an extraordinarily high pitch—a B-flat two octaves above middle C, well beyond the range of most tenor saxophonists. "Yesterdays" was a safe choice as well because Hawkins had been using the tune regularly at Kelly's. "I remember very distinctly," says Leonard Gaskin, "because he always used to go up and make that out-of-the-range note." "Rainbow Mist"—a transparent revisiting of "Body and Soul," with composer credit to Hawkins—was likewise a sure bet, capitalizing on the fact that Victor had allowed the original Bluebird recording of "Body and Soul" to go out of print. With one foot firmly

EX. 56.
"Bu-Dee-Daht" (1944), interlude, mm. 1–8.

planted in his past, Hawkins was ready to move into new territory. As Gaskin put it, "He was looking for a new identity. He had to come up with something other than 'Body and Soul.' "

The remaining tunes were original compositions, emphasizing Hawkins's taste for pungent harmonies and an ostentatiously modern idiom. Some of the harmonic devices were hardly groundbreaking. The bridge to "Bu-Dee-Daht," by Budd Johnson and Clyde Hart, is dominated by diminished seventh chords, reminiscent of both the second chorus of Ben Webster's famous 1940 solo on Duke Ellington's "Cotton Tail" and the bridge to Hampton's "Flying Home." A later passage in "Bu-Dee-Daht" (music example 56) relies on a favorite jam session trick: interrupting a tune, usually "I Got Rhythm," with a chord that seems impossibly remote, only to move rapidly back to the tonic via the circle of fifths.[4] But other passages show a shrewd awareness of that most basic contrivance of bebop harmony, the tritone substitution.

"Bu-Dee-Daht" again provides a good example. Its opening phrase, in C major (music example 57), updates the well-worn "I Got Rhythm" pattern by replacing the middle two chords of the usual I–vi–ii–V root movement (C–A–D–G) with chords with roots a tritone distant (E-flat and A-flat). The same mildly chromatic progression provides the underpinning for the opening section of "Feeling Zero" (music example 58), a ponderous ballad written by Hawkins for the occasion, one that recalls

4. Billy Kyle, pianist for the John Kirby band, had immortalized this device in 1938 with a tune called, appropriately, "From A-flat to C" (Decca 2216, recorded 28 October 1938). Its use as a jam session trick is documented on Don Byas's version of "I Got Rhythm" (recorded 9 June 1945, first released on Commodore FL 20029, later anthologized on the *Smithsonian Collection of Classic Jazz*).

EX. 57.
"Bu-Dee-Daht" (1944), theme and bass line, mm. 1–4.

EX. 58.
"Feeling Zero" (1944), theme and bass line, mm. 1–5.

his harmonic experiments from the previous decade ("A Strange Fact," "Queer Notions").

All of this amounted to a codification of the common practice at Minton's (see chapter 5), now aimed at the general public. In an after-hours jam session, of course, harmonic substitutions had served as a kind of obstacle course—a way of training and challenging musicians away from the public eye. Recording sessions provided the incentive to transform these fluid oral strategies into a more formal musical language. "This was the beginning for this stuff being put down on paper," Budd Johnson has said of the Apollo sessions. "The cats used to just play it and teach each other—you make the riff and I find it. But, see, we started to writing it, and when you start to write it, you got to get the right voicings, and you gotta really know a little something about the harmonic devices."

The tune that most closely reflects the new harmonic thinking is Gillespie's "Woody'n You." "Woody'n You" (later retitled "Algo Bueno") is a self-conscious exploration of the half-diminished chord. As Gillespie later remembered, "The tune just popped out on a record date I had with Coleman Hawkins. . . . On this Coke break, I started fooling around with the piano. I had been playing the progressions a long time, and I said, 'I'll make a tune outta this, right now.' Bam! The melody turned out great, and after hearing the melody, I found it easy to write down a countermelody. The song came right from the chords."

Gillespie's account must be taken with more than a grain of salt. Budd Johnson remembered the tune being part of the repertory of the Onyx Club combo ("We had been playing it, but Dizzy wrote an arrangement for Hawk"). Leonard Gaskin recalled it from Kelly's. And, as its title suggests, Gillespie had worked up an arrangement of it for Woody Herman some time before (and collected his customary $100). But the tune did come "right from the chords." Like many other tunes in the early bop repertory, it features a sequential chain of ii⁷–V⁷ chords, with pungent alterations: the ii⁷ chords have become half-diminished chords, and the dominant sevenths are topped with raised ninths (music example 59).

The point of these alterations was not harmonic freakishness for its own sake, but an attempt to bridge the gulf between harmonic background and improvisation. The new chromatic harmonies suggested and justified a more chromatic style of soloing. Both the half-diminished chord and the altered dominant seventh offered ways of supporting the lowered sixth and seventh degrees of the scale as a literal expression of the harmonic background. Indeed, with the inclusion of the lowered second degree that results from the tritone substitution to the dominant,

EX. 59.
"Woody'n You" (1944), theme and countermelody, mm. 1–8.

chromatic dissonances that had previously seemed to be eccentric "off notes" were absorbed into a comprehensive musical vocabulary.

Hawkins clearly found this musical environment invigorating. Although his solo on "Woody'n You" closely shadows Gillespie's melody, adding little dissonance not already implicit in the tune, his improvisation on "Disorder at the Border" makes an earnest, almost ostentatious use of "off notes" within the framework of the twelve-bar blues. As usual, the overall effect is cumulative, with each chorus ratcheting the level of intensity up yet another notch. The "off notes" for the most part are the usual passing and neighbor tones, resolving almost immediately to chord tones. But as the solo heats up, they are given uncommon emphasis, falling squarely on the beat for maximum dissonant effect. The climax of the fourth and final chorus (music example 60) is a shouted-out "flatted fifth"—an e-natural against the tonic B-flat⁷ chord (measure 4).

Gillespie's solo on "Disorder at the Border" (music example 61), by contrast, is sly and elusive, bypassing obvious harmonic effects for rhythmic flexibility and unpredictability. He begins on muted trumpet with a simple rifflike figure that sounds at first like a response to the "call" of the riff melody of the tune (which continues underneath him in octaves). The pairs of eighth notes are crisply articulated, closer to dotted eighth and sixteenth than the usual swing triplet subdivision—the better to throw the accents of the weak or "back" part of the beat in sharp relief. In the second chorus Gillespie takes the lead: he removes his mute, the

EX. 60.
"Disorder at the Border" (1944), Coleman Hawkins solo, chorus 4, mm. 1–12.

band switches to riff figures that are clearly intended to serve as background, and Max Roach moves to the shimmering cymbal sound that Gillespie favored as accompaniment. There are enough harmonic tricks in the line to keep it sounding modern—an e-natural against the tonic harmony in measure 15, the implied chromatic passing chord ($\flat$III^7 or C-sharp minor^7) in measure 20 (soon to be a bop cliché)—but the real emphasis is on the constantly shifting pattern of accents, sometimes on the on-beat, sometimes on the off-beat.

The third chorus begins a sudden clarion call: a tricky, obviously well-rehearsed pattern, worthy of an Indian tabla drummer (measures 25–28). From this base, Gillespie launches into an extremely fast double-time passage—the kind of brilliant display that was making him the most talked-about trumpet player in musicians' circles. Even this rhythmic effect is less straightforward than it may appear, for Gillespie's line is not always as closely tied to the underlying pulse as notation might suggest. Toward the end of the passage—at the beginning of measure 31—the flow of notes slows down *just* enough for an eighth note to disappear. This goes by too fast to register in consciousness (at least for my ears; to capture this passage in notation, I resorted to the expedient of playing back the passage at half-speed), but it adds another subtle element to the already disorienting effect of the solo. By the fourth beat of the measure, Gillespie is crisply back on track, ready to make a seamless decompression to a slower rhythmic gear.

Following Leonard Feather's example in *Inside Be-Bop*, the Apollo recordings have been routinely referred to as the first bebop recording session.[5] On the face of it, this is an inadequate, even misleading description. Despite the brilliant solos by Gillespie, the recordings still featured a large arranged band with Hawkins's booming tenor the dominant voice, quite different in character from either of the small combos then performing nightly at the Onyx Club or Kelly's Stable.

Nevertheless, these recordings represented a landmark in the emergence of bebop for a number of reasons. Hawkins's sponsorship of the music (the band was officially Coleman Hawkins and His Orchestra)

5. "[T]he first strictly bebop unit ever assembled for records" (Feather 1949, 29); "first modern-jazz studio-recording session" (Gillespie 1979, 505); "generally recognized as the first bop record session" (Gitler 1974, 75); "the first formal statement of the new music on record" (Gitler 1985, 122); "the records generally considered the first bop records" (Collier 1978, 356).

EX. 61.

"Disorder at the Border" (1944), Dizzy Gillespie solo, mm. 1–36.
(Continued on following page)

EX. 61 *(continued).*

served as a catalyst, offering musicians who had operated on the periphery of the music industry the chance to take advantage of the new business climate. Gillespie and Budd Johnson were veteran big-band arrangers
who would have been on the lookout for similar opportunities in any
case, although the circumstances of the recording session (a group nominally led by Hawkins, but composed largely of musicians associated with
Gillespie and Johnson) gave them an unusual degree of leeway. The remainder were mostly young locals with very limited experience. Some
would remain obscure, but others would shortly emerge as major figures
in their own right. As a musician who had grown up in the Swing Era,
Max Roach naturally assumed that he would someday play with the big
bands. The Apollo recordings showed that he could fulfill his artistic
ambitions and achieve a degree of fame without having to leave New
York and 52nd Street. Roach's name appeared prominently on the record
label, along with those of Hawkins, Gillespie, Clyde Hart, and Oscar
Pettiford. "My first record date . . . was the result of Dizzy introducing
me to Hawkins," Roach reflected later. "And that was the beginning of a
whole new world for me, musically and also creatively."

As documents placed in commercial circulation, the Apollo recordings
were also capable of carrying Dizzy Gillespie's distinctive voice far beyond Harlem or 52nd Street. The Apollo recordings were not for everyone. They sold at a premium price ($1.35 direct from Apollo, discounted
as much as $.30 at some stores, but well above the $.35 to $.50 for main-

stream records before the ban), and they enjoyed limited distribution. Nevertheless, the recordings were released promptly and in due course found their way into the hands of those who could make the most use of them. Apollo 751 ("Woody'n You"/"Rainbow Mist") was snapped up by Miles Davis of East St. Louis, who had just turned eighteen. It was one of the few records he owned, along with Jay McShann's "Hootie Blues": "That's where I first heard Diz and Bird, and I couldn't believe what they were playing." Pianist Al Haig was fortunate enough to hear a rare broadcast of Gillespie's Onyx Club band in Boston. While the music was intriguing (he remembered hearing "A Night in Tunisia"), there was only so much he could carry in his memory. The next day he asked whether anyone in his band knew Dizzy Gillespie. "Sure," came the reply, "you can buy his records." "When I bought the records I got into the harmonic part of it which was different, and the drummer—all parts of the group sounded different, too. . . . I started learning those tunes."

Significantly, although the label clearly credited Coleman Hawkins, both Miles Davis and Al Haig thought of the Apollo recordings as "Dizzy's records." It is impossible to say how many others at the time made the same imaginative leap; not enough, certainly, to bring any immediate benefit to the young trumpet player's career. Gillespie would still have to earn a reputation in the arena of live performance, either in the cramped clubs of 52nd Street or back out on the road with one of the swing dance orchestras. Which of these formats offered the best prospects for success was a question that he and other members of his circle struggled with throughout 1944. The answer helped to determine the subsequent shape of jazz.

9 · ECKSTINE AND HERMAN

A Contrast in Fortunes

We knew that the white guy was only copying
what he'd heard the black guys do. The way that
we played—that's what they copied. And the
way that we—our harmony, our rhythm, our
figures and everything—they copied everything.
DIZZY GILLESPIE

After I heard what Dizzy was doing, I said, "Shit,
I can do that!" HOWARD MCGHEE

In 1944 there was, as yet, no such thing as "bebop." Yet what would soon be recognized as the bebop movement had already gathered momentum. Charlie Parker and Dizzy Gillespie had emerged as among the most promising young soloists and arrangers of their generation, and their repute (at least within the musicians' community) began to give them the leverage they needed to pursue their projects to their logical conclusion. Doors that would previously have been closed to them, whether in the recording studio or in nightclubs on 52nd Street, were starting to inch open. The rhythmic and harmonic innovations that made their music "difficult" also set it apart and helped win the attention of other young musicians as well as canny veterans of the music scene.

From the longer perspective that only history can afford—the equivalent of a cinematic long shot—the thrust of all this activity seems clear: to establish a small-combo jazz idiom as the alternative to the commercial entertainments of the swing dance orchestras, and in the process to reassert the spontaneity and complex dialogic rhythms of the jam session as the essence of jazz. From the Apollo sessions to the first definitive bop recordings, from the Onyx Club in 1943 to the Three Deuces in 1945, was but a small step.

A close-up reveals a different picture: more complicated, more richly nuanced, and therefore more ambiguous in its implications. Certain details are inconsistent with the main storyline and therefore tend to escape notice. Reintroducing them into the narrative opens the possibility for fresh modes of interpretation.

For example: the musician most involved in bringing experimental small-group jazz before a paying public in 1944 was Coleman Hawkins. It was Hawkins, not Gillespie or Parker, who worked consistently on New York's 52nd Street with the likes of Thelonious Monk, Oscar Pettiford, and Howard McGhee; who made the first recording of "Salt Peanuts" and presided over Monk's commercial recording debut; and who in general was best positioned, artistically and professionally, to give the new music instant credibility. Had Hawkins been sufficiently motivated to exploit the situation, he could easily have become the public face of bebop.

Dizzy Gillespie and Charlie Parker, meanwhile, spent much of the year on the road. Their energies, surprisingly, were directed toward the very institution that the bebop generation was supposedly bent on escaping: the swing dance orchestra. The Billy Eckstine band of 1944 is well known in jazz lore for its astonishing concentration of talent. Among the musicians passing through the band during its first year, in addition to Parker and Gillespie, were Art Blakey, Sarah Vaughan, Dexter Gordon, Fats Navarro, Howard McGhee, Gene Ammons, and Lucky Thompson. The impact of these musicians playing together was such that Miles Davis, who heard and sat in with the band as a teenager in his hometown of St. Louis, chose to begin his autobiography nearly half a century later with a tribute to "the greatest feeling I ever had in my life." When asked to substitute for an ailing trumpet player, the shaky high school graduate found himself at the center of a musical hurricane:

> When I heard Diz and Bird in B's band, I said, "What? What is this!?" Man, that shit was so terrible it was scary. I mean, Dizzy Gillespie, Charlie "Yardbird" Parker, Buddy Anderson, Gene Ammons, Lucky Thompson, and Art Blakey all together in one band and not to mention B: Billy Eckstine himself. It was a motherfucker. Man, that shit was all up in my body. Music all up in my body, and that's what I wanted to hear. The way that band was playing music—that was *all* I wanted to hear. . . .
>
> B's band changed my life. I decided right then and there that I had to leave St. Louis and live in New York City where all these bad musicians were. . . .
>
> I've come close to matching the feeling of that night in 1944 in music,

when I first heard Diz and Bird, but I've never quite got there. . . . I'm always looking for it, listening and feeling for it, though, trying to always feel it in and through the music I play every day.

And yet the Billy Eckstine band occupies a peculiar position in the genesis of bebop. It seems to have been a puzzling, and ultimately unsatisfying, detour. Its first months were spent touring the Jim Crow South, exposed to the horrors of racism and playing before black audiences who preferred the blues to big-band arrangements of "A Night in Tunisia" and "Salt Peanuts." The few recordings from 1944 contain only oblique hints of the musical revolution to come. While Eckstine soldiered on in the elusive pursuit of commercial success, Parker and Gillespie decided they had had enough. By the end of the year, they turned their attention to the radically streamlined small-group setting of the bebop combo.

The Eckstine band thus stands as a symbol of frustration and thwarted ambition. To understand the implications of this ill-starred project for the history of bebop, we must reexamine the cultural politics of race. Specifically, I mean the institutionalized bias of the music business discussed earlier: the patterns of discrimination that restricted the commercial potential of black musicians while automatically favoring their white counterparts. Accordingly, this chapter contrasts the fortunes of Eckstine's band with the band led by white clarinetist Woody Herman.

The "politics of race" also suggests something subtler, however: the ways in which ethnicity was projected and shaped by the marketplace. Here the crucial focus is the blues—a genre virtually synonymous with African-American cultural identity, but one with which black jazz musicians often had an uneasy relationship. For better or for worse, the blues symbolized certain restrictive social realities that the younger musicians in particular were anxious to escape or transform.

But before taking up these issues, we must first return to Coleman Hawkins, who continued to build an audience for bebop on 52nd Street while his younger colleagues went on the road.

On the Bean: Hawkins and Bebop, 1944

In 1944 Hawkins's professional fortunes were surprisingly promising. Four years earlier, after the collapse of his dance band, his embrace of small combos had seemed a retreat. Having given up hope of attaining mainstream success, he had resigned himself to a career on the fringes of the music business, playing to a modest audience: to those who re-membered "Body and Soul" or knew something of his reputation among musicians. But in the intervening years, that niche had become, in both artistic and financial terms, unexpectedly rewarding. Hawkins now had no difficulty finding the kind of work he wanted: lengthy residences in nightclubs, occasional lucrative one-nighters (in August, Hawkins's small band drew over a thousand dancers on a one-nighter in Connecticut). Jazz concerts—soon to be an important new venue—were just on the horizon. Recording companies contended for his services, keeping his fees high and his music constantly before the jazz-loving public. It was a comfortable and gratifying existence. Without having to leave his adopted hometown of New York, he made a decent wage and was treated with the deference befitting a master. Night after night he played for only as long as he wanted—often only one or two numbers a set. When restless, he simply left the stand, hanging out in the kitchen of Kelly's or wandering down the block to the White Rose to enjoy his whiskey.

Yet he was restless in other ways. He was just short of forty—old enough to count as an elder statesman of jazz, but young enough to feel keenly the need to keep up with the most conspicuously modern of trends. For the next year and a half, he made a conscious effort to expand and deepen the association with members of the bebop generation that had begun with the Apollo recording session.

There was, undoubtedly, a practical side to this. The bop pioneers were readily available and eager to work. Disenchanted with the tedious round of touring with the swing bands, they tended to resurface in New York and were generally open to accepting far less than they would have earned on the road for the privilege and convenience of playing on 52nd Street. If any of Hawkins's young charges felt restless or dissatisfied with subordinate status (as Gillespie did in late 1943), it was easy enough to find someone else to take his place.

But the distinctive character of Hawkins's musical activities from 1944 until well into 1945 was not simply the result of opportunism or ser-endipity. Inspired by what he heard in both the Pettiford-Gillespie band and the Clark Monroe group at Kelly's Stable, he shaped the personnel of his bands carefully. After lingering on the sidelines for several years, he now knew what he wanted.

Standing alongside Hawkins in the front line for much of 1944 was fellow saxophonist Don Byas. On the face of it, another tenor saxophonist was an odd choice—if only because redundancy of instrumentation was something that small combos instinctively avoided. But Byas was an ideal bridge to the new musical language. Born in 1912, he was clearly Hawkins's junior, but he shared with Hawkins more than a decade of experience in the swing bands (he was playing with Walter Page's Blue Devils as early as 1929). Of the many tenor saxophonists emerging from Hawkins's shadow in the 1930s, Byas was among the most secure harmonically; as he put it later, "I was about the only one of that sort of Hawkins school who had modern ideas with it." Hawkins, who had noticed him as a soloist with Count Basie in 1941, included him, along with Lester Young and Ben Webster, among the dozen tenor players he most admired. Byas was also a fierce competitor, "a rough man in any cutting session," who transformed the potential monotony of back-to-back tenor solos into an electrifying confrontation. Byas would play "unbelievable choruses" on Charlie Parker's favorite harmonic obstacle course, "Cherokee," leaving Hawkins to follow in his wake. Hawkins once complained (with an obvious undertone of pride), "There's no need for a man my age to work as hard as this fool from Oklahoma wants me to!"

As a mainstay of Dizzy Gillespie's Onyx Club band, Byas brought with him firsthand experience of the new repertory that Hawkins was eager to assimilate. But Byas was valuable in yet another respect: he remained close enough to Hawkins in sound, approach, and even physical appearance (although of rather different builds, both were dapper men sporting elegant, thin mustaches) to serve as a surrogate on the frequent occasions that Hawkins preferred to be elsewhere. "The place would be packed," remembered bassist John Simmons. "People would be sitting there with the assumption that they were listening to Hawkins, when they were listening to Don. And Hawk would get up and play his number, his specialties, and walk off."

Even more startling than Byas was Hawkins's choice of pianist. At the time Thelonious Monk was scarcely known outside the circles at Minton's and Monroe's. Musicians and audiences alike were used to judging pianists by their facility and virtuosity, with Art Tatum the nearly impossible standard. By this measure, Monk's style seemed at best merely adequate and at worst distractingly peculiar. He carried the additional burden of a reputation as an unreliable eccentric. "Everybody wanted him but everybody was afraid of him," Teddy Hill reminisced in 1948. "He was too undependable. He'd just rather mess around at home." Hawkins took justifiable pride in championing Monk when no one else would.

"One of the worst things I went through in those days was with Monk, when he was working in my group," he said later. "I used to get it every night—'Why don't you get a piano player?' and 'What's that stuff he's playing?' " Today, Hawkins's taste for Monk's pungent harmonies seems prescient, and in the short run his willingness to risk Monk's unpredictability paid off. Monk proved to be dependable enough to remain an integral part of Hawkins's rhythm section for the rest of 1944 and off and on for the next several years.

Hawkins hired a succession of trumpet players during 1944. The first was Little Benny—Benny Harris. A native of New York, Harris had a long acquaintance with many of the principal bop pioneers. He grew up in the same neighborhood as Monk and struck up a friendship with Dizzy Gillespie in 1937, when the latter returned from Europe with Teddy Hill's band. He was part of the inner circle at Minton's and Monroe's and enthusiastically proselytized for the new musical ideas ("Dizzy was always preaching Benny Carter till I got him to hear Bird"). By 1944 Harris was a veteran of various dance bands (he had been part of the clique of young progressives who convinced Earl Hines to hire Gillespie and Parker in 1943). Several years of reaching for high notes night after night had injured his lip ("he'd fluff a few notes every now and then," Hawkins admitted), and he was eager to make the transition to the small-combo scene in New York.

Having surrounded himself with these remarkable musicians, Hawkins concentrated on developing a distinctive repertory. Monk, of course, was a composer, but so was Benny Harris, whose reworking of "How High the Moon" was later retitled "Ornithology." The band remained more or less intact (with some changes in the rhythm section) through trips to Boston and Toronto, as well as a move down the block from Kelly's Stable to the new Downbeat Club.[1] Perhaps for the first time as a bandleader, Hawkins was roused into a conscious effort to mold the band into a finely honed unit. "We used to rehearse every day," he recalled with some pride. "Everything we played was all written down, outside of the very solos themselves." Taking a page from the Gillespie-Pettiford book, he had the three horns play intricate, convoluted lines in stark octaves. The effect,

---

1. When Hawkins's band began playing at 66 West 52nd Street on April 28, the club was called the Yacht Club ("World's Greatest Saxophonist at Yacht Club Nitely," *New York Amsterdam News*, 13 May 1944, 7B). When the Yacht Club folded and was rechristened the Downbeat, the band stayed on.

by all accounts, was unusual and striking. It may have bewildered some. Advertisements seemed designed to prepare customers for an unfamiliar experience with their references to "the interpretive music of Coleman Hawkins." But in the trade press, the band received rave reviews. Citing the "amazing unison jump scorings," a reviewer for *Down Beat* had no problem identifying the beginnings of a new progressive movement in jazz, with Hawkins at its forefront: "With three horns creating fast-moving riff figures remarkable for their fresh inventive quality, the listener is almost convinced that a new jazz form is being built. Here it's interesting to note that Hawk is not content with the direction jazz is taking. Dissatisfied with the riff cliches used by big bands, he does like Ellington, though he thinks of the Duke as a tone color expert, not as a pioneer in tomorrow's musical idiom."

The "new jazz form," of course, was bebop: the streamlined unison "heads," the emphasis on speed and flexibility, the defiantly modernist stance are all recognizable from this account. Hawkins's band was certainly not the first to play in this idiom on 52nd Street, nor necessarily the best (although, by any standard, the conjunction of Hawkins, Byas, and Monk would be well worth hearing). But by lending his name to the new style, Hawkins did more than anyone during 1944 to prepare for its viability in the marketplace.

What relationship did Hawkins's version of the "new jazz form" have to the bop style that emerged a year later? Unfortunately, the kind of evidence one would like does not exist. Despite Hawkins's vogue as a recording artist (from May to mid-June, he led or co-led five different sessions for Savoy, Apollo, and Keynote) and the obvious care he put into shaping his latest musical project, he made no studio recordings with the Byas-Harris-Monk band.

One reason for this curious lack, ironically, was Hawkins's unusually secure position in the jazz business. Normally, the point of making recordings was to stimulate demand for live performance: since black acts were virtually closed off from radio, they needed a hit record to draw crowds to 52nd Street. But Hawkins already had hit records. The Apollo recordings from February were out and doing well, and "Body and Soul," rereleased by Victor in early June, immediately earned a spot on *Billboard*'s "Harlem Hit Parade," where it competed successfully with records by Nat Cole, Louis Jordan, and the Ink Spots through the end of the summer.[2] Fame and prosperity (both relative, of course) came to Hawkins with little additional effort. His reputation, burnished by half a decade in Europe and reinforced by the perennial popularity of "Body and Soul," continued to precede him, filling the narrow rooms of 52nd Street and giving him the luxury to experiment and to associate with eccentric unknowns like Thelonious Monk.

His new recordings, meanwhile, were driven by different market forces. Keynote and Savoy liked to assemble "all-star" groups that could never have existed outside the studio. They aimed their products at jazz enthusiasts who responded not just to the reputation of a bandleader, but to all the musicians on a given record. (To underscore the point, all the performers were carefully listed in fine print on the face of the label.) Under these circumstances, it made far more sense to pair Hawkins not with Thelonious Monk but with Teddy Wilson, not with Benny Harris but with Roy Eldridge or Charlie Shavers, not with Stan Levey or Denzil Best (his drummers during 1944) but with Sid Catlett or Cozy Cole. Moreover, the small companies had neither the production capacity nor the distribution networks to market all of their recordings successfully. The idea was to build an inventory that could be held in reserve for months or even years. Many of the recordings that Hawkins made in 1944 were not released until 1945.

Hawkins accepted these ground rules and apparently made no effort to bring his well-rehearsed sextet and its book of original tunes into the studio. One has to assume this, at any rate. It strains credulity to imagine Harry Lim of Keynote, who wrote glowingly of Hawkins's innovations for *Metronome* in May ("Hawk is a musician who is still continuously advancing his playing, whose harmonic ideas become more daring with every recording date") and even proposed a concert tour for the saxophonist, turning down a serious offer from him. As it was, in 1944 Hawkins recorded with Don Byas only in the context of an all-star "Sax Ensemble" (rounded out by alto saxophonist Tab Smith and Ellington stalwart Harry Carney on baritone), and with Benny Harris or Thelonious Monk not at all.

Nor does much survive of the band's unusual repertory. The tunes recorded by Hawkins in the spring were ordinary fare: popular songs,

2. " 'Harlem' Hit Parade," *Billboard* 56 (15 July 1944): 15. *Harlem* in this case referred to seventeen strategically placed stores in black neighborhoods in New York, Chicago, Cincinnati, Atlanta, and Richmond.

most dutifully copyrighted (although *Metronome* sharply criticized Hawkins for evading royalty payments on "How High the Moon" by disguising it as "Bean at the Met"),[3] and "originals" based on generic jam session routines. There were, however, a few hints of what Hawkins's band might have been playing on 52nd Street. Perhaps the most striking is "Father Co-operates," from a February 22 session for Keynote by the Cozy Cole All-Stars—a group featuring Hawkins, trombonist Trummy Young, and (as the title suggests) Earl "Father" Hines.

The chord progression of "Father Co-operates" is unexceptional—yet another reworking of "I Got Rhythm," albeit at an uncommonly brisk tempo (approximately $\downarrow$ = 250). But the angular riff that precedes the solos (music example 62) is not. It is aggressively dissonant, leaning heavily and insistently on the lowered sixth and second degrees of the scale. At the end of the performance it is transmuted into a variant "outchorus" (music example 63), with running eighth notes recalling the "fast-moving riff figures" that so caught *Down Beat*'s fancy. Trummy Young is the composer of record for "Father Co-operates," but its preoccupation with chromatic dissonance strongly suggests Hawkins. On each of the four surviving takes, Hawkins's two-chorus solo restates and amplifies its characteristic dissonances, especially the lowered sixth degree, G-flat. Hawkins's four solos show a strong degree of similarity, as if the saxophonist had carefully mapped out his improvisation in advance. The climax of each comes at the bridge of the second chorus, with a strident and harshly dissonant sequential figure (music example 64) closely related to the bridge of Dizzy Gillespie's "Salt Peanuts" (music example 65).[4]

Did Hawkins simply appropriate this idea from Dizzy? After all, he recorded "Disorder at the Border" with the young trumpet player on the same day. But the issue is muddied. As we have seen, the first recording of "Salt Peanuts" was made not by Gillespie but by Hawkins—in May 1944, well before either Gillespie version from 1945. Yet Gillespie had been playing the tune on 52nd Street, where both Hawkins or Charlie

3. "Nancy Hamilton and Morgan Lewis, who wrote 'How High the Moon,' and Chappell, who published it, will be intrigued to hear how this number has now been rewritten for this record. Well, that isn't quite what really happened; Hawk devised a riff chorus on the well-known chords of 'Moon,' and Harry Lim is right in there for half the credit. Maybe he didn't read our August editorial [decrying the practice]" ("Record Reviews," *Metronome* 61 [October 1944]: 25).
4. On the second take of "Father Co-operates," Hawkins miscalculates and plays this figure during the *first* chorus. The mistake is obvious: at the end of the chorus, he plays the outchorus riff figure (music example 63), clearly expecting the other horns to join in. They don't, and he continues for another chorus.

EX. 62.
"Father Co-Operates" (1944), theme, mm. 1–8.

EX. 63.
"Father Co-operates" (1944), outchorus, mm. 1–4.

EX. 64.
"Father Co-operates" (1944), Coleman Hawkins solo, take 3, chorus 2,
mm. 17–25.

Shavers (the trumpet player for the 1944 date) would certainly have
heard it.[5] The early version is clearly Dizzy's tune: it carries his name
(along with that of collaborator Kenny Clarke) on the composer credit

5. On at least one occasion in April 1944 Shavers was seen sitting in with the Gillespie–
Budd Johnson combo at the Yacht Club (*Pittsburgh Courier*, 22 April 1944, 15).

and follows his transposition of the "I Got Rhythm" changes from B-flat to F, presumably to accommodate the range of the "novelty" vocal ("Salt peanuts, salt peanuts!"). But the distinctive chromatic double-neighbor cadence in the bridge is a melodic device that Hawkins had internalized long before. When Hawkins plays the bridge (by himself, as if filling in space between arranged ensembles), it sounds like an improvisation (music example 66). Who is to say who influenced whom?

By the summer's end, Hawkins allowed his group to evaporate. Neither Byas nor Benny Harris could be expected to work as support personnel indefinitely, and each left to pursue his own career. Hawkins retained Monk but made no effort to duplicate the unusual two-tenor-saxophone lineup, working instead only with a trumpet player. As a replacement for

EX. 65.
"Salt Peanuts" (May 1945), theme, mm. 17–23 (transposed from original key of F major for comparison).

EX. 66.
"Salt Peanuts" (1944), theme, mm. 17–24.

Harris, he drew once again from the pool of musicians associated with Clark Monroe, tapping Vic Coulsen.

With Coulsen in tow, Hawkins played a week at the Apollo Theatre in early September as the headline act for the usual revue of comedians and dancers. That Hawkins got his name on the Apollo marquee with a "cocktail combo act" was in itself a sign of the times. Art Tatum and Nat "King" Cole, each backed only by a trio, were also considered viable "attractions" on the strength of the popularity of their recordings. But Hawkins apparently made no special effort to adjust to the venue: the band showed up on stage, played its usual set, and left. Such nonchalance undoubtedly puzzled the Apollo regulars, who were used to more flamboyant entertainment. Even Leonard Feather, who showed his awareness of new currents in a knowing reference to "Vic Coulsen's Gillespie-ish trumpet," felt uncomfortable with the band's backroom 52nd Street manner. "Hawk needed a build-up announcement and a little stagecraft," he complained. "To present talent like his so baldly was to throw it away."

The same diffidence characterized the one time during 1944 that Hawkins brought his working rhythm section—including Thelonious Monk—into the studio.[6] On October 19, he recorded four tunes for a new label owned and named after the veteran music publisher Joe Davis. On the whole it is not a very revealing session. Coulsen is absent, and the recording quality is so poor that Denzil Best's drumming is almost inaudible. It was Monk's first commercial recording session, and his solo on "On the Bean" can be read, in retrospect, as a pastiche of early bebop (music example 67). Sinuous, rhythmically elusive passages that would not sound out of place coming from a bop saxophonist (measures 9–12) contrast with Monkian idiosyncrasies: whole-tone scales (measures 7–8) and repetitive figures that make no attempt to escape the gravitational pull of the downbeat (measures 1–2). The distinctive rhythmic hook from "Salt Peanuts" (measures 3–4) leads directly into a line foreshadowing Monk's composition "I Mean You" (measures 5–6). Hawkins later claimed the composer credit for "I Mean You" on a 1946 recording, and he undoubtedly had this and other Monk tunes in his book. But no Monk tunes were recorded on October 19. Instead, all of the nondescript compositions were credited to the recording director for the date, saxophonist Walter "Foots" Thomas.

Still, just how far Hawkins had been drawn into the bebop orbit can

6. These recordings were not released until mid-1945 ("Record Reviews," *Billboard* 57 [16 June 1945]: 27, 66; "Advance Record Releases," *Billboard* 57 [11 August 1945]: 21).

EX. 67.

"On the Bean" (1944), Thelonious Monk solo (right hand only), mm. 1–12.

be gauged by comparing his improvisation with a solo recorded a year earlier on "Stumpy"—a tune that, like "On the Bean," was based on the chord progression of the jam session standard "Whispering" (music example 68). The later improvisation is strikingly more modern in conception. Harmonically, Hawkins's solo on "On the Bean" shows a deeper reliance on chromatic dissonance, especially in the pervasive use of harmonic substitutions: the implied displacement of the expected dominant harmonies with chords either a half step higher (D-flat[7] for C[7] in measure 7, G-flat[7] for F[7] in measure 10) or a tritone distant (F-flat[7] for B-flat[7] in measure 12). Its rhythmic shape is a continuous string of eighth notes, punctuated by ascending upbeat triplets, sixteenth-note ornaments, and the telltale two-note "bebop" motive at the ends of phrases (e.g., measure 9). In a riff blues recorded the day before for Keynote ("El Salon de Gutbucket"), Hawkins launches into an extended up-tempo double-time solo that recalls Dizzy Gillespie's startling flight on "Disorder at the Border" from the Apollo sessions. There can be little doubt that Hawkins was paying close attention to Gillespie, Monk, Byas, Harris, Coulsen, and other younger musicians and absorbing whatever he could into his own style.

Hawkins's reluctance to push his proto-bebop orientation more forcefully into the commercial sphere during 1944 may seem peculiar, but only in retrospect. He was in no hurry. As long as his musical curiosity was engaged by what he was playing on the bandstand, it mattered little whether it was made available to the wider public (and posterity). He

EX. 68.
Top line: "Stumpy" ["Whispering"] (1943), Coleman Hawkins solo, mm. 5–13.
Bottom line: "On the Bean" ["Whispering"] (1944), Coleman Hawkins solo, chorus 2, mm. 5–13 (transposed from original key of A-flat).

already had what the bebop generation craved—a degree of security within the music business that afforded him the freedom to pursue his professional and artistic goals. By the end of the year, roused by his own restlessness and the specter of competition, he would finally make an effort to put his more frankly experimental side before the public. All along, his younger rivals had had no choice.

Mr. B's Blues

Like Hawkins, Gillespie started the year on 52nd Street, but in a far less auspicious position. The group he co-led with Oscar Pettiford was not a headline act, but one of several acts rounding out a larger bill. As with most such acts, the pay was not much more than union scale.[7] ("The average Swing Street nitery owner doesn't want to spend any more than is absolutely necessary," noted *Billboard* in 1945.) Moreover, while Hawkins was clearly his own boss, the Gillespie-Pettiford combo was a loose cooperative venture yoking the ambitions of distinct and often conflicting personalities. Inevitably, tension surfaced. One evening, after an inebriated Pettiford staggered in from an intermission spent at the White Rose, Gillespie accused the bassist of being a "prima donna." This taunt apparently touched a nerve, and their partnership was sundered. Pettiford retained his position at the Onyx, where he remained until midsummer.

Gillespie, for his part, struggled to keep his enterprise together. Retaining his partnership with Budd Johnson (who served as "business manager") and Clyde Hart, and hiring Leonard Gaskin as the bassist, he secured a job at the Yacht Club across the street. Most accounts say that Max Roach was also part of the band, but Gaskin does not remember him being there. Roach spent much of the year with Benny Carter, unable to resist the opportunity to tour with a major dance band (he had just turned twenty), and he may have left as early as the beginning of March. With two-thirds of his original rhythm section (Roach and Pettiford) gone, Gillespie worked hard to recapture the spirit of the Onyx Club arrangements. He rehearsed difficult tunes like the minor-mode showpiece later titled "Be-Bop" at lightning-fast tempos, hectoring one of several new drummers, Jackie Mills, to learn the arrangements and to fit into the ensemble style. Mills "had the feeling to start with," according to Gaskin, but Gillespie "actually *taught* him. He showed Jackie how to drop those bombs, how to keep the tempo, how to fit in the accents."[8]

Exhilarating as it may have been to work out these details on 52nd Street, Gillespie probably sensed that he needed a change. Even had he been able to keep the job indefinitely, he was earning no more than he had at the Onyx Club—about $75 a week. By the end of April, his engagement at the Yacht Club had run out. To make ends meet Gillespie worked once again as a sideman, substituting for Charlie Shavers with the tightly arranged small combo led by John Kirby.

All of this prompted Gillespie to turn his back on 52nd Street to take

7. Pettiford and Gillespie received $75 per week each, Byas $60, the rest "around $50" (Feather 1949, 28).
8. Gaskin has said he also remembered Karl Kiffe playing with the band (Leonard Gaskin, interview with author, 1993). A notice in the *Music Dial*, announcing that Gillespie was replacing drummer Johnny Morris with Shadow Wilson, adds two other possible names to the personnel (Jimmy Butts, "The Music Box," *Music Dial* 1 [May 1944]: 12).

his chances with yet another dance orchestra. But this time the terms were different: he would not simply be an employee in the trumpet section, but on salary as music director with the responsibility of building the band from the ground up. The vehicle for this ambition was "Mr. B"—singer Billy Eckstine.

On the face of it, Eckstine made an unlikely champion of bebop. He was a superlative singer of romantic popular song, a genre barely touched by the innovations of the new music. As a youth, he was inspired by the stentorian resonance of Paul Robeson and, without benefit of any formal training, began acquiring experience as a singer. He soon matured into a rich baritone. Although he had imitated Cab Calloway's exuberant persona well enough as a teenager to win an amateur contest at Washington's Howard Theater, his professional reputation was founded on his smooth but faithful rendering of ballads.

Yet this handsome and seductive figure, soon to emerge as a pop idol rivaling Frank Sinatra, harbored the ambition to be a jazz musician of the progressive stripe. Perhaps the turning point came sometime after Eckstine was hired as the vocalist for Earl Hines's band in 1939. Meredith Willson—later the composer of *The Music Man*—heard the singer over the radio and invited him to perform with his choral group:

> They handed me a sheet of music and I couldn't sight-read it. And I'm the only black there! The director turned around and said, "Oh, we thought you could read, I'm sorry."
>
> So I went back over on the South Side, and I was reeling because I was so embarrassed. I was so hurt! When I told Budd [Johnson], he set me down. He said, "Well, Old Gal"—the guys in the band called our roommates "Old Gal"—"Well, Old Gal, what you got to do is learn to sight-read." So when we were on the road, Budd would take a manuscript and drill me on all the different notes and rhythms. . . . And then I bought a trumpet from another fellow—paid twelve bucks for it—and started studying the trumpet. . . .
>
> So that is how I really got started, got my foot in the door with studying, learning.

Eckstine took his playing seriously—he was soon capable enough to fill in on the fourth trumpet parts in the Hines band when needed—and he began to live the musician's life. He took an apartment in Harlem on Seventh Avenue, in a "musicians' building," and made the acquaintance of his upstairs neighbor, Dizzy Gillespie, who spent his spare time working out harmonies on his upright piano. Benny Harris, a fixture of the Hines trumpet section as early as 1941, kept him abreast of the latest developments. By the time Budd Johnson left the Hines band at the end of 1942, Eckstine was already in the habit of taking his trumpet to Monroe's Uptown House after hours to jam. It was through Eckstine's urging that Hines came uptown to hear Charlie Parker and hired him as Johnson's replacement. While Parker and Gillespie were in the Hines band, Eckstine cemented his relationship with what he called "my gang"—the younger generation with whom he shared musical tastes.

Although Eckstine was a ballad singer who could also play the trumpet (and later the valve trombone), in the early 1940s his claim to fame was as a reluctant blues singer. On long tours of the South with the Hines band, through dances in tobacco warehouses where two flatbed trucks sometimes served as a stage, Eckstine learned to adapt to the tastes of his audiences. "Down there, you had to play plenty of blues." With the help of band members adept at constructing head arrangements, he borrowed liberally from the repertory of Kansas City blues singer Joe Turner: "Cherry Red," "Piney Brown Blues." At a 1940 recording session for Victor, the band found itself with time for another song after the company rejected an instrumental. "Why don't you play some kind of blues," the A & R (Artists and Repertory) man suggested. "They sell down South." Eckstine retreated to scrawl a set of lyrics on a used brown envelope and came up with the opening hook when he overheard a scrap of casual conversation at an open phone booth: "Hello, baby, I had to call you on the phone."

Hines and Budd Johnson hastily worked out an arrangement. The resultant blues, titled "Jelly, Jelly," became the hit record of the session. The combination of Eckstine's suave delivery and urbane good looks with the suggestive and earthy blues text proved irresistible in theaters and on jukeboxes in black neighborhoods. The record boosted his earning power—he began with the Hines band at about $10 a night and was earning as much as $30 a night when he left in 1943[9]—and it launched his career as a singer.

9. Eckstine says he began at $8 a night, but graduated to $30 a night without ever having to ask for a raise (Southern 1979, 190). According to Budd Johnson, that was because he and Eckstine handled the fiscal affairs of the Hines band and gave themselves raises as the financial health of the band permitted. It was in 1942, when Johnson found by perusing payroll records that Eckstine had been raised to $25, that he quit the Hines band (Budd

Fame came at a cost, however. Like so many other black performers with a proven draw in the "race" market, Eckstine quickly became type-cast and systematically excluded from other kinds of repertory. "Blues tunes have been good for me," he said later, "but I know that white folks want to label all Negroes as blues singers. . . . The white man thinks that blues is all a black man should sing. He doesn't want you to do roman-tic stuff." Publishing companies insisted that Hines record their latest ballads as instrumentals, on the transparently specious grounds that the "Southern accents" of black singers made the words unintelligible. ("What Southern accent are you talking about?" Eckstine wondered. "The only South I know is the South Side of Pittsburgh!") Hines called their bluff. "If you don't understand his words," he countered, "I'll pay for the arrangements myself." But despite the encouraging sales of tunes like "Skylark," a new Hoagy Carmichael ballad recorded by Eckstine with the Hines band in 1942, Eckstine the blues singer overshadowed every-thing else, much to his frustration. "I hate blues," he was quoted later as saying. "You can't do anything with them."

By the summer of 1943, when Hines announced yet another tour of the South, Eckstine had had enough. "I told him, 'Hell, no! I don't want to go down South any more.' I'd just gotten married, so I said: 'I think I'm going to stay around in New York.' "[10] But his options were limited. Although his voice was ideally suited for the stage, he knew he had no future on Broadway: black singers either "[did] rag . . . or sang 'Old Man River,' " he later recalled. "You couldn't sing a love song." Like so many other black artists, he found work on 52nd Street, as part of a bill first at the Yacht Club, then at the Onyx. But since "the only thing audiences knew about him was 'Jelly, Jelly,' " his inclination toward ballads like "You Don't Know What Love Is" and the melodramatic "Water Boy" elicited as much puzzlement as enthusiasm.

Eckstine turned for advice to John Hammond, who recommended him to Billy Shaw of the William Morris Agency. Shaw tested the waters, sending telegrams to several dozen promoters announcing the possibility of Eckstine as a touring act. More than half responded, wanting to know when the singer might be available. Shaw's first inclination was to send

Johnson, National Endowment for the Arts /Smithsonian Institution Jazz Oral History Project).
10. At the time the *Music Dial* hinted that "there is more behind the resigning of Vocalist Billy Eckstine from the Earl Hines band than they want the public to know" (J. [Gibby] Gibson, "It Wasn't Told to Me—I Only Heard," *Music Dial* 1 [September 1943]: 10).

Eckstine on the road accompanied by the St. Louis–based band led by George Hudson, a veteran black trumpet player with experience dating to the early 1930s in Kansas City and elsewhere. But Dizzy Gillespie and Budd Johnson, consulted by Eckstine for advice, dissuaded him. Once the tour was finished, they pointed out, Eckstine would come back to New York no better off than when he started. Why not assert some control over his life? Why not form a new band?

The argument had some merit. There was still plenty of room at the top of the music business for name bands toward the end of the war. Demand remained artificially high, and manpower shortages prevented more than a handful of potential bandleaders from launching new enterprises. The risks were great: payroll and transportation costs were punishing, and few new ventures survived long enough to establish the reputation needed to crack the most lucrative jobs. Yet the potential rewards were too enticing to ignore. Determined to make something of Eckstine's proven popularity, Shaw shifted to a different strategy: perhaps the vocalist could work with a band in the commercially proven style of a Count Basie. "They wanted me to sing, and play 'One O'Clock Jump' . . . in other words, let the band copy other successful things and you sing." But Eckstine held out for greater autonomy. He saw the opportunity to build his new band on the talents of his "gang" and hired Dizzy Gillespie as his music director.[11] With the spitball incident still a vivid memory, Shaw was dubious. He reportedly called Gillespie into his office for a lecture: "If you do well, this'll be your big chance to straighten out."

Gillespie's first responsibility was to staff the band. Convincing black musicians to undergo a grueling regimen of travel during wartime was no easy task—especially since the band initially would have to go through the South. Tours of the South were a necessary evil for even the more established black bands and virtually inescapable for lesser or new ones. Ironically, wartime transportation difficulties had created new op-

11. Budd Johnson consistently maintained that he had a long-standing agreement with Eckstine that should the latter ever field a dance orchestra, he would be music director and chief arranger. In exchange for these responsibilities, he would receive 20 percent of the income. When Eckstine began negotiating with the William Morris Agency, this proposal (not surprisingly) was rejected out of hand: "they cut me out right away" (in Gillespie 1979, 200; Dance 1977, 216). It was only at this point, according to Johnson, that Gillespie was brought in as music director (not on a percentage basis, but on a flat salary). Needless to say, the Eckstine band would have been quite a different organization had the saxophonist been more realistic in his demands, or had Eckstine felt more stubbornly loyal to his longtime associate from the Earl Hines band. Without the opportunity to take charge, Gillespie might not have been interested in subjecting himself once again to life on the road.

portunities in the South. Because the white name bands wanted to avoid any travel, the top black bands gained entrée to many lucrative one-nighters north of the Mason-Dixon line and thus cut back their southern touring. Meanwhile, increasingly prosperous southern black audiences clamored for entertainment. The vacuum was filled by perennially marginal bands like vocalist Tiny Bradshaw's or the all-female International Sweethearts of Rhythm, both of which prospered in 1944. But the potential for profit was greatest for attractions that catered to southern black tastes. Cootie Williams's band normally spent much of its time at the Savoy Ballroom, but in 1944, riding the success of alto saxophonist Eddie Vinson's bluesy vocals on "Cherry Red Blues" and "Somebody's Gotta Go" (both of which landed on the Harlem Hit Parade), the trumpeter headed out on the road in combination with Ella Fitzgerald and the Ink Spots, earning a respectable guaranteed minimum of $750 per engagement from Roanoke to Pensacola to Fort Worth.

Eckstine's reputation as a blues singer made him a natural for the South, with its dense concentration of "Negro-patronized spots where he made a name as former vocalist with Earl Hines." As an unproven bandleader, he had no choice. The proposed itinerary for the summer of 1944 began on June 9 in Delaware, continued to Washington, D.C., and then rapidly cut a swath through the heart of the South—North Carolina, South Carolina, Georgia, Florida, Alabama, Louisiana, Texas, Oklahoma, Missouri—before coming to rest in a residency in St. Louis.

Given the reluctance of black musicians to leave New York for any reason, it is remarkable that Eckstine was able to assemble a band at all. But his vision of the band as a haven for progressive trends had its practical side. With Gillespie in place, Eckstine hastily traveled to Chicago to secure Charlie Parker's services in the reed section. The chance to work once again alongside Parker and Gillespie lured most of the brass players from the Hines band of 1943: trumpeters Gail Brockman and Shorty McConnell; trombonists Gerry Valentine, Bennie Green, and Howard Scott. Saxophonist Junior Williams and trumpeter Buddy Anderson were drawn from Parker's circle in the McShann band. Still others joined from 52nd Street. Leo Parker, who had been playing alto saxophone with Clark Monroe at Kelly's Stable, switched to baritone. The rhythm section came from the group accompanying Trummy Young at the Yacht Club: bassist Tommy Potter, guitarist Connie Wainwright, and pianist John Malachi.

As spring came to an end, the personnel continued to shift. Some positions were easy to restock: when former Hines saxophonist Tommy Crump was drafted, he was quickly replaced by Lucky Thompson, already an experienced soloist. But Eckstine had no such luck with his drummer. He had lined up his close friend and former Hines colleague Shadow Wilson, an experienced big-band drummer who was a habitué of Minton's and a favorite of Gillespie's. But Wilson was inducted just as the band was about to go on tour. With Kenny Clarke in the army and Max Roach on tour with Benny Carter, there were few palatable alternatives. According to John Malachi, Eckstine used a white drummer for the first few gigs, but had to leave him behind after Washington, D.C. As soon as his replacement drummer tasted life under segregation in North Carolina he fled for New York, making up a story about being called for induction to cover his embarrassment. For the remainder of the southern tour Eckstine had to rely on largely unsatisfactory local substitutes.[12] Not until Art Blakey was able to catch up with the band in St. Louis did Eckstine finally secure an explosive drummer in the new bebop manner to complement the rest of the band.

The Eckstine band of 1944—inevitably prefaced with the adjective *legendary*—is central to the history of modern jazz. It was the "first big bop band": the obvious precursor to Dizzy Gillespie's big bands and the logical culmination of efforts by Gillespie, Parker, and other young firebrands to parlay their hard-won innovations into something resembling conventional commercial success. The launching of the Eckstine band drew like-minded musicians into a single unit. Its touring schedule carried the music deep into the heartland, where it lured still others to the movement.

But the legacy of the early Eckstine band cannot be limited to the triumphal march of bebop. For Eckstine himself, the band was a bridge to the mainstream market as a pop singer. In this, his success was part of a broader trend. The notion that a singer had to be one part of a larger entertainment package including dance music and instrumental virtuosity was a relic of the Swing Era. By 1944 singers like Frank Sinatra and Jo Stafford had already begun to assert their independence from the bands that had formerly employed them. Within a few years, the Swing Era was displaced by the "era of the 'big singer,' " led by the likes of Bing

12. Eckstine recalls getting by with no drummer for the first job in Wilmington, Delaware, and hiring an ailing substitute named Joe in Tampa, who died in his hotel room in New Orleans (*Melody Maker* 30 [28 August 1954]: 13). Another report indicated that drummer George Jenkins would join the band in the South (Jimmy Butts, "The Music Box," *Music Dial* 2 [July 1944]: 24).

Crosby, Perry Como, Eddie Fisher, and Patti Page. Black artists had a more difficult time joining these ranks. Like Nat "King" Cole, who left his piano trio (and its string of successes on the Harlem Hit Parade) behind him once mainstream success beckoned in the late 1940s, Eckstine eventually severed connections with instrumental jazz, although he struggled along with the anachronism of a full-service entertaining dance orchestra until 1947. "People still talk today about that legendary Billy Eckstine band," he later remarked. "Man! The legendary Billy Eckstine was about to starve with that motherfucker, so I decided to break it up." Dizzy Gillespie inherited the band's library, uniforms, and music stands: "I don't ever want to see this shit again," Eckstine told him. "I decided the best thing was to do a single and go hear Dizzy for kicks."

Before either Eckstine or his youthful cohorts could fulfill their ambitions, however, the band had to pass a crucial test. For the first full year of its existence, the Eckstine band played almost exclusively for black audiences.[13] Its financial survival depended on satisfying the tastes of the "race" market—the newly prosperous (in relative terms) and increasingly independent working-class black audience that was to become the core constituency for rhythm and blues.

"Educating" the Masses: Blues and the Black Audience

As we have seen, wartime defense work pulled huge numbers of black men and women into the industrial economy for the first time. With money in their pockets, they asserted their taste for entertainment that leaned heavily toward the blues through their patronage at dance halls, jukeboxes, and theaters. Within a few years, a new musical idiom, eventually dubbed rhythm and blues (R & B), would break off from both the world of Tin Pan Alley and large dance orchestras and from older forms of "race" music. By the end of the decade, this thriving new idiom would be supported by its own structures: independent labels like Savoy, King, Specialty, and Chess specializing in R & B artists and radio stations catering to vast new black consumer markets across the South and Midwest (WXLW in St. Louis, WOKJ in Jackson, WDIA in Memphis), giving R & B recordings the exposure they needed.

None of this was in place in 1944. The music industry was only beginning to awaken to the changing tastes and increased purchasing power

13. See, for example, the report on the Eckstine band finally securing a date in a "white" theater: "Crew since organization has confined itself to race dances and colored theaters" ("Billy Eckstine to Have First White Theater," *Down Beat* 12 [15 November 1945]: 1).

of black audiences. Still, the signs were clear for those who cared to read them. An aggressively populist approach was paying off handsomely for bandleaders like Lionel Hampton, Cootie Williams, Erskine Hawkins, Lucky Millinder (who had just hired blues shouter Wynonie Harris in April), and Louis Jordan (a former sideman with Chick Webb's orchestra whose small combo called the Tympany Five placed a string of records on the Harlem Hit Parade beginning in 1942). "I loved playing jazz with a big band," Jordan later recalled. "Loved singing the blues. But I really wanted to be an entertainer—that's me—on my own. I wanted to play for millions, not just a few hep cats." Of the beboppers he said, "Those guys . . . really wanted to play mostly for themselves, and I still wanted to play for the people. I just like to sing my blues and swing."

The musicians of the Eckstine band, from their leader on down, were decidedly more ambivalent about the necessity of playing to the blues-oriented public. Indeed, one could argue, as W. T. Lhamon does, that a complex and often strained relationship between black jazz musicians and the mass appeal of the blues extended back to the experience of Hawkins's generation with the classic blues recordings of the 1920s. "Jazz is . . . an art that has welcomed into all its styles the splinters and clods of blues, but skeptically, as when urban combos answered downhome remorse with exaggerated horn boohoos." Part of the discomfiture, certainly, was technical—the predictable reaction by urbane musicians to unstudied rural modes of expression. The disdain Hawkins felt for the "plain blues" was shared by many younger musicians as well, and they reacted by adding an ironic layer of complexity that (not incidentally) flaunted their special skills. "Bebop is a highly sophisticated form of music; the blues is very simple, in form," commented Dizzy Gillespie. "The bebop musicians wanted to show their virtuosity. They'd play the twelve-bar outline of the blues, but they wouldn't blues it up like the older guys they considered unsophisticated. They busied themselves making changes, a thousand changes in one bar."

The variety of stances toward the blues in Swing Era jazz are almost infinite in nuance—from the well-oiled dance music of Kansas City to the elegant concert transmutations of Duke Ellington, from the unseemly rush to embrace the rough, pounding strains of boogie-woogie in the late 1930s to the smoothly focused shuffle blues of Louis Jordan in the 1940s. Eckstine's blues recordings with Earl Hines map out their own distinctive territory. On "Jelly, Jelly" his rendering of the straight, old-fashioned three-line blues (as opposed to the more densely packed poetic stanzas that Jordan was already perfecting) is effortlessly urbane. Behind him, the band is at great pains to hold its virtuosity in check. Hines thumps out a groove, the horns sustain quiet chords, an electric guitar wails sympathetically. The whole effort verges on the parodic—city slickers signifying on their country cousins. Yet it worked. As country blues singer Baby Doo Caston explained:

> Billy Eckstine came out with Earl Hines's band singing, "Jelly, jelly, jelly stays on my mind," and most everybody bought the record because a big band was right behind it. But if it had been somebody like Sonny Boy Williamson with his harp and somebody playing them old guitars behind him, an old bass, and beating on a drum, they wouldn't have bought it because it was kind of a gutbucket thing. It's just the style of it, it was a class.

Instead of parody, black audiences around the country heard a sophisticated updating of the old blues sound, and they clamored for more.

Four years later, the backers of the new Billy Eckstine band were determined to give it to them. In an effort to stimulate demand for live appearances, a recording date was arranged in April, well before either the personnel or the repertory of the new band had solidified. The recording company was the New Jersey–based DeLuxe, remembered today, if at all, as a footnote in the history of rhythm and blues—a "pioneer" label that was absorbed in 1947 by the more successful King label. Like many other independent companies of the time, DeLuxe initially hedged its bets in an uncertain market by simultaneously exploring several different "specialty" niches. Its first recordings were in the country field (then known as Western or hillbilly), with sessions in February and March by Tex Grande and his Range Riders. Not surprisingly, DeLuxe saw in Eckstine a way of initiating its "race" catalog.

Billy Eckstine, accompanied by the DeLuxe All-Stars, recorded three tunes on April 13, 1944. "I Got a Date with Rhythm," paired with a gospel quartet number ("I Couldn't Hear Nobody Pray") on DeLuxe 1003, was not released for nearly two years. The remaining pair of tunes—"Good Jelly Blues" and "I Stay in the Mood for You"—were blues performances aimed straight at the "race" market, as the trade press recognized on their release as DeLuxe 2000 at the end of May. "The sepia entry into the swooning sweepstakes, Eckstein [Eckstine did not alter the spelling of his name until the end of the summer] goes race instead of romantic with two standard blues back to back," announced *Billboard*. "Phono appeal, because of the song selections, will undoubtedly be greatest at the race locations. On that score, both sides will count heavily for the production of coins."

Both tunes echo the basic formula of the "Jelly, Jelly" success. On each, Eckstine is well in the foreground, his reading of the slightly salacious text ("not exactly polite," noted *Billboard*, "but sure to create beaucoup juke box following") suave and clearly enunciated over a placid, medium-slow tempo. But if the vocalist faithfully sticks to the same script, the instrumental response is both more insolent and up-to-date. Rich sustained chromatic harmonies enhance and deepen the romantic mood; jeering double-time unison riffs undermine and mock it, signifying on traditional blues pitch-bending gestures with intricately chromatic and rhythmically abrupt figures (music examples 69 and 70). The riffs came straight from the New York musicians' underground—so advanced that the horn players had trouble reading the sixteenth-note notation for "Good Jelly Blues" and had to have Gillespie sing it to them ("Talk about be-bop, we were *beeeee*-boppin' behind him!" he crowed). The in-group signifying was not limited to blues or jazz. The opening of "Good Jelly Blues" (music example 71)—later recycled as the standard introduction to bebop performances of Jerome Kern's "All the Things You Are"—is a hip caricature of the ponderous opening of Rachmaninoff's Prelude in C-Sharp Minor, a staple of every piano bench of the time and probably the

EX. 69.
"Good Jelly Blues" (1944), riff figure, chorus 3, mm. 11–12.

EX. 70.
"Good Jelly Blues" (1944), riff figure, chorus 4, mm. 3–4.

best-known motive in classical music after the first four notes of Beethoven's Fifth.

Who or what was being advertised by these recordings? The reviewer
for *Billboard* was equally impressed by the "round-up of sepia instrumental aces," each of whom was dutifully listed on the face of the record
label. As it turned out, the DeLuxe recordings captured the Eckstine project in flux. Only a fraction of those on the recording ended up with the
band when it hit the road two months later. Charlie Parker's absence is
striking and particularly regrettable, since he was best positioned to
bridge the yawning gulf between the "plain blues" and the emergent
modern sensibility. Instead, the only solo on either record belongs to
Gillespie. On the final chorus of "I Stay in the Mood for You" (music
example 72), he announces himself with a brilliant flurry of thirty-second
notes before launching into a longer phrase containing a strategically
placed flatted fifth. "You forget about changes when you play the blues,"
Gillespie once said, "but every now and then you put in a little lick in
there to let 'em know, 'Here's where I'm at, really.' " Gillespie's solo was
full of such markers. Indeed, all of his contributions to the recording were
an oblique commentary on the blues that made it clear to those in the
know "where [he was] at, really."

The beboppers' frustration with the technical limitations of the older
blues style was easily overcome. By fusing traditional blues gestures with
a speeded-up double-time feeling and couching their language in chromatic dissonance, they imposed a new feeling of swing on the old. But
Gillespie has also alluded to a different and deeper uneasiness with the
blues, one that was social, rather than musical, in origin: "The bebop
musicians didn't like to play the blues. They were ashamed. The media
had made it shameful."

EX. 71.
"Good Jelly Blues" (1944), introduction, mm. 1–4.

EX. 72.

"I Stay in the Mood for You" (1944), Dizzy Gillespie solo, mm. 4–8.

That sense of shame was shared by the black political and cultural leadership of the time, who were embarrassed by the frankly lower-class orientation of traditional blues. Guitarist Danny Barker—whose wife, Blue Lu, had recorded a risqué blues song, "Don't You Feel My Legs," in 1938 (under the title "Don't You Make Me High")—describes a political rally in Harlem he attended at which Franklin Roosevelt was to appear. On the grandstand were Walter White, Bill Robinson, Mary McLeod Bethune, Marian Anderson, and Eleanor Roosevelt. As they stood waiting, the operator of a truck rigged out with sound equipment used by the Savoy Ballroom to publicize its performances saw an opportunity to tweak the establishment by blaring out Blue Lu's latest effort:

> And he slowed down the truck and he passed by mischievously, and finally went by. And you could hear, "Listen at that filthy record . . . "
> "It's filthy!"
> "Get that record!"
> Somebody shouted, "Stop that truck and get that record!"
> Some of the people were laughing, some of them were embarrassed: a song like this showed the vulgarity of the black mind. It was a disgrace. Yet at their houses, probably half of them had that record, and played it at their parties. But they said, "Get that record!"

Today, such a hysterical overreaction to the earthy humor of the blues seems hypocritical. But the anxiety was real, and felt not just by social climbers or politicians but by musicians as well. As upwardly mobile professionals, they distanced themselves from the rural blues milieu even as they trafficked in its gestures and techniques. Their distancing, however, was no retreat. The progressive urge—in social and cultural terms as well as musical—demanded that musicians take responsibility for elevating the taste of the people they entertained. Their very existence as a professional elite gave the lie to the stereotype of the unlettered Negro singing lewd blues to his guitar. Every sharp, impeccably pressed outfit, every intricate phrase executed with faultless intonation and technique, was a challenge to white assumptions of cultural supremacy and to black resignation to social inferiority. Milt Hinton, touring the South with the Cab Calloway band in the 1930s, felt that Calloway fought a losing battle "trying to educate the Southern black people. . . . All they wanted was dirty records . . . old dirty blues. . . . So they didn't dig nothing. . . . I guess I got the idea from [Cab] that this kind of thing kept the black mind in the South down":

> The music we played was completely different from what blacks usually heard. In most Southern towns there'd be a small radio station catering to a black audience. The music they'd play was real trash—blues, but with lyrics that had sexual messages. "You got bad blood, mama, I think you need a shot," "Now my needle's in you, honey," those kinds of lines. . . .
>
> Southern black people seemed to be kept ignorant, poor, and fighting among themselves. But Cab was like a breath of fresh air. . . . It was beautiful to see and it also showed that black people could be dignified.

According to Hinton, "They wanted [Calloway] to sing, but he would never sing the blues or any of those bad things. He said, 'I feel obligated to try to show these people that there's a better way of life—that entertainment is higher than this.' "

This internecine debate over style, pitting the calculated urbanity of northern-based black musicians like Calloway (or later Eckstine and Gillespie) against the stubbornly rural ethos of the masses, is often overlooked in the history of jazz because it does not fit the prevailing paradigm. In contemporary criticism, the blues is more often than not celebrated as the center of an essentialist conception of black identity. It is (in Baraka's words) "the purest expression of Negro life in America," asserting its legitimacy and autonomy from the white-dominated marketplace by staying in continual touch with "the most honestly *contemporary* expression of the Negro soul." There is little room for ambivalence or ambiguity in such a formulation. One is either at the center of what it means to be black or in some dangerous (because *"impure," "dishonest"*) purgatory reserved for those shamed by the frank reality of the blues.

But the expression of ethnicity through art is never so uncomplicated. It is always inflected by class, regional difference, the warp and woof of the marketplace, the infinite variety of individual experience. For black jazz musicians of the 1940s, the blues was less a cultural essence to be embraced or rejected than a nexus, a point of exchange, between artist and audience. It is hard to imagine the hardened crew of malcontents in Eckstine's band sharing Calloway's concern with the moral tone of entertainment, blushing as their leader extolled the virtues of "that real fine jelly roll." But as brash New Yorkers with an attitude, they were keenly aware that the blues embodied a certain social inertia, a rural passivity, that they were determined to overcome. They also knew that the white-controlled culture industry was only too happy to stereotype them as blues musicians as an excuse for restricting their sphere of influence to the "race market" (siphoning off the lion's share of the profits in the process). For the bop generation, the blues was both opportunity and obstacle.

As professionals, they accepted without complaint the obligation to satisfy their audiences. In the first leg of the band's tour through the South, Parker helped the band supply what he called "rice-and-beans music" for blues-oriented audiences. In the Midwest, "colored audiences liked it but the whites didn't." There can be little doubt that playing before sympathetic black audiences was an inspiration. "You know how they were playing for them black folks at the Riviera," said Miles Davis of the nightclub where he first heard the Eckstine band. "Because black people in St. Louis love their music, but they want their music right. So you *know* what they were doing at the Riviera. You know they were getting *all* the way *down*."

Having to accompany Eckstine on some "dumb blues lyric" night after night may not have been the most gratifying part of the bargain. But other situations gave plenty of room for the exercise of personal creativity and professional skill. The Eckstine band faced its first several gigs with perilously few written arrangements in its book. Charlie Parker and Dizzy Gillespie staved off disaster by keeping dancers on the floor with an endless succession of bluesy riffs, spontaneously fleshed out into head arrangements by the band. Jury-rigged arrangements like "Blue 'n Boogie," which begins with a soaring Dizzy Gillespie lick scored for the trumpet section (music example 73), provided a refreshing and up-to-date alternative to blues-based dance music in the Basie mold. "They're not particular about whether you're playing a flatted fifth or a ruptured 129th as long as they can dance," Gillespie later said.

Still, the musicians insisted on their prerogative to "educate" their public. Even the intricate, ironic backgrounds for Eckstine's vocals were designed to demonstrate that the blues idiom could bear the weight of a new kind of wit, audacity, and virtuosity. ("Whatever you go into, go into it *intelligently*.") But Eckstine typically sang no more than one or two numbers per set. More and more time was devoted to instrumental music of uncompromising complexity. Gillespie continued adding arrangements to the band's book, including full-band versions of some of his "double-time specials" from 52nd Street ("Salt Peanuts," "Max Is Making Wax"). For variety, Eckstine brought out a "little band" that featured Parker, Gillespie, and Lucky Thompson. Such music demanded that audiences suspend, or at least reevaluate, their habitual responses: "People were used to patting their feet and dancing. This was new, and it was like they were going around educating people. In some of the places, the younger people were so amazed at the virtuosity of the instrumentalists. And they were showcased with these new types of ar-

EX. 73.
"Blue 'n Boogie" (1945), introduction, mm. 1–7.

rangements. A lotta younger people were more flexible. Man, they were awed. They would stand there and just go crazy. But nobody was dancing."

The absence of dancing was in itself nothing startling. Ever since gawking teenaged crowds had flocked to the front of the bandstand while Benny Goodman played the Palomar, swing music had sold itself as spectacle. Every band had its "flagwavers," theatrically flashy arrangements that offered instrumental virtuosity as entertainment. The up-tempo bop numbers followed this tradition. "Diz made an arrangement of 'Max Is Makin' Wax' which was way up there, featuring him and Bird," recalled Eckstine. "You couldn't dance to that at all, but people would stand there and watch." The difficulty was that none of this music was promoted through the media. Audiences knew of the band only through its blues recordings. Such a marketing strategy mitigated *against* versatility as a selling point, which made the band's policy of playing a varied and unusual repertory seem deliberately confrontational—a refusal to give audiences what they expected and wanted. "[The crowds] came in to hear Billy Eckstine," Gillespie later recounted. "They'd start screaming where they hear, 'Jelly, jelly, jelly.' But for 'A Night in Tunisia' and 'Salt Peanuts' and things like that, they didn't." At dances, Sarah Vaughan remembered, the few who understood the music "would be in a corner, jitterbugging forever, while the rest just stood staring at us. . . . We were just trying to play some music for the people, that we knew was together. We were trying to educate them. And it took a while!"

Throughout its tour of the South, the Eckstine band endured the provocations of entrenched racist custom. They rode in Jim Crow railroad cars, where even having chicken bones tossed their way or being forced to sleep in the dust and hay of the baggage car did not dampen their brash spirit. ("We got some smart 'uns dis time, suh!" reported one black porter to his white superior on the goings-on in the Jim Crow car.) Every black band touring the South put up with similar trials. But the Eckstine band had no older authority figure like Hampton, Kirk, or Basie to counsel patience and discretion. Indeed, at the Plantation Club, a white gangster-run nightclub in St. Louis that paid "terrif dough" to black bands, it was Eckstine himself who insisted on courting disaster by entering through the front door, forcing a hasty change of venue to the black-owned Riveria club. Some of that swagger and barely repressed anger was sublimated into the music. "Regardless of what problem we had during the day, there's our chance to let it out," Eckstine asserted.

"And baby, some of the times when we've had the worst problems during the day, we'd get on the stand at night, and man, you never heard a band play like that in your life. We'd be wailing."

At the heart of this resilience was Charlie Parker. The Eckstine band was Parker's swan song as a dance band musician, and by all accounts he was deeply involved. As leader of the reed section, he ran endless rehearsals and set riffs for head arrangements, and he proved a sensitive accompanist for vocalists: his obbligato behind Sarah Vaughan on "I'll Wait and Pray" stopped the show at Chicago's Regal Theater in August. As a soloist, Parker was a revelation. "I remember sometimes the other musicians would forget to come in on time because they was listening to Bird so much," said Miles Davis. "They'd be standing up there on the stage with their mouths wide open. Goddamn, Bird was playing some shit back then." Not all of his influence was benign, of course: the example of his drug addiction ate away like a cancer through the ranks of the band from the beginning. But the fierce dedication he inspired to the discipline of art provided some compensation for chaos. It became a point of pride to play the most difficult charts from memory: "You had a music stand there, but the music was under the stand, baby." Even the drummer, Art Blakey, felt free to contribute to an exhilarating creative enterprise: "It was like a small combo. . . . You don't go to Duke's band and play Art Blakey, you go into Duke's band and play Duke Ellington. You go to Count Basie's band, you play Count Basie. You don't go and try to stick your influence in there. The only way I had a chance to stick my influence is in Billy Eckstine's band, because it was that type of thing. It was like a combo. But [for] the rest of the bands, you're the timekeeper."

The Eckstine band survived its grueling first months in surprisingly good financial shape. Its gross income for the latter half of 1944 was $103,000—far less than the figures earned for the entire year by Cab Calloway ($750,000), Duke Ellington ($600,000), or Count Basie ($400,000), but competitive with such long-established bands as those of Louis Armstrong ($250,000), Andy Kirk ($150,000 to $200,000), and Fletcher Henderson ($100,000). After playing more than seventy one-nighters in its tour of the South and Midwest, it graduated to the more prestigious and lucrative circuit of black theaters. In his debut at the Apollo as bandleader in September, Eckstine proved so popular that the band played seven shows a day, earning a bonus from a grateful management. Such success kept the band going and laid the foundation for Eckstine's later popularity as a singer.

But for all this, the Eckstine band had not escaped the marginal status automatically accorded it on the basis of race. Eckstine's voice could be heard on jukeboxes in black neighborhoods but not on the radio. The unusual instrumentals could be heard only in live performance in the archipelago of ballrooms and theaters catering to black consumers across the country. As with other midlevel black bands, the Eckstine band's modest prosperity depended on a punishing schedule of personal appearances that sapped the energy of the most dedicated musicians. Eckstine made every effort to publicize his extraordinary instrumentalists (the official billing was "Romantic Singing Maestro, Billy Eckstine, and his sensational New Orchestra featuring Dizzy Gillespie, King of the Trumpet"), but the spotlight was barely big enough for himself.

Inevitably, key contributors became discouraged. Charlie Parker had already left the band in August, fed up with travel and eager to return to New York. Gillespie didn't last much longer. Sensing little further advantage to staying with the band, he gave Eckstine his notice in the fall, recruiting twenty-one-year-old Fats Navarro (then playing alongside Howard McGhee in the Andy Kirk trumpet section) as his replacement.[14] With Gillespie scheduled to leave, there was no point in devoting any new recordings to his music, so a session for DeLuxe in early December highlighted the efforts of ongoing members of the band. Half of the six sides were given over to ballads composed and sung by Eckstine. "Opus X" was written by the band's pianist, John Malachi. "Blowing the Blues Away," featuring a "tenor battle" between Dexter Gordon and Gene Ammons, was credited to Eckstine and Jerry Valentine. DeLuxe apparently wanted the last side to be another blues, but the band protested, threatening to walk out unless Sarah Vaughan had an opportunity to record "I'll Wait and Pray," a new ballad composed by Malachi. Gillespie played a few solos on these recordings, but otherwise held his music in reserve. By the end of the year, he was once again on his own.

14. Eckstine has said that Gillespie left his band during an engagement at the Club Bali, in Washington, D.C., and recommended Navarro, then playing at the Louisiana Club, as his replacement (*Melody Maker* 30 [4 September 1954]: 5). The Club Bali engagement lasted for two weeks beginning 20 October ("Music Grapevine," *Billboard* 56 [30 September 1944]: 14). Since Gillespie was still with the band at the time of the DeLuxe recordings, however, it seems more likely that he did not end his relationship with the band until it returned to New York at the end of the year for a week-long engagement at the Apollo Theatre beginning 22 December 1944.

A Question of Race: Woody Herman's "First Herd"

One of the durable axioms of bebop can be found in a story related by Mary Lou Williams. At some point before Thelonious Monk began working at Minton's, he supposedly tried to organize a big band. More than a dozen musicians spent their evenings running through arrangements by Monk and Bud Powell in a basement. Nothing came of the venture, which seems to have been forgotten by everyone else involved. It is remembered today only for the words that Williams attributes to Monk: "We are going to get a big band started. We're going to create something that they can't steal because they can't play it."

Interestingly, nowhere in this anecdote does Williams raise the issue of race. She rails instead against the power of "paid-for publicity," arguing that "most anybody can become a great name if he can afford enough of it." ("In the end," she says, "the public believes what it reads. So it is difficult for the real talent to break through.") Nevertheless, Monk's comment is almost always interpreted along racial lines, with *they* understood to refer to the white musicians who would, given the chance, "steal" bebop just as they had stolen swing (and jazz and ragtime).

This interpretation has had a perennial appeal because it offers an easily grasped motivation for bebop's bristling complexity. But taken more literally as a plan of action, Monk's comments seem either desperate or naive. Music can never be theft-proof. Whatever animus the bop generation may have harbored against white Americans as a whole, and however much they may have belittled the musical ability or taste of the white majority, they knew that a strategically placed handful of white musicians were capable of keeping pace musically.

They knew this because their paths crossed continually. Descriptions of Minton's are haunted by images of predatory white musicians surreptitiously jotting down riffs on their cuffs, to be smuggled downtown for commercial exploitation, much as white comics like Milton Berle used to steal material from black comics. But most of the exchange was out in the open. Charlie Parker, according to Benny Harris, had "just as many white friends as colored. He liked company." Dizzy Gillespie counted white musicians like Stan Levey and Al Haig among his inner circle of devotees. Howard McGhee befriended a young Red Rodney in Philadelphia ("Howard started showing me things, teaching me things and how this went to that. . . . the conception, how the music was played and the chord progressions"), and Gillespie took Rodney to New York to hear Charlie Parker. The consequences of such largesse must have been obvious, but in the short term the benefits of free exchange outweighed the risks. Budd Johnson remembered his dismay at watching Gillespie's gregarious nature at work with the white Boyd Raeburn band (which eventually had the honor of making the first big-band recording of "A Night in Tunisia" in early 1945):

> Dizzy would sit in the bands and show the trumpet players how to play the parts. I used to get a little peeved with him about that. I'd say, "Man, what are you doing, showing these cats?" But he got a kick out of it. . . . Of course, he had made the arrangement, so he wanted his arrangement to sound good. And he showed them. They would get hung up on the fingering, when they'd get up above high C. Diz would show them how to do that.

The issue, then, was not theft per se, but an economic landscape so distorted by racism that white musicians enjoyed an automatic and insuperable advantage. In the competition to parlay the latest jam session innovations into a commercially viable big-band style, the results were predictable. By the end of 1944, Billy Eckstine was still touring the hinterland, struggling to get his music heard. In the end-of-the-year poll for readers of *Down Beat*, Eckstine garnered only 45 votes in the category of best swing band, earning him twenty-fifth place (behind such swing powerhouses as Hal McIntyre, Del Lucas, and Charlie Spivak). Ellington won the poll with 1,673 votes, but only by a narrow 67-vote margin. His close competitor, another bop-flavored band staffed with young musicians, would win the next swing band poll easily and be hailed in the jazz press as "historically and musically with the half-dozen greatest bands in jazz since the beginning of jazz: Duke, the early Lunceford, the early Goodman and Basie and Hampton. . . . probably the most consistently progressive band there has ever been." The band? White bandleader Woody Herman's famous "First Herd."

The parallels between Billy Eckstine and Woody Herman are striking. In 1944 the two bandleaders had just entered their early thirties (Eckstine was born in 1914, Herman the previous year), and both had recently made a point of surrounding themselves with much younger musicians. Each fulfilled his bandleader's duties as both vocalist and instrumentalist. And although both men were comfortable with romantic ballads, they were indelibly associated in the public eye with the blues. Indeed, according to Herman, his first band (formed in 1936 at the outset of the initial swing boom) was known as "The Band That Played the Blues" for the simple reason that "playing the blues was the best thing we knew how to do musically."

But the differences between the two men were as stark as black and white. One might say that the blues chose Billy Eckstine, but Woody Herman chose the blues. Once Eckstine showed an aptitude for singing the blues, he had no choice but to continue doing so ("The white man thinks that blues is all a black man should sing"). Herman sang and played the blues because it intrigued him. Like many white jazz musicians of his generation, he studied black idioms carefully—the orchestrations of Duke Ellington, the saxophone playing of Coleman Hawkins—and made a specialty of playing them effectively. This transgression of racial boundaries in his choice of repertory and manner of delivery carried some risk, at least early on. Herman liked to tell the story of the note he received on a gig in Texas in the 1930s: "Will you kindly stop singing and playing those nigger blues." Over time, however, his musical proclivities paid off. His 1939 recording for Decca of "Woodchopper's Ball," a simple riff tune, hit the jackpot, and Herman became a name band at the height of the Swing Era.

Like other swing bands, Herman's was a versatile outfit, taking advantage of the varied venues open to successful white dance orchestras. It could play energetic swing, but also accommodate dancers in staid hotel ballrooms like the Hotel Pennsylvania in New York or the Hotel Sherman in Chicago. In 1938 Herman began traveling to California to appear in movies, which "helped to make the band more identifiable" with a mass audience. The band recorded steadily and prolifically for Decca: more than 150 titles in the three and a half years preceding the recording ban of 1942, including pop songs of all kinds (often with a female vocal) and cover versions of best-selling records ("Frenesi," "A String of Pearls," "Boogie Woogie Bugle Boy").

But one distinctive feature of the band continued to be Herman's enthusiastic evocation of black idioms. In itself, this was nothing new. Swing had always trafficked in such images (at least some of the millions clamoring for "Stomping at the Savoy" had to know where the Savoy was). But for certain kinds of blues-oriented material, Herman crafted an outlandish stage persona that made its "otherness" more explicit. On such tunes his otherwise smooth vocal quality coarsened, disintegrating at moments of intensity into growls and falsetto squeaks. There is an element of parody in Herman's "black" persona that lies not so much in mannered exaggeration, which after all was endemic to the style (if any-thing, his performances are mild compared with Louis Jordan's eye-popping comic mask or Eddie "Cleanhead" Vinson's ecstatic squeals), as in the mere fact of its appropriation by a mainstream white bandleader. Stripped of its ethnic context, the blues becomes a species of good-humored farce—a strategic move, needless to say, that was only available to white musicians.

Herman chose his material shrewdly. Some of it continued to be drawn from the older "race record" blues repertory, albeit cleaned up for mass consumption. Like Eckstine, Herman sang about "jelly," but he substi-tuted carnivalesque jiggling for thinly veiled references to sex ("It must be jelly 'cause jam don't shake like that / Oh Mama, you're so big and fat!"). His version of the time-worn "hokum" blues standard "Four or Five Times" alludes not to sexual athleticism, but to more innocent pur-suits ("Kiss her again / Four or five times"). On the other hand, the sanc-tified gospel atmosphere of "Amen" (complete with back-beat handclaps, plagal cadences, and shouts of "Brother!" "Sister!") is brought down to earth through hoary blues stereotypes:

A two-faced woman and a jealous man
The cause of trouble since the world began
Take my chicken and my ham gravy too
But I draw the line when it comes to Bessie!
Amen!

In exploiting the appeal of such material in the early 1940s, Herman was riding the crest of the wave. Crossover hits like Louis Jordan's "Is You Is Or Is You Ain't (My Baby)," already positioned on the shifting border between black and white, were promptly covered by the Herman band in stylish swing arrangements. It was a delicate balancing act, and on at least one occasion the NAACP felt that he crossed the line. Her-man's 1944 hit "Who Dat Up Dere?," recorded for Decca with Ben Web-ster as soloist, apparently hit a raw nerve with its use of dialect. The pressure was directed not at Herman, however, but at Duke Ellington, who had loaned Webster for the recording and whose "Black and Tan Fantasy" was conspicuously quoted in the opening bars of "Who Dat Up Dere?" (Herman says ambiguously that "Ellington had something to do with the writing of [it].") Herman found that his newly "diversified" repertory gave him an entrée to black audiences. Although he rarely employed black musicians at the time (he did so regularly later in his career), his was one of the few white bands, along with Charlie Barnet's, to play such black theaters as the Apollo.[15]

For Herman (or any white musician) the black persona was a mask that could be put on or taken off at will. And its implications were deliberately ambiguous. Hipsters of both races could revel in Ellington references, the "jive" slang, and titles like "Basie's Basement" and "125th Street Prophet." The permanently unhip could enjoy such eccentricities as harmless, if irreverent, nonsense.[16] Besides, Herman never lingered in one mode for long. A zany blues tune was sure to be followed by a swing instrumental or one of the dreamy romantic ballads that "Woody Herman fans dancing by" at the Hotel Pennsylvania "always ask for" (the Herman band managed to earn twelfth place in the "sweet band" category of the *Down Beat* poll). By mid-1944 the up-tempo instrumentals were more likely than not to have a bop tinge.

In his association with bebop, Woody Herman resembled Earl Hines more than Billy Eckstine. More a father figure than "one of the boys," he drifted into the boppers' orbit almost inadvertently. During the war, the draft forced a rapid turnover of his personnel, leading to crucial new hires. In late 1943 he took on bassist Chubby Jackson. Jackson had been working with the Charlie Barnet band, where he had played alongside Howard McGhee and Oscar Pettiford[17] and heard Charlie Parker when McGhee did—in late 1942, playing "Cherokee" with Jay McShann. From that point on, Jackson cast his lot with the emergent bop idiom: "It was cooking, but it was so strange, and it seemed that you had to play double time all the time to get any kind of a raised eyebrow from anybody. I fell in love with it." A naturally gregarious personality, Jackson kept tabs

15. Dizzy Gillespie played briefly with the band during one of its engagements at the Apollo (Herman and Troup 1990, 40). For much of 1944, Herman used Carl "Bama" Warwick, a close friend of Gillespie's, in the trumpet section. But Warwick was one of several light-skinned African-American musicians who "passed" for white in order to secure more lucrative jobs (Gillespie 1979, 164). The black-owned *Music Dial* accused such musicians of "ignoring former buddies," adding: "Carl (Bama) Warwick, the members of your home town local 274 are turning thumbs down on you. 'Straighten up Jackson' " (Happy Caldwell, "In Old Philly," *Music Dial* 2 [August 1944]: 25).

16. Pop singer Allan Jones, in announcing a 1944 radio broadcast, seemed to express the bemused tolerance of the mainstream audience: "Woody Herman sure can dig up some of the goofiest titles for tunes! Remember 'Who Dat'? '125th Street Prophet'? 'It Must be Jelly'? Well, the one coming up is 'Basie's Basement'! Explain that, will you Woody?" (Old Gold Broadcast, 20 September 1944).

17. Howard McGhee remembered that Jackson and Pettiford "got an act together. . . . We used to call them 'salt and pepper,' 'cause they would sing a little bit, then they would dance a little bit, and they played the bass. But Pettiford played so much bass, he turned Chubby into a nervous wreck" (Gitler 1985, 94).

EX. 74.
"Down Under" (1942), interlude for guitar and bass, mm. 1–8.

on the best available musicians and provided recommendations to a grateful Herman. Over the next year, Herman hired a fiery stable of young soloists, including tenor saxophonist Flip Phillips and trombonist Bill Harris.

Dizzy Gillespie had written several arrangements for the Herman band as early as 1942 ("[He] said I was the first guy to pay him $100 for an arrangement," Herman remembered). Herman recorded "Down Under," a fast minor-mode piece with "Salt Peanuts" rhythmic fragments (music example 74), shortly before the recording ban. A year or two later, when Gillespie offered an arrangement of "Woody'n You" he was both pleased and flattered to discover that musicians in the band had been paying attention to the new sound. Some white bands, he noted, struggled to play his charts with the proper articulation, but Herman's band "had no trouble, because the guys were getting into the music and they wanted to really play bebop. . . . All the trumpet players in the band wanted to play like me."

Foremost among the Gillespie disciples in the trumpet section was Neal Hefti, who had been following Gillespie since the Cab Calloway band came through his hometown of Omaha in the late 1930s. A gifted arranger as well as instrumentalist, Hefti helped bridge the gap between 52nd Street and the swing band. When in New York between jobs, he made a point of searching out Gillespie and eagerly absorbed the latest developments, including the proto-bop unison ensembles of Coleman Hawkins's combo of early 1944.[18] He soon had some of the essentials of the idiom under his fingers and firmly planted in his mind.

18. "[Neal] Hefti was fascinated by the experiments made on 52nd Street, like Coleman Hawkins's ingenious riffs played by a blend of two tenor horns, trumpet, and three

EX. 75.
"Red Top" (1944), riff figure, mm. 1–5.

These new ideas often made their way into Herman's repertory through the back door—not in formal arrangements but through the spontaneous synergy of the jam session. "On one-nighters, Woody would often leave in the middle of the last set," according to Chubby Jackson. "Flip Phillips would start to play, endlessly. Meanwhile, Neal would add figures. Then Bill Harris, and finally the ensemble. The next night, I would say to Woody, 'We got one for you.' " As these head arrangements coalesced, they were offered to the public as unbuttoned entertainment. By the end of the summer, one lick, unmistakably borrowed from Gillespie, surfaced as a soaring unison figure for the entire trumpet section in "Red Top" (music example 75). In other tunes, the Gillespie influence was subtler, but still obvious. "There's a record of Woody's called 'Apple Honey,' " Gillespie has indicated. "Everybody just *knew* that I had arranged that for Woody Herman. I said, 'No, I didn't do it.' It was just the followers, you know."

All of this places the Woody Herman band in the thick of the competition to translate the emergent bop idiom to the more marketable medium of the large dance orchestra. There is no doubt his musicians were, in Gillespie's words, "followers"; but they caught up fast. "Unquestionably, Gillespie and Eckstine's arranger Gerry Valentine inaugurated the new style *on records*," argues Gunther Schuller. "But Woody Herman, with Jackson's and Hefti's ears close to the ground, picking up the new vibrations from Harlem and Minton's was certainly not far behind." By the beginning of 1945, it was Herman's band, not Eckstine's,

---

rhythm" (Frank Stacy, "Key Men, New Ideas Set Herman Style," *Down Beat* 12 [1 April 1945]: 3).

that captured public attention with startling up-tempo bop-flavored arrangements like "Caldonia." "We were the only band doing that sort of thing at the time," boasted Herman, "and it gave us something different to say."

Woody Herman's band was, of course, *not* the only one doing "that sort of thing." But he may be forgiven for not knowing about the head arrangements concocted by the Billy Eckstine band, for like the rest of the country, he had no opportunity to hear them. The whole country, meanwhile, knew about Woody Herman. At the end of July, his band landed a spot as the musical entertainment on a prime-time radio program sponsored by Old Gold Cigarettes. For the next eleven weeks, Herman's "load of sweet and hot stuff" was heard coast to coast on the CBS network. There was plenty of opportunity to air the new head arrangements, the very titles of which celebrated both the radio show and its commercial sponsor. "Red Top" referred to the popular sports announcer, Red Barber, who hosted the show. "Apple Honey" was a cigarette additive regularly advertised on the program: "Apple Honey literally ties on to the natural moisture of every particle of Old Gold tobacco. Helps keep it from evaporating, and so helps it deliver the aroma and flavor that Mother Nature puts into it. Apple Honey helps bring you a fine cigarette at concert pitch."

Herman had less luck with recordings—at least, initially. He remained committed to Decca, and when the company settled with the union in the fall of 1943, he resumed his usual busy schedule, recording more than two dozen tunes over a six-month period. But Decca, faced with the same limited production capability as other record companies, lost interest in Woody Herman. By the end of 1944, only a handful of these recordings had been released.[19] (Many would not be issued for several years.) Frustrated, Herman turned to Columbia Records, which had just resolved its dispute with the union, and worked out a deal that gave his band maximum exposure:

> "Don't worry about guarantees," I told Columbia. "Just give me as much publicity as your top two artists." The top two Columbia artists then were

19. In February, Herman complained that Decca was not "pushing bands" and that only four sides had been released since the previous September: Decca 18641, "Saturday Night" (recorded 11–12 December 1944)/"I Didn't Know About You" (recorded 5 April 1944); Decca 18619, "Who Dat Up Dere?" (recorded 8 November 1943)/"Let Me Love You Tonight" (recorded 29 July 1942) ("Woody Herman Leaves Decca for Columbia Disks; Other Leaders Are Seething Openly," *Billboard* 57 [17 February 1945]: 17).

Frank Sinatra and Dinah Shore. Every time Columbia put an ad in a trade paper, I got one. That drove the other bandleaders crazy—Les Brown, Harry James. They couldn't figure it out. Sinatra would be on one page, Dinah Shore on the other, and I would be on the next: "Columbia Records presents. . . ." We became Number One in the country because of that as much as anything. It pushed us to the very peak of popularity.

"Laura" was the first side we recorded on our first Columbia date [19 February 1945], and it was also our first release. . . . Harry James was Columbia's big band then, and he thought he had it sewed up. He recorded it a few days after us, but Columbia scrapped his and released ours. . . . It became a smash hit. Columbia had a gold record made as a special gift to me, even though the record hadn't really sold a million copies. It couldn't because the companies weren't allowed to press that many.

Woody Herman's appeal as a romantic vocalist (as well as that of his "girl singer," Frances Wayne) was carefully balanced by the novelty of his hard-driving instrumental music. Along with "Laura" came "Apple Honey," "Northwest Passage," and "Caldonia"—all recorded within the first two weeks of the band's contract with Columbia and promptly released. "Caldonia" was yet another Louis Jordan tune, transformed in Herman's reading from a sly, unpretentious blues burlesque to a hard-edged virtuoso showpiece. ("He did his own thing," Jordan later remembered. "He did it up real fast. Mine was medium tempo—bump-be-dump-ee, bump-be-dump be-doo-be-doo.") Jordan's astonishing falsetto yodel on the chorus ("Caldon-*ia!* Caldon-*ia!*"), rocketing more than an octave to land unerringly on the upper tonic, is gone, displaced by discordant, almost jeering shouts from the band. The focus shifts instead to the instrumental commentary—improvised solos and riffs, culminating in the famous full-chorus unison trumpet passage that cemented Herman's status as a harbinger of bop (music example 76). The immediate source for this passage was Neal Hefti, who had worked it out as a solo routine on another blues, "Woodchopper's Ball," before folding it into the head arrangement on "Caldonia." But its obvious inspiration, as Hefti freely admitted, was Dizzy Gillespie. Backed by Columbia's formidable publicity machine, "Caldonia" became a hit.

It would be misleading to call Woody Herman's band a *bop* band. Indeed, this term does not fit any large jazz orchestra before Gillespie's band of 1946. As with other swing bands, the success of Herman's band depended on the combination of disparate elements—smooth pop singing, high-spirited virtuoso playing, and more than a touch of smart-ass

EX. 76.
"Caldonia" (1945), riff figure, mm. 1–11.

hipster humor.[20] This was also essentially the formula that the Billy Eckstine band pinned its hopes to. Eckstine's broadcasts from California in early 1945 over the Armed Forces Radio Service show an engaging and eclectic mixture. Bop-flavored charts are prominently featured ("Blue 'n Boogie" was the band's theme), but they are carefully blended in with romantic vocals by Eckstine and Sarah Vaughan, more danceable swing fare, and scripted comic banter with emcee Ernie "Bubbles" Whitman. The mix was not perfect. Although the band never lacked outstanding soloists, it missed the electrifying presence of Charlie Parker and the irrepressible stage personality of Dizzy Gillespie. Unable to gain access to the latest pop hits like "Laura," Eckstine had to either offer his own compositions or plunder the backlog of standards (his first commercial success came with songs made famous years before by vocalist Russ Columbo). Still, the Eckstine band sounds every bit as polished and ready to entertain as any jazz-oriented dance band of the mid-1940s.

20. Herman's recording of "Your Father's Moustache" (Columbia 36870, recorded 5 September 1945) contains a sly reference to European music. Just before the parodic vocals ("Ahhhhhhhhh . . . yer fadder's moustache!"), the trumpet section quietly intones an unsyncopated phrase that turns out to be a quotation from Stravinsky's *Petrouchka*. The difference between this and the Rachmaninoff quotation in the opening bars of Eckstine's "I Stay in the Mood for You" is that the butt of the joke is not the "classical" repertory, but the squares who (obviously) wouldn't know Stravinsky if they heard it. Just a few months later, Stravinsky returned the favor by writing the *Ebony Concerto* for the Herman band.

All of this makes the contrast in fortunes between the two organizations particularly stark. By the end of 1945, Herman was "on the gravy train" and morale was high. His band had landed another prime-time radio show, this time sponsored by hair-tonic manufacturer Wildroot (a new instrumental, "Wild Root," celebrated the connection), and recordings were selling well. Much of the year was spent in lengthy theater engagements, and while on the road, the band had the luxury of playing concerts as well as dances. By contrast, the Eckstine band continued to struggle through endless southern tours. Its first anniversary was marked in a tobacco warehouse somewhere in South Carolina. Fed up and restless, the musicians got drunk and acted out their frustration. "Half the band was playing and the other half was out on the floor dancing with the chicks, and then they'd switch," recalled Dexter Gordon. "The promoter wigged. He said, 'Goddamn, what kind of fuckin' band is this? You guys are screwy.' . . . There was no discipline on the stand at all." Years later, the mere thought of the disparity was enough to rouse Eckstine to bitter resentment: "Shit, Woody Herman, get a load of his things—'Northwest Passage.' All those things were nothing but a little *bit* of the music that we were trying to play. All of those things. . . . Shit, but they got the *Down Beat* number one band, yap, yap, yap, all of this kind of shit, but Woody better not have lit nowhere near where my band was. Nowhere."

Such righteous anger only increases the temptation to cast Woody Herman as the villain of a morality play in black and white: the imitator and exploiter, parlaying a cheaply acquired veneer of bop experimentation into commercial gain, with black innovators once again left without credit or reward. But such a judgment, however emotionally satisfying, would miss the point. Woody Herman was in no way undeserving of the success and critical acclaim that came his way. His was an excellent band, with its own unique resources (the elegant arrangements of Ralph Burns, for example) and an appealing overall personality.

Nor did the band somehow come by its bebop orientation dishonestly—not with Gillespie and others openly encouraging the spread of new ideas in all directions. Besides, the Woody Herman and Billy Eckstine bands were not the only ones playing the game. Intimations of bebop can be found scattered elsewhere in recordings and broadcasts in 1944. Cootie Williams (with Bud Powell on piano) recorded Thelonious Monk's "'Round Midnight" in August. Issued as the flip side of the blues hit "Somebody's Gotta Go," it found a place in black jukeboxes across the nation. Earlier in the year, a sextet led by Williams had recorded an ingenious and delightfully off-center version of "Honeysuckle Rose"

EX. 77.
"Honeysuckle Rose" (1944), theme, mm. 1–8.

EX. 78.
"New Orleans Jump" (1944), interlude (incorporating introduction
to Dizzy Gillespie's "Be-Bop"), mm. 1–13.

(music example 77), which also, presumably, bore the influence of Powell
and Monk. Howard McGhee, working with Andy Kirk, grafted Gillespie's
"Be-Bop" onto an arrangement with the unlikely title "New Orleans
Jump" (music example 78), ingeniously superimposing its F minor passages as a bluesy commentary on the prevailing F major tonality. None

of this rivaled the more systematic policy of Herman or Eckstine, but it shows that the boundary between 52nd Street or Minton's and the swing bandstand was fluid.

Still, the question remains: what would have happened had Billy Eckstine not been hedged in by the barriers of racism? Eckstine, after all, did eventually manage to shatter those barriers on his own. His crowning achievement, on signing with MGM in 1949, was finally to be allowed to sing the heavily promoted "number one" pop songs of the moment. So, in his own way, did Gillespie break through—albeit at the cost of positioning himself (or allowing himself to be positioned) as a somewhat subversive eccentric. Only with time and age would the subcultural implications of Gillespie's persona fade away, leaving his famous popped cheeks as the trademark of yet another American celebrity.

It is easy enough to read bebop as a radical critique of commercial culture: in its rejection (or radical transformation) of popular song and dance music or its opaque, apparently meaningless titles ("Ko Ko," "Anthropology," "Salt Peanuts"). But had the Eckstine band succeeded in its aim of bringing the talents of Gillespie, Parker, and other young progressives to a wide audience through conventional professional channels, the history of modern jazz might have taken a different turn. (Perhaps "Salt Peanuts" would have been picked up as a theme song for Planters Peanuts.) Throughout the brief career of the Eckstine band, the bop generation tried hard to do what jazz musicians had always done: find a musical style and format that pleased the public as well as themselves. And as the success of Woody Herman's "First Herd" shows, that goal was attainable—at least for a white band.

The failure of the bop generation to achieve such a breakthrough forced their hand. Sensing no realistic alternative, they returned to the starting point—the small jam-session-based combo—and built from there.

10 · SHORT STAY IN THE SUN

*[Coleman Hawkins and I] had an understanding
that we were both learning the new kind of
music. And we just went from there.*
HOWARD MCGHEE

In the history of bebop, 1945 was the decisive year. At its outset Dizzy
Gillespie and Charlie Parker were still edgy young professionals, fighting
against the odds to make names for themselves in a crowded field. By
year's end they were not much better known—not, at least, by the general public—but they had proved that an idiosyncratic form of jazz entertainment could carve out a new niche on the periphery of the music
business. On 52nd Street, in concerts in New York's Town Hall, and at
Billy Berg's new Hollywood nightclub, Gillespie and Parker found paying
audiences for an idiom that showcased their finely honed virtuosity—
not within the usual contexts of dance or popular song, but in defiantly
dissonant and disorienting original compositions.

And, of course, they made recordings. Their efforts in the studio from
the first months of 1945 constitute a permanent record, rich in detail, of
the new music's emergence as public phenomenon and commercial commodity. These recordings include the earliest surviving versions of much
of its core repertory—"A Night in Tunisia," "Be-Bop," "Groovin' High,"
"Blue 'n Boogie," "Dizzy Atmosphere," "Salt Peanuts" (all Gillespie compositions)—as well as the first collaborations between Gillespie and
Charlie Parker in the small-combo format.

Many of these early recordings were obscure when released and remain
obscure today. The first recording of "Groovin' High," for example, had

such a limited run that in 1976, when the Smithsonian produced a special edition of Gillespie's recordings, only one battered copy of the original 78 rpm recording could be found. Immediately after the transfer to tape, Martin Williams reported melodramatically, "the walls of one of its grooves broke down forever."

Others, however, have long since earned a firm place in the jazz canon. Performances like "Shaw 'Nuff" (recorded May 11 for Guild) and "Ko Ko" (November 26 for Savoy) are now enshrined on the *Smithsonian Collection of Classic Jazz* as "definitive statements of the new music." What is being celebrated here is not simply artistic achievement. There are, after all, many other fine recordings by Gillespie and Parker. But there is only one pivotal, defining moment: the birth of modern jazz. One can look ahead and see, as Gary Giddins does, all of jazz modernity flowing from this moment ("Ko Ko," he writes, "was the seminal point of departure for jazz in the postwar era"). Or one can cast an eye backward and see the first bop recordings as the desired, and probably inevitable, outcome of a tortuous struggle for self-expression and artistic autonomy, the permanent achievement that marked the end of the Swing Era and announced a new musical age. "With them," James Lincoln Collier has written, "the bop revolution was complete."

That a handful of commercial recordings should stand metonymically in these assessments for all that the bop generation sought to achieve is hardly surprising. Recordings are jazz's enduring artifacts, analogous in this respect to the published compositions of the European "classical" tradition. Because they constitute virtually the only surviving evidence of artistic activity, it is natural to exaggerate their importance as an official record of musicians' intentions. Much of this is wishful thinking. We may understand that improvisation is an inherently volatile act, more process than product; that the recording studio is a poor stand-in for the usual social contexts in which the music was heard; and that the economics of recording affects the process of documentation in myriad, mostly unhelpful ways. Still, we hope that the result faithfully represents reflexes honed by countless hours of working together on the bandstand and that only the most ingenious and effective routines have been selected for preservation. We have faith that it is truly a *record* of a certain musical reality and that a history of recordings therefore constitutes a history of the music.

It would be a mistake to underestimate the importance of the medium of recording for bebop. Once committed to disc, the music could be carried far beyond the constricted social and professional world of the black jazz musician. Whether encountered in a record shop listening booth, over the air on one of "Symphony Sid" Torin's Friday night radio shows in New York, or pressed into someone's hands by an enthusiastic friend, the first releases by Manor, Savoy, and Guild had the capacity to bewilder, intimidate, annoy, or enthrall those who had never heard of Charlie Parker, let alone heard him in person. As historical documents, these recordings remain infinitely more compelling than the bare facts of chronology they supplement. The history of early bebop is rightly focused on them.

At the same time, one must not overestimate the role that recording played in the professional lives of musicians of the 1940s. Their work in the recording studio was less an end in itself than a means toward an end. The real money lay in live performance. Recordings were ephemeral commodities, placed into circulation essentially as a form of advertisement. Booking agents and club owners were understandably skeptical that young musicians with reputations for eccentricity could be viable box-office attractions. Having a few records in the jukebox offered tangible evidence of a mass audience willing to pay cash to see them in person.

If the bebop generation seemed to pour a great deal of energy into making records, that is because they sensed new opportunities. A few years earlier, a Dizzy Gillespie could have gained access to the media only through a handful of well-worn avenues: on recordings and broadcasts as a featured soloist with an existing dance band or, less probably, as the leader of a new band in a high-risk, capital-intensive venture. The chaotic state of the recording industry in the mid-1940s changed all that. As we have seen, the partial lifting of the recording ban in 1943 fostered a speculative atmosphere in which the doors to recording studios were thrown open to all manner of low-stakes projects. The only proviso was that expenses be kept to an absolute minimum. This was the opening that any number of musicians—established professionals like Coleman Hawkins as well as the bebop generation—set out systematically to exploit.

Recordings offered an unusual creative outlet for professionals struggling to find a satisfactory relationship to an industry that granted only partial reward for their talents. The uneven results reflected the varied temperaments of the performers, as well as their power vis-à-vis the recording companies. For Charlie Parker, his low-key debut as a freelance soloist for Savoy Records in the fall of 1944 provides the only opportunity we now have to assess his improvising style in the period immediately preceding the public emergence of bebop. For Coleman Hawkins, recordings were part of a conscious strategy whereby he hoped to position himself in 1945 as the leader of a new "progressive" movement in jazz. He used Asch, an obscure independent label, to document the band's more frankly experimental repertory, while striking a more cautious stance in his dealings with a major commercial enterprise, Los Angeles–based Capitol Records.

No one, however, used the recording studio to further his artistic and professional ambitions more ingeniously than Dizzy Gillespie. Determined to make the most of the limited resources available to him in early 1945, Gillespie made the momentous decision to concentrate on the small-group format, adroitly tailoring his repertory of original compositions to that idiom. The landmark recordings with Charlie Parker were designed to announce a new musical approach that could be heard nightly at the Three Deuces during their historic residency on 52nd Street.

That these recordings proved singularly effective as advertisements was certainly their creators' intention. That they have subsequently become exemplars of an uncompromising modernism and have influenced the course of twentieth-century music is a result they could scarcely have suspected. Gillespie eventually grew comfortable with his role as the founding father of modern jazz, much as the nascent field of jazz criticism came to treasure these prickly and admittedly imperfect performances as "masterpieces." At the time, however, Gillespie's ambitions lay elsewhere; the outcome subsequently labeled bebop and absorbed into an overarching narrative as the next step in the evolution of jazz was one of several possibilities that would have satisfied his desire to make a mark on the field of American popular music.

This chapter does not attempt to provide a comprehensive overview of the opening moments of bebop's "short stay in the sun." It is, instead, a series of glimpses, following up some of the biographical threads initiated in other chapters and focusing on the recordings that define, in retrospect, the early history of bebop.

King of the Underground: Charlie Parker's Savoy Recordings

By the end of August 1944, Charlie Parker had drifted back to New York. After quitting the Eckstine band, he was no longer anyone's featured soloist and had no obvious outlet for his virtuosity apart from the still-insular world of the jam session. For the next several months, he devoted himself to a round of activities that made him nearly invisible outside the black musicians' underground.

Parker's outward appearance did not match the stereotype of a young virtuoso on the rise. Miles Davis, soon to be a leading apostle of the importance of looking hip, was taken aback to find him in Harlem "dressed in these baggy clothes that looked like he had been sleeping in them for days." He cut the same poor figure on the occasions that he came down to 52nd Street. Stan Levey, who played drums with Hawkins's band at the Downbeat Club, vividly remembered Parker sitting in: "He looked like a used pork chop—so bad it was ridiculous. You never saw anything like him. None of his clothes fit. His horn was all rubber bands and cellophane." But his playing belied his dishevelment. "I was amazed at how Bird changed the minute he put his horn in his mouth," said Davis. "Shit, he went from looking real down and out to having all this power and beauty just bursting out of him."

Davis had arrived from St. Louis in the fall, ostensibly to study at Juilliard. He spent his first several weeks in New York in a fruitless search for Charlie Parker. Even other musicians who knew Parker well enough to understand why Davis was looking for him had no idea how to find him. Davis haunted the clubs on 52nd Street, hoping to spot anyone he recognized from his brief stint with the Eckstine band. While at the Downbeat, Coleman Hawkins wandered by his table during a break between sets. Davis introduced himself and, with characteristic effrontery, tried to enlist the elder saxophonist in his search. Hawkins did his paternalistic best to dissuade him. Such an obviously well-bred (and presumably socially ambitious) young man had little to gain, and much to lose, by associating with a self-destructive junkie, no matter how talented: "My best advice to you is just to finish up your studies at Juilliard and forget Bird." This remark only enraged Davis. "I got a real bad temper, so the next thing I know I'm saying to *Coleman Hawkins* something like, 'Well, you know where he is or not?' Man, I think Hawk was shocked by a young little black motherfucker like me talking to him like that." Hawkins suggested trying one of several small Harlem clubs: "Bird loves to jam in those places."

Hawkins was right. It was at the Heat Wave, a neighborhood club on West 145th Street, that Miles Davis finally caught up with Parker. Started up only two years before, the Heat Wave was too modest an operation to open its doors to the public more than one or two nights a week, but it had carved out a niche by making its facilities available to special groups at certain times. Tuesday nights and Sunday afternoons were set aside for jam sessions. Parker was a regular. Rare photographs from the fall of 1944 document his presence at musical occasions at the club hosted by the black-run trade magazine the *Music Dial*. Davis got word that Parker might show up one evening and spotted him on the sidewalk outside. As Parker walked in the door, "everybody greeted him like he was the king, which he was."

Outside of the Harlem jam session scene, Parker was less a king than yet another irregularly employed saxophonist looking for work. Exactly when and under what circumstances he began playing on 52nd Street is not clear. Ben Webster, one of his early champions, reportedly offered him a gig shortly after his arrival. He is also said to have formed a combo with Stan Levey, pianist Joe Albany, and bassist Curley Russell. That such accounts are confused and difficult to confirm is unsurprising. The clubs on 52nd Street were eager for unheralded and inexpensive talent to fill out their bills, but they were indifferent to their continual shifts in personnel and little inclined to give them the kind of publicity that would leave some trace in the historical record.

The real significance of Parker's presence on 52nd Street in late 1944 is that it led to his appearance on a Savoy recording session, under the leadership of guitarist Lloyd "Tiny" Grimes, on September 15. Not only was this his first commercial recording session since the Jay McShann days, but it remains the only sonic evidence of Parker's playing between the private hotel room recordings from early 1943 (see chapter 6) and the bebop sessions of 1945.

Tiny Grimes was the classic jazz autodidact. He had already bluffed his way into the music business on drums and piano before picking up a tipple, the small four-string guitar popular with Harlem novelty acts. Left to his own resources ("I've learned everything I know by *myself.* No one ever learned me *nothing!*"), he devised a "system" of chording so idiosyncratic that it wedded him to the four-string guitar for the remainder of his career.

As an instrumentalist Grimes was decidedly limited. He survived on an entertainer's knack for ingratiating himself with his audiences and a certain nervy determination to better himself musically: "I had quick ears, the desire to play and be in the fast crowd." When Art Tatum made a bid for wider popular appeal in 1943 by marketing himself, à la Nat Cole, as the leader of a trio, he hired the novice guitarist. Grimes was out of his depth musically and knew it: "The only thing that kept me with them . . . [was that] they knew I was trying *so* hard." But he also formed a bridge between Tatum's formidable virtuosity and the mass audience, delighting crowds by peppering his solos with outrageously inapposite quotations from "Yankee Doodle" or "The Campbells Are Coming."[1]

At the end of the summer of 1944, the Tatum trio temporarily disbanded while the pianist underwent eye surgery. Grimes took advantage of the hiatus to launch his own career as a bandleader. His new fame allowed him to attract top-flight musicians: the adaptable Clyde Hart and, for a time, bassist Oscar Pettiford rounded out the trio. Initially, however, the bassist was Jimmy "The Face" Butts—an energetic figure, popular in Harlem for his Bert Williams–style clowning, who divided his time between performing and reporting on the black music scene for *Down Beat* and the *Music Dial*.

The venue was a rarity on 52nd Street—a black-owned and operated club, Tondaleyo's, named after the black dancer (née Wilhelmina Gray) who fronted the club with money provided by her husband, John Levy.[2] Perhaps the mere existence of a black-operated club in the heart of midtown piqued Charlie Parker's curiosity or made him feel more comfortable. In any event, Parker began sitting in with the Grimes trio often enough to become a shadow member of the group, even staying around after hours to rehearse.[3]

The genesis of the Savoy recording session is straightforward enough. Savoy's proprietor, Herman Lubinsky, was desperate for new artists to record and hired Buck Ram, an experienced black arranger, to scout 52nd Street for talent. Tiny Grimes, thanks to his association with the popular Tatum trio, was an obvious prospect. Charlie Parker was not. Neither

1. Predictably, musicians were less impressed with his musical quotations. "It bugged me that he'd get a bigger rise out of the crowd than anything the great Tatum did," grumbled pianist Johnny Guarneri (in Arnold Shaw 1977, 305). But the equally great Charlie Parker was also inordinately fond of quotation.

2. John Levy—not to be confused with the bassist by the same name—was, despite his name, an African American. Levy was later photographed with Billie Holiday, with whom he had a sordid affair. "Without those pictures," wrote Holiday later, "a lot of people might never know he was a Negro. Nobody ever took me for Irish on account of my name. But with him it was different" (1975, 154).

3. There is some confusion about where the Grimes trio was performing at the time of the Savoy recordings. Jimmy Butts remembered working with Grimes at the Spotlite—the Clark Monroe–owned club that didn't open until December (Gitler 1985, 145)—but it is conceivable that he mistook one black-owned club for another. James Patrick (1978) identifies the venue as the Downbeat Club, but it seems clear that Grimes took up the engagement at the Downbeat later in the fall (Arnold Shaw 1977, 328).

particularly well known nor a regular member of Grimes's group, he was added, according to Grimes, over the company's vigorous objection—not surprisingly, since the notoriously tightfisted Lubinsky had to absorb the expense of an extra musician.

Historians of bebop have often been discomfited by Parker's debut for Savoy on 15 September 1944. These recordings serve as an embarrassing reminder that bebop was initially entangled in the mundane world of entertainment. Only two of the four tunes recorded on that day in the Nola Studios on 52nd and Broadway present Parker as we would prefer to hear him—as the leader (in fact if not in name) of a streamlined jam session ensemble. The remainder feature Grimes as vocalist on his own compositions—a romantic ballad ("I'll Always Love You Just the Same") and a humorous novelty number ("Romance Without Finance")—with Parker's contribution restricted to brief solos and faint obbligatos. For this intrusion of "commercialism," Ross Russell's widely distributed biography of Parker blames the misplaced ambitions of the guitarist. "Grimes had somehow convinced Savoy he was destined for fame as a ballad singer," Russell writes with thinly veiled sarcasm. "[He] was not really a professional singer. He simply wanted to be." Grimes has hotly disputed this interpretation; the emphasis on vocals, he argues, was the record company's idea. A glance at Savoy's recording log for 1944 bears him out. In addition to devoting numerous recording sessions to vocalists (Miss Rhapsody, the Three Riffs, Helen Humes), Savoy regularly encouraged instrumentalists like Hot Lips Page and Earle Warren to sing.[4]

Russell's account of the Savoy session, with its manufactured internal dialogue ("The session did not sound very promising to him. . . . Still, the thirty dollars would come in handy"), is at pains to distance Parker from the project and to make his involvement seem, at best, reluctant. The recordings suggest the opposite. Here, after all, was Parker's first real opportunity to practice the art of phonography—a medium that, as Evan Eisenberg argues, is as distinct from live performance as film is from theater, requiring of its practitioners new techniques and new stances toward their material. There is an engaging innocence with which Parker throws himself into the task of making the most of these unpretentious, low-budget productions. The framing instrumental passages (the fruit,

---

4. On two 1944 sessions for Savoy (June 14 and September 12), five of the eight numbers featured Hot Lips Page as vocalist. Similar sessions include saxophonists Pete Brown on August 1 (one vocal out of four) and Earle Warren on April 18 (two of four), and violinist Stuff Smith on September 26 (four of four).

presumably, of those after-hours rehearsals) bear his unmistakable stamp: the head to "Red Cross" (music example 79), the two different outchoruses for "Tiny's Tempo" (music examples 80 and 81), and the introduction (and ending) of "Romance Without Finance" (music example 82) all display his dual fascination with chromatic substitute harmonies and rhythmic intricacy. During "I'll Always Love You," he dutifully remains well off-mike so that his elaborate obbligatos do not overwhelm the vocal, until the moment arrives for him to step up to the mike and deliver the kind of heart-felt solo that must have stopped the show at the Regal Theater a month earlier. He does what he can to maintain an atmosphere of zany hilarity through five tedious takes of "Romance Without Finance." And on the instrumental tunes, his is always the first solo (a year of working with Tatum having probably inured Grimes to the habit of deferring to his musical betters).

Phonography offered Parker the opportunity to hone his persona as jam session virtuoso. The mythos of the jam session celebrates superabundance—the improviser spinning out endless choruses on the blues and rhythm changes. What Parker sounded like in jam sessions in 1944 is, of course, impossible to know. But live recordings from later in his career suggest that Parker played quite differently than he did on his better-known studio recordings. Caught up in the momentum of public ritual, Parker was inclined to be more prolix. With a real audience to provoke, startle, and delight, his playing was more disjunct, relying more for its effect on unexpected juxtapositions, intertextual references (i.e., his penchant for quotation), and occasional jarring dissonance.[5] But commodification demanded concision and the paradoxical projection of spontaneity in a carefully staged moment. As a veteran of the swing bands, Parker had already internalized the necessity of making the most of his brief time in the spotlight—concentrated gesture instead of cumulative intensity. ("I can play all I know in eight bars.")

As the leadoff soloist in a small-combo recording—still constrained by the three-minute limit of 78 rpm records but unencumbered by orches-

5. Even in his Jay McShann days, Parker displayed a knack for translating audience interaction into music. The signal, according to bassist Gene Ramey, was timbre. "Sometimes on the dance floor, while he was playing, women who were dancing would perform in front of him. Their attitudes, their gestures, their faces, would awaken in him an emotional shock that he would express musically in his solos. *As soon as his tones became piercing*, we were all so accustomed to his reactions that we understood at once what he meant" (in Reisner 1977, 187; emphasis added).

EX. 79.
"Red Cross" (1944), theme, mm. 1–8.

EX. 80.
"Tiny's Tempo" (1944), outchorus 1, mm. 1–2.

EX. 81.
"Tiny's Tempo" (1944), outchorus 2, mm. 1–2.

EX. 82.
"Romance Without Finance" (1944), introduction, mm. 1–8.

tral arrangements—Parker was given a relatively generous amount of time: a full chorus on "Red Cross" (based on "I Got Rhythm"), three up-tempo choruses of the blues on "Tiny's Tempo." For "Red Cross," there are two versions: the first unissued (and preserved for decades in Savoy's archives), the second commercially released. Ross Russell hears both performances as evanescent and unrepeatable—"pure improvisation" ("played off the top, and against the clock at that") resulting, miraculously, in unique, autonomous creations. "Each of the solos on 'Red Cross,' " he insists, "is shaped to provide its own design, with a beginning, a middle, and an end. Each is a work of art in miniature." Yet a comparison of the two takes (music example 83) suggests that Parker came in with a surprisingly clear idea of how he wanted to fill the slot assigned to him—a detailed "rhetorical plan," in Lawrence Gushee's phrase. Despite the appearance of spontaneity, each performance is skillfully molded to the same last.

Consider, for example, the first eight-bar phrase. Parker begins each solo with a pungent blues gesture—identical in its opening, although diverging after a few notes. Its "bluesiness" is announced through a variety of familiar means: the pentatonic scale (expressed diatonically, as in take 1, or through the trademark flatted degrees or "blue notes" in take 2); scooped or "bent" attacks to individual notes; a tendency to drag slightly behind the beat or to float ambiguously above it. All of these qualities are packed into a pithy, self-contained phrase that fills most, but not all, of the first four bars. What follows has a different feeling: a longer phrase, without the blues markers, that cleanly articulates the chromatic voice-leading implied by the chord progression (I⁷–IV–flat-IV–I) in measures 5–7. Remarkably, this complex phrase is almost identical in the two takes, as if the formula "blues gesture plus cadential phrase" pulled out the same, apparently spontaneous, constellation of notes and rhythms.

In the second eight bars, the two takes begin quite differently, only to converge again at the end. The commercially issued second take begins with another succinct blues gesture, answered a measure later by an off-hand flurry of sixteenth notes—as if Charlie Parker were both blues singer and virtuoso accompanist. The continuation is another cadential phrase, but grafted onto a rhythmically intricate, punning blues lick in measure 14 (the d-flat' is both a harmonically astute reaction to the local harmony—IV⁷—and the "blue" third degree of the scale).

The unissued version takes a different tack for measures 9–16: Parker launches into a startling, out-of-the-chord-progression sequence of diminished seventh chords. This is a jam session trick, related to the well-

EX. 83.
"Red Cross" (1944), Charlie Parker solo, comparison of take 1 and take 2. *(Continued on following page)*

worn device of jumping at the beginning of a phrase to an impossibly distant chord, only to ride the circle of fifths to resolution on the tonic (see chapter 8). Parker's version is subtler and more individual, but no less formulaic: it appears again, almost verbatim, in his solo on "Dizzy Atmosphere" and later in the year in the famous coda to "Ko Ko," where the absence of chordal accompaniment makes the chromatic meanderings all the more disorienting. By measure 13, Parker has safely returned

EX. 83 *(continued).*

to his harmonic home base, steering his line to the same cadential phrase that closed out the other version.

The bridge, with its distinctive up-and-down arpeggiations, is even more obviously worked out down to the smallest detail. Moreover, the same routine surfaces eight months later in the bridge to "Shaw 'Nuff." All of which makes one wonder: what can it mean to hold up performances such as this as exemplars of "pure improvisation"?

My point is not simply to undermine the cliché, usually offered as the highest praise, that Charlie Parker "never played the same thing twice." This claim, of course, is literally true. Even subtle differences in dynamics, timbre, and articulation can make otherwise identical passages sound individual—as every classical musician knows. But the proposition that Parker never repeated himself can easily slip into something quite different: that he was *incapable* of repeating an idea. The two versions of "Red Cross," with their meticulously wrought similarities, give the lie to this belief. Parker's reputation as an endlessly inventive improviser emerged from the jam session, where the paramount concern was unbroken momentum. The recording studio required him to think intensively rather than extensively, to concentrate his creative thought into the brief space allotted him. What Louis Armstrong once said of King Oliver could be applied to Charlie Parker: "When he started makin' records, he started bein' a writer."

The degree of premeditation revealed in "Red Cross," though, is atypical. More common is the variety one finds in the different versions of Parker's three-chorus solo on the blues "Tiny's Tempo," which proves far less easy to reduce to a single underlying plan. This is not to say that one does not find pervasive similarities in both subtle detail and broader design both within and among these solos. The fact that Parker systematically repeated himself is a basic insight that jazz musicians long ago discovered for themselves. It must be emphasized, however, that this repetition is meaningful. Melodic formulas are not evidence of faltering imagination, but reference points for a larger, if highly flexible, design.

The most striking instances of repetition in "Tiny's Tempo" involve the coincidence of melodic formulas with specific points in the harmonic-rhythmic cycle of the blues. Measure 8 of each chorus, for example (music example 84), is more often than not filled out with descending arpeggios neatly outlining the chord progression iii⁷–♭iii⁷ (in the key of B-flat, Dm⁷–D-flatm⁷). The various ways in which Parker subtly alters this figure do not disguise its formulaic nature. It is a pre-cadence figure, designed to arrive strongly on the upper tonic (b-flat') on the downbeat of measure 9—the beginning of the last four-bar phrase. From this point, the line invariably descends, stepwise, toward resolution on the lower tonic. (This resolution is often not reached, but the *potential* for closure, however provisional, is clearly implied.)

A different kind of formula occurs in measure 5—i.e., the beginning of the second four-bar phrase (music example 85). Here, Parker typically gives his line a distinctly bluesy turn. The melodic goal is d-flat', the lowered third degree of the scale and the flatted seventh of the underlying subdominant harmony. Its bluesiness is usually enhanced by a scooped attack and the throaty timbre available in the lower register of the alto saxophone. The sense of arrival at this juncture is strengthened by voice-leading. Parker is generally careful in the preceding measure (measure 4) to emphasize a-flat', the lowered seventh degree—a "blue note," but also clearly the dissonant seventh of a secondary dominant leaning toward a resolution on the new harmony, IV.

EX. 84.
"Tiny's Tempo" (1944), Charlie Parker solo, comparison of different
approaches to m. 8 of the twelve-bar blues cycle.

These two formulaic moments are closely related through a kind of
rhetorical opposition—between blues gestures and "nonblues" material
derived from the harmonic progression. Measure 5 serves as the logical
locus for bluesiness within the twelve-bar cycle, since the arrival of the
subdominant harmony in that bar is perhaps the one irreducible element
of blues harmony: a constant in nearly every variant harmonization, no
matter how encrusted with chromatic accretions. Measure 8, on the other

EX. 85.
"Tiny's Tempo" (1944), Charlie Parker solo, comparison of different
approaches to m. 5 of the twelve-bar blues cycle.

hand, is given over to a descending chromatic progression that is independent from, and incompatible with, traditional blues gestures. The notes of the iii^7 (D-minor^7) arpeggio—especially a', the *un*flatted leading tone—are resolutely diatonic and unbluesy; the chord tones of the ♭iii^7 chord make sense only as chromatic passing tones resolving to ii^7 in the following bar. The musical space in between these moments is a kind of transition zone: the reappearance of a' (the leading tone) or d' (the unaltered third degree) signals a shift away from the blues gestures toward harmonically based cadential material.

Strikingly, in neither "Tiny's Tempo" nor "Red Cross" does Parker make the kind of ostentatious use of chromatic dissonance for which bebop was soon to be infamous. There are numerous chromatic tones, but most are clearly either blue notes or simple passing tones. Such chromatic wizardry as one can find in "Tiny's Tempo" is tucked away in measure 4 of the blues cycle, where the shift from I to IV is occasionally intensified through a dizzying flurry of dissonances, including the oft-cited flatted fifth.[6] It is Parker's band mates who make a show of their modernism: pianist Clyde Hart's whole-tone scales on the bridge of "Red Cross" (music example 86), Tiny Grimes's aggressive dissonances in the tradition of Coleman Hawkins (music example 87).

The revolutionary character of Parker's music, as evidenced on these recordings, lies not in its unremitting modernism, but in his determination to bridge the widening gulf between the new musical currents and the blues. As always, his playing delights in sudden and disorienting shifts of rhetoric: bluesy "rice-and-beans" gestures, which would have satisfied dancers in the South, linked seamlessly to the esoteric arabesques of the improvising virtuoso, at a speed that makes the whole process seem abrupt and startling. It is this synthesis that Parker's contemporaries found compelling. It upped the ante of virtuosity in a way

6. In his essay on Charlie Parker in *The Reluctant Art*, Benny Green focuses on the opening phrase of the second take of "Red Cross," citing Parker's use of the "flatted fifth" as the fourth note of the phrase as symbolic of the bop revolution itself: "Acceptance or rejection of that note, and the nature and degree of the acceptance and rejection of that note, was a kind of litmus test. . . . In other words, a few uses of that note from 'Red Cross' and Charlie Parker had lopped away a huge percentage of jazz followers from the body of the music itself" (1991, 166–167). But this note—f-flat'—is clearly a bluesy inflection, resolving immediately to e-flat'. The classic flatted fifth is quite different—a chromatic dissonance, usually embedded in a dominant seventh chord and often unresolved, suggesting a slippery kind of polytonality: the "tritone substitution" (see chapter 2). It is exemplified by the lowered second degree in the "Night in Tunisia" cadence (see music example 35 in chapter 6). The opening gesture of "Tiny's Tempo" is a piquant dissonance that may have riled a few ears, but it should not be confused with the classic flatted fifth.

EX. 86.
"Red Cross" (1944), Clyde Hart solo, mm. 17–19.

EX. 87.
"Red Cross" (1944), Tiny Grimes solo, mm. 1–9.

that caught even the most confident professional soloists by surprise, while suggesting a way that such a music might ultimately find a broader audience.

As invaluable as these recordings seem in retrospect, they had surprisingly little immediate relevance to Parker's career. *Down Beat* made no mention of the saxophonist in its review of "Tiny's Tempo" and "I'll Always Love You Just the Same" (paired as Savoy 526 at the end of the year), citing Grimes's improvising as the "main attraction on these sides." Parker made more purposive use of the recording studio only months later, as part of a concerted effort by his far more determined colleague, Dizzy Gillespie (see below). Not until 1946 were recordings issued under his name, as a result of the famous November 1945 session for Savoy that yielded "Ko Ko," "Billie's Bounce," and "Now's the Time."

Too Wild and Too Rough: Clyde Hart's Hot Seven

Even as Coleman Hawkins advised Miles Davis to "forget Bird," he kept a close eye on other experimentally minded musicians of Parker's generation who were making a strong bid to turn the new musical currents into something commercially viable. Conveniently, he could do so without leaving 52nd Street. In the fall of 1944 Harlem entrepreneur Clark Monroe finally realized his dream of gaining a foothold in midtown Manhattan. He opened his own club, the Spotlite, at 56 West 52nd Street and continued to associate with the best available progressive talent. By November his house band boasted Oscar Pettiford, Benny Harris, Clyde Hart, and Budd Johnson. For Pettiford and Harris, the two youngest members of the band, the lure of 52nd Street won out over competing opportunities. Both abandoned high-profile (and presumably lucrative) positions with white bandleader Boyd Raeburn when faced with the prospect of a southern tour, retreating instead to the relative security of New York.

On the night that a reviewer from *Billboard* happened into the club, the house band was playing one of three nightly floor shows. Its role was to fill in the space between appearances by the club's headline acts, including the "zany antics" and "nonsensical gibberish" of Harry "the Hipster" Gibson, a white pianist whose energetic contortions and easy command of black slang were beginning to gain notoriety. In its brief moments in the spotlight, the band was careful to showcase individual talents. Benny Harris began playing the melody to "How High the Moon," but after a show-stopping cadenza launched into his own melodic line on the same chord progression, later made famous under the title "Ornithology." Bass solos were still rare in 1944, but Oscar Pettiford displayed his "strumming-thumping wizardry" on the challenging changes of "Body and Soul." Budd Johnson reprised what must have been his regular moment of glory at the Onyx Club, taking an extended solo on Dizzy Gillespie's "Be-Bop."

All of this was duly noted by *Billboard*'s reviewer. But while freely acknowledging the wealth of individual talent, he had sharp criticism for the band as a whole. "For dancing or listening," he wrote, "they are just too wild, too rough, and as a crew, unjelled." Was this just another uninformed rejection of early bebop? Perhaps—among the things singled out for complaint was the "excessive drumming" behind Budd Johnson's solo. But there is other evidence to consider.

A few weeks later, on December 19, the core of the Spotlite band, augmented by white musicians Herbie Fields and Chuck Wayne, and billed as Clyde Hart's Hot Seven, recorded four tunes for Savoy Records. Half of the tunes ("Smack That Mess" and "Shoot the Arrow to Me, Cupid") were novelty numbers, presumably aimed at the black jukebox market. The remainder were instrumentals officially credited to members of the band: "Dee Dee's Dance," written by drummer Denzil Best (borrowed for the occasion from Coleman Hawkins's band), and the eponymous "Little Benny" by Benny Harris.

If the point of the instrumentals was to advertise the musicians involved in a timely fashion, they can hardly be accounted a success. Like so much other music hastily recorded during this period, these recordings were held for some time by Savoy before being released—so long, in fact, that Clyde Hart had succumbed to tuberculosis in the meantime. But their value for the historian is inestimable. Here, finally, is some hard evidence for the "amazing unison jump scorings" that had been the talk of 52nd Street for nearly a year. The tunes in question are hardly classics of the genre (although "Little Benny" would enjoy some currency in Charlie Parker's repertory under the title "Crazeology"). But they exhibit some of the distinctive qualities of the bebop "head": phrases ending abruptly with the trademark pair of eighth notes (*be-bop*); a certain chromatic harshness exemplified by the tritone-laden bridge to "Dee Dee's Dance" and in the use of the "Night in Tunisia" cadence in both tunes; and the challenging harmonic progression of "Little Benny," with an unexpected modulation in the fifth bar from the home key of B-flat to the distant key of F-sharp. The manner of articulation—the way of "getting from one note to another"—also shows some of Charlie Parker's characteristic influence. Upbeats are swallowed or "ghosted," subtly creating accents that coincide with melodic peaks to form a shifting, polyrhythmic pattern—as in the opening bars of "Little Benny" (music example 88).

Why, then, are these recordings not regularly adduced in the history of bebop? Why have they remained obscure to this day? The answer,

EX. 88.
"Little Benny" (1944), theme, mm. 1–8.

perhaps, is that virtuoso material demands virtuoso execution. This particular constellation of musicians was clearly not equal to the task. Both tunes are played at breakneck speeds (nearly 280 quarter notes a minute on "Dee Dee's Dance") that pushed Benny Harris's technique to the breaking point. In some passages of the intricate outchorus to "Dee Dee's Dance," he fluffs so many notes that the intended melodic contour can only be guessed at. "Rough" and "unjelled," as it turns out, is neither an unfair nor inaccurate description of these performances. This innovative small-combo idiom required musicians better equipped to realize its evident potential.

Such, at any rate, is the conclusion that Coleman Hawkins seems to have drawn as the year came to an end. His extended engagement at the Downbeat Club, just a few doors away from the Spotlite, left him ample opportunity to study the competition. He heard nothing in what the younger generation had to offer that he could not easily handle, and he was not above appropriating what he liked. "Hawk's bunch and the one at the Spotlite play many of the same head arrangements of riffs," reported Leonard Feather in December, "and it's amusing to jump from door to door and compare the performances." When the opportunity arose for him to travel to California and present a new face to the public, Hawkins took even more decisive steps to align himself professionally with the emergent progressive sound.

Mississippi with Palm Trees

For nearly two years, Hawkins had been firmly ensconced in New York on 52nd Street, leaving town only to play brief residencies in other East Coast cities. For the next several years he would continue to use 52nd Street as a home base, returning for virtually guaranteed employment at one club or another. But the cramped brownstone basement clubs had lost much of their allure. A few years earlier, reported *Billboard*, top-flight jazz instrumentalists were "beating [their] brains out" for the luxury of being paid to play small-combo jazz night after night in the heart of Manhattan. The most sought-after performers now had other, more lucrative options. Roy Eldridge, for example, had shared the bill with Hawkins at the Downbeat, but left in October 1944 to take a position as a featured soloist with Artie Shaw. Some, like Art Tatum and Billie Holiday, found work in other cities. The 52nd Street clubs fought back with high fees for headline acts (Art Tatum commanded the unheard-of figure of $1,150 a week early in 1945), but with their tiny seating capacities, they could ill afford such exorbitant rates. In any case, many well-established performers found they could command better money and more pleasant working conditions elsewhere.

One such place was Los Angeles. With wartime travel restrictions easing, southern California reemerged as a realistic and attractive alternative to the East Coast for many musicians. The engine of the local entertainment economy, of course, was the motion picture industry, which made Los Angeles second only to New York as a center for mainstream entertainment. But the movies were a tightly centralized business, notorious for offering few places to black jazz musicians. Blacks tended to find other niches in the culture industry. In both recordings and radio, where African-American musicians were reasonably well represented, the stakes were relatively low and the issue of race neutralized by the absence of visual representation. By contrast, movies were both high-profile and capital-intensive. A handful of celebrities (Louis Armstrong, Fats Waller, Cab Calloway, Billie Holiday) appeared on the screen, but their musical talents were either isolated from the main plot line or obscured in stereotype. Black faces were even rarer behind the scenes in studio orchestras (although Lester Young's younger brother, Lee, was employed by Columbia Pictures by 1945).

The black community, however, offered its own support to musicians. As the only major city on the West Coast with a sizable black population, Los Angeles had been an early point of migration for black entertainers since the 1920s. The first recording by a black jazz band, led by New Orleans trombonist Kid Ory ("Ory's Creole Trombone"), had been made there in 1922. Coleman Hawkins passed through the following year as part of a vaudeville revue with Mamie Smith. The black population of Los Angeles grew steadily, from about 15,000 in 1920 to nearly 40,000 in 1930. By 1940 the population had reached 64,000, its entertainment district concentrated in characteristically Angeleno fashion in the "linear neighborhood" along Central Avenue. And then came the war. The lure of defense jobs in the Los Angeles basin added another 75,000 African-American workers, swamping the former "Little Tokyo" and creating almost overnight "one of the largest [black communities] in the country" as well as a booming market for musical entertainment of all sorts. As Ted Gioia has noted, jazz was only one piece of the mosaic that was Central Avenue nightlife, taking its place alongside "R&B, song-and-dance, comedy, blues, reviews, shake dancing, vaudeville and the like." Not surprisingly, postwar black Los Angeles became a seedbed for rhythm and blues, the home base of such labels as Specialty, Modern, and Aladdin.

When Coleman Hawkins came to Los Angeles, however, it was not to Central Avenue. Instead, his music found a place on the shifting boundary line between black and white, in "mainstream" venues like Billy Berg's and the Philharmonic Auditorium, where it was offered as a challenge to the prevailing atmosphere of racial hostility.

Hawkins was invited to California by Billy Berg, a veteran of the Los Angeles nightclub scene. Berg was a former vaudevillian and an inveterate gambler who had previously owned the Capri Club and the Trouville. In late 1944 he had just sold his latest venture, the Swing Club, for $50,000. Casting about for a new investment, he decided to take over Slapsy Maxie's on Beverly Boulevard. His plan was to turn it into a West Coast analogue to Café Society, New York's liberal mixed-race entertainment enclave.

This step was a bold move in a city that struggled unsuccessfully to contain its rising racial tensions. The $15.8 billion worth of defense contracts in California attracted to Los Angeles not just African Americans eager to gain a foothold in the industrial economy, but even greater numbers of similarly marginalized white laborers from the rural South and Midwest, who made no effort to disguise their naked contempt for their black coworkers. Added to this were white servicemen in such numbers that it seemed to the black novelist Chester Himes that the armed services had "chosen Los Angeles as the ideal place in which to give white southerners leave." Like the protagonist of his 1945 novel, *If He Hollers Let Him Go*, Himes had moved to Los Angeles in 1940 to work in the defense plants. Later he wrote:

> Los Angeles hurt me racially as much as any city I have ever known—much more than any city I remember from the South. It was the lying hypocrisy that hurt me. Black people were treated much the same as they were in an industrial city of the South. They were Jim-Crowed in housing, in employment, in public accommodations, such as hotels and restaurants. . . . The difference was that the white people of Los Angeles seemed to be saying, "Nigger, ain't we good to you?"

Not without reason did some musicians refer to Los Angeles as "Mississippi with Palm Trees."

Berg's willingness to challenge the racial status quo was undoubtedly fostered by a Harlem upbringing and a genuine liking for black music—as well as his experience that "in the cash register people prefer Negro entertainers." Whatever his inclination, he was sparked into action by Norman Granz, a Los Angeles native and UCLA graduate who officially enlisted jazz in the war against intolerance. Granz grew up in racially mixed neighborhoods, where he developed an abhorrence of racial prejudice, and became entranced by jazz as a youthful record collector in the late 1930s. He was relentless, uncompromising, and disarmingly clean-cut. Lee Young remembered him as "a real Joe College type, with the brown-and-white shoes, the open collar, the sweater, and the general Sloppy Joe style. . . . We'd drink malteds together." Troubled that Hollywood nightclubs excluded black patrons, Granz formulated a plan to use informal jam sessions as a wedge against segregation. Shortly after his discharge from the army in 1943, he approached Billy Berg with the idea of hiring prominent black musicians to play in Berg's club on otherwise idle nights—on the condition that black customers be admitted. Berg agreed, as did several other nightclub owners. Granz soon had a circuit of public jam sessions filling most of the nights of the week.

Emboldened by his success, Granz soon left the cramped confines of the nightclub behind. In February 1944 he held his first jazz concert, attracting a "mixed audience, noticeably minus the drunken jitterbugs" to a local auditorium called Music Town. On July 2, he secured the most prestigious venue in town, drawing nearly two thousand jazz fans to the first of several jazz programs at the Los Angeles Philharmonic Auditorium. Although subsequent "Jazz at the Philharmonic" concerts were strictly commercial enterprises, music was firmly aligned with racial politics for the opening concert, with all proceeds donated to the Sleepy Lagoon Defense Fund.

Granz later admitted he knew little about the Sleepy Lagoon case. He was still in the army when a group of Hispanic youths were falsely charged and convicted for a murder committed during the summer of 1942. "I don't even remember where Sleepy Lagoon was," he recalled, "and I didn't know what the hell was going on with the case, but it did seem to be a prejudice case, and this was a chance to try out one of my ideas, which was to put on a jazz concert at the Philharmonic." He may have still been away from Los Angeles in June 1943, when the "zoot-suit riots" spread throughout the city, including his old neighborhood of Boyle Heights. Rampaging servicemen hunted down zoot-suit-wearing *pachucos* to beat them, strip them, and destroy their elaborate Cab Calloway–style finery. Although most of the victims of the riot were

Hispanic rather than black, Chester Himes recognized the motivation for their ritual humiliation as racial. "What could make the white people more happy than to see their uniformed sons sapping up some dark-skinned people?" he wrote in the pages of the *Crisis*. "The outcome is simply that the South has won Los Angeles."

Jazz at the Philharmonic concerts did not need the open link to current events to be controversial. The ritual enactment of racial harmony on the stages of concert halls, and the racially mixed audiences that inevitably flocked to listen, were enough to unsettle the establishment. The management of the Hollywood Bowl declined Granz's overtures to stage a concert there (while accepting Frank Sinatra and Dinah Shore), sniffing that it objected to "the use of the word 'jazz' in connection with events presented at the Bowl." Granz's attitude earned him the praise of the jazz press as a "protagonist of racial unity," but eventually wore out his welcome at the Philharmonic Auditorium. The manager of the Philharmonic began insisting that no more than 50 percent of the musicians be black (a demand that Granz ignored), and he finally severed relations with Granz, refusing "to play host to an audience that could not be handled without police protection." Granz simply took his show, and the Philharmonic's name, on the road.

Granz's crowds were youthful and often unruly, reveling in the simulated combat of a staged jam session, expressing their approval with ear-splitting whistles and cheers. Billy Berg lacked either Granz's outspoken convictions or his vision of an entirely new concert format for jazz. He simply wanted to offer entertainment that would appeal to a liberal, mixed-race Hollywood audience. Coleman Hawkins was an ideal candidate for his opening act. Like Duke Ellington, Hawkins was dignified, worldwise, and unmistakably hip, with a following among well-behaved sophisticates of both races. Berg heard Hawkins during a talent-scouting trip to New York and secured his services after his contract at the Downbeat Club ended in mid-November. The news was the last straw for the Downbeat's owner, Chick Goldman, who promptly sold the club: "With the tough time I have trying to get acts, it's not worth the trouble."

As it turned out, talk of Hawkins's departure was premature. On his return to Los Angeles, a furious Berg discovered that Slapsy Maxie's had been leased to someone else. While Berg scrambled for a new venue, Hawkins had no trouble continuing on at the Downbeat. Quick negotiations with the club's new owners brought him a $150 raise and a tentative return engagement in the spring for $900 a week. In the meantime, Berg acquired an empty supermarket on Vine Street, which he first wanted to saddle with the unfortunate name Cornegie Hall. Ultimately, he settled on the more sensible expedient of naming it after himself. Hawkins was now committed for an opening at Billy Berg's in February 1945.

With the California trip secure, Hawkins set about reshaping his band. Thelonious Monk declined to leave his family in New York, although he apparently gave the matter some thought (an early press release announced "Delonious" Monk as pianist). His replacement was "Sir" Charles Thompson, a self-described "utility piano player" on 52nd Street. The rhythm section was rounded out by Oscar Pettiford, whom Hawkins lured away from the Spotlite Club band with the prospect of national exposure. Hawkins had hoped to convince Don Byas to rejoin him in the front line, but the tenor saxophonist was unavailable. Instead, he took Pettiford's recommendation on a young trumpet player who had just drifted into town: Howard McGhee.

"Like Freedom": The Asch Recordings

When Howard McGhee walked out on Andy Kirk's band in the summer of 1944 rather than ride the Jim Crow car, he did not have to look long for work. Veteran white saxophonist Georgie Auld needed a "high-note" soloist for his dance band and hired McGhee on the spot. For several months McGhee enjoyed both the high salary and increased attention that came with playing with a white band, and his "McGhee Special" received favorable notices in theaters across the country. Johnny Sippel, the Chicago editor for *Down Beat*, wrote a feature article on McGhee in September. A few months later, Sippel presciently cited him (along with Dizzy Gillespie, Charlie Parker, and Art Blakey) as the "hope for the future" in jazz. As McGhee said later: "I thought I had it made."

But the good times ended abruptly. At the beginning of December, Auld's band hit one of the snags that periodically plagued neophyte bandleaders. After an engagement at the Tune Town Ballroom in St. Louis, a contract dispute with his booking agent, William Morris, left him short on cash and unable to meet his payroll. The interruption was not serious for Auld, who changed agents and was back on the road within a few months. But for McGhee, the incident rankled. "He ain't paid me nothing! To this day he still owes me," he complained in 1980. Left suddenly without income, he couldn't afford to wait. He drifted back to Chicago, where a girlfriend offered temporary shelter. There he found pleasant work substituting in the trumpet section of the Billy Eckstine band during its engagement at the Regal Theater. When Eckstine moved on, McGhee contacted Philadelphia club owner Nat Segal, who offered him a spot as the guest soloist with his regular trio at the Down Beat Swing Room. "He gave me peanuts. But I mean, I didn't have nothing else to turn to."

For a time McGhee commuted to Philadelphia from New York. But one night, on 52nd Street, his old friend Oscar Pettiford introduced him to Coleman Hawkins: "He told Hawk that I was a damn good trumpet player, and he thought I could make the grade. And Hawk said [imitating gruff, gravelly voice] 'You want to play with me?' [Laughs.] And I said, 'Well, most overcertainly, most overcertainly,' because I'd heard him play 'Body and Soul' and I thought that was beautiful."

The meeting was providential for both parties. Hawkins needed an experienced improviser, able to step in at a moment's notice. McGhee was available to take over the following night. "That's how fast things was happening in New York at that time," he remembered: "We didn't re-hearse, we just went on the bandstand and played. Which was a ball, man, because I knew a lot of the tunes by working with Dizzy and Bird . . . like 'Lady Be Good.' [Hawkins] had a different melody [sings head to 'Rifftide']. So Hawk said, 'Let's play "Lady Be Good." ' I said, 'OK.', so he lit out, and I went right with him."

For McGhee, the sudden opportunity to play with a top-flight band on 52nd Street was exhilarating: "Like freedom, you know what I mean? We didn't have to do anything special with the tune; we'd just go and play it." The prospect of traveling to southern California was also ap-pealing. Partly it was a matter of escaping New York in January: Mc-Ghee's earlier experiences with North Dakota winters had left him with a morbid fear of cold climates. But, like other Americans, he was also influenced by the popular image of Los Angeles as a palm-tree-lined paradise: "[Hawkins] said, 'You like California?' I says, 'I love California, you kidding?' And I did, at the time. I thought California was like heaven on earth."

Best of all was a feeling of being an equal partner in a hip, up-to-date enterprise. After hearing Charlie Parker, McGhee knew he wanted to be involved in the new music. After hearing Dizzy Gillespie, he felt sure he could handle it. "I was saying, 'That's the kind of music I should be playing, what them cats is playing.' " It didn't surprise him that Hawkins felt the same way. "He hipped me to a lot of music. . . . I had to get hip to what Monk's tunes were, and whatever else they was playing up at

Minton's. . . . We had an understanding that we were both learning the new type of music. And we just went from there."

The departure date for California loomed, but continuing delays in the opening of the new Billy Berg's caused Hawkins to put it off. He was expected for a theater engagement in Chicago on January 5 and a jam session concert in Los Angeles on January 17. He missed them both. Instead, he concentrated on the next task: making records with the new band. "He had the date planned," according to McGhee, "but he just didn't have the right thing that he wanted to present. So when I got in the band, he said, 'Yeah, now we can make the record.' "[7]

The repertory for the session was hastily thrown together. Hawkins had some material ready, but eagerly accepted ideas from other members of the band. Sir Charles Thompson wrote "Ladies Lullaby," a misspelled tribute to Billie Holiday ("Lady Day"), while McGhee contributed a moody ballad entitled "Ready for Love" and a melodic line that he and Pettiford had written to suit the harmonic progression of "Lullaby in Rhythm": "[Hawk] used to play 'Lullaby in Rhythm' . . . so the first couple of nights I played it down, and Hawk said, 'Yeah—what's that you're playing?' I said, 'I'm playing "Lullaby in Rhythm," but this is just a different melody to it.' And he said, 'Yeah, I like that! Play it again!' So the next night [that] he came to work, he had it. And he said, 'Yeah, I worked it out.' "[8]

The choice of Asch Records for the session is rather surprising. Moses Asch's company had previously specialized in the folk music revival, with Leadbelly, Woody Guthrie, Burl Ives, and Pete Seeger on its roster, and had only just begun to branch out into jazz. But Hawkins was at this point in danger of being overexposed. Over the past twelve months, he had already made records for eight different independent companies, including the leaders in the jazz field (Commodore, Savoy, Keynote). Each was glad to have material by Coleman Hawkins in its catalog but unlikely to want more, especially with new releases facing competition from all

7. Standard discographies list a date of January 11, but McGhee remembered two recording dates with slightly different personnel. Aural evidence suggests that while Hawkins's regular bassist Eddie Robinson performed on "Night Ramble," "Bean Stalking," and "Leave My Heart Alone," Oscar Pettiford was the bassist for "Sportsman's Hop," "Ready for Love," and "Ladies Lullaby."
8. McGhee and Pettiford's line covered only the A section of "Lullaby in Rhythm." The melody for the bridge was supplied later by Sir Charles Thompson, who eventually received composer credit (Howard McGhee, interview with author, 1980).

the other labels. Hawkins, who had recorded for Asch Records in mid-December as a guest soloist with Mary Lou Williams, probably settled on the label as a useful alternative. Besides, as Williams had discovered, Asch had a refreshingly hands-off attitude in the studio. "He never told a performer how to record or what to do. If you only burped, Moe recorded it."

Asch's inexperience in the jazz field was all too evident. To judge from the sound quality of the recordings, its engineers were ill equipped to handle the more complex acoustics of a jazz band. The melody instruments sound thin and distant, and the drumming of Denzil Best is nearly inaudible. But Asch gave Hawkins what he really wanted: the freedom to record whatever he pleased, no matter how unconventional.

Just how unconventional is a matter for debate. The Asch recordings are anomalous in the history of early bebop. On the one hand, they capture many of the essential ideas of the movement—knotty, dissonant chord progressions; tricky unison themes and transitional passages; break-neck displays of virtuosity—but not the aggressive, interactive drumming of a Max Roach or Kenny Clarke. (According to McGhee, Denzil Best "played free and easy, but he didn't drop any bombs.") They also suffer by the obvious comparison with the Gillespie-Parker collaborations that came only a few months later. Had Hawkins been able to retain the services of Thelonious Monk as his pianist, these recordings would have attracted more attention, if only because they would probably have included the first recordings of one or more Monk compositions. As it is, the hastily arranged session for Asch represents *Coleman Hawkins's* take on the new musical currents—a vision that would soon be superseded by Dizzy Gillespie's more energetic efforts later in the year.

The point requires amplification because the usual assumption is that bebop held no place for Hawkins's ponderous rhythmic approach. It is certainly true that the young progressives offered a particular approach to virtuosity that Hawkins couldn't match. "He couldn't play like Charlie Parker, let's face it," commented Howard McGhee. "He didn't play that type of horn. 'Cause Bird had no polish on his wings—like he just— *brrrrrrrr* [fast, whirring sound], whatever he felt like doing, he could *do*." But did Hawkins need to play *like* Charlie Parker to fit in? Tenor saxophonists more or less in the Hawkins mold—Don Byas, Big Nick Nicholas, Lucky Thompson, Dexter Gordon—*were* prominent in early bebop, their booming resonance serving as an effective foil to the more mercurial treble instruments. Even as the professional paradigm for the timbre of the alto saxophone was transformed almost overnight from the creamy richness of a Benny Carter or a Johnny Hodges to Parker's hard-edged brilliance, the tenor sax retained its heavier sonic identity for some time to come. As Ben Webster complained after hearing Parker play the tenor in 1943, "That horn ain't s'posed to sound that fast."

Hawkins was confident that he could keep up with the youngsters: there was no tempo too fast, no chord progression too outrageous for him to negotiate. If there was no place in the bop movement for him, it was not for want of trying (as these and other recordings from the period show, he was an eager follower of trends). It was because he had no intention of yielding an inch of his hard-won professional preeminence. We now automatically think of bebop as Charlie Parker or Dizzy Gillespie music, but for Hawkins, any new music he was to be associated with had to be identifiable, first and foremost, as *Coleman Hawkins* music. He was incapable of accepting a subordinate role or submerging himself in a movement. And since he did not think of himself as being in competition with Dizzy Gillespie or Charlie Parker—who were, in 1944, profession-ally insignificant by comparison—he saw no reason to do so.

The most ostentatiously "modern" piece on the Asch recordings is a Hawkins composition, specially designed to keep potential competitors at bay. "The Night Ramble" is a harmonic minefield, full of diminished chords, tritone substitutions, and "Night in Tunisia" cadences, restlessly oscillating between C major and E-flat major (music example 89). "Bean said [imitating a gruff voice], 'Let me see these cats play this jive,' " remembers McGhee. "Nobody touched it, except us on the record date. . . . You got two beats on the tonic key, then you're off into something else. . . . Boy, oh boy, I sat up all night trying to think out what I'm going to play on those changes."

Other tunes from the recording date are more workable and scarcely less ambitious harmonically. "Sportsman's Hop" (the name given to the reworking of "Lullaby in Rhythm") is based, like "Little Benny," on an abrupt half-step-up modulation (music example 90). Halfway through

EX. 89.
"The Night Ramble" (1945), theme, mm. 1–4.

the tune, a carefully worked-out transitional passage ingeniously trans-
mutes the usual circle-of-fifths jam session trick into something fresh
(music example 91). McGhee's "Ready for Love" uses an ambiguity between major and minor mode as a way of interpolating the lowered sixth
and seventh degrees of the scale (music example 92).

The improvising within these ingenious and intricate frameworks is
aggressively modern as well. Hawkins's "Bean Stalking," based on the
chord progression of the pop song "Idaho," provides the requisite up-
tempo showpiece. At the bracing tempo of ♩ = 280, Hawkins is clearly
more comfortable than McGhee, whose attempts at upper-register trumpet passages are smeared and indistinct. ("For the Asch records, I hadn't
gotten myself together too good," he explains, "'cause I wasn't hip to
New York that much.") But McGhee will soon enough make a specialty
of soloing fluently at much higher speeds (e.g., ♩ = 340 on "Trumpet at

EX. 90.
"Sportsman's Hop" (1945), theme, mm. 1–8.

EX. 91.
"Sportsman's Hop" (1945), interlude, mm. 1–8.

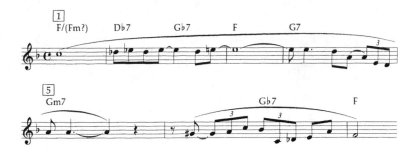

EX. 92.
"Ready for Love" (1945), theme, mm. 1–7.

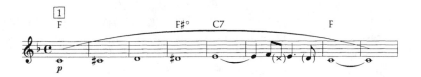

EX. 93.
"Bean Stalking" (1945), theme, mm. 1–8.

Tempo" and "High Wind in Hollywood," both from 1946). Meanwhile, on the recording, the two work together splendidly in the "fast-moving riff figures" the new style called for. After the opening theme of "Bean Stalking" is stated—a quiet, chromatically rising line in whole notes (music example 93)[9]—the second chorus begins with crisp and energetic riffs, with expertly shaded dynamics in the classic bop manner (music example 94).

At Billy Berg's

The trip to California began in upstate New York, where, to McGhee's consternation, it was so cold that "the cabs wouldn't run." Nor were the surroundings particularly glamorous. Hawkins's combo shared a floor show at a Buffalo nightclub with the "amazing mentalist" Princess Garnett and Tracy the "unicycle specialist"; afterward, the audience was in-

9. The unusual opening melody to "Bean Stalking" may have had its origins as an improvised countermelody. Hawkins plays a similar line, *pianissimo*, as a counterpoint to McGhee's embellished statement of the verse to "Stardust" on the 23 February 1945 recording for Capitol.

EX. 94.
"Bean Stalking" (1945), chorus 2, mm. 1–8.

vited to "dance to the tunes of this marvelous orchestra—then join his jam session." But with the Billy Berg's opening looming, the band moved quickly on. After brief gigs in Detroit and Chicago they boarded a train to Los Angeles, reportedly helped at the Chicago station by a small mob of red-cap porters eager to meet the famous saxophonist. The band arrived in southern California in time to play a dance at the Elks Ballroom on South Central Avenue on February 11. There Hawkins met an eager Norman Granz, who convinced him to appear the following night at Philharmonic Auditorium. A week later, Hawkins returned to the stage of the Philharmonic as part of a large cast of black musicians in a "jam-swing concert" benefit sponsored by the black musicians' union to combat tuberculosis.

The February 13 debut at Billy Berg's went on as scheduled, even though Berg had found the task of converting the supermarket into a nightclub more difficult than he had expected. On opening night the club still lacked such basic amenities as carpeting and a functional kitchen. But, as *Down Beat*'s Los Angeles correspondent noted, it had decent acoustics, ample seating for several hundred, "and—thank goodness— no dance floor." A radio wire made it possible for the band to broadcast locally for about half an hour every night at midnight.

The club did a brisk business during Hawkins's tenure on the bandstand, despite the calculated novelty of his music. "People didn't know what we were playing when we opened at Billy Berg's," according to McGhee, "but they knew it was good, and they accepted the band for *that* fact. . . . The joint was packed every night." Still, McGhee overheard some of Hawkins's older fans asking plaintively, "Why don't he play like he used to play? This ain't the same."

Those who had trouble grasping the point of Hawkins's music could take refuge in the more accessible antics of singer and guitarist Slim Gaillard, who shared the bill at Billy Berg's. Gaillard, who had settled in Los Angeles at the beginning of the war, had made his reputation by writing and recording such successful novelty songs as "The Flat Foot Floogie" and "Chicken Rhythm." Although he was a passable improviser, fond of hammering out choruses on thinly disguised versions of "I Got Rhythm," Gaillard's real talent lay in comedy. Like Harry "the Hipster" Gibson (who played at Billy Berg's later in the year), he staked out a position on the boundary of the jazz musicians' community, offering a kind of farcical translation of otherwise impenetrable subcultural codes for mainstream white audiences. Like Cab Calloway, he presented creative enactments of stereotype, laced with a manufactured nonsense dialect that parodied the "jive" slang of the black inner city. What he lacked in instrumental brilliance he made up for with slapstick humor and sharp-edged lampoons of sentimental popular crooners and Yiddish song. Audiences unaccustomed to imagining the black jazz musician as an aloof, self-confident virtuoso felt comfortable with Gaillard's clever nightclub shtick.

Today, it may be easier to see Gaillard as an innovator in his own right. One recent overview of the Los Angeles hip-hop scene reaches back to claim him as an ancestor, a verbal virtuoso "expanding the tradition of scatting . . . into a new language that reflected the urban scene." But neither Gaillard nor Gibson has earned more than a passing contemptuous reference in jazz history. Jazz discourse has traditionally emphasized instrumental virtuosity, disdaining "mere" entertaining. McGhee coldly describes Gaillard as "an entertainer. . . . I mean, he really wasn't playing no music. All he had was a bass player, a piano, a drummer, and him. And he didn't play nothing, he just filled in the times."

Jazz instrumentalists' indifference to Gaillard and Gibson at times shaded into hostility. When Dizzy Gillespie came to Billy Berg's later in the year, he also shared the stage with Gaillard. One evening, when asked how he liked California, Gillespie loudly complained backstage about the " 'Toms' and musical nothings" that plagued his existence. He didn't mention Gaillard by name, but didn't need to. Such a generalized insult is a classic example of the African-American rhetorical trope known as signifying. A comment ostensibly aimed at no one in particular is, in fact, designed to smoke out a reaction from anyone who might happen to hear it. To respond to the provocation is in itself acknowledgment of guilt, proof that the taunt has found its home—i.e., "if the shoe fits, wear it."

Gaillard recognized himself in Gillespie's jibe in spite of its calculated indirection ("Man, I ain't even mentioned your name since I been out here!" protested Gillespie). An angry confrontation in the washroom quickly escalated to violence, with Gillespie landing a solid punch before the two were separated.

In the longer run, such resentment was not so easy to resolve. Like Coleman Hawkins before them, the bebop pioneers initially showed little interest in developing a public persona to go along with their music. Their personal idiosyncrasies were colorful enough (and would eventually provide overeager popularizers with all the copy they needed), but their onstage demeanor was unnervingly cool, reflecting the studied nonchalance of the jam session. In the absence of competing visual images of its own, bebop—at least in California—inevitably absorbed some of the subcultural deviance that was Gaillard and Gibson's stock-in-trade.

Indeed, reports on the new musical trend in the mainstream press in early 1946 characterized it less as a brilliant updating of instrumental jazz than as a wave of subversion spearheaded by Gaillard, whose 1945 "Cement Mixer" proved so popular that the independent label Cadet was unable to press any other recordings, and Gibson, who "titillated" audiences with "a surreptitious mention of marijuana, and not such a sneaking mention of bennies, and how everybody was high." The new catch-phrase *bebop* became inseparable from such goings-on: Gaillard was advertised as the "be-bop bombshell" (and his band as the "be-bop barbarians from Billy Berg's beanery"). According to *Time*, bebop was "hot jazz overheated, with overdone lyrics full of bawdiness, references to narcotics and doubletalk." Los Angeles radio station KMPC indignantly banned all bebop from its airwaves. While such scandalized disapproval earned bebop musicians some attention, it also wedged their music into a difficult-to-escape marginal status defined by the racial stereotype of social deviance.

"Hollywood Stampede": The Capitol Recordings

For Coleman Hawkins, the path was considerably smoother. When a screenwriter at Universal penciled in scenes featuring jazz in the script for *The Crimson Canary*, the studio hired Hawkins and his combo for the part. Much more impressive was the news that Hawkins had signed an exclusive contract with Capitol Records. In so doing, he moved from the fringes of the recording industry toward its center and positioned himself for another bid for mainstream success.

Founded in the spring of 1942, Capitol was one of many labels springing up in the shadows of "the majors." By early 1945 it had prospered
so efficiently that it was clearly in the same class as Columbia, Decca,
and Victor. Capitol's success was attributable in part to good timing. Several of its first releases, recorded just before the AFM ban, became major
hits, and the partial settlement of the ban in late 1943 kept two of its
largest competitors, Columbia and Victor, on the sideline for most of the
following year. But Capitol also benefited at the outset from its close ties
to the entertainment industry. Its co-owners were Johnny Mercer, a veteran lyricist who contributed the words to such profitable tunes as "That
Old Black Magic" (1942) and "Ac-cent-tchu-ate the Positive" (1944), and
Glenn Wallichs, owner of a thriving Los Angeles record store. One of its
principal investors was Buddy DeSylva, executive producer in charge of
production at Paramount Studios. Capitol could well afford to pay Hawkins the "biggest fee of his twenty-year career" to join its ranks.

The man responsible for bringing Hawkins to Capitol was Dave Dexter.
Dexter began his career as a journalist, first with a Kansas City newspaper, then from 1938 to 1942 with the Chicago-based *Down Beat*. Like
many other jazz fans in the profession, he made no pretense of objectiv-
ity. As editor at *Down Beat*, he used all the powers at his disposal—
personal contacts, record reviews, feature articles, and photographs—to
generate favorable publicity for bands he had "adopted." Jay McShann
was among the early beneficiaries of Dexter's enthusiasm. The cub reporter for the Kansas City *Journal-Post* placed a rave review in *Down
Beat* and wrote letters to Decca urging them to record the then-unknown
local band. McShann returned the favor years later by titling one of the
tunes on his first recording session "Dexter Blues." Dexter also knew the
featured soloist on "Dexter Blues," Charlie Parker, but had little inclination to work with him. During his apprentice years, when Parker
"played alto sax ineptly and hung around all the bands and combos bug-
ging the musicians to allow him to sit in and blow," he nicknamed the
reporter "Dexterious" and hit him up for cigarettes and small change. "I
never liked him as a person," admitted Dexter, adding, "Nor did many
of the black Kansas City musicians."

Dexter shared the enthusiast's passion to become involved in as many
aspects of jazz production as possible. In 1939 John Hammond invited
him to sit in on a Count Basie recording session, which opened his eyes
to the joys of hands-on involvement with the music and the artistic authority of the control booth. On his way home from the studio, he kept
thinking, "*Hammond gets paid doing the thing he enjoys most.*" He also

became fascinated with jazz history. Early in his career, he compiled a notebook on Kansas City jazz; in Chicago, he sought out obscure blues singers. Soon Decca took him up on his suggestion to produce a series of historical anthologies, supplemented by new recordings of Kansas City jazz.

In early 1943 Dexter moved to Los Angeles, joining the staff of the newly formed Capitol Records. His work centered on public relations—one of his main responsibilities was editing and publishing the company newsletter, *Capitol News*. But he relished every opportunity to work directly with musicians in the studio. Among his projects was a "History of Jazz," which purported to provide a "panoramic recreation [*sic*] of the music from its early days" through more than three dozen new recordings by such artists as Paul Whiteman, Red Nichols, Rex Stewart, and Capitol regulars Nat "King" Cole and Stan Kenton.

Coleman Hawkins's first appearance in California in twenty years was, for Dexter, yet another opportunity to articulate the past glories of jazz in the present. Hawkins was an artist he had "dreamed of recording for many years." With the saxophonist under contract, Dexter set about shaping the music to his satisfaction. Although Hawkins had worked without a rhythm guitarist for the past several years, Dexter insisted on adding one to the combo. Allan Reuss, then working with Harry James, was one of the best in the business, but his steady 4/4 chunking beat was an anachronism increasingly out of favor on 52nd Street. Nevertheless, Hawkins agreed to this change. "I found Hawkins easy to work with," Dexter remembered later. "He had no objection to my bringing in Allan Reuss on guitar. He was in good humor, and accepted my tune suggestions eagerly."

None of this sat well with Howard McGhee, who watched in dismay as Dexter reshaped the band's musical concept to suit his tastes:

> Dexter was supervisor of the date, so Hawk tried to please him. In fact we got in an argument about that, him trying to please Dave Dexter. 'Cause I said to Hawk, "Man, you don't need Dave Dexter, you're Coleman Hawkins. What do you need Dave Dexter for?" And he said, "Maggie, you don't understand, this is business." I said, "But what do you need him for?" And he [Dexter] heard me say that, so he didn't like me to start out with.

The clash of wills between Dexter and McGhee came to a head during a seven-hour recording session on March 2. Each remembered the incident differently. According to Dexter, McGhee showed up "belligerent and uncooperative" and patently incapable of proceeding through the session. Dexter suspected drugs—a not unreasonable supposition, since McGhee had probably begun experimenting with narcotics a few years before.[10]

At some point the band set to work on "Too Much of a Good Thing," based on the chord progression to "Fine and Dandy." McGhee stumbled helplessly on the relentless string of eighth notes in the opening unison melody, prompting Hawkins to pull him from the lineup. In "sheer desperation" and with Hawkins's approval, Dexter made a late-night phone call to the veteran cornetist Red Nichols.

Nichols owed Dexter a favor. Although he had made hundreds of records of small-combo jazz in the late 1920s and early 1930s as Red Nichols and His Five Pennies, he had virtually "dropped out of sight" until Dexter revived his career by signing him to Capitol. Within twenty minutes, he was in the studio, ready to work. But Nichols proved even less capable of negotiating the difficult arrangement than McGhee. "It wasn't Red's kind of music and I should have known that," Dexter admitted in his autobiography. "Nichols felt bad, I felt worse, and Hawkins laughed at both of us." In a private communication to John Chilton, Dexter described himself as "humiliated" by the experience.

But was McGhee's alleged drug use the proximate cause? McGhee sounds perfectly in control of his instrument on "Hollywood Stampede," recorded during the same session. "Too Much of a Good Thing" may simply have bedeviled him. A week later, when the group retackled it, Dexter rejected more than two dozen takes spoiled by McGhee's fluffs before settling on a mildly flawed version for commercial release.

Significantly, Hawkins's telling of the story in 1946 bypassed musical explanations altogether. "I was making a record date for Capitol out on the Coast," he began, "and Dave Dexter couldn't get along with Howard McGhee." This observation suggests that Dexter may have been looking for an excuse to replace a musician he considered "belligerent and uncooperative." One might have expected Hawkins to stick up for his young trumpet player. But Hawkins continued his policy of passively assenting to Dexter's personnel decisions. For him, the episode was a humorous

10. In an interview with the author, McGhee alluded to a woman he had met while touring with the Andy Kirk band who "had turned me on to something I hadn't knew about before. . . . I was sick, and I was shivering, [while] everyone else was sweating." He consulted a doctor, who cured his "problem" with bed rest, vitamins, and plenty of fluids.

parable illustrating the futility of trying to hold back progress. "Finally Dexter put in an old-time Dixieland trumpet player," Hawkins reminisced, "one he thinks is one of the world's greatest, to play the trumpet part on a modern number. This trumpet player was so completely lost, he couldn't do a thing, and Howard forgot he was mad and almost killed himself laughing."

McGhee may have been laughing, but he was still mad. To be benched in favor of a has-been—a white has-been, at that—was an affront to his pride. "Dave Dexter thought Red Nichols could do anything, that he could outplay anybody," he remembered. "But that's how far his mind went back." Slumped in his chair, McGhee took great pleasure in watching Dexter's plans disintegrate:

> Hawk had a tune that Red Nichols couldn't play in no kind of way. I was just sitting there waiting to see what was going to happen. And [Nichols] had the nerve to turn around and tell me, "Maggie, you shouldn't feel bad, that's a hard tune to play." I said, "Well, I can play it. Definitely. I didn't say I couldn't play it." He said, "You can play that?" I said, "Yeah." He said, "Well, man, you're the one that should be on this date, not me." . . .
>
> And Pettiford cracked up laughing when [Nichols] started to play, and that made Dave Dexter mad. You know, here we are laughing at a white boy. He couldn't figure that out. But he had no business putting Red in there in the first place. Red didn't know what our band was like. He didn't know what kind of music we were playing.

There were plenty of other tunes on the Capitol sessions with which Nichols would have felt perfectly at home, however. Even with McGhee restored to the front line, these recordings show a decidedly conservative side of the Hawkins band. Of the twelve tunes, seven were familiar standards, none published more recently than 1933. Such tunes had long been in Hawkins's repertory, but remained underrepresented in his recordings because of the pressure by smaller companies to record only "originals." Finally in the embrace of a major company that could afford to pay composer royalties, Hawkins allowed himself the luxury of openly stating copyrighted melodies. The ballads in particular—"Star Dust," "It's the Talk of the Town," "Someone to Watch Over Me"—are superbly performed and recorded. Even by modern standards, the quality of the state-of-the-art engineering at C. P. MacGregor Studios is remarkable, capturing with surprising fidelity the wide range of Hawkins's timbral nuances, from the intimate, breathy gestures of the opening measures to the inevitable booming climax. Later in life, Hawkins remembered studios pressuring him to "do another one like 'Body and Soul.' " With that lucky "accident" only a little more than five years behind him, Hawkins could not have been unmindful of the possibility of lightning striking twice.

The remaining tunes provide glimpses of Hawkins's bebop-inspired repertory. "Rifftide"—based on the changes to "Oh! Lady Be Good"— is credited to Hawkins, but later claimed by Thelonious Monk, who recorded the tune under the title "Hackensack." The latter attribution is the more persuasive: in the opening pair of riffs (music example 95), the angular punning on the third degree of the scale (brought out a bit more in Monk's later version) is reminiscent of Monk's "Straight, No Chaser," while the bridge ends with an unresolved half-step-up maneuver that seems quite uncharacteristic of Hawkins (music example 96). Given Hawkins's admiration for Monk's music, and the common practice of bandleaders appropriating tunes written by their sidemen, the only surprise is that more of Monk's tunes did not end up under Hawkins's name.

The other original compositions are peppered with mannerisms that must have been common practice on 52nd Street. Decorative triplets and sixteenth notes are everywhere, as are the abrupt phrase endings that suggest the syllables *be-bop* (music example 97). The opening rhythmic gesture of "Bean Soup" recalls Dizzy Gillespie's "Groovin' High," as does

EX. 95.
"Rifftide" (1945), theme, mm. 1–4.

EX. 96.
"Rifftide" (1945), theme, mm. 23–25.

EX. 97.
"Hollywood Stampede" (1945), theme, mm. 1–4.

EX. 98.
"Bean Soup" (1945), theme, mm. 1–5.

EX. 99.
"Too Much of a Good Thing" (1945), theme, mm. 1–5.

EX. 100.
"Hollywood Stampede" (1945), outchorus, mm. 21–32.

the interpolation of a chromatic passing chord between iii and ii (music example 98). Similar chromatic side-stepping can be found in the opening of "Too Much of a Good Thing" (music example 99). All of this falls under the category of shared musical language, but more explicit inter-textual borrowings underscore how fluid the boundary lines between different "compositions" could be in a repertory that was transmitted orally. For the outchorus of "Hollywood Stampede," someone—presumably McGhee, to judge by his earlier appropriation of Dizzy Gillespie's "Be-Bop" for Andy Kirk's "New Orleans Jump" (music example 78 in chapter 9)—fits both the opening riff of Benny Harris's "Ornithology," the introduction to "Be-Bop," *and* a characteristic Gillespie triplet run into the chord progression of "Sweet Georgia Brown" (music example 100).

A reviewer for *Down Beat* heard an unmistakable "Gillespie influence" in the "catch unison work" on the Capitol recordings. The reference was undoubtedly not only to the telltale borrowings, but also to the distinctive phrasing and articulation that brought them to life. In this realm, McGhee was clearly the adept and Hawkins the willing pupil. Through a skillful shading of volume—ghosting certain notes to throw a subtle emphasis on the notes that follow—the trumpet player brings out the irregular, elusive quality of the phrases at the end of "Hollywood Stampede." It is McGhee's solos, as well, that strike the proper tone, for they make far more effective use of ambiguity and irony than does Hawkins's earnest manner.

Consider, for example, the first few phrases of McGhee's solo on "Bean Soup," a reworking of the 1920s pop song "Tea for Two" (music example 101). The opening gesture is sly and bluesy, dragging slightly behind the beat at the beginning and emphasizing the ambiguous dissonance of the second degree of the scale against the tonic harmony. Still, when the harmony takes a chromatic detour in the fourth bar (the passing ♭iii chord, B minor[7] in the key of A-flat major), McGhee unerringly spells out the passing dissonant chord tones (*"a little lick in there to let 'em know, 'Here's where I'm at, really' "*). The phrase ends abruptly, and with deceptive simplicity, in measure 5. At first one might think that McGhee is simply articulating the local harmony, in which case a-flat' and f' in measure 5 are understood as dissonances that will move on when the harmony shifts from ii[7] to V[7] in the following measure. But after a full measure of silence (measure 6) in which the notes do *not* resolve, one is forced to rehear measure 5 as a premature arrival on the tonic, with the

EX. 101.
"Bean Soup" (1945), Howard McGhee solo, mm. 1–9.

relaxed, semidissonant sixth degree (f′) as almost an afterthought. Just as the phrase seems to end early, the next begins unexpectedly with a sudden *forte* burst in the upper register. McGhee is clearly an improviser in the Hawkins tradition, someone who makes a point of "know[ing]— not just feel[ing]" what he is doing when choosing notes in relationship to the underlying (or implied) harmonic background. At the same time, irony and disconcerting shifts of rhetoric are as essential to the effect here as in the solos of Lester Young, whom McGhee deeply admired, and Charlie Parker, whom he hoped to emulate.

The partnership between Hawkins and McGhee ended as precipitously as it began. One night at Billy Berg's, while Hawkins launched into a performance of "Body and Soul," McGhee wandered backstage to the kitchen. There, on a meat-chopping table, he saw an open briefcase. His curiosity piqued, he idly flipped through the documents. The briefcase, it turned out, had been accidentally left behind by a representative from Moe Gale, the agency handling Hawkins's affairs. Inside were a stack of contracts for more than a dozen one-nighters from Los Angeles back to New York. McGhee was astonished at how much Hawkins was earning. Armed with this information, he confronted his employer after the gig:

I said to Hawk, "Look, I seen how much money you're making. I think I deserve a raise, 'cause that little $35 you're paying me ain't saying much."

So he said, "How much do you want?"

I told him, "I want at least $75 a night."

He says, "Well, no, no, no, no, no, I can't pay you that much. I might be able to give you 50."

I said "No, I want 75." And I knew what he was making there. He could've afforded to pay *all* of us $75 a night.

Underlying the dispute over money was the same generational struggle that had spoiled Hawkins's relationship with Dizzy Gillespie two years earlier (see chapter 7). With a small combo, Hawkins could not easily claim the same magisterial authority he commanded when leading a full-size dance orchestra. The jam session format was by its nature more informal and egalitarian, distributing artistic responsibility throughout the ensemble. As the reviewer from *Down Beat* noted approvingly on opening night at Billy Berg's, "Hawk doesn't hog the solos; he features the others as much as himself." The situation might have been different several years before, when Hawkins staffed his bands with musicians awestruck simply to share the same stage with the undisputed master of the saxophone. But McGhee knew how heavily Hawkins had relied on his young employees to keep up to date with the latest 52nd Street currents. He was shocked to discover that Hawkins did not acknowledge the collaborative nature of the enterprise where it counted—in the paycheck:

He said he couldn't afford it. He was jiving, he wasn't telling the truth. . . . I feel like—I'm playing with him, me and him supposed to be sharing things alike. I figured that he was on my side, but he wasn't; he was for Coleman Hawkins. . . .

He wanted us to do [the] work for him. 'Cause we were the band, let's face it. He only played one line. So I told Sir Charles about it, and he wanted the same thing, so Hawk decided to bust up the whole band rather than give up $75 a night.

Hawkins's intransigence was rooted in his conviction that he could always find someone else to take McGhee's place. "I'll get Joe Guy," he responded airily—but Guy was not interested. To a reporter for *Down Beat*, he speculated out loud (and rather impractically) about hiring Roy Eldridge. But in the end, he settled for Bill Coleman, a veteran trumpet player Hawkins's own age. Coleman had found himself temporarily unemployed after coming to Los Angeles with John Kirby's combo and was happy to take over McGhee's spot. For several more weeks, Hawkins stayed on in Los Angeles at Shepp's Playhouse, a nightclub in the Little Tokyo district. But when Oscar Pettiford quit and John Kirby lured Bill Coleman back East, Hawkins decided to cut his losses and leave California behind him. Less than a week after closing out at Shepp's Playhouse, he was back on 52nd Street, where his job at the Downbeat Club was waiting for him.

For his own part, Howard McGhee had called Hawkins's bluff because his own future looked reasonably bright. A brief overview of McGhee's professional activities provides a further example of how a career in the early years of bebop might unfold.

Two months of playing alongside Coleman Hawkins had raised McGhee's stock, and guest appearances at Granz's Jazz at the Philharmonic concerts had earned him a local reputation as an up-and-coming trumpet virtuoso. As soon as the engagement at Billy Berg's ended in mid-April, he set about forming his own band, recruiting local talent such as Teddy Edwards, whom he heard in a blues band and convinced to switch from alto to tenor saxophone. "They were unknowns—just people who lived out there, you know. But they could play, and we molded the shit together, with different types of arrangements Hawk and I had." At first he retreated to the resources of the black community, playing at the Downbeat Club on Central Avenue. By August he was under the management of a local agency that promised to promote him as a "name cocktail" act. For the remainder of the year, he played more prestigious (and presumably more lucrative) venues on Hollywood Boulevard: the Swing Club, the Streets of Paris, and the "incredibly ornate" Jade Palace Cafe.

The music McGhee played was bop—or so, at least, is the after-the-fact consensus, since the term *bop* was not yet in circulation. (Ted Gioia, for example, states that "Howard McGhee's pioneering bebop band [was] the first modern jazz ensemble on the West Coast, predating the more heralded arrival of Parker and Gillespie by several months.") The key factors were tempo and drumming style. McGhee used many of the same charts he had used with Coleman Hawkins, but he pushed the speed up to the limit of his playing abilities—as well as the ability of his audience to comprehend. At the Jade Palace, where he played opposite a New Orleans revival group led by trombonist Kid Ory, McGhee reveled in the disorienting effect of his tempos: "We used to play some tempos, man, that they wouldn't believe. Them old guys would be sitting there looking at us with their mouths wide open. We used to play that 'Hollywood Stampede' like: [sings head, ♩ = 320]. And Hawk would play it: [♩ = 200]. They'd go along with *that*, but the way we would play it, man, they couldn't understand it."

The powerful, disruptive drumming was the province of Roy Porter, who joined McGhee's group while it was still on Central Avenue. A native of Colorado, Porter was still a struggling teenaged musician when he arrived in New York in the summer of 1943—just in time to witness the Harlem riots and the first public stirrings of the bop movement. One night he dropped in at Minton's, where he gaped in wonder at Kenny Clarke's novel approach to the drumset. At the time, he "wasn't quite hip to it" or to other drumming techniques that "completely turned me around musically." But by the time he moved to Los Angeles in 1944 and decided that playing the drums on Central Avenue was infinitely preferable to his day gig as a gardener in Bel Air and Beverly Hills, he had absorbed the new sounds to the point that older styles of drumming no longer satisfied him. "The drummers in Los Angeles were just playing swing drums, rudiments, paradiddling and ratamacuing," he remembered. "They just weren't happening." With McGhee's band, he was free to work out his own version of the style he had heard at Minton's. Not everyone appreciated it, of course. The Los Angeles stringer for *Metronome* tersely reported, "That drummer with Howard McGhee at the Swing Club is the loudest and worst on the Boulevard."

McGhee would, by the late 1940s, become one of the most successful trumpet players in the bop idiom, earning a spot in three consecutive *Down Beat* all-star bands (including first place in 1949); but in 1945 he had to struggle to make an impression on the Los Angeles scene. He did everything he could to attract attention, even borrowing a contrived battle of the tenor saxes from his former boss, Andy Kirk. Kirk had a number that featured his three tenor players: as one took a solo, the others complained to Kirk with comically frantic stage gestures that the man was "hogging the mike." The routine satisfied even Leonard Feather, who was normally resistant to such overtly "commercial" ploys: "It was good music," he wrote, "but it proved again that showmanship pays off, too." One of those tenor players, James D. King, surfaced in Los Angeles the following year, and brought the routine to McGhee's new band:

Well, Teddy [Edwards] was playing tenor; and J.D. [King] would be waiting to play, and he would get the people on his side, because every time he
goes to play, Teddy would say, "No, no" and push him over. He'd do this a
couple of times. See? So J.D. gets mad, and when he finally comes on in and
starts to play he jumps off the floor at the end of the bridge—and you'd
think an atomic bomb hit. People would holler and scream, "Yeeaaah, that's
what we're talking about, that's what we want." That's showmanship. You
have to do that, too, you know. I mean, you can be serious, but just don't
overdo it. If the people ain't happy with what they hear, the man don't *need*
you. They can get somebody else to make them feel good.

Meanwhile, McGhee did his best to gain access to the media. For a
time, his performances from the Streets of Paris were broadcast locally
late on Friday nights. He also made numerous recordings for various Los
Angeles–based independent labels—some with a bop combo, some with
a twelve-piece band ("McGhee Special" once again), still others with blues
singers. But he was completely unaware of the recording that would
transform his career. One day he was walking down the street when he
was stopped short by a familiar sound wafting from a nearby record store:
"I said, 'Doggone, that sounds like me.' So I go into the store, and say,
'Hey, man, what's that record?' He says, 'Oh, we just got that in today,
it's a new Jazz at the Philharmonic.' That rang a bell. I said, 'Well, I'll be
damned!' "

The trumpet player on the record was, indeed, McGhee. Without his
knowledge, Norman Granz had made a recording of an extended jam
session at one of his concerts at Philharmonic Auditorium in early 1945.[11]
After shopping the recordings around to Keynote, Granz eventually released them on the Asch label, which distributed the performances of the
jam session staples "How High the Moon" and "Lady Be Good" over six
78 rpm sides. When pressured by McGhee, Granz (who had boasted on
the liner notes that "musicians will be paid a wage commensurate with
their abilities") sent him a check for the usual one-time recording fee.

As it turned out, the Jazz at the Philharmonic album, featuring
McGhee's sparkling two-chorus solo on "How High the Moon," became

11. Although the date of this recording does not appear in standard discographies, it was
probably 5 March 1945. Three of the performers on the recording—Gene Krupa, Willie
Smith, and Illinois Jacquet—were also scheduled to play that particular concert ("Jazz Concerts Rock the Coast," *Down Beat* 12 [15 March 1945]: 6). Granz had earlier recorded
extensive portions of his first Philharmonic concert on 2 July 1944, which were eventually
released commercially.

a minor best-seller, establishing his reputation as a leading trumpet virtuoso. But McGhee, firmly settled into the relative isolation of the West Coast club scene, knew none of this: "I was working with my band, so I wasn't really going *hungry* or nothing, but I didn't know how big the record was." The situation gave Coleman Hawkins, who delighted in understated "signifying," a chance to get back at his impudent former employee: "Coleman Hawkins knew about it, but he wouldn't even pull my coat. He was supposed to be my buddy, but he would never tell me nothing. 'How're you doing, Maggie?' I said, 'Well, I'm doing all right.' He said, 'OK, 'long as you're doing all right, everything's cool.' I'm not knowing that I could've been getting $1,750 a night for five pieces on my own . . . out [in New York]. Gee!"

McGhee made his move to national prominence in 1947, sharing the stage with Hawkins as one of the featured artists in the touring version of Jazz at the Philharmonic. By this time bebop had become well established both as an artistic movement and a commercial antidote to the waning public interest in swing. That same year, Dizzy Gillespie (with guest artists Charlie Parker and Ella Fitzgerald) played to a packed house at Carnegie Hall in "a triumphant recognition of what is today America's most vital music form—bebop." The foundation for that success had been laid earlier, while both Hawkins and McGhee were still in California.

Lemonades and Malarkeys: Gillespie in the Studio

Dizzy Gillespie left the Billy Eckstine band in December 1944. Like Charlie Parker several months before, he faced the immediate challenge of making a transition from salaried employee to freelance virtuoso on the make. Unlike Charlie Parker, he was not inclined to make either his whereabouts or his intentions a secret. A brief notice in *Billboard* announced that Eckstine's erstwhile "King of the Trumpet" was forming his own small combo. But the famous combo with Charlie Parker at the Three Deuces that would unmistakably announce bebop as an artistic force did not materialize for another four months, until mid-April. In the meantime, Gillespie poured all of his energies into the recording studio, in projects designed to display his multiple talents as soloist, arranger/composer, and bandleader.

Within just a few weeks of leaving Eckstine, Gillespie had talked his way into the studios of four different record companies. Continental, Manor, Guild, and Black & White were all firms founded in the wake of the recording ban. Faced with a struggle for survival in an increasingly crowded marketplace (*Variety* counted 130 companies by mid-1945), each looked to the ferment in urban black culture at the end of the war for some musical commodity on which to ride to financial security. Jazz was part of that ferment, and many small companies hedged their bets by maintaining an active jazz catalog. But with the exception of a few labels like Keynote and Commodore, they saw jazz not as a separate genre (and certainly not as an art form), but as one manifestation of the broader phenomenon of "race music"—touching at various points on the decades-old category of blues, the current swing mainstream, and the nascent rhythm-and-blues revolution.

The attitude of these companies toward jazz was both casual and opportunistic. Their ideal jazz artist was someone on whom they need expend no extra effort or expense, someone whose reputation alone could be counted on to sell records: an Art Tatum, a Coleman Hawkins. By 1945 such artists tended to be overexposed, overpriced, or unavailable. Further exploitation of the jazz specialty market fell to those dedicated enough, or desperate enough, to scout out new talent for themselves, typically relying on the expert opinion of hired intermediaries with access to the musicians' grapevine. In this way, a handful of labels stumbled onto bebop.

Dizzy Gillespie was a likely enough prospect—especially after February, when his rising status was confirmed by a critic's poll in *Esquire* proclaiming him the "New Star" of the trumpet. Shortly thereafter Guild Records took the bait, signing Gillespie to an "exclusive" contract and expending scarce resources publicizing its association with the "New Ace of trumpeters."[12] Guild did its best to hitch its precarious fortunes to Gillespie's rising star. Its breathless advertising copy from later in the year seems surprisingly prescient in situating him at the forefront of a new movement: "He's the newest excitement in the band business . . . creator of a brand new, excitingly different jazz kick. . . . that's Dizzy Gillespie, tops of the new trumpeters, and a national jive fad! And of course, he records exclusively for Guild Records."

But whether Gillespie was a sound investment for Guild is difficult to say. By the end of the year, after having released only three of his records (Guild 1001: "Groovin' High"/"Blue 'n Boogie"; Guild 1002: "Shaw

12. The "exclusive" contract did not impede Gillespie from recording on a competing label for blues singer Albinia Jones on April 14. He was listed under the pseudonym "John Kildare," although advertisements clearly identified him as " 'Dizzy' Gillespie" (*Billboard* 57 [19 May 1945]: 26).

'Nuff"/"Lover Man"; Guild 1003: "Salt Peanuts"/"Hot House"), the company was bankrupt, its catalog absorbed by the larger Musicraft label.

In due time, other companies would take up the role of championing the "new jazz kick" with conspicuously more success. By early 1946 Savoy's Herman Lubinsky, frustrated that his recordings of Coleman Hawkins, Slam Stewart, Lester Young, Ben Webster, and other marketable veterans had to compete with recordings by the same artists on several dozen other labels, turned his attention to cornering the market on "the rebob [sic] stuff—'modern jazz.' " In February of that year, Gillespie and Parker joined forces for the debut recording session of Dial Records, a new enterprise launched by Ross Russell in Hollywood. Savoy and Dial were to emerge by the late 1940s as aggressive and prolific supporters of bop, flooding the market with small-combo recordings targeting the bop aficionado.

But in the mid-1940s, before "bebop" emerged as a marketable commodity, young freelancers like Gillespie and Parker, with only modest reputations and no immediate ties to dance bands, were distinct anomalies. To the extent they were noticed at all, record companies treated them as bit players, useful for their versatility within the broad rubric of "race music." Record producer Teddy Reig summed up Gillespie's early forays in phonography as an "obstacle course":

> He always used to wind up with all the lemonades, and malarkeys. . . . He overcame more obstacles that were thrown in his way. Maybe they were the politics of a record company, maybe they were politics of friendship—the guy with the record company or the A & R man had a friend he had to use—all kinda reasons unbeknown to us; let's leave it at that. . . . But there were so many others that could have been on his early records if Dizzy were given more freedom. When it said "All Star Sextet," it never was that. I mean they were all good players, but not the guys he could have used. And you see, in those days, it was a different kind of scene. For the average black musician to get a record date, he made them with a blues singer.

Perhaps the most obvious failing of Gillespie's early recordings lay in their personnel. The makeup of the rhythm section was conspicuously unstable: on five recording dates from December to May, he used five different bassists, five different drummers, and four different pianists, most of them either now-obscure white musicians (Irv Kluger, Frank Papparelli, Murray Shipinksi, Jack Lesberg) or well-known black musicians firmly associated with swing (Cozy Cole, Sid Catlett, Clyde Hart,

Slam Stewart).[13] The front line for the January session for Manor included swing veterans Trummy Young and Don Byas. It is hard not to view some of these names as interlopers—competent, even excellent musicians, but so out of sync with the emergent bop style that their presence in the studio with Gillespie is inappropriate, incoherent.

Where, one might ask, were the more appropriate musicians? Although, as we shall see, there is good reason to suspect contingency and compromise in the making of these recordings, there are simpler explanations. Many musicians Gillespie might have preferred to use were unavailable in early 1945. Drummers in particular were in short supply: Kenny Clarke was still in the army; Art Blakey was playing with Billy Eckstine; and Max Roach, who would rejoin Gillespie by midyear, was on the road with Benny Carter. Pianist Bud Powell was out of commission—beaten senseless while in Philadelphia with the Cootie Williams band, his head injuries were so severe that for some time he required institutionalization. Bassist Oscar Pettiford lent his efforts to Gillespie's first date in January, but probably only as a quid pro quo for Gillespie's participation in his session on the same day (see below); he was not likely to want to work regularly for a man who had called him a "prima donna." Charlie Parker himself spent most of January and February working steadily in Cootie Williams's reed section. The "obstacles" that impeded the progress of bebop were, to some extent, logistical.

In any case, Gillespie had a practical, even cautious, streak. He was a vocal admirer of Bud Powell's fire and Thelonious Monk's originality, but preferred support personnel who were more loyal, reliable, and tractable. His durable association with Clyde Hart is a case in point. Hart, some eight years Gillespie's senior, was a pianist and arranger with experience dating back to the Kansas City scene in the late 1920s. Gillespie got to know him as an upstairs neighbor in his apartment building on Seventh Avenue in the early 1940s and drew him into his combo at the Onyx Club in early 1944. Hart had an exceptionally keen ear—while in Kansas City, he is supposed to have copied a rival dance band's recorded arrangements by feeding nickels into a jukebox and transcribing them on the spot. "Though he didn't play in our style, like Bud Powell," Gillespie

---

13. Ira Gitler argues that Irv Kluger was the drummer for the 9 January 1945 date for Manor Records—not, as reported in the standard discographical literature, Shelley Manne (Gitler 1974, 75). If so, there were only four drummers on the five dates: Morey Feld (31 December 1944), Kluger (9 January and 9 February 1945), Cozy Cole (February/March 1945), and Sid Catlett (11 May 1945).

admitted, "Clyde knew everything—all the changes we played." His death from tuberculosis in mid-March, just weeks after a recording session, severed a relationship that may well have continued on into the bop era.

Hart's considerable experience and maturity came in handy on Gillespie's early recording sessions, a few of which had the distinct smell of disaster. On January 9, both were part of an impressive studio band that recorded Gillespie's arrangement of Oscar Pettiford's "Max Is Making Wax" (retitled "Something for You") for Manor. Billed as "Oscar Pettiford and His 18 All Stars," the recording session may have been intended to test the commercial potential of the bassist as swing bandleader. (Perhaps this explains why the arrangement, used by the Eckstine band as a blisteringly fast showpiece, was recorded at an eminently danceable tempo—although it is quite possible that the musicians may have not been able to sight-read it any faster.)

The remainder of the session, however, verged on chaos. No one, apparently, had remembered to bring any other arrangements. Panicked at the prospect of having nothing to show for the extraordinary expense of eighteen musicians, Gillespie and Hart decided to take the path of least resistance and do what black bands always did when strapped for material: play the blues. Someone contacted Henry "Rubberlegs" Williams, a veteran of the Theater Owners' Booking Association (TOBA) stage, whose blustery style of delivery as a blues singer suggested possible competition for the likes of Eddie "Cleanhead" Vinson. While the band cooled its heels in the hallway, Gillespie and Hart hastily scrawled out an accompaniment. "The band backed him singing the blues," remembered drummer Shelley Manne, " 'cause it was easy to do."

Rubberlegs Williams was later at the center of an even more spectacular fiasco—a recording session for Continental in which the singer, wildly disoriented after unwittingly ingesting an enormous dose of Benzedrine, screeched his way through several numbers. The anecdote is interesting because it combines a notorious preoccupation with drugs with another striking characteristic of the bop generation: their cool contempt for older forms of blues entertainment. A dancer and sometime female impersonator, Rubberlegs Williams was the embodiment of the raucous style that had dominated the black variety stage earlier in the century. Even by contemporary standards, the repertory for the session was almost defiantly old-fashioned: tunes recorded by Bessie Smith nearly two decades earlier[14] and thinly updated versions of blues clichés (from "4-F Blues": "Girls, whatcha gonna do when Uncle Sam takes your 4-F man to war? / Some of you gonna drink muddy water, sleep in a hollow log"). But the date was Clyde Hart's; presumably eager to keep his friends steadily employed, he stocked the backup band with young progressives, including Gillespie, Don Byas, and Charlie Parker, making his first appearance in a recording studio since September.[15]

Parker and Gillespie, of course, had spent the previous summer together staking out a pointedly ironic stance to material considerably less ripe for parody than this. So it is quite believable that the incident may have been a prank. According to Gillespie, he and Charlie Parker deliberately spiked the singer's coffee as a way of enlivening what looked to be a dull day's work. But several other eyewitness accounts, including those of trombonist Trummy Young and Parker himself, insist the overdose was accidental. The session was held at ten in the morning, and Parker had gotten off his job with Cootie Williams at the Savoy only hours before. To fortify himself, he pried open a Benzedrine inhaler ("he was a genius for getting them open," remembered Teddy Reig admiringly), pulled out the wick saturated with the powerful amphetamine, and set it in a cup of coffee to steep. When Rubberlegs Williams entered the studio, half-drunk, someone grabbed the spiked coffee by mistake and urged it on the singer. Williams complained repeatedly about the bitter taste. Parker, meanwhile, sipping from an ordinary cup, wondered aloud why his usual jolt didn't seem to faze him.

Everyone agrees on what happened next. As the concentrated dose of Benzedrine began to take its effect, Williams unraveled. Panic-stricken and sweating profusely, he complained that the studio lights were too hot and ordered the studio plunged into darkness. Most of all, however, he lashed out at Parker and Gillespie. With the deft maliciousness of *banderilleros,* they were amusing themselves by punctuating the increasingly hysterical vocals with double-time obbligatos and rhythmically off-center riffs. Dizzy's ostentatious dissonances in particular enraged the

14. "What's the Matter Now?" and "I Want Ev'ry Bit of It" were recorded on 5 March 1926, with Clarence Williams accompanying Smith on piano, and released together as Columbia 14129-D.

15. According to Bobby Shad, who helped produce the session, Parker's period of absence from the studio had to do with the fact that he was in arrears to three different locals (Kansas City, Chicago, New York) of the musicians' union: "I phoned Al Knopf, who was then head of 802, and guaranteed to take X dollars out of his recording dates and pay off all the locals. It was the weirdest deal I ever made" (in Arnold Shaw 1978, 141).

singer ("Miss Gillespie, you keep playing those wrong notes behind me, I'm going to beat your brains"), but even Parker's more mild modernisms (the descending chromatic sequence he liked to use in measure 8 of the blues form, for example) clashed against the straight I–IV–V chord progression Williams favored. But by the end of the session, Williams was beyond caring. On the aptly named "That's the Blues," he is literally out of control: his voice cracking to the breaking point, he roars out such clichés as, "I got the blues—I got the blues so bad it hurts my tongue to talk / I got the blues so bad it hurts my feet to walk!" After one particularly heartfelt plea ("if you can have mercy on anybody, please distribute a little bit on me!"), one of the musicians—probably Gillespie—screams with ecstatic delight.[16]

"Tunisia" and "Salt Peanuts"

Gillespie's rapid rise in 1945 as the putative leader of a "national jive fad" depended in large part on the shrewd husbanding of his musical resources. He fought to maintain some control over the creation and marketing of his artistic productions, insisting on the inseparability of his playing and his music. As a hungry freelancer, he had every incentive to sell his services to all comers for short-term gain—especially in the early months of the year, when recording fees undoubtedly bulked large in his income. But Gillespie showed little inclination to market himself as a soloist-for-hire, available to play a few choruses of a jam session standard on someone else's record in exchange for a flat fee.[17] Nor was he content to fade behind the scenes as arranger and composer—despite well-intentioned advice by Woody Herman to do just that.

By the outset of 1945, Gillespie had compiled an impressive catalog of compositions and arrangements: "A Night in Tunisia," "Salt Peanuts," "Dizzy Atmosphere," "Blue 'n Boogie," "Be-Bop," "Max Is Making Wax." Most remained unrecorded. Among his most urgent priorities, therefore, was to commit this repertory to disc, preferably in performances that would unmistakably project the music's novelty while simultaneously affirming him as its foremost interpreter.

But with what instrumental resources? For some time, Gillespie had been struggling to find the center of gravity in his career. Such progress

16. The recordings from this session were not released until early 1946 (advertisement, *Billboard* 58 [16 February 1946]: 24).
17. Exceptions are his appearance on January 12 with the Joe Marsala Sextet for Black & White and on June 6 with the Red Norvo Sextet for Comet.

as he had made had involved tacking back and forth between the margins and the center—between the artistic freedom and inherent flexibility of the small-combo/jam session format and the ongoing momentum of his work with large dance orchestras. To escape the dead-end drudgery of freelancing with the big bands after leaving Cab Calloway, he had formed the combo at the Onyx Club in 1943. When 52nd Street itself looked like a dead end, he had helped build up the Eckstine orchestra. In early 1945 he aimed once again at gaining a foothold on 52nd Street. All along, he continued to adapt, adjust, and expand his repertory to meet his immediate needs.

Consider, for example, the convoluted histories, both on the bandstand and in the studio, of two of Gillespie's most famous compositions: "A Night in Tunisia" and "Salt Peanuts."

"A Night in Tunisia" dates back to Gillespie's first stint on 52nd Street, with Benny Carter, in the winter of 1941–42. By his own account, it arose out of his restless regimen of harmonic experimentation: "I sat down at the piano to improvise some chord changes. Actually, they were thirteenth chords—A-thirteenth resolving to D minor. I looked at the notes of the chords as I played the progression and noticed that they formed a melody. All I had to do was write a bridge, put some rhythm to it, and I was over. . . . We played the tune on Fifty-second Street and called it 'A Night in Tunisia.' "

From the outset, "Tunisia" occupied a place of honor in Gillespie's repertory. When he joined the Earl Hines band, it was scored for full orchestra and served as a flashy vehicle for his high-register virtuosity as well as an exotic, even topical novelty (the early months of 1943 saw fierce fighting for control of Tunisia at the climax of the North Africa campaign). The AFM ban probably prevented Hines from recording it. Although "Tunisia" was also a staple of the Eckstine band the following year, any opportunity to record it passed when Gillespie left at the end of 1944. Almost immediately, it entered the repertory of white bandleader Boyd Raeburn, to whom Gillespie continued to sell arrangements ("I had to do it," Gillespie apologized later; "I wasn't making enough money").[18] It was Raeburn who in late January ended up with the honor

---

18. Several months later, a review of Raeburn's band at the Hotel New Yorker complained that "some of his efforts, penned by hot trumpeter Dizzy Gillespie, tend to show off his seven-man brass section too loudly" (Bill Ely, "On the Stand: Boyd Raeburn," *Billboard* 57 [12 May 1945]: 20).

of first recording the fully orchestrated version of "Tunisia," with Gillespie as guest soloist.

An even earlier recording for Continental Records, however, reveals that Gillespie had devised an alternative plan for "A Night in Tunisia." For months, vocalist Sarah Vaughan had languished in the shadow of her employer, Billy Eckstine. When Vaughan left Eckstine in late December of 1944 to strike out on her own, Gillespie immediately saw the possibilities in yoking his ambitions with hers. The vehicle he chose was "Tunisia," fitted with words and retitled "Interlude." Armed with a rough demonstration record of the tune with Vaughan as vocalist, he spent the waning days of 1944 trying, without much success, to persuade some company to record it.

While hawking his project on 52nd Street, Gillespie ran into Leonard Feather. The meeting is hardly surprising. Feather, in the words of historian John Gennari, was "*the* ubiquitous presence on the '40s New York jazz scene." In his zealous work as "jazz gate-keeper and missionary" he wore "half a dozen hats" as journalist, author, songwriter, radio-show host, publicist, and record producer. As it turned out, Feather was equally enthusiastic about Sarah Vaughan's talent and commercial potential, and he made the project as much his own as Gillespie's. He quickly secured a recording date with Continental and surrounded Gillespie and Vaughan with an "all-star" group of white musicians, reflecting his professional circle of acquaintances as well as his passionate advocacy of racial integration. To cut down on expenses, Feather assigned himself the role of pianist.[19]

Leonard Feather is best known today as a jazz critic, but his successes in the recording studio in the mid-1940s had encouraged him to think of himself as a songwriter and producer with a knack for the blues. Recordings of his raucous, idiomatic material ("Salty Papa Blues," "Evil Gal Blues") had helped launch Dinah Washington's career just the year before. For Sarah Vaughan, he pulled together two new compositions, displaying his taste for both modern jazz and the "plain blues." "Signing Off" was a sinuous, chromatic ballad laden with tritone substitutions,

19. The remaining personnel included tenor saxophonist Georgie Auld, a bandleader in his own right and arguably the only "all-star" in the group; drummer Morey Feld, who was working regularly with Benny Goodman; clarinetist Aaron Sachs, who would be a member of Goodman's band by February; and bassist Jack Lesberg, who had been playing in the New York City Symphony Orchestra. Only guitarist Chuck Wayne had at this time any regular contact with the black bebop pioneers, having recorded earlier in the month with Oscar Pettiford and Benny Harris for Savoy.

specially designed to exploit Vaughan's impeccable intonation and savvy harmonic sense. By contrast, "No Smokes" was a straightforward twelve-bar blues offering commentary on the wartime cigarette shortage, the kind of tune that every black singer was expected to toss off.

Feather later expressed regret at having monopolized valuable studio time with his "trivial" blues tune—much as he also apologized to posterity for not letting Gillespie solo on a blues date under his supervision several years earlier. His error, of course, is evident only in retrospect and greatly exaggerated by the subsequent course of events. With Gillespie safely canonized as one of the towering figures in modern jazz, anything that infringed on his autonomy in the studio is now likely to be construed as an "obstacle"—yet more evidence of commercial interference. But Gillespie's ambitions for this Continental recording date were no less obviously commercial. His version of the standard "East of the Sun" (perhaps a revision, for reduced forces, of the version he had written for the Eckstine band) is no jam session vehicle, but a straightforward arrangement featuring Vaughan as pop vocalist. Its few harmonic modernisms are discreetly blended into the background, and Gillespie's uncharacteristically restrained solo is limited to ten bars.

Even more striking is the recasting of "A Night in Tunisia" as "Interlude." In the process of transforming the fiery trumpet showcase into a brooding torch song ("I thrill as your arms would unfold me / A kiss of surrender set the mood / Then heaven fell down when you told me / Love's a passing Interlude"), Gillespie drops the tempo and the dynamic level so low that no trace of Latin rhythmic excitement remains: even the trademark syncopated bass line is sacrificed. The performance is more sketch than finished product, the texture at times painfully thin. (It doesn't help matters much that Feather, as pianist, struggles to negotiate the complex chord changes.) But both tempo and mood are expertly tailored to Vaughan's strengths. Gillespie remained committed to selling himself as a virtuoso instrumentalist. But "Interlude" shows him wistfully searching for that elusive and characteristically American goal—a hit pop song.

The more familiar version of "A Night in Tunisia" did not surface until early 1946, when Gillespie recorded the tune with a septet under his leadership for Victor. As the recording shows, even with more limited forces, Gillespie retained as much as possible of the big-band version, including its complex structure (with a lengthy opening vamp and several connecting passages) and a few hints of a fuller orchestration.[20] Still, it is through this pared-down version, playable by any combination of instruments in a jam session format, that "Tunisia" entered the bop repertory and became one of the most enduring of modern jazz standards.

Compared with "A Night in Tunisia," "Salt Peanuts" is much less prepossessing. It began as a polyrhythmic figure (probably a drum lick by Kenny Clarke, credited as co-composer) that attracted, as if by gravitation, a melodic contour from the oral tradition.[21] Gillespie first thought of it as a riff figure to "set" behind a soloist in a big-band context, and he used it in this way on a recording as early as 1942 (Lucky Millinder's "Little John Special"). Somewhat later—probably in time for the Onyx Club band—he began to think of it as a distinct tune, performable by a small combo.

"Salt Peanuts" seems like the ideal jam session vehicle—an ingenious and witty way of introducing "I Got Rhythm" changes (albeit in F, not B-flat, and with a slightly different bridge), with the added attraction of the nonsense catchphrase in the title, a bit of Dada humor guaranteed to puzzle the unhip. It was in this form (complete with nonsense vocal) that it caught Coleman Hawkins's attention in 1944. But that same year a fully orchestrated version of "Salt Peanuts" also surfaced in the Eckstine band's repertory. On the stages of theaters across the country, "Salt Peanuts" was heard as a humorous novelty number that showed off the bad-boy humor and brilliant trumpet playing of the band's music director.

Within a few weeks after leaving the Eckstine band, Gillespie recorded "Salt Peanuts" for Manor Records on January 9, 1945—his first date as leader of a recording session. The sextet was staffed primarily with colleagues from his stint the previous year on 52nd Street (Don Byas, Clyde Hart, and Oscar Pettiford from the Onyx Club band, Trummy Young from the Downbeat). The "Salt Peanuts" theme may have started as an

20. The most obvious ways in which the 1946 sextet used its limited resources to suggest a fuller orchestration are the undulating saxophone riff in the opening vamp, dutifully played as a single line by Don Byas, and the chromatic connecting passage before Byas's solo, in which the guitar joins the horns to create a three-part harmony. A more subtle instance is Gillespie's rare use of the mute. In the full band arrangement, the opening melody is given to the trombone—suggesting a parallel with valve trombonist Juan Tizol's role on such Latin-influenced exotica as "Conga Brava" and "Caravan" with Duke Ellington. To provide a similar contrast in timbre between the theme statement and the trumpet solo that immediately follows, Gillespie plays the opening theme muted, steps aside for a few bars during the intervening interlude to remove the mute, and launches into his solo with open horn.
21. Martin Williams has traced various parts of the "Salt Peanuts" melody to Louis Armstrong's 1930 recording "I'm a Ding Ding Daddy" (OKeh 41442, recorded 21 July) as well as to characteristic piano figures by Count Basie (Williams 1976).

EX. 102.
"Salt Peanuts" ["Salted Peanuts"] (January 1945); top line: introduction; middle and bottom lines: composed interludes.

unpretentious scrap of an idea, but by 1945 it had become embedded in a complex arrangement that, in its ingenuity and almost obsessive concern with textural variety, strongly suggests a big-band provenance. As one would expect of any small-combo recording, the composed theme and the improvised solos that follow make up the bulk of the performance. But the theme statement is double: after a full chorus scored for ensemble, the melody line of the A section is divided between an instrumental "call" and a vocal "response" ("Salt peanuts, salt peanuts").[22] An elaborate introduction also serves as a coda: a drum solo, unmistakably sounding out the "Salt Peanuts" theme in rhythmic outline, followed by a quirky, eight-bar stop-time passage (music example 102, top line). At strategic points Gillespie interpolates unusual and somewhat disorient-

22. The Coleman Hawkins version, by contrast, has only a single theme statement. The "Salt peanuts!" chant appears only once, thrown in at the end of the first A section as a humorous aside while the theme continues to be played.

EX. 103.
"Little John Special" (1942), "Salt Peanuts" riff figure, mm. 1–4.

EX. 104.
"Salt Peanuts" ["Salted Peanuts"] (January 1945), theme, mm. 17–20.

ing connecting passages, each followed by a dramatic unaccompanied "break" to launch the next solo (music example 102, middle and bottom lines).

Although the routine is well suited to a small combo, echoes of the big-band texture are especially resonant in the few places where the three-horn January 9 version diverges from the more familiar two-horn Guild version (featuring Charlie Parker) recorded four months later. In its earlier incarnation as a big-band riff, the "Salt Peanuts" theme (played by the trumpet section) was answered by a low-tonic pedal point by the trombones, entering with a conspicuous syncopation on the last beat of the second bar (music example 103)—an effect similar to the trombone pedal points in the famous "fade-out" chorus of "In the Mood." On the January recording for Manor, trombonist Trummy Young takes over this extra part, sustaining the tonic while Don Byas and Gillespie play the octave leap. In the corresponding passage of the Guild recording, the pedal point is gone, and the necessary syncopated accent is assigned instead to the piano and drums.[23] A few measures later

23. On the Coleman Hawkins version, the horns simply absorb the lower note into their line.

in the Manor version, the monophonic line of the theme briefly opens up into three-part harmony, again suggesting the fuller orchestration (music example 104). By contrast, the Guild version dispenses with such harmonized passages (if one excepts the oddly exposed, dissonant intervals of the introduction and second interlude). As with "A Night in Tunisia," it is the later, sparer version, with its musical energy concentrated into fleet, superbly executed unison lines, that has survived as an icon of early bop.

Bebop Heads

Many other tunes recorded by Gillespie in the early months of 1945 have some direct or indirect connection with large dance bands. "Blue 'n Boogie," like "Salt Peanuts," comes from a riff that was expanded into a head arrangement for the Eckstine band. "Good Bait" is a pared-down version of the Tadd Dameron arrangement, also part of the Eckstine band's repertory. "All the Things You Are," an otherwise straightforward rendering of Jerome Kern's song, borrows as its introduction the Rachmaninoff parody from the opening of "Good Jelly Blues." "Be-Bop," with its fiendishly difficult opening passages, seems to strain the resources of the jam session idiom; while I know of no evidence for an earlier orchestrated version, the riffing behind Don Byas's first solo chorus reflects at least the habit of working in a big-band context.

Still, the outlines of a new genre are apparent. In these recordings Gillespie moved steadily toward the streamlined method of presentation that came to characterize bebop in particular: the convoluted melodic lines, or "heads," played immediately before and after the improvised solos on familiar chord progressions. These ingenious melodic and rhythmic creations are ideally suited to the small combo, making a virtue of its limited resources and contributing to the sense of a distinct bebop aesthetic.

The effect of the bebop head does not lie in ingenuity of orchestration. It is simply a melody played in bare octaves or unison by all available melody instruments. The practice arose out of the jam session, in which skeletal riffs provided a frame for the necessarily more unpredictable improvising that made up the bulk of the performance. The themes to some of Gillespie's early recordings, including "Dizzy Atmosphere," "Blue 'n Boogie," and "Salt Peanuts" (and to a lesser extent "Good Bait," "Groovin' High," and "Be-Bop"), are riffs: intricate, ingeniously off-balance, and unmistakably modern, to be sure, but riffs nevertheless. As such, they shared a tendency toward repetition and/or sequence, with surface complexities ultimately yielding to predictable, easy-to-follow patterns.

The bebop head differs from the Swing Era riff in its unpredictability. Within its brief confines, bop musicians concentrated all that was most novel and disorienting in their new musical language. By placing it *first*— before the listener could situate the improvisation within some recognizable context—the beboppers made it impossible to hear their music as a version, a "jazzing," of some other repertory. The effect was unnerving even to fellow professionals, as in this oft-quoted reaction by drummer Dave Tough to hearing Gillespie and Parker for the first time on 52nd Street: "As we walked in, see, these cats snatched up their horns and blew crazy stuff. One would stop all of a sudden and another would start for no reason at all. We never could tell when a solo was supposed to begin or end. Then they all quit at once and walked off the stand. It scared us."

Complex, asymmetric riff figures were not unknown before bop, but they characteristically came toward the end, rather than the beginning, of a performance. On any number of small-group recordings from the Swing Era, the verbatim restatement of the opening theme that normally follows the string of solos is displaced, wholly or in part, by elaborately worked-out passages or outchoruses. Flashy closing riffs, often played in unison at blinding speed, were a trademark of the famous early 1940s Benny Goodman Sextet that featured guitarist Charlie Christian,[24] and obviously influenced the Tiny Grimes recordings from 1944.

Not surprisingly, the most startling composed-out passages on many of Dizzy Gillespie's early recordings are the outchoruses. Compare, for example, the opening to the outchorus of Tadd Dameron's "Good Bait." The head (music example 105) begins squarely on the beat, unfolding in metrically unambiguous sequences. The outchorus (music example 106), on the other hand, is out of kilter from the start. It opens with a dissonance (the seventh degree of the scale) on the second beat of the measure; the descending four-beat arpeggio that follows strongly suggests a shift of accents from the main beats to the backbeats (two and four) of the measure. No sooner has this rhythmic wrinkle ironed itself out than the

---

24. Examples of Goodman Sextet tunes with outchoruses include "Till Tom Special"/ "Gone With 'What' Wind" (Columbia 35404, recorded 7 February 1940), "Six Appeal" (Columbia 35553, recorded 20 June 1940), and "Good Enough to Keep (Air Mail Special)" (Columbia 36099, recorded 13 March 1941).

EX. 105.
"Good Bait" (1945), theme, mm. 1–5.

EX. 106.
"Good Bait" (1945), outchorus, mm. 1–8.

phrase abruptly terminates with the trademark *be-bop* figure: a pair of eighth notes landing on a dissonant flatted fifth (measure 2). The rest of the passage is similarly disjunct and asymmetric. It is striking precisely because it is *not* a riff. Indeed, the avoidance of patterning, even the expected wholesale repetition at the level of the eight-bar phrase, is willfully perverse.

"Dizzy Atmosphere" adds to this asymmetry the dizzying element of speed. The head (music example 107) is an unpretentious scrap of melody, flying by with a certain flip charm. But the outchorus (music example 108), played in octaves by Gillespie and Parker, is an elaborate tour de force. It begins with an ascending sequence, firmly on the beat, if subtly accenting the backbeat; but it quickly disintegrates into choppy phrases that rely on discontinuity and skillfully unresolved dissonance to toss the implied accent around the measure. There are rifflike fragments, such as the pair of phrases in measures 7–10 (later reworked by Gillespie into

EX. 107.
"Dizzy Atmosphere" (1945), theme, mm. 1–4.

EX. 108.
"Dizzy Atmosphere" (1945), outchorus, mm. 1–16.

"Oop-Bop-Sh'Bam"), but nothing sticks around long enough to add up to a predictable pattern. The chorus combines the best of both improvisation and composition: the apparent spontaneity of its erratic rhythms and the obvious care with which the whole is conceived, rehearsed, and executed.

The catalyst for this new approach, presumably, is Charlie Parker. The opening gesture of the outchorus on "Dizzy Atmosphere" echoes one of his favorite licks (music example 109), while the off-center beginning of the outchorus to "Good Bait" is built around the sort of rhythmic displacement that was his trademark (music example 110). By early 1945

EX. 109.
Top line: "Dizzy Atmosphere" (1945), outchorus, mm. 1–3. Bottom line: "Ko Ko" (1945), Charlie Parker solo, chorus 2, mm. 1–3.

EX. 110.
Top line: "Good Bait" (1945), outchorus, mm. 1–2. Bottom line: "Ko Ko" (1945), Charlie Parker solo, chorus 2, mm. 33–34.

both Gillespie and Parker were in New York and at liberty to work out new musical ideas together, such as the lengthy, intricate passagework they devised for outchoruses. It is hardly surprising to find such material foregrounded in their May recording session for Guild, featuring the Three Deuces quintet (Gillespie, Parker, Al Haig, Curley Russell, and Sid Catlett substituting for drummer Stan Levey, who had just left to play with Woody Herman's orchestra). In the new version of "Salt Peanuts," a characteristically angular eight-bar unison passage is shoehorned in as an interlude between the two opening statements of the theme (music example 111). But in "Shaw 'Nuff" and "Hot House" (the latter by Tadd Dameron), the disjunct, asymmetrical passagework has *become* the theme. The package was now complete: virtuoso playing framed by origi-nal compositions, both startlingly new.

EX. 111.
"Salt Peanuts" (May 1945), interlude, mm. 1–8.

What did Gillespie hope to advertise with his early 1945 recordings? In the short term, the obvious answer is the Three Deuces quintet, which played the same tunes for paying audiences on 52nd Street. January was by no means too early to make records for an April nightclub debut. Even under the best of circumstances, several months normally elapsed between the time of recording and the release date. In wartime it often took much longer. Manor 5000 ("Be-Bop"/"Salted Peanuts"), from early January, did not surface until midsummer, and Guild 1001 ("Groovin' High"/"Blue 'n Boogie"), recorded in early February, was probably not released until some time in May.[25]

Ultimately, the vagaries of record production combined with the vagaries of Gillespie's career to keep new recordings from lining up neatly with current performing projects. By the time the first Manor and Guild sides were released, they were outdated. According to a knowledgeable reviewer for *Downbeat*, Don Byas on tenor saxophone is a poor substitute for Charlie Parker: his resonant tone fails to blend well with Gillespie's trumpet and "isn't right for that kind of fast stuff." The riffs on Guild 1001 "are not new, except to one who has never dug Dizzy's stuff before," while Manor 5000 "will undoubtedly give many listeners the wrong im-

25. Guild 1001 was advertised in *Billboard* in May (*Billboard* 57 [12 May 1945]: 21) and reviewed in *Downbeat* in June ("Diggin' the Discs," *Down Beat* 12 [15 June 1945]: 8). Guild 1003 ("Salt Peanuts"/"Hot House") was advertised in *Billboard* in September (*Billboard* 57 [8 September 1945]: 29). Guild 1002 ("Shaw 'Nuff"/"Lover Man") was not released until December, when it was reviewed in *Downbeat* ("Diggin' the Discs," *Down Beat* 12 [15 December 1945]: 8) and *Billboard* ("Record Reviews," *Billboard* 57 [22 December 1945]: 78). The remaining Guild sides—"Dizzy Atmosphere"/"All the Things You Are"—were released later by Musicraft.

pression as to what Dizzy and Charlie Parker and their crew had been putting down on 52nd Street."

Indeed, by midsummer Gillespie had left 52nd Street behind him. He was justifiably proud of the artistic achievement of the Three Deuces quintet (he later called it "the height of the perfection of our music"). He also had something to show for his efforts financially: as the group's leader, he earned $200 a week, substantially more than the $66 he had settled for the year before. But he was not content to stay indefinitely in the noisy, cramped confines of a nightclub, waiting for audiences to find him.

The nascent phenomenon of the jazz concert (see chapter 7) offered one attractive alternative. In early March, Gillespie had appeared in one of a series of jazz concerts organized by Bill Randle in Detroit on the same bill as drummer Cozy Cole and boogie-woogie pianist Meade Lux Lewis. In June he joined forces with Don Byas, Sid Catlett, and Slam Stewart for a jam session concert sponsored by Philadelphia's Nat Segal. Such concerts were potentially lucrative—*Billboard* speculated that the participants in the Detroit concert probably earned as much in a single night as they normally would all week. But the inherent risks and logistical difficulties of such undertakings were still daunting.

Just how difficult it was for Gillespie to find alternative venues for his music is evident from the two concerts he gave in Town Hall on May 17 and June 22. Located on 43rd Street, less than ten blocks from the Three Deuces, Town Hall offered prestige, good acoustics, and 1,500 comfortable seats available to paying customers at premium prices. By 1945 it had been in use as a venue for jazz for several years, with guitarist Eddie Condon, the gruff but genial host of a series of freewheeling jam sessions, the most regular tenant. Gillespie's sponsor in the enterprise was a group called the New Jazz Foundation, organized by promoter Monte Kay and disk jockey "Symphony Sid" Torin. Torin did his best to promote Gillespie's new releases on his Friday night show on WHOM and acted as master of ceremonies for the occasion.

The concerts were designed to showcase the Gillespie-Parker quintet. For the May concert, the quintet opened with a strong set featuring its most impressive routines: "Shaw 'Nuff," "A Night in Tunisia," "Groovin' High," "Be-Bop," "'Round Midnight," and "Salt Peanuts." To vary the program and to fill out time, other well-known jazz acts were announced. This strategy backfired badly. According to Torin, the other performers were offered a paltry $25 for their services, an amount that scarcely sufficed to secure a commitment from busy freelancers. Several acts scheduled to appear at the first concert (including Count Basie, Georgie Auld, and Teddy Wilson) failed to show up. As an emergency measure, the quintet dug further into its modest repertory of arrangements, playing "Blue 'n Boogie," "Dizzy Atmosphere," "Confirmation," and Parker's favorite pop song showpiece, "Cherokee," but a visibly embarrassed Gillespie spent much of his valuable stage time peering anxiously into the wings. The June concert didn't go much better. This time, the no-shows included Slam Stewart and Coleman Hawkins. The jazz trade press, while enthusiastic about the music ("the most original breath of fresh air that the jazz world has known since Benny Goodman started an entire generation jumping back in the mid-thirties"), harshly condemned the chaos onstage and the "stupid" emceeing of Symphony Sid. Dizzy Gillespie decided to shift gears once again.

Making It as Bandleader

The collaboration of Dizzy Gillespie and Charlie Parker looms so large in the history of bebop that it is surprising to realize how briefly they worked together on 52nd Street. It struck some of their contemporaries that way, too. "Dizzy's quitting the group shocked everybody in the music world, and upset a lot of musicians who loved to hear them play together," remembered Miles Davis. "Now, everybody realized that it was over and we weren't going to hear all that great shit they did together no more, unless we heard it on record."

Gillespie's sudden move, according to Davis, was motivated in large part by his exasperation at Parker's drug-induced irresponsibility ("Dizzy didn't believe in missing gigs"). Later in the year, when the group was temporarily reconstituted to play at Billy Berg's in California, Gillespie made sure to bring an extra soloist (his "prized pupil," Milt Jackson) to cover for Parker's inevitable absences. But in all likelihood it was a move that had been planned all along.[26] No matter how exhilarating the experience of working with a small group, Gillespie had no interest in relying on that format indefinitely.

The physical and psychic trials of working with the Billy Eckstine band had not been enough to extinguish Gillespie's aspirations to succeed in conventional terms—with his own dance orchestra. At the outset of his

---

26. Tenor saxophonist Charlie Rouse, who played in the Eckstine band in 1944 and left about the time Gillespie did, had the distinct impression that Gillespie had every intention at that time of forming his own dance band. Gillespie advised Rouse that when the band was ready, he would "send for" the saxophonist—which he in fact did about half a year later (Gitler 1985, 158–159).

career, his ascent was steep: from local territory bands to a job with a top-rank national band in just four years. Losing his job with Cab Calloway was a humiliating detour, but he kept up his professional stock by toiling for several years as a freelance soloist and arranger. As music director of the Eckstine band, he proved his ability to impose a musical personality on a fractious group of musicians under difficult circumstances. Now, with some recordings under his own name, he felt poised to take the ultimate step: leading his own large band.

In the long run, Gillespie's stubborn insistence proved justified. The Dizzy Gillespie orchestra, launched in 1946, thrived in the late 1940s even as well-established swing bands failed; by translating the modern idiom to the powerful sound of a full-size jazz orchestra, it firmly established Gillespie's presence in the marketplace at the high-water mark of bebop. But his first band, in 1945, was a disaster from the start, its misfortunes exceeding even those of the initial Eckstine tour, recalling Marx's maxim that history is experienced first as tragedy, then as farce.

Gillespie had his champions. Billy Shaw of the William Morris Agency (immortalized in the title of "Shaw 'Nuff") had worked with Gillespie in starting up the Eckstine band and was determined to find a way to make the trumpet player's obvious talents pay off commercially. His son, Milt, agreed to serve as Gillespie's road manager. In planning Gillespie's maiden tour as a bandleader, they decided not to offer the band as a single act but as part of a varied package of entertainment—an arrangement that had worked earlier for the combined forces of the Ink Spots, Cootie Williams's dance band, and Ella Fitzgerald. In addition to the Dizzy Gillespie orchestra, the stars of the "Hepsations of 1945" were the Nicholas Brothers, Fayard and Harold, fresh from their astonishing acrobatic dancing in the film *Stormy Weather*. Rounding out the show were June Eckstine (Billy's wife), the rotund comedians Patterson and Jackson, shake dancer Lovey Lane, and a chorus line.

Although preoccupied with the Three Deuces quintet, Gillespie began putting his band together. The arranger Walter "Gil" Fuller remembered walking into Minton's one night and hearing eight musicians rehearsing arrangements. According to Fuller, he interceded on Gillespie's behalf with Shaw and son, insisting that the fledgling band be given a budget for paid rehearsals and a suitable rehearsal space downtown.[27]

---

27. Whether Fuller's account should be taken literally is an open question. According to Budd Johnson, Fuller was a "sharp operator" notorious for claiming more credit than was his due (Gitler 1985, 134–135).

Fuller and Gillespie then sat down to work out a strategy for the band's repertory. With the Guild and Manor records just beginning to hit the jukeboxes, it made sense to concentrate on arrangements of tunes the Three Deuces combo had been playing. Some of these, like "Salt Peanuts" and "A Night in Tunisia," already existed as big-band arrangements, but it is likely that they were reworked, if not completely rethought.

For Gillespie faced new competition. By 1945 Woody Herman had stolen much of Dizzy's fire. Thanks to hit recordings like "Caldonia," the public was more likely to associate soaring double-time trumpet lines with the Herman band than with Gillespie, leaving the originator of the style in the uncomfortable position of apparent imitator. The solution was to fight fire with fire, to further exaggerate Gillespie's already sharply drawn musical profile. He and Fuller revisited "Be-Bop," recorded earlier in the year. "Why give them the royalties off of 'Bebop' when we don't control the publishing . . . and they don't pay you anyhow," argued Fuller. "Let's write something new, another melody on top of it." Later retitled "Things to Come," this number became a staple of the Gillespie band. The ultimate frantic up-tempo showpiece, it was played at such a blinding speed that it was barely under control.

Armed with such material, Gillespie hoped to draw audiences interested in "just sitting and listening to music." Not that he didn't consider his own music danceable. "I could dance to it," he later asserted. "I could dance my ass off to it. . . . Jazz should be danceable." But many swing bands at the time attracted listeners with dance music, prompting one trade press reporter to ask: "Are you a square if you dance at a dance?" When the Woody Herman band opened at the prestigious Hotel Pennsylvania in New York in the summer of 1945, the reporter noted, it was rare to see anyone "actually dancing; they were all out on the floor, standing in front of the band and just plain diggin'." Emboldened by this reaction, the Herman band soon planned a series of concerts, trying to "get away with as little commercial stuff as possible." Gillespie, Herman's inspiration and putative competitor, aimed for nothing less.

Of course, a young black band—especially one so untried that its own management felt the need to surround it with dancers and comedians—could not expect to gain access to such prestigious and lucrative gigs. Gillespie was resigned to the usual series of one-nighters through the South, rationalizing the hardship as the necessary next step: "To attract a mass audience to bebop," he later wrote, "we had to first establish a feeling for the music among the large black population of the South by touring the southern states." But he still hoped to do things his way, apparently bolstered by assurances from Billy Shaw that the engagements would be billed as concerts.

Whatever the intentions, the reality turned out very different. Only an active campaign of arm-twisting on Gillespie's behalf could have convinced black venues in the South to offer something other than the usual bluesy entertainment. Shaw may well have tried his best to book concerts and found the task impossible. In any event, according to Gillespie, Shaw farmed out most of the one-nighters to a white intermediary, who bypassed local promoters by hiring his own black representatives in each locality to handle logistics. Not surprisingly, these middlemen did not share Gillespie's missionary zeal. So, to his "chagrin and surprise," the only part of the show that audiences expected to enjoy while seated was the vaudeville part. Either before or after that show, they expected to dance, and they counted on the new bandleader with the funny nickname to provide hard-driving dance music. Each leg of the journey brought Gillespie face to face with "unreconstructed blues lovers down South who couldn't hear nothing else but the blues."

The results were predictable. Fayard Nicholas remembered a typical one-nighter from somewhere in the Deep South:

> Now, this opening night, they had the dance before the show, and everybody was there, all the people. The place was packed, and the band was onstage and the curtains were closed. So they opened the curtains, and then they saw the band. They were running up to the bandstand, saying "Yeah . . . !"
>
> There was a voice from backstage saying, "Now, ladies and gentlemen, Dizzy Gillespie and his Orchestra." So Dizzy strikes up with "Bebop." They were playing like mad. Everybody was listening. They were dumbfounded at first, and then they said, "Oh, man, you a drag!" and walked away. Ha! Ha!

"They wouldn't even listen to us," fumed Gillespie later. "After all these years, I still get mad just talking about it. . . . When we got back to New York, I broke up that big band almost immediately."

Nevertheless, the Hepsations of 1945 proved to be a valuable learning experience for Gillespie. When the tour began, Gillespie had no experience as a public figure. Urged by the Nicholas Brothers to step up to the microphone, he would "clam up" and make "stiff, awkward bows." Eventually, he developed a rapport with his audiences. "People always thought I was crazy, so I used that to my advantage." As he became more comfortable onstage, he drew upon his natural ebullience, his keen-edged wit, and his improviser's knack for timing to develop a stage persona that leavened the uncompromising difficulty of his music. He offered easily comprehended comedy (his favorite shtick: the announcement, "Now, I'd like to introduce the band," followed by the spectacle of saxophonists and trombonists standing up to shake hands with each other) and good-natured singing ("I sing about one new song every five years to accompany my music—tunes like 'Oop-Pop-A-Dop [sic],' 'Ooop-Bop-Sh'-Bam [sic],' 'I'm Beboppin' Too,' 'You Stole My Wife, You Horsethief,' 'Swing Low, Sweet Cadillac' ").

None of this fits either the insider-craftsman ideal of studied nonchalance or the modernist insistence on the autonomy of high art from the ephemera of popular culture. Gillespie may have disliked what he perceived as the obsequious tone of older forms of black entertainment, including Louis Armstrong's "grinning in the face of white racism," but in reaching beyond the circumscribed world of the jazz virtuoso to the broader sphere of commercial entertainment, he discovered his own accommodation with audience expectation—what he later called "my own way of 'Tomming.' " Drawing on his experiences in show business, he offered an updated, idiosyncratic version of Cab Calloway's urban hipster (it is not very far from "hi-de-ho" to "ooop-bop-sh'bam") or of Louis Armstrong, the original artist-as-entertainer. In short, Gillespie became a "personality," within the bounds allowable to African Americans at midcentury. This strategy put a public face on bebop and undoubtedly helped to neutralize the impression of racial antagonism that many audiences may have drawn from the sight of black instrumentalists determined not to entertain. Even as sympathetic an observer as Martin Williams, who heard Gillespie and Parker's quintet at Billy Berg's while on shore leave from the navy, remembered: "I'm a southern kid. I've still got all that latent stuff in me [about race] that I haven't dealt with. I'm living in this paradox. That [bebop] sounded arrogant, uppity. . . . [When I] saw Bird's combo, what struck me even more than the music was the *attitude* coming off the bandstand—self-confident, aggressive. It was something I'd never seen from black musicians before."

Gillespie's efforts to soften that impression naturally discomfited his allies in the jazz critical establishment, who increasingly couched their espousal of bebop in modernist terms and scorned even the appearance of compromise with "commercialism." Barry Ulanov, writing for *Metronome*, complained about the "senseless screams," the "endless quotations of trivia," and the "frantic clowning" of Gillespie's brand of modern jazz entertainment. Even Armstrong found Gillespie's antics too much during his 1947 debut in Carnegie Hall. "You're cutting the fool up there, boy," he admonished. "Showing your ass."

But Gillespie did not look back. He was rewarded, finally, by a degree of commercial acceptance. His next big band, launched out of Clark Monroe's Spotlite Club in 1946, survived yet another southern tour of the "watermelon circuit" and then, like Eckstine's band, received far more sympathetic attention when allowed to play in major urban areas. In 1948 the band made a concert tour of Europe, followed by a series of critically acclaimed concerts across the United States. Feeling "like a young, hip black Santa Claus," Gillespie treated himself to a pair of ostrich-leather shoes. He had good reason to celebrate. Through ingenuity, persistence, and sheer force of artistic personality, he had accomplished what he had set out to do when he joined the music business as a hungry newcomer in the mid-1930s. He had made it as a bandleader.

EPILOGUE

Unfinished Business

*Some guys said, "Here's bop." Wham! They
said, "Here's something we can make money
on!" Wham! "Here's a comedian." Wham!
"Here's a guy who talks funny talk."*
CHARLIE PARKER

*If you want to make a living at music, you've got
to sell it.* DIZZY GILLESPIE

The meanings of bebop are not easily exhausted, as Ralph Ellison discovered when he struggled to make sense of this "revolution in culture"
after the fact. In his elegiac essay on Minton's Playhouse, first published
in 1958, Ellison reflected on the process by which memory is transmuted
into history:

> [Of] those who came to Minton's . . . no one retained more than a fragment
> of its happening. Afterward the very effort to put the fragments together
> transformed them—so that in place of true memory they now summon to
> mind pieces of legend. They retell the stories as they have been told and
> written, glamorized, inflated, made neat and smooth, with all incomprehen-
> sible details vanished along with most of the wonder.

The task of the historian is always to impose order on chaos—to assemble
the shards of experience into coherent patterns. In some ways, this task
is made easier by the passage of time. Ellison had to account for the
mutable nature of living memory. ("With jazz," he wrote, "we are not
yet in the age of history, but linger in that of folklore.") The modern
historian can rely instead on the relative certainties of the historical rec-

437

ord. Yet the writing of history is never a straightforward lining up of facts, nor is it ever complete.

What kind of story does bebop make? Success or failure? Tragedy or triumph? As Ellison suggests, bebop is not one story, but many: the sum total of all the lives involved in its creation, whose meanings are infinitely variegated and often at odds. A thorough consideration of this legacy is well beyond the scope of this book. Still, it seems appropriate to consider, by way of conclusion, some of the ways in which the subsequent history of bebop played itself out. In the process, we can come to appreciate bebop as both success and failure—as an art that touches on both the best and the worst of what it means to be American.

Bop and the Postwar Market

Toward the end of his recent book *Swing Changes*, the historian David Stowe suggests that bebop was more "swing *redux*" than a radical departure in popular music. This is a provocative argument. Swing and bebop have habitually been construed as "polar opposites"—with bebop as a "small-group art music" created by African Americans as an alternative to the functional, white-dominated commercial music of swing. Stowe asks us to understand bop instead as *part* of swing: not (as some jazz historians would have it) as its inexorable musical outgrowth, but in social and economic terms as the "final surge" in the cultural forces that launched the Swing Era in 1935 and sustained it for more than a decade. This way of framing the problem has the virtue of reminding us that, whatever its subcultural origins, once bebop entered well-worn commercial channels it followed a familiar pattern of exploitation for a mass consumer audience. For this, there is no better illustration than Dizzy Gillespie's rapid ascent to celebrity in the late 1940s.

Like swing before it, Gillespie's bebop represented the successful mass marketing of musical (and cultural) practices that had previously circulated in a much narrower ambit. Even when transformed into mainstream entertainment, bebop was still a music with a strong subcultural resonance. The very term (like *swing*) came from black musicians' oral culture, as did many of the nonsensical or ironic song titles ("Oop-Pop-A-Da," "Groovin' High," "Salt Peanuts," "Ornithology"). The insider atmosphere was part of the new music's commercial appeal. Enthusiasm for the music often went hand in hand with a taste for its unorthodox sartorial style: Gillespie's widely-imitated beret, horn-rimmed glasses, and goatee added a bohemian flair to the usual drape suits of the day.

Bebop was not just for its devotees, however. Those who found the music and its trappings bewildering and threatening could still have their curiosity piqued by a publicity campaign, skillfully guided by Gillespie's manager, Billy Shaw, that relied on "promotional techniques devised in the late 1920s for Ellington by Irving Mills and institutionalized during swing's heyday." For all its musical novelty, Gillespie's band was a familiar sight: the latest in a long series of name bands to parlay some striking idiosyncrasy into instant recognizability.

Moreover, Gillespie's band continued to serve the musicians' community in the same way that the swing dance orchestras had always done: as advanced professional training for the up-and-coming. The system that had provided formative experiences for Gillespie, Parker, and McGhee in bands led by Cab Calloway, Earl Hines, Lionel Hampton, Jay McShann, and Andy Kirk continued to work for a new generation of African-American musicians. Such future jazz stars of the 1950s and beyond as Ray Brown, John Coltrane, Kenny Dorham, Paul Gonsalves, Jimmy Heath, Milt Jackson, Yusef Lateef, John Lewis, James Moody, and Sonny Stitt all played for Gillespie from 1948 to 1949. For many, it was their first real exposure to top-flight musical standards. "It was a band," remembered baritone saxophonist Cecil Payne, "that, if you made a mistake reading your music, you felt bad. Immediately." For all, it was an important step up the professional ladder, a valuable credential for their careers.

But even as Gillespie's breakthrough demonstrated the durability of swing as an institution, his rapid fall from commercial favor by 1950 signaled its ultimate demise. Unlike Benny Goodman in 1935, Gillespie did not pull along new bands in his wake; there was no new, lucrative phase in the dance band business. All too quickly, Gillespie found himself up against "the old bebop dilemma" that the brief but heady success of his big band had only postponed: "whether jazz is primarily a music for dancing or listening." Postwar audiences looking for music that "made it easy to dance close and screw" provided a poor base for his synthesis of progressive instrumental music and entertainment.

Like Coleman Hawkins a decade earlier, Gillespie had little to show for his fling as a bandleader. By 1950, with "no band, no recording contract, and no definite plans for the future," he resigned himself to the life of the freelance jazz instrumentalist. Apart from the anomalous revival of his big band in the mid-1950s (underwritten by the State Department for overseas tours in the service of cold war propaganda), this was the niche he occupied for the remainder of his long career.

The failure of Gillespie's bid for commercial success had many under-lying causes, not least of which was the prevailing racial climate. Even sympathetic coverage in the trade press tended to look beyond Gillespie to a "progressive" jazz that, in Bernard Gendron's words, would be "more cerebral, more influenced by European avant-garde music, and, in con-trast to bebop, less embroiled in showmanship, unusual argot and dress, and suspect life-styles. . . . Faced with a bebop movement dominated by African-American musicians, the virtually all-white jazz journals seemed always to be in search of 'great white hopes'—white modernists, like [Lennie] Tristano and [Stan] Kenton, with whom a mostly white read-ership would feel more at home."

In the mainstream press, the general public was given a less nuanced and informed view. Bebop, for many, was at best arrant foolishness, a farrago of nonsense syllables and noisy, incomprehensible music. At worst it was a musical practice that hinted darkly of an underground of drug users, antisocial deviants, and racial militants. Both impressions, needless to say, were informed by racially grounded stereotypes. The infamous photo spread on the bebop movement in *Life* mostly empha-sized silliness, but in showing Gillespie and Benny Carter giving each other an elaborate (and wholly fictitious) secret handshake, Gillespie's Afro-Cuban drummer Chano Pozo "shouting incoherently" in a "bebop transport," and (a still-Christian) Gillespie bowing toward Mecca, it sug-gested something peculiar going on in contemporary Negro popular cul-ture that might at any moment jump the traces of propriety. Gillespie later regretted the publicity stunt, especially the ersatz Islam ("They tricked me into committing a sacrilege"), realizing too late that any ex-pression of high-spirited frivolity by an African American at midcentury would be instantly and willfully misread.

But race was hardly the sole obstacle to the successful pursuit of a bebop career; it merely lengthened the odds in an already parlous eco-nomic climate. In the postwar era, the economy as a whole and the music business in particular faced a painful period of contraction and readjust-ment. Wages had been driven to artificially high levels during the war by inflation and the scarcity of experienced musicians. At the war's end, many large dance bands were simply unable to draw large enough crowds to meet their payrolls. The ensuing crisis made the entire system of large touring orchestras suddenly vulnerable. By late 1946 a number of promi-nent bandleaders, including Tommy Dorsey and Woody Herman, re-sponded to these pressures by downsizing their orchestras, reducing personnel and lowering salary scales. In retrospect, it was the beginning of the end of the Swing Era.

Against this backdrop, the modest successes of a few low-budget enterprises in the postwar years were especially striking. The very factors that had pushed larger bands to the brink worked in the favor of musicians who had already learned to make do with less. The Nat "King" Cole Trio, Louis Jordan and his Tympany Five, and Illinois Jacquet's sextet surprised industry observers by earning "big band coin" with a fraction of the payroll costs. Jazz at the Philharmonic was another success story for similar reasons. The overhead for presenting jam-session-style jazz in concert form was low, and the amount that could be charged at the door of a prestigious auditorium high, allowing Granz to lure a host of well-known jazz artists, including Coleman Hawkins, Roy Eldridge, Lester Young, Ella Fitzgerald, and Charlie Parker, onto a single stage. Granz and Eddie Condon were soon joined by a host of imitators, raising the jazz concert from an occasional curiosity to a legitimate, if highly specialized, part of the music business. As *Variety* reported in late 1946: "The highest paid sidemen in the music business today are working in these travelling jazz concert units and a number of bandleaders have actually folded their orchestras in order to get on this gravy train. Few swing bands pay sidemen as much as $250 a week for one-nighters, yet in [Eddie] Condon's fourteen-man group the lowest paid man received this salary, with some receiving as much as $500 weekly."

Once bebop began to register (for good or ill) in the public consciousness, it was logical for the music industry to imagine it as a potential antidote for its distress. As a result, as Gendron has noted, bebop became "burdened with the obligation to save jazz from its economic miseries." Two avenues suggested themselves. The first, exemplified by Gillespie's big band, lay in exploiting the undeniable novelty of bop to jump-start the slumping dance orchestra field. In this effort, Gillespie's race was a distinct liability, especially when faced with competition by Stan Kenton, Woody Herman, and other white progressives. By 1949 even Benny Goodman, while admitting that "I still don't know what bop is," had donned a beret and surrounded himself with twenty-somethings in a conscious attempt to make bebop seem "respectable and amusing, while keeping its musical flavor and controversial approach." The attempt was doomed to failure. Such tactics helped to put bebop briefly in vogue, but virtually guaranteed its obsolescence.

The second route was more practical, if less glamorous: promoting bop

in its original, jam-session-style format as a kind of specialized entertainment for the jazz aficionado, a market already tolerant of the racial
mixing prevalent in the bop scene. At first bebop promised a dramatic
revitalizing of the jazz nightclub scene. Sensing the potential of the new
style to revitalize business, *Down Beat* threw in its support, doubling the
number of articles devoted to bebop. There were signs of a recovery. In
New York, 52nd Street had entered an irreversible decline by the late
1940s, its famous clubs either shuttered or converted to burlesque houses
and Chinese restaurants; but new venues devoted to bebop sprang up a
few blocks away on Broadway: the Royal Roost (a chicken restaurant that
turned to modern jazz in 1948), Bop City, and the Clique. When the last-
named of these failed in 1949, it reopened in mid-December as Birdland.
Opening night featured the club's namesake, Charlie "Bird" Parker, finally taking his place as one of the leading figures of the movement. Even
in this sphere, however, the success of bebop was short-lived. Of the New
York clubs just mentioned, only Birdland thrived, or even lasted more
than a few years.

   As a freelance, Dizzy Gillespie adjusted to the new environment as best
he could. The work was often not very remunerative—"I just couldn't
seem to make very much money in those days," he said of his early 1950s
sextet—but there were at least a few alternatives. He began selling his
services: first to his putative rival, Stan Kenton, and then to Jazz at the
Philharmonic. The latter, he admitted, "wasn't much musically because
Norman Granz got his nuts off by sending two or three trumpet players
out there to battle one another's brains out on the stage. And he'd just
sit back and laugh." But Granz's commitment to racial equality was gratifying, and the high wages Gillespie earned helped subsidize more interesting musical pursuits. "I'd break up the little band . . . go out with JATP
and make some money, then come back and organize another small
band."

   Meanwhile, other contexts for his life's work had begun to emerge:

Not long after Charlie Parker died [in 1955], our efforts to establish a proper
place in U.S. society and in the world for our music began to bear fruit. We
started receiving more recognition from American musicians and musicol-
ogists who'd been interested before almost exclusively in symphonic music.
They could see now, after jazz and classical musicians in Europe welcomed
modern jazz with such enthusiasm, how vital as a creative force it was and
how essential to the development of modern music of all kinds. . . .

   I've struggled to establish jazz as a concert music, a form of art, not just

music you hear in clubs or places where they serve whiskey. I did a lot of
playing along those lines in the late 1950s and early 1960s.

Before Gillespie had turned forty, jazz had loosened its ties to mass entertainment and cast its lot with art.

Bebop in Jazz History

Contemplating the vagaries of the history of science, Thomas Kuhn
warned that "the temptation to write history backwards is both omnipresent and perennial." One might reply that there is no other way to
go about it. History is not the passive imprint of the past but an active
search for meaning, a creative reading of the past to suit the needs of the
present.

With jazz, the writing of history has largely been driven by the efforts
of a shifting (and often uneasy) coalition of musicians and critics to make
jazz a "concert music" or "a form of art," to push it to the far side of the
"Great Divide" separating art in the modernist mold from "an increasingly consuming and engulfing mass culture." Not surprisingly, this project has left its mark on the interpretation of bebop, which emerges in
historical accounts less as a short-lived form of mass entertainment than
as the apotheosis of jazz as art.

With bebop, we are repeatedly told, jazz took an irrevocable step. No
longer would its complex and demanding virtuosity be offered, under
false colors, to the public as a creature of the marketplace—a dance music,
a subspecies of vaudeville, a medium for purveying popular song, yet
another popular expression adrift on the tides of fashion. The artistic
achievement of bebop announced that jazz had finally transcended its
sometimes squalid social and economic origins to take its place in American culture as a creative expression of unassailable integrity. In its wake,
all of jazz must be properly understood as an autonomous art, governed
by its own laws and judgeable only by its own criteria. And that meant,
as Martin Williams argued in his influential book, *The Jazz Tradition*, "a
change in even the function of the music": "The music of Charlie Parker
and Dizzy Gillespie represented a way for jazz to continue. . . . From now
on it was somehow a music to be listened to, as many of its partisans had
said it should have been all along. We will make it that, Parker seemed
to say, or it will perish."

The ambiguous aftermath of bebop did much to undermine such wishful thinking. Jazz did not perish, but neither did it thrive. Over the longer

term, jazz (the label *bop* was hurriedly jettisoned in the early 1950s) settled into an uncomfortable purgatory, accepted neither as popular music (especially as rock 'n' roll gathered irresistible momentum) nor as officially sanctioned art. Having abandoned the dance hall (or ceding it to newer idioms), jazz performance was pushed to the periphery of the music industry. Jazz nightclubs, springing up like mushrooms in major cities (and vanishing just as rapidly), functioned as seedy surrogates for the concert hall, lacking the social prestige and economic subsidy that automatically accrues to the European art tradition. Even as optimistic a champion of the idiom as Martin Williams came reluctantly to the conclusion that "the failure to establish a new function and milieu for jazz was, more than anything else, the personal tragedy of the members of the bebop generation."

Much has changed in recent years, however. The position jazz occupies in American culture at the end of the twentieth century continues to be tenuous and fraught with contradiction, but there is little doubt that in recent years it has made substantive steps toward becoming "America's classical music." Jazz is now a staple of college curricula, both in liberal arts universities and conservatories. Its listening audience is roughly the size of that for European "classical" music, and equally weighted toward the upper end of the scale of education and income. It is finding a place in what is familiarly known as "music appreciation"—a category that encompasses educational outreach both within the classroom and beyond it: public broadcasting, government-subsidized concerts, museum exhibits, and the like. The narrative sweep of jazz history, so self-consciously modeled on that of European music in its succession of stylistic "periods" and pantheon of master musicians, and yet so thoroughly grounded in modern black modalities, grants prestige while relocating its source from the aristocratic Europe of the past to democratic twentieth-century America. It may well be, as the film scholar Krin Gabbard has suggested, that jazz is in the same position as another vernacular art form, film, was a generation ago: on the verge of becoming absorbed into official academic culture.

Perhaps, then, the time has come to reconsider the legacy of bebop. Perhaps the story of Charlie Parker and Dizzy Gillespie is best told, in the historian Hayden White's terms, in the metanarrative of Romance: the unqualified triumph of "good over evil, of virtue over vice, of light over darkness." And indeed, this avenue of interpretation has a great deal to recommend it. There is real justice in the belated embrace of bebop by the establishment, in the acceptance of apparent outcasts (or "outcats," in Francis Davis's clever neologism) as important American musicians. Parker did not live to see the end of the story; but others, like Gillespie, Max Roach, and Billy Taylor, came to comfortably inhabit new roles as educators and elder statesmen. The progress of jazz from the margins to the center serves as a powerful and resonant symbol for racial progress, as when Gillespie returned to Cheraw, South Carolina, in 1959 to play for the first integrated audience in his hometown's history[1] or accompanied a Southern peanut-farmer-turned-president singing "Salt Peanuts" at the White House in 1978. Such optimism, in short supply in late twentieth-century America, is not lightly set aside.

Yet some caution is required. A certain pessimism, grounded in a recognition of the perdurability of racism and the necessity to struggle against adversity, is as ineluctably part of bebop as it is deeply embedded in the fabric of African-American history. It is hard to imagine the Parker or Gillespie of 1945 expecting a glorious outcome to their life's work—not because they lacked faith in the worth of their music, but because they had little reason to believe that social respect and economic reward would be forthcoming in their lifetimes. In the 1940s every attempt to advance, to rectify the injustices of the past, met with entrenched resistance—if not directly through the legalized machinery of segregation, then through the subtler but no less effective cultural mechanisms that systematically undermined and undervalued African-American dignity and effort. Bebop remains a product of its time, an improvised and audacious attempt to make the most of a bad situation. Some of its spirit is suggested by a contemporary stage routine by Jackie "Moms" Mabley, a comedian similarly conditioned by long experience in show business to recognize the absurdities of a "success" constrained by racism:

> I was ridin' along in my Cadillac, you know, goin' through one of them little towns in South Carolina. Pass through a red light. One of them big cops come runnin' over to me, say, "Hey woman, don't you know you went

1. On another occasion, Gillespie remembered a "Dizzy Gillespie day" in Cheraw, for which he was honored by a cocktail party hosted by the mayor. When, however, he tried to get his hair cut, he found the "colored" barbershops full and was refused service by a white barber. "Later, I got a letter from Cheraw asking me if I would mind if they put up a sign on the outskirts saying Dizzy Gillespie was born there. I said I would mind—it would embarrass me if someone I knew came through and wanted a haircut and couldn't get it. But later I relented" (Whitney Balliett, "Profiles: Dizzy," *New Yorker*, 17 September 1990, 54).

through a red light." I say, "Yeah, I know I went through a red light." "Well, what did you do that for?" I said, "'Cause I seen all you white folks goin' on the green light. . . . I thought the red light was for us!"

The musical triumphs of bebop are unquestioned. As preserved on recordings or reinterpreted by contemporary musicians, bebop is a thing of beauty, a victory of wit and pluck over circumstance, and a continual inspiration to excellence. But an appreciation for its intricacy and ingenuity, as well as for its perennial relevance to the modern craft of jazz, should not blind us to the frustration embedded in its core.

The most obvious outward manifestation of that frustration was drug addiction. Long before heroin flooded urban black neighborhoods to plague the lives of average working-class African Americans, musicians sought in narcotics an avenue of escape. Charlie Parker's example was undoubtedly decisive. It is a commonplace that younger musicians mistook his voracious appetite for stimulation (Hampton Hawes once watched Parker drink "eleven shots of whiskey, pop a handful of bennies, then tie up, smoking a joint at the same time") for the wellsprings of his creativity. Parker was widely imitated, to his evident distress, and the tide of addiction continued to rise, unchecked by the harrowing spectacle of victims like trumpeter Fats Navarro, withering away to "skin and bones" before his death in 1950. Howard McGhee, among others, began his slide into addiction that same year. He was not to emerge until the end of the 1950s, and he never came close to regaining his prior professional and commercial stature.

For Miles Davis, heroin use was explicitly tied to a deepening sense of alienation. In the spring of 1949 he made his first trip overseas for a week-long festival in Paris. There, like so many other African-American musicians before him, he experienced the adulation of European fans and an unexpected and overwhelming sense of "freedom" in being treated offstage "like a human being." On his return to New York, his newfound sense of confidence immediately began to crumble. As he struggled to find work, he developed a keen awareness of the persistence of racism: "I started noticing things that I hadn't noticed before, political stuff—what was really happening to black people." Before long, he fell into a depression and joined others of his generation—Dexter Gordon, Art Blakey, Sonny Rollins, Jackie McLean—who had turned to heroin. "To realize that you don't have any power to make things different is a bitch," he said later. "I lost my sense of discipline, lost my sense of control over my life, and started to drift." No passing fad, heroin became virtually the "endemic curse of the jazz profession," a symptom of an underlying despair that took its toll on both body and soul.

This aspect of the bebop story should not be forgotten; but neither should it be brooded over. Heroin killed Charlie Parker, but Miles Davis summoned the strength to kick the habit on his father's farm in Illinois. Gillespie was never touched by it. He and many others persevered, continuing to find new ways to ply their trade as virtuoso instrumentalists as the Swing Era, and the promise it once embodied, faded into distant memory.

In the process, jazz became something altogether different. To consider the subsequent and ongoing transformation of the profession by new venues (e.g., jazz festivals), technologies (long-playing records), artistic and political developments (the jazz avant-garde and the rise of black nationalism) would require another book. But some sense of the issues involved may be gleaned by returning, in conclusion, to the career of Coleman Hawkins.

Coda: The Last Days of Coleman Hawkins

Coleman Hawkins had little need for bop. As one of the best-known freelance jazz musicians of the late 1940s, his career was going quite well. Although he occasionally burnished his reputation as a progressive by seeking out the up-and-coming generation of musicians (Fats Navarro, J. J. Johnson, Max Roach, Miles Davis, Milt Jackson, Hank Jones) for recording sessions, he spent most of his time with Granz's Jazz at the Philharmonic, crisscrossing the country at the head of an all-star cast that at various times also included Charlie Parker and Howard McGhee. On his own, he made several triumphal return tours of Europe. On one such trip, he responded disdainfully to a reporter's questions: "Bop? Man, I ain't never heard of bop! What is this bop? . . . I don't know any bop music. I only know one music—the music that's played. There's no such thing as bop music, but there is such a thing as progress. What you are talking about is probably a commercial phrase, huh? A phrase that has been used to make something sell. . . . It's just music, and we go along with it."

The rapid decline of bebop, however, signaled a corresponding narrowing of Hawkins's options. He continued to work regularly in the United States and Canada, often as a soloist with a pickup rhythm section, but found engagements harder to come by and less personally rewarding. In

1954, as he turned fifty, he complained that while the musical language of jazz continued to show progress, public comprehension had failed to keep pace: "The state of the music business now is just as bad as, or even worse, than it's ever been. The musicians today are fine, the music today is great, but I don't think we have a listening public. . . . All through the war people were very attentive, but when the war ended the trend started changing." To Leonard Feather he was blunter, and uncharacteristically bitter about his chosen profession: "I wouldn't ever want any child of mine to get into anything as rotten as this business. I hate the music business."

By mid-decade, things began to turn around. The emergence of outdoor festivals, such as the Newport Jazz Festival, added lucrative and well-publicized work in the summer months for talent of Hawkins's stature (although he had to put up with Roy Eldridge's needling: "Bet you never thought you'd be back playing carnivals again, did you, Bean?"). Hawkins found a substitute for 52nd Street in the Metropole, a noisy midtown Manhattan bar that employed several small combos for a full day's schedule of jazz. It was a peculiar venue, with the stage so narrow that the band had to play ranged in a line. But the work was steady, and Hawkins had plenty of intermission time to relax at a nearby neighborhood tavern.

In his last decade Hawkins settled on a style of life that suited his advancing years and his sense of what he had accomplished over the course of a distinguished career. He spent more time closer to home in New York, venturing out for concerts and tours only when the money tempted him ("I'd play in Timbuktu if they paid me"). And the money was usually good. "I never played for $5 a night in my life," he bragged in 1962. "I was always a rich musician." He was a shrewd enough businessman to hold out for top dollar—much to the frustration of his erstwhile co-bandleader, Roy Eldridge, who complained: "That man's done me out of a lot of work. If Hawk don't like the bread, he won't take the gig. And he don't know no word but *thousand dollars*!" When Hawkins died in 1969, he was not only respected and mourned but, in the assessment of his biographer, "a wealthy man." For vocalist Thelma Carpenter, the image of wealth conveys not just Hawkins's material affluence, but his very sense of who he was and what he deserved: "He was very sensitive, a very proud man, and he'd been treated like royalty in Europe. . . . And it's almost like—if you're terribly rich, you think everybody's rich. 'Cause I know that when I went to the East Side, and met all of these fantastically rich people, they assumed that if you were with them, you were rich, too. So with Hawk—not so much monetarily, but he was a millionaire. He was the rich man."

There the story might end, on a satisfyingly affirmative note. But there is a sad epilogue. In the mid-1960s Hawkins began systematically drinking himself to death. It took several years for his strong constitution and hearty appetite to be worn down by a steady diet of brandy and little else, but in the end he was so frail and unkempt that friends who had not seen him for years scarcely recognized him.

Just why anyone, let alone a proud artist like Hawkins, would embark on a path of self-destruction is a mystery about which it seems presumptuous to speculate. But his fall is eerily reminiscent of what biologists have called intropunitive behavior: a "self-destruct process" triggered when an individual is excluded socially from a group. One has the sense that Hawkins no longer felt at home in the professional world he had helped to create. To return to Thelma Carpenter's thoughts: "I imagine it's like the fall of 1929, and you have all this money, or whatever, your possessions, and for him it was his music. And all of a sudden you have a crash. It was all good until it got up into the '60s. . . . He lost his pride."

Toward the end, Hawkins began complaining about the jazz avant-garde: "I don't hear anything in what they're playing, just noise and crap." The issue cut deeper than aesthetics. Hawkins, after all, was a staunch modernist who claimed to have been listening to Stravinsky since he was a kid and who always prided himself on being ahead of the curve. But the avant-garde movement of the 1960s brought with it an assault on the very assumptions of professionalism and craft, of "precise playing," that had been the foundation of his career for four decades. The bebop revolution made sense to him, but not what journalists called the "New Thing." "They're playing 'Freedom' and they're playing 'Extensions,' whatever these things are," he said in 1964. "Man, I don't know what they are. These guys are looking for a gimmick, a short cut. There is no short cut."

One cannot help but wish for a more satisfactory conclusion to this story. Hawkins and jazz began the century together. If only Hawkins had not succumbed to his demons and had carried his career further toward the century's end (and it is worth noting that his mother lived to be ninety-six), he might well have found a new place in an art world that has continued to change. Perhaps he would have slipped into the role of pedagogue: in 1967 he mused, "Some kind of way I've got to start teaching, got to teach these boys how to play."

Yet many individual lives in jazz—in American culture—are unsatisfying and incomplete, even tragic. For every Dizzy Gillespie, basking in later years in the autumnal glow of a life well led, there is a Charlie Parker, leaving behind a tangle of unfulfilled ambition. Coleman Hawkins's story reminds us that jazz itself is unfinished business, undergoing the painful process of outliving its own time and watching its social and aesthetic meanings drift into new, unfamiliar formations as the original context for its creation disappears. As Gary Taylor has recently argued, cultural memory begins with death: the death of the creator. The search for meaning is left to the survivors. It is up to us to decide how to tell the story, how best to represent the struggle and achievement of artists whose lives belong to the past but whose music continues to live in the present. In the process, we will decide what "jazz" will mean in the century ahead.

Notes

Note: The abbreviation *JOHP* refers to the National Endowment for the Arts / Smithsonian Institution Jazz Oral History Project, currently owned and housed by the Institute of Jazz Studies, Rutgers University, Newark.

Introduction: Stylistic Evolution or Social Revolution?

"A most inadequate word": Ellison 1966, 202.

"A momentous modulation": ibid., 200.

As the musicologist Carl Dahlhaus: Dahlhaus 1983, 56.

"that great revolution": Gendron 1994, 159.

"across the time and space": Russell 1959, 195–196.

as Hugues Panassié continued to do: Panassié 1942, 73–74.

"maintains its identity": Dahlhaus 1983, 44.

no single workable definition of jazz: Gridley, Maxham, and Hoff 1989.

"We were the first generation": Hawes and Asher 1979, 8.

"Modern jazz did not burst": Gridley 1988, 143.

Bebop "spurted beyond": Ulanov 1952, 273.

"Although the beginnings of bop": Stearns 1958, 155.

"Any contemporary style": Russell 1959, 188.

as Bernard Gendron has recently noted: Gendron 1995.

"The critics and jazz amateurs": Russell 1959, 188.

"Jazz is a classical music": Tirro 1996, 23.

"All pieces of music": Crawford 1993, 43.

"Any time you hear": Chernoff 1979, 61.

"If an old man": ibid., 65.

"We must abandon": Nettl 1974, 19.

"records not only disseminated": Eisenberg 1987, 144.

"Commercialism [is]": Blesh 1946, 11–12.

"The very omnipresence": Hobsbawm 1993, 303.

Jazz "was . . . so deeply embedded": ibid., 302–303.

"The story of bop": Feather 1949, 45.

"The war against": Russell 1959, 202.

"What [Charlie] Parker and bebop": Williams 1993, 136.

"threadbare" and "aging": Russell 1959, 188.

"harmonic and melodic blind alley": Feather 1960, 30.

"death by entropy": Hsio 1959, 187.

"billion-dollar rut": Feather 1949, 4.

"crisis theory" of twentieth-century European music: Treitler 1989, 124.

"new branch of jazz": Feather 1960, 30.

"Bebop musicians were trying to raise": Tirro 1993, 290.

"commercial and contractual relations": Ross 1989, 70.

"A note don't care who plays it": in Wilmer 1970, 103.

"Black musicians dominated bop": Collier 1993, 209–210.

"As soon as the rigid segregation": Feather 1960, 23.

"jazz, originally the music": Feather 1959, 53.

"[jazz] stemmed from a specific social environment": Feather 1960, 23.

"the Great Music Robbery": Baraka and Baraka 1987, 328–332.

"no warm welcome of blacks": ibid., 331.

"no study of jazz can be complete": Feather 1959, 39.

"'You must not know where Bop comes from'": Hughes 1961, 118–119.

"They were Guilds, Manors, Savoys"; "Be Bop. A new language": Baraka 1984, 57–58.

"single upward stroke to socialism": Baraka and Baraka 1987, 331.

Although its continuous and rigorous attack: Bürger 1984, chapter 3.

Exhibiting a urinal: ibid., 51–52.

"The substantial distance": Gabbard 1991, 96.

"life tone and cultural matrix": Baraka and Baraka 1987, 319.

"Without blues": Baraka and Baraka 1987, 264.

"a discourse about color": Ross 1989, 69–70.

a *"willfully harsh, anti-assimilationist" music:* L. Jones [Baraka] 1963, 181.

"nothing succeeds like rebellion": Ellison 1966, 246.

"Today the white audience expects": ibid., 222.

"a fresh form of entertainment": ibid., 245.

"why go to a white recording studio": Allen Tinney, in Patrick 1983, 169.

"Between the thirties and the end of World War II": L. Jones [Baraka] 1963, 179.

"the bridge into the mainstream": ibid., 179.

"the sense of resentment": ibid., 178.

"forgotten years of the Negro revolution": Dalfiume 1971.

"Bebop was intimately if indirectly related": Lott 1995, 246.

"raised themselves by their talents": Hobsbawm 1993, 56.

"the least political of men": Ellison 1966, 245.

"about politics and race": in Gitler 1985, 225.

"We liked Marcantonio's ideas": Gillespie 1979, 287.

"A symbol to the Negro people?": in Reisner 1977, 51.

"People made bebop": L. Jones [Baraka] 1968, 16.

Charlie Parker being "called upon": Williams 1993, 136; emphasis added.

"overlaps 'style' ": Treitler 1989, 35.

Chapter 1: Progress and the Bean

"In spite of all that is written": Johnson 1912, 148.

"There's no such thing as bop music": in Mike Nevard, " 'Man, I Ain't Never Heard of Bop!' Said Coleman Hawkins," *Melody Maker* 25 (17 December 1949): 3.

"Man, it was a great day for me": in Doug Ramsey, liner notes for Cannonball Adderley, *What I Mean*, Milestone M-47053 (LP). Adderley was

born in September 1928, so this incident must have occurred before his sixth birthday.

"Man, I told him Hawkins was supposed to make him nervous": in Hentoff 1975, 47.

"Coleman Hawkins was the saxophonist": in Shapiro and Hentoff 1955, 336.

"Hawk was most highly respected": in ibid., 362.

"logical rhythmic change": Williams 1993, 6.

"the most gifted and original improviser": ibid., 122.

"Hawk was the master": in Russell 1959, 212.

"Get up, pussycat"; "Yes, Hawkins was king": Shapiro and Hentoff 1955, 292–293; M. Jones 1987, 192.

"primal torch-passing scenes": Rasula 1995, 141.

"Hawkins had the great taste": in Berger, Berger, and Patrick 1982, 195.

"most creative man of the era": Hinton in Shapiro and Hentoff 1955, 362.

one of its most prominent "role models": Chip Stern, "Sonny Rollins: The Rose and the Cross," *Musician* 115 (May 1988): 90.

The museum-like quality of the "classical" European repertory: Burkholder 1983.

the nickname "Greasy": Chilton 1990, 15.

"naively believed their music better": Hodeir 1956, 27.

"It's like a man thinking back": in Leonard Feather, "The Blindfold Test," *Metronome* 62 (November 1946): 30.

"That's amazing to me": ibid.

the animating purpose of Kuhn's study: Kuhn 1970, 208.

"normal science": ibid., 10–42.

"the first great soloist": Schuller 1968, 89–133.

"jazz musicians spent": Williams 1987, 19.

"reconstitution of the field": Kuhn 1970, 85.

"I do not think": Williams 1993, 139.

"stands for the entire constellation": Kuhn 1970, 175.

"disciplinary matrix": ibid., 182.

"the network of people": Becker 1978, x.

America . . . was a bleak landscape: Meier 1971, 161–162.

black Americans had historically turned away: ibid., 24.

the sixty-dollar organ: Southern 1983, 308–309.

the rosewood piano: Meier 1971, 104.

Full-time professional musicians: Leiter 1953, 11.

Scott Joplin's lessons: Berlin 1994, 7.

cello lessons: Chilton 1990, 4.

"family band": Lester Young: Schaap, 1991, 6–8; Marshal Royal: Marshal Royal, JOHP.

a craze for dance music: Erenberg 1981, 146–175.

James Reese Europe's Clef Club: Badger 1995, 52–77, 83–85; Charters and Kunstadt 1962, 24–26; Southern 1983, 287–289.

"aristocracy" of the black musical world; "bigwigs who played Miami Beach"; "rank and file": Stewart 1991, 90.

"every hamlet had its dance hall": ibid., 91.

"fancy wall decorations": Bernhardt 1986, 149–150.

"In New York you had a whole bunch of dance halls": Foster 1971, 138.

"As a comedian, Morton is grotesque": Gushee 1985, 402.

vaudeville acts "were very important": Stewart 1991, 90.

"introduction to the big time": ibid., 37.

[Hawkins] slap-tongued his saxophone: Bernhardt 1986, 33.

"At that time, I didn't really think of myself as a jazz musician": Basie 1985, 56.

Holiday . . . required to put on blackface: Holiday 1975, 59–60; Basie 1985, 205–206.

"That's why so many kids in New Orleans took up music": in Shapiro and Hentoff 1955, 26.

"He was born about 1900": Hsio 1959, 174.

"both musical and in the larger sense, social": ibid., 177.

"surely one of the most disparaged social groups": Ross 1989, 76.

social standing had traditionally been defined: Frazier 1949, 273–305.

cultural orientation of the black elite: Myrdal 1962, 690–693.

"Waltzes was popular then in Harlem": Bernhardt 1986, 120.

They wielded their fierce pride . . . as a weapon: Peretti 1992, 58–64.

"The worst Jim Crow around New Orleans": Foster 1971, 65.

As numerous biographers have pointed out: Collier 1987, 7; Tucker 1991, 4–15; Hasse 1993, 29–33.

"center of Negro 'society' ": Frazier 1957, 197.

"I don't know how many castes of Negroes there were": Ellington 1973, 17.

"an opportunity for artistic exploration": Hennessey 1994, 495.

for . . . J. C. Higginbotham: J. C. Higginbotham, JOHP.

Fletcher Henderson's decision: Schuller 1968, 246, 252–253; Charters and Kunstadt 1962, 165–166.

"the music took over": Jimmy Jones, JOHP.

"It is not uncommon for a Negro . . . to rise": Myrdal 1962, 694.

he struggled with several unskilled . . . jobs: Bernhardt 1986, 27–32, 36–44.

"You are making a start now": ibid., 48.

"big colored people": ibid., 42.

"during the time some black doctors": ibid., 87.

"a way to 'make it' ": Hennessey 1994, 10.

"The artist sprung from the unskilled poor": Hobsbawm 1993, 170.

black jazz musicians gradually receded in importance: ibid., 174–176.

"know how to talk to people": Barker 1986, 176.

"make-believe" . . . of the black bourgeoisie: Frazier 1957, 153.

"anyone who could claim 'professional' status": Malcolm X 1964, 41.

"I wouldn't have dared to bother the man": ibid., 49–50.

"the Negro class system": Myrdal 1962, 694.

"If you don't come from Fisk": Carner 1989, 119.

"The jazz business deals in the distribution": Hobsbawm 1993, 158.

Efforts to extend the benefits of education: Southern 1983, 283.

Sissieretta Jones: ibid., 242–243.

"Blind Tom" Bethune: ibid., 246–247.

Joseph Douglass: ibid., 278–279.

Will Marion Cook: ibid., 268–269, 297–299; Badger 1995, 24.

W. C. Handy: Southern 1983, 336–338.

James Reese Europe: Badger 1995.

Major N. Clark Smith: Southern 1983, 284–285; Hinton and Berger 1988, 22–24.

Lionel Hampton . . . remembered him: Hampton and Haskins 1989, 20–21.

Dr. Mildred Bryant Jones: Hinton and Berger 1988, 22.

workhorses of the light classic repertory: Gene Ramey, JOHP; Pearson 1987, 18, 44; Shapiro and Hentoff 1955, 190; Ellison 1966, 191.

"as a black, or Negro": Benny Carter, JOHP.

"Go out and make some money": Marshal Royal, JOHP.

The modern drum set: T. Brown 1976.

"Nobody taught guitar then": John Collins, JOHP.

"We used to jazz up the marches": Trummy Young, JOHP.

"I don't want to go to the conservatory": in M. Tucker 1991, 105.

"We've got to help him": Dance 1977, 264.

one Kansas City band prefaced its rehearsals: Pearson 1987, 156.

"There were a number of trade tricks": Artie Shaw 1952, 106–107.

"The most important thing I learned": ibid., 105–106.

"What [these abilities] represent is not natural impulse": Murray 1976, 98.

"the essence of ethnicity": Hall 1977, 82.

"Breakdown music was the best": Davin 1964, 50.

"damn-it-to-hell bass": Waters 1975, 147.

"too sophisticated . . . I think it should": Hawkins 1956.

"Don't think for a minute that it's easy": ibid.

"The trick was less": Lhamon 1990, 77.

"As urbane jazz musicians": ibid., 57.

"the picture of the Negro in the white world": Teddy Wilson, JOHP.

"Never before has any branch of music": Leonard Feather, "Jazz Is Where You Find It," *Esquire* 21 (February 1944): 129.

"comfortable retirement"; "Styles are changing very fast in jazz": Leonard Feather, "Jazz Symposium: Does Life End at Forty for Jazz Musicians?" *Esquire* 23 (March 1945): 85.

"Jazz is like baseball": ibid.

"He's been around twenty years": ibid.

"I always did want to be heard": Nat Hentoff, "The Hawk Talks," *Down Beat* 23 (14 November 1956): 13, 50.

"I always did work with kind of a stiff reed": Coleman Hawkins, "The Jazz Scene Today," *Down Beat* 21 (17 November 1954): 8.

his prized Capehart phonograph: Charles Graham, "Stereo Shopping with Coleman Hawkins," *Down Beat* 33 (7 April 1966): 39; George "Big Nick" Nicholas, interview with author, 1986.

alto saxophonist Rudy Wiedoeft: Russell 1971, 147, 233; Gee 1986, 24–25. See also Schuller 1989, 313, 428, 474, 627, for the influence of Wiedoeft on such saxophonists as Don Redman, Georgie Auld, Stump Evans, and Jimmy Dorsey.

"Coleman—on tenor—took over": Stewart 1991, 67–68.

"You either had more or less tone": in Shapiro and Hentoff 1955, 362–363.

"I heard that sound": George "Big Nick" Nicholas, JOHP.

"[He] seemed to have everything": ibid.

"I used to ask": Nicholas, interview with author, 1986.

"We called him Bean": Budd Johnson, JOHP.

"In the three to four months": George Duvivier, JOHP.

"a year with Hawkins": in Travis 1983, 212.

"college of music"; "The greatest musicians": Sir Charles Thompson, JOHP.

"scales, exercises, study": Coleman Hawkins, "Playing Tenor," *Melody Maker* 10 (14 April 1934): 11.

"Nobody had taught me anything": Hinton and Berger 1988, 51.

"There [were] many musicians": Carter, JOHP.

"depended on you playing the right chord progressions": Thompson, JOHP.

"I don't know anything about chords": Higginbotham, JOHP.

"confines you too much": Lee Young, JOHP, reprinted in L. Porter 1991, 36.

a skilled pianist himself: Stewart 1972, 67.

"I just listen to piano players": Hawkins 1956.

"He was a very studious person": Leonard Gaskin, interview with author, 1986.

"Oh, yeah, it sounds good": Cozy Cole, JOHP.

"They didn't make the changes good": Hawkins 1956.

"They really inspired me": in Ulanov 1952, 238.

he had memorized Hawkins's solo: Hentoff 1957, 297.

"played more like a saxophone did": in ibid., 300.

"I was full of ideas": in Ulanov 1952, 238.

"We would try running these chords": Gillespie 1979, 51–52.

The Philadelphia-based Frankie Fairfax band: W. O. Smith 1991, 38.

"That was supposed to be one of the hardest things": in Gillespie 1979, 56–57.

"The crucial thing about the bebop style": Williams 1993, 137–138.

Chapter 2: The Making of a Virtuoso

Louis Armstrong made a bad first impression: Shapiro and Hentoff 1955, 202; Allen 1973, 124–125.

"the kind that policemen wear": Kaiser Marshall, in Allen 1973, 125.

"the boys" looked "a little stuckup": in Shapiro and Hentoff 1955, 204.

clomping around in heavy policeman's shoes: ibid., 206.

"medley of beautiful Irish waltzes": ibid., 203–204.

"By the Waters of Minnetonka": Louis Armstrong, "Goffin manuscript," Institute of Jazz Studies, Rutgers University (used with permission).

"cut loose"; "all of the band boys just couldn't play": Armstrong, ibid.

the "hot solo," formerly a moment of incidental excitement: Collier 1993, 32–36.

"There were thousands of dancers": Robert Goffin, "Jazzmen's Greatest Kicks," *Esquire* 22 (August 1944): 142.

"I don't think Louis influenced Coleman Hawkins": in Chilton 1990, 30–31.

he actively resisted his debt to Armstrong: ibid., 30.

the tutelage of Peter Davis: Giddins 1988, 66–67.

"inventiveness and musical integrity"; "the highest order": Schuller 1968, 90, 89.

"He undoubtedly used the term": Giddins 1988, 41.

"figured out how to make his music": ibid., 110.

"an artist who happened to be an entertainer": ibid., 32.

"He announces 'When You're Smiling' ": Irving Kolodin, in Giddins 1988, 116.

"studied virtuoso": Giddins 1988, 111.

the only salary . . . Henderson guaranteed: Chilton 1990, 57.

routinely cited in jazz criticism: Heckman 1991, 260; Williams 1993, 74.

"the first important example": Schuller 1989, 431.

"self-conscious act": Kenney 1993, 36.

Dave Peyton: Lax 1974, 115; Kenney 1993, 56–58.

"faking" and "bad habits"; "sloppy New Orleans hokum": in Allen 1973, 168.

"It was like we were emulating white folks": in Lax 1974, 118.

Great Day flopped: Allen 1973, 228–232.

"out of the pit and on the stage": Giddins 1988, 110.

"fusion theory" of the origins of jazz: Brothers 1994, 479.

"off notes": Hawkins 1956.

[blues] as a modal system: Titon 1979, 138–177.

Gunther Schuller [transcription]: Schuller 1989, 168.

"sense of infinite plasticity": Crouch 1990, 73.

"consists more in the manner of saying": Johnson 1912, 172.

"plain blues": Chilton 1990, 140.

"I was just like a clarinet player": in Porter and Ullman 1993, 60.

"I used to tell him": Hawkins 1956.

Jimmy Noone and Johnny Hodges: Schuller 1989, 431; Williams 1993, 73.

"When I was playing one note": Hawkins 1956.

"Hawk, like the rest of us": Stewart 1972, 68, 182.

"machine-gun style": Russell 1959, 208.

"It is as if in making all the chords": Williams 1993, 73.

"between the rhythmic cracks": Schuller 1989, 435.

"Back in the 'thirties—I can't think of nothing": in Feather 1957, 173.

"a giant, wrestling with a large problem": Schuller 1989, 435.

average of $150 a week; billed as "Cole Hawkins, World's Greatest Saxophonist": Chilton 1990, 95, 76.

"I am interested in coming to London": Hawkins 1956.

sharp attack . . . by James Lincoln Collier: Collier 1988.

life as an expatriate: Chilton 1990, 92–155.

"When we were working at the Casino": in Goddard 1979, 288.

"kind of thing [that] gives you the courage to go on": in Ulanov 1972, 151.

"the first time in my life": Stewart 1991, 182.

tour of Scandinavia: Chilton 1990, 118–119.

"Girls were his hobby": in ibid., 142.

"Europe was really Europe then": in Balliett 1983, 46.

"a long, honorable tradition of clowning": Hampton and Haskins 1989, 36.

his improvisations "sounded as classics": Chilton 1990, 123.

"They jotted the chorus down": Hawkins 1956.

"Five years abroad have done Hawkins no good": Walter Schaap, "Jazzmen Abroad," *Jazz Information* 1 (24 November 1939): 2, 4.

"Hawkins's performances on stage": Spike Hughes, "Swing Gem without a Setting," *Melody Maker* 14 (3 December 1938): 5.

"Most of the time, except for a piano chorus or two": Schaap, "Jazzmen Abroad," *Jazz Information* 1 (24 November 1939): 2, 4.

primitivism [in] writing on jazz: Gioia 1988, 19–37.

jazz "exhibit[ed] no intellectual complexities": Sargeant 1946, 256–257.

"For years jazz musicians had played": Panassié 1942, 66.

Panassié's work . . . an "oddity": Collier 1988, 60.

concert at the Salle Rameau with Hawkins: Chilton 1990, 115–116.

preferred to "present things neatly packaged": Schuller 1989, 381.

"make his music part of a larger presentation": Giddins 1988, 110.

"I don't think I started playing 'Body and Soul' ": Hawkins 1956.

He continued to feature ["Body and Soul"] regularly: W. O. Smith 1991, 82–83.

"chorus after chorus and no two alike": "Band Reviews: Coleman Hawkins Orchestra," *Variety* 136 (11 October 1939): 49.

"going into his seventh straight chorus": "The Hawk Takes Off," *Down Beat* 6 (1 November 1939): 18.

"his ten-minute solos of 'Body and Soul' ": D. F., "Westchester Hepsters Hear Stars Jamming," *Metronome* 55 (December 1939): 11.

sales, estimated at nearly 100,000 copies: "Coleman Hawkins to Guest Star," *New York Amsterdam News,* 22 June 1940, 3B.

"Thelonious Monk said to me": Hawkins 1956.

"he plays all of the chords": in Nat Hentoff, "An Afternoon with Miles Davis," *Jazz Review* (December 1958): 12.

"the special declamatory drama of the concert singer": Williams 1993, 78.

"First, you have to tell them the story": Thelma Carpenter, interview with author, 1986.

"You greet the song": Thelma Carpenter, in Chilton 1990, 158.

"that's when you're having the orgasm": Carpenter, interview with author, 1986.

"put the question in the ladies' minds": in Davin 1964, 61.

"the people you've got to please": Hawkins 1956.

"I started to play": ibid.

"We always looked on that simply as a half-step": Gillespie 1979, 92.

"That is 'Body and Soul' ": Hawkins 1956.

"It was through ['Body and Soul']": Sir Charles Thompson, JOHP.

"the superimposition of a single harmonic zone": Schuller 1989, 230.

"Now, there's a whole lot of things I could do here": Gene Ramey, JOHP.

"by the devious means of omission": B. Green 1991, 97.

"occupy an ambiguous place between consonance and dissonance": Brothers 1994, 493.

[sixth degree as] chameleon note: van der Merwe 1989, 230–232.

Chapter 3: Out of Step with Swing

"The truth is that the public will absorb": Paul Eduard Miller, " 'Money Invested in Swing Music Will Keep it Alive,' Says Miller," *Down Beat* 7 (15 April 1940): 6.

"Few colored bands of today": in Bob Locke, " 'I'm Through with the Road,' Says the Hawk," *Down Beat* 9 (15 January 1942): 4.

trend toward larger and more organized bands: Collier 1989, 28–44.

"Harlem's newest dance craze": Allen 1973, 252.

As Howard Spring persuasively argues: Howard Spring, "Swing and the Lindy Hop: Dance, Venue, Media, and Tradition," *American Music* (forthcoming).

"Jazz had by 1932": Schuller 1989, 3.

Hodeir's "classic period": Hodeir 1956, 30.

Swing Era [as] a system of economic interdependence: Stowe 1994, 94–140.

Tin Pan Alley: Hamm 1979, 284–325.

licensing fees wherever their songs were performed: Sanjek 1988, 32–56; Ryan 1985.

giant vaudeville circuits: Sanjek 1988, 16–21.

Theater Owners Booking Association: ibid., 58–59; Southern 1983, 291–295.

"race recordings": Sanjek 1988, 30–31, 64–65; Southern 1983, 365–372

sound recordings . . . rival . . . sheet music in sales: Hamm 1979, 336–337.

royalties for "mechanical reproduction": Sanjek 1988, 22.

national [radio] networks: ibid., 74–90.

Vaudeville fell into an irreversible collapse: ibid., 57–61.

recording industry [decline and rise]: ibid., 117–146.

"Big Three": "Phonograph Records," *Fortune* 20 (September 1939): 100.

territory bands: Hennessey 1994, 44–66, 103–121.

Henderson band was a national band: ibid., 82–98.

Henderson band resembled the prominent white bands: Allen 1973, 173; McDonough 1979, 11.

fondness for fast, expensive automobiles: Allen 1973, 221; Chilton 1990, 56; Stewart 1972, 24.

Henderson . . . continued to handle the engagements: Allen, 221; Stewart 1972, 24.

William Morris Agency: "Put Their Name Up in Lights," *Fortune* 18 (August 1938): 67–73.

Music Corporation of America: Walker 1972, 233–239.

handful of giant booking agencies: Kolodin 1941; "Local Bookers Important," *Variety* 126 (14 April 1937): 59.

shrewd strategy of . . . Irving Mills: Hennessey 1994, 125–126; Hasse 1993, 88–92, 118–129.

"a piece of the action": Kolodin 1941, 73.

"exploited by the small timers": Hammond 1981.

"You know what used to happen during the depression?": in Shapiro and Hentoff 1955, 198.

"property" of Irving Mills: Allen 1973, 291.

structure of the dance band business: Hennessey 1994, 155–156.

"I don't think we even had a waltz": Basie 1985, 173.

"adapting . . . to the white dances": Souchon 1964, 28.

his [King Oliver's] repertory; "[Other black bands]": Bernhardt 1986, 96.

"My idea of a band": Earl Hines, "The Critics in the Doghouse," *Down Beat* 5 (August 1938): 13.

"I used to get letters": Earl Hines, Bloch Lectures, University of California, Berkeley, Spring 1982.

"It seems to be congenitally impossible": "Introducing Duke Ellington," *Fortune* 8 (August 1933): 90.

encouraged—or required—to conform: Kirk 1989, 73–74.

"The contrast of jazz and erudition": in Allen 1973, 177.

"Somewhere in the vaults": Stewart 1991, 119.

"The highest grade of Negro entertainment": "Introducing Duke Ellington," *Fortune* 8 (August 1933): 48.

"The Swing Era didn't open up ballrooms": Wells 1991, 43.

jukeboxes accounted for over half of all record sales: Sanjek and Sanjek 1991, 52–53.

music was the attraction: Hennessey 1994, 128.

"a virtual show in itself": Kolodin 1941, 77.

"Nearly all of them have": in A. Green and Laurie 1951, 459.

a "compromise version of vaudeville": "$100,000,000 Band Biz Czar," *Variety* 135 (16 August 1939): 35.

dance orchestras generated nearly $100 million: ibid., 1.

"The bands of today": ibid., 1, 35.

Fletcher Henderson's band saw a revival: Allen 1973, 330–356.

"more or less in the same category": "Musicians in the Money," *Billboard* 50 (31 December 1938): 63.

"By 1934, it was axiomatic": A. Green and Laurie 1951, 412–413.

"Rippling Rhythm" of Shep Fields: Walker 1972, 73.

"As it is now, musical worth is measured": Artie Shaw with Bob Maxwell, "Music Is a Business," *Saturday Evening Post* 212 (2 December 1939): 15.

"We still didn't realize how big a reputation": Basie 1985, 217–218.

"Spots which never before went in for name strength": "Niteries, Hotels

Splurging on Names; Not Enough B.O. Orchs to Go Around," *Variety* 126 (2 June 1937): 46.

"Sudden spurt in one-nighter business": "7800 Spots in U.S. for Touring Bands; Competition and Showmanship Aids," *Variety* 127 (21 July 1937): 55.

not enough orchestras with proven national reputations: "Big Business, Orchestras," *Variety* 130 (27 April 1938): 49.

the handsome salary of $275 per week: "Gene Krupa Mulls Idea of Own Band; Top-Priced Drummer," *Variety* 126 (21 April 1937): 48.

base salary had reportedly risen to $500: "Gene Krupa Leaves Goodman; Own Band," *Variety* 129 (9 March 1938): 48.

"cash in on the name": "Gene Krupa Mulls Idea . . . ," *Variety* 126 (21 April 1937): 48.

Goodman alumni leading their own bands: "Four Former Goodman Guys Begin Bands," *Metronome* 55 (February 1939): 7, 45.

"hysterical activity in the forming of new orchestras": "Many New Bands Forming," *Variety* 135 (5 July 1939): 39–40.

"Never before in the history of dance bandom. . . . For years, mild-mannered Theodore": "Wanted: Side-men!" *Metronome* 56 (September 1939): 26.

Alexander contacted Hawkins: "Coleman Hawkins to Have American Band," *Down Beat* 6 (August 1939): 2; "Coleman Hawkins Back," *Variety* 135 (9 August 1939): 41; Chilton 1990, 155.

he assumed that he would be able to surround himself: "Too Many Aces Spoil Hawk's Dream of Having Own Band," *Down Beat* 6 (15 October 1939): 2.

"that young guy is blowing up a storm": in Chilton 1990, 126.

"That boy's wonderful!": "Too Many Aces . . . ," *Down Beat* 6 (15 October 1939): 2.

"Hawk had been away a long time": ibid.

"jam outfit": ibid., 5.

"small combination": "Band Reviews: Coleman Hawkins Orchestra," *Variety* 136 (11 October 1939): 49.

one of two singers for . . . Teddy Wilson: Bill Chase, "All Ears," *New York Amsterdam News,* 14 October 1939, 21.

"I just thought I'd take a chance": Thelma Carpenter, interview with author, 1986.

a jazz newsletter referred: "Coleman Hawkins with New Band Opens Thursday at Kelly's Stable," *Jazz Information* 1 (3 October 1939): 1.

"Joe Guy was playing their way": Stanley Dance, "Hawk Talk," *Down Beat* 29 (1 February 1962): 17.

Hawkins himself "showed up almost an hour late": W. O. Smith 1991, 88.

nickname of drummer Harold "Doc" West: Kermit Scott, interview with author, 1983.

"[Hawkins] reached over some place": in Chilton 1990, 163.

"aural mark of identification": A. Green and Laurie 1951, 413.

"body and soul of the saxophone": "Over 1500 Fans Hear Jam 'Sesh,' " *New York Amsterdam News,* 22 June 1940, 21.

"radiantly brassy tone": Schuller 1989, 746.

"Coleman Hawkins is the surprise of the entire poll": "Eleven Leaders on Down Beat's All-American 1939 Band," *Down Beat* 7 (1 January 1940): 12.

Among his new acquisitions: "Hawkins to Leave Kelly's Stable," *Jazz Information* 1 (7 November 1939): 8.

"He'd show me how to hold notes out": Gillespie 1979, 68.

"Why he took me I can't understand": Scott, interview with author, 1983.

"He used to sound like Hawk": in Gillespie 1979, 218.

"He had me sit up right next to him": Scott, interview with author, 1983.

"Don't Start a Band Now!"; "Suppose you started a band": "Don't Start a Band Now!" *Metronome* 56 (October 1939): 20.

engagement at the Arcadia Ballroom: Carpenter, interview with author, 1986.

"It seems to be a custom": George Simon, "Dance Band Reviews: Teddy Hill," *Metronome* 51 (July 1935): 15.

"Gale affects the life of every Negro maestro"; "Because the average Negro": Maurice Zolotow, "Harlem's Great White Feather," *Saturday Evening Post* 214 (27 September 1941): 37.

cavernous, 25,000-square-foot spot: "Harlem's New Golden Gate Promises Stiff Competish [sic] for Savoy," *Billboard* 51 (28 October 1939): 10.

room for five thousand on the dance floor: "Harlem's New Ballroom," *Variety* 136 (25 October 1939): 39.

doubled as [a dance hall and] a roller skating rink: "Jay Faggen Operates Negro Rink-Hoofery," *Variety* 136 (20 September 1939): 44.

[Faggen] joined forces with Moe Gale: Zolotow, "Harlem's Great White Father," *Saturday Evening Post* 214 (27 September 1941): 40.

"one of the most ambitious ballroom policies": "Harlem's New Golden Gate . . . ," *Billboard* 51 (28 October 1939): 10.

promised to keep "the hope of work alive": "Chick Dies and Drums Cease Roll," *New York Amsterdam News,* 30 December 1939, 13.

[Hawkins] a client of Consolidated Radio Artists: "Down Beat's 1939 All-American Swing Band," *Down Beat* 7 (1 January 1940): 1.

1940 Miss Harlem contest: advertisement, *New York Amsterdam News,* 27 January 1940, 20.

"Rhythm Rodeo": "New York Gossip," *Down Beat* 7 (15 February 1940): 5.

gimmick commemorating Leap Year Day: Leonard Feather, "New York News," *Down Beat* 7 (15 March 1940): 2, 20.

one of the biggest "kicks" in his career: Dance 1974, 147.

loss of the ballroom's beer license: Feather, "New York News," *Down Beat* 7 (15 March 1940): 2, 20.

ballroom went into bankruptcy: "Savoy Ballroom Owners to Run Golden Gate as Independent," *Down Beat* 7 (15 April 1940): 3.

"social ballroom": Basie 1985, 237.

"It's Czar Moe Gale in Harlem Now": "It's Czar Moe Gale in Harlem Now," *Metronome* 57 (May 1940): 34.

"self-service nightclub": Richard Decker, "Three Bands and Dinner for 60 Cents," *Billboard* 52 (13 April 1940): 16–17.

"Since the Danceteria is primarily a restaurant": ibid.

"swing on the soft side": "Coleman Hawkins Refuses to Play Mickey Mouse," *Metronome* 57 (June 1940): 8.

"Mine isn't a Mickey Mouse band": " 'No Mickey Mouse for Me'— Hawkins," *Down Beat* 7 (1 June 1940): 3.

"If they want that kind of music": "Coleman Hawkins Refuses . . . ," *Metronome* 57 (June 1940): 8.

Hawkins . . . joining Moe Gale's fold: "Coleman Hawkins on Moe Gale List," *Variety* 139 (12 June 1940): 33.

Count Basie appeared at the Apollo Theatre: "Satchmo Raids Hawkins' Band," *Down Beat* 7 (15 June 1940): 1.

Hawkins "nearly started a riot": "Two 'Hawks,' Barnet, Carter, Jam with Basie Band," *New York Amsterdam News,* 1 June 1940, 17.

Hawkins . . . at the Apollo Theatre: "Over 1500 Fans . . . ," *New York Amsterdam News,* 22 June 1940, 21.

invaluable radio exposure for Hawkins: "Coleman Hawkins to Guest Star," *New York Amsterdam News,* 22 June 1940, 3B.

Hawkins's band could be heard three nights a week: "Hawkins' Paris Home Bombed," *Down Beat* 7 (15 July 1940): 1.

"on the theory that a Negro": Zolotow, "Harlem's Great White Father," *Saturday Evening Post* 214 (27 September 1941): 68.

"unholy alliance": E. Berger 1993, 47.

Not until late 1943: "802 Hikes Savoy Scale to $50; Ends Old Feud," *Billboard* 55 (6 November 1943): 14.

long, hard hours: E. Berger 1993, 47.

"They used to say to us": ibid.

"The idea was that playing the Savoy": in M. Berger, E. Berger, and Patrick 1982, 188.

"To work the Savoy would lift up": Hal Mitchell, in Carner 1989, 123.

annual popularity contest: "Complete Totals of All Bands in Contest," *Metronome* 57 (August 1940): 15.

opportunities to get away from the Savoy: George Kelly, in Deffaa 1992, 213.

The two bands traded sets: "Hawkins and Cooper on 'Double-Feature' Tour," *Billboard* 52 (7 September 1940): 17.

"I think we went all through the South": Scott, interview with author, 1983.

"We covered a lot of miles": in Chilton 1990, 183.

"race prom" in Kansas City: Bob Locke, "Big Hawk Homecoming in Kaycee," *Down Beat* 7 (1 November 1940): 19; "On the Stand," *Billboard* 52 (16 November 1940): 13.

Savoy Ballroom in Chicago: "Chicago," *Jazz Information* 2 (25 October 1940): 1.

"small jam band": "The Hawk's Ork Disbands," *Down Beat* 8 (15 March 1941): 1; "What's New in Jazz," *Jazz Information* 2 (8 November 1940): 3–5.

"you could hear a pin drop": in E. Berger 1993, 43.

"Now Hawk is playing with five men": R. L. Larkin, "Are Colored Bands Doomed as Money Makers?" *Down Beat* 7 (1 December 1940): 2.

"He doesn't seem concerned": "The Hawk's Ork Disbands," 1.

college crowd drifted on to other fashions: "Swing Flunks Its Finals," *Billboard* 52 (1 June 1940): 9–10.

tried-and-true dances as the waltz: "Leaders Note Further Retreat from Swing as Waltz Requests Increase," *Variety* 138 (24 April 1940): 1.

"sweet-hot": "Swing Kings Tapering Off?" *Variety* 136 (15 November 1939): 1.

"swing-sweet"; "white man's style of swing": Bernie Woods, "Swing Knocked Itself Out," *Variety* 137 (24 January 1940): 35.

"degenerated into a cold business proposition": Miller, " 'Money Invested in Swing . . . ,"* Down Beat* 7 (15 April 1940): 6.

"Every new band that's formed": Bernie Woods, "The Dance Band Parade," *Variety* 137 (3 January 1940): 125.

"The practice is drawing a knife": ibid.

"Where are all those bands going to work?": "Wanted: Side-men!" *Metronome* 56 (September 1939): 26.

Agents offering clients at low prices: "Inside Stuff: Bands," *Variety* 134 (26 April 1939): 32.

Venues with "wires" . . . lower their fees: Bernie Woods, "Bands' Bad Biz Methods," *Variety* 138 (1 May 1940): 39.

bandleaders . . . absorb cost of "wires": "Many New Bands in Need of Buildup Favoring Night Club Managements," *Variety* 136 (25 October 1939): 39.

"unfair competition" and "working under scale": "If Band Pays Own Line, It's Bye-Bye," *Variety* 137 (7 February 1940): 33.

"We take a young guy with a new band": Dave Dexter, "What Are the Chances for all the Sidemen Now Starting Bands?" *Down Beat* 8 (15 May 1941): 5, 23.

"Since the supply of dance orchestras": "Offices Killing Own Bands," *Metronome* 56 (June 1940): 7, 10.

"the acceptance of swing music": Henry Johnson [John Hammond], "The Negro and the Jazz Band," *New Masses* 21 (17 October 1936): 15.

"competition from the Dorseys": "Ofay Bands Out-heating Colored Swing Stars, Cutting In on 'Em at B .O.," *Variety* 131 (24 August 1938): 39.

employment for black entertainers generally had declined: "Negro Employment Down," *Billboard* 52 (23 November 1940): 3, 13.

"when a Negro band is on the sidelines": "Chick Dies . . . ," *New York Amsterdam News,* 30 December 1939, 12.

"It is rather . . . curious": Kolodin 1941, 79; emphasis added.

Louis Armstrong's . . . radio broadcast: "Negro Employment Down," *Billboard* 52 (23 November 1940): 13.

hiring of Count Basie by a major New York hotel: "Hotel Lincoln, N.Y., Books First Negro Band (Basie)," *Variety* 151 (1 September 1943): 37.

Radio networks and hotel operators: Kolodin 1941, 80.

Calloway . . . earning more than $6,000 a week: " 'Cab' Averages $6000 a Week," *Down Beat* 4 (September 1937): 21.

Ellington was able to charge at least two to three times more: Collier 1987, 214.

sending musicians into black neighborhoods: "Negro Employment Down," *Billboard* 52 (23 November 1940): 3, 13.

"blare of the jam cellar": "Pleasing the 'Cats,' Customers at Same Time Is Tough," *Down Beat* 4 (November 1937): 12.

"The truth is that the public": Miller, "Money Invested in Swing . . . ," *Down Beat* 7 (15 April 1940): 6, 12.

"personality"; "high-note appeal"; "Basie's high-powered jump style": ibid.

"practically out of the picture": ibid.

MCA took in $19,000 in commissions: "Asserts That MCA Makes $19,000 Profit While Basie Band $11,000 into Red," *Variety* 140 (6 November 1940): 43.

"We haven't had a location job": " 'I'll Break Up My Band,' Basie Says," *Down Beat* 7 (15 November 1940): 1, 23.

overhead . . . wiped out any profits: "Basie Band Won't Break Up," *Down Beat* 7 (15 December 1940): 2.

Basie threatened publicly to dissolve his band: Basie 1985, 245.

"natural limitations": "Asserts That MCA . . . ," *Variety* 140 (6 November 1940): 43.

Basie finally paid a $10,000 penalty: Ed Flynn, "Basie Pays 10Gs for His Release," *Down Beat* 8 (15 January 1941): 1.

rejoining Willard Alexander: Basie 1985, 247.

"that's where our records had sold best": Kirk 1989, 88.

50,000 miles a year: ibid.

"People may wonder if we were exploited": ibid., 93–94.

"You always hear about one-nighters": ibid., 89.

"Kirk is still playing one-nighters": Danny Baxter, "Guitar Is Burr in Kirk Band's Pants," *Down Beat* 6 (June 1939): 8.

"How long can Kirk": Larkin, "Are Colored Bands Doomed . . . ," *Down Beat* 7 (1 December 1940): 23.

bandleader willing to accept any one-nighter: "William Morris Gets Lunceford Band," *Variety* 160 (24 October 1945): 47.

In a typical month, May, 1940: "Band Bookings," *Variety* 138 (17 April 1940): 40.

"We were out there all the time": Trummy Young, JOHP.

"We were full of cold": ibid.

"He called it mutiny": Trummy Young, in Dance 1977, 224.

using the money he had carefully saved: Teddy Wilson, JOHP.

"During one month": "Wanted: Side-men!" *Metronome* 56 (September 1939): 26.

"Pennsylvania, country's prime dance date location": "Ofay Bands . . . ," *Variety* 131 (24 August 1938): 39.

"They had an equal rights law": Leonard Feather, "Jazz Symposium: How Have Jim Crow Tactics Affected Your Career?" *Esquire* 22 (September 1944): 93.

"the typical black jazz band": Wilson, JOHP.

"Perhaps it needed more flash": Simon 1967, 484.

"The Teddy Wilson band was so polished": Leonard Gaskin, interview with author, 1987.

"Teddy's band was too white": Carpenter, interview with author, 1986.

Wilson . . . [at] the new Golden Gate Ballroom: "Harlem's New Ball-room," *Variety* 136 (25 October 1939): 39.

"that broke the spine of the band": Al Hall, interview with author, 1987.

"Things look so bad": Leonard Feather, "Teddy Wilson Reveals He May Drop his Band," *Down Beat* 7 (1 May 1940): 2.

"the type of band his advisers": "Teddy Wilson Reduces Band; Goes to Work," *Metronome* 57 (July 1940): 7.

Wilson earned only $100 a week: Wilson, JOHP.

"mystery man": "Ozzie Nelson Moves Out of Schmalz Rut," *Down Beat* 7 (15 August 1940): 14.

"Carter could be the best": Larkin, "Are Colored Bands Doomed . . . ," *Down Beat* 7 (1 December 1940): 23.

"The audiences wanted good music": Hampton and Haskins 1989, 82.

Gladys Hampton ruthlessly kept expenses as low as possible: ibid., 74.

"[Lionel Hampton]sort of had an attitude": in Deffaa 1992, 254.

"Why should you give it up to them": in Carner 1989, 131.

"Goodman offered me a job": Dave Dexter, Jr., "Hines Hits Broadway and Tears It Apart!" *Down Beat* 8 (15 February 1941): 3.

"Hawkins differs from the usual": Stewart 1972, 61.

"He was a person people were afraid to talk to": in Balliett 1986, 112–113.

Friends described him as shy, private: Major Holley, in Balliett 1986, 114.

"To get him to talk": in Travis 1983, 418.

"You could sit with him for hours": Carpenter, interview with author, 1986.

"Hawkins was a very taciturn man": Stern, "Sonny Rollins . . . ," *Musician* 115 (May 1988): 90.

"In him we have a person": Stewart 1972, 66.

"They were good friends": Carpenter, interview with author, 1986.

"Well, I guess I'd better call": in Stewart 1972, 66.

the same trick with "Red" Allen: Horace Henderson, JOHP.

[Hawkins] enjoyed disconcerting band members: Dance 1974, 143.

"a very strange man": in Chilton 1990, 230.

"There come the two bosses": Johnny Simmen, "Sandy Williams: A Portrait," *Storyville* 116 (December 1984/January 1985): 55.

"He was the first leader": Wells 1991, 64.

"I was concentrating on written arrangements": Wilson, JOHP.

"the 'Hawk' seemed to bear the brunt": "On the Stand," *Billboard* 52 (16 November 1940): 13.

"He had such great confidence": in Chilton 1990, 170.

"aggressive, progressive, showman-minded maestros": John Hurley, "$80,000,000 Dance Cost," *Variety* 129 (29 December 1937): 1, 40.

"I'd have to say": Carpenter, interview with author, 1986.

"limited market stuff"; "for swing collectors": "Record Reviews," *Variety* 139 (31 July 1940): 130.

"good, but not for average": "Record Reviews," *Variety* 140 (2 October 1940): 46.

"Many of his admirers": Whitey Baker, "Hawk Slipping? Reporter Says 'Bean' a Dud in Washington!!" *Down Beat* 7 (1 February 1940): 19.

"To hep cats": "On the Stand," *Billboard* 52 (16 November 1940): 13.

"He was giving them a show": Carpenter, interview with author, 1986.

"His biggest problem was getting to work on time": in Chilton 1990, 170.

"The most he'd do on the bandstand": in ibid., 168.

"the better part of a dollar"; "He disappeared entirely": Duane Woodruff, "Coleman Hawkins Is Declining!" *Music and Rhythm* 1 (December 1940): 30.

"always up in the clouds": in Chilton 1990, 179.

"wouldn't give a quarter": Stewart 1972, 63.

"He didn't care about the band": Carpenter, interview with author, 1986.

"He was a very sensitive man": ibid.

"a weird sight ambled across Boston Common": Stewart 1972, 65.

a *"shitty place"*: Carpenter, interview with author, 1986.

"swing brilliance personified": George T. Simon, "Lunceford and Norvo Really Shell Out!" *Metronome* 57 (July 1940): 17.

"I'm tired of a big band": Locke, " 'I'm Through with the Road!' . . . ," *Down Beat* (15 January 1942): 4.

Chapter 4: Spitballs and Tricky Riffs

"With bop, you had to know": McGhee, interview with author, 1980.

"The older musicians did what they had to do": Enstice and Rubin 1992, 178–179.

Feather's publisher convinced him to change the title: Feather 1977, "Introduction to New Edition" (n.p.).

"world was swinging with change": Ellison 1966, 199.

"integrated professionals": Becker 1978, 228–233.

"tasteless commercialism"; "drag [jazz] outside the mainstream": L. Jones [Baraka] 1963, 181, 184.

"the political economy of jazz": Gennari 1991, 491–492.

"Almost always the men who achieve": Kuhn 1970, 90.

"I was all-ways bad, you know": Richard O. Boyer, "Profiles: Bop," *New Yorker* 24 (3 July 1948): 31.

the *"head and hands"* of bebop: M. Davis 1989, 64.

"like a man dismembering himself": Ellison 1966, 223.

"Bird was great and a genius": M. Davis 1989, 65.

"No jazzman, not even Miles Davis": Ellison 1966, 222.

"See, Dizzy was a comedian": McGhee, interview with author, 1980.

"He'd play a phrase": in Gitler 1974, 34.

"The alto saxophone was just a metal pipe": John Malachi, JOHP.

"Bird paid strict attention": in Gillespie 1979, 119.

"I'm not what you call a 'blues' player": ibid., 310.

coaching drummers: Kenny Clarke, JOHP.

pounding out chord voicings: Budd Johnson, JOHP.

singing the proper phrasing: John Malachi, JOHP.

"[Bird] was so spontaneous": in Shapiro and Hentoff 1955, 352.

John Malachi has related an anecdote; *"Just play the tune"*: Malachi, JOHP.

"Oh, oh, I've got to learn it": Gillespie 1979, 28.

"never . . . be embarrassed again": ibid., 55.

"Sonny Matthews had shamed me once": ibid., 32.

listen to the remote broadcast: ibid., 33.

"It really hurt me": ibid., 34.

"like a blessing from the blue": ibid., 39.

"I knew how to play, I figured"; *"The first thing they started playing"*: recorded interview with Marshall Stearns and James T. Maher, May 1950, Marshall Stearns collection, Institute of Jazz Studies, Rutgers University (used with permission); see also Giddins 1987, 38; Koch 1988, 14–15.

a *"nothing saxophone player"*: Gene Ramey, JOHP.

"Bird couldn't play much in those days": ibid.

practicing . . . over twelve hours a day: taped interview with John Fitch and Paul Desmond, WHDH-FM, January 1954.

"Bird . . . startled everybody": Ramey, JOHP.

"Pinstripes, pegged pants, drapes": Gillespie 1979, 49.

"that little dizzy cat": ibid.

"cut out like a real musician": ibid., 60.

"Trying to survive in New York": ibid.

frequenting the Savoy Ballroom: ibid., 63.

"Being able to read and play well": ibid., 65.

"Shad Collins, Dicky Wells": ibid., 66–67.

"Today, I'm a world-renowned trumpet player": ibid.

"Get yourself somebody like Rex Stewart": ibid., 81.

He had failed to get a job: ibid., 49–50.

audition for the Edgar Hayes band; "Fess, now take it down again": Bernhardt 1986, 138–139.

"I'd play chord changes": Gillespie 1979, 54.

"Edgar Hayes really respected my knowledge": ibid., 91.

he would stop and laugh out loud: Bill Dillard, in Deffaa 1992, 161.

"Like a mischievous kid": Bernhardt 1986, 139.

"if you want your glasses"; "Man, my hand was bloody": Gillespie 1979, 97.

The Cotton Club abandoned its Harlem location: Haskins 1977, 113–157.

"I saw the handwriting on the wall": Calloway and Rollins 1976, 151–152.

"Cab could get anybody he wanted": Gillespie 1979, 109.

athletic display of somersaults: McCarthy 1977, 210–211.

"As long as I'm with you": in Calloway and Rollins 1976, 175.

an "unrelenting, stubborn black son of a bitch": ibid., 7.

"Discipline! That was the word": Gillespie 1979, 108.

"On the stand he was a tyrant": Bushell 1988, 90.

"It was the best job": Gillespie 1979, 107–108.

two-week paid vacation for Christmas: Barker 1986, 163–166.

"There's never been any band": in Calloway and Rollins 1976, 146.

When fired by Calloway: Barker 1986, 173.

"I was out of Chicago": Milt Hinton, in Gillespie 1979, 113.

"We were in this big social band": Milt Hinton, JOHP.

"Musical nothings": Gillespie 1979, 243.

"wasn't interested in developing any musicians": ibid., 109.

"young, vigorous, and restless": Barker 1986, 164.

"Dizzy would take me up there": in Gitler 1985, 58.

"raved" about substitute chords: Jonah Jones, JOHP.

inserting double-time passages in arrangements: Calloway and Rollins 1976, 160.

"He would play a solo": Hinton, in Gillespie 1979, 130.

"I was always into something else": ibid., 110.

filling in of the diatonic scale with chromatic tones: Schuller 1989, 366.

"I worked hard while I played with Cab": Gillespie 1979, 128.

"And, of course, when he came off": Hinton, in Gillespie 1979, 131.

"The spitballs would go ping": Calloway and Rollins 1976, 160.

In Hartford, a spitball landed: Gillespie 1979, 128–133; Hinton and Berger 1988, 94–96.

According to Jonah Jones: Jonah Jones, JOHP.

"That's the guy who cut Cab, right?": ibid.

"Despite losing the 'good job' with Cab": Gillespie 1979, 152.

"the best thing in the world": ibid., 157.

playing with a sextet . . . at Martin's-On-The-Plaza: Koch 1988, 18; Ramey, JOHP.

"conservative" white nightclub: Pearson 1987, 168.

cut a taxi driver with his knife: Giddins 1987, 50; Koch 1988, 19.

"the raggedest guy you'd want to see": in Shapiro and Hentoff 1955, 353.

"just digging New York, period": Jay McShann, in Gitler 1985, 67.

seedy dime-a-dance halls: Koch 1988, 20; Russell 1973, 102–106.

"I didn't even know Bird played saxophone": John Collins, JOHP.

"You got to hear this guy play": Budd Johnson, in Gitler 1985, 61.

"Bird liked my playing": Biddy Fleet, in Gitler 1985, 70.

"he used to come out in the spotlight": Fleet, ibid., 69.

"Nobody paid me much mind then": Michael Levin and John S. Wilson, "No Bop Roots in Jazz: Parker," *Down Beat* 16 (9 September 1949): 12.

Dave Dexter and . . . Walter Bales: Pearson 1987, 168–169.

"When we came out of there": in ibid., 171.

"He set a riff, I took the thirds": Bernhardt 1986, 69.

"You playin' my note?": Eddie Durham, in Dance 1980, 63.

"camp meeting": Ramey, JOHP.

"The other guys would have to harmonize": ibid.

McShann depended on alto saxophonist John Jackson: Giddins 1987, 60.

"But when we did a head tune": Jay McShann, JOHP.

"He was an interested cat": McShann, in Dance 1980, 252–253.

McShann played a variety of tunes: Ramey, JOHP; Reisner 1977, 150; Pearson 1987, 176.

McShann came under Moe Gale's management: "Gale Grabs Jay McShann for Savoy," *Down Beat* 9 (1 February 1942): 2.

"What in the hell have we got here?": John Tumino, in Pearson 1987, 177.

"We're going to send you hicks": Ramey, in ibid., 178.

"When Jay turned his boys loose": Bernhardt 1986, 146.

sharp uniforms: ibid., 151.

"Jay didn't give a damn": ibid., 154.

Parker . . . solo in his stocking feet: Shapiro and Hentoff 1955, 357; Dance 1980, 253–254.

passed out cold on stage: Bernhardt 1986, 154.

"I know it's gonna out me one of these days": in ibid.

"When Bird started getting into this other thing": McShann, JOHP.

"When I came to New York": in Feather 1949, 15.

His first exposure to organized music: McGhee, interview with author, 1980.

attributed his agility as a trumpet player: ibid.; Johnny Sippel, "Faster Trumpet Work Tabs 'McGhee' Special," *Down Beat* 11 (15 September 1944): 4.

McGhee's climb up the ladder: McGhee, interview with author, 1980.

Gene Coy . . . "didn't pay nobody": Howard McGhee, JOHP.

he contracted pleural pneumonia: McGhee, interview with author, 1980.

"It was kind of mean": ibid.

Gradually, McGhee drifted east: ibid.

"I got so I could play as fast as Roy": ibid.

"His feature was 'Body and Soul' ": George "Big Nick" Nicholas, JOHP.

Club Congo in Detroit: McGhee, interview with author, 1980.

"a thing that featured me": ibid.

"[Hampton] came through and he heard me": ibid.

"He wanted me and Ernie [Royal]": in Gitler 1985, 87.

"Me, like a dummy": McGhee, JOHP.

"Shit, I ain't goin' to New York broke": in Gitler 1985, 87.

shortly thereafter: Feather gives a date of November 1941 for McGhee joining Kirk: Feather 1960, 327.

Kirk "was working all the time": McGhee, interview with author, 1980.

"I don't like to talk about it": McGhee, JOHP.

"We played a lot of white dances": McGhee, interview with author, 1980.

his salary increased: McGhee, JOHP.

"You know, cause sitting back there": McGhee, interview with author, 1980.

"He said, 'Maggie, can you write this up' ": ibid.

"I didn't know you could do that with music": ibid.

McGhee . . . noticed by the trade press: Barry Ulanov, "Kirk Provides Theatre's Best Show," *Metronome* 58 (August 1942): 16.

Gillespie . . . came to hear him at Loew's State: McGhee, interview with author, 1980.

"raised ninths and flatted fifths": ibid.

"I said to myself, this is where I belong": ibid.

"I had just come in after we came off the stage": ibid.

"I could hear what he was doing": McGhee, JOHP.

"I mean, here's a guy who's playing everything": McGhee, interview with author, 1980.

Chapter 5: The Jazzman's True Academy

"Wherever there was good musicians": Bernhardt 1986, 88.

"modulation into a new key of musical sensibility": Ellison 1966, 200.

"Many a big-time commercial sideman": Dick Rogers, "I Love Jam Sessions," *Music and Rhythm* 1 (January 1941): 24.

"This is the music they are not permitted to play": Panassié 1942, 69.

"almost like the beginnings of modern American writing": L. Jones [Baraka] 1963, 198.

playing "dance music for money": Cameron 1954, 177.

"recreational rather than a vocational activity": ibid.

"a chance to get the taste of commercial music": ibid., 178.

"For outsiders, the intensity of distaste": ibid., 178, 180.

"Jazz is at once radical and idealistic": ibid., 180.

"jazzmen as romantic outsiders": Leonard 1975.

"deviant" lifestyle: see Becker (1963, 79–119) for a description of "dance musicians" as a "deviant group."

"jazz selects blacks; whites select jazz": Nanry 1979, 248.

isolated, self-sufficient subculture: Merriam and Mack 1960.

Bert Hall: Barker 1986, 113.

"strictly a musicians' club": Wells 1991, 34.

They could play cards, shoot pool: Cozy Cole, JOHP; Sharon A. Pease, "Rivera's Clever Pianistics Send Calloway Crew," *Down Beat* 11 (1 February 1944): 14.

"I'm from 802": Arnold Shaw 1977, 63–65.

"primarily for whites": W. O. Smith 1991, 66.

On Monday afternoons: Barker 1986, 113.

"The guys used to gather": Al Hall, interview with author, 1987.

"You could call at any hour": Mezzrow and Wolfe 1946, 207–208.

Ben Webster . . . was counseled by Count Basie: Dance 1970, 127.

"A lot of guys used to bring their instruments": Basie 1985, 78.

"the thing about the Rhythm Club": ibid.

"What I saw and heard I will never forget": Barker 1986, 113.

"washing away"; "trumpet battle": ibid., 114.

professional baseball players: Will 1990.

"On the New York gossip scene": Barker 1986, 145.

"always wash you away": Sonny Greer, in Dance 1970, 69.

Hoofer's Club: Wells 1991, 24–25; Stewart 1972, 144–145.

"You had to graduate to get down there": Wells 1991, 33.

"Anyone could go": ibid., 24.

"What you're calling today a jam": Hawkins 1956.

"Through all these friendly but lively competitions": Mezzrow and Wolfe 1946, 230.

"The Rhythm Club sessions were a good way": Basie 1985, 78.

"These contests taught the musicians": Mezzrow and Wolfe 1946, 231.

"If a guy came into town": Trummy Young, JOHP.

"the jazzman's true academy"; "It is here": Ellison 1966, 206–207.

"The young musicians could be found jamming": Clayton 1987, 89.

"We had a session going at all times": Al Hall, JOHP.

"In those days we had several means": Gillespie 1979, 134.

contests between Roy Eldridge and Rex Stewart: ibid., 58.

"We'd go down to the Village": ibid., 64.

"We'd go in a place and find out": ibid., 62.

"safe" place in Harlem: Malcolm X 1964, 90.

"holes": Wells 1991, 33.

accessible only through a dingy boiler room: Arnold Shaw 1977, 62.

"night people": Wells 1991.

"conglomeration of artists, taxi drivers": Stewart 1991, 76.

"The average musician hated to go home": Sonny Greer, in Dance 1970, 69.

"When you were in this category": Jo Jones, JOHP.

he threw his high-hat cymbal on the floor: Giddins 1987, 40; Koch 1988, 15; Russell 1973, 85.

"oriental keys": Reig 1990, 14.

"After I finally had gotten a little better control": Benny Carter, JOHP.

"'Mr. Smith, I know this tune' ": Stewart 1991, 54; original read: "A sharp to A flat."

Modulating up a half-step each chorus: Cole, JOHP; Arnold Shaw 1977, 228; W. O. Smith 1991, 38; Gus Johnson, JOHP.

"If a guy came in [to Monroe's Uptown House]": Al Tinney, in Patrick 1983, 157–158.

"Guys used to come in when we were playing at the Onyx": Cole, JOHP.

"I got up there and looked at the sheet music": Basie 1985, 134.

"phalanx of tenors": E. Berger 1993, 437.

"He lost quite a few people at that point": George Duvivier, JOHP.

"I don't know anything about anybody challenging Hawkins": Basie 1985, 149.

The development of modern jazz drumming by Kenny Clarke: see A. Brown 1990, 41–44.

"I always concentrated on accompaniment": Kenny Clarke, JOHP.

"I knew exactly what they were playing": ibid.

"They said, 'Oh, that little guy is crazy' ": ibid.

"It just happened sort of accidentally": ibid.

"Man, we can't use 'Klook' ": in Gillespie 1979, 100.

"After he became manager of this club": Clarke, JOHP.

Nick Fenton . . . also a veteran of the Hawkins band: "Hawkins' Bass Man Cut in Brawl at Bar," *Down Beat* 7 (1 August 1940): 1.

a bar in front, a back room for music: Duke Jordan, in Chilton 1990, 187.

tables with white linen tablecloths: M. Davis 1989, 53.

"Showplace of Harlem": advertisement, *Music Dial* 1 (May 1944): 24.

[Minton's] was a legitimate nightclub: Kermit Scott, interview with author, 1983.

"Teddy Hill treated the guys well": Gillespie 1979, 139.

Hill would shatter the cozy ambience: Scott, interview with author, 1983.

interaction of Clarke and . . . Christian [at Minton's]: see also A. Brown 1990, 45–46.

"Man, that little cat is modern"; "That was the biggest sendoff": Clarke, JOHP.

[Catlett] taught [Clarke] Armstrong's repertory: ibid.

"every kind of job you can think of": Cuscuna 1983.

"I wanted to play my own chords": in ibid.

"He'll come in here anytime and play for hours"; "One reason for it": Ira Peck, "The Piano Man Who Dug Be-Bop," *PM*, 22 February 1948.

Monk began composing in earnest: Sales 1960; Cuscuna 1983; Patrick 1983, 174.

"He got me hired on piano": Sales 1960.

a "freaky sound": Hampton and Haskins 1989, 54.

"The first time I heard [the chord]": Gillespie 1979, 135.

"Let's change the changes to 'I Got Rhythm' ": Milt Hinton, in Gitler 1985, 58.

"I couldn't see going up there": in Shapiro and Hentoff 1955, 343.

"[Monk] generally started playing strange introductions": Barker 1986, 171–172.

"Diz was there every night": Scott, interview with author, 1983.

"That was about the best rhythm section": Howard McGhee, interview with author, 1980.

"He said, 'Hey, Maggie, do you really dig this?' ": ibid.

"the nucleus of bop": in Patrick 1983, 166.

Malcolm X worked there as a waiter: Malcolm X 1964, 80.

the area between 133rd and 135th Streets: Erenberg 1981, 255.

"to entertain and jive the white night crowd": Malcolm X 1964, 87.

"Especially after the nightclubs downtown closed": ibid., 111–112.

"I first saw the drama cleverly enacted": Barker 1986, 134.

the decline of Harlem: Haskins 1977, 110–111.

"America's Casbah": Malcolm X 1964, 83.

prompting some black musicians to wonder: Barker 1986, 142.

"The guys used to kid him": Leonard Gaskin, interview with author, 1987.

"he was the most beautiful man": Holiday 1975, 100.

"He was an outspoken, dapper, colorful dude": Gaskin, interview with author, 1987.

"Clark Monroe had a warm feeling for musicians": Gillespie 1979, 140.

"Clark was very business-like": Barker 1986, 145.

an unprepossessing basement club: Gaskin, interview with author, 1987.

Lana Turner and John Garfield frequented the club: Ray Abrams, interview with author, 1988.

semi-improvisational format called ups: Barker 1986, 137.

"some kind of noise": Gaskin, interview with author, 1987.

"Musicians used to go there and battle": in Gillespie 1979, 218.

"When those guys came in to play": Abrams, interview with author, 1988.

Allen Tinney [early biography]: Patrick 1983, 150–153.

Tinney's presence attracted other musicians: Patrick 1983, 154–155; Gitler 1985, 78–80.

"You had these people coming in": Gaskin, interview with author, 1987.

"When I put my foot in the door": in Patrick 1983, 157.

"When 'Every Tub' . . . came out": Gaskin, interview with author, 1986.

a careful selection of obscure tunes: Gaskin, interview with author, 1987.

"'How High the Moon' was a ballad": ibid.

"He was really the innovator": ibid.

"He didn't have a lot of range": in Gitler 1985, 79.

"had a tendency to be very evil": in Patrick 1983, 165.

"He did have one problem": Gaskin, interview with author.

Coulsen had become a "wino": Gitler 1985, 79.

"Ray always had a piece of junk car": Gaskin, interview with author, 1986.

Covan's Morocco: Gaskin, interview with author, 1987.

78th Street Taproom: Abrams, interview with author, 1988; Gitler 1985, 77.

"Naturally, we were eighteen": Abrams, interview with author, 1988.

"I was undecided": Gaskin, interview with author, 1987.

"We used to kid each other": ibid.

"We used to have mental rehearsals": ibid.

"Actually, what we were doing was swinging so hard": ibid.

Chapter 6: Wartime Highs—and Lows

"Hard Times, as though by some twentieth-century alchemy": Terkel 1984, 7.

A. Philip Randolph's bold threat: Blum 1976, 185–188.

"We shall not call upon our white friends": in Sidran 1971, 100.

"There is no power in the world": in Buchanan 1977, 31.

"the Wailing Wall for minorities": Sitkoff 1971, 676.

Interracial violence reached a peak in 1943: ibid., 671–675.

"the seeds of the protest movements": Charles Silberman, in Dalfiume 1971, 299; Polenberg 1972, 99–130; Lingeman 1976, 323–331.

"The treatment accorded the Negro": in Dalfiume 1971, 420.

jazz as an "indigenous American art": Howard Taubman, "The 'Duke' Invades Carnegie Hall," *New York Times Magazine,* 17 January 1943, 10.

"Entertainment and sports are the greatest antidote": in Carl Cons, "The Effect War Is Having on the Music World," *Down Beat* 9 (1 January 1942): 22.

Industry observers had always expected: "Good Times Ahead for Bands as War Shock Wears Off; Biz Booms," *Down Beat* 9 (15 January 1942): 2.

"Normal moral repressions may vanish": Cons, "The Effect War . . . ," *Down Beat* 9 (1 January 1942): 22.

a sharp increase in earning power: Joe Shoenfeld, "Bands at Theatre B.O. Peaks," *Variety* 148 (7 October 1942): 41; "Colored Bands' Bonanza," *Variety* 150 (17 March 1943): 33.

Shellac . . . was needed for such military applications: "Priorities Hit Disks," *Billboard* 54 (18 April 1942): 19.

stringent quotas on [shellac and recycling]: Lingeman 1976, 119–120.

Eckstine band on the DeLuxe label: John Malachi, JOHP.

shortage of rubber: Polenberg 1972, 14–18; Lingeman 1976, 235–243.

"The best bet is a hotel": Cons, "The Effect War . . . ," *Down Beat* 9 (1 January 1942): 19; see also " 'Hit the Road' Now a Big Headache!" *Down Beat* 9 (15 March 1942): 19.

Hotel ballrooms expanded their music offerings: "Orks Name Own Prices," *Billboard* 54 (26 September 1942): 1, 5.

from a peak of thirty to forty: John C. Flinn, "Bands No. 1 Theatre B.O.," *Variety* 145, 12 (25 February 1942): 1, 46.

over fifty by the end of 1942: Schoenfeld, "Bands at Theatre . . . ," *Variety* 148 (7 October 1942): 41.

fees rose by an estimated 25 percent: "Agencies, AFM Seek Government Ruling on Legality of Raising Band Prices," *Variety* 150 (12 May 1943): 41.

"out-and-out seller's market": "Orks Name Own Prices," *Billboard* 54 (26 September 1942): 1.

"even more fantastically crowded on weekends": "Pleasure Ban on Bands, Too," *Down Beat* 10 (1 February 1943): 3.

"super-names": "Blues in the One-Nights," *Billboard* 54 (21 February 1942): 20.

able to pick and choose their jobs: "Total Ban on Pleasure Driving Lethal Blow to Medium Bands and Agencies," *Variety* 149 (13 January 1943): 39–40.

James . . . in midtown Manhattan: "Three N.Y. Engagements Thru 19 Weeks Won't Take Harry James off 1 Block," *Variety* 147 (8 July 1942): 1.

income from network radio contracts: "Seek Washington Sympathy on Tires for Band, Important in Soldier Diversion," *Variety* 146 (8 April 1942): 41–42.

appearances in motion pictures: Dave Dexter, Jr., "Bands' Big Bonanza in '42 on Movie Screens!" *Down Beat* 9 (15 March 1942): 6.

top tier of bands expanded their rosters: "Buyers Influence Big Band Rosters," *Variety* 153 (23 February 1944): 37.

"Band bookers are constantly complaining": "Inside Stuff—Orchestras," *Variety* 147 (19 August 1942): 35.

infiltration of teenagers: "Despite Draft, Replacements Still Easy for Dance Orchestras," *Variety* 147 (19 August 1942): 35.

some increased opportunities for women: Dahl 1984, 58.

ambitious musicians could evade wage limits: "Musicians: Have a Head as Well as a Heart!" *Metronome* 59 (January 1943): 42.

"An independent attitude": "Inside Stuff—Orchestras," *Variety* 148 (30 September 1942): 40.

Wages rose steeply: "High Salary Demands by Individual Musicians Seen Crippling Medium Bands," *Variety* 149 (23 December 1942): 37.

insuperable obstacle to the formation of new bands: "New Band Snags Too Tough," *Variety* 153 (16 February 1944): 37.

(ODT) issued a preliminary edict: "Delay on Chartered Busses Is Won; Tours Tough; Negroes Hit Worst," *Variety* 146 (3 June 1942): 39, 43.

protested by bookers Moe Gale and Joe Glaser: "Two Managers of Negro Bands May Merge," *Variety* 147 (17 June 1942): 41.

by Cab Calloway: "Calloway with Walter White Urges Bus Leeway for Negro Bands to Avoid Jim Crow Embarrassments," *Variety* 147 (1 July 1942): 41.

by . . . John Hammond: "ODT Gives Negro Bands 3-Month Trial Respite on Bus Ban, But Limits Tours Strictly to Southern Territory," *Variety* 147 (26 August 1942): 41.

Fats Waller's Lincoln sedan: Mezzrow and Wolfe 1946, 207.

a few [black] bands . . . owned [buses]: "Bus-Owning Bands Able to Continue While Tires Do; Much Envious Talk," *Variety* 147 (5 August 1942): 44.

"Without busses to play one-nighters": "Delay on Chartered Busses . . . ," *Variety* 146 (3 June 1942): 39, 43.

commandeering of rail lines: "Busses Yanked, Leaving Negro Bands Jim-Crowed on One-Night Stands," *Variety* 147 (24 June 1942): 41.

trucks had to be hired: "Negro Bands' Transportation Costs Doubled by Railroad Jumps," *Variety* 147 (22 July 1942): 31.

increasing the bill for transportation . . . 25 to 50 percent: "Negro

Bands Can Forget about Busses; ODT Must Say 'Nix,' " *Billboard* 54 (11 July 1942): 19.

grueling tours for little financial gain: "Touring Gets Still Tougher," *Variety* 149 (17 February 1943): 31.

government agreed to lend five buses: "Mapping Negro Bands' 3-Month Bus Sked," *Variety* 148 (9 September 1942): 31.

bands were required to entertain: "USO Shows a Must for Negro Bands," *Metronome* 58 (October 1942): 5.

similar deal . . . for white territory bands: "USO-ODT Plan Revives One-Nighters," *Metronome* 58 (November 1942): 9.

buses were denied to all bands: "ODT Refuses Renewal of Busses for Negro Bands Touring South," *Variety* 149 (13 January 1943): 40; "Negro Bands Lose Busses," *Metronome* 59 (February 1943): 5.

"It's Our Country, Too!": Walter White, "It's Our Country, Too!," *Saturday Evening Post* (14 December 1940): 27.

blacks were barred entirely: Polenberg 1972, 123; Blum 1976, 184.

induction proceeded slowly: "Colored Bands Hit by Draft for First Time," *Variety* 148 (16 September 1942): 41; "Negro Units Riding High," *Billboard* 55 (19 June 1943): 18.

"The War Department cannot ignore": in Polenberg 1972, 124.

black officers could rise no higher: ibid.

glorified stevedore work: Terkel 1984, 275.

such basic privileges as use of the PX: ibid., 341–346; 149.

Race riots broke out: Sitkoff 1971, 668–669; Polenberg 1972, 126.

less likely to be placed in a military band: "Service Bands Pass Negroes; Colored Musicians Have Slim Chance to Play in Uniform," *Down Beat* 9 (1 November 1942): 2.

"big chain down to his knees": Büchmann-Moller 1990, 117.

Buck Clayton . . . induction: Clayton 1987, 115–118.

"I want to get sent down South": Malcolm X 1964, 106.

"Man, why should I fight?": Howard McGhee, interview with author, 1984.

"They started asking me my views": Gillespie 1979, 120.

"I felt like if I was going in the military," "let 'im have it": Malachi, JOHP.

"came in with their own thinking": Kirk 1989, 109.

"even those called for feature spots": "Band Reviews: Andy Kirk," *Billboard* 56 (25 March 1944): 26.

"What's the matter with you fellows?"; *"You know something's wrong"*: Kirk 1989, 109.

zoot suits . . . subverted the War Production Board's rationing: Cosgrove 1984, 80.

More and more talented musicians disengaged: Major Robinson, "Critic Sees Dismal Days Ahead for Negro Bands," *Chicago Defender*, 25 July 1942, 22.

"slept almost a whole year": in Dance 1974, 90.

Clyde Bernhardt . . . left the band: Bernhardt 1986, 159.

"Doc" Cheatham . . . hospitalized: Deffaa 1992, 35–36.

"They'd take all the prices down": Reig 1990, 9.

" 'axle-grease fried chicken' ": Stewart 1991, 133.

"We traveled through the South all day": in Enstice and Rubin 1992, 21.

"In that whole section of the country": Hampton and Haskins 1989, 75.

Musicians have warmly acknowledged: Travis 1983, 232–233; Kirk 1989, 89, 94–96.

"We had a hard way to go": Milt Hinton, JOHP.

"Look, them niggers are from New York": ibid.

"big red-faced man"; *"Blackie that was all right"*; *"my first command performance"*; *" 'My gawd!' "*: Stewart 1991, 109–110; the incident probably took place about 1930.

"public, theatrical" expression of racism: Peretti 1992, 178.

"In those days, when we were traveling"; *"When I was with Fletcher Henderson"*: Wells 1991, 49, 50.

"You just be a gentleman and do your thing": Horace Henderson, JOHP.

Charlie Parker reputedly played the stuttering Negro rube: Giddins 1987, 62–63.

"There was a message to our music": in Gillespie 1979, 142.

"Remember how Cincinnati and Washington used to be": Dan Burley, "Dan Burley's Back Door Stuff," *New York Amsterdam News*, 13 November 1943, 6-B; ellipses in original.

"Of course, the whites were sitting back": in Travis 1983, 505.

"You had to ride in the first car": McGhee, interview with author, 1980.

"*He gives us a list of one-nighters*": ibid.

"*very strange*" *four weeks:* Gillespie 1979, 184.

"*I'd hang out with him all night*": McGhee, interview with author, 1980.

"*Out on the road with Earl*"; "*His crowd, the people he hung out with*": Gillespie 1979, 176.

"*a very good section man*": in Reisner 1977, 114.

"*one of the fastest guys*": Gillespie 1979, 175.

"*flatted fifth chords and all the modern harmonies*": in Dance 1977, 290.

Hines's offerings: ibid.

an all-female string section: Dance 1977, 96.

"*a black entertainer from the old school*": Early 1989, 267.

"*he'd look up and keep playing*": Gillespie 1979, 176.

"*make a man of him*": Giddins 1987, 69.

learning to fall asleep on the bandstand: Russell 1973, 149.

fellow band members . . . ganged up on him: Benny Harris, in Reisner 1977, 188.

"*I frankly admit that I never had to worry*": Barnet 1984, 3.

Barnet openly modeled his music on his favorite black bands: ibid., 77.

"*The fact is that very few white bands*": Malcolm X 1964, 49.

"*I never made a point of hiring black musicians*": Barnet 1984, 122.

"*We were losing more and more men*": ibid., 117.

"*White bands, you got better gigs*": McGhee, interview with author, 1980.

Another advantage to working with white bands: Gillespie 1979, 158.

"*Yeah, of course. For money I'd go with King Kong*": in Gitler 1985, 90.

Young . . . earned about $50 more per week: Trummy Young, JOHP.

"*When you work for a millionaire*": McGhee, interview with author.

"*I hardly ever ate*": Holiday 1975, 73.

"*When I finally did get in*": in Feather 1959, 48–49.

McGhee had clowned and sung: Barry Ulanov, "Kirk Provides Theatre's Best Show," *Metronome* 58 (August 1942): 16.

"*Charlie Shavers heard me*": in Gitler 1985, 90–91.

"*he used to take me with him*": McGhee, interview with author, 1980.

He once fired the entire band; "*everybody fired*": ibid.

"*[Gibson] came out of the car like Jesse Owens*": Barnet 1984, 101.

"Often, when I'd find myself strapped": Gillespie 1979, 165, 168.

"Boy, I'd love to have you in my band": in Enstice and Rubin 1992, 178; see also Gillespie 1979, 209–210.

"Man, this thing is too big": in Shapiro and Hentoff 1955, 356.

"pretty notes": Wilson Levy, "No Bop Roots," *Down Beat* 16 (9 September 1949): 12.

"I think I was a little more advanced": Gillespie 1979, 177, 232; ellipsis after "never" in original.

"compound function": Seeger 1966, 130–131.

"I can play all I know in eight bars": McGhee, interview with author, 1980.

"Stop that crazy boppin' and a-stoppin' ": in Shapiro and Hentoff 1955, 351.

"creat[e] his Hawkins music": Schuller 1989, 433.

"had a rich sarcasm about them that immunized them": Francis Davis, "Man with a Horn," *Atlantic* (March 1992): 116.

"Could the new style survive alone": Gillespie 1979, 173.

Chapter 7: Showcasing the Real Stuff

"There was a warmness about New York": Jimmy Jones, JOHP.

his sidemen scattered: Chilton 1990, 187–188.

a bill that included comedians, singers, and a chorus line: "Hawkins Cuts Two Sides with Basie Band," *Down Beat* 8 (1 May 1941): 15; Rob Roy, "Chicago Hails Coleman Hawkins and His Orchestra," *Chicago Defender*, 26 April 1941, 20.

contract was extended indefinitely: "Coleman Hawkins to Start Tour of West," *Chicago Defender*, 27 September 1941, 21.

Hawkins ... received the highest salary: Al Monroe, "Swingin' the News," *Chicago Defender*, 14 June 1941, 21.

year-end poll: "Duke Ellington Wins Number 1 Band Contest Second Time," *Chicago Defender*, 7 February 1942, 20.

Hawkins decided to leave the Swingland: "Coleman Hawkins to Start Tour ...," *Chicago Defender*, 27 September 1941, 21; Al Monroe, "Swingin' the News," *Chicago Defender*, 29 November 1941, 20.

Hawkins did not get very far: Travis 1983, 418; Chilton 1990, 192–193.

Hawkins . . . take[s] up residency at . . . White's Emporium: Bob Locke, " 'I'm Through with the Road!' Says the Hawk: Ace Negro Saxophonist Building Jump Combo in Chicago," *Down Beat* 9 (15 January 1942): 4; Al Monroe, "Swingin' the News," *Chicago Defender*, 21 February 1942, 21; "Coleman Hawkins Now a Fixture at White's," *Chicago Defender*, 7 March 1942, 21.

married a local woman: Chilton 1990, 190.

In his public pronouncements: Locke, " 'I'm Through with the Road!' . . .," *Down Beat* 9 (15 January 1942): 4; "Coleman Hawkins Now a Fixture . . .," *Chicago Defender*, 7 March 1942, 21.

had to brace himself against . . . the grand piano: Eddie Johnson, in Travis 1983, 418.

"I remember he detested playing 'Body and Soul' ": ibid.

Poor business and political complications: Onal Spencer, "Three Chicago Sepia Spots Fold in Panic," *Down Beat* 9 (1 June 1942): 23.

Hawkins moved briefly to Cleveland: Al Monroe, "Swingin' the News," *Chicago Defender*, 4 July 1942, 22; "Hawk in Cleveland," *Down Beat* 9 (15 July 1942): 26.

arranging several recording dates: Gene Cooper, "Hawk Setting Disc Date," *Down Beat* 9 (1 August 1942): 9.

"Hawkins is now reportedly rebuilding": "Chicago Band Briefs," *Down Beat* 9 (15 September 1942): 5.

"Coleman Hawkins, in keeping with the times": "Pertinent Facts: Small Bands and Cocktail Units," *Billboard* 54 (26 September 1942), "Band Year Book" supplement: 124–129.

"cocktail lounge" . . . field: "Moe Gale Adds Cocktail Department," *Down Beat* 9 (15 November 1942): 3; "Negro Makes Advances," *Billboard* 55 (9 January 1943): 6.

two-week engagement in Cedar Rapids: "The Bean in Cedar Rapids," *Down Beat* 9 (15 November 1942): 21.

standing-room-only crowds: Chilton 1990, 195.

"didn't want to spend a weekend in a hick town": Travis 1983, 209.

Duluth, Minnesota: "Off the Cuff," *Billboard* 54 (5 December 1942): 18.

"Hawkins is back in town out of work": "Chicago Band Briefs," *Down Beat* 9 (1 December 1942): 4.

another engagement at Kelly's Stable: Barry Ulanov, "Coleman Hawkins Better Than Ever," *Metronome* 59 (March 1943): 20.

collectors of commercially available recordings: see S. Smith 1939; C. E. Smith 1944; Hoefer 1944.

"hot clubs"—in Los Angeles: "Swing Stuff," *Variety* 121 (22 January 1936): 57, and David Hyllon, letter to the editor, *Metronome* 52 (February 1936): 17; *in Detroit:* Frank Sidney, "Detroit's Concert Too Much Like Dance Date," *Down Beat* 5 (May 1938): 20; *in Philadelphia:* "Philadelphia Hot Club Formed," *Jazz Information* 1 (1 December 1939): 1; *in Boston:* "Boston Hot Club's First Meeting," *Jazz Information* 1 (16 February 1940): 1, 4; *in San Francisco:* "Frisco Hot Club Holds Jam Session," *Jazz Information* 1 (2 February 1940): 1, 4.

Milt Gabler [and] . . . the Commodore Record Shop: Millstein 1975; Gabler 1988; Arnold Shaw 1977, 231–236, 243–250; "Saga of Milt Gabler and His Commodore Record Shop," *Down Beat* 14 (13 August 1947): 15.

"in an effort to promote the sale of jazz records": Arnold Shaw 1977, 245.

"The original idea was to give the fans": "Swing Stuff," *Variety* 122 (1 April 1936): 48.

golden age of the "swing concert": DeVeaux 1989.

"correct method of listening to swing"; "There was naught but reverential quiet": Cecelia Ager, "Jam What Am, Dished Up Sunday; Swingo Session 'Sends' Sobbie," *Variety* 126 (17 March 1937): 43.

Musicians in Pittsburgh picked up the habit of jamming: "Union Raps Cuffo Swing," *Variety* 126 (21 April 1937): 47.

"There's always been a strict union rule": "Jamming Is Crazy Fad, Says Philly Union Chief," *Down Beat* 5 (April 1938): 4.

"The local is really clamping down": Jan Berger, "A Bob Crosby Man Was Fined for Jamming," *Down Beat* 4 (March 1937): 32.

"as plentiful as fleas": Dan Burley, "Why Musicians Are Jobless," *New York Amsterdam News,* 9 November 1940, 21.

"We went out there that night": Cozy Cole, JOHP.

Stockton, California; Harrisburg, Pennsylvania; Worcester, Massachusetts: "Hot Men Gather at Cool Corners," *Down Beat* 8 (15 February 1941): 16; Sidney Repplier, "Jams Until Late; Mother Scolds; Saxist Kills Self," *Down Beat* 8 (15 March 1941): 3; Merrill M. Hammond, "Mixed Bash Held Sundays in Worcester," *Down Beat* 8 (1 January 1941): 20.

Harry Lim . . . jam sessions in New York: "New York," *Jazz Information* 1 (1 March 1940): 1, 4.

series at the Hotel Sherman: "Jam Sessions Held Every Sunday in Chi," *Down Beat* 7 (15 October 1940): 2; "Jam Sessions in Chicago," *Jazz Information* 2 (15 October 1940): 6–7.

Ralph Berton . . . jam sessions: "Ralph Berton's Jam Sesh," *Variety* 141 (1 January 1941): 32.

Milt Gabler . . . series at Jimmy Ryan's: "Milt Gabler's Concerts," *Variety* 141 (22 January 1941): 48.

Admission ranged from $.50 to $1.50: "Jam Sessions Butter Bread of Some," *Variety* 142 (12 March 1941): 37.

Gabler's sessions featured two bands: Arnold Shaw 1977, 246–248.

"The problem was to get [them] to bring their wives": ibid.

"We would go uptown to Minton's": Reig 1990, 5.

"There were sessions going on": Gillespie 1979, 213.

The sessions at Kelly's ended abruptly: Arnold Shaw 1977, 205–206; Jimmy Butts, "Harlem Speaks," *Jazz Record* 10 (1 July 1943): 5.

"Naturally, it had to do with the black-white thing": in Arnold Shaw 1977, 206.

house band . . . led by Kenny Clarke: Kenny Clarke, JOHP.

Monk played intermission piano: Cuscuna 1983; Al Hall, interview with author, 1987.

Hawkins played there at least once: Reig 1990, 7.

[Hawkins] at a Boston jam session: " 'I Thought I Heard . . . ,' " *Jazz Record* 2 (1 March 1943) 2.

modern notion of jazz as concert music: DeVeaux 1989.

Promoters were quick to realize: ibid., 17–18.

Eddie Condon concerts: Kenney 1983.

"pure and righteous jive": "Righteous Jazz Strikes Gold at Last; Concerts!" *Billboard* 54 (25 April 1942): 21.

the William Morris Agency announced plans: "Lining Up Unit of 'Hot' Groups," *Variety* 150 (28 April 1943): 45.

individual groups would be available for one-nighters: "Jazz to Be Road Shown," *Billboard* 55 (1 May 1943): 20; "Morris to Organize Jazz Tour," *Jazz Record* 6 (1 May 1943): 2.

[Hawkins] in Toronto and Boston: "Mezzrow at Kelly's Stable," *Jazz Record* 7 (15 May 1943): 5; "Bean Romps in Beantown," *Down Beat* 10 (1 July 1943): 23.

"monster jam session": "Hawk to Head Monster Bash," *Down Beat* 10 (1 June 1943): 12.

quickly retreated to Kelly's Stable: Butts, "Harlem Speaks," *Jazz Record* 10 (1 July 1943): 5; "Jazz Flows Again in Swing Lane," *Down Beat* 10 (15 August 1943): 15.

dissolved the band: Butts, "Harlem Speaks," *Jazz Record* 13 (October 1943): 10.

"long, low-ceilinged, narrow": "Where to Go in New York," *Jazz Record* 6 (1 May 1943): 8.

"All the clubs were shaped like shoe boxes": in Arnold Shaw 1977, 280.

"It had such a big reputation": M. Davis 1989, 55.

Hawkins . . . [made] only a few magisterial appearances: Ulanov, "Coleman Hawkins Better . . . ," *Metronome* 59 (March 1943): 20.

as Max Roach is fond of pointing out: Gillespie 1979, 232–233; Gitler 1985, 77–78.

later reduced to 20 percent: "Youth Is on March Cadence in Fast One," *Down Beat* 11 (15 June 1944): 10.

"a public performance for profit": Johnny Sippel, "Music Affected by New Tax Measure," *Down Beat* 11 (1 May 1944): 1.

large "NO TAX" signs: "Spots Shutter as Panic over Tax Continues," *Down Beat* 11 (15 May 1944): 1.

"Since the decline of the one-nighter business": "Most Newcomers from Harlem," *Billboard* 55 (30 October 1943): 22.

"sure-fire attractions": Paul Ross, "Disks a Must for 52nd St. Click," *Billboard* 56 (24 June 1944): 23.

black artists were consistently paid less: Leonard Feather, in Arnold Shaw 1977, 282–283; Billy Taylor, in ibid., 173.

Billie Holiday earned $175 a week: Holiday 1975, 96.

reported income was $1,250: "Swing Street Not Jivin' at the B.O.," *Variety* 164 (13 November 1946): 40.

Fats Waller drew $300: "Negro Units Riding High," *Billboard* 55 (19 June 1943): 18.

Art Tatum . . . trio grossed over $1,000: "I Ran Into . . . ," *Jazz Record* 14 (November 1943): 2; "Name-itis Hits 52d Street," *Billboard* 57 (17 February 1945): 24.

characterized 52nd Street as a "plantation": Holiday 1975, 94.

the "plantation owners . . . found they could make money": ibid., 96.

"I resented the exclusion of black people": in Arnold Shaw 1977, 279–280.

unpleasant and occasionally violent harassment: "Gendarmes Halt Racial Skirmish," *Down Beat* 11 (15 June 1944): 1; "Racial Hatred Rears Its Ugly Mug in Music," *Down Beat* 11 (1 August 1944): 1; Gillespie, 210–211.

inexpensive drinks . . . [and] free hors d'oeuvres: Leonard Gaskin and Ray Abrams, interview with author, 1988.

"The tourists didn't have a chance": Slim Gaillard, in Arnold Shaw 1977, 227.

"petty and sordid crime": "Thief Loots Home Next to Mayor's in 'Crime Region,' " *New York Times,* 10 November 1941, 1, 10.

"another Harlem riot" . . . *"mugging":* "Crime Outbreak in Harlem Spurs Drive by Police," *New York Times,* 7 November 1941, 1, 15.

"The so-called recent crime wave": in "Thief Loots Home Next to Mayor's in 'Crime Region,' " *New York Times,* 10 November 1941, 1, 10.

"Harlem night life": Herb Golden, "Crime Wave Publicity Deals Harlem's Night Life 'Comeback' a Severe Blow," *Variety* 144 (12 November 1941): 1, 62.

Harlem was declared off-limits: New York World-Telegram, 11 August 1942, in Schoener 1979, 173.

the Savoy Ballroom was closed for six months: "Stompin' at the Savoy," *Metronome* 59 (June 1943): 5; "Harlem Feet Happy Again, Track Jumps," *Down Beat* 10 (15 November 1943): 2.

"the real reason was to stop Negroes": Malcolm X 1964, 113.

night of August 1, 1943 [Harlem riot]: Sitkoff 1971, 675; James, Breitman, and Keemer 1980, 281–287; Buchanan 1977, 53–56.

"Hell, man, it just exploded": Ellison 1972, 529.

"They did it themselves": ibid., 536.

"the crash of men against men": ibid., 540.

"hoodlums, vandals, and irresponsible elements": James, Breitman, and Keemer 1980, 284.

"Numerous stories have been told": New York Amsterdam News, 7 August 1943, in Schoener 1979, 177–178.

Murrain's: Gaskin, interview with author, 1986.

Clark Monroe and His Funsters: Butts, "Harlem Speaks," *Jazz Record* 9 (15 June 1943): 5.

"Being such a ham": Gaskin, interview with author, 1987.

[joining] Local 802: ibid.

Monroe's group provided accompaniment: Butts, "Harlem Speaks," *Jazz Record* 14 (November 1943): 11.

"strictly on an Ellington kick": ibid.

"it was just a long honeymoon": Gillespie 1979, 153.

"'Look, you're gonna miss a trumpet player' ": ibid.

"They paid Coleman the money he asked for": ibid.

he had quit the profession: Gitler 1974, 153.

[McGhee] arranged for the bandleader [Barnet] to hear Pettiford: Gitler 1985, 93–94.

[Pettiford] replaced Nick Fenton: Butts, "Harlem Speaks," *Jazz Record* 8 (1 June 1943): 5.

playing with Roy Eldridge at the Onyx: Gitler 1974, 155.

first place in . . . poll: Miller 1944, 108–130.

Gillespie was struck . . . by his melodic imagination: Gillespie 1979, 137.

Gillespie . . . would be co-leader: Arnold Shaw 1977, 257; Gillespie 1979, 203; Feather 1949, 28.

"the birth of the bebop era": Gillespie 1979, 202.

[Gillespie] wanted Charlie Parker: Gitler 1985, 123; Gillespie 1979, 202.

Lester Young . . . worked with the band: Büchmann-Moller 1990, 110–111.

Count Basie . . . fired tenor saxophonist Don Byas: Butts, "Harlem Speaks," *Jazz Record* 15 (December 1943): 7.

Byas . . . drifted into rehearsals: Gillespie 1979, 202.

He may have used Harold "Doc" West: Büchmann-Moller 1990, 110.

Gillespie considered using Bud Powell: Max Roach, in Gillespie 1979, 206; Billy Taylor, in Arnold Shaw 1977, 171.

reportedly used Thelonious Monk: Butts, "Harlem Speaks," *Jazz Record* 15 (December 1943): 7.

"We didn't need a strong piano player": Gillespie 1979, 207.

Onyx Club [repertory]: Billy Taylor, in Gitler 1985, 123.

easier . . . singing it with scat syllables: Budd Johnson, in ibid., 119.

"I put down a lot of things for Oscar Pettiford": ibid. Elsewhere, Johnson says, "Monk actually had tunes down on paper" (Gillespie 1979, 218).

two horns playing in unison or octaves: Feather 1949, 29; Gitler 1974, 155; George Hoefer, "The First Bop Combo," *Down Beat* 30 (20 June 1963): 19, 37.

"I noticed that Coleman Hawkins was often present": Bernie Savodnick, letter to the editor, *Down Beat* 11 (1 July 1944): 10.

Chapter 8: The Rush to Record

recording ban [background]: DeVeaux 1988.

"a whole chapter, even a whole volume": Rust 1978, i.

"By about 1942, it was clear": Collier 1978, 355.

"We'd do that kind of thing in 1942": Gillespie 1979, 135.

improving business conditions were largely to blame: DeVeaux 1988, 144–145.

jazz records "take up shellac": Mike Levin, "Recording Sliced One-Third," *Down Beat* 9 (1 May 1942): 1.

"Unless record fans rise up in arms": John Hammond, "John Hammond Says," *Music and Rhythm* 2 (June 1942): 26.

"the music wasn't called bop at Minton's": in Shapiro and Hentoff 1955, 350.

"the real thing happened up in Harlem": M. Davis 1989, 55.

"Jamming at Minton's and Monroe's": Gillespie 1979, 186–187.

fifteen publishing companies accounted for 90 percent: Ryan 1985, 101.

dispute between ASCAP [and BMI]: Ryan 1985, 77–100.

Membership was strictly controlled: ibid., 56–63.

Meade "Lux" Lewis . . . became a member: Dave Dexter, Jr., "ASCAP Moguls Fluff Off Lux Lewis' Bid for a Card," *Down Beat* 8 (1 December 1941): 1; Dave Dexter, Jr., "Big ASCAP Official to Bat for Meade Lux," *Down Beat* 9 (1 January 1942): 1.

Scott Joplin was admitted: Ryan 1985, 65.

"the illegal pooling of most of the desirable copyright music": ibid., 95.

independents: DeVeaux 1988, 146–148.

audience for jazz was small but dedicated: ibid., 144–145, 152–154.

Keynote Records had offered an odd assortment: B. Porter 1986.

"small but lucrative jive-loving and jazz-collecting field": "Keynote Set to Invade Longhair Jive Disk Field," *Billboard* 56 (4 March 1944): 15.

Savoy Records [early history]: Ruppli 1980, xv–xvii.

seemed determined to record every musician: "Stuff Smith's Violin Recorded by Savoy," *Down Beat* 11 (15 October 1944): 5.

"Apparently all that is required": Wanda Marvin, "Waxing Is Everybody's Biz," *Billboard* 56 (22 April 1944): 12.

Record companies estimated they could sell ten times: "Postwar Deluge of Diskers," *Billboard* 55 (2 October 1943): 1.

with an eye to creating backlogs: "AFM Record Ban Assists Minor Platter Firms," *Down Beat* 11 (15 May 1944): 9.

"disk educated": Paul Ross, "Disks a Must for 52nd St. Click," *Billboard* 56 (24 June 1944): 23.

Union regulations mandated: "Hats On!" *Metronome* 61 (April 1944): 18.

"whatever the traffic would bear": Reig 1990, 90; "Small Wax Firms under 802 Eye," *Down Beat* 12 (15 February 1945): 2.

they demanded, and received, higher fees: Leonard Feather, "Waxing Furious," *Metronome* 61 (June 1944): 18; "Inside Hot Jazz Disking Pays Plenty Over-scale Dough," *Billboard* 58 (12 January 1946): 14.

"It was 'monkey see, monkey do' ": Reig 1990, 35.

Under existing copyright laws: Patrick 1978.

companies set themselves up as "publishers": DeVeaux 1988, 155.

"You don't read or write music yourself": Leonard Feather, "Rhythm Section," *Esquire* 24 (September 1945): 82.

Feather . . . traced the figure to Charlie Parker: Feather 1949, 26.

he'd "dive in with all four feet": Ray Abrams, interview with author, 1988.

taking Hawkins fishing: Tiny Grimes, JOHP.

"Hawkins usually thinks about something": Charles Graham, "Stereo Shopping with Coleman Hawkins," *Down Beat* 33 (7 April 1966): 39.

"That's what they should've been playing": Hawkins 1956.

"Charlie Parker and Dizzy were getting started": in Dance 1974, 145.

aimed generally at "the colored market": Feather, "Waxing Furious," *Metronome* 61 (June 1944): 18.

Gottlieb later claimed: Robert Levin, "Just Messin' Around with Diz and the Hawk," *Village Voice,* 10 April 1957, 5.

four-hour Saturday afternoon "Swing Concert": "1200 Fans Hear Prof. Burton's Jazz Concert at Savoy," *New York Amsterdam News,* 16 January 1943, 15.

"I remember very distinctly": Leonard Gaskin, interview with author, 1988.

"He was looking for a new identity": in Chilton 1990, 209.

"This was the beginning for this stuff being put down": in Gillespie 1979, 215.

"The tune just popped out": Gillespie 1979, 185–186.

"We had been playing it": in ibid., 214.

Gaskin recalled it from Kelly's: Gaskin, interview with author, 1993.

Gillespie had worked up an arrangement: Gitler 1985, 189.

Max Roach naturally assumed: "Max Roach: No Boundaries," *Modern Drummer* 17 (August 1993): 24.

Roach's name appeared prominently on the record label: record label for "Woody'n You" reproduced in Schoener 1979, 202.

"My first record date": in Gillespie 1979, 220.

They sold at a premium price: advertisement, *Down Beat* 11 (1 May 1944): 8.

recordings were released promptly: Dan Burley, "Back Door Stuff," *New York Amsterdam News*, 29 April 1944, 6B.

"That's where I first heard Diz and Bird": M. Davis 1989, 7.

"Sure, you can buy his records"; "When I bought": in Gitler 1985, 143.

Chapter 9: Eckstine and Herman

"We knew that the white guy was only copying": in Enstice and Rubin 1992, 177.

"After I heard what Dizzy was doing": McGhee, interview with author, 1980.

"the greatest feeling I ever had in my life": M. Davis 1989, 7.

"When I heard Diz and Bird in B's band": ibid., 7, 9, 10.

a one-nighter in Connecticut: "Hawkins 5-Man Unit Solid One-Nighter Draw," *Billboard* 56 (2 September 1944): 13.

"I was about the only one": Valerie Wilmer, "The Big Noise from Muskogee," *Jazz Beat* 2 (1965): 4.

included him along with Lester Young: *Music and Rhythm* (August 1941), in Chilton 1990, 191.

"a rough man in any cutting session": Reig 1990, 14.

"unbelievable choruses": Billy Taylor, in Gitler 1985, 141.

"There's no need for a man my age": Reig 1990, 14.

"The place would be packed": John Simmons, JOHP.

"Everybody wanted him but everybody was afraid": Ira Peck, "The Piano Man Who Dug Be-Bop," *PM,* 22 February 1948.

"One of the worst things I went through": in Feather 1957, 172.

"Little Benny" Harris [background]: Dick Hadlock, "Benny Harris and the Coming of Modern Jazz," *Metronome* 78 (October 1961): 18–20.

"Dizzy was always preaching Benny Carter": in Reisner 1977, 107; see also Feather 1949, 26; for Harris's proselytizing, see Johnny Carisi, in Gitler 1985, 84; Billy Taylor, in Gitler 1985, 100; Dexter Gordon, in Gitler 1974, 90.

"he'd fluff a few notes": Hawkins 1956; see also Dance 1977, 290.

"We used to rehearse every day": Hawkins 1956.

"the interpretive music of Coleman Hawkins": advertisement, *New York Amsterdam News* 35 (27 May 1944): 6B.

"amazing unison jump scorings"; "With three horns creating fast-moving riff figures": "Combos Collared by Groovy Gothamites," *Down Beat* 11 (1 June 1944): 14.

Apollo recordings out and doing well: Pittsburgh Courier, 13 May 1944, 15.

"Body and Soul" rereleased by Victor: "Hawk's Apollo Disc Stirs Victor Issue," *Down Beat* 11 (15 May 1944): 9.

"Hawk is a musician": Harry Lim, "Hawk!" *Metronome* 61 (May 1944): 16.

tapping Vic Coulsen: Jimmy Butts, "Harlem Speaks," *Jazz Record* 21 (June 1944): 13; " 'New Faces' Tops [sic] Swing St. Fare," *Down Beat* 11 (1 September 1944): 3; Jimmy Butts, "The Music Box," *Music Dial* 2 (August 1944): 17.

Hawkins . . . at the Apollo Theatre: "Coleman Hawkins Starts Run at Apollo Theatre," *New York Amsterdam News* 35 (9 September 1944): 9B.

Art Tatum and Nat "King" Cole . . . [as] "attractions": Bill Smith, "Vaude Opening to Combos," *Billboard* 56 (28 October 1944): 24.

"Vic Coulsen's Gillespie-ish trumpet"; "Hawk needed a build-up announcement": Leonard Feather, "Stage Show Reviews: Reynolds-Hawkins," *Metronome* 61 (October 1944): 30.

"The average Swing Street nitery owner": "Name-itis Hits 52d Street," *Billboard* 57 (17 February 1945): 24.

Gillespie accused the bassist of being a "prima donna": Gillespie 1979, 211; Arnold Shaw 1977, 258.

Pettiford retained his position at the Onyx: Herman Rosenberg, "Manhattan Melange," *Record Changer,* September 1944, 52.

Budd Johnson . . . served as "business manager": Budd Johnson, JOHP.

may have left as early as the beginning of March: Leonard Gaskin, interview with author, 1988; Carter's band played in New York at Loew's State Theater during the last week of February 1944 and subsequently went on the road, ending up in Los Angeles by May: Bill Smith, "Vaudeville Reviews: State, New York," *Billboard* 56 (25 March 1944): 26; *Down Beat* band bookings.

Mills "had the feeling to start with": Gaskin, interview with author, 1988.

about $75 a week: ibid.

Billy Eckstine [background]: Southern 1979, 183–188.

"They handed me a sheet of music": ibid., 194.

a "musicians' building": Gitler 1985, 60; Travis 1983, 318.

Eckstine . . . [at] Monroe's Uptown House: Shapiro and Hentoff 1955, 353.

"my gang": Southern 1979, 196.

dances in tobacco warehouses: Earl Hines, Bloch Lectures, University of California, Berkeley, Spring 1982.

"Down there, you had to play plenty of blues": Billy Eckstine, "Crazy People Like Me," *Melody Maker* 30 (21 August 1954): 5.

borrowed liberally from . . . Joe Turner: Southern 1979, 190; Dance 1977, 241.

band found itself with time for another song: Eckstine, "Crazy People . . . ," *Melody Maker* 30 (21 August 1954): 5.

"Why don't you play some kind of blues": in Travis 1983, 313.

Eckstine retreated to scrawl a set of lyrics: Southern 1979, 190.

"Blues tunes have been good for me": in Travis 1983, 316.

"What Southern accent are you talking about?": in ibid.

"If you don't understand his words": in Southern 1979, 189.

"I hate blues": Metronome 64 (October 1947), in Simon 1967, 185.

"I told him, 'Hell, no! I don't want to go' ": Eckstine, "Crazy People . . . ," *Melody Maker* 30 (21 August 1954): 5.

black singers either "[did] rag": in Southern 1979, 196.

he found work on 52nd Street: "Eckstein Crosses 52d Street," *Billboard* 56 (29 April 1944): 15; John R. Gibson, "It Wasn't Told to Me—I Only Heard," *Music Dial* 1 (May 1944): 14.

"the only thing audiences knew about him": Gaskin, interview with author, 1993.

his inclination toward ballads: *Pittsburgh Courier*, 15 April 1944, 13; *Pittsburgh Courier*, 22 April 1944, 15.

Eckstine turned for advice: Billy Eckstine, "Billy Eckstine Writes about Crazy People Like Me," *Melody Maker* 30 (28 August 1954): 13.

George Hudson: McCarthy 1977, 120–121.

Dizzy Gillespie and Budd Johnson ... dissuaded him: Eckstine, "Billy Eckstine Writes ...," *Melody Maker* 30 (28 August 1954): 13.

There was still plenty of room at the top: "Nut Cuts Number of Newies," *Billboard* 56 (22 July 1944): 15, 30.

"They wanted me to sing, and play 'One O'Clock Jump' ": Gitler 1985, 126.

"If you do well, this'll be your big chance": Feather 1949, 30.

gained entrée to many lucrative one-nighters: Paul Secon, "More $$ for Negro Musickers," *Billboard* 57 (3 February 1945): 13.

$750 per engagement from Roanoke to Pensacola: ibid., 15.

"Negro-patronized spots where he made a name": ibid.

proposed itinerary: John Malachi, JOHP.

Eckstine hastily traveled to Chicago: Eckstine, "Billy Eckstine Writes ...," *Melody Maker* 30 (28 August 1954): 13.

Shadow Wilson ... a habitué of Minton's and a favorite of Gillespie's: Gillespie 1979, 146, 247.

Wilson was inducted: Butts, "The Music Box," *Music Dial* 2 (August 1944): 17; Eckstine, "Billy Eckstine Writes ... ," *Melody Maker* 30 (28 August 1954): 13.

Eckstine used a white drummer: Malachi, JOHP.

"the first big bop band": George Hoefer, "The First Big Bop Band," *Down Beat* 32 (24 July 1965): 23.

the "era of the 'big singer' ": Hamm 1979, 387.

"People still talk today": in Travis 1983, 318.

"I don't ever want to see this shit again": in ibid.

"I decided the best thing was to do a single": in Simon 1967, 185.

dubbed rhythm and blues: George 1988, 15–58; Gillett 1970, 135–195.

radio stations catering to vast new black consumer markets: George 1988, 40–41.

had just hired . . . Wynonie Harris: Pittsburgh Courier, 15 April 1944, 13.

"I loved playing jazz with a big band": in Arnold Shaw 1978, 66.

"Those guys really wanted to play mostly for themselves": in Keil 1966, 64.

"Jazz is . . . an art that has welcomed": Lhamon 1990, 110–111.

"Bebop is a highly sophisticated form of music": Gillespie 1979, 371.

"Billy Eckstine came out with Earl Hines's band": in Titon 1981, 22.

"pioneer" label: Arnold Shaw 1978, xvii, 133.

absorbed in 1947 by the more successful King label: Ruppli 1985, vol. 2, xiii.

first recordings were in the country field: ibid., 483.

"The sepia entry into the swooning sweepstakes": M. H. Orodenker, "Popular Record Reviews," *Billboard* 56 (3 June 1944): 19.

"not exactly polite": ibid.

"Talk about be-bop, we were beeeee-boppin' ": Dance 1977, 261.

"round-up of sepia instrumental aces": Orodenker, "Popular Record Reviews," *Billboard* 56 (3 June 1944): 19.

"You forget about changes when you play the blues": Gillespie 1979, 371.

"The bebop musicians didn't like to play the blues": ibid.

"And he slowed down the truck": Barker 1986, 159–160; as a result of the incident, Decca was pressured to stop production of the recording.

"trying to educate the Southern black people": Milt Hinton, JOHP.

"The music we played was completely different": Hinton and Berger 1988, 122.

"They wanted [Calloway] to sing, but he would never sing the blues": Hinton, JOHP.

"the purest expression of Negro life in America"; "the most honestly contemporary expression": L. Jones [Baraka] 1963, 119.

"rice-and-beans music": Red Rodney, in Gitler 1985, 225–226.

"colored audiences liked it": in Feather 1949, 31.

"You know how they were playing for them black folks": M. Davis 1989, 9.

some *"dumb blues lyric":* Eckstine, in Gitler 1985, 129.

Charlie Parker and Dizzy Gillespie staved off disaster: Malachi, JOHP.

"They're not particular": "Bird Wrong; Bop Must Get a Beat: Diz," *Down Beat* 16 (7 October 1949): 1.

"Whatever you go into": in Gillespie 1979, 142.

Eckstine typically sang no more than one or two numbers: Leonard Feather, "Billy Eckstine," *Metronome* 61 (January 1945): 2.

"double-time specials": "Eckstine Spots Strong Trumpets," *Down Beat* 11 (1 September 1944): 1.

"little band" that featured Parker, Gillespie, and Thompson: "Billy Eckstine's Ork Hailed," *Pittsburgh Courier,* 19 August 1944, 13.

"People were used to patting their feet": Bob Redcross, in Gillespie 1979, 198.

"Diz made an arrangement of 'Max Is Makin' Wax' ": in ibid., 190.

"[The crowds] came in to hear Billy Eckstine": in Enstice and Rubin 1992, 181.

"would be in a corner, jitterbugging forever": in Gillespie 1979, 192, 193.

chicken bones tossed their way: ibid., 193.

dust and hay of the baggage car: Gitler 1985, 128.

"We got some smart 'uns dis time": Gillespie 1979, 188.

paid "terrif dough" to black bands: Secon, "More $$ . . . ," *Billboard* 57 (3 February 1945): 15.

courting disaster by entering through the front door: Davis 1989, 8; Gillespie 1979, 188; Reisner 1977, 51.

"Regardless of what problem we had": Eckstine, in Gitler 1985, 129.

his obbligato behind Sarah Vaughan: Johnny Sippel, "Bands Dug by the Beat: Billy Eckstine," *Down Beat* 11 (1 October 1944): 4. Art Blakey says the number was "You Are My First Love": Reisner 1977, 51.

"I remember sometimes the other musicians": M. Davis 1989, 9.

"You had a music stand there": Sonny Stitt, in Enstice and Rubin 1992, 248.

"It was like a small combo": Art Blakey, in ibid., 21–22.

gross income for the latter half of 1944: Secon, "More $$ . . . ," *Billboard* 57 (3 February 1945): 13, 15.

debut at the Apollo: *Pittsburgh Courier*, 7 October 1944, 13.

official billing was "Romantic Singing Maestro": Feather, "Billy Eckstine," *Metronome* 61 (January 1945): 2.

DeLuxe apparently wanted the last side: Malachi, JOHP.

"We are going to get a big band started": in Shapiro and Hentoff 1955, 340–341; M. Jones 1987, 200.

"most anybody can become"; "In the end, the public believes": in Shapiro and Hentoff 1955, 340–341.

jotting down riffs on their cuffs: M. Jones 1987, 201.

white comics like Milton Berle: Watkins 1994, 274.

"just as many white friends as colored": in Reisner 1977, 107.

"Howard started showing me things": in Gitler 1985, 136.

"Dizzy would sit in the bands": in Gillespie 1979, 217.

end-of-the-year poll: "Spivak Gets Crown from TD, Duke Wins; Bing Is New Voice," *Down Beat* 12 (1 January 1945): 1, 13.

[Herman] would win the next swing band poll: "Woody & TD Win, Ten New All-Stars," *Down Beat* 13 (1 January 1946): 1.

"historically and musically with the half-dozen greatest bands": Barry Ulanov, "Woody!" *Metronome* 61 (December 1945): 14.

"playing the blues was the best thing": Herman and Troup 1990, 21.

"The white man thinks that blues": in Travis 1983, 316.

"Will you kindly stop singing and playing": Herman and Troup 1990, 29.

"helped to make the band more identifiable": ibid., 50.

"Ellington had something to do with the writing": ibid., 46–47.

"diversified" repertory: ibid., 47.

"Woody Herman fans dancing by": introduction to "Sweet Lorraine," Old Gold broadcast, Hindsight HRS 134.

twelfth place in the "sweet band" category: "Spivak Gets Crown . . . ," *Down Beat* 12 (1 January 1945): 13.

"It was cooking, but it was so strange": in Gitler 1985, 189.

"[He] said I was the first guy to pay him $100": Herman and Troup 1990, 39.

Herman's band "had no trouble": Gillespie 1979, 168–169.

had been following Gillespie: Gitler 1985, 189.

he made a point of searching out Gillespie: ibid., 192.

"On one-nighters, Woody would often leave": in Herman and Troup 1990, 52.

"There's a record of Woody's": in Enstice and Rubin 1992, 177.

"Unquestionably, Gillespie and Eckstine's arranger": Schuller 1989, 737–738.

"We were the only band doing that": Herman and Troup 1990, 59.

Herman's "load of sweet and hot stuff": Old Gold broadcast, 13 September 1944, Hindsight HRS134.

"Apple Honey literally ties on": advertisement, Old Gold broadcast, 20 September 1944, Hindsight HRS134.

"'Don't worry about guarantees' ": Herman and Troup 1990, 58.

"He did his own thing": in Arnold Shaw 1978, 69–70.

The immediate source for this passage: Gitler 1985, 192; Lees 1995, 109.

as Hefti freely admitted: Lees 1995, 110.

Herman was "on the gravy train": "Woody Enters Concert Field Next Spring," *Down Beat* 12 (1 November 1945): 1.

"Half the band was playing": in Gitler 1985, 132.

"Shit, Woody Herman, get a load of his things": in ibid., 127.

Eckstine . . . allowed to sing . . . "number one" pop songs: Southern 1980, 58; Ulanov 1952, 268.

Chapter 10: Short Stay in the Sun

"[Coleman Hawkins and I] had an understanding": Howard McGhee, interview with author, 1980.

"the walls of one of its grooves": Williams 1976.

"definitive statements of the new music": Gitler 1974, 26.

"Ko Ko was the seminal point of departure": Giddins 1987, 88.

"With them, the bop revolution was complete": Collier 1978, 359.

"short stay in the sun": Gendron 1994.

leading apostle of the importance of looking hip: M. Davis 1989, 110–111.

"dressed in these baggy clothes": ibid., 57.

"He looked like a used pork chop": Burt Korall, "Stan Levey: Bop Pioneer," *Modern Drummer* 11 (May 1987): 7.

"I was amazed at how Bird changed": M. Davis 1989, 58.

While at the Downbeat, Coleman Hawkins wandered by his table: ibid., 56. Davis identifies the club as the Onyx, but Hawkins was at the Downbeat in the fall of 1944.

"My best advice to you": ibid.

Heat Wave was too modest an operation: "Business Men of the Profession—A Monthly Review: The Heat Wave," *Music Dial* 2 (August 1944): 30.

Rare photographs: Music Dial 2 (October 1944): 2, 32; (November 1944): 2.

"everybody greeted him like he was the king": M. Davis 1989, 57–58.

Ben Webster . . . offered him a gig: Priestley 1984, 26; Koch 1988, 43.

combo with Stan Levey, pianist Joe Albany, and bassist Curley Russell: Gitler 1974, 25 (at the Famous Door); Russell 1973, 166–167 (at the Three Deuces).

"I've learned everything I know by myself": in Dance 1974, 361.

"I had quick ears": in ibid.

"The only thing that kept me with them": in ibid., 364.

peppering his solos with . . . quotations: Arnold Shaw 1977, 328.

[Tatum] underwent eye surgery: Nick Necles, "Nick Necles 'Says,' " *Music Dial* 2 (September 1944): 5; " 'New Faces' Tops [*sic*] Swing St. Fare," *Down Beat* (September 1944): 3.

Clyde Hart and . . . Oscar Pettiford: Herman Rosenberg, "Manhattan Melange," *Record Changer,* October 1944, 70; Jimmy Butts, "The Music Box," *Music Dial* 2 (October 1944): 14.

black-owned and operated club, Tondaleyo's: Butts, "The Music Box," *Music Dial* 2 (August 1944): 17.

Parker . . . become a shadow member: Jimmy Butts, in Gitler 1985, 145.

Buck Ram: Morgenstern 1976.

[Parker] was added . . . over the company's vigorous objection: Tiny Grimes, JOHP.

"Grimes had somehow convinced Savoy": Russell 1973, 167–168.

the emphasis on vocals . . . was the record company's idea: Grimes, JOHP.

"The session did not sound very promising": Russell 1973, 167.

art of phonography: Eisenberg 1987, 109–159.

"I can play all I know": quoted by McGhee, interview with author, 1980.

"pure improvisation": Russell 1973, 170.

"rhetorical plan": Gushee 1991, 250.

"When he started makin' records": in Eisenberg 1987, 144.

basic insight that jazz musicians long ago discovered: Berliner 1994, especially 170–242.

coincidence of melodic formulas with specific points in the harmonic/ rhythmic cycle: see also Koch 1975.

the "main attraction on these sides": Down Beat 12 (15 January 1945), in Patrick 1978.

He opened his own club, the Spotlite: Arnold Shaw 1977, 268.

house band boasted Oscar Pettiford, Benny Harris, Clyde Hart, and Budd Johnson: Pittsburgh Courier, 25 November 1944, 13.

Both had abandoned . . . Boyd Raeburn: "Raeburn and Slack Re-organize Bands," Down Beat 11 (1 November 1944): 5, 9; "Two Plan Crew," Down Beat 11 (1 December 1944): 2.

"zany antics": "Night Club Reviews," Billboard 56 (2 December 1944): 26.

later made famous under the title "Ornithology": Feather 1949, 32.

"strumming-thumping wizardry": "Night Club Reviews," Billboard 56 (2 December 1944): 26.

"For dancing or listening, they are just too wild": ibid.

"excessive drumming": ibid.

"amazing unison jump scorings": "Combos Collared by Groovy Goth-amites," Down Beat 11 (1 June 1944): 14.

"Hawk's bunch and the one at the Spotlite": Leonard Feather, "New York Roundup: The Street," Metronome 61 (December 1944): 14.

"beating [their] brains out": "Swing Street Hard Pressed for Name At-tractions," Billboard 56 (4 November 1944): 24.

Art Tatum commanded . . . \$1,150 a week: "Name-itis Hits 52d Street," Billboard 57 (17 February 1945): 24.

movies . . . offering few places for black jazz musicians: Stowe 1994, 137–140.

first recording by a black jazz band: Nordskog 3009 ("Ory's Creole

Trombone"/"Society Blues"), recorded June 1922 in Los Angeles by Spikes' Seven Pods of Pepper Orchestra.

"linear neighborhood": Gioia 1992, 3.

"one of the largest [black communities]": Frazier 1949, 271.

booming market [in black Los Angeles]: "Growing L.A. Sepia Clubs Offer 15G Weekly Market," *Billboard* 57 (10 February 1945): 23.

"R&B, song-and-dance, comedy, blues": Gioia 1992, 4.

former vaudevillian and an inveterate gambler: ibid., 16–17.

sold . . . the Swing Club, for $50,000: Milton Benny, "Hollywood Periscope," *Metronome* 61 (October 1944): 28.

he decided to take over Slapsy Maxie's: "Hawk Roosts in New L.A. Nitery," *Down Beat* 11 (1 November 1944): 6.

West Coast analogue to Café Society: "New Slapsy Maxie Op Opens with Hawkins," *Billboard* 56 (30 September 1944): 25.

$15.8 billion worth of defense contracts: Lingeman 1976, 69.

armed services had "chosen Los Angeles": Himes 1973, 221.

"Los Angeles hurt me racially": Himes 1972, 73–74.

"Mississippi with Palm Trees": Barry Ulanov, "California Dialogue," *Metronome* 62 (March 1946): 22.

"in the cash register people prefer Negro entertainers": "Berg Finds Negro Bands Click Best in Cash Register," *Ebony* 3 (April 1948): 30.

"a real Joe College type": in Feather 1974, 177.

plan to use informal jam sessions: ibid., 176–178.

"mixed audience, noticeably minus the drunken jitterbugs": "Granz Inaugurates L.A. Sunday Swing Shows," *Down Beat* 11 (1 March 1944): 6.

first of several jazz programs at the Los Angeles Philharmonic: "Granz Prepares Big L.A. Session," *Down Beat* 11 (1 July 1944): 11; "L.A. Jam Session Attracts Crowd," *Down Beat* 11 (15 July 1944): 6; "L.A. Session Heps Kids; Granz to Do Second One," *Down Beat* 11 (1 August 1944): 12.

"I don't even remember where Sleepy Lagoon was": in Feather 1974, 178.

"zoot-suit riots": Cosgrove 1984; Mazón 1984; A. G. Mezerik, "Justice, California Style," *New Republic,* 31 January 1944, 132–133; Heinz H. F. Eulau, "The Sleepy Lagoon Case," *New Republic,* 11 December 1944.

"What could make the white people more happy": reprinted in Himes 1973, 225.

"the use of the word 'jazz' ": "Bowl Fluffs Jazz; But Sinatra, Shore OK," *Down Beat* 12 (15 June 1945): 1.

"protagonist of racial unity": "Granz Prepares . . . ," *Down Beat* 11 (1 July 1944): 11.

no more than 50 percent of the musicians: " 'Jazz All Right in Its Place'—Sympho Head," *Down Beat* 12 (1 December 1945): 16.

refusing "to play host to an audience": "L.A. Sympho Hall Closed to Jazz after Disorders," *Down Beat* 13 (25 February 1946): 1.

Berg . . . secured his services: "Music Grapevine," *Billboard* 56 (30 September 1944): 14; "Personalities in the News," *Metronome* 61 (November 1944): 12.

"With the tough time I have": "Goldman Turns over Downbeat to New Owners," *Billboard* 56 (18 November 1944): 22.

$150 raise: ibid.

tentative return engagement in the spring: "Downbeat Buys Tatum at $1,150 and 2G Advance," *Billboard* 56 (30 December 1944): 14.

"Cornegie Hall": "Eddie, Billy, Play L.A.," *Metronome* 62 (February 1945): 21; Benny, "Hollywood Periscope," *Metronome* 62 (March 1945): 11.

"Delonious" Monk: "Hawk Roosts . . . ," *Down Beat* 11 (1 November 1944): 6.

"utility piano player": Sir Charles Thompson, JOHP.

Hawkins had hoped to convince Don Byas: Chilton 1990, 221–222.

Auld needed a "high-note" soloist: McGhee, interview with author, 1980.

feature article about McGhee: Johnny Sippel, "Faster Trumpet Work Tabs 'McGhee' Special," *Down Beat* 11 (15 September 1944): 4.

"hope for the future": Paul Eduard Miller, "Jazz Symposium: Who Are the No. 1 Challengers of the Winners of Esquire's All-American Jazz Band?" *Esquire* 23 (February 1945): 75.

"I thought I had it made": McGhee, interview with author, 1980.

The interruption was not serious for Auld: "Flash!" *Metronome* 62 (January 1945): 8; "Flash!" *Metronome* 62 (February 1945): 8.

"He ain't paid me nothing!": McGhee, interview with author, 1980.

guest soloist with . . . trio at the Down Beat Swing Room: "Off the Cuff," *Billboard* 56 (23 December 1944): 23.

"He gave me peanuts": McGhee, interview with author, 1980.

"*He told Hawk that I was a damn good trumpet player*": ibid.

"*That's how fast things was happening*": McGhee, interview with author, 1982.

"*Like freedom, you know what I mean?*": ibid.

"*[Hawkins] said, 'You like California?' *": ibid.

"*I was saying, 'That's the kind of music' *": ibid.

"*He hipped me to a lot of music*": Howard McGhee, JOHP.

"*We had an understanding*": McGhee, interview with author, 1982.

theater engagement in Chicago: Phil Feathergill, "Chicago Telescope," *Metronome* 62 (January 1945): 11.

jam session concert in Los Angeles: Charles Emge, "Coast Esquire Bash Misses on Jazz; Too Heavy," *Down Beat* 12 (1 February 1945): 6.

"*He had the date planned*": McGhee, interview with author, 1982.

"*[Hawk] used to play 'Lullaby in Rhythm' *": ibid.

"*He never told a performer how to record*": in M. Jones 1987, 202.

Denzil Best "played free and easy": McGhee, interview with author, 1982.

"*He couldn't play like Charlie Parker*": McGhee, interview with author, 1980.

"*That horn ain't s'posed to sound that fast*": in Shapiro and Hentoff 1955, 356.

"*Bean said . . . 'Let me see these cats play this jive' *": McGhee, interview with author, 1980.

"*For the Asch records, I hadn't gotten myself together*": McGhee, interview with author, 1982.

"*the cabs wouldn't run*": in Chilton 1990, 222.

"*amazing mentalist*" *Princess Garnett:* advertisement, *Buffalo Evening News*, 29 January 1945, 16.

"*dance to the tunes of this marvelous orchestra*": advertisement, *Buffalo Evening News*, 26 January 1945, 23.

small mob of red-cap porters: Feathergill, "Chicago Telescope," *Metronome* 62 (March 1945): 10.

dance at the Elks Ballroom: "Coleman Hawkins and Orchestra at Elks," *California Eagle*, 8 February 1945, 12.

Granz . . . [concert] at Philharmonic Hall: Benny, "Hollywood Periscope," *Metronome* 62 (March 1945): 11.

"jam-swing concert" benefit: "Blow Charity Tunes," *California Eagle,* 15 February 1945, 12; "Sell-out Looms for T.B. Jam-Swing Concert Sunday," *California Eagle,* 15 February 1945, 18; "Candid Comments," *California Eagle,* 22 February 1945, 13.

"and—thank goodness—no dance floor": Hal Holly, "Los Angeles Band Briefs," *Down Beat* 12 (1 March 1945): 6.

broadcast locally . . . every night at midnight: Ulanov, "California Dialogue," *Metronome* 62 (March 1946): 23.

"People didn't know what we were playing": McGhee, interview with author, 1980.

"Why don't he play like he used to play?": McGhee, JOHP.

Gaillard . . . had settled in Los Angeles: Peter Budge, "A Matter of Taste," *Wire* no. 2 (1982): 8; Steve Voce, "Slim Gaillard," *Jazz Journal International* 35 (1982): 20.

verbal virtuoso "expanding the tradition of scatting": Cross 1993, 5.

Gaillard as "an entertainer": McGhee, interview with author, 1980.

" 'Toms' and musical nothings": Gillespie 1979, 243.

"signifying": see Mitchell-Kernan 1981.

"if the shoe fits, wear it": Kochman 1981, 89–96.

"Man, I ain't even mentioned your name": Gillespie 1979, 243.

Cadet was unable to press any other recordings: "Gaillard's 'Mixer' Cadet's Gold Mine," *Billboard* 58 (6 April 1946): 20.

"a surreptitious mention of marijuana": Ulanov, "California Dialogue," *Metronome* 62 (March 1946): 21.

"be-bop bombshell": advertisement, *Billboard* 58 (13 April 1946): 25.

"hot jazz overheated": in Gillespie 1979, 279.

KMPC . . . banned all bebop: "Bop KMPC for Banning 'Be-Bops,' " *Billboard* 58 (23 March 1946): 5, 56.

studio hired Hawkins and his combo: Chilton 1990, 223.

same class as Columbia, Decca, and Victor: "Diggin' the Discs," *Down Beat* 12 (1 January 1945): 8; "Small Diskers Bag Plenty Names," *Billboard* 57 (24 March 1945): 15.

Buddy DeSylva: Dexter 1976, 85.

"biggest fee of his twenty-year career": Benny, "Hollywood Periscope," *Metronome* 62 (April 1945): 10.

he used all the powers at his disposal: Dexter 1976, 62.

Jay McShann was among the early beneficiaries: ibid., 28.

Parker "played alto sax ineptly"; "I never liked him": ibid., 28.

"Hammond gets paid doing the thing he enjoys most": ibid., 56.

compiled a notebook on Kansas City jazz: ibid., 29.

sought out obscure blues singers: ibid., 45–46.

a series of historical anthologies: ibid., 58–60.

Among his projects was a "History of Jazz"; "panoramic recreation": ibid., 103.

"dreamed of recording for many years": ibid., 106.

"I found Hawkins easy to work with": in Chilton 1990, 229.

"Dexter was supervisor of the date": McGhee, interview with author, 1982.

"belligerent and uncooperative": in Chilton 1990, 227.

"sheer desperation": in ibid.

with Hawkins's approval: Dexter 1976, 106.

Red Nichols had "dropped out of sight": Milton Benny, "Red Nichols Rides Again," *Metronome* 61 (December 1944): 15, 32.

"It wasn't Red's kind of music": Dexter 1976, 106.

"humiliated" by the experience: in Chilton 1990, 227.

Dexter rejected more than two dozen takes: ibid., 228–229.

"I was making a record date for Capitol": Leonard Feather, "The Blindfold Test," *Metronome* 63 (November 1946): 30.

"Finally Dexter put in an old-time Dixieland trumpet player": ibid.

"Dave Dexter thought Red Nichols could do anything": McGhee, interview with author, 1982.

"Hawk had a tune": ibid.

"do another one like 'Body and Soul' ": Hawkins 1956.

"Gillespie influence": "Diggin' the Discs," *Down Beat* 12 (15 July 1945): 8.

"a little lick": Gillespie 1979, 371.

"I said to Hawk, 'Look, I seen how much money' ": McGhee, interview with author, 1980.

"Hawk doesn't hog the solos": Holly, "Los Angeles Band Briefs," *Down Beat* 12 (1 March 1945): 6.

"He said he couldn't afford it": McGhee, interview with author, 1980.

"I'll get Joe Guy": in Chilton 1990, 230.

he speculated . . . about getting Eldridge: Holly, "Los Angeles Band Briefs," *Down Beat* 12 (15 April 1945): 13.

Coleman found himself temporarily unemployed: Coleman 1991, 149.

Hawkins stayed on . . . at Shepp's Playhouse: "C. Hawkins in Opening at Shepp's April 19," *California Eagle,* 12 April 1945.

job at the Downbeat Club was waiting: "Hawk, Holiday Apple Hold-overs; Tatum Due," *Down Beat* 12 (15 June 1945): 1.

guest appearances . . . had earned him a local reputation: Eddie Burbridge, "No Fooling," *California Eagle,* 5 April 1945, 13.

engagement at Billy Berg's ended: "McGhee Builds Own Combo on Coast," *Down Beat* 12 (15 April 1945): 13.

"They were just unknowns": McGhee, interview with author, 1980.

playing at the Downbeat Club: Holly, "Los Angeles Band Briefs," *Down Beat* 12 (15 May 1945): 6.

"name cocktail" act: "Gervis-Wald Signs Howard McGhee to Front Own Band," *Billboard* 57 (4 August 1945): 17.

the Swing Club: Holly, "Los Angeles Band Briefs," *Down Beat* 12 (1 August 1945): 6; (15 September 1945): 6.

Streets of Paris: Holly, "Los Angeles Band Briefs," *Down Beat* 12 (15 November 1945): 6.

"incredibly ornate": Ulanov, "California Melodies," *Metronome* 61 (July 1944): 17.

Jade Palace Cafe: Ulanov, "California Melodies," *Metronome* 62 (September 1945): 19.

"Howard McGhee's pioneering bebop band": Gioia 1992, 5.

"We used to play some tempos": McGhee, interview with author, 1980.

"wasn't quite hip to it"; "completely turned me around musically": R. Porter 1991, 48, 50.

"The drummers in Los Angeles": ibid., 54.

"That drummer with Howard McGhee": Benny, "Hollywood Periscope," *Metronome* 62 (September 1945): 13.

three consecutive Down Beat all-star bands: "Stan, Duke, Hamp Tops," *Down Beat* 14 (31 December 1947): 1; "Duke Sweeps '48 Poll," *Down Beat* 15 (29 December 1948): 1; "Woody, Shearing Win '49 Poll," *Down Beat* 16 (30 December 1949): 1. Since Gillespie was at the time technically a "bandleader," he did not compete with McGhee in this category.

"hogging the mike"; "It was good music": Leonard Feather, "Stage Show Reviews: Andy Kirk," *Metronome* 61 (July 1944): 28.

"Well, Teddy [Edwards] was playing tenor": McGhee, interview with author, 1980.

performances from the Streets of Paris were broadcast: Holly, "Los Angeles Band Briefs," *Down Beat* 12 (1 December 1945): 6.

"I said, 'Doggone, that sounds like me' ": McGhee, interview with author, 1980.

shopping the recordings around: Leonard Feather, "Manhattan Kaleidoscope," *Metronome* 62 (August 1945): 10.

"I was working with my band": McGhee, interview with author, 1980.

"Coleman Hawkins knew about it": ibid.

"a triumphant recognition": "Bebop to Carnegie Hall Sept. 29," *Down Beat* 14 (24 September 1947): 5.

A brief notice in Billboard: "Off the Cuff," *Billboard* 57 (13 Jan 1945): 29.

combo . . . did not . . . materialize for another month: "Off the Cuff," *Billboard* 57 (21 April 1945): 28.

Variety counted 130 companies: "Recording Outfits, 130 of 'Em, Face Battle for Survival in Postwar," *Variety* 159 (27 June 1945): 42.

"New Star" of the trumpet: Leonard G. Feather, "All-American Jazz Ballot, 1945," *Esquire* 23 (February 1945): 28.

"New Ace of trumpeters": advertisement, *Billboard* 57 (3 March 1945): 88.

"He's the newest excitement in the band business": advertisement, *Billboard* 57 (3 November 1945): 31; ellipses in original.

"the rebob stuff": "Savoy Sights on Exclusive Artist Pacts," *Billboard* 58 (5 January 1946): 19.

"He always used to wind up with all the lemonades": in Gillespie 1979, 300.

Bud Powell . . . beaten senseless: Dance 1970, 109.

got to know him as an upstairs neighbor: Gillespie 1979, 124.

copied a rival dance band's recorded arrangements: Gitler 1985, 107; Budd Johnson, JOHP.

"Though he didn't play in our style": Gillespie 1979, 213.

blisteringly fast showpiece: ibid., 190.

"The band backed him singing the blues": in Gitler 1985, 151–152.

deliberately spiked the singer's coffee: Gillespie 1979, 284; see also Russell 1973, 192.

Trummy Young and Parker himself: Trummy Young, JOHP; Charlie Parker, recorded interview with Marshall Stearns and James T. Maher, 1950; Marshall Stearns collection, Institute of Jazz Studies, Rutgers University.

"he was a genius for getting them open": Reig 1990, 131.

Everyone agrees on what happened next: Trummy Young, JOHP; Gitler 1985, 149–150; Reig 1990, 13; Arnold Shaw 1978, 141.

"Miss Gillespie, you keep playing those wrong notes": Trummy Young, JOHP.

well-intentioned advice by Woody Herman: Herman and Troup 1990, 40.

"I sat down at the piano": Gillespie 1979, 171.

"I had to do it": ibid., 252.

Armed with a rough demonstration record: ibid., 204.

"the ubiquitous presence on the '40s New York jazz scene": Gennari 1993, 183; see also 181–193 for more on Feather.

"jazz gate-keeper and missionary": ibid., 183.

"half a dozen hats": Feather 1987, 187.

he pulled together two new compositions: Feather 1987, 100–101; Gillespie 1979, 204–205.

his "trivial" blues tune: Feather 1987, 101.

not letting Gillespie solo on a blues date: Gillespie 1979, 204; Feather 1987, 181.

version he had written for the Eckstine band: Gitler 1985, 128.

he began to think of it as a distinct tune: Gillespie 1979, 170–171.

"As we walked in, see": in Stearns 1958, 159.

Levey . . . had just left to play with Woody Herman: Korall, "Stan Levey . . . ," *Modern Drummer* 11 (May 1987): 76.

"isn't right for that kind of fast stuff": "Diggin' the Discs," *Down Beat* 12 (15 June 1945): 8.

"are not new, except to one who has never dug": ibid.

"will undoubtedly give many listeners the wrong impression": "Diggin' the Discs," *Down Beat* 12 (1 August 1945): 8.

"the height of the perfection of our music": Gillespie 1979, 231.

he earned $200 a week: Feather 1949, 33.

jazz concerts organized by Bill Randle in Detroit: "Jazzmen Dig Plenty Dough via Midwest Concert Dates," *Billboard* 57 (17 March 1945): 29.

jam session concert sponsored by . . . Nat Segal: "Philly Set to Try Swing-Jam Concert," *Billboard* 57 (26 May 1945): 15.

probably earned as much in a single night: "Jazzmen Dig Plenty Dough . . . ," *Billboard* 57 (17 March 1945): 29.

Eddie Condon . . . the most regular tenant: Kenney 1983.

New Jazz Foundation: Feather 1949, 34.

Torin . . . promote[d] Gillespie's new releases: Gitler 1985, 6; Chambers 1985, 84.

other performers were offered a paltry $25: Reisner 1977, 220.

quintet dug further into its modest repertory: Barry Ulanov, "Dizzy Dazzles for an Hour; Rest of Concert Drags," *Metronome* 61 (June 1945): 22.

visibly embarrassed Gillespie: "Gillespie Bash Drags as Cats Fail to Show," *Down Beat* 12 (1 June 1945): 1.

"the most original breath of fresh air": ibid.

the "stupid" emceeing of Symphony Sid: "Jazz Stars Absence Drags Gillespie Bash," *Down Beat* 12 (15 July 1945): 1; Leonard Feather, "Again, Stars Fail to Appear at Jazz Foundation Concert," *Metronome* 61 (July 1945): 26.

"Dizzy's quitting the group shocked everybody": M. Davis 1989, 68.

"Dizzy didn't believe in missing gigs": ibid.

Gillespie made sure to bring an extra soloist: Arnold Shaw 1977, 261.

his "prized pupil," Milt Jackson: Gillespie 1979, 242.

Gillespie had his champions: ibid., 222–223; 228.

the Ink Spots, Cootie Williams's dance band, and Ella Fitzgerald: Paul Secon, "More $$ for Negro Musickers," *Down Beat* 12 (3 February 1945): 15.

According to Fuller, he interceded on Gillespie's behalf: Gillespie 1979, 223–224.

"Why give them the royalties off of 'Bebop' ": in ibid., 224. On another occasion, Fuller said he wrote "Things to Come" in 1946: ibid., 254.

"just sitting and listening to music"; "I could dance to it": Gillespie 1979, 223.

"Are you a square if you dance at a dance?": "Cats Square to Dance to Jazz—If They Can!" *Down Beat* 12 (1 August 1945): 3.

"get away with as little commercial stuff as possible": "Woody Enters Concert Field Next Spring," *Down Beat* 12 (1 November 1945): 1.

"To attract a mass audience to bebop": Gillespie 1979, 223.

Shaw farmed out most of the one-nighters: ibid., 224.

"chagrin and surprise": ibid., 223.

"unreconstructed blues lovers": ibid.

"Now, this opening night"; *"They wouldn't even listen to us"*; *"When we got back to New York"*: ibid., 228–229, 223, 230.

he would "clam up": ibid., 229.

make "stiff, awkward bows": Feather 1949, 34.

"People always thought I was crazy": Gillespie 1979, 303.

"I sing about one new song every five years": ibid., 304.

"grinning in the face of white racism": ibid., 295.

"my own way of 'Tomming' ": ibid., 296.

"I'm a southern kid": Gennari 1993, 11.

couched their espousal of bebop in modernist terms: Gendron 1994, 145–147.

"senseless screams": in ibid., 145.

"You're cutting the fool up there": Gillespie 1979, 312.

"watermelon circuit": ibid., 309.

"like a young, hip black Santa Claus": ibid., 343.

Epilogue: Unfinished Business

"Some guys said, 'Here's bop' ": in *Down Beat* 16 (9 September 1949): 12.

"If you want to make a living at music": in "Good By, Bop," *Newsweek*, 4 September 1950, 76.

"[Of] those who came to Minton's": Ellison 1966, 200.

"With jazz. . . . we are not yet in the age of history": ibid., 203.

"swing redux": Stowe 1994, 202.

"polar opposites": ibid., 204.

the "final surge": ibid., 16.

"promotional techniques devised in the late 1920s": ibid., 216.

"It was a band that, if you made a mistake": Gitler 1985, 228.

"the old bebop dilemma": Gillespie 1979, 356.

"made it easy to dance close": ibid., 359.

"no band, no recording contract": ibid., 363.

"more cerebral, more influenced by European avant-garde music": Gendron 1994, 145, 147.

infamous photo spread: "Life Goes to a Party: Bebop," *Life,* 11 October 1948, 138–142.

"shouting incoherently" in a "bebop transport": ibid., 141.

"They tricked me into committing a sacrilege": Gillespie 1979, 293.

large dance bands . . . unable to . . . meet their payrolls: "Bands Scramble for Survival," *Variety* 163 (24 July 1946): 49; "Bands Wary of B.O. Slide," *Variety* 164 (30 October 1946): 47; "Whose Goose Is Golden or the Egg and They," *Down Beat* 14 (29 January 1947): 10.

prominent bandleaders . . . downsizing their orchestras: Mike Levin, "Music Biz Just Ain't Nowhere!" *Down Beat* 13 (18 November 1946): 1; Bill Gottlieb, "Big Payrolls, Loud Brass Must Go," *Down Beat* 13 (12 August 1946): 1; "Les Brown First Top Name to Break Up Orchestra Due to Inflated Costs," *Variety* 164 (6 November 1946): 47.

Nat "King" Cole Trio: "King Cole's $8700 in K.C., St. Loo One-Niters," *Variety* 164 (11 September 1946): 50.

Louis Jordan and his Tympany Five: "P.C. Trailerizes Jordan, 55-Minute Follow Planned," *Variety* 161 (13 February 1946): 41.

Illinois Jacquet's sextet: "Jacquet's Grosses Top Even His High Notes," *Down Beat* 14 (12 February 1947): 3.

"big band coin": "P.C. Trailerizes Jordan . . . ," *Variety* 161 (13 February 1946): 41.

"The highest paid sidemen in the music business": "Hot Jazz a Surprisingly Potent B.O. Bonanza in Longhair Concert Halls," *Variety* 164 (16 October 1946): 46.

"burdened with the obligation to save jazz": Gendron 1994, 158.

"I still don't know what bop is": "B. G. and Bebop," *Newsweek,* 27 December 1948, 66.

"respectable and amusing": Stowe 1994, 202.

doubling the number of articles devoted to bebop: Gendron 1994, 152–153.

52nd Street had entered an irreversible decline: Arnold Shaw 1977, 349–352.

new venues devoted to bebop: Gendron 1994, 152; Sorrentino 1963, 76–80.

"I just couldn't seem to make very much money": Gillespie 1979, 366.

"wasn't much musically because Norman Granz": ibid., 405.

"I'd break up the little band": ibid., 367.

"Not long after Charlie Parker died"; "I've struggled to establish jazz as a concert music": ibid., 403, 448.

"the temptation to write history backwards": Kuhn 1970, 138.

"an increasingly consuming and engulfing mass culture": Huyssen 1986, vii.

"a change in even the function of the music"; "The music of Charlie Parker": Williams 1993, 137.

"the failure to establish a new function": ibid., 152.

Its listening audience: DeVeaux 1995, 2–3, 9–10, 16–19.

Krin Gabbard has suggested: Gabbard 1995, 4.

triumph of "good over evil": White 1973, 9.

"outcats": F. Davis 1990.

Gillespie returned to Cheraw: Gillespie 1979, 440–441.

"I was ridin' along in my Cadillac": in Watkins 1994, 392.

heroin flooded urban black neighborhoods: Courtwright, Joseph, and Des Jarlais 1989, 14–19.

"eleven shots of whiskey": Hawes 1979, 14.

to his evident distress: Chambers 1985, 139.

"skin and bones": M. Davis 1989, 134; Wilmer 1970, 134.

McGhee . . . began his slide into addiction: Wilmer 1970, 133–142.

first trip overseas for a week-long festival: Chambers 1985, 115–117.

"freedom" in being treated offstage "like a human being": M. Davis 1989, 126.

"I started noticing things": ibid., 128.

"To realize that you don't have any power": ibid., 129.

the "endemic curse of the jazz profession": Lees 1991, 131.

"Bop? Man, I ain't never heard of bop!": Mike Nevard, " 'Man, I Ain't Never Heard of Bop!' Said Coleman Hawkins," *Melody Maker* 25 (17 December 1949): 3.

"The state of the music business now": *Down Beat* (17 November 1954), in Chilton 1990, 273.

"I wouldn't ever want any child of mine": in Chilton 1990, 269.

"Bet you never thought you'd be back": in ibid., 289.

with the stage so narrow: ibid., 284.

"I'd play in Timbuktu": in ibid., 322.

"I never played for $5 a night": "Play the Way You Feel," *Time*, 31 August 1962, 61.

"That man's done me out of a lot of work": in Crow 1992, 181.

"a wealthy man": Chilton 1990, 389.

"He was very sensitive, a very proud man": Thelma Carpenter, interview with author, 1986.

hearty appetite: Stewart 1972, 62.

friends . . . scarcely recognized him: Chilton 1990, 369–373.

intropunitive behavior: a "self-destruct process": Bloom 1995, 54–55.

"I imagine it's like the fall of 1929": Carpenter, interview with author, 1986.

"I don't hear anything in what they're playing": in M. Jones 1987, 57.

listening to Stravinsky since he was a kid: "In Between, the Adventure," *Down Beat* 28 (13 April 1961): 15.

"precise playing": "Play the Way You Feel," *Time*, 31 August 1962, 61.

"They're playing 'Freedom' ": in Chilton 1990, 358.

"Some kind of way I've got to start teaching": in M. Jones 1987, 57.

cultural memory must begin with death: Taylor 1996, 3–20.

Selected Bibliography

Allen, Walter C. 1973. *Hendersonia: The Music of Fletcher Henderson and His Musicians.* Highland Park, N.J.: Walter C. Allen.

Badger, Reid. 1995. *A Life in Ragtime: A Biography of James Reese Europe.* New York: Oxford University Press.

Balliett, Whitney. 1983. *Jelly Roll, Jabbo, and Fats: Nineteen Portraits in Jazz.* New York: Oxford University Press.

———. 1986. *American Musicians: Fifty-six Portraits in Jazz.* New York: Oxford University Press.

Baraka, Amiri [LeRoi Jones]. 1984. *The Autobiography of LeRoi Jones.* New York: Freundlich Books.

Baraka, Amiri [LeRoi Jones], and Amina Baraka. 1987. *The Music: Reflections on Jazz and Blues.* New York: William Morrow.

Barker, Danny. 1986. *A Life in Jazz.* New York: Oxford University Press.

Barnet, Charlie. 1984. *Those Swinging Years: The Autobiography of Charlie Barnet.* With Stanley Dance. Baton Rouge: Louisiana State University Press.

Basie, Count. 1985. *Good Morning Blues: The Autobiography of Count Basie.* With Albert Murray. New York: Random House.

Becker, Howard S. 1963. *Outsiders: Studies in the Sociology of Deviance.* London: Collier-Macmillan.

———. 1978. *Art Worlds.* Berkeley: University of California Press.

Berger, Edward. 1993. *Bassically Speaking: An Oral History of George Du-vivier.* With a foreword by Benny Carter; musical analysis by David Chevan. Studies in Jazz, no. 17. Metuchen, N.J.: Institute of Jazz Studies, Rutgers University, and Scarecrow Press.

Berger, Morroe, Edward Berger, and James Patrick. 1982. *Benny Carter: A Life in American Music.* 2 vols. Metuchen, N.J.: Scarecrow Press and Institute of Jazz Studies, Rutgers University.

Berlin, Edward A. 1994. *King of Ragtime: Scott Joplin and His Era.* New York: Oxford Unviersity Press.

Berliner, Paul F. 1994. *Thinking in Jazz: The Infinite Art of Improvisation.* Chicago: University of Chicago Press.

Bernhardt, Clyde E. 1986. *I Remember: Eighty Years of Black Entertainment, Big Bands, and the Blues.* With Sheldon Harris. Philadelphia: University of Pennsylvania Press.

Blesh, Rudi. 1946. *Shining Trumpets: A History of Jazz.* New York: Alfred A. Knopf.

Bloom, Howard. 1995. *The Lucifer Principle: A Scientific Expedition into the Forces of History.* New York: Atlantic Monthly Press.

Blum, John Morton. 1976. *V Was for Victory: Politics and American Culture during World War II.* New York: Harcourt Brace Jovanovich.

Bowen, José A. 1993. "The History of Remembered Innovation: Tradition and Its Role in the Relationship between Musical Works and Their Performances." *Journal of Musicology* 11:139–173.

Brothers, Thomas. 1994. "Solo and Cycle in African-American Jazz." *Musical Quarterly* 78:479–509.

Brown, Anthony. 1990. "Modern Jazz Drumset Artistry." *Black Perspective in Music* 18:39–58.

Brown, Theodore Dennis. 1976. *"A History and Analysis of Jazz Drumming to 1942."* Ph.D. dissertation, University of Michigan.

Buchanan, A. Russell. 1977. *Black Americans in World War II.* Santa Barbara, Cal.: Clio Books.

Büchmann-Moller, Frank. 1990. *You Just Fight for Your Life: The Story of Lester Young.* New York: Praeger.

Bürger, Peter. 1984. *Theory of the Avant-Garde.* Translated by Michael Shaw. Minneapolis: University of Minnesota Press.

Burkholder, Peter. 1983. "Museum Pieces: The Historicist Mainstream in Music of the Last Hundred Years." *Journal of Musicology* 2:115–134.

Bushell, Garvin. 1988. *Jazz from the Beginning.* As told to Mark Tucker. Ann Arbor: University of Michigan Press.

Calloway, Cab, and Bryant Rollins. 1976. *Of Minnie the Moocher and Me*. New York: Thomas Y. Crowell.

Cameron, William Bruce. 1954. "Sociological Notes on the Jam Session." *Social Forces* 33:177–182.

Capeci, Dominic J. 1977. *The Harlem Riot of 1943*. Philadelphia: Temple University Press.

Carner, Gary. 1989. "Conversation with Hal Mitchell: Jazz Patriarch of Newark." *Black Perspective in Music* 17:109–134.

Chambers, Jack. 1985. *Milestones: The Music and Times of Miles Davis*. University of Toronto Press, 1983 *(Milestones I: The Music and Times of Miles Davis to 1960)*; 1985 *(Milestones II: The Music and Times of Miles Davis since 1960)*. Reprint, New York: William Morrow.

Charters, Samuel B., and Leonard Kunstadt. 1962. *Jazz: A History of the New York Scene*. Garden City, N.Y.: Doubleday.

Chernoff, John Miller. 1979. *African Rhythm and African Sensibility: Aesthetics and Social Action in African Musical Idioms*. Chicago: University of Chicago Press.

Chilton, John. 1990. *The Song of the Hawk: The Life and Recordings of Coleman Hawkins*. London: Quartet Books.

Clayton, Buck. 1987. *Buck Clayton's Jazz World*. Assisted by Nancy Miller Elliott; discography by Bob Weir. New York: Oxford University Press.

Coleman, Bill. 1991. *Trumpet Story*. Boston: Northeastern University Press.

Collier, James Lincoln. 1978. *The Making of Jazz: A Comprehensive History*. Boston: Houghton Mifflin.

———. 1987. *Duke Ellington*. New York: Oxford University Press.

———. 1988. *The Reception of Jazz in America: A New View*. I.S.A.M. Monographs, no. 27. Brooklyn: Institute for Studies in American Music.

———. 1989. *Benny Goodman and the Swing Era*. New York: Oxford University Press.

———. 1993. *Jazz: The American Theme Song*. New York: Oxford University Press.

Cosgrove, Stuart. 1984. "The Zoot-Suit and Style Warfare." *History Workshop* 18:77–91.

Courtwright, David, Herman Joseph, and Don Des Jarlais. 1989. *Addicts Who Survived: An Oral History of Narcotic Use in America, 1923–1965*. With a foreword by Claude Brown. Knoxville: University of Tennessee Press.

Crawford, Richard. 1993. *The American Musical Landscape*. Berkeley: University of California Press.

Cross, Brian. 1993. *It's Not about a Salary: Rap, Race, and Resistance in Los Angeles*. New York: Verso.

Crouch, Stanley. 1990. "Jazz Criticism and Its Effect on the Art Form." In *New Perspectives in Jazz*, edited by David N. Baker, 71–87. Washington, D.C.: Smithsonian Institution Press.

Crow, Bill. 1992. *From Birdland to Broadway: Scenes from a Jazz Life.* New York: Oxford University Press.

Cuscuna, Michael. 1983. "Thelonious Monk: The Early Years." Jacket notes. For *The Complete Blue Note Recordings of Thelonious Monk*. Mosaic Records MR4–101. LP.

Dahl, Linda. 1984. *Stormy Weather: The Music and Lives of a Century of Jazzwomen.* New York: Pantheon Books.

Dahlhaus, Carl. 1983. *Foundations of Music History.* Translated by J. B. Robinson. Cambridge, England: Cambridge University Press.

Dalfiume, Richard M. 1971. "The 'Forgotten Years' of the Negro Revolution." In *The Black Americans: Interpretive Readings,* edited by Seth M. Scheiner and Tilden G. Edelstein, 420–436. New York: Holt, Rinehart and Winston.

Dance, Stanley. 1970. *The World of Duke Ellington.* New York: Charles Scribner's Sons.

———. 1974. *The World of Swing.* Vol. 1. New York: Charles Scribner's Sons.

———. 1977. *The World of Earl Hines.* Vol. 2 of *The World of Swing.* New York: Charles Scribner's Sons.

———. 1980. *The World of Count Basie.* New York: Charles Scribner's Sons.

Davin, Tom. 1964. "Conversations with James P. Johnson." In *Jazz Panorama: From the Pages of the Jazz Review,* edited by Martin Williams, 44–61. New York: Collier Books.

Davis, Francis. 1990. *Outcats: Jazz Composers, Instrumentalists, and Singers.* New York: Oxford University Press.

Davis, Miles. 1989. *Miles: The Autobiography.* With Quincy Troupe. New York: Simon and Schuster.

Deffaa, Chip. 1992. *In the Mainstream: Eighteen Portraits in Jazz.* Studies in Jazz, no. 11. Metuchen, N.J.: Scarecrow Press and Institute of Jazz Studies, Rutgers University.

DeVeaux, Scott. 1988. "Bebop and the Recording Industry: The 1942 AFM Recording Ban Reconsidered." *Journal of the American Musicological Society* 41:126–165.

———. 1989. "The Emergence of the Jazz Concert, 1935–1945." *American Music* 7:6–29.

———. 1991. "Constructing the Jazz Tradition: Jazz Historiography." *Black American Literature Forum* 25:525–560.

————. 1995. *Jazz in America: Who's Listening?* Research Division Report, National Endowment for the Arts, no. 31. Carson, Cal.: Seven Locks Press.

Dexter, Dave. 1976. *Playback: A Newsman/Record Producer's Hits and Misses from the 30s to the 70s.* New York: Billboard Publications.

Early, Gerald. 1989. *Tuxedo Junction: Essays on American Culture.* Hopewell, N.J.: Ecco Press.

Eisenberg, Evan. 1987. *The Recording Angel: The Experience of Music from Aristotle to Zappa.* New York: Penguin Books.

Ellington, Duke. 1973. *Music Is My Mistress.* Garden City, N.Y.: Doubleday.

Ellison, Ralph. 1966. *Shadow and Act.* New York: New American Library.

————. 1972. *Invisible Man.* New York: Vintage Books.

Enstice, Wayne, and Paul Rubin. 1992. *Jazz Spoken Here: Conversations with Twenty-two Musicians.* Baton Rouge: Louisiana State University Press.

Erenberg, Lewis A. 1981. *Steppin' Out: New York Nightlife and the Transformation of American Culture, 1890–1930.* Chicago: University of Chicago Press.

Feather, Leonard. 1949. *Inside Be-bop.* New York: J. J. Robbins, 1949.

————. 1957. "Coleman Hawkins." In *The Jazz Makers,* edited by Nat Shapiro and Nat Hentoff, 163–174. New York: Grove Press.

————. 1959. *The Book of Jazz.* New York: Meridian Books.

————. 1960. *The Encyclopedia of Jazz.* New York: Bonanza Books.

————. 1974. *From Satchmo to Miles.* London: Quartet Books.

————. 1977. *Inside Jazz.* New York: Da Capo Press.

————. 1987. *The Jazz Years: Earwitness to an Era.* New York: Da Capo Press.

Foster, Pops. 1971. *Pops Foster: The Autobiography of a New Orleans Jazzman.* Introduction by Bertram Turetzky; interchapters by Ross Russell; discography by Brian Rust. Berkeley: University of California Press.

Frazier, E. Franklin. 1949. *The Negro in the United States.* New York: Macmillan.

————. 1957. *Black Bourgeoisie.* Glencoe, Ill.: Free Press.

Gabbard, Krin. 1991. "The Quoter and His Culture." In *Jazz in Mind: Essays on the History and Meanings of Jazz,* edited by Reginald T. Buckner and Steven Weiland, 92–111. Detroit: Wayne State University Press.

————. 1995. "Introduction: The Jazz Canon and Its Consequences." In *Jazz among the Discourses,* edited by Krin Gabbard, 1–28. Durham: Duke University Press.

Gabler, Milt. 1988. "The Commodore Story: An Interview with Milt Gabler." Jacket notes. For *The Complete Commodore Jazz Recordings, Vol. 1.* Mosaic Records NR23–123. LP.

Gee, Harry R. 1986. *Saxophone Soloists and Their Music, 1844–1985: An Annotated Bibliography.* Bloomington: Indiana University Press.

Gendron, Bernard. 1994. "A Short Stay in the Sun: The Reception of Bebop, 1944–1950." In *The Bebop Revolution in Words and Music,* edited by Dave Oliphant, with an introduction by Richard Lawn, 137–159. Austin: Harry Ransom Humanities Research Center, University of Texas at Austin.

———. 1995. " 'Moldy Figs' and Modernists: Jazz at War (1942–1946)." In *Jazz among the Discourses,* edited by Krin Gabbard, 31–56. Durham: Duke University Press.

Gennari, John. 1991. "Jazz Criticism: Its Development and Ideologies." *Black American Literature Forum* 25:449–523.

———. 1993. *"The Politics of Culture and Identity in American Jazz Criticism."* Ph.D. dissertation, University of Pennsylvania.

George, Nelson. 1988. *The Death of Rhythm and Blues.* New York: Pantheon Books.

Giddins, Gary. 1987. *Celebrating Bird: The Triumph of Charlie Parker.* New York: William Morrow.

———. 1988. *Satchmo.* New York: Doubleday.

Gillespie, Dizzy. 1979. *To Be, or Not . . . to Bop: Memoirs.* With Al Fraser. Garden City, N.Y.: Doubleday.

Gillett, Charlie. 1970. *The Sound of the City: The Rise of Rock and Roll.* New York: Outerbridge and Dienstfrey.

Gioia, Ted. 1988. *The Imperfect Art: Reflections on Jazz and Modern Culture.* New York: Oxford University Press.

———. 1992. *West Coast Jazz: Modern Jazz in California, 1945–1960.* New York: Oxford University Press.

Gitler, Ira. 1974. *Jazz Masters of the Forties.* The Macmillan Jazz Masters Series. New York: Collier Books.

———. 1985. *Swing to Bop: An Oral History of the Transition in Jazz in the 1940s.* New York: Oxford University Press.

Goddard, Chris. 1979. *Jazz Away from Home.* New York: Paddington Press.

Green, Abel, and Joe Laurie, Jr. 1951. *Show Biz: From Vaude to Video.* New York: Henry Holt.

Green, Benny. 1991. *The Reluctant Art: Five Studies in the Growth of Jazz.* Expanded edition. New York: Da Capo Press.

Gridley, Mark C. 1988. *Jazz Styles: History and Analysis.* Third edition. Englewood Cliffs, N.J.: Prentice-Hall.

Gridley, Mark, Robert Maxham, and Robert Hoff. 1989. "Three Approaches to Defining Jazz." *Musical Quarterly* 73:513–531.

Gushee, Lawrence. 1985. "A Preliminary Chronology of the Early Career of Ferd 'Jelly Roll' Morton." *American Music* 3:389–412.

———. 1991. "Lester Young's 'Shoe Shine Boy.' " In *A Lester Young Reader*, edited by Lewis Porter, 224–254. Smithsonian Readers in American Music. Washington, D.C.: Smithsonian Institution Press.

Hall, Edward T. 1977. *Beyond Culture*. Garden City, N.Y.: Anchor Books.

Hamm, Charles. 1979. *Yesterdays: Popular Song in America*. New York: W. W. Norton.

Hammond, John. 1977. *John Hammond on Record: An Autobiography*. With Irving Townsend. New York: Penguin Books.

———. 1981. Jacket notes. For *The Fletcher Henderson Story: A Study in Frustration*. CBS CBS66423. LP.

Hampton, Lionel, and James Haskins. 1989. *Hamp: An Autobiography*. New York: Warner Books.

Harvey, Mark S. 1991. "Jazz and Modernism: Changing Conceptions of Innovation and Tradition." In *Jazz in Mind: Essays on the History and Meanings of Jazz*, edited by Reginald T. Buckner and Steven Weiland, 128–147. Detroit: Wayne State University Press.

Haskins, Jim. 1977. *The Cotton Club*. New York: Random House.

Hasse, John Edward. 1993. *Beyond Category: The Life and Genius of Duke Ellington*. With a foreword by Wynton Marsalis. New York: Simon and Schuster.

Hawes, Hampton, and Dan Asher. 1979. *Raise Up Off Me: A Portrait of Hampton Hawes*. New York: Da Capo Press.

Hawkins, Coleman. 1956. *Coleman Hawkins: A Documentary*. Riverside Records RLP 12–117/118. LP.

Heckman, Don. 1991. "Pres and Hawk: Saxophone Fountainheads." In *A Lester Young Reader*, edited by Lewis Porter, 255–263. Smithsonian Readers in American Music. Washington, D.C.: Smithsonian Institution Press.

Hennessey, Tom. 1994. *From Jazz to Swing: African-American Jazz Musicians and Their Music, 1890–1935*. Detroit: Wayne State University Press.

Hentoff, Nat. 1957. "Roy Eldridge." In *The Jazz Makers*, edited by Nat Shapiro and Nat Hentoff, 296–315. New York: Grove Press.

———. 1975. *The Jazz Life*. New York: Da Capo Press.

Herman, Woody, and Stuart Troup. 1990. *The Woodchopper's Ball: The Autobiography of Woody Herman*. New York: E. P. Dutton.

Himes, Chester. 1945. *If He Hollers Let Him Go*. Garden City, N.Y.: Doubleday.

———. 1972. *The Autobiography of Chester Himes*. Garden City, N.Y.: Doubleday.

———. 1973. *Black on Black: Baby Sister and Selected Writings*. Garden City, N.Y.: Doubleday.

Hinton, Milt, and David Berger. 1988. *Bass Line: The Stories and Photographs of Milt Hinton*. Philadelphia: Temple University Press.

Hobsbawm, Eric. 1993. *The Jazz Scene*. Revised edition. New York: Pantheon Books.

Hodeir, André. 1956. *Jazz: Its Evolution and Essence*. Translated by David Noakes. New York: Grove Press.

Hoefer, George. 1944. "Collectors: Personalities and Anecdotes." In *Esquire's Jazz Book*, edited by Paul Eduard Miller, with an introduction by Arnold Gingrich, 69–78. New York: Smith and Durrell.

Holiday, Billie. 1975. *Lady Sings the Blues*. With William Dufty. London: Abacus.

Hsio Wen Shih. 1959. "The Spread of Jazz and the Big Bands." In *Jazz: New Perspectives on the History of Jazz by Twelve of the World's Foremost Jazz Critics and Scholars*, edited by Nat Hentoff and Albert J. McCarthy, 171–187. New York: Holt, Rinehart and Winston.

Hughes, Langston. 1961. *The Best of Simple*. Illustrated by Bernhard Nast. New York: Hill and Wang.

Huyssen, Andreas. 1986. *After the Great Divide: Modernism, Mass Culture, Postmodernism*. Bloomington: Indiana University Press.

James, C. L. R., George Breitman, and Ed Keemer. 1980. *Fighting Racism in World War II*. Edited by Fred Stanton. New York: Monad Press.

Johnson, James Weldon. 1912. *The Autobiography of an Ex-colored Man*. Boston: Sherman, French.

Jones, LeRoi [Baraka, Amiri]. 1963. *Blues People: Negro Music in White America*. New York: William Morrow.

———. 1968. *Black Music*. New York: William Morrow.

Jones, Max. 1987. *Talking Jazz*. London: Macmillan.

Keepnews, Orrin. 1958. "Charlie Parker." In *The Jazz Makers*, edited by Nat Shapiro and Nat Hentoff, 202–217. New York: Grove Press.

Keil, Charles. 1966. *Urban Blues*. Chicago: University of Chicago Press.

Kenney, William Howland. 1983. "Jazz and the Concert Halls: The Eddie Condon Concerts, 1942–1945." *American Music* 1:60–72.

———. 1993. *Chicago Jazz: A Cultural History, 1904–1930*. New York: Oxford University Press.

Kirk, Andy. 1989. *Twenty Years on Wheels*. As told to Amy Lee. Ann Arbor: University of Michigan Press.

Knauss, Zane. 1977. *Conversations with Jazz Musicians*. Detroit: Gale Research.

Koch, Lawrence O. 1975. "Ornithology: A Study of Charlie Parker's Music (Part Two)." *Journal of Jazz Studies* 2:61–85.

———. 1988. *Yardbird Suite: A Compendium of the Music and Life of Charlie Parker.* Bowling Green, Ohio: Bowling Green State University Popular Press.

Kochman, Thomas. 1981. *Black and White Styles in Conflict.* Chicago: University of Chicago Press.

Kolodin, Irving. 1941. "The Dance Band Business: A Study in Black and White." *Harper's Magazine,* 183:72–82.

Kuhn, Thomas. 1970. *The Structure of Scientific Revolutions.* Second edition, enlarged. International Encyclopedia of Unified Sciences, vol. 2, no. 2. Chicago: University of Chicago Press.

Kukla, Barbara J. 1991. *Swing City: Newark Nightlife, 1925–1950.* Philadelphia: Temple University Press.

Lax, John. 1974. "Chicago's Black Jazz Musicians in the Twenties: Portrait of an Era." *Journal of Jazz Studies* 1:107–127.

Lees, Gene. 1991. *Waiting for Dizzy.* New York: Oxford University Press.

———. 1995. *Leader of the Band: The Life of Woody Herman.* New York: Oxford University Press.

Leiter, Robert D. 1953. *The Musicians and Petrillo.* New York: Bookman Associates.

Leonard, Neil. 1975. "Some Further Thoughts on Jazzmen as Romantic Outsiders." *Journal of Jazz Studies* 2:42–52.

Lhamon, W. T., Jr. 1990. *Deliberate Speed: The Origins of a Cultural Style in the American 1950s.* Washington, D.C.: Smithsonian Institution Press.

Lingeman, Richard R. 1976. *Don't You Know There's a War On?: The American Home Front, 1941–1945.* New York: Capricorn Books.

Lott, Eric. 1995. "Double V, Double-time: Bebop's Politics of Style." In *Jazz among the Discourses,* edited by Krin Gabbard, 243–255. Durham: Duke University Press.

Malcolm X [Malcolm Little]. 1964. *The Autobiography of Malcolm X.* As told to Alex Haley. New York: Grove Press.

Mazón, Mauricio. 1984. *The Zoot-Suit Riots: The Psychology of Symbolic Annihilation.* Austin: University of Texas Press.

McCarthy, Albert. 1977. *Big Band Jazz.* New York: Berkley Publishing.

McDonough, John. 1979. "Coleman Hawkins." Jacket notes. For *Coleman Hawkins.* Time-Life Records. LP.

Meier, August. 1971. *Negro Thought in America, 1880–1915: Racial Ideologies in the Age of Booker T. Washington.* Ann Arbor: University of Michigan Press.

Merriam, Alan P., and Raymond W. Mack. 1960. "The Jazz Community."
  Social Forces 38:211–222.

Mezzrow, Milton "Mezz," and Bernard Wolfe. 1946. *Really the Blues.* New
  York: Random House.

Miller, Paul Eduard, ed. 1944. *Esquire's Jazz Book.* With an introduction by
  Arnold Gingrich. New York: Smith and Durrell.

Millstein, Gilbert. 1975. "The Commodore Shop and Milt Gabler." In *Eddie
  Condon's Treasury of Jazz,* edited by Eddie Condon and Richard Gehman,
  80–100. Westport, Conn.: Greenwood Press.

Mitchell-Kernan, Claudia. 1981. "Signifying." In *Mother Wit from the
  Laughing Barrel: Readings in the Interpretation of Afro-American Folk-
  lore,* edited by Alan Dundes, 310–328. Critical Studies on Black Life and
  Culture, vol. 7. New York: Garland Publishing.

Morgenstern, Dan. 1976. "The Changing Face of Harlem." Jacket notes. For
  The Changing Face of Harlem: The Savoy Sessions. Savoy Records SJL
  2208. LP.

Murray, Albert. 1976. *Stomping the Blues.* New York: McGraw-Hill.

Myrdal, Gunnar. 1962. *An American Dilemma: The Negro Problem and
  Modern Democracy.* Twentieth anniversary edition. In collaboration with
  Richard Sterner and Arnold Rose. New York: Harper and Row.

Nanry, Charles. 1979. *The Jazz Text.* With Edward Berger. New York: D. Van
  Nostrand.

Naremore, James. 1995. "Uptown Folk: Blackness and Entertainment in
  Cabin in the Sky." In *Representing Jazz,* edited by Krin Gabbard, 169–
  192. Durham: Duke University Press.

Nettl, Bruno. 1974. "Thoughts on Improvisation: A Comparative Approach."
  Musical Quarterly 60:1–19.

Owens, Thomas. 1974. *"Charlie Parker: Techniques of Improvisation."* Ph.D.
  dissertation, University of California, Los Angeles.

———. 1995. *Bebop: The Music and Its Players.* New York: Oxford University Press.

Panassié, Hugues. 1942. *The Real Jazz.* Translated by Anne Sorrelle Williams.
  Adapted for U.S. publication by Charles Edward Smith. New York: Smith
  and Durrell.

Patrick, James. 1978. "The Music of Charlie Parker." Jacket notes. For *Charlie
  Parker: The Complete Savoy Studio Sessions.* Savoy Records 5500. LP.

———. 1983. "Al Tinney, Monroe's Uptown House, and the Emergence of
  Modern Jazz in Harlem." *Annual Review of Jazz Studies* 2:150–179.

Pearson, Nathan W., Jr. 1987. *Goin' to Kansas City.* Urbana: University of
  Illinois Press.

Peretti, Burton W. 1992. *The Creation of Jazz: Music, Race, and Culture in Urban America*. Urbana: University of Illinois Press.

Polenberg, Richard. 1972. *War and Society: The United States*. Philadelphia: J. B. Lippincott.

Porter, Bob. 1986. "Keynote: The Label and It's [*sic*] Producer." Jacket notes. For *The Complete Keynote Collection*. Nippon Phonogram 18PJ-1051/1071. LP.

Porter, Lewis, ed. 1991. *A Lester Young Reader*. Washington, D.C.: Smithsonian Institution Press.

Porter, Lewis, and Michael Ullman. 1993. *Jazz: From Its Origins to the Present*. With Ed Hazell. Englewood Cliffs, N.J.: Prentice-Hall.

Porter, Roy. 1991. *There and Back: The Roy Porter Story*. With David Keller. Baton Rouge: Louisiana State University Press.

Priestley, Brian. 1984. *Charlie Parker*. Tunbridge Wells, England: Spellmount.

Rasula, Jed. 1995. "The Media of Memory: The Seductive Menace of Records in Jazz History." In *Jazz among the Discourses*, edited by Krin Gabbard, 134–162. Durham: Duke University Press.

Reig, Teddy. 1990. *Reminiscing in Tempo: The Life and Times of a Jazz Hustler*. In collaboration with Edward Berger. Studies in Jazz no. 10. Methuchen, N.J.: Scarecrow Press and Institute of Jazz Studies, Rutgers University.

Reisner, Robert George. 1977. *Bird: The Legend of Charlie Parker*. New York: Da Capo Press.

Ross, Andrew. 1989. *No Respect: Intellectuals and Popular Culture*. New York: Routledge.

Ruppli, Michel, comp. 1980. *The Savoy Label: A Discography*. With assistance from Bob Porter. Discographies, no. 2. Westport, Conn.: Greenwood Press.

———, comp. 1985. *The King Labels: A Discography*. Westport, Conn.: Greenwood Press.

Russell, Ross. 1959. "Bebop." In *The Art of Jazz*, edited by Martin Williams, 187–214. New York: Oxford University Press.

———. 1971. *Jazz Style in Kansas City and the Southwest*. Berkeley: University of California Press.

———. 1973. *Bird Lives: The High Life and Hard Times of Charles "Yardbird" Parker*. London: Quartet Books.

Rust, Brian. 1978. *Jazz Records 1897–1942*. Vol. 1. New Rochelle, N.Y.: Arlington House.

Ryan, John. 1985. *The Production of Culture in the Music Industry: The ASCAP-BMI Controversy.* Lanham, Md.: University Press of America.

Sales, Grover. 1960. "I Wanted to Make It Better: Monk at the Black Hawk." *Jazz: A Quarterly of American Music* 5:31–41.

————. 1984. *Jazz: America's Classical Music.* Englewood Cliffs, N.J.: Prentice-Hall.

Sanjek, Russell. 1988. *From 1900 to 1984.* Vol. 3 of *American Popular Music and Its Business: The First Four Hundred Years.* New York: Oxford University Press.

Sanjek, Russell, and David Sanjek. 1991. *American Popular Music Business in the Twentieth Century.* New York: Oxford University Press.

Sargeant, Winthrop. 1946. *Jazz: Hot and Hybrid.* New and enlarged edition. New York: E. P. Dutton.

Schaap, Phil. 1991. "Young Lester Young." In *A Lester Young Reader,* edited by Lewis Porter, 4–15. Washington, D.C.: Smithsonian Institution Press.

Schoener, Allon, ed. 1979. *Harlem on My Mind: Cultural Capital of Black America, 1900–1978.* With an introduction by Nathan Irvin Huggins. New York: Dell.

Schuller, Gunther. 1968. *Early Jazz: Its Roots and Musical Development.* Vol. 1 of *The History of Jazz.* New York: Oxford University Press.

————. 1989. *The Swing Era: The Development of Jazz, 1930–1945.* Vol. 2 of *The History of Jazz.* New York: Oxford University Press.

Seeger, Charles. 1966. "Version and Variants of the Tunes of 'Barbara Allen' " *Selected Reports of the Institute of Ethnomusicology* 1:120–163.

Shapiro, Nat, and Nat Hentoff, eds. 1955. *Hear Me Talkin' to Ya: The Story of Jazz as Told by the Men Who Made It.* New York: Rinehart.

Shaw, Arnold. 1977. *52nd Street: The Street of Jazz.* With a foreword by Abel Green. New York: Da Capo Press.

————. 1978. *Honkers and Shouters: The Golden Years of Rhythm and Blues.* New York: Macmillan.

Shaw, Artie. 1952. *The Trouble with Cinderella (an Outline of Identity).* New York: Farrar, Straus, and Young.

Sidran, Ben. 1971. *Black Talk.* New York: Holt, Rinehart and Winston.

Simon, George T. 1967. *The Big Bands.* With a foreword by Frank Sinatra. New York: Macmillan.

Sitkoff, Harvard. 1971. "Racial Militancy and Interracial Violence in the Second World War." *Journal of American History* 58:661–681.

Smith, Charles Edward. 1944. "Collecting Hot." In *Esquire's Jazz Book,* edited by Paul Eduard Miller, with an introduction by Arnold Gingrich, 24–29. New York: Smith and Durrell.

Smith, Stephen W. 1939. "Hot Collecting." In *Jazzmen*, edited by Frederic Jr. Ramsey and Charles Edward Smith, 287–299. New York: Harcourt Brace Jovanovich.

Smith, W. O. 1991. *Sideman: The Long Gig of W. O. Smith*. Nashville: Rutledge Hill Press.

Sorrentino, Gilbert. 1963. " Remembrances of Bop in New York, 1945–1960." *Kulchur* 10:70–82.

Souchon, Edmond. 1964. "King Oliver: A Very Personal Memoir." In *Jazz Panorama: From the Pages of the Jazz Review,* edited by Martin Williams, 21–30. New York: Collier Books.

Southern, Eileen. 1979. "Conversation with William Clarence 'Billy' Eckstine: 'Mr. B' of Ballad and Bop." *Black Perspective in Music* 7:182–198.

———. 1980. "Conversation with William Clarence 'Billy' Eckstine: Part 2." *Black Perspective in Music* 8:54–64.

———. 1983. *The Music of Black Americans: A History.* Second edition. New York: W. W. Norton.

Stearns, Marshall. 1958. *The Story of Jazz.* New York: Oxford University Press.

Stewart, Rex. 1972. *Jazz Masters of the Thirties.* New York: Macmillan.

———. 1991. *Boy Meets Horn.* Edited by Claire P. Gordon. Ann Arbor: University of Michigan Press.

Stowe, David. 1994. *Swing Changes: Big-Band Jazz in New Deal America.* Cambridge, Mass.: Harvard University Press.

Susman, Warren I. 1984. " 'Personality' and the Making of Twentieth-Century Culture." In *Culture as History: The Transformation of American Society in the Twentieth Century,* 271–285. New York: Pantheon Books.

Taruskin, Richard. 1992. "Tradition and Authority." *Early Music* 15:311–325.

Taylor, Gary. 1996. *Cultural Selection.* New York: Basic Books.

Terkel, Studs. 1984. *"The Good War": An Oral History of World War Two.* New York: Ballantine Books.

Tirro, Frank. 1993. *Jazz: A History.* Second edition. New York: W. W. Norton.

———. 1996. *Living with Jazz: An Appreciation.* Fort Worth: Harcourt Brace College Publishers.

Titon, Jeff Todd. 1979. *Early Downhome Blues: A Musical and Cultural Analysis.* Urbana: University of Illinois Press.

———, comp. and ed. 1981. *Downhome Blues Lyrics: An Anthology from the Post–World War II Era.* Boston: Twayne Publishers.

Travis, Dempsey. 1983. *An Autobiography of Black Jazz.* With a foreword by Studs Terkel. Chicago: Urban Research Institute.

Treitler, Leo. 1989. *Music and the Historical Imagination*. Cambridge, Mass.: Harvard University Press.

Tucker, Bruce. 1989. " 'Tell Tchaikovsky the News': Postmodernism, Popular Culture, and the Emergence of Rock 'n' Roll." *Black Music Research Journal* 9:271–95.

Tucker, Mark. 1991. *Ellington: The Early Years*. Urbana: University of Illinois Press.

Ulanov, Barry. 1952. *A History of Jazz in America*. New York: Viking Press.

———. 1972. *Duke Ellington*. New York: Da Capo Press.

van der Merwe, Peter. 1989. *Origins of the Popular Style: The Antecedents of Twentieth-Century Popular Music*. Oxford: Clarendon Press.

Walker, Leo. 1972. *The Wonderful Era of the Great Dance Bands*. Garden City, N.Y.: Doubleday.

Waters, Ethel. 1975. *His Eye Is on the Sparrow*. With Charles Samuels. New York: Pillar Books.

Watkins, Mel. 1994. *On the Real Side: Laughing, Lying, and Signifying— the Underground Tradition of African-American Humor That Transformed American Culture, from Slavery to Richard Pryor*. New York: Simon and Schuster.

Wells, Dicky. 1991. *The Night People: The Jazz Life of Dicky Wells*. As told to Stanley Dance; with a foreword by Count Basie. Washington, D.C.: Smithsonian Institution Press.

White, Hayden. 1973. *Metahistory: The Historical Imagination in Nineteenth-Century Europe*. Baltimore: Johns Hopkins University Press.

Will, George F. 1990. *Men at Work: The Craft of Baseball*. New York: Macmillan.

Williams, Martin. 1976. Jacket notes. For *Dizzy Gillespie: The Development of an American Artist*. Washington, D.C.: Smithsonian Collection R 004. LP.

———. 1987. "Jazz Music: A Brief History." Jacket notes. For *The Smithsonian Collection of Classic Jazz*. Revised edition. Washington, D.C.: Smithsonian Collection R033 A5 19477. CD.

———. 1993. *The Jazz Tradition*. Second revised edition. Oxford: Oxford University Press.

Wilmer, Valerie. 1970. *Jazz People*. New York: Bobbs-Merrill.

Recordings Cited

"All the Things You Are": Dizzy Gillespie Sextet, Musicraft 488, recorded 29 February 1945, New York.

"Amen": *see* "Yeah, Man"

"Apple Honey": Woody Herman and His Orchestra, Columbia 36803, recorded 19 February 1945, New York.

"Basie's Basement": Woody Herman and His Orchestra, first released on Hindsight HRS134 (LP), recorded 20 September 1944, New York.

"Bean and the Boys": Coleman Hawkins and His Orchestra, Sonora 3024, recorded December 1946, New York.

"Bean at the Met": Coleman Hawkins Quintet, Keynote 610, recorded 31 January 1944, New York.

"Bean Soup": Coleman Hawkins and His Orchestra, Capitol 15855, recorded 9 March 1945, Los Angeles.

"Bean Stalking": Coleman Hawkins and His Orchestra, Asch 3552, recorded January 1945, New York.

"Beat Me Daddy, Eight to the Bar": Will Bradley and His Orchestra, Columbia 35530, recorded 21 May 1940, New York.

"Be-Bop": Dizzy Gillespie Sextet, Manor 5000, recorded 9 January 1945, New York.

"Begin the Beguine": Artie Shaw and His Orchestra, Bluebird B-7746, recorded 24 July 1938, New York.

"Billie's Bounce": Charlie Parker's Reboppers, Savoy 573, recorded 26 November 1945, New York.

"Blowing the Blues Away": Billy Eckstine and His Orchestra, DeLuxe 2001, recorded 5 December 1944, New York.

"Blue 'n Boogie": Billy Eckstine and His Orchestra, broadcast, first released on Spotlite 100 (LP), recorded c. February/March 1945, Hollywood.

"Blue 'n Boogie": Dizzy Gillespie Sextet, Guild 1001, recorded 9 February 1945, New York.

"Body and Soul": Chu Berry and His "Little Jazz" Ensemble, Commodore 1502, recorded 11 November 1938, New York.

"Body and Soul": Coleman Hawkins and His Orchestra, Bluebird B10523, recorded 11 October 1939, New York.

"Boogie Woogie Bugle Boy": Woody Herman and His Orchestra, Decca 3617, recorded 22 January 1941, New York.

"Bu-Dee-Daht": Coleman Hawkins and His Orchestra, Apollo 752, recorded 16 February 1944, New York.

"Caldonia": Woody Herman and His Orchestra, Columbia 36789, recorded 26 February 1945, New York.

"Caldonia": Louis Jordan and His Tympany Five, Decca 8670, recorded 19 January 1945, New York.

"Cement Mixer (Put-Ti-Put-Ti)": Slim Gaillard Trio, Cadet 201, recorded 1 December 1945, Los Angeles.

"Cherokee": Charlie Parker (accompanied by unidentified musicians), first released on Spotlite 120 (LP), recorded c. 1942, New York.

"Cherry Red Blues": Cootie Williams and His Orchestra, Hit/Majestic 7084, recorded 6 January 1944, New York.

"Chicken Rhythm": Slim Gaillard and His Flat Foot Floogie Boys, Vocalion 5138, recorded 15 September 1939, New York.

"Chocolate Shake": Duke Ellington and His Famous Orchestra, Victor 27531, recorded 26 June 1941, Hollywood.

"Christopher Columbus": Fletcher Henderson and His Orchestra, Vocalion/OKeh 3211, recorded 27 March 1936, Chicago.

"Confessin' the Blues": Jay McShann and His Orchestra, Decca 8559, recorded 30 April 1941, Dallas.

"Cotton Tail": Duke Ellington and His Famous Orchestra, Victor 26610, recorded 4 May 1940, Hollywood.

"Crazy Rhythm": Coleman Hawkins and His All-Star Jam Band, His Master's Voice K-8511, recorded 28 April 1937, Paris.

"Cupid's Nightmare": Cab Calloway and His Orchestra, OKeh 6035, recorded 28 August 1940; broadcast (from the Meadowland Ballroom), first released on Alamac QSR2407 (LP), recorded 27 July 1940, Cedar Grove, New Jersey.

"The Day You Came Along": Coleman Hawkins and His Orchestra, Parlophone R-1685, recorded 29 September 1933, New York.

"Dee Dee's Dance": Clyde Hart's Hot Seven, recorded 19 December 1944, Savoy 598, New York.

"Dexter Blues": Jay McShann and His Orchestra, Decca 8583, recorded 30 April 1941, Dallas.

"Disorder at the Border": Coleman Hawkins and His Orchestra, Apollo 753, recorded 22 February 1944, New York.

"Dizzy Atmosphere": Dizzy Gillespie Sextet, Musicraft 488, recorded 29 February 1945, New York.

"Don't You Make Me High": Blue Lu Barker (accompanied by Danny Barker's Fly Cats), Decca 7506, recorded 11 August 1938, New York.

"Down Under": Woody Herman and His Orchestra, Decca 18544, recorded July 24 1942, Los Angeles.

"East of the Sun": Sarah Vaughan and Her All-Stars, Continental 6031, recorded 31 December 1944, New York.

"Epistrophy": *see* "Fly Right"

"Every Tub": Count Basie and His Orchestra, Decca 1728, recorded 16 February 1938, New York.

"Evil Gal Blues": Dinah Washington with the Lionel Hampton Sextet, Keynote K605, recorded 29 December 1943, New York.

"Exactly Like You": *see* "Kerouac"

"Father Co-operates": Cozy Cole All Stars, Keynote K1301, recorded 22 February 1944, New York.

"Feeling Zero": Coleman Hawkins and His Orchestra, Apollo 753, recorded 22 February 1944, New York.

"Fine Dinner": Coleman Hawkins and His Orchestra, Bluebird B-10523, recorded 11 October 1939, New York.

"The Flat Foot Floogie": Slim and Slam, Vocalion 4021, recorded 17 February 1938, New York.

"Fly Right" ["Epistrophy"]: Cootie Williams and His Orchestra, first released on CBS C3L-38 (LP), recorded 1 April 1942, Chicago.

"Flying Home": Lionel Hampton and His Orchestra, Decca 18394, recorded 26 May 1942, New York.

"Four or Five Times": Woody Herman and His Orchestra, first released on Hindsight HRS134 (LP), recorded 30 August 1944, New York.

"4-F Blues": Clyde Hart's All Stars, Continental C6020, recorded January 1945, New York.

"Frenesi": Woody Herman and His Orchestra, Decca 3427, recorded 27 September 1940, New York.

"Good Bait": Dizzy Gillespie Sextet, Manor 1042, recorded 9 January 1945, New York.

"Good Jelly Blues": Billy Eckstine with the DeLuxe All-Stars, DeLuxe 2000, recorded 13 April 1944, New York.

"Groovin' High": Dizzy Gillespie Sextet, Guild 1001 (matrix 554), recorded 9 February 1945, New York.

"Groovin' High": Dizzy Gillespie Sextet, Guild 1001, recorded February/ March 1945, New York.

"Hackensack": Thelonious Monk Quartet, Columbia CL2038, recorded 6 November 1962, New York.

"Hayfoot, Strawfoot": Duke Ellington and His Famous Orchestra, Victor 20– 1505, recorded 28 July 1942, Chicago.

"High Wind in Hollywood": Howard McGhee Sextet, Dial 1012, recorded 18 October 1946, Hollywood.

"Hollywood Stampede": Coleman Hawkins and His Orchestra, Capitol 10036, recorded 2 March 1945, Los Angeles.

"Honeysuckle Rose": Fletcher Henderson and His Orchestra, Columbia 2732-D, recorded 9 December 1932, New York.

"Honeysuckle Rose": Cootie Williams and His Orchestra, Hit 8088, recorded 6 January 1944, New York.

"Honky Tonk Train Blues": Meade Lux Lewis, Paramount 12896, recorded December 1927, Chicago.

"Hootie Blues": Jay McShann and His Orchestra, Decca 8559, recorded 30 April 1941, Dallas.

"Hot and Anxious": Fletcher Henderson and His Orchestra, Columbia 2449-D, recorded 19 March 1931, New York.

"Hot House": Dizzy Gillespie All Star Quintet, Guild 1003, recorded 11 May 1945, New York.

"How High the Moon (parts 1 and 2)": Jazz at the Philharmonic, Asch 4531, probably recorded 5 March 1945, Los Angeles.

"How High the Moon (part 3)": Jazz at the Philharmonic, Asch 4532, probably recorded 5 March 1945, Los Angeles.

"I Got a Date with Rhythm": Billy Eckstine with the DeLuxe All-Stars, DeLuxe 1003, recorded 13 April 1944, New York.

"I Mean You": Coleman Hawkins and His Orchestra, Sonora 3027, recorded December 1946, New York.

"I Stay in the Mood for You": Billy Eckstine with the DeLuxe All-Stars, DeLuxe 2000, recorded 13 April 1944, New York.

"If I Could Be With You One Hour Tonight": Louis Armstrong and His Sebastian New Cotton Club Orchestra, OKeh 41448, recorded 19 August 1930, Los Angeles.

"I'll Always Love You Just the Same": Tiny Grimes Quintet, Savoy 526, recorded 15 September 1944, New York.

"I'll Wait and Pray": Billy Eckstine and His Orchestra, DeLuxe 2003, recorded 5 December 1944, New York.

"In a Mist": Bix Beiderbecke, OKeh 40916, recorded 9 September 1927, New York.

"In the Mood": Glenn Miller and His Orchestra, Bluebird B10416, recorded 1 August 1939.

"Interlude (A Night in Tunisia)": Sarah Vaughan and Her All-Stars, Continental 6031, recorded 31 December 1944, New York.

"Is You Is Or Is You Ain't (My Baby)": Woody Herman and His Orchestra, first released on Hindsight HRS134 (LP), recorded 2 August 1944, New York.

"Is You Is Or Is You Ain't (My Baby)": Louis Jordan and His Tympany Five, V-Disc 158, recorded 22 November 1943, Hollywood.

"It Don't Mean a Thing (If It Ain't Got That Swing)": Duke Ellington and His Orchestra, Brunswick 6265, recorded 2 February 1932, New York.

"It Must Be Jelly": Woody Herman and His Orchestra, first released on Hindsight HRS134 (LP), recorded 2 August 1944.

"It's the Talk of the Town": Coleman Hawkins and His Orchestra, Capitol 15853, recorded 9 March 1945, Los Angeles.

"It's the Talk of the Town": Fletcher Henderson and His Orchestra, Columbia 2825-D, recorded 22 September 1933, New York.

"I've Got to Sing a Torch Song": Horace Henderson and His Orchestra, Columbia CB-701, recorded 3 October 1933, New York.

"Jelly, Jelly": Earl Hines and His Orchestra, Bluebird B-11065, recorded 2 December 1940, Hollywood.

"Jersey Bounce": Les Hite and His Orchestra, Hit 7001, recorded c. January 1942, New York.

"Kerouac" ["Exactly Like You"]: The Monroe's Jam Sessions, first released on Smithsonian Collection R 004 (LP), recorded c. May 1941, New York.

"Ko Ko": Charlie Parker's Reboppers, Savoy 597, recorded 26 November 1945, New York.

"Ladies Lullaby": Coleman Hawkins and His Orchestra, Asch 3552, recorded January 1945, New York.

"Lady Be Good": Jones-Smith Incorporated, Vocalion 3459, recorded 9 October 1936, Chicago.

"Laura": Woody Herman and His Orchestra, Columbia 36785, recorded 19 February 1945, New York.

"Little Benny": Clyde Hart's Hot Seven, recorded 19 December 1944, Savoy 598, New York.

"Little John Special": Lucky Millinder and His Orchestra, Brunswick 03406, recorded 29 July 1942, New York.

"Love Cries": Coleman Hawkins (accompanied by The Berries), Parlophone B-35512, recorded April 1936, Zurich.

"Main Stem": Duke Ellington and His Famous Orchestra, Victor 20–1556, recorded 26 June 1942, Hollywood.

"The Man I Love": Coleman Hawkins's Swing Four, Signature 9001, recorded 23 December 1943, New York.

"Max Is Making Wax": *see* "Something for You"

"McGhee Special": Andy Kirk and His Twelve Clouds of Joy, Decca 4405, recorded 14 July 1942, New York.

"McGhee Special": Howard McGhee and His Orchestra, Modern Music 136, recorded September 1945, Hollywood.

"Meet Doctor Foo": Coleman Hawkins and His Orchestra, Bluebird B-10477, recorded 11 October 1939, New York.

"Mop Mop": Coleman Hawkins accompanied by Leonard Feather's Esquire All Stars, Commodore 548, recorded 4 December 1943, New York.

"My Buddy": Benny Carter and His Orchestra, Decca F-42136, recorded 18 August 1937, The Hague.

"My Buddy": Lionel Hampton and His Orchestra, Victor 26608, recorded 21 December 1939, New York.

"New King Porter Stomp": Fletcher Henderson and His Orchestra, OKeh 41565, recorded 9 December 1932, New York.

"New Orleans Jump": Andy Kirk and His Twelve Clouds of Joy, first released on Swing House SWH39 (LP), recorded c. 1944, Los Angeles.

"A Night in Tunisia": Dizzy Gillespie Septet, Victor 40–0132, recorded 22 February 1946, New York.

"A Night in Tunisia": Boyd Raeburn and His Orchestra, Guild 107, recorded 26 January 1945, New York.

"The Night Ramble": Coleman Hawkins and His Orchestra, Asch 3552, recorded January 1945, New York.

"No Smokes": Sarah Vaughan and Her All-Stars, Continental 6061, New York.

"Northwest Passage": Woody Herman and His Orchestra, Columbia 36835, recorded 1 March 1945, New York.

"Now's the Time": Charlie Parker's Reboppers, Savoy 573, recorded 26 November 1945, New York.

"Oh! Miss Jaxson": Charlie Barnet and His Orchestra, Decca 18547, recorded 17 July 1942, New York.

"On the Bean": Coleman Hawkins Quartet, Joe Davis 8251, recorded 19 October 1944, New York.

"One Hour": Mound City Blue Blowers, Victor V-38100, recorded 14 November 1929, New York.

"125th Street Prophet": Woody Herman and His Orchestra, first released on Hindsight HRS134 (LP), recorded 13 September 1944, New York.

"One O'Clock Jump": Count Basie and His Orchestra, Decca 1363, recorded 7 July 1937, New York.

"Oop-Bop-Sh'Bam": Dizzy Gillespie Sextet, Musicraft 383, recorded 15 May 1946, New York.

"Opus X": Billy Eckstine and His Orchestra, DeLuxe 2002, recorded 5 December 1944, New York.

"Ory's Creole Trombone": Spikes' Seven Pods of Pepper Orchestra, Nordskog 3009, recorded June 1922, Los Angeles.

"Queer Notions": Fletcher Henderson and His Orchestra, Vocalion 2583-A, recorded 18 August 1933, New York.

"Rainbow Mist" ["Body and Soul"]: Coleman Hawkins and His Orchestra, Apollo 751, recorded 22 February 1944, New York.

"Ready for Love": Coleman Hawkins and His Orchestra, Asch 3553, recorded January 1945, New York.

"Red Cross": Tiny Grimes Quintet, Savoy 12001, recorded 15 September 1944, New York; alternate takes first released on Savoy 5500 (LP).

"Red Top": Woody Herman and His Orchestra, V-Disc 382, recorded 5 September 1944, New York.

"Rifftide": Coleman Hawkins and His Orchestra, Capitol 15335, recorded 23 February 1945, Los Angeles.

"Romance Without Finance": Tiny Grimes Quintet, Savoy 532, recorded 15 September 1944, New York.

"'Round Midnight": Thelonious Monk, Riverside RLP12–235, recorded 12 April 1957, New York.

"'Round Midnight": Cootie Williams and His Orchestra, Hit/Majestic 7119, recorded 22 August 1944, New York.

"El Salon de Gutbucket": Charlie Shavers's All-American Five, Keynote K619, recorded 18 October 1944, New York.

"Salt Peanuts": Auld-Hawkins-Webster Saxtet, Apollo 755, recorded 17 May 1944, New York.

"Salt Peanuts": Dizzy Gillespie All Star Quintet, Guild 1003, recorded 11 May 1945, New York.

"Salted Peanuts" ["Salt Peanuts"]: Dizzy Gillespie Sextet, Manor 5000, recorded 9 January 1945, New York.

"Salty Papa Blues": Dinah Washington with the Lionel Hampton Sextet, Keynote K606, recorded 29 December 1943, New York.

"Shaw 'Nuff": Dizzy Gillespie All Star Quintet, Guild 1002, recorded 11 May 1945, New York.

"She's Funny That Way": Coleman Hawkins and His Orchestra, Bluebird B-10477, recorded 11 October 1939, New York.

"Shoot the Arrow to Me Cupid": Clyde Hart's Hot Seven, recorded 19 December 1944, Savoy 542, New York.

"Signing Off": Sarah Vaughan and Her All-Stars, Continental 6024, recorded 31 December 1944, New York.

"Skylark": Earl Hines and His Orchestra, Bluebird B-11512, recorded 19 March 1942, New York.

"Smack That Mess": Clyde Hart's Hot Seven, recorded 19 December 1944, Savoy 542, New York.

Smithsonian Collection of Classic Jazz: revised edition, Smithsonian Collection R033 A5 19477 (CD).

"Somebody's Gotta Go": Cootie Williams and His Orchestra, Hit/Majestic 7119, recorded 22 August 1944, New York.

"Someone to Watch Over Me": Coleman Hawkins and His Orchestra, Capitol 15853, recorded 9 March 1945, Los Angeles.

"Something For You" ["Max Is Making Wax"]: Oscar Pettiford and His 18 All Stars, Manor 1034, recorded 9 January 1945, New York.

"Sportsman's Hop": Coleman Hawkins and His Orchestra, Asch 3553, recorded January 1945, New York.

"The Stampede": Fletcher Henderson and His Orchestra, Columbia 654-D, recorded 15 May 1926, New York.

"Stardust": Coleman Hawkins and His Orchestra, Capitol 15854, recorded 23 February 1945, Los Angeles.

"Straight, No Chaser": Thelonious Monk, Blue Note BLP1511, recorded 23 July 1951, New York.

"A Strange Fact": Coleman Hawkins (accompanied by The Ramblers), Decca F42127, recorded 27 April 1937, Casino Hamdorff, Laren.

"A String of Pearls": Woody Herman and His Orchestra, Decca 4176, recorded 28 January 1942, New York.

"Stumpy": Coleman Hawkins and His Orchestra, Signature 28102, recorded 8 December 1943, New York.

"Sweet Georgia Brown": Coleman Hawkins and His All-Star Jam Band, His Master's Voice K-8511, recorded 28 April 1937, Paris.

"Sweet Georgia Brown": The Redcross Recordings, first released on Stash ST-260 (LP), recorded 15 February 1943, Chicago.

"Sweet Lorraine": King Cole Trio, Decca 8520, recorded 6 December 1940, Los Angeles.

"Sweet Lorraine": Thelonious Monk, first released on Xanadu 107 (LP), recorded c. 1941, New York.

"Swing to Bop" ["Topsy"]: first released on Everest FS-219 (LP), recorded c. 1941, New York.

"Swinging the Blues": Count Basie and His Orchestra, Decca 1880, recorded 16 February 1938, New York.

"That's the Blues": Clyde Hart's All Stars, Continental C6013, recorded January 1945, New York.

"Things to Come": Dizzy Gillespie Orchestra, Musicraft 447, recorded 9 July 1946, New York.

"This Time the Dream's On Me": Artie Shaw and His Orchestra, Victor 27609, recorded 2 September 1941, New York.

"Tiny's Tempo": Tiny Grimes Quintet, Savoy 526, recorded 15 September 1944, New York; alternate takes first released on Savoy 5500 (LP).

"Too Much of a Good Thing": Coleman Hawkins and His Orchestra, Capitol 15855, recorded 9 March 1945, Los Angeles.

"Topsy": see "Swing to Bop"

"Trumpet at Tempo": Howard McGhee Jam Band, Dial 1005, recorded 29 July 1946, Hollywood.

"Tuxedo Junction": Erskine Hawkins and His Orchestra, Bluebird B-10409, recorded 18 July 1939, New York.

"Underneath the Harlem Moon": Fletcher Henderson and His Orchestra, Columbia 2732-D, recorded 9 December 1932, New York.

"Until the Real Thing Comes Along": Andy Kirk and his Twelve Clouds of Joy, Decca 809, recorded 2 April 1936, New York.

"Who Dat Up Dere?": Woody Herman and His Orchestra, Decca 18169, recorded 17 November 1943, New York.

"Wild Root": Woody Herman and His Orchestra, Columbia 36949, recorded 16 November 1945, New York.

"Woodchopper's Ball": Woody Herman and His Orchestra, Decca 2440, recorded 12 April 1939, New York.

"Woody'n You": Coleman Hawkins and His Orchestra, Apollo 751, recorded 16 February 1944, New York.

"Yeah, Man" ["Amen"]: Woody Herman and His Orchestra, V-Disc 519, recorded August 1944, New York.

"Yesterdays": Coleman Hawkins and His Orchestra, Apollo 752, recorded 16 February 1944, New York.

"Zigeuner": Artie Shaw and His Orchestra, Bluebird B-10127, recorded 23 January 1939, New York.

Index

and education/training, 59–60; and entertainer role, 48–49, 126–27, 135–36, 156, 300; Hawkins's attempt to reject, 86; late Swing Era competition, 127, 145–46, 160; and music industry, 16, 118, 127, 1940s decline of black, 151–56; and professional identity, 48, 49; and stereotypes, 135–36; and unitary popular culture, 300; white domination of, 18, 47, 146–47; working conditions, 49, 248–52; and World War II, 239, 253. *See also* Bandleader roles; Swing Era; *specific bands and musicians*
Dance, Stanley, 12, 159
Daniels, Billy, 290
"Danny Boy," 125
Dan Wall's Chili House (Harlem), 189–90
Dave's Swingland (Chicago), 275
Davis, Francis, 269, 445
Davis, Joe, 329
Davis, Lem, 284n
Davis, Meyer, 47
Davis, Miles, 101, 317; on black audience reaction, 346; on commodification of bebop, 299; death of, 2; drug abuse, 446–47; on Eckstine band, 319–20, 349; on 52nd Street clubs, 284; on Gillespie, 172, 431; on Hawkins, 101, 368; and Parker, 173, 368–69
Davis, Peter, 74
"Day You Came Along, The," 85
Debussy, Claude, 107
Decca Records, 121, 192, 353, 358; and AFM recording ban, 297, 302, 303
"Dee Dee's Dance," 383, 384
"Deep in the Heart of Texas," 199
DeLuxe All-Stars, 341, 344
DeLuxe Records, 341–43, 344, 350
Depression: and advancement opportunities, 121–23; McGhee's career during, 196; and music industry, 86, 116, 120–21, 123; and World War II, 236
DeSylva, Buddy, 399

Dexter, Dave, 145, 190, 399–402
"Dexter Blues," 399
Dial Records, 413
Dicky Wells' (Harlem), 213
Dillard, Bill, 136, 160, 161
Discography, 40, 296
"Disorder at the Border," 313–14, 315–16, 326, 330
Dissonance, defined, 79–80; and Gillespie, 260, 416, 425; and Hawkins, 92–95, 97, 102, 110, 330; and Parker, 192, 262, 264, 372, 380; and whole-tone scales, 107; and Young, 113–14. *See also* Harmony; "Off Notes"
"Dizzy Atmosphere," 364, 424, 426–27, 428, 429n, 431
Dorham, Kenny, 439
Dorsey, Jimmy, 259, 260
Dorsey, Tommy, 128, 141, 148, 150, 241, 440
Douglass, Joseph, 55
Down Beat, 399, 442
Downbeat Club (Los Angeles), 408
Downbeat Club (New York), 323, 370n, 384, 388
Down Beat Swing Room (Philadelphia), 390
"Down By the Old Mill Stream," 254
"Down Under," 254, 356
Dozens, the, 210–11
Drug abuse: and black alienation/frustration, 446–47; Coulsen, 233; and Gillespie's early 1945 recordings, 415, 416; McGhee, 401, 446; Parker, 173, 175, 194, 254, 349, 431, 446; and World War II draft, 247
Du Bois, W. E. B., 245
Duchamp, Marcel, 22
Duvivier, George, 65–66, 141, 143, 216
Dynamics, 264, 395, 396, 420

Earle Theater (Philadelphia), 139
Early, Gerald, 26n
Earnings: arranging, 199, 257, 259; and Barnet band, 257; and Bernhardt, 53; and Calloway band, 181; concert format, 430, 442; dance orchestras, 86,

Parker, Charlie *(continued)*
   recordings, 413; political views of, 26;
   and professional identity, 188, 191–
   92, 194–95; and racial boundary
   crossing, 19, 351; rhythm, 70, 192,
   261–62, 263, 264–65, 307, 372, 427;
   Savoy recordings (1945), 381; and
   southern tours, 250–51; "Sweet Georgia Brown," 260, 261–63, 264–67,
   268–69; Three Deuces quintet, 367,
   428–30. *See also* Bebop pioneers;
   Parker Savoy recordings (1944)
Parker, Leo, 309, 337
Parker Savoy recordings (1944), 366–67,
   369, 370–81; and anticommercial
   rhetoric, 371; Parker's attitude to-
   wards, 371–72; premeditation in,
   374–80
Patrick, James, 370n
Pay. *See* Earnings
Payne, Cecil, 169n, 233, 439
Pentatonic scale, 374
Peretti, Burton, 250
Performance: vs. composing, 9–12, 40,
   104; vs. jam sessions, 202; and recording technology, 11, 40; and sexu-
   ality, 103–4. *See also* Dance music;
   Entertainer role
Performance/composing dichotomy, 9–
   12, 40, 298, 305, 372–77
Performance rights organizations, 120,
   299, 301–2, 305
Perlman, Itzhak, 172n
Petrillo, James, 295–96
Pettiford, Oscar: age of, 169n; Barnet
   band, 257, 355; Commodore recordings, 306; and Gillespie's early 1945
   recordings, 414, 415, 421; and
   Grimes, 370; and Hawkins, 38, 309,
   319; and Hawkins's small combos,
   389, 390, 391, 402, 408; and small
   combos, 285; Spotlite house band,
   382; "Sweet Georgia Brown," 260; on
   youth of musicians, 63. *See also* Gillespie-Pettiford band
Peyton, Dave, 77
Philharmonic Auditorium (Los Ange-

les), 386, 387, 388, 396, 410. *See also*
   "Jazz at the Philharmonic"
Philips, Flip, 356
"Piney Brown Blues," 334
Pinkard, Maceo, 301
Pla-Mor Ballroom (Kansas City), 190
Plantation Club (St. Louis), 348
Pods's and Jerry's (Harlem), 228
Poet and Peasant Overture (von Suppé),
   56
Polyphony, 2, 101, 265, 293
Popular songs, 67, 120, 268, 300, 305,
   420; and Eckstine band, 333, 335,
   360; Hawkins, 89, 99, 309, 325–26,
   402; Herman band, 353, 355; Hines
   band, 254; and jam sessions, 203. *See
   also specific songs*
Porter, Cole, 300
Porter, Roy, 409
Potter, Tommy, 169n, 337
Powell, Adam Clayton, Jr., 287
Powell, Bud, 18, 169n, 231, 292, 361–
   62, 414
Pozo, Chano, 440
Primitivism, 91, 204, 205
Professional identity, 28; and advancement opportunities, 16, 52; and anticommercial rhetoric, 12, 170; and appearance, 72, 182, 188, 245; and
   assimilation, 50; and avant-garde
   stance, 449; bebop pioneers, 170–71;
   and dance orchestras, 48, 49; and edu-
   cation/training, 55–61; and entertainer role, 183; Hawkins's search for,
   86, 87–92; and jam sessions, 207; vs.
   jazz as art, 44–45; and performance/
   composing dichotomy, 9–12; and racism, 26, 46–47; struggle for autonomy, 12, 17, 27–28, 118, 122, 242,
   298, 336
Professional intermediaries, 122, 129–
   30, 137; and advancement opportunities, 122–23; and bus controversy,
   243–43; and Eckstine band, 335–36,
   341; exploitation by, 144–45, 152; and
   Gillespie orchestra (1945), 432–34;
   and Hawkins Orchestra, 138, 139,

Designer:	Steve Renick
Compositor:	Impressions Book and Journal Services, Inc.
Text:	10/13 Aldus
Display:	Frutiger
Printer and binder:	IBT